SYNGRESS®

COVERS ALL 100% CERTIFIED EXAM OBJECTIVES

MCSE

Exam 70-296: Planning, Implementing and Maintaining a Windows Server 2003 Environment for an MCSE Certified on Windows 2000

STUDY GUIDE & DVD TRAINING SYSTEM

Laura E. Hunter

Brian Barber

Melissa Craft

Norris L. Johnson, Jr.

Tony Piltzecker, Technical Editor

KEY	SERIAL NUMBER
001	TH33SLUGGY
002	Q2T4J9T7VA
003	82LPD8R7FF
004	Z6TDAA3HVY
005	P33JEET8MS
006	3SHX6SN$RK
007	CH3W7E42AK
008	9EU6V4DER7
009	SUPACM4NFH
010	5BVF3MEV2Z

PUBLISHED BY
Syngress Publishing, Inc.
800 Hingham Street
Rockland, MA 02370

Planning, Implementing and Maintaining a Windows Server 2003 Environment for an MCSE Certified on Windows 2000 Study Guide & DVD Training System

Printed in the United States of America

1 2 3 4 5 6 7 8 9 0

ISBN: 1-932266-57-7

Technical Editors: Tony Piltzecker

Technical Reviewer: Jeffery A. Martin
Acquisitions Editor: Catherine A. Nolan
DVD Production: Michael Donovan

Cover Designer: Michael Kavish
Page Layout and Art by: Patricia Lupien
Copy Editor: Darlene Bordwell
Indexer: J. Edmund Rush
DVD Presenter: Tony Piltzecker

Acknowledgments

We would like to acknowledge the following people for their kindness and support in making this book possible.

Karen Cross, Meaghan Cunningham, Kim Wylie, Harry Kirchner, Kevin Votel, Kent Anderson, Frida Yara, Jon Mayes, John Mesjak, Peg O'Donnell, Sandra Patterson, Betty Redmond, Roy Remer, Ron Shapiro, Patricia Kelly, Andrea Tetrick, Jennifer Pascal, Doug Reil, David Dahl, Janis Carpenter, and Susan Fryer of Publishers Group West for sharing their incredible marketing experience and expertise.

The incredibly hard working team at Elsevier Science, including Jonathan Bunkell, AnnHelen Lindeholm, Duncan Enright, David Burton, Rosanna Ramacciotti, Robert Fairbrother, Miguel Sanchez, Klaus Beran, and Rosie Moss for making certain that our vision remains worldwide in scope.

Will Schmied, the President of Area 51 Partners, Inc. and moderator of www.mcseworld.com for sharing his considerable knowledge of Microsoft networking and certification.

David Buckland, Wendi Wong, Daniel Loh, Marie Chieng, Lucy Chong, Leslie Lim, Audrey Gan, and Joseph Chan of Transquest Publishers for the enthusiasm with which they receive our books.

Kwon Sung June at Acorn Publishing for his support.

Jackie Gross, Gayle Voycey, Alexia Penny, Anik Robitaille, Craig Siddall, Darlene Morrow, Iolanda Miller, Jane Mackay, and Marie Skelly at Jackie Gross & Associates for all their help and enthusiasm representing our product in Canada.

Lois Fraser, Connie McMenemy, Shannon Russell, and the rest of the great folks at Jaguar Book Group for their help with distribution of Syngress books in Canada.

David Scott, Annette Scott, Delta Sams, Geoff Ebbs, Hedley Partis, and Tricia Herbert of Woodslane for distributing our books throughout Australia, New Zealand, Papua New Guinea, Fiji Tonga, Solomon Islands, and the Cook Islands.

Winston Lim of Global Publishing for his help and support with distribution of Syngress books in the Philippines.

A special thanks to Daniel Bendell from Assurance Technology Management for his 24x7 care and feeding of the Syngress network. Dan manages our network in a highly professional manner and under severe time constraints, but still keeps a good sense of humor.

Contributors

Laura E. Hunter (CISSP, MCSE, MCT, MCDBA, MCP, MCP+I, CCNA, A+, Network+, iNet+, CNE-4, CNE-5) is a Senior IT Specialist with the University of Pennsylvania, where she provides network planning, implementation, and troubleshooting services for various business units and schools within the University. Her specialties include Microsoft Windows NT and 2000 design and implementation, troubleshooting and security topics. As an "MCSE Early Achiever" on Windows 2000, Laura, was one of the first in the country to renew her Microsoft credentials under the Windows 2000 certification structure. Laura's previous experience includes a position as the Director of Computer Services for the Salvation Army and as the LAN administrator for a medical supply firm. She also operates as an independent consultant for small businesses in the Philadelphia metropolitan area and is a regular contributor to the TechTarget family of websites.

Laura has previously contributed to the Syngress best-seller *Configuring Symantec Antivirus, Corporate Edition* (ISBN: 1-931836-81-7). She has also contributed to several other exam guides in the Syngress Windows 2003 MCSE/MCSA DVD Guide and Training System series as a DVD presenter, contributing author and technical reviewer. Laura holds a bachelor's degree from the University of Pennsylvania and is a member of the Network of Women in Computer Technology, the Information Systems Security Association, and InfraGard, a cooperative undertaking between the U.S. Government other participants dedicated to increasing the security of United States critical infrastructures.

Brian Barber (MCSE/W2K, MCSA/W2K, MCSE/NT 4, MCP+I, MCNE, CNE-5, CNE-4, CNA-3, CNA-GW) is a Senior Consultant with Sierra Systems Consultants Inc. in Ottawa, Canada who specializes in multiplatform infrastructure and application architecture. His focus is on Web-based electronic service delivery through directory services and messaging, and on IT service management. In over 10 years of experience in IT, he has held numerous positions, including Senior Technical Analyst with MetLife and Senior Technical Coordinator with LGS Group Inc. (now a part of IBM Global Services). Brian has contributed to the other following Syngress

Products, including *Configuring and Troubleshooting Windows XP Professional* (ISBN: 1-928994-80-6). He would like to thank Glen Donegan at Microsoft Canada for providing the software he needed and also his family for all of their patience, love, and support.

Melissa Craft (CCNA, MCNE, MCSE, Network+, CNE-3, CNE-4, CNE-GW, CNE-5, CCA) is the Vice President and CIO for Dane Holdings, Inc., a financial services corporation in Phoenix, AZ, where she manages Web development, and the LAN and WAN for the company. During her career, Melissa has focused her expertise on developing enterprise-wide technology solutions and methodologies focused on client organizations. These technology solutions touch every part of a system's lifecycle, from assessing the need, determining the return on investment, network design, testing, and implementation to operational management and strategic planning.

In 1997, Melissa began writing magazine articles on networking and the information technology industry. In 1998, Syngress hired Melissa to contribute to an MCSE certification guide. Since then, Melissa has continued to write about various technology and certification subjects. She is the author of the best-selling *Configuring Windows 2000 Active Directory* (Syngress Publishing, ISBN: 1-928994-60-1), and *Configuring Citrix MetaFrame for Windows 2000 Terminal Services* (Syngress, ISBN: 1-928944-18-0).

Melissa holds a bachelor's degree from the University of Michigan and is a member of the IEEE, the Society of Women Engineers, and American MENSA, Ltd. Melissa currently resides in Glendale, AZ with her family, Dan, Justine, and Taylor.

Norris L. Johnson, Jr. (MCSA, MCSE, CTT+, A+, Linux+, Network +, Security+, CCNA) is a technology trainer and owner of a consulting company in the Seattle-Tacoma area. His consultancies have included deployments and security planning for local firms and public agencies, as well as providing services to other local computer firms in need of problem solving and solutions for their clients. He specializes in Windows NT 4.0, Windows 2000, and Windows XP issues, providing consultation and implementation for networks, security planning and services. In addition to consulting work, Norris provides technical training for clients and teaches for area community and technical colleges. He is co-author of many Syngress publications, including the best selling *Security+ DVD Training & Study Guide* (ISBN: 1-931836-72-8), *SSCP Study Guide and DVD Training System* (ISBN: 1-931836-80-9), *Configuring and Troubleshooting Windows XP Professional* (ISBN: 1-928994-80-6), and *Hack Proofing Your Network, Second Edition* (ISBN: 1-928994-70-9). Norris has also performed technical edits and reviews on *Hack Proofing Windows 2000 Server* (ISBN: 1-931836-49-3) and *Windows 2000 Active Directory, Second Edition* (ISBN: 1-928994-60-1). Norris holds a bachelor's degree from Washington State University. He is deeply appreciative of the support of his wife, Cindy, and three sons in helping to maintain his focus and efforts toward computer training and education.

Technical Editor, Contributor, and DVD Presenter

Tony Piltzecker (CISSP, MCSE, CCNA, Check Point CCSA, Citrix CCA), author of the *CCSA Exam Cram,* is the IT Operations Manager for SynQor, Inc., where he is responsible for the network design and support for multiple offices worldwide. Tony's specialties include network security design, implementation, and testing. Tony's background includes positions as a Senior Networking Consultant with Integrated Information Systems and a Senior Engineer with Private Networks, Inc. Tony holds a bachelor's degree in Business Administration, and is a member of ISSA. Tony currently resides in Leominster, MA with his wife, Melanie, and his daughter, Kaitlyn.

Technical Reviewer

Jeffery A. Martin (MCSE, MCDBA, MCT, MCP+I, MCNE, CNI, CCNP, CCI, CCA, CTT, A+, Network+, I-Net+, Project+, Linux+, CIW, ADPM) has been working with computers and computer networks for over 15 years. Jeffery spends most of his time managing several companies that he owns and consulting for large multinational media companies. He also enjoys working as a technical instructor and training others in the use of technology.

MCSE 70-296 Exam Objectives Map and Table of Contents

All of Microsoft's published objectives for the MCSE 70-296 Exam are covered in this book. To help you easily find the sections that directly support particular objectives, we've listed all of the exam objectives below, and mapped them to the Chapter number in which they are covered. We've also assigned numbers to each objective, which we use in the subsequent Table of Contents and again throughout the book to identify objective coverage. In some chapters, we've made the judgment that it is probably easier for the student to cover objectives in a slightly different sequence than the order of the published Microsoft objectives. By reading this study guide and following the corresponding objective list, you can be sure that you have studied 100% of Microsoft's MCSE 70-296 Exam objectives.

Exam Objective Map

Objective Number	Objective	Chapter Number
1	**Planning & Implementing Server Roles and Server Security.**	
1.1	Configure security for servers that are assigned specific roles.	8
1.2	Plan Security for Servers that are assigned specific roles. Roles might include domain controllers, Web servers, and mail servers.	8
1.2.1	Deploy the security configuration for servers that are assigned specific roles.	8
1.2.2	Create custom security templates based on server roles.	8
2	**Planning Implementing and Maintaining a Network Infrastructure.**	
2.1	Plan a host name resolution strategy.	1
2.1.1	Plan a DNS namespace Design.	1
2.1.2	Plan zone replication requirements.	1

Objective Number	Objective	Chapter Number
2.1.3	Plan a forwarding configuration.	1
2.1.4	Plan for DNS Security.	1
2.1.5	Examine the interoperability for DNS with third-party DNS solutions.	1
3	**Planning, Implementing, and Maintaining Server Availability.**	
3.1	Plan services for high availability.	
3.1.1	Plan a high availability solution that uses clustering services.	11
3.1.2	Plan a high availability solution that uses Network Load Balancing.	11
3.2	Plan a backup and recovery strategy.	11
3.2.1	Identify appropriate backup types. Methods include full, incremental, and differential.	11
3.2.2	Plan a backup strategy that uses volume shadow copy.	11
3.2.3	Plan system recovery that uses Automated System Recovery (ASR).	11
4	**Planning and Maintaining Network Security**	
4.1	Plan secure network administration methods.	10
4.1.1	Create a plan to offer Remote Assistance to client computers.	10
4.1.2	Plan for remote administration by using Terminal Services.	10
4.2	Plan security for Wireless Networks.	9
4.3	Plan security for data transmission.	8
4.3.1	Secure data transmission between client computers to meet security requirements.	8
4.3.2	Secure data transmission by using IPSec.	8
5	**Implementing PKI in a Windows 2003 Network**	
5.1	Configure Active Directory directory services for certificate publication.	4
5.2	Plan a public key infrastructure (PKI) that uses Certificate Services.	4

Objective Number	Objective	Chapter Number
5.2.1	Identify the appropriate type of certificate authority to support certificate issuance requirements.	4
5.2.2	Plan the enrollment and distribution of certificates.	4
5.2.3	Plan for the use of smart cards for authentication.	4
5.3	Framework for planning and implementing security.	4
5.3.1	Plan for Security Monitoring	4
5.3.2	Plan a change and configuration management for security.	4
5.4	Plan a security update infrastructure. Tools might include Microsoft Baseline Security Analyzer and Microsoft Software Update Services.	4
6	**Planning and Implementing an Active Directory Infrastructure.**	**2**
6.1	Plan a strategy for placing global catalog servers.	
6.1.1	Evaluate network traffic considerations when placing global catalog servers.	2
6.1.2	Evaluate the need to enable universal group caching.	2
6.2	Implement an Active Directory directory service forest and domain structure.	2
6.2.1	Create the forest root domain.	2
6.2.2	Create a child domain.	2
6.2.3	Create and configure Application Data Partitions.	2
6.2.4	Install and configure an Active Directory domain controller.	2
6.2.5	Set an Active Directory forest and domain functional level based on requirements.	2
6.2.6	Establish trust relationships. Types of trust relationships might include external trusts, shortcut trusts, and cross-forest trusts."	2

Objective Number	Objective	Chapter Number
7	**Managing and Maintaining an Active Directory Infrastructure.**	
7.1	Manage an Active Directory forest and domain structure.	3
7.1.1	Manage trust relationships.	3
7.1.2	Manage schema modifications.	3
7.1.3	Add or remove a UPN suffix.	3
7.2	Restore Active Directory directory services.	3
7.2.1	Perform an authoritative restore operation.	3
7.2.2	Perform a nonauthoritative restore operation.	3
8	**Planning and Implementing User, Computer, and Group Strategies.**	
8.1	Plan a user authentication strategy.	5
8.1.1	Plan a smart card authentication strategy.	5
8.1.2	Create a password policy for domain users.	5
9	**Planning and Implementing Group Policy.**	
9.1	Plan Group Policy strategy.	6
9.1.1	Plan a Group Policy Strategy by using Resultant Set of Policy (RSoP) Planning mode.	6
9.1.2	Plan a strategy for configuring the user environment by using Group Policy.	6
9.1.3	Plan a strategy for configuring the computer environment by using Group Policy	6
9.2	Configure the user environment by Using Group Policy.	6
9.2.1	Distribute software by using Group Policy.	6
9.2.2	Automatically enroll user certificated by using Group Policy.	6
9.2.3	Redirect folders by using Group Policy.	6
9.2.4	Configure user security settings by using Group Policy.	6
10	**Managing and Maintaining Group Policy**	**7**
10.1	Troubleshoot issues related to Group Policy application deployments. Tools might include RSoP and the gpresult command.	7
10.2	Troubleshoot the application of Group Policy security settings. Tools might include RSoP and the gpresult command.	7

Contents

Foreword

What is Exam 70-296?

So you want to be a Microsoft Certified Systems Engineer for Windows Server 2003? Not a bad idea. To stay competitive in today's competitive IT world, you must not only possess the knowledge necessary to do your job, but you must also be able to prove to your employer (or potential employer) that you have the abilities and knowledge. The best way to prove this is through certifications. If you are reading this book, you have already achieved the status of Microsoft Certified Systems Engineer on Windows 2000. This is not a bad title to have, but unfortunately (or, fortunately depending on how you look at it) times have to change. As Microsoft continues to improve upon its Windows products, you will be required to keep up with this evolving technology. The good news is, the path from MCSE on Windows 2000 to MCSE on Windows Server 2003 is a relatively short one, as you are only required to take two exams for certification. The other good news is that unlike the upgrade path from Windows NT 4.0 to Windows 2000, this isn't a one-time shot, you are allowed to take this exam as many times as necessary – although we think you'll have everything you need in this book to pass it the first time. Let's talk a little more about the this exam, and the requirements to sit for the exam.

Requirements for the 70-296 Exam

Exam 70-296, *Planning, Implementing, and Maintaining a Microsoft Windows Server 2003 Environment for an MCSE Certified on Windows 2000*, is the second exam offered by Microsoft in the Upgrade Exam for Windows 2000 MCSE series. Prior to taking this exam, you must possess a current Windows 2000 MCSE designation, which means you have taken and passed all the exams necessary as stated my Microsoft. Unfortunately, if you are a Windows NT 4.0 MCSE, you are not allowed to take this exam. If you are unsure if you meet the requirements to take this exam, more information is available on the Microsoft MCP Web site at www.microsoft.com/traincert/mcp/mcse/windows2003/#3.

What Do I Need to Know Before I take this Exam?

As we stated earlier, the MCSE on Windows Server 2003 upgrade exams are only available to those candidates who currently certified an MCSE on Windows 2000. Although Microsoft states that the MCSE for Windows Server 2003 credential is intended for IT professionals that work in medium to large computing environments, even smaller companies still have a need for many of the features and benefits that come with Windows Server 2003. Officially, however, Microsoft states that candidates should have experience implementing and administering a network operating system in environments that have the following characteristics:

- 250 to 5,000 or more users
- Three or more physical locations
- Three or more domain controllers
- Network services and resources such as messaging, database, file and print, proxy server, firewall, Internet, intranet, remote access, and client computer management
- Connectivity requirements such as connecting branch offices and individual users in remote locations to the corporate network and connecting corporate networks to the Internet

In addition, candidates should have experience in the following areas:

- Implementing and administering a desktop operating system
- Designing a network infrastructure

Once again, even if you don't have the experience in an environment that Microsoft has laid out, it does not mean that you should close this book and pass on upgrading your MCSE status. In fact, quite the contrary; once you have read this book, you will not only be able to manage a small network environment, you will be prepared to take on larger environments when the opportunity arises.

Path to MCSE 2003

The path to the MCSE for Windows Server 2003 is a short one indeed, when you consider that it requires only two new exams to reach the certification. However, you already know that to get to your Windows 2000 MCSE certification was not easy. For clarity, lets recap the credentials that were required for the Windows 2000 MCSE and how they translate to the Windows Server 2003 MCSE:

- **Networking** An MCSE on Windows 2000 has the option to take Exams 70-292 and 70-296 instead of the four core network exams. However, an MCSE on Windows 2000 can choose to take all four core network exams.
- **Client** An MCSE on Windows 2000 has already passed Exam 70-210 or 70-270, which also satisfies the client requirement for MCSE on Windows Server 2003; therefore, no action is required.
- **Design** The design skills required of an MCSE on Windows Server 2003 do not differ significantly from those required of an MCSE on Windows 2000; therefore, no action is required.
- **Elective** Elective exams are required so that candidates prove technical breadth, interoperability skills, or additional technical depth. For MCSEs on Windows 2000, the current MCSE credential satisfies the elective requirement for Windows Server 2003 because it proves the ability to support another version of the platform; therefore, no further action is required.

Once you have met all of the above requirements, you have completed the path to your Windows Server 2003 certification. If you need more information on the MCSE certification track, you can always visit the Microsoft MCSE Web site at www.microsoft.com/traincert/mcp/mcse/default.asp. Not only can you get information about the 70-296 exam, you can find out more information about the other exams offered to Windows Server 2003 MCSEs.

A Note on Exam 70-292

Before we move, lets take a moment to discuss the other MCSE for Windows Server 2003 upgrade exam. Exam 70-292, *Managing and Maintaining a Microsoft Windows Server 2003 Environment for an MCSA Certified on Windows 2000*. If you haven't taken this exam yet, you're probably wondering why you need to take an MCSA exam. Well, the 70-292 exam covers a direct subset of job tasks that are included in typical

MCSE skills. The skills tested by the MCSA upgrade exam are expected to be part of an MCSE's job tasks, and therefore Microsoft requires this exam to be taken as well. By taking the 70-292 exam, you also become a certified MCSA on Windows 2003. To those of you who have taken the exam and passed, congratulations on your new certification – you're half way to completing you MCSE for Windows Server 2003!

Where Do I Take My Test?

MCP exams are administered by two third-party organization, VUE and Thompson-Prometric. You can register for the exam online or via telephone. Currently, MCP exams cost $125 each, but make sure to check with your testing center of choice prior to registering for your exam. There contact information for the two testing organization is as follows:

- **VUE** www.vue.com, (800) 837-8734 in the United States and Canada. See www.vue.com/contact/ms for contact numbers outside of the U.S. and Canada.
- **Thompson-Prometric** www.2test.com, (800) 755-EXAM (3926) in the U.S. and Canada. See www.prometric.com/candidates for contact numbers outside of the U.S. and Canada.

Exam Day Experience

If you are unfamiliar with the examination process and format, taking your first MCP exam can be quite an experience. You should plan on arriving at your testing center at least 15 minutes before your scheduled exam time. Remember to bring two forms of identification with you, as testing centers are required by the vendor (Microsoft in this case) to verify your identity.

Types of Questions

You should expect to see a variety of question types on this exam, as Microsoft tends to use multiple question types to further discourage cheating on exams. Some types of questions that you may encounter include:

- **Multiple Choice** This is the standard exam question followed by several answer choices. You will see questions that require only one correct answer and also questions that require two or more correct answers. When multiple answers are required, you will be told this in the question, such as "Choose all correct answers" or "Choose three correct answers."

- Hot Area This type of exam question presents a question with an accompanying image and requires you to click on the image in a specific location to correctly answer the question. CompTIA regularly uses this type of question on the A+ exams.
- **Active Screen** This type of question requires you to configure a Windows dialog box by performing tasks to change one or more elements in the dialog box.
- **Drag-and-Drop** This type of exam question requires you to select objects and place them into the answer area as specified in the question.

Exam Experience

The exam itself is delivered via a computer. You will be allowed to use the Windows calculator at all times during the exam, but all other functions of the testing computer are locked out during the testing process. The testing center will have some means in place to monitor the testing room, either via video camera or one-way mirror glass, to discourage cheating. Before starting the exam, you may be asked to complete one or more short surveys. The time spent completing these surveys is separate from the time you will be allotted to complete the exam itself. If you are not taking the exam in English you may be entitled to extra testing time, make sure you talk to the testing center personnel about this issue. You may also be asked to complete one or more surveys following the exam. Again, any surveys you are asked to complete after the exam will not take away from your exam time. You will know immediately after completion of the exam whether or not you have passed and will receive an official score report from the testing center. However, it will take several business days for your online transcript to be updated on Microsoft's Web site. You can access your online transcript at www.microsoft.com/traincert/mcp/mcpsecure.asp.

About the Study Guide and DVD Training System

In this book, you'll find lots of interesting sidebars designed to highlight the most important concepts being presented in the main text. These include the following:

- **Exam Warnings** focus on specific elements on which the reader needs to focus in order to pass the exam.
- **Test Day Tips** are short tips that will help you in organizing and remembering information for the exam.
- **Configuring & Implementing** contain background information that goes beyond what you need to know from the exam, providing a deep foundation for understanding advanced design, installation, and configuration concepts discussed in the text.
- **New & Noteworthy** discussions and explanations of features and enhancements to Windows Server 2003.
- **Head of the Class** discussions are based on the author's interactions with students in live classrooms and the topics covered here are the ones students have the most problems with.

Each chapter also includes hands-on exercises. It is important that you work through these exercises in order to be confident you know how to apply the concepts you have just read about.

You will find a number of helpful elements at the end of each chapter. For example, each chapter contains a *Summary of Exam Objectives* that ties the topics discussed in that chapter to the published objectives. Each chapter also contains an *Exam Objectives Fast Track,* which boils all exam objectives down to manageable summaries that are perfect for last minute review. *The Exam Objectives Frequently Asked Questions* answers those questions that most often arise from readers and students regarding the topics covered in the chapter. Finally, in the *Self Test* section, you will find a set of practice questions written in a multiple-choice form that will assist you in your exam preparation These questions are designed to assess your mastery of the exam objectives and provide thorough remediation, as opposed to simulating the variety of question formats you may encounter in the actual exam. You can use the *Self Test Quick Answer Key* that follows the *Self Test* questions to quickly determine what information you need to review again. The *Self Test Appendix* at the end of the book provides detailed explanations of both the correct and incorrect answers.

Additional Resources

There are two other important exam preparation tools included with this Study Guide. One is the DVD included in the back of this book. The other is the concept review test available from our Web site.

- **Instructor-led training DVD provides you with almost two hours of virtual classroom instruction.** Sit back and watch as an author and trainer reviews all the key exam concepts from the perspective of someone taking the exam for the first time. Here, you'll cut through all of the noise to prepare you for exactly what to expect when you take the exam for the first time. You will want to watch this DVD just before you head out to the testing center!
- **Web based practice exams.** Just visit us at **www.syngress.com/certification** to access a complete Windows Server 2003 concept multiple choice review. These remediation tools are written to test you on all of the published certification objectives. The exam runs in both "live" and "practice" mode. Use "live" mode first to get an accurate gauge of your knowledge and skills, and then use practice mode to launch an extensive review of the questions that gave you trouble.

- Anthony Piltzecker
Technical Editor

Chapter 1

MCSA/MCSE 70-296

Implementing DNS in a Windows Server 2003 Network

Exam Objectives in this Chapter:

2.1 Plan a host name resolution strategy.

2.1.1 Plan a DNS namespace design.

2.1.2 Plan zone replication requirements.

2.1.3 Plan a forwarding configuration.

2.1.4 Plan for DNS security.

2.1.5 Examine the interoperability for DNS with third-party DNS solutions.

- ☑ Summary of Exam Objectives
- ☑ Exam Objectives Fast Track
- ☑ Exam Objectives Frequently Asked Questions
- ☑ Self Test
- ☑ Self Test Quick Answer Key

Introduction

As a Windows 2000 MCSE, you understand how crucial a properly designed and configured host name resolution strategy is for your Windows network to run properly. In Windows Server 2003, the way you plan your host name resolution strategy is (in some ways) even more crucial than before. As we've seen in recent years, the Domain Name System (DNS) has become a victim to several attacks. Initially, DNS was designed as an open protocol, a fact that has now left it open to various threats, including footprinting, denial-of-service (DoS) attacks, data modification, and DNS redirection. Windows Server 2003 has made strides in preventing these types of attacks on your infrastructure through various security features, which we discuss at length within this chapter.

In addition to these new security features, Microsoft has added several other new features to DNS in the 2003 family, including:

- Stub zones
- DNS zone replication in Active Directory enhancements
- Round-robin enhancements
- Enhanced logging for debugging
- EDNS0
- Automatic name service record registration

Each of these new features will enhance your ability to provide a solid, functional DNS architecture for your environment. As with the new security features, we discuss each of these additional enhancements at length within this chapter to provide you with the information you need—not only to pass the 70-296 exam but to assist you with the development of your DNS architecture. Before we get started, you need to ask yourself several questions prior to designing your DNS namespace:

- Will this DNS namespace be used for internal (private) use or for the Internet (public)?
- If this namespace will be used for the Internet, have I chosen and registered a DNS domain name?
- If this namespace will be used for my internal network, will it interact with Active Directory?
- Will this namespace need to interact with any namespaces on a third-party DNS platform?
- Will this namespace need to interact with any namespaces on a legacy (non-Windows Server 2003) DNS platform?

- Do I have any constraints in choosing domain names? Constraints could be industry-related (military or government, for example) or based on company requirements (physical location, parent organizations, and the like).

Don't worry if you don't know the answers to all these questions just yet. Simply keep these questions in mind as you read this chapter and plan your domain name resolution strategy.

Reviewing the Domain Name System

DNS is a great place to start the coverage of objectives for the 70-296 exam, simply because it is the lifeline of the Windows networking environment. As with Windows 2000, Active Directory cannot function without DNS installed somewhere in your environment. Some things have changed in Windows Server 2003 from previous versions of Windows, but the basic functionality of DNS has remained the same. Before we step through the exam objectives, let's review how DNS came into existence, the basic concepts of DNS, and a brief overview of the new features of DNS in a Windows Server 2003 network environment.

A Brief History of DNS

DNS is much like the yellow pages phone directory you might have sitting on your desk. DNS is a hierarchical system of user-friendly names that can be used to locate computers and other resources on your network or networks abroad such as the Internet. Although you can find systems and resources by using their IP addresses, most people prefer to use "friendly," more easily understood names. Generally, it is much easier to remember www.syngress.com than it is to remember 216.238.8.44. This is why we need DNS. DNS is defined under requests for comment (RFCs) 1034 and 1035 (found at www.ietf.org/rfc/rfc1034.txt and www.ietf.org/rfc/rfc1035.txt, respectively) and is used on Windows networks and on the Internet to provide a standard naming convention for translating friendly names to their corresponding IP addresses. Before we had DNS, we used HOSTS files to translate friendly names to IP addresses. Names and IP addresses were entered into the HOSTS files, and computers used copies of these files for name resolution.

DNS Namespaces

Both DNS and the older method of HOSTS files function in a namespace. A *namespace* is a grouping in which names are used to represent other types of information, such as IP addresses, and define rules to determine how names can be created and used. A DNS namespace is *hierarchical*, which means that it is structured and provides rules that allow it to be divided into subsets of names for distribution and delegation of its different parts.

HOSTS file namespaces, on the other hand, can't be divided and can only be distributed as a whole. For this reason, HOSTS files created a problem for networking professionals as the number of IP-based nodes on the Internet (and internal networks) continued to grow. Because of the incredible growth, updating and distributing HOSTS files were becoming difficult, if not impossible. DNS replaced these HOSTS files by using a distributed database that implemented a hierarchical naming system (see Figure 1.1).

Figure 1.1 A Sample DNS Hierarchy

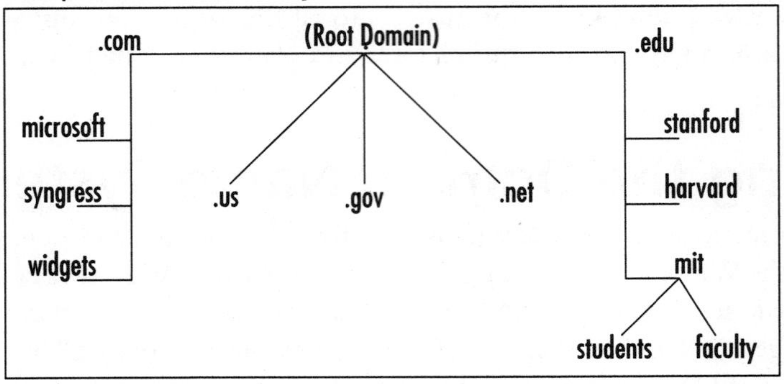

The DNS Structure

As we just mentioned, DNS uses a hierarchical system to manage the resolution of friendly names to IP addresses. Obviously, there has to be some sort of management in order to keep DNS from becoming a database of useless records. In Figure 1.1, you'll notice that the top level is represented by a dot (.). This is known as the *root* of the namespace, or the *null record*. Root servers are controlled by groups known as *registrars*, and they contain entries in their zone files that represent top-level domains. Some examples of top-level domains are:

- **.edu** Educational organizations
- **.biz, .com** Commercial organizations
- **.gov** Government organizations
- **.mil** Military organizations
- **.us** Sites based in the United States (other countries are represented by a two-letter top-level domain as well)
- **.org** Nonprofit organizations (Though this has become a gray area)
- **.net** Typically, Internet-related organizations (although this has become a gray area as well)

As the number of organizations connecting to the Internet continues to increase, new top-level domains continue to become available.

Head of the Class...

Using "Private" Top-Level Domains

In Windows 200*x*, you can create your own top-level domains for your internal networks. It's a very good idea, when applicable, to create top-level internal domains that do not exist outside your internal network. Using a top-level domain such as .home or .work makes it difficult for users outside your network to resolve IP addresses for computers inside your private network, since these top-level domains do not exist in the public DNS system.

For example, let's say that you are the network administrator for a company called High Tech Satellites. High Tech Satellites has a Web presence under the parent domain of hightechsats.com. Within this domain, you host a Web server and an e-mail server. Rather than using hightechsats.com for the top-level domain of your internal network, you could use hightech.sats. So, essentially, your domains would break down like this:

- www.hightechsats.com (external Web server)
- mail.hightechsats.com (external mail server)
- dc1.hightech.sats (internal domain controller)
- apps.hightech.sats (internal application server)
- user001.hightech.sats (internal user workstation)

Using this configuration, external entities will be able to resolve the .com servers but will not be able to discover the .sats servers and workstations.

Below these top-level domains are second-level domains represented by syngress.com (or microsoft.com, mit.edu, and so forth) in Figure 1.1. Since second-level domains are only concerned with hosts inside their domain, such as the syngress.com domain, they are considerably smaller and easier to maintain than top-level domains. An example of hosts within a second-level domain is www.syngress.com or ftp.syngress.com. If you were to verbalize the first one, it would say "host *www* inside the second-level domain *syngress,* which is part of the top-level domain *com.*" The top-level domain is always placed at the end (far right) of a host name. Because of all the second-level domains that exist on the Internet, the DNS hierarchy has taken on a shape that represents an upside-down tree. Let's take a look at how DNS works within the Windows 2000/2003 operating systems.

DNS in Windows Operating Systems

Although DNS server functionality existed in previous versions of Windows such as Windows NT 4.0, it didn't play a prominent part in the operating system until the release of Windows 2000. Since you are a Windows 2000 MCSE, you are familiar with the need for DNS within a Windows 2000 network. For starters, you cannot run a Windows 2000 domain without having a DNS server available. Planning the DNS namespace for your forest was (and is) extremely crucial for a successful Active Directory implementation. Microsoft did a fantastic job implementing DNS in Windows 2000 and has built on the DNS functionality by adding new features in Windows Server 2003.

Now that we've taken a moment to discuss the history of DNS, let's move on and take a look at the new features of DNS in Windows Server 2003.

New Features in Windows Server 2003 DNS

Microsoft has continued to build on the functionality and integration of DNS in Windows Server 2003 that existed in Windows 2000, offering new and enhanced features in Windows Server 2003. Since DNS for Windows 2000 was developed, new technologies and developments have occurred. For example, vulnerabilities in DNS since Windows 2000 have resulted in many DNS-based denial of service (DoS) attacks. Let's take a look at some of the changes in Windows Server 2003 DNS, starting with conditional forwarders.

Conditional Forwarders

A *conditional forwarder* is a new feature that is used to forward DNS queries based on the DNS domain name used in a lookup query. For instance, a DNS server can forward all the name resolution queries it receives for names ending with internal.syngress.com to an IP address of one (or more) DNS servers that manage the internal.syngress.com zone. We'll cover conditional forwards in much more depth later in the chapter, when we discuss objective 2.1.3, DNS forwarding.

Stub Zones

A *stub zone* is a representation of a DNS zone that contains records necessary to identify the authoritative DNS servers for that particular zone. Especially helpful when dealing with discontinuous domain names, stub zones can be used to allow parent domains to remain aware of DNS servers that host a primary or secondary copy of a child DNS zone. They can also be used to keep DNS zone transfer traffic minimized over WAN links. For instance, a small office may need to resolve FQDNs from several different zones within the organization. However, the number of queries does not warrant secondary copies of the zone database being transferred and maintained on a local DNS server. Stub zones can be implemented to minimize the number of queries necessary to locate an authoritative DNS server for the zone. This reduction in recursion maximizes the efficiency of queries to these zones. Stub zones contain only NS, A and SOA records.

Active Directory Zone Replication

In Windows Server 2003, DNS zones can be stored within the domain or in Active Directory data structures used for replication purposes, known as *application directory partitions*. (These are also used by developers for purposes other than DNS; however this is beyond the scope of the 70-296 exam.) Actice Directory Zone replication can be of four different scopes:

- All DNS servers in the Active Directory forest
- All DNS servers in the Active Directory domain
- All domain controllers in the Active Directory domain
- All domain controllers in a specified application directory partition

These zone replication *scopes* allow for better management of Active Directory integrated zones within your enterprise. Later in this chapter, we will discuss replication for Active Directory integrated zones and zone transfers for standard zones when we discuss objectives 2.1.2 and 2.1.5, zone replication.

Enhanced Security

Because of the different threats to DNS, Windows Server 2003 DNS can be configured to reduce some of the vulnerabilities that existed in previous Windows versions. In Windows Server 2003, you can configure DNS to secure DNS clients, secure your DNS namespace, protect the services that run DNS on the Windows server, secure DNS zone transfers by implementing *dynamic updates,* and DNS resource records. We will discuss the enhancements to DNS security at the end of this chapter when we cover objective 2.1.4, DNS security.

Enhanced Round Robin

Round robin is a load-balancing system DNS uses to distribute workloads between network resources. You can use round robin to rotate all types of resource record types (A, CNAME, MX, NS, etc.) used within a query answer if multiple resource records exist. By default, Windows DNS performs round-robin rotation for all types of resource records. You can specify the types of resource records that are not to be used in a round-robin rotation in the Registry. In Windows Server 2003, you can change Registry settings that will disallow the use of round-robin functionality altogether, even in the presence of multiple resource records.

Enhanced Logging

In Windows Server 2003, most debugging options remain unchanged. However, the GUI to configure them has been greatly enhanced and is much easier to use. When debug logging options are enabled, DNS can perform additional trace-level logging of certain events for troubleshooting and debugging purposes. In Windows Server 2003, Microsoft now allows us to control which packets are logged through filtering. They also provide new options to control the level of DNS logging in the Event Viewer utility.

DNSSEC

Along with the aforementioned security enhancements, Microsoft has implemented another security feature into Windows Server 2003. Windows Server 2003 DNS now provides support for the DNS Security Extensions (DNSSEC) protocol. In the past, hackers have been able to exploit specific security holes in DNS to spoof Web sites. DNSSEC prevents these spoofing attacks by allowing Web sites to verify their domain names and IP addresses through the use of digital signatures and public key encryption. Public key encryption is covered at length in Chapter 5, "Managing User Authentication."

Configuring & Implementing...

Beware of Extensive Logging!

Whenever you are doing any type of extensive debug logging, the process can be resource intensive, which will affect your overall server performance and can eat up massive amounts of disk storage space. For these reasons, you should only use debug logging on a temporary basis, typically with an operator on hand to stop it should server performance degrade to a point at which logging must be disabled. You will also want to make sure that your server has sufficient memory and hard drive space when you turn on debug logging. The extra memory is needed to support the additional overhead of the debugging process so that the server's daily processing requirements are not affected by the potential degradation. The hard drive space is directly correlated to the amount of data you will be logging. Depending on the size of your environment, if you are planning to keep logging on for more than 60 minutes, you may need to have several gigabytes of hard drive space available. It's also important to note that you *do not* want to save log files to hard drives that are used for virtual memory swap files, since these drives are already being taxed by the swapping process. When it is possible, you might also want to perform debugging outside of business hours so as not to affect users within your environment.

EDNS0

Using Extension Mechanisms for DNS (EDNS0), you can allow DNS requestors to advertise the size of their UDP packets and control the transfer of UDP packets that are larger than 512 octets. When a request is sent to a DNS server from a DNS requestor, it identifies the requestor's UDP packet size and adjusts the response to contain as many resource records as possible within the UDP packet size that was specified by the DNS requestor.

Resource Registration Restriction

Windows Server 2003 DNS allows you to restrict which servers and zones are allowed to register name server (NS) resource records. Using the *dnscmd* command-line tool, you can set your environment to allow NS resource records to be created only by specific domain controllers. Likewise, you can use the *dnscmd* command-line tool to specify servers that you *do not* want to be able to create NS resource records.

EXAM 70-296 OBJECTIVE 2.1 2.1.1

Planning a DNS Namespace

Planning the key components in your Windows Server 2003 environment is a theme you will see over and over again throughout this book. Planning is the key to a successful implementation and can greatly reduce the number of post-implementation "fires" that you will need to extinguish. Planning your environment prior to implementation also gives you a better understanding of how your environment will look after a major change, such as the creation of a DNS namespace.

Planning a DNS namespace prior to implementation is incredibly important, requiring consideration of a large number of factors. Some of the questions you will have to answer prior to implementation include:

- Have I chosen a domain name?
- Will this domain name be the same as my Internet domain name?
- How many servers will I need?
- Where will my servers reside?
- Will I be using DNS with Active Directory?

Let's begin this section with a look at some different name resolution strategies.

EXAM 70-296 OBJECTIVE 2.1.1

Resolution Strategies

The first step towards planning your DNS namespace is to get a snapshot of your entire organization. This can help you develop a picture of what your DNS structure needs to look like.

Let's say you work for a company called Widgets Inc., the worldwide leader in making widgets, with offices spread all over the United States and in several countries (see Table 1.1). How do you plan to handle DNS name resolution for the different U.S. offices? What about the offices in other countries?

Table 1.1 Widgets Inc. Office Locations

Continent	Country	City
North America	United States	Boston (headquarters)
North America	United States	Chicago
North America	United States	Los Angeles
North America	United States	Miami
North America	United States	Phoenix
North America	Canada	Quebec
Europe	United Kingdom	London
Europe	France	Paris
Europe	Germany	Frankfurt
Europe	Spain	Barcelona
Asia	Japan	Tokyo
Asia	India	New Delhi
Asia	China	Beijing

Obviously, having a user in China resolve DNS names on a server in the Boston office isn't a very good idea. Connection speed, reliability, and other factors make hosting a single DNS server in the Boston office for all remote offices a poor strategy. A better strategy might be to create *subdomains* off your parent (first) domain—one for each continent, and then another below that for each country, followed by a third subdomain for each city (see Figure 1.2).

Now that you have an idea of how your DNS structure will look, we should probably take a step back to decide what the parent domain name should be.

Figure 1.2 Widgets Inc. DNS Naming Strategy

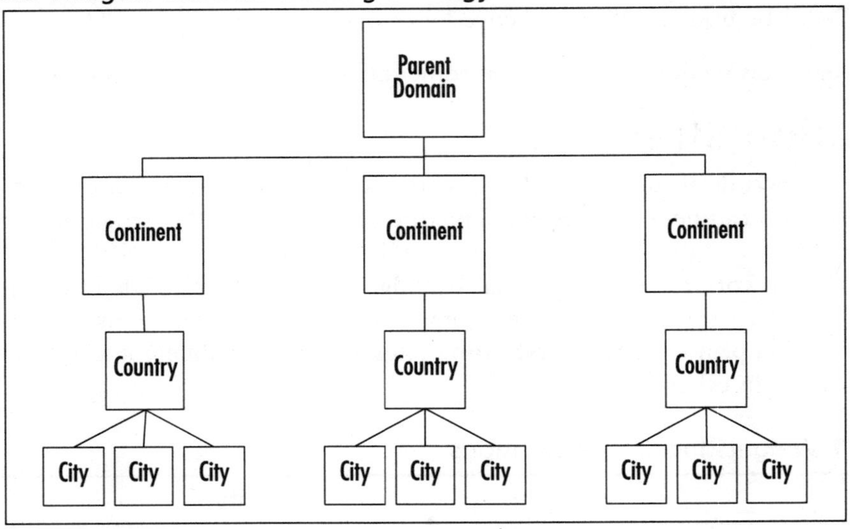

Choosing Your First DNS Domain Name

Choosing your first DNS domain name is an important decision. You'll want to choose something that represents your organization, but you also want to choose a parent domain name that isn't overly difficult for you and your users to deal with. For example, if your company name is Pharmazeutisch Pharmaceuticals, *pharmazeutischpharmaceuticals.com* probably isn't the best choice. (*Pharmazeutisch* is "pharmaceuticals" in German.) Getting back to our Widgets Inc. example, we want to choose a domain name that fits our organization. Let's assume that Widgets already has a Web site, www.widgets.com. Widgets also has an e-mail server (mail.widgets.com), an FTP server (ftp.widgets.com), and several other servers that are accessible via the Internet. Certainly, we can use the widgets.com domain name for our top-level Windows Server 2003 domain name, but, as we discussed earlier, this isn't always the best solution. Sometimes it's better to separate internal DNS namespaces from external DNS namespaces. Let's take a moment to look at how internal and external (Internet) namespaces can be implemented.

Head of the Class...

It's Like Picking a Name for a Child —Everybody Has a Suggestion...

While working as a networking consultant, I was given the task of assisting an organization with its migration from Windows NT 4.0 to Windows 2000. A "migration committee" was created, consisting of myself, two of my coworkers, and several of the customer's IT senior staff members. One of the most difficult hurdles to get over during the migration process was the politics of choosing a parent domain name. Part of the difficulty was that the child companies of the parent company did not always share the same company name, typically because they had been acquired or they offered a different product line. At the conclusion of a meeting that took about four hours, we finally came up with a parent domain name that everyone could be happy with. The moral of the story is, if these types of politics exist within your organization (and they typically do), make sure to discuss any proposed namespaces prior to implementation. The last thing you want is to be in the middle of the implementation and have it come to a screeching halt because someone is unhappy with the name that was chosen.

Internal Domains versus Internet Domains

In creating an internal namespace, you have a great deal of flexibility that you do not have when you're creating an Internet (external) namespace. When you're creating an Internet namespace, you have to conform to one of the predefined top-level domains (such as .com, .net, etc.). When you're creating an Internet domain space, using these predefined top-level domains is the only way that you can name your IP-based nodes if you want them to be seen via the Internet through the use of fully qualified domain names (FQDNs). On the other hand, if you are creating an internal DNS namespace that will be used only for your own internal network, you are not restricted as to how it is designed or implemented.

Getting back to our Widgets Inc. example, let's say that based on the fact that widgets.com is already registered by your company for its Internet servers, you decide that you want to have a separate, internal namespace. After discussing different namespace suggestions, you decide on widgets.home as your parent domain name. At the time of this writing, .home is not a top-level domain currently in use (or planned) on the Internet. Therefore, Internet users will not be able to resolve IP-based nodes within your internal network without access to your internal DNS server records. However, there may come a time that you need to provide either full DNS resolution for the Internet or referral to an external namespace. (You can learn more about integrating internal and external namespaces in the Windows Server 2003 Resource Kit at www.microsoft.com/windowsserver2003/techinfo/reskit/deploykit.mspx.) Although we've said that we will be using widgets.home for the parent domain for Widgets Inc., let's take a look at some of the naming standards that you should adhere to when you're selecting your first domain name.

Naming Standards

There are many standards when it comes to computer networking. There are standards for protocols, standards for addressing, and even standards for cabling. There is also a standard set of characters that are permitted for use in DNS host naming. This standard of characters for DNS host naming is defined in RFC 1123 (www.ietf.org/rfc/rfc1123.txt). According to RFC 1123, all numbers 0 through 9, lowercase letters *a* through *z*, all uppercase letters *A* through *Z*, and hyphens (-) can be used within a domain name. Therefore, we could have chosen any of the following as our domain name for Widgets Inc. instead of widgets.home:

- Widgets123.home
- widgets.123
- widgets-inc.home
- widgets1.home
- WIDGETSINC.HOME

There are vast numbers of combinations that you could use for your namespace. In fact, Windows Server 2003 DNS even allows you to use characters outside the recommended character set. In Windows Server 2003, Microsoft has expanded DNS character support to include enhanced default support for UTF-8, which is a Unicode transformation format. The UTF-8 protocol allows for use of extended ASCII characters and translation of UCS-2, which is a 16-bit Unicode character set that encompasses most writing standards. By including UTF-8, Windows Server 2003 DNS enables a much wider range of names than you can get using ASCII or extended ASCII encoding alone.

New & Noteworthy...

Nonstandard DNS Names and Legacy Operating Systems

You might want to stick with using standard DNS names if you are planning for interoperability with legacy operating systems such as Windows NT 4.0. Although Windows NT 4.0 can handle the RFC 1123 standards for host naming, it cannot handle the expanded DNS naming capabilities in Windows Server 2003. If you must use a naming convention that falls outside the RFC 1123 naming standard, legacy operating systems can use NetBIOS names to communicate with Windows Server 2003 hosts. In Windows Server 2003, NetBIOS hostnames are derived from the first 15 characters of the FQDN. For example, if the FQDN of your Chicago Exchange server is chicagoexchange.widgets.home, the NetBIOS name would be CHICAGOEXCHANGE. However, if the FQDN of the Chicago Exchange server is chicagoexch.widgets.home, the NetBIOS hostname would be CHICAGOEXCH.

Now that we know what our parent domain will be, let's go ahead and build our DNS structure. To keep things simple, we will follow the RFC 1123 naming standard. For Widgets Inc., we will follow the convention of *city.country.continent.widgets.home.* Table 1.2 expands on Table 1.1 to show the domain names for each office, and Figure 1.3 shows the widgets.home DNS tree. In Exercise 1.01, we will create our new DNS namespace in a Windows Server 2003 network.

Test Day Tip

If your exam contains questions that give you the names of several offices and/or domains and subdomains, draw them out on the piece of scrap paper provided for you. It's a lot easier to visualize an environment if you see it sketched out.

Table 1.2 Widgets Inc. Namespace

Continent	Country	City	Domain Names
North America	United States	Boston (headquarters)	boston.us.na.widgets.home
North America	United States	Chicago	chicago.us.na.widgets.home
North America	United States	Los Angeles	losangeles.us.na.widgets.home
North America	United States	Miami	miami.us.na.widgets.home
North America	United States	Phoenix	phoenix.us.na.widgets.home
North America	Canada	Quebec	quebec.ca.na.widgets.home
Europe	United Kingdom	London	london.uk.eu.widgets.home
Europe	France	Paris	paris.fr.eu.widgets.home
Europe	Germany	Frankfurt	frankfurt.gr.eu.widgets.home
Europe	Spain	Barcelona	barcelona.sp.widgets.home
Asia	Japan	Tokyo	tokyo.jp.as.widgets.home
Asia	India	New Delhi	newdelhi.in.as.widgets.home
Asia	China	Beijing	beijing.ci.as.widgets.home

Figure 1.3 Widgets Inc. DNS Namespace

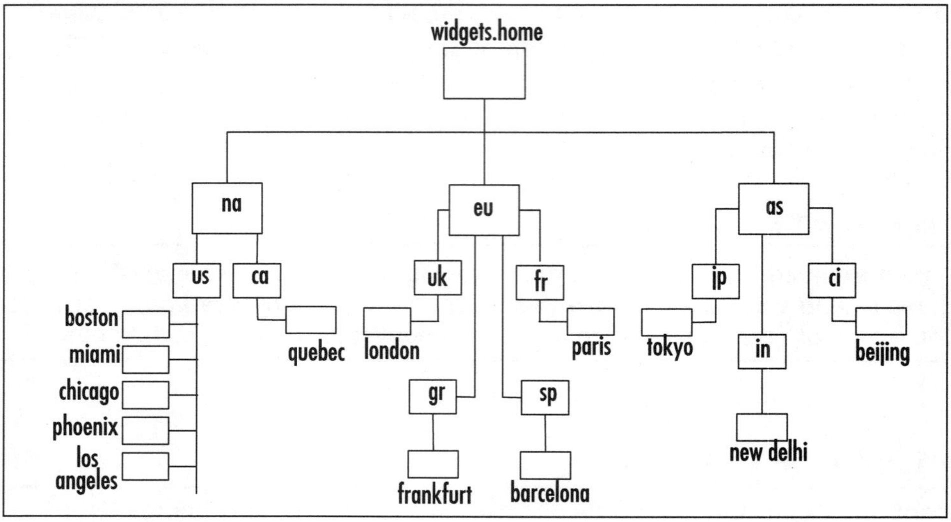

Exercise 1.01

Creating a Windows Server 2003 DNS Namespace

In this exercise, we walk through the steps for creating the Widgets Inc. parent domain. To complete this exercise, you need a PC running Windows Server 2003 Server Edition. Insert the Windows 2003 Server CD-ROM into your CD-ROM drive, and let's begin our exercise:

1. If the CD-ROM starts automatically, cancel out of the autorun by clicking the **Exit** button.
2. Click **Start | Control Panel**, and choose **Add or Remove Programs**.
3. Click the **Add/Remove Windows Components** icon.
4. Scroll down the list of components until you come to the Network Services component, and highlight it. After you highlight it, click the **Details** button.
5. In the list of Network Services Subcomponents, highlight **Domain Name System (DNS)** and then place a check in the empty check box next to it (see Figure 1.4). Next, click **OK** to continue. When the Network Subcomponents window closes, click the **Next** button. The DNS service will begin to install.

Figure 1.4 The Network Services Subcomponents Screen

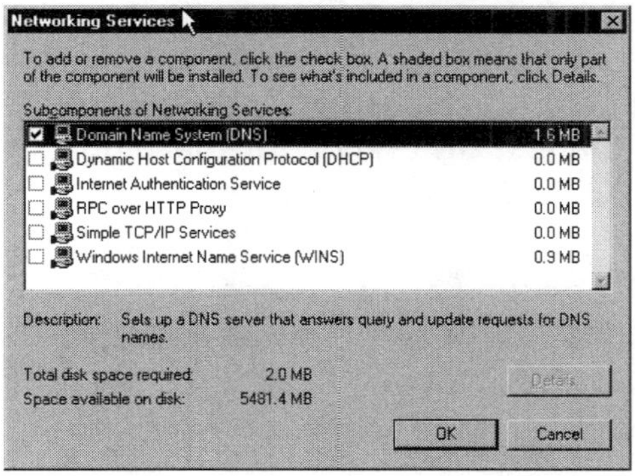

6. Click **Finish** when the install has finished.
7. Next, click the **Start** button again, and then click **Administrative Tools | DNS**.
8. If prompted to connect to a DNS server, click **This Computer** and then click **OK**. The DNS Management console will open (see Figure 1.5).

Figure 1.5 DNS Management Console

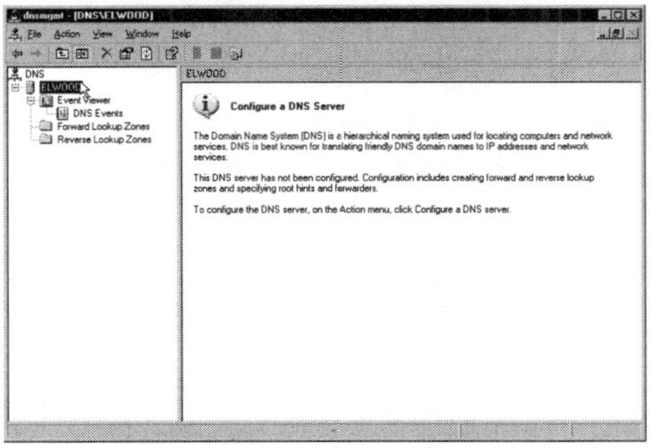

9. Right-click the server name (in this case, **Elwood**) and select **Configure a DNS server** from the context menu.
10. When the Configure a DNS Server Wizard window appears, click **Next**.
11. When prompted to select a type of server to configure, choose **Create forward and reverse lookup zones** and click **Next**.
12. When asked if you want to create a forward lookup zone now, choose **Yes, create a forward lookup zone now** and click **Next**.

13. You will be prompted to select a zone type. Choose **Primary Zone** and click **Next**. (Zone types are explained later in the chapter.)

14. When prompted for the name of the zone, enter **widgets.home**, since this will be the first DNS server for the widgets.home domain (see Figure 1.6). Click **Next** to continue.

Figure 1.6 Selecting a Zone Name

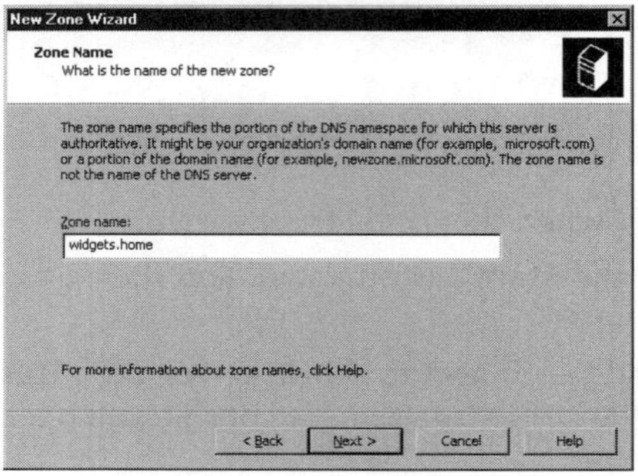

15. When prompted for the zone filename, leave the default filename (**widgets.home.dns**) and click **Next**.
16. When prompted to allow dynamic updates, leave this setting on the default of **Do not allow dynamic updates** and click **Next**. (We discuss dynamic updates and secure dynamic updates later in this chapter in our discussion of objective 2.1.4, DNS security.)
17. Select **Yes, create a reverse lookup zone** when asked if you want to create a reverse lookup zone now, and then click **Next**.
18. Again, this will be a primary zone, so click **Primary Zone** and then click **Next** when asked to select a zone type.
19. When prompted to enter a network ID, you will want to enter the first three IP octets of the subnet that this DNS zone will be used to resolve. For example, we use 192.168.0 for the first three octets (see Figure 1.7). Notice that the reverse lookup zone name is entered for you. Click **Next**.

Figure 1.7 Entering the Reverse Lookup Zone Name

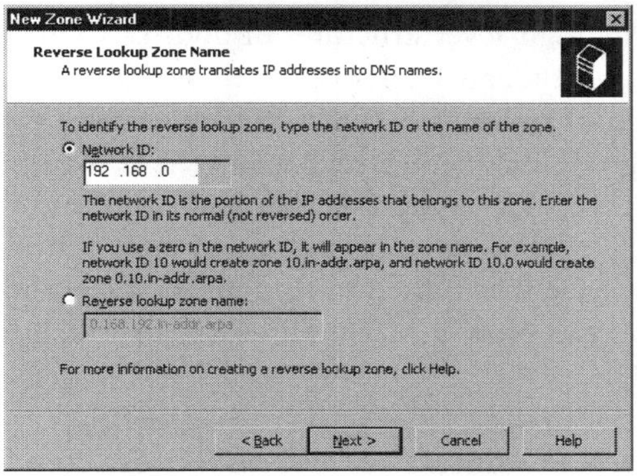

20. You will be prompted to create a reverse lookup zone file. Leave the default filename and click **Next**. The default filename should be 0.168.192.in-addr.arpa.dns if you followed our IP address schema.
21. Again, choose **Do not allow dynamic updates** and click **Next** to continue.
22. Next you will be prompted about forwarders; we discuss forwarders later in this chapter. For now, when asked if this DNS server should forward queries, select **No, it should not forward queries** and click **Next**.
23. Click **Finish** to complete the DNS zone configuration process. Your parent domain namespace has been created. We delegate the zones to the various offices later, in Exercise 1.02.

DNS Namespace and Active Directory Integration

Being a Windows 2000 MCSE, you are familiar with the integration between Active Directory and DNS. In many ways, they are very similar and appear to work as one, but they are also very different. That said, since DNS is an industry standard, it runs on several different operating systems (Windows, UNIX, Linux, etc.), and it does not require Active Directory in order to run on Windows Server 2003. However, Active Directory does need DNS to function. If you've ever run *dcpromo* on a Windows 2000 or 2003 server, you know that the installation of Active Directory searches for a DNS server that is capable of dynamic updates. If it doesn't find one, the installation will pause and ask if you would like to install and configure this server as part of your Active Directory installation, or configure a DNS server manually after the installation has completed. Active Directory is covered in greater detail in Chapters 2 and 3. In this next section, we look at the similarities and differences between DNS and Active Directory as well as how DNS integrates with Active Directory.

How DNS Integrates with Active Directory

If you were to compare the high-level structures of both DNS and Active Directory, you would see that they are almost identical. Active Directory domain names are derived from DNS names, but DNS names and Active Directory names serve two different purposes. DNS is used for resolving resource names, such as servers or workstations. If you wanted to find the IP for the Web server www.syngress.com, you could run the command-line utility *nslookup* to resolve the server name to an IP address, as shown in Figure 1.8. Active Directory is a directory service that is used to find information about a user, group, or resource. For example, you can browse Active Directory to search for users with the first name Bill (see Figure 1.9).

Figure 1.8 Resolving the IP Address for www.syngress.com

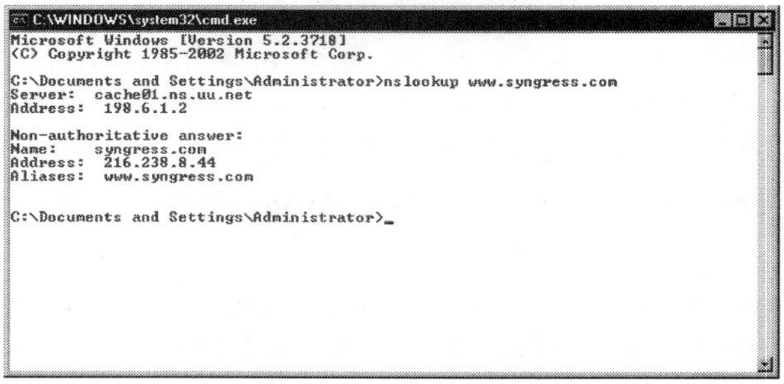

Figure 1.9 Active Directory Search Results for Users Named Bill

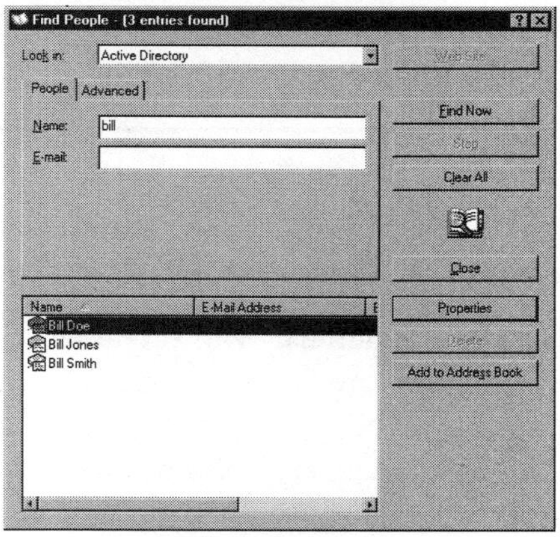

As stated previously, Active Directory relies heavily on DNS for all types of functionality, especially since they take complementary roles in the environment. For example, Active Directory uses DNS as a locator service to resolve the names and IP addresses of servers that run certain services, such as the KDC service for domain authentication. The preferred resolution method for a Windows 2000 or later computer to use when logging on to a Windows 2003 Active Directory domain is DNS, but older methods such as WINS are still supported for legacy clients to use. This is how the request for a domain controller takes place for a Windows 2000 or later client using DNS:

1. The Net Logon service running on the client collects the required logon information and sends a query to the DNS server.
2. The DNS server responds with a list of the closest domain controllers belonging to the client's domain, including the FQDN and IP address of the domain controller.
3. The client contacts the domain controllers to verify that they are online.
4. The first domain controller that responds to the client is the domain controller that will be used for the clients' logon process.
5. The Net Logon service on the client caches the information for the domain controller for the duration of the client's network session so that the location process does not need to occur again.

Exam Warning

You can expect a question on how a client requests a domain controller from the DNS server. Remember the five steps involved in the request process.

This is just one way that Active Directory and DNS interact, but as you can see, they both play very important roles in Windows Server 2003.

DNS also picks up some additional functionality through integration with Active Directory. One of the biggest advantages from the perspective of DNS is the ability to use Active Directory for the storage and replication of your DNS zones as well as the ability to process secure dynamic updates. We cover DNS zones next in our discussion of zone replication, and we talk about DNS security (objective 2.1) later in this chapter.

Benefits of Integration

We briefly discussed some of the major benefits to integrating DNS with Active Directory, but let's quickly run through some of the other advantages of integration:

- **Speed** Directory replication is much faster when DNS and Active Directory are integrated. This is because Active Directory replication is performed on a *per-property* basis, limiting the amount of data transferred to only what has changed. Additionally, when replication takes place between sites, Active Directory may use compression to further reduce traffic size.

- **Integrated management** Anytime you can reduce the number of management consoles that you have to work with, thereby reducing the amount of time needed to manage information, it is an advantage. Without integrating DNS and Active Directory, you would have to manage your Active Directory domains and DNS namespaces separately. This makes management more time-consuming and creates more opportunity for mistakes. As your network continues to grow and become more complex, managing two separate entities becomes more involved. By integrating Active Directory and DNS, you reduce your management consoles, giving you the ability to view them together as one single entity.
- **Automatic synchronization** When a new domain controller is brought online, networks that have integrated DNS and Active Directory have the advantage of automatic synchronization. Even if a domain controller will not be used to host the DNS service, the Active Directory integrated zones can still be replicated, synchronized, and stored on the new domain controllers.

Now that you have developed an implementation plan, have run through the steps of implementing your DNS namespace into your Windows Server 2003 environment in Exercise 1.01, and understand the features and benefits of DNS and Active Directory integration, let's move on to the topic of DNS zone replication.

EXAM 70-296 OBJECTIVE 2.1.2 2.1.5

Zone Replication

Before we begin discussing DNS zone replication, let's take a step back to define DNS zones. The DNS system is a collection of zone files that are spread throughout the Internet as well as private networks. Internet zone files break up the DNS namespace into smaller pieces that can be easily managed. Zones allow for the distribution of data but also for the management of localized DNS databases. By managing local DNS databases, you can manage your own zone files by defining your own zone boundaries and selecting DNS settings that will only affect your own resource records. By dividing your parent domain and subdomains into smaller zones, you improve the performance and manageability of your DNS structure.

Using our Widgets Inc. example, we can break our widgets.home parent domain and its subdomains into several zones. We could, in fact, create a separate zone for each office, making the local administrators responsible for the management of their own DNS names within these zones. Another idea is to create separate zones based on the continent on which the offices reside; however, this might not be the best idea based on communication issues. This is because if you decided to make the Paris office the managing zone file for eu.widgets.home and all its subzones, the quality and speed of communications were poor, the London, Frankfurt, and Barcelona subzones would all feel the impact. However, if the London, Frankfurt, and Barcelona offices are relatively small and without the proper IT staff, you might indeed want to make the Paris office the manager for separate DNS zone for london.uk.eu.widgets.home, frankfurt.gr.eu.widgets.home, and barcelona.sp.widgets.home. You need to decide how best to break up your DNS zones within your environment. Some things you need to take into consideration when planning DNS zones are:

- **Traffic patterns** You can use the System Monitor to get DNS server statistics and review DNS performance counters. You will also want to review client-to-server traffic to see how much of the traffic is DNS related, especially when the queries are running over WAN connections.
- **Link speed** What types of links exist between the DNS servers? Are these links running 24/7 or only at particular times of the day?
- **Caching-only versus full DNS server** If an office is a small, remote office, does it need its own server or can it use a *caching-only server*? A caching-only server is a DNS server that does not host any DNS zones but still performs name resolution and stores the results in its own cache. By default all Windows Server 2003 servers become caching-only servers when DNS is first installed.

EXERCISE 1.02

DELEGATING DNS ZONES

In Exercise 1.01, we created our parent domain namespace for Widgets Inc. In this exercise, we build on our parent domain and delegate the zones to the various Widgets offices. In Exercise 1.02, we delegate phoenix.us.na.widgets.home to the Phoenix, Arizona, office. Don't worry if you do not have a PC to use as the DNS server for the Phoenix office; you will still be able to delegate authority, even if there is no physical server to connect to. Let's begin:

1. Click **Start | Administrative Tools | DNS**.
2. If prompted to choose a DNS server to connect to, click **This Computer** and then click **OK**. The DNS Management console will open.
3. When the console opens, expand the forward lookup zones by clicking the + symbol next to **Forward Lookup Zones** and right-click **widgets.home** (see Figure 1.10).
4. From the drop-down menu, click **New Delegation.**
5. When the **Welcome to the New Delegation Wizard** opens, click **Next.**
6. Enter the domain name that will be delegated to another DNS server in the Delegated Domain text box. In our example, we use **phoenix.us.na.widgets.home** (see Figure 1.11). Click **Next** to continue.

Figure 1.10 Selecting the widgets.home Domain in the DNS Management Console

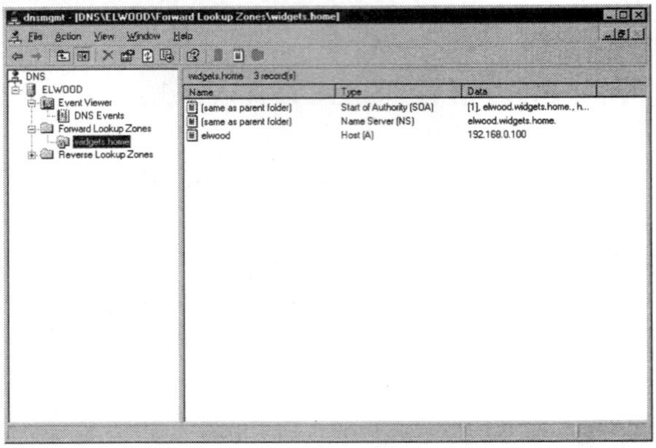

Figure 1.11 Entering a Domain Name to Delegate

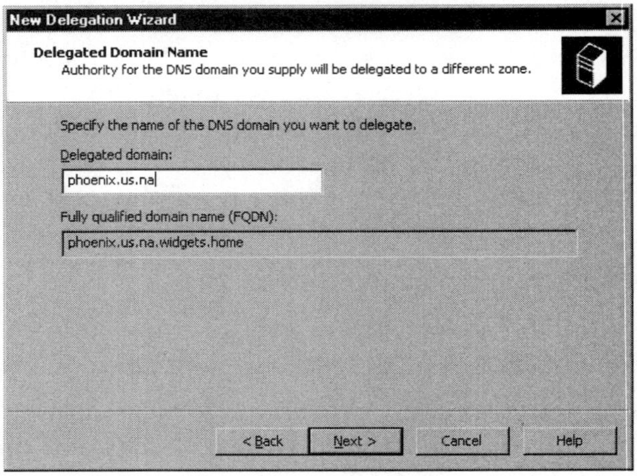

7. You now need to enter the DNS servers that will be assigned to host the zone you are delegating. Click the **Add** button on the Name Servers screen to add a DNS server.
8. Type the FQDN for the DNS server in the Phoenix office, **phxdns1.phoenix.na.us.widgets.home**.
9. Type the IP address for phxdns1; we will use **192.168.2.100** (see Figure 1.12). Click **Add** to save the IP address, and then click **OK** to exit the New Resource Record window.

Figure 1.12 Adding a Resource Record for Zone Delegation

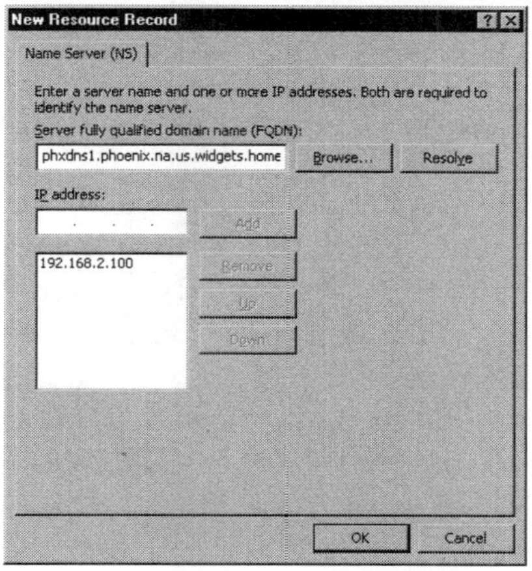

10. At this point you can add another DNS server to be delegated to, or you can click **Next**.
11. Click **Finish** to complete the zone delegation. The DNZ zone for the Phoenix office has now been delegated to the phxdns1 server.

When you return to the DNS management console, take a look at your DNS forward lookup zone tree. You will notice that you can now drill down further into the *na* and *us* subdomains. If you open the *phoenix* delagated subdomain, you will see the resource record (NS) for the DNS server in the Phoenix office that has been delegated the phoenix.na.us.widgets.home zone.

A reasonable question to ask at this point is, "Why are zone replication and zone transfer necessary?" Since DNS and DNS zones play such significant roles in the Windows Server 2003 environment, we have to provide a level of fault tolerance to our DNS services. Let's say that the Boston office for Widgets Inc. had just a single DNS server. If that server were to become unavailable for any reason, DNS queries and updates would not be possible. For this purpose, DNS zone transfers are necessary for the replication and synchronization of the resource records stored within a zone.

Transfer Types

When using Active Directory integrated zones, all zone replication takes place as part of Active Directory replication. When standard zones are in use, Windows Server 2003 uses three different modes to transfer zone information between DNS servers:

- **Full Transfer** When you bring a new DNS server online and configure it to be a secondary server for an existing zone in your environment, it will perform a full transfer of all the zone information in order to replicate all the existing resource records for that zone. Older implementations of the DNS service also used full transfers whenever updates to a DNS database needed to be propagated. Full zone transfers can be very lengthy and resource intensive, especially in situations in which there is not sufficient bandwidth between a primary and secondary DNS servers. For this reason, incremental DNS transfers were developed.

- **Incremental Transfer** When using incremental zone transfers, the secondary server retrieves only resource records that have changed within a zone so that it remains synchronized with the primary DNS server. When incremental transfers are used, the databases on the primary server and the secondary server are compared to see if any differences exist. If the zones are identified as the same (based on the serial number of the *start of authority* resource record), no zone transfer is performed. If, however, the serial number on the primary server database is higher than the serial number on the secondary server, a transfer of the delta resource records commences. Because of this configuration, incremental zone transfers require much less bandwidth and create less network traffic, allowing them to finish faster. Incremental zone transfers are often ideal for DNS servers that must communicate over low-bandwidth connections.
- **DNS Notify** The third method for transferring DNS zone records isn't actually a transfer method at all. To avoid the constant polling of primary DNS servers from secondary DNS servers, DNS Notify was developed as a networking standard (RFC 1996) and has since been implemented into the Windows operating system. DNS Notify allows a primary DNS server to utilize a "push" mechanism for notifying secondary servers that it has been updated with records that need to be replicated. Servers that are notified can then initiate a zone transfer (either full or incremental) to "pull" zone changes from their primary servers as they normally would. In a DNS Notify configuration, the IP addresses for all secondary DNS servers in a DNS configuration must be entered into the notify list of the primary DNS server (as shown in Figure 1.13) to pull, or request, zone updates.

Each of the three methods has its own purpose and functionality. How you handle zone transfers between your DNS servers depends on your individual circumstances.

Test Day Tip

Remember that full and incremental transfers actually transfer the data between the DNS servers and that DNS Notify is used to notify a secondary server that new records are available for transfer.

Figure 1.13 The Notify List on a Primary DNS Server

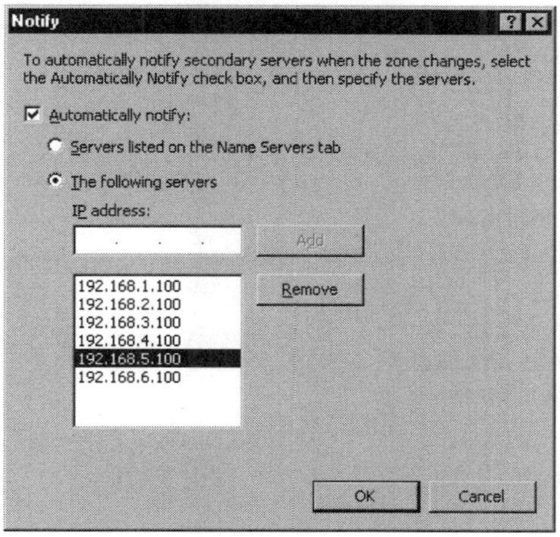

Based on the considerations we discussed for implementing zone replication and understanding the types of zone transfer types that you can use within Windows Server 2003, you should begin to see how your DNS namespace needs to be implemented in a working environment. The next logical step is to take a look at the types of zones that you can use within your Windows Server 2003 DNS environment, how they differ from one another, and why you might want to consider one type over another. At this point, let's move on to discuss the two types of non-Active Directory integrated zones, known as *standard primary* and *standard secondary* zones.

EXAM 70-296 OBJECTIVE 2.1.5

Non-Active Directory Integrated Zones

Two zone types can be used outside the Active Directory integrated world; these are known as non-Active Directory integrated zones, or *standard* zones. The first type of standard zone, *standard primary zones,* are the master servers in a zone replication scheme. DNS master servers replicate a copy of their zones to one or more servers that host *secondary zones*, thereby providing fault tolerance for your DNS servers. DNS standard zones are the types of zones you need to use if you do not plan on integrating Active Directory with your DNS servers. For example, if you wanted to isolate your DNS servers that supply name resolution for your Internet-facing hosts (such as public Web servers, e-mail servers, etc.), you might want to place these DNS servers in your demilitarized zone (DMZ). Assuming that you do not plan to implement Active Directory in your DMZ, you can configure these DNS servers as standard primary and standard secondary servers (refer back to Figure 1.8). For additional fault tolerance, you could place one of the DNS servers in one office (for example, the home office in Boston) and a second DNS server in a remote office, as shown in Figure 1.14.

Figure 1.14 Using Multiple DNS Servers in Remote Offices

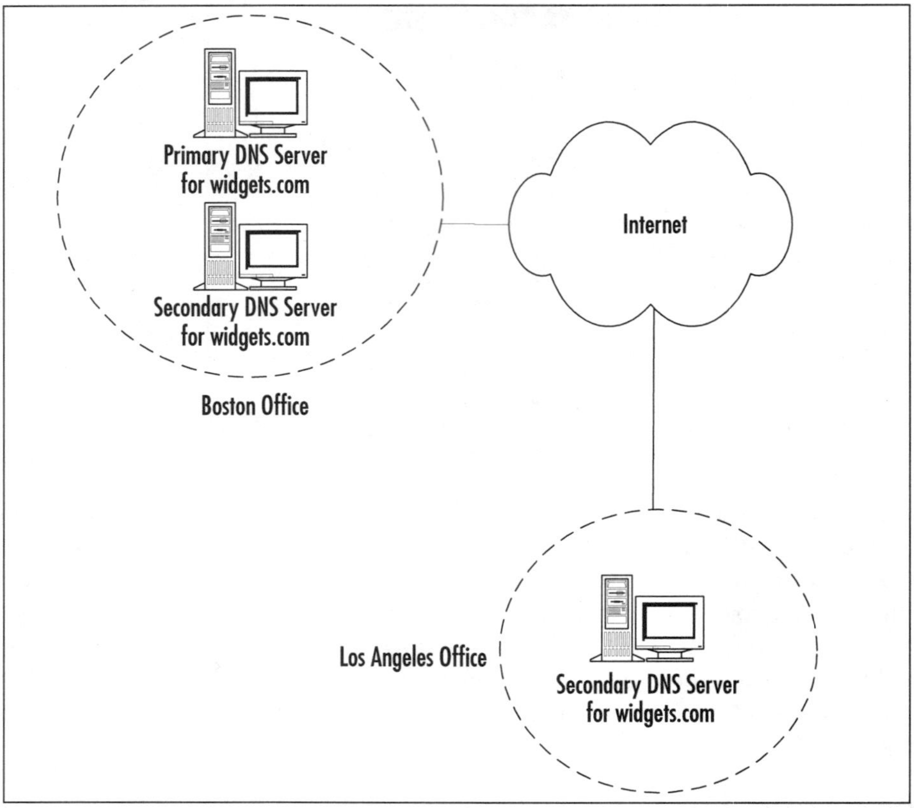

Head of the Class...

Using Multiple DNS Servers in Multiple Locations

Keeping secondary zones on DNS servers that are physically remote from their primary servers is, quite often, a lifesaver. On one occasion, I was working for a company that was moving our office into a new building. We had already set up a new DNS server at the new office as well as having set up all the cabling, connectivity, and other preparations necessary to move all the servers and network infrastructure to the new office. A few days before the move, we notified our domain name registrar of our new DNS server address. However, rather than moving all our DNS servers over to the new office, we left one at our old building while the move was occurring. We also kept the secondary DNS record at our domain name registrar the same, pointing to the remaining DNS server at our old office—and it's a good thing we did. As we were bringing servers online in the new office, we realized that we had forgotten one key element: sufficient electricity. As we kept bringing servers

Continued

online, we kept popping circuit breakers. Eventually, we had to make the decision to only bring "critical" systems online until we could get an electrician in to give us additional power outlets. Because we left the record for the secondary server unchanged with our domain name registrar, we were able to shut down the DNS server at our new office while still providing DNS name resolution. I learned two things from this experience: First, It's always a good idea to have a secondary DNS server offsite. Second, always check to make sure you have sufficient electricity before moving into a new office building.

Exercise 1.03

Replicating Primary and Secondary Zones

In Exercise 1.03, we set up replication for the boston.us.na.widgets.home zone to secondary servers within the Boston, Massachusetts, office. We will look at the configuration changes for both the primary server and the secondary server. In order to complete this exercise, you need two physically separate computers running Windows Server 2003 with DNS installed. If you do not have the resources available to complete this exercise, you can still follow along by completing most of the steps in the exercise, but you will not be able to replicate the zone files. In addition, note that you can follow these same steps to transfer a reverse lookup zone. First, let's take a look at the changes for the primary server:

1. To begin, click **Start | Administrative Tools | DNS**.
2. If prompted to choose a DNS server to connect to, click **This Computer** and then click **OK**. The DNS Management console will open.
3. The first step is to create resource records for the secondary DNS server. First, we will create a new A record for the secondary servers. Click **Action** from the DNS management console, and select **New Host (A).**
4. In the New Host window, enter the name of the secondary server; we use **bosdns02**.
5. Enter the IP address for bosdns2; we use **192.168.0.101**. You can also create an associated pointer record (PTR) if you have created a reverse lookup zone for the Boston zone. Click the **Add Host** button when you are done. Notice the new resource record in boston.us.na.widgets.home for the bosdns2 server.
6. Next, we need to create an NS resource record for the bosdns2 server. To do this, right-click the **boston.us.na.widgets.home forward lookup zone**, and click **Properties**. When the properties window opens, click the **Name Servers tab** (see Figure 1.15).

Figure 1.15 The Name Servers Tab

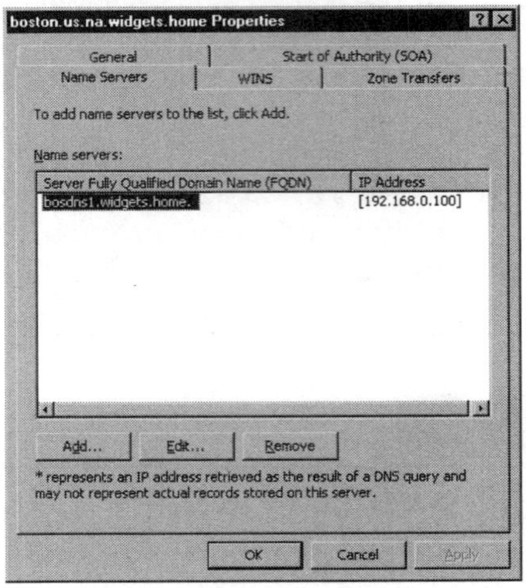

7. Click the **Add...** button to add a name server to the list.
8. Type the FQDN (**bosdns2.boston.us.na.widgets.home**), then click the **Resolve** button to resolve the IP address (192.168.0.101) for the bosdns2 server, and click **OK**.
9. Notice that a new NS record has been created in the boston.us.na.widgets.home zone.
10. Reopen the zone properties for the zone, and click the **Zone Transfers tab**.
11. Notice that **Allow zone transfers** is checked and is configured to allow only the name servers listed on the Name Servers tab (see Figure 1.16). Alternatively, you could select **Only to the following servers** and enter the IP addresses for the DNS servers you want to allow for zone transfers. Since we will be using the name servers listed in the Name Servers tab, you can just click **OK** or **Cancel** to exit the Properties screen.

The primary server is now configured and ready to accept zone transfer requests from secondary servers. Next, we need to configure our secondary server, bosdns2.

Figure 1.16 The Zone Transfers Tab

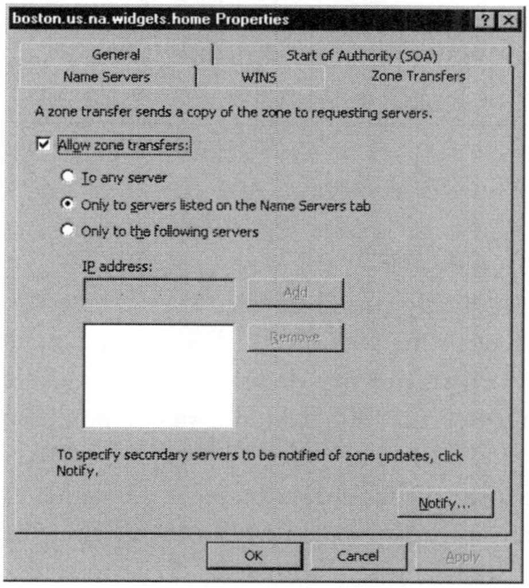

1. Open the DNS management console on bosdns2, and click **Action**. Select **New Zone** from the drop-down list.
2. At the Welcome to the New Zone Wizard screen, click **Next**.
3. Type the **boston.us.na.widgets.home** when asked for the name of the zone, and click **Next**.
4. In the Master DNS Servers window, enter the IP address of the primary server for the boston.us.na.widgets.home zone, and click **Add**. In this case, the IP address is 192.168.0.100 (see Figure 1.17). Click **Next**.
5. To complete the secondary zone wizard, click **Finish**.

Figure 1.17 The Master DNS Properties Window

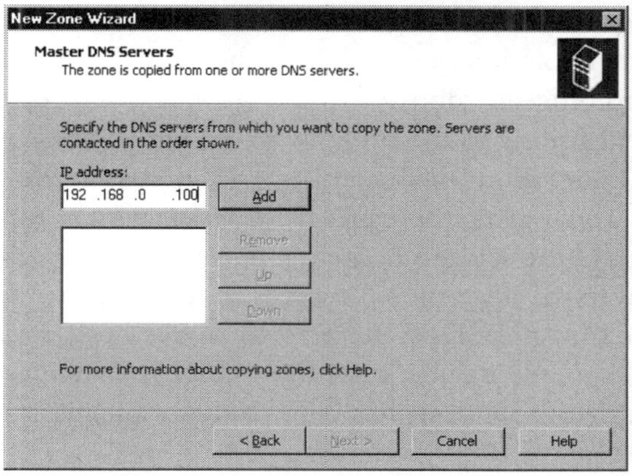

You need to wait a few moments for the zones to replicate. Once the zones have replicated, you can check the data in the boston.us.na.widgets.home zone to see if all the records have replicated properly. As an additional test, you can go back to the bosdns1 server and create a new record to see if it transfers.

Configuring Stub Zones

Centralized management is typically the preferred way to ease the administrative burden. However, it can be helpful from time to time to delegate authority to others while still retaining overall authority. With this in mind, Microsoft has developed a third type of DNS zone that is new in Windows Server 2003, called a *stub zone*. A stub zone contains only certain resource records that are required in order to locate the DNS server that is authoritative for a particular zone. Using stub zones, enterprise administrators have the ability to delegate child zones to other administrators in remote offices while still keeping overall authority of the parent zones. Stub zones consist of three records:

- An SOA record
- An NS record
- A special type of A record, known as a *glue A resource record*

The glue A resource record is used for locating the authoritative DNS servers for a delegated zone and is used to "glue" zones together to create a more effective referral path for name resolution. Stub zones are used not only to improve name resolution but also to simplify DNS administration.

For example, we know that Widgets Inc. is planning to delegate each subdomain for its company to DNS servers in the respective field offices. However, administrators in each office have complete control over their servers and can typically make network changes without the Boston HQ staff's approval. The Chicago office has experienced incredible growth over the past six months and has added several new employees. The DNS server that is currently functioning in the Chicago office is becoming overburdened and needs a secondary server to offload some of the name resolution queries. When the second DNS server is brought online, queries from the Chicago office are directed to the secondary server, but all requests from the other offices are going exclusively to the primary server. This is because the parent domain for widgets.home does not know about the secondary DNS server in the Chicago office. By configuring the widgets.home parent domain's DNS server with a stub zone for chicago.us.na.widgets.home, the widgets.home server can query the master server at the Chicago office for discovery of any new NS records for authoritative servers that exist in the Chicago zone. Using the stub zone, DNS administration overhead is reduced because the administrator at the Chicago office doesn't need to inform the administrator of the Boston HQ office of new authoritative DNS servers being brought online.

Another type of DNS zone transfer that you must consider, outside Windows DNS standard zones and stub zones, is the integration of Windows DNS zones with third-party DNS solutions such as Berkeley Internet Name Domain, or BIND. One of the objectives of the 70-296 exam is to examine the interoperability for DNS with third-party DNS solutions, so let's take a look at how Windows Server 2003 zones (standard and Active Directory integrated) work with third-party solutions.

EXAM WARNING

Expect a trick question on the exam about stub zones. The exam might present a scenario in which both stub zones and conditional forwarders are possible answers. Remember that with a stub zone, certain records exist on the DNS server hosting the stub zone, whereas a conditional forwarder is used to forward DNS resolutions to specific DNS servers based on domain name.

EXAM 70-296 OBJECTIVE 2.1.5

Using Windows DNS with Third-Party DNS Solutions

BIND is arguably the most widely implemented DNS solution in use today. It is a DNS software package that runs on the *nix (UNIX, Linux, etc.) operating systems that has been implemented in many corporations for quite some time. Although BIND can support basic DNS functionality (such as primary and secondary DNS zone transfers), in some cases it cannot handle Active Directory. This is because older versions of BIND (as well as other third-party DNS solutions) do not offer support for service location (SRV) resource records or Dynamic DNS. If you want to continue using BIND in your Windows Server 2003 environment, you have to upgrade to BIND version 8.1.2 or later in order to support the additional requirements of Active Directory Integrated DNS. If you do not plan on supporting Active Directory integrated zones, Microsoft has certified that Windows Server 2003 DNS will interoperate with the following versions of BIND:

- BIND 4.9.7
- BIND 8.1.2
- BIND 8.2
- BIND 9.1.0

If you plan to use Windows DNS along with an existing third-party DNS server implementation that does not support Active Directory, Microsoft has come up with two solutions for designing your DNS namespace: creating a new single subdomain as your Active Directory root or creating multiple subdomains and zones for Active Directory.

EXAM WARNING

Remember that for a Windows Server 2003 Active Directory integrated DNS server to replicate with a BIND server, it must be version 8.1.2. or higher.

Creating a Single Subdomain

You can create a new single subdomain in your existing DNS implementation that will serve as the root for your Active Directory domain. For example, if widgets.home were already implemented within the Widgets Inc. network environment using a BIND DNS server, you could create a subdomain called ad.widgets.home and delegate authority for ad.widgets.home to the Windows Server 2003 server running DNS for your environment. Using this method, you can still manage the parent domain of widgets.home with the BIND server while offering Active Directory integrated DNS zones for your Windows.

Creating Multiple Subdomains

When you create a single subdomain in an existing third-party DNS hierarchy, all the Active Directory integrated zones fall below the single subdomain in a "tree" configuration. Alternatively, you can create multiple subdomains for Active Directory integrated zones directly off the parent domain. For example, if widgets.home was the parent domain and was being served by BIND, you could create multiple domains and delegate the authority of these subdomains to your Windows Server 2003 servers. This is similar to the single subdomain configuration, except that it is more a "flat" configuration than a hierarchy.

Now that we've discussed how Windows Server 2003 can interact with other third-party DNS packages, let's begin our discussion of Active Directory integrated zones and how they work.

Active Directory Integrated Zones

In our earlier discussion about namespace planning and Active Directory integration, we compared and contrasted Active Directory and DNS. We saw how the two work in conjunction in a Windows Server 2003 domain, and we noted the advantages of having an Active Directory integrated zone. In this section, we discuss how zones are replicated when Active Directory and DNS are combined, storing zones, and replication scopes, and we walk through configuring DNS integration with Active Directory. Before we attempt to integrate DNS with Active Directory, let's talk about how DNS zones are stored in an integrated zone.

Zone Storage

In a standard zone configuration, DNS zones are stored in the c:\windows\system32\dns folder inside a .dns file. Each .dns zone file corresponds to a zone that is stored on a particular DNS server. For example, the zone file for the Beijing office of Widgets Inc would be beijing.ci.as.widgets.home.dns.

Active Directory integrated zones, on the other hand, store their zone data in the Active Directory tree under the domain or application directory partition. Each zone is stored in a container object known as a *dnsZone* container, which is identified by the name of the zone that has been created. In an integrated zone configuration, only primary zones can be stored within Active Directory. If your DNS server is going to host a secondary zone, it will continue to store the primary Active Directory integrated zone in a dnsZone container within Active Directory, but any secondary zones will be stored in standard text files. This occurs due to the *multimaster replication model* of Active Directory, which removes the need for secondary zones when all zones are stored in Active Directory. In the multimaster replication model, any authoritative DNS server can be designated a primary source for a DNS zone. Because the zone file is stored in the Active Directory database, any DNS server that is also a domain controller can update it. Since any domain controller can update the master DNS database within Active Directory, there is no need to create a secondary DNS zone for Active Directory integrated zones. This is also a good time to mention the fact that the DNS Notify feature in Windows Server 2003 does not apply to Active Directory integrated DNS zones, simply because there will never be a secondary DNS server for a primary DNS server to notify.

TEST DAY TIP

Don't get confused about zone storage. If you get a question that relates to zone storage of Active Directory zones, remember that Active Directory integrated zones are always stored in dnsZone containers within Active Directory. However, a server that contains an Active Directory integrated zone can still host a standard primary or secondary zone; these zone files will be stored in c:\windows\system32\dns, even though the Active Directory integrated zones are stored in Active Directory.

In our earlier discussion about DNS namespaces, we mentioned that the three major advantages to integration are speed, integrated management, and automated synchronization. Each of these three advantages is realized due to the way DNS is stored within the Active Directory structure. A fourth advantage, which we discuss in the DNS security section, is the ability to have secure dynamic updates in your environment. All these features exist simply due to the way DNS is stored in Active Directory in an integrated configuration.

Let's take a moment here to stop and integrate DNS into Active Directory. You might want to bookmark this exercise and come back to it after reading Chapters 2 and 3. If not, let's begin Exercise 1.04, integrating DNS with Active Directory.

Exercise 1.04

Integrating DNS with Active Directory

In this exercise, we integrate the boston.us.na.widgets.home domain into Active Directory. This exercise requires you to install Active Directory onto your server. As mentioned, you might want to wait until after you read Chapters 2 and 3 to perform this exercise. If not, you can run *dcpromo* from a command prompt and follow the defaults.

In this example, let's assume that the widgets.home parent domain is hosted in the Boston headquarters and the Elwood DNS server supports name resolution for widgets.home and boston.us.na.widgets.home in order to save resources for the company. Do the following:

1. Open the DNS management console on your DNS server—in our case, **Elwood**—and click **Action**.
2. Select **New Zone** from the drop-down list, and click **Next** at the Welcome to the New Zone Wizard window.
3. Select **Primary Zone**. Notice that the **Store the zone in Active Directory** check box is no longer grayed out (see Figure 1.18). However, remove the check from the check box for the purposes of this exercise and then click **Next**.

Figure 1.18 The Zone Type Configuration Window

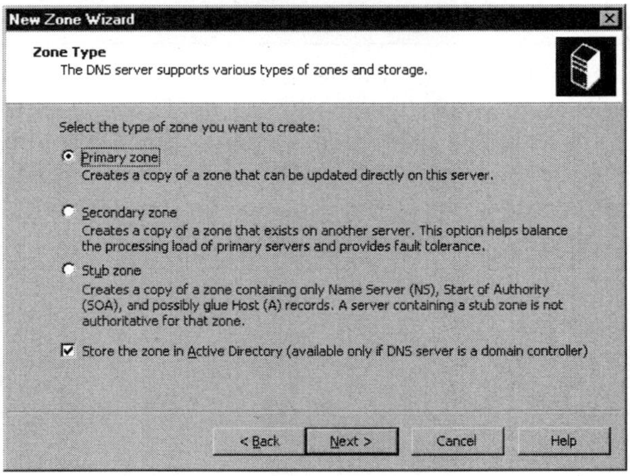

4. Select **Forward Lookup Zone** from the zone type window and click **Next**. (You could also complete this exercise using reverse lookup zones.)

5. Enter **boston.us.na.widgets.home** for the zone name, and click **Next**.
6. Use the default zone file, and click **Next**.
7. Click **Next** at the dynamic updates window.
8. Click **Finish** to finish the creation of the zone.

We have just created a standard primary forward zone for the Boston office of Widgets Inc. We've done this several times before. However, this time we're creating it on a server with Active Directory installed. Imagine that you had been using a BIND secondary server for the Boston office that was running an older version of BIND. You decided to upgrade your BIND server to 8.1.2 to support Active Directory integrated zones, and now you can make the boston.us.na. widgets.home zone an Active Directory integrated zone. Let's convert the zone to being stored within Active Directory:

1. Open the DNS Management console.
2. Right-click the **boston.us.na.widgets.home** zone, and click **Properties**.
3. In the **General** tab, notice that the zone type shows up as *Primary* (see Figure 1.19).

Figure 1.19 The General Tab

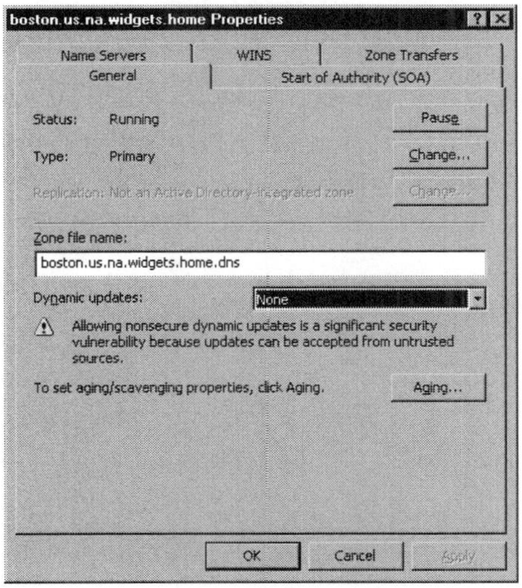

4. Click the **Change** button directly across from the Type field.
5. Place a check in the **Store the zone in Active Directory** check box, and click **OK**. You will be prompted to verify that you want to convert the zone to an Active Directory integrated zone, as shown in Figure 1.20. Click **Yes**.

Figure 1.20 DNS Zone Change Verification Window

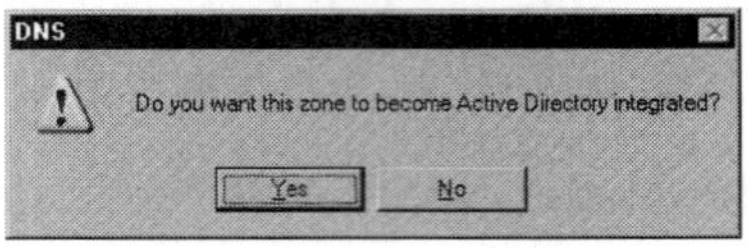

6. Notice that the Type field in the General properties tab has now changed from Primary to Active Directory Integrated.

Scopes

Depending on your enterprise configuration, you need to decide on a scope for replication when you use Active Directory integrated zones. Microsoft has four replication scenarios that you can use within an Active Directory integrated configuration.

- DNS servers within an Active Directory domain
- DNS servers within an Active Directory forest
- Domain controllers within an Active Directory domain
- Domain controllers within an application directory partition

The biggest factor in choosing a scope to use in your environment comes down to one thing: bandwidth. Certain scopes require greater bandwidth capacities in order to complete the replication process; others might only affect local LAN traffic. Let's begin our discussion of scopes with the default, *All DNS servers in the Active Directory domain.*

Configuring All DNS Servers within an Active Directory Domain

In the configuration of all DNS servers in an Active Directory domain, DNS zones are replicated to all DNS servers running on domain controllers in the Active Directory domain. For example, if the Chicago office staff of Widgets Inc. wanted to replicate all DNS zone information to all Windows Server 2003 DNS servers within its local domain (chicago.us.na.widgets.home), they would select this replication scope. As mentioned, this is the default scope for Windows Server 2003 DNS servers and would not require change in this scenario.

Configuring DNS Servers within an Active Directory Forest

In configuring DNS servers in an Active Directory forest, DNS zone information is replicated to all DNS servers running on domain controllers in the Active Directory forest. Using our Chicago office example, the DNS zone would in fact be replicated to *all* the DNS servers throughout the widgets.home hierarchy. Although this method can be very useful for fault tolerance and speed of name resolution, you definitely need to take bandwidth into consideration before making this change.

Configuring Domain Controllers within an Active Directory Domain

Essentially, configuring domain controllers in an Active Directory domain is the same as configuring DNS servers within an Active Directory Domain, except that this scope allows replication to Windows 2000 DNS servers as well. If you plan to keep active DNS servers within your Windows Server 2003 enterprise, you need to select this scope.

Configuring Domain Controllers within an Application Directory Partition

In configuring domain controllers in an application directory partition, DNS zone information that is stored within an application directory partition is replicated based on the replication scope of the application directory partition. For a zone to be stored in the specified application directory partition, the DNS server hosting the zone must be enlisted in the specified application directory partition. Application directory partitions are covered in Chapter 2.

EXAM WARNING

Remember the four scopes and where they are to be used within an environment. If you get a question that mentions Windows 2000, the correct answer will always be *domain controllers within an Active Directory domain*.

EXERCISE 1.05

CHANGING REPLICATION SCOPE

In this exercise, we change the replication scope from all DNS servers in an Active Directory domain to domain controllers within an Active Directory domain on the Elwood server. The Elwood server must be able to replicate with Windows 2000 DNS servers while the rest of the company is being converted from Windows 2000 to Windows Server 2003. Do the following:

1. Open the DNS management console on your DNS server—in our case, **Elwood**.
2. Right-click the **widgets.home** zone, and click **Properties**.
3. On the **General** tab, notice that the replication type is *All DNS servers in the Active Directory domain* (see Figure 1.21). Click the **Change** button directly across from the replication type.

Figure 1.21 The General Tab of the widgets.home Zone

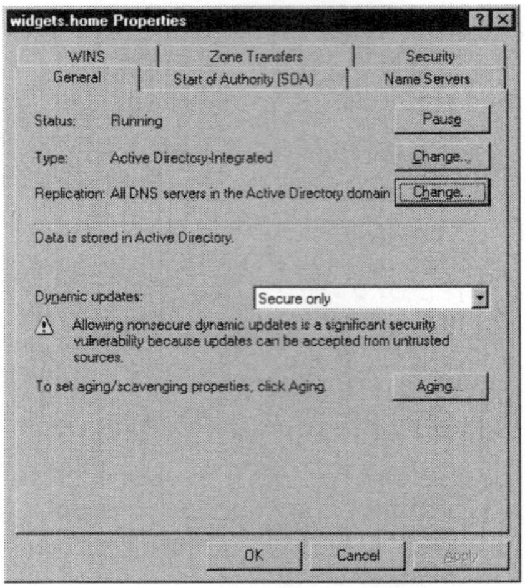

4. In the Change Zone Replication Settings window, select **To all domain controllers in the Active Directory domain widgets.home** (see Figure 1.22), and click **OK**.

Figure 1.22 The Change Zone Replication Settings Window

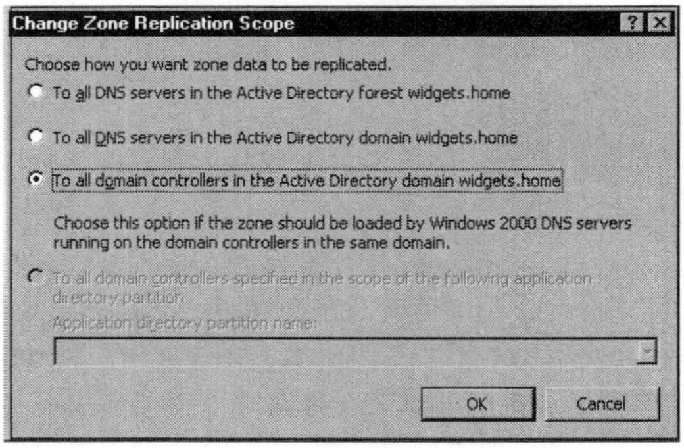

5. Notice that the replication setting on the General tab has changed to **All domain controllers in the Active Directory domain**.

EXAM 70-296 OBJECTIVE 2.1.3

DNS Forwarding

In many cases, reducing the amount of contact that your internal servers have with external entities (such as the Internet) is a good idea. This is true not only from a network security standpoint but also from a network and Internet bandwidth perspective. In the case of DNS name resolution, using *DNS forwarders* adds security and reduces the amount of traffic passing from your internal network to the outside world.

A DNS forwarder acts as a *proxy server* by accepting all queries forwarded from internal DNS servers that cannot be resolved internally and resolves them on behalf of the internal DNS server. In this section, we review the concept of DNS forwarders, discuss how they can be used, and look at how to configure a DNS forwarder using Windows Server 2003 DNS. We also discuss a new concept of DNS forwarding in Windows Server 2003, known as *conditional forwarders.* Let's begin now with an overview of how forwarders work within a network environment.

Understanding Forwarders

The simplest definition of a forwarder is a DNS server that is configured to forward DNS queries for external DNS resources (such as Internet Web sites) to DNS servers outside that DNS server zone. A DNS server becomes a forwarder by configuring the internal DNS servers in a network to forward to the DNS forwarder any queries that they cannot resolve themselves. DNS servers that do not have DNS forwarders configured send queries outside the network to untrusted, external servers using their root hints. Allowing your internal DNS servers to function with this forwarder configuration creates a large amount of network traffic that can bog down Internet and WAN bandwidth and is a security hazard because it exposes your internal DNS servers to the outside world.

TEST DAY TIP

Remember that a DNS forwarder is a server that is used to resolve queries for resources that exist outside the client's domain.

In a typical configuration, DNS forwarders sit on the outside of your firewall, typically in a DMZ. DNS traffic is limited on the firewall so that it can only pass to and from the internal DNS servers and the DNS forwarder in the DMZ. By allowing the DNS traffic to pass only between the internal DNS servers and DNS forwarder outside of your firewall, you are keeping would-be hackers from gaining critical network information from your DNS server. We'll further discuss the security aspects of DNS later in this chapter under objective 2.1.4, DNS security. At this point, let's discuss exactly how forwarders behave when DNS queries have been forwarded to them.

Forwarder Behavior

Three components play a part in DNS resolution using DNS forwarders:

- DNS client(s)
- Internal DNS server(s)
- External DNS forwarder server(s)

For DNS forwarders to be used properly, DNS clients must be first configured to point to the internal DNS servers for *all* DNS traffic, both internal and external to their network. When a client makes a request to the internal DNS server, the server will attempt to resolve the request internally. If the internal DNS server cannot resolve the IP address, it will forward a *recursive query* to the first DNS forwarder that has been designated in its forwarders list. Unlike a simple (iterative) query, in which a name server provides the best response based on what the server knows from its on zone files or caching, a recursive query forces the DNS server to take the workload of the query from the client by requesting further information from other DNS servers in order to complete the query request.

The internal DNS server waits for a response from the first forwarder, and if no response is received, it continues down its list of DNS forwarders until a response is received from a forwarder.

A forwarder builds up a large cache of external DNS information because all the external DNS queries in the network are resolved through it. In a short amount of time, a forwarder will resolve a good portion of external DNS queries using this cached data and thereby decrease the Internet traffic over the network and the response time for DNS clients. When the internal DNS server receives the response from the forwarder, it returns a nonauthoritative answer to the client who made the initial request.

Exercise 1.06

Configuring Windows Server 2003 Servers for Forwarding

Widgets Inc. has a DNS server, Jake, outside its firewall for all name resolution of the company's Internet-accessible servers, which are part of the widgets.com domain. In order to resolve all Internet DNS names, the Elwood server must forward external queries to the Jake server. In this exercise, we configure the Elwood server to use forwarders to forward the external queries:

1. Open the DNS management console on the Elwood server.
2. Right-click the **Elwood** server, and click **Properties**.
3. Click the **Forwarders** tab in the Elwood Properties window.
4. Select **All other DNS domains** in the DNS Domain window (see Figure 1.23); this will likely be the only choice.

Figure 1.23 The Forwarders Tab of the Elwood Server Properties Window

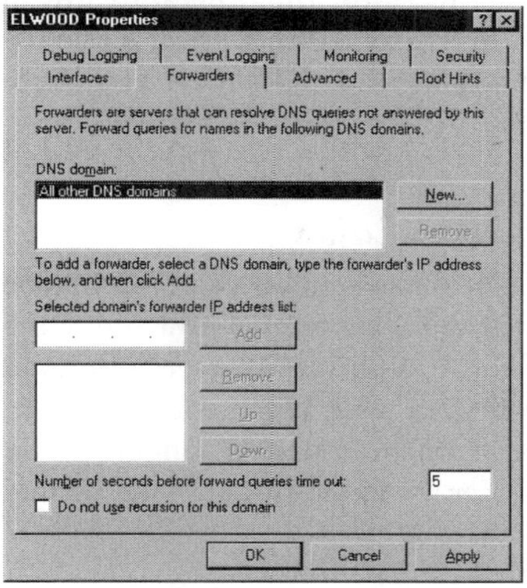

5. Enter the IP address of an external DNS server in the selected domain's forwarder IP address list. The IP address for the Jake server in this exercise is **10.0.0.1**. Click the **Add** button to add the IP address to the forwarder list. Click **OK** to save your changes. Your forwarder is now complete!

Conditional Forwarders

A new feature in Windows Server 2003 DNS is the ability to use *conditional forwarders*. Conditional forwarders can be configured on Windows Server 2003 DNS servers to forward DNS queries based on specific domain names. With conditional forwarders, a DNS server can forward queries to specific DNS servers based on the specific domain names that are being requested within the queries instead of having the DNS servers follow the typical resolution path all the way to the root domain. Conditional forwarders improve upon regular forwarding by adding a name-based condition to the forwarding process.

When a DNS client sends a query to a DNS server, the DNS server looks at its own database to see if the query can be resolved using its own zone data. If the DNS server is configured to forward for the domain name designated in the query, the query is forwarded to the IP address of the DNS forwarder that is associated with that domain name. If the DNS server has no forwarder listed for the name designated in the query, it attempts to resolve the query using standard recursion. You can use conditional forwarders to enhance and improve upon both internal and external name resolution. Let's take a look at how conditional forwarders can be used in either situation.

TEST DAY TIP

Remember that a conditional forwarder only forwards queries for a specific domain that is defined in the forwarders list. If a conditional forwarder does not exist, the query will be send to the default forwarder.

Understanding Intranet Resolution

Let's say that the Miami office of Widgets Inc. is constantly in communication with the Quebec office. Rather than always having to query the root servers of widgets.home, a conditional forwarder can be configured to forward all queries for quebec.ca.na.widgets.home to the authoritative DNS server for that zone. Using conditional forwarders in this scenario cuts unnecessary necessary network traffic to the widgets.home root server, especially considering that the widgets.home root server sits in the Boston headquarters.

Understanding Internet Resolution

The same advantages to using conditional forwards in your intranet exist in Internet resolution using conditional forwarders. Let's say that Widgets Inc. uses Worldwide Distribution Inc. as the main distributor of its product worldwide. Employees at Widgets Inc. constantly use Internet servers at Worldwide Distribution to manage product distribution, order fulfillment, and other business-related needs. Rather than having to contact the Internet root servers for resolution of the servers at worldwide-distribution.com, the internal DNS servers at Widgets Inc. can directly contact the DNS servers at Worldwide Distribution.

EXERCISE 1.07

CONFIGURING CONDITIONAL FORWARDING FOR INTERNET RESOLUTION

In this exercise, let's use our example of Widgets' partnership with Worldwide Distribution Inc. You need to set up your DNS servers to forward DNS name resolution for Worldwide Distribution resources directly to the Worldwide DNS servers. Worldwide Distribution has three DNS servers:

- dns1.worldwide-distribution.com (172.16.1.1)
- dns2.worldwide-distribution.com (172.16.1.2)
- dns3.worldwide-distribution.com

In this exercise, we point the Elwood server directly to the three servers at Worldwide Distribution:

1. Open the DNS management console on the Elwood server.
2. Right-click the **Elwood** server, and click **Properties**.
3. Click the **Forwarders** tab in the Elwood Properties window.
4. Click the **New** button in the DNS Domain window (shown previously in Figure 1.23).
5. Enter the name of the domain for Worldwide Distribution, **worldwide-distribution.com** (see Figure 1.24) and click **OK**.

Figure 1.24 The DNS Domain Name for a Conditional Forwarder

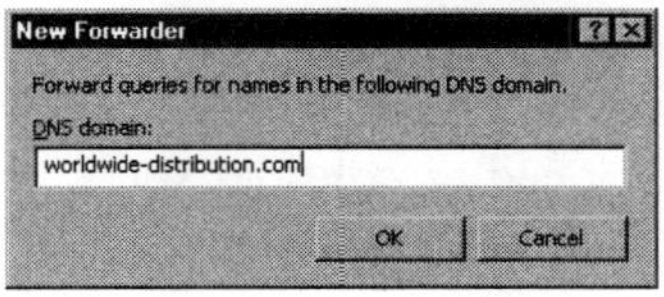

6. Notice that the worldwide-distribution.com domain has been added to the DNS domain list. Highlight the **worldwide-distribution.com** domain.
7. Type the IP addresses—**172.16.1.1**, **172.16.1.2**, and **172.16.1.3**—for the three DNS servers for worldwide-distribution into the selected domain's forwarder IP address list.
8. Click **OK** to activate your conditional forwarder for Worldwide Distribution.

Forward-Only Servers

Another way that a DNS server can be configured is to not perform recursion should forwarders fail to resolve a query request. In a regular DNS configuration that is set to use forwarders, the DNS server attempts to resolve the query using standard recursion should a forwarder fail to resolve a request. With forward-only servers, the server does not attempt any further recursive queries to resolve the name. Instead, if the DNS server does not receive a successful response from a forwarder, it fails the query. If all forwarders for a name in the query do not respond to a forward-only DNS server, that DNS server will not attempt recursion.

Forward-only servers can be used in a situation in which security requirements are high and DNS resolution should only occur on either a local DNS server or the predefined forwarders. For example, say that Widgets Inc. has a highly secured data center that has both physical and logical access restrictions in place. Clients and servers inside the data center need to be able to resolve DNS names within their data centers via their internal DNS servers as well as specific hosts outside the data centers. The administrator can configure the DNS server in the data center as a forward-only server so that it will forward any external lookups to a specified Widgets Inc. DNS server outside the data center. If that external DNS server is unable to successfully respond to the query, the DNS server in the data center will fail the request and the client in the data center will not be able to resolve the name or IP address.

Directing Queries Through Forwarders

In planning your DNS namespace, you will encounter situations in which you might need to use any of the types of forwarders that we discussed. The way you configure your forwarders within your environment will affect how well queries are answered. If your forwarding scheme is poorly designed, it will affect your ability to properly direct and resolve these queries. For this reason, you need to consider some issues prior to implementing forwarders into your environment:

- **Keep it simple** Implement only as many forwarders as necessary for optimum resolution performance. If possible, don't overload internal DNS servers with dozens of DNS forwarders. Keep in mind that every time a DNS server attempts to process a query, it first attempts to resolve it locally, and then it forwards it sequentially through its list of known DNS forwarders. This creates additional overhead by using system resources to complete the query request.
- **Balance is key** One common mistake in using DNS forwarders is pointing multiple internal DNS to a single, external DNS forwarder. This practice simply creates a bottleneck within your environment. To keep a DNS forwarder from becoming a bottle neck—and a single point of failure—consider creating more than one DNS forwarder and load-balance your forwarding traffic.
- **No "chains of love"** Unless it is completely unavoidable, do not chain your DNS servers together in a forwarding configuration. In other words, if you are configuring your internal DNS servers to forward requests for www.widgets.com to server X, do not configure server X to forward requests for www.widgets.com to server Y, and so on. Doing so will just create additional overhead and increase the amount of time it takes to resolve a query.
- **Know your forwarders** In our discussion of conditional forwarders, we mentioned how they could be used for Internet resolution outside your environment. If you plan to use conditional forwarders in this manner, make sure that you know where these forwarders are and who is managing them. For example, make sure that company XYZ isn't using a third-party DNS hosting company (like www.mydns.com) to host their DNS names. These servers can potentially be anywhere in the world and run by any number of people.

- **Remember the big picture** Keep your entire infrastructure in mind when you are configuring a forwarding scenario. In our Widgets Inc. example, it wouldn't make sense to forward requests from the London office to the Boston office, considering that the query would have to "cross the pond" from England to the United States. Since there are many network "hops" between England and the United States, this would be inefficient. Examine your network bandwidth prior to implementing DNS forwarders, and even when sufficient bandwidth exists, try to keep your DNS forwarders in the same physical location as your internal DNS servers.

By following these simple guidelines, you will make client query requests much more streamlined and avoid creating administration nightmares for yourself.

EXAM 70-296 OBJECTIVE 2.1.4

DNS Security

Whenever you expose your system to the outside world, you are leaving your environment open to attacks by hackers. To an attacker, a DNS server is just as fair game as a Web server, a mail server, or any other server that is accessible to the outside world. To take it a step further, we all know very well that attackers do not await us only on the Internet. Chances are that probably at least one employee in your organization is unhappy with his or her position, the company, or life in general. Since information is readily available on the Internet on how to perform all different types of network-based attacks, it doesn't take an elite computer guru to figure out how to bring down your network.

Whether you're dealing with attackers on the Internet, attackers on your internal network, or—most likely—both, Microsoft has made some great strides in incorporating security features into Windows Server 2003 DNS. In Windows Server 2003, you can configure DNS to secure DNS clients, secure your DNS namespace, protect the services that run DNS on the Windows server, secure DNS zone transfers by implementing secure dynamic updates, and secure DNS resource records. Lastly, one of the greatest advancements in Windows Server 2003 is the implementation of DNSSEC.

DNS Security Guidelines

Before we start discussing what you can do within Windows Server 2003 DNS, let's take a few moments to talk about some general security concepts that you can implement whether you are using Windows NT DNS, Windows 2000 DNS, BIND, or another DNS solution.

One of the easiest and most common things that you can do is split your DNS namespace into *internal* and *external* zones. In cases in which you want to keep the Internet-standard DNS top-level domain structure (.com, .net, .edu, etc.), you can do this quite easily by creating a child domain off your parent domain and managing that zone on an internal DNS server.

For example, if the think tank at Widgets Inc. decides that they want to keep the widgets.com domain name constant throughout their internal and external networks, they can create a zone called *internal* off their DNS server that hosts widgets.com and delegate authority to an internal DNS server that will manage internal.widgets.zom. Of course, you could always take this a step further, as we did earlier in this chapter, and create an internal domain that does not directly comply with Internet standards, such as our widgets.home internal DNS namespace.

Now, once the internal DNS server has been configured inside your network and the DNS database has been populated, you will want to have the two DNS servers possess the ability to communicate with one another. However, since you are making the effort to separate your internal and external DNS namespaces, you definitely don't want outsiders to be able to get access to your internal DNS servers. The best (and easiest) way to keep outsiders from gaining access to your internal DNS server is to configure your firewall to *explicitly* allow only UDP and TCP port 53 communications between the servers (see Figure 1.25). By doing so, you are restricting DNS queries to and from the internal DNS server and the outside world to flow *only* through the external DNS server.

Exam Warning

If you get a question on communication issues between internal and external servers that are separated by a firewall, remember that port 53 must be open for the servers to communicate.

Figure 1.25 Communicating Between an Internal and an External DNS Server

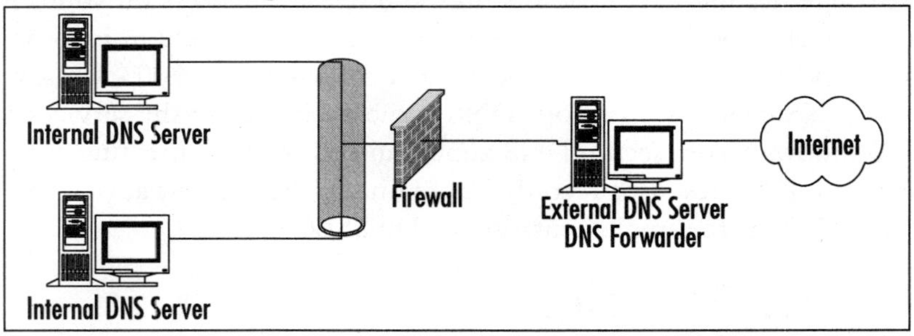

Next, configure your internal DNS server to forward all queries for external names to your external DNS server. In the previous section, you learned how to configure forwarders in Windows Server 2003 DNS, and this is a great place to apply those concepts. Lastly, once you have configured your internal DNS server to point to your external DNS server, you need to configure your clients to point to the internal DNS server for name resolution. By doing this, you are restricting all DNS queries to pass from the client to the internal DNS server and then to the external DNS server. Of course, you will want to keep your internal DNS server from being a single point of failure, so setting up a second internal (and external) DNS server is a good idea.

The previous scenario is a very general yet very easy way to secure your DNS servers. It's also a very good baseline for adding security to your name resolution strategy. In the sections to come, we discuss some of the concepts and features that Microsoft has put forth to relating specifically to DNS and DNS security within Windows Server 2003. In the next section, we discuss the three levels of security that Microsoft has defined for DNS.

Levels of DNS Security

DNS security, like many other forms of security, is a relative term. For some, simply implementing a firewall and placing their DNS server behind it is sufficient security. For others, only the latest and greatest, top level of security will satisfy their needs. To assist you with your DNS security configurations for Windows Server 2003, Microsoft has broken security into three separate levels for comparison purposes:

- Low level
- Medium level
- High level

As you apply different security features to your Windows 2000 DNS namespace, you systematically move from a lower level of security to a higher level. To make a real-world analogy, you can compare it to security clearances that are in place in the U.S. Government. Classification of documents and material within the U.S. Government falls into one of five categories:

- Unclassified
- Sensitive but classified (SBC)
- Confidential
- Secret
- Top secret

As you go from unclassified to top secret, the criticality of information security becomes more and more severe. Obviously, knowing what the *U.S.S. Nimitz* will be serving for lunch is (probably) much less a security risk than knowing what types of ammunition are stored on the ship. Microsoft's definition of security levels for DNS follows much of the same patterns. Things such as DNS access to the Internet, dynamic updates, zone transfer limitation, and root hint configurations take on different aspects as you increase in security level from low to high. Let's begin by running through the implementation and configuration settings for a DNS server with a low level of security.

Low-Level Security

Low-level security, as defined by Microsoft, is basically using the default configuration settings when DNS for Windows Server 2003 is installed. Typically, you do not want to run a DNS server under this configuration due to the fact that it is so wide open. The characteristics of a DNS server set for low-level security are as follows:

- **Full exposure to the Internet** Your DNS namespace is completely exposed to the Internet, meaning that Internet users can perform DNS lookups on any PC within your infrastructure. Typically, port 53 is open bi-directionally on your firewall.
- **Zone transfer** Your DNS servers can transfer zone information to any server.
- **DNS root hints** Your DNS servers are configured with root hints that point to the root server on the Internet.
- **DNS listener configuration** Your DNS servers have been configured to listen to all and any IP addresses configured for the server. For example, if you have a server running on two subnets, it will listen for requests on either subnet.
- **Dynamic update** Dynamic update is allowed on your DNS server. This means that users are allowed to update their resource records at will.

Medium-Level Security

Typically, a medium-level configuration is what you will see and typically implement into an environment. The medium-level characteristics offer a higher level of protection than low-level security while not becoming so restrictive that it makes it difficult to operate. The characteristics of a DNS server set for medium-level security are as follows:

- **Limited exposure to the Internet** Only certain DNS traffic is allowed to and from your DNS server. Typically, port 53 traffic is only allowed to and from certain external DNS servers. The external DNS servers typically sit on the outside of your firewall. DNS lookups for external IP addresses are first forwarded to these external DNS servers.
- **Zone transfer** Your DNS servers can only transfer zone information to servers that have NS records in their zones.
- **DNS root hints** Internet DNS root hints are only present on the DNS servers on the outside of your firewall.
- **DNS listener configuration** Your DNS servers have been configured to listen only on specified IP addresses.
- **Dynamic update** Dynamic update is disabled on your DNS servers.

High-Level Security

The high-level configuration characteristics are very similar to those of the medium level configuration. However, one key difference between medium and high levels is that a high-level configuration contains a domain controller as well as a DNS server, and the DNS zone information is also stored within Active Directory. The other key differences between the medium-level configuration for DNS and the high-level configuration for DNS are as follows:

- **No exposure to the Internet** Your DNS server does not communicate with the outside world under any circumstances.
- **DNS root hints** DNS root hints for your internal servers point exclusively to internal DNS servers that host root information for your internal namespace.
- **Dynamic update** Dynamic update is allowed, but only when your domain is configured for secure dynamic updates. (We cover dynamic updates and secure dynamic updates in the "Using Secure Updates" section.)

There is no management console in Windows Server 2003 to select whether your DNS server will function on a low, medium, or high level of security. These are simply guidelines that you can use in developing your DNS infrastructure. You should match your DNS configuration to the three levels to determine if the security of your DNS server meets the security needs of your organization.

One constant in computer networks is that now matter what type of security you implement in your environment, your environment will never be completely secure. There will always be someone out there who wants to see if he or she can penetrate the safeguards you have put into place in your network. Knowing what threats exist and being diligent in keeping your network secure from known and recently discovered threats are your best bet for maintaining a secure environment. Let's take the next few pages to discuss threats to a DNS server and what you can do to mitigate those threats.

Understanding and Mitigating DNS Threats

Those who cannot remember the past are condemned to repeat it. That famous quote has been repeated many times throughout history by many influential people. It's also a quote that applies itself well to network security. If you are not aware of security threats (such as DNS spoofing, DoS attacks, or DNS footprinting) that already exist and do not protect yourself against them, you are setting yourself up to be a victim of these threats. In this case, understanding the known DNS security threats, how they are performed, and how to protect yourself against them will pay dividends in the end—even if you can't see how right now. In this section, we discuss some of the more common DNS attacks as well as some tips on how to protect against them.

DNS Spoofing

DNS spoofing occurs when a DNS server uses information from a host that has no authority to pass along that information. DNS spoofing is a form of *cache poisoning,* in which intentionally incorrect data is added to the cache of a DNS server. Spoofing attacks can cause users to be directed to an incorrect Internet site or e-mail servers to route e-mails to mail servers other than that for which they were originally intended.

DNS query packets have a 16-bit ID associated with them that is used to determine the original query. Although later revisions have worked around this issue, earlier versions of DNS sent out sequential ID numbers. In other words, you could run a query that would generate an ID number. Then the next query to the DNS server would generate another ID number, which would be the previous ID number plus one. This made it easy for a would-be hacker to determine the next ID number in the series, making the request easier to predict and spoof.

Due to the nature of a DNS spoofing attack, it can carry on for a long time without being noticed. You can use tools such as DNS Expert (www.menandmice.com/2000/2100_dns_expert.html) to check for DNS spoofing and other DNS vulnerabilities. If you don't want to purchase software, you can easily test your DNS server to see if it is susceptible to DNS spoofing attacks. You can do this by sending several queries to your DNS server. You can then analyze the results of the query to determine whether or not it is possible to guess the next ID number. If you can successfully determine the next query ID, your server is vulnerable to DNS spoofing attacks, particularly *DNS cache poisoning*. Cache poisoning occurs when a DNS server is sent an incorrect mapping with a high Time To Live (TTL). When a "poisoned" DNS server is queried for the address of a host, it returns the invalid IP information, misinforming the requestor. The good news is that Microsoft has implemented the functionality as a default to prevent your DNS servers from cache pollution. Within the properties of the DNS server, you can select (or remove) **Secure cache against pollution** to prevent a would-be attacker from polluting the cache of your DNS server with false resource records (see Figure 1.26). Basically, you would never want to remove this from your server options. We've made it a point to show you this detail because in Windows 2000 DNS servers, the option was not enabled by default.

Denial of Service

A DoS attack occurs when a hacker attempts to "deny" the availability of domain name resolution by overloading a DNS server with multiple recursive queries. A recursive query occurs when a DNS server is used as a proxy for DNS clients that have requested resource record information outside their domain. When a recursive query is sent to the DNS server, it issues additional queries to external DNS servers, acting on behalf of the client, and returns the query information to the client once it obtains the information. As the attacker floods the

DNS server with more and more queries, the CPU on the server eventually becomes overloaded with requests until it reaches its maximum capacity, causing the DNS Server service to become unavailable. Once the DNS server becomes overwhelmed with these queries, it becomes unavailable to read DNS queries, causing the server to deny client requests.

Figure 1.26 Securing a Server Against Cache Pollution

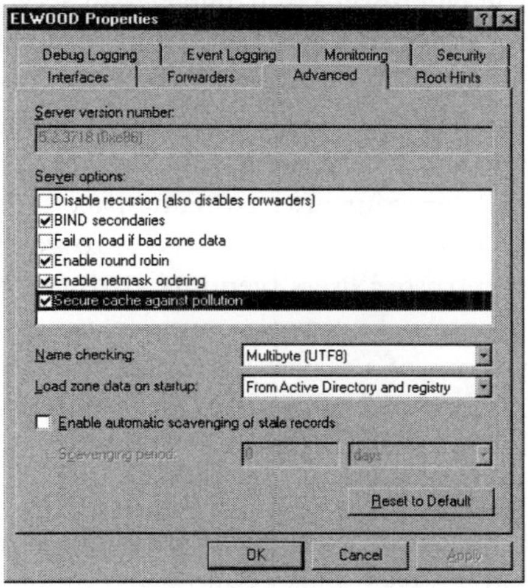

In Windows Server 2003, you can configure your DNS server to disable recursion. Unlike cache pollution, recursion is not disabled for the DNS Server service by default. You can disable DNS recursion in the Advanced Properties dialog box of the DNS server (see Figure 1.27).

Figure 1.27 Disabling DNS Recursion

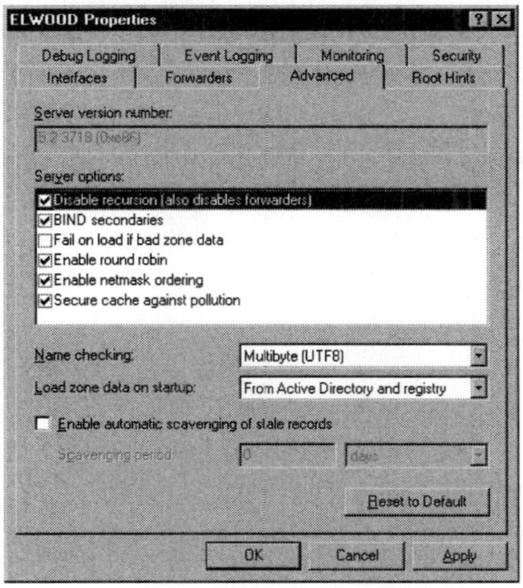

DNS Footprinting

Unlike a DoS attack, *DNS footprinting* is a *passive* attack. DNS footprinting occurs when a hacker obtains DNS zone information from your DNS server in order to gather naming and IP information for resources within your network. Typically, host names represent the type of function of a particular resource. For instance, exchange.boston.us.na.widgets.home can easily be interpreted as the Microsoft Exchange e-mail server for the Boston office of Widgets Inc. In a footprinting attack, the attacker begins to diagram, or *footprint,* the network based on the IP addresses and DNS names of the resources. Typically, footprinting is used for gathering information that will be used in further attacks on your network, such as a DNS spoofing attack. The best way to prevent your network from being a victim of a DNS footprinting attack is to keep your internal namespace separated from the Internet and secured behind a firewall. If you must provide access to your internal namespace to external users or if you have untrusted users (vendors, partners, customers, etc.) who will be physically connecting to your internal network, consider using a naming convention that does not give obvious descriptions of a server. For example, instead of using exchange.boston.us.na.widgets.home, use ex001.boston.us.na.widgets.home.

Using Secure Updates

Since you are a Windows 2000 MCSE, you should certainly familiar with the concept of dynamic DNS updates. Dynamic DNS updates allow a computer on your network to register and update its DNS resource records whenever a change occurs, such as a change of computer name. Dynamic DNS updates were intended to reduce the amount of administrative work in terms of updating DNS databases each time a machine was brought online, moved, or renamed.

In Windows Server 2003, Microsoft has taken the concept of dynamic DNS updates a step further. When a DNS zone is integrated with Active Directory, it has the added advantage of utilizing secure dynamic updates. When DNS is configured to use secure dynamic updates, only computers that have been authenticated to the Active Directory domain can perform dynamic updates. In Windows Server 2003, dynamic DNS updates have been disabled by default when standard zones are used; however, when a zone becomes an Active Directory integrated zone, secure dynamic DNS updates are turned on by default. If you want to allow clients to be able to use nonsecure DNS updates on an Windows Server 2003 DNS server (using either standard or Active Directory integrated zones), you need to turn this option on manually (see Figure 1.28).

Figure 1.28 Properties for Unsecured Dynamic DNS Updates

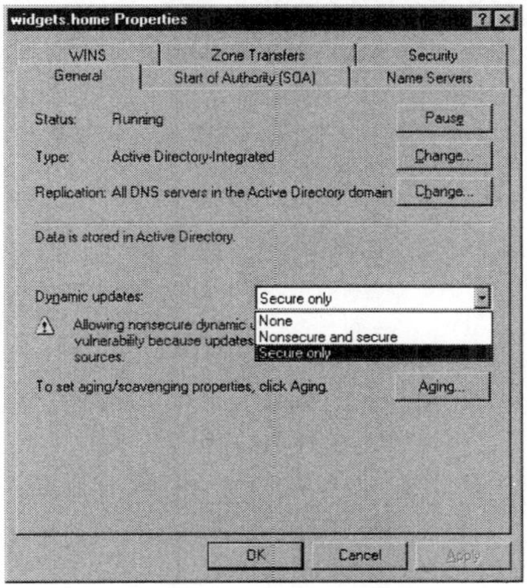

Configuring & Implementing...

Managing a DNS Access Control List

To further enhance security for a Windows Server 2003 DNS server with Active Directory integrated zones, you can adjust the security settings in the discretionary access control list (DACL). The DACL can be accessed through the DNS Management console under the Security tab of the zone properties. DACL properties for a DNS zone are similar to DHCP and sharing security properties, with which you should already be familiar. You can use the DACL to specify full control, read, write, create all child objects, delete child objects, or special permissions for users and/or groups.

The default setting for authenticated users is *Create All Child Objects*, which is the minimum permission required for a user to use secure dynamic updates. For more information on adjusting DACL security settings, visit www.microsoft.com/technet/treeview/default.asp?url=/technet/prodtechnol/windowsserver2003/proddocs/datacenter/sag_DNS_pro_ModifySecurityZone.asp.

Exam Warning

Remember that dynamic updates can only be configured as Secure Only for Active Directory integrated zones.

New & Noteworthy...

Using Unsecured Dynamic DNS Updates with Active Directory Integrated Zones

Be mindful of turning on unsecured dynamic DNS updates on Windows Server 2003 servers that are configured with Active Directory integrated zones. When a client attempts to update his or her resource record information using dynamic updates, the client will first attempt to connect to the DNS server via unsecured dynamic update. Only when the client is able to connect using the unsecured method will it bother to try to use the secure dynamic update method. For example, older clients such as Windows 95 and Windows NT, as well as third-party clients like Macintosh OS or Linux that do not support. Windows Server 2003 DHCP offers proxy dynamic registration for secure dynamic updates, as Windows 2000 did for proxy registration of unsecured dynamic DNS registration. Therefore, there really is no overwhelming reason why unsecured dynamic DNS updates should be used.

The DNS Security Extensions Protocol

The last topic that we discuss in this chapter is support for the DNS Security Extensions (DNSSEC) protocol. DNSSEC is a set of extensions to DNS that adds the ability to authenticate resource records and was designed to protect the Internet from certain attacks. DNSSEC uses public key cryptography with digital signatures to provide a process for a requestor of resource information to authenticate the source of the data. DNSSEC offers reliability that a query response can be traced back to a trusted source, either directly or through a hierarchy that can extend all the way to the parent DNS server.

In DNSSEC, a DNS zone has its own public and private key pair, which is used to encrypt and decrypt digital signatures. DNSSEC works by adding into DNS two additional record types, KEY and SIG, which will be used for authentication:

- The KEY record stores the *public key* information for a host or zone.
- The SIG record stores a *digital signature* associated with each set of records.

When a resource record in a zone is signed using a private key, DNSSEC-aware resolvers containing the secured zone's public key can authenticate whether resource information received from the zone is authentic. If a resolver receives an unsigned record set when it expects a signed one, it can identify that there is a problem and will not accept the information that has been retrieved. A typical DNSSEC-enabled query occurs as follows:

1. First, the resolver must query the root servers using the root server's public key (which is well known) to find out the DNS server authoritative for a particular zone as well as the public key for that zone.
2. The resolver then sends a DNS query to the authoritative server for the zone for which it had requested the public key in Step 1.

3. The DNS server receives the query and responds to the resolver with the requested information as well as the SIG record that corresponds to the DNS zone.
4. The resolver receives the resource record as well as the SIG record and authenticates the resource record using the known public key (which was obtained in Step 1).
5. If the resolver can authenticate the resource record and SIG, it will accept the resource record information. If it cannot authenticate the information, it will discard it.

NOTE

Public key encryption, key pairs, and digital signatures are all covered in depth in Chapter 4, "Implementing PKI in a Windows Server 2003 Network."

You might be asking yourself what happens if a DNS server does not have a resource record for a particular query in its database. For this purpose, a third type of record has been added to DNS as part of the DNSSEC implementation—the NXT (next) record. When a DNS server responds to a query that it does not have a matching record for, the DNS server sends a NXT record. The NXT record contains the name of the next DNS entity that exists in the zone as well as a list of the types of records (NS, SOA, MX, etc.) present for the current name. The purpose of the NXT record is to not only inform the requestor that a particular resource record does not exist, but it also prevents the DNS server from becoming a victim of a *replay attack*. In a replay attack, a third party that is sitting in the middle of two separate parties replays information to the second party that it has previously received from one of the parties.

So, what does the NXT record do in preventing a replay attack? As we mentioned, the NXT record contains the name of the next record that exists within a zone. So, let's say that the following records exist in the phoenix.us.na.widgets.home domain:

- alpha.phoenix.us.na.widgets.home
- beta.phoenix.us.na.widgets.home
- delta.phoenix.us.na.widgets.home
- omega.phoenix.us.na.widgets.home
- zeta.phoenix.us.na.widgets.home

Frank, who is a very unhappy mail clerk at Widgets Inc., is familiar with the concept of a DNS replay attack. Frank makes a request to a DNSSEC-enabled DNS server for the resource record of kappa.phoenix.us.na.widgets.home. Since this host does not exist in our table, Frank is sent a NXT record for delta.phoenix.us.na.widgets.home, since it is the record just *prior* to where *kappa* would exist. This NXT record contains the name of the next existing server in the zone, which is omega.phoenix.us.na.widgets.home.

Frank decides that he wants to cause a little havoc within the Phoenix office. He performs a replay attack on his coworker Karen. Karen sends a query to the same DNS server for the IP address of alpha.phoenix.us.na.widgets.home. Before the DNS server can respond to Karen's query, Frank sends his stored NXT record to Karen. Since the NXT record was signed by the DNS server, Karen's computer verifies the record as authentic. However, when Karen's computer views the NXT record, it sees that the NXT record is that of delta.phoenix.us.na.widgets.home, and since *alpha* does not fall between *delta* and *omega*, Karen's computer can assume that the record is invalid and discard it.

To learn more about DNSSEC, visit www.dns.net/dnsrd/rfc/rfc2535.html, which is the original RFC on DNSSEC. You might also want to check out www.dnssec.net, which is a great portal for Web sites relating to DNSSEC.

Using DNSSEC

As far as Windows Server 2003 support for DNSSEC, we have some good news and some bad news. First, the bad news: It does not support all the features listed in RFC 2535. The good news is that it does cover "basic support" for DNSSEC as described in RFC 2535. The basic support functionality as described in the RFC states that a DNS server must possess the ability to store and retrieve SIG, KEY, and NXT resource records. Any secondary or caching server for a secure zone must have at least these basic compliance features.

EXAM WARNING

Expect at least two questions on the exam relating to DNSSEC. Remember the new keys (SIG, KEY, and NXT) and the functions they perform. Also remember that a Windows Server 2003 DNS server can only function as a secondary DNSSEC server.

Server Support

Because Windows Server 2003 only meets the basic support functionality for DNSSEC, it can only be configured to operate as a secondary DNSSEC-enabled DNS server. This means that a Windows Server 2003 DNS server cannot perform such functionality as signing zones or resource records or validating SIG resource records. When a Windows Server 2003 DNS server receives a zone transfer from a DNSSEC-enabled DNS server that has resource records, it writes these records to the zone storage as well as the standard DNS resource records. When the Windows Server 2003 DNS server receives a request for a DNSSEC resource record, it does not verify the digital signatures; rather, it caches the response from the primary server and uses it for future queries.

Client Support

In Windows Server 2003 (and Windows XP professional), the DNS client cannot read or store a key for a trusted zone, nor can it perform authentication or verification. When a Windows 2003/XP client initiates a DNS query and the response contains DNSSEC resource records, the DNS client returns these records and caches them in the same manner as any other resource records. However, at the current time this is the maximum amount of support that Windows Server 2003 and Windows XP clients have for DNSSEC.

Summary of Exam Objectives

As you can see, planning a DNS namespace resolution strategy requires a great deal of planning and consideration prior to implementation. Getting the "big picture" of your corporate environment and building that into your namespace resolution strategy is the baseline for which all additional features and configuration decisions will be made. Whenever possible, try to include other resources from the IT staff during the decision-making process, including staff at other offices and staff internal to your office. It's always best to table environment-altering decisions prior to implementation rather than going back later to make changes because a key element was forgotten or overlooked. Decisions that should be tabled prior to implementation include top-level domain name use (private versus Internet standard), parent domain name, DNS zone delegation, and security requirements.

The next step in planning your Windows Server 2003 DNS namespace is zone configuration and replication. The decisions you made in your namespace planning will not be implemented into your DNS zone structure. However, you must now make the decision whether to use standard primary, standard secondary, or Active Directory integrated zones. You need to understand the features and benefits of Active Directory integration, including storage, scopes, and secure updates. You also have to make decisions on issues such as the use of caching servers and DNS stub zones, where they are applicable. You will also have to decide how you will handle the forwarding of name resolution queries for external DNS resources. A strategy for securing recursive lookups through the use of internal and external DNS servers needs to be realized and implemented enterprisewide. You also need to decide if conditional forwards can (and should) be used for either frequent internal or external name resolution.

Finally, you need to make sure that your namespace is properly secured. Does it make sense to use secure dynamic updates, use unsecured dynamic updates, or disable dynamic updates altogether? What level of security configuration does your namespace fall into—low? Medium? High? Does this level meet the security requirements of your organization?

Planning a DNS namespace is not particularly difficult as much as it is time consuming and requires quite a bit of planning and detailed information prior to implementation. By understanding the features and configuration options you have available when you're using Windows Server 2003, you are well on your way to being able to plan the best namespace design for your company.

Exam Objectives Fast Track

Reviewing the Domain Name System

☑ The Domain Name System, or DNS, is a hierarchical system of user-friendly names that can be used to locate computers and other resources on an your network or networks abroad, such as the Internet.

☑ A namespace is a grouping in which names are used to represent other types of information such as IP addresses and define rules to determine how names can be created and used.

☑ Since second-level (parent) domains are only concerned with hosts inside their domains, such as the syngress.com domain, they are considerably smaller and easier to maintain than top-level domains.

Planning a DNS Namespace

☑ The first step to planning your DNS namespace is to get a snapshot of your entire organization.

☑ Choose a parent domain name that represents your organization but isn't overly difficult for you and your users to understand or use.

☑ Often it's better to separate internal DNS namespaces from external DNS namespaces.

☑ A standard set of characters is permitted for use in DNS host naming, as defined in RFC 1123.

☑ In Windows Server 2003, Microsoft has expanded DNS character support to include enhanced default support for UTF-8, which is a Unicode transformation format.

Zone Replication

☑ Three considerations when planning DNS zones are traffic patterns, link speed, and server type.

☑ There are three transfer types in Windows Server 2003: full transfer, incremental transfer, and DNS Notify.

☑ There are four types of zones in Windows Server 2003: standard primary, standard secondary, stub zones, and Active Directory integrated zones.

☑ If you want to continue using BIND in your Windows Server 2003 environment, you have to upgrade to BIND version 8.1.2 or later in order to support the additional requirements of Active Directory Integrated DNS.

DNS Forwarding

☑ A forwarder is a server configured with the DNS service that is used to forward DNS queries for external DNS names to DNS servers outside a private network.

- ☑ In a typical configuration, DNS forwarders sit on the outside of your firewall, typically in a demilitarized zone (DMZ).
- ☑ When a client makes a request to the internal DNS server, the server attempts to resolve the request internally. If the internal DNS server cannot resolve the IP address, it forwards a recursive query to the first DNS forwarder that has been designated in its forwarders list.
- ☑ Conditional forwarders are DNS servers that can be used to forward queries based on specific domain names.

DNS Security

- ☑ There are three defined levels of DNS security: low, medium, and high.
- ☑ Active Directory integrated zones can realize the benefits of secure dynamic updates.
- ☑ A Windows Server 2003 DNS server can function as a secondary DNS server in a DNSSEC-enabled environment.

Exam Objectives Frequently Asked Questions

The following Frequently Asked Questions, answered by the authors of this book, are designed to both measure your understanding of the Exam Objectives presented in this chapter, and to assist you with real-life implementation of these concepts. You will also gain access to thousands of other FAQs at ITFAQnet.com.

Q: What should be the first step in planning my DNS namespace?

A: First, take a look at your company as a whole. Do you have remote offices? Will they need to have DNS servers? Will these DNS servers need to have administrative control over their DNS zones? Once you have determined your corporate needs, you can take other issues into consideration, including the separation of internal and external namespaces, Active Directory integration, and third-party DNS server support.

Q: Is there any advantage to upgrading my Windows 2000 DNS servers to Windows Server 2003?

A: Absolutely. The addition of new features in Windows Server 2003, including conditional forwarders, stub zones, and secure dynamic updates, alone makes the change to Windows Server 2003 DNS important. It also makes sense to upgrade your DNS servers to Windows Server 2003 if you plan to upgrade your Active Directory infrastructure to Windows Server 2003.

Q: I do not want to invest the extra capital into separating my internal and external DNS namespaces using internal and external DNS servers. Do I really need to do this?

A: It depends on your definition of the word *need*. You do not need to do this from an architectural standpoint, meaning that Windows Server 2003 DNS will function just fine forwarding recursive lookups to an ISP DNS server. However, you need to do this if you want to properly secure your internal network from outside influences.

Q: DNS Notify seems like a really cool feature in Windows Server 2003 DNS; however, the chapter text says that it can't be used with Active Directory integrated DNS. Since I'm going to be integrating my DNS with Active Directory, why would I need DNS Notify?

A: One scenario for using DNS Notify would be for a company with two "headquarters"—for instance, one in the United States and one in Germany. The U.S. office is the primary standard zone DNS server for the U.S./English-based Internet-facing resources as well as the secondary DNS server for the German-based Internet-facing resources. Likewise, the German office is the primary standard zone DNS server for the German-based Internet-facing resources and the secondary server for the U.S./English-based Internet-facing resources. Rather than having the secondary servers in the two offices constantly polling the other office's primary servers (which is eating up lots of bandwidth), the primary servers can notify the secondary servers. Since these servers are standard servers, they can utilize the advantages of DNS Notify.

Q: You mentioned several enhancements to Windows Server 2003 DNS but only covered some of them within the text of the chapter. What about the other features?

A: The other features (enhanced DNS logging, enhanced round robin, EDNS0, etc.) are certainly important, but they do not play a direct role in meeting the exam objectives for the 70-296 exam. If you want to learn more about these features, visit Microsoft's Technet Web site at www.microsoft.com\technet.

Self Test

1. Stephen is creating a standard primary zone for his company on a Windows Server 2003 DNS server. Stephen wants to enable secure-only dynamic DNS updates on his standard primary zone for clients within his office. Stephen opens the DNS management console and opens the Properties window of the primary zone. He notices that the only options available for dynamic updates are None and Nonsecure and Secure. Why can't Stephen enable secure-only dynamic DNS updates on this zone?

   A. Stephen cannot use secure-only dynamic DNS updates unless his zone is an Active Directory integrated zone.

   B. The Secure Dynamic Updates feature is not available in Windows Server 2003.

   C. After creating the zone, Stephen must stop and restart the DNS server service.

   D. Stephen can just use the Nonsecure and Secure option, since clients will attempt to use secure dynamic updates first.

2. Your manager is concerned that the DNS servers in your network could be susceptible to name spoofing and wants to implement DNS security in your environment. He asks you to research the implementation of DNSSEC onto your existing Windows Server 2003 DNS servers. After researching DNSSEC, you explain to your boss that your Windows Server 2003 DNS servers can only act as secondary servers while running DNSSEC. Why is this so?

   A. A Windows Server 2003 DNS server can only run as a secondary server when using DNSSEC because it only meets the basic requirements of DNSSEC.

   B. A Windows Server 2003 DNS server can only run as a secondary server when using DNSSEC because a DNSSEC primary server can only run on BIND.

   C. A Windows Server 2003 DNS server can only run as a secondary server when using DNSSEC because you must purchase the additional DNSSEC module for Windows Server 2003 in order for your server to function as a primary DNS server.

   D. A Windows Server 2003 DNS server can indeed run as a primary or secondary server when using DNSSEC, as long as it is configured correctly.

3. One of your coworkers, Sam, has been tasked with finding various ways to reduce the amount of network traffic that passes over your wide area network. Sam comes to you with the idea of setting up DNS Notify for your Active Directory integrated DNS zones. You tell Sam that although this is a good idea for reducing DNS traffic, it will not work in your environment. Why is this true?

A. DNS Notify is used to notify secondary servers of changes to the DNS database on the primary server. Since secondary servers do not exist in Active Directory integrated zones, DNS Notify cannot be implemented.

B. DNS Notify is not available on the Windows Server 2003 operating system; however, an Active Directory integrated zone can function as a secondary server using DNS Notify on a BIND server that functions as the primary server.

C. DNS Notify cannot run on your Windows Server 2003 server *unless* you place your zone files into an application directory partition.

D. This is not true. You can use DNS Notify in your environment as long as you add the list of secondary servers to notify in the properties of the primary server.

4. You are configuring your parent DNS server to delegate authority for your child domains to authoritative DNS servers in remote offices. However, you want to know about any additional DNS servers brought online in these remote offices without having to manually enter resource records for the DNS servers. What can you create in your parent DNS server to support this scenario?

   A. Conditional forwarders

   B. Primary zone

   C. Secondary zone

   D. Stub zone

5. You have just started a new job as the network administrator for a software development company. You are reviewing the resource records in the Windows Server 2003 DNS server and notice that there are NXT and SIG resource records in the zone file. Upon further research, you discover that this server is functioning as a secondary server. What else would this DNS server need to have configured in order to produce these types of records?

   A. Stub zones

   B. Secure dynamic updates

   C. Conditional forwarders

   D. DNSSEC

6. DNS spoofing occurs when a DNS server uses information from a host that has no authority to pass along resource information. In this scenario, the unauthorized host is intentionally supplying incorrect data to be added to the cache of the DNS server. What type of attack is DNS spoofing a form of?

   A. Footprinting

   B. Cache poisoning

   C. Cache implantation

   D. Cache registration

   E. None of the above

7. On occasion, clients need to resolve DNS records for external resources. When this occurs, the client sends its query to its appropriate internal DNS server. The DNS server sends additional queries to external DNS servers, acting on behalf of the client, and returns the query information to the client once the server obtains it. What type of query occurs when a DNS server is used as a proxy for DNS clients that have requested resource record information outside their domain?

   A. Recursive query

   B. Iterative query

   C. Reverse lookup query

   D. External query

8. Kaitlyn wants to change the replication scope of her Active Directory integrated DNS zones so that they can replicate with Windows 2000 DNS servers. Which replication scope does she need to use in order for her Windows Server 2003 servers to replicate with Windows 2000 servers?

   A. DNS servers within an Active Directory domain

   B. DNS servers within an Active Directory forest

   C. Domain controllers within an Active Directory domain

   D. Domain controllers within an application directory partition

9. Michael is creating a new standard primary zone for the law firm that he works for, Jones and Associates, using the domain jones.firm. Michael creates the zone through the DNS management console, but he wants to view the corresponding DNS zone file, jones.firm.dns. Where would Michael need to look in order to find this file?

   A. Michael cannot view the zone file because it is stored in Active Directory.

   B. Michael can look in the C:\Windows\system32\dns folder.

   C. Michael cannot view the DNS file except by using the DNS management console.

   D. The DNS zone file is actually just a key in the Windows Registry. Michael needs to use the Registry Editor if he wants to view the file.

10. Windows Server 2003 offers legacy support for NETBIOS names. If the fully qualified domain name for a Windows Server 2003 fileserver were fileserv1.parentdomain.com, what could the corresponding NETBIOS name be?

    A. FILESERV1

    B. FILESERV1PARENT

    C. FILESERV

    D. Whatever you want it to be

11. David is planning his DNS namespace for his new Windows Server 2003 network and is deciding what top-level domain to use for his internal network. He has decided that he will use a top-level domain that falls outside the Internet standard. Which of the following top-level domains should David use if he isn't going to use one of the Internet standard top-level domains?

    A. .com

    B. .biz

    C. .net

    D. .corp

12. Before DNS was developed, DNS resolution was controlled via special files to translate friendly names to IP addresses. Names and IP addresses were entered into these files, and computers used copies of these files for name resolution. What is the name of these files?

    A. DNS zone text

    B. LMHOSTS

    C. HOSTS

    D. WINS

13. Active Directory integrated zones store their zone data in the Active Directory tree under the domain or application directory partition. Each zone is stored in a container object, which is identified by the name of the zone that has been created. What is the name of this type of container object?

    A. dnsZone

    B. dns-Zone

    C. .dnsZone

    D. Active Directory zone

14. Active Directory uses DNS as a locator service to resolve domains, sites, and service names to their corresponding IP addresses. In order to log onto a computer that is part of an Active Directory domain, the client must send a message to his or her DNS server to obtain the address of an available domain controller. What is the name of the message that is sent to the DNS server?

    A. Broadcast request

    B. DNS query

    C. DC query

    D. Recursive query

15. David is planning his DNS zones for his company. The company has 12 regional offices within the United States, with smaller branch offices that report to the regional offices. Three key issues David will need to take into consideration when planning DNS zones are which of the following? (Choose all that apply.)

    A. Use of caching-only servers

    B. The version of Windows DNS that is being used in the regional offices

    C. Link speed

    D. Traffic patterns

    E. Use of conditional forwarders

    F. Client configuration

Self Test Quick Answer Key

For complete questions, answers, and explanations to the Self Test questions in this chapter as well as the other chapters in this book, see the Self Test Appendix.

1. **A**
2. **A**
3. **A**
4. **D**
5. **D**
6. **B**
7. **A**
8. **C**
9. **B**
10. **B**
11. **D**
12. **C**
13. **A**
14. **B**.
15. **A**, **C**, **D**

Chapter 2

MCSA/MCSE 70-296

Planning and Implementing an Active Directory Infrastructure

Exam Objectives in this Chapter:

6.1	Plan a strategy for placing global catalog servers.
6.1.1	Evaluate network traffic considerations when placing global catalog servers.
6.1.2	Evaluate the need to enable universal group caching.
6.2	Implement an Active Directory service forest and domain structure.
6.2.1	Create the forest root domain.
6.2.2	Create a child domain.
6.2.3	Create and configure application data partitions.
6.2.4	Install and configure an Active Directory domain controller.
6.2.5	Set an Active Directory forest and domain functional level based on requirements.
6.2.6	Establish trust relationships. Types of trust relationships include external trusts, shortcut trusts, and cross-forest trusts.

Introduction

It can be said with little disagreement that Active Directory was the most significant change between Windows NT 4.0 and Windows 2000. Active Directory gave administrators the flexibility to configure their network to best fit their environment. Domain structures became much more understandable and flexible, and the task of managing users, groups, policies, and resources became less overwhelming.

As wonderful a tool as Active Directory appeared to be, it did not come without its own set of issues. Failing to properly plan an Active Directory structure prior to implementation became a nightmare for many administrators who were used to simple implementation processes for older operating systems such as Windows NT 4.0. There were also questions revolving around the best migration path from Windows NT 4.0 to Windows 2000 Active Directory: Do you upgrade? Do you rebuild your domain from scratch? What are the pros and cons of each choice? What is the cost associated with either choice? Not choosing the best migration path and poor planning were the growing pains of moving to the latest and greatest operating system from Microsoft.

Now, as you face the decision to move to Windows Server 2003, you must face many of these questions again. The good news is, your experience with planning your Windows 2000 environment will make this transition that much easier. That said, there is still a great deal of work to be done and a lot of planning that must take place before you actually sit down at your servers to take that leap. We begin this chapter by laying out our Active Directory hierarchy.

EXAM 70-296 OBJECTIVE 6.2 6.2.1 6.2.2

Designing Active Directory

Active Directory is all about relationships between the domains it consists of and the objects each domain contains. As you probably already know, users, groups, printers, servers, and workstations, along with a host of other types of network resources and services, are represented in Active Directory domains as *objects*. Each object contains information that describes the individuality of that particular user or computer, and so forth. The design of the domains in Active Directory are placed in tree structures that form a *forest*. Moreover, the objects in each domain can be organized in a hierarchical structure through which the objects relate to each other.

Through a solid design, Active Directory can facilitate administration of the entire network—from password management to installs, moves, adds, and changes. Therefore, the choice to have a single or multiple forests, the design of domains contained within those forests and their tree structures, and the design of the objects within each domain are critical to a well-functioning network.

Evaluating Your Environment

Before you design your future network, you must have a good understanding of the network already in place. The network includes not only the existing servers and protocols but everything down to the wired (or wireless) topology. Let's look at the elements that you should gather in evaluating your environment.

Network topology is the physical shape of your network. Most networks have grown over time and thus have become hybrids of multiple types of topologies. Not only must you discover the shape of the network at each level, but you must also find out the transmission speed of each link. This information will help you in placing the Active Directory servers, called *domain controllers*, throughout the network.

The easiest way to start is to look at an overall 10,000-foot view of the network, which generally displays the backbone and/or wide area network links. Then you will drill down into each geographical location and review each building's requirements, if there are separate buildings. Finally, you will look at every segment in those buildings. Exercise 2.01 uses an example network to evaluate a WAN in anticipating an Active Directory design.

EXERCISE 2.01

EVALUATING A WAN ENVIRONMENT

Let's look at an example network, which we use throughout this chapter. Our example company has an existing internetwork that connects three separate offices in Munich, Germany; Paris, France; and Sydney, Australia. The headquarters of the company are located in Munich. Both the networks in Paris and Sydney connect directly to Munich, and all traffic between Paris and Sydney is transmitted through the Munich office. The connections are all leased E1 lines with a 2.032Mbps transmission speed. Figure 2.1 shows this configuration.

Figure 2.1 A High-Level View of the Example WAN

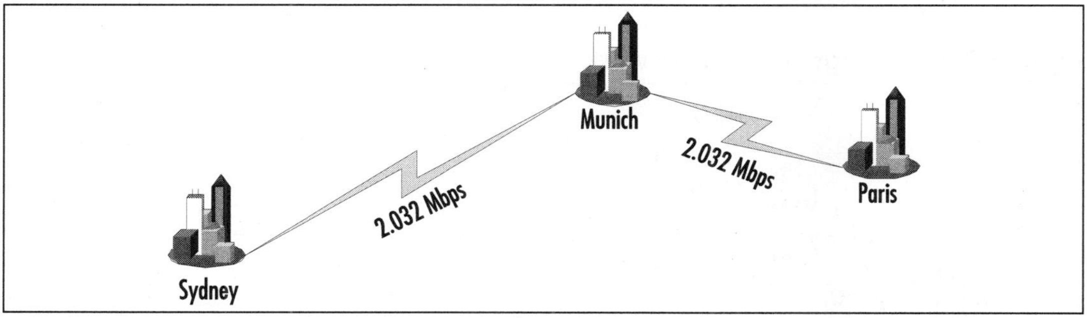

At this point, you might think, "Cool, done with that." But you're not done yet. Now you need to look at the networks within each location. In the Munich location, three buildings are connected by a fiber optic ring running Fiber Distributed Data Interface (FDDI) at 100Mbps. Neither the Paris location nor the Sydney locations have multiple buildings. The Munich location is configured as shown in Figure 2.2.

Figure 2.2 General Layout of the Munich Campus Network

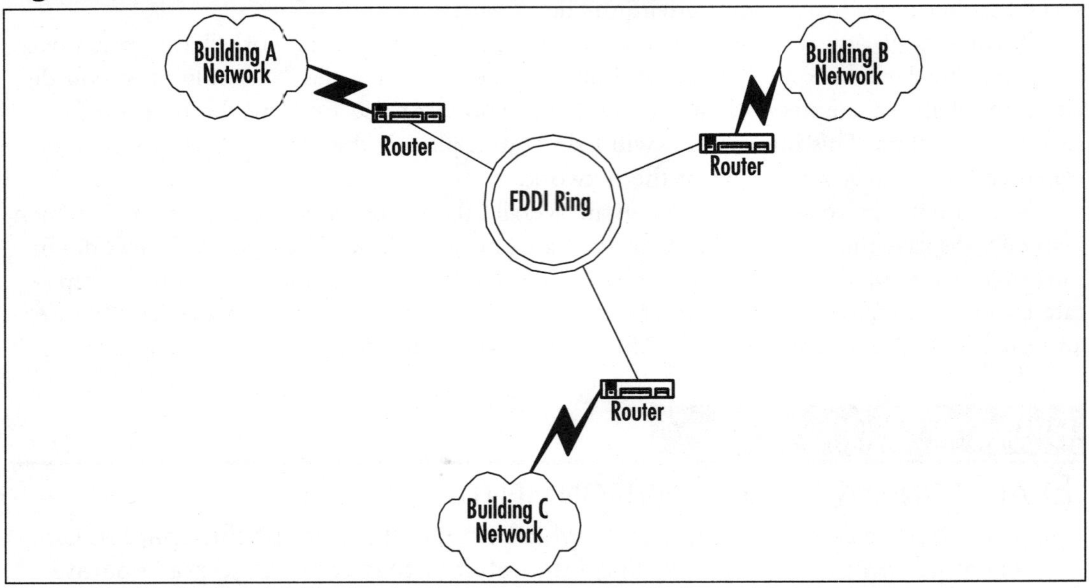

The buildings in the Munich network are named A, B, and C. Both Buildings A and B have been upgraded to Gigabit Ethernet throughout over CAT6 copper cabling. Building A houses the servers for the entire Munich campus on a single segment. Both of these buildings have three segments each, connected by a switch, which is then routed into the FDDI ring, as shown in Figure 2.3.

Figure 2.3 Buildings A and B Network Configuration

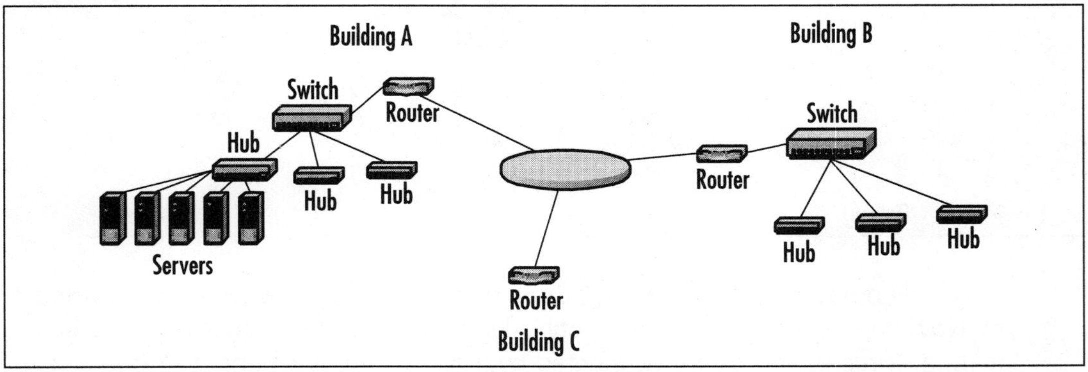

Building C in Munich uses a single Token Ring network segment at 16Mbps and two Ethernet segments running 10BaseT. This is displayed in Figure 2.4.

Figure 2.4 The Building C Network in Munich Has Older and Slower Networking Equipment Than Buildings A and B

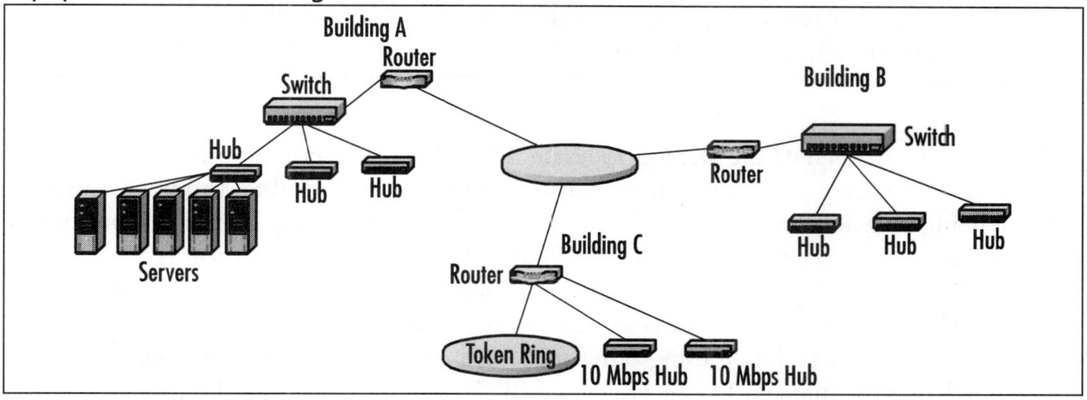

The Paris location and Sydney location, although being far apart, have nearly identical configurations. Each location has two segments of 100BaseT Ethernet, both with servers, and the Ethernet segments are connected to each other by a switch. A router is connected to one segment that leads to the Munich location. This topology is depicted in Figure 2.5.

Figure 2.5 Sydney and Paris Have Nearly Identical Network Topologies

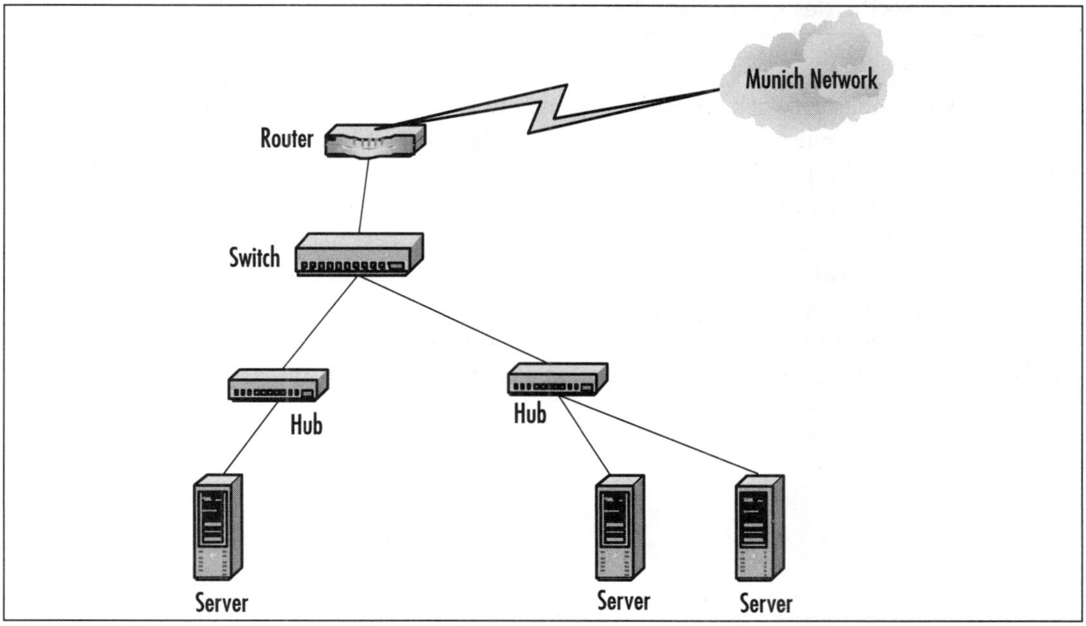

When describing the physical topology of a network, you could find that a single drawing that attempts to include all the items within the network is too confusing. By breaking the process down and looking at different portions of the network, you can make it easy to document an entire internetwork.

Notice that in each of the areas in Exercise 2.01 we have described routers and the types of topology they are routing from and to. In addition, you need to know what protocols are being routed across the internetwork. The network will likely be using Transmission Control Protocol/Internet Protocol (TCP/IP) and it's likely that it is version IPv4. It is possible that the network could be using IPv6, which is routed differently than IPv4, and it's just as possible that the network is using both IPv4 and IPv6 on various segments. In addition, the network could be using other routable protocol stacks, such as Internetwork Packet Exchange/Sequenced Packet Exchange (IPX/SPX) or AppleTalk. Unroutable protocol stacks such as NetBIOS Enhanced User Interface (NetBEUI) will not need to be routed but will affect bridging configurations and overhead on the data transmitted.

Exam Warning

The exam will test your knowledge of how to use environment-specific information to design an Active Directory infrastructure. Rather than being asked how to evaluate an environment, you might be asked what network document would influence a specific design decision based on a given scenario.

For our example network, the network already uses TCP/IP with IPv4 addresses. The network administrator uses Network Address Translation (NAT) for connecting to the Internet, so it uses the private IP Class B addresses of 172.10.0.0 through 172.10.255.255 inside the network that are then translated to a Class C address for any computer communicating on the Internet. NAT provides the translation process between an IP address used on an external network and an IP address used on an internal network. NAT typically uses a set of IP addresses both internally and externally, but it is capable of sharing a single external IP address among multiple internal hosts using different internal IP addresses. TCP/IP is used throughout the internetwork. The Munich location has two NetWare

Figure 2.6 Protocols Can Be Mapped to the Segments That Require Them

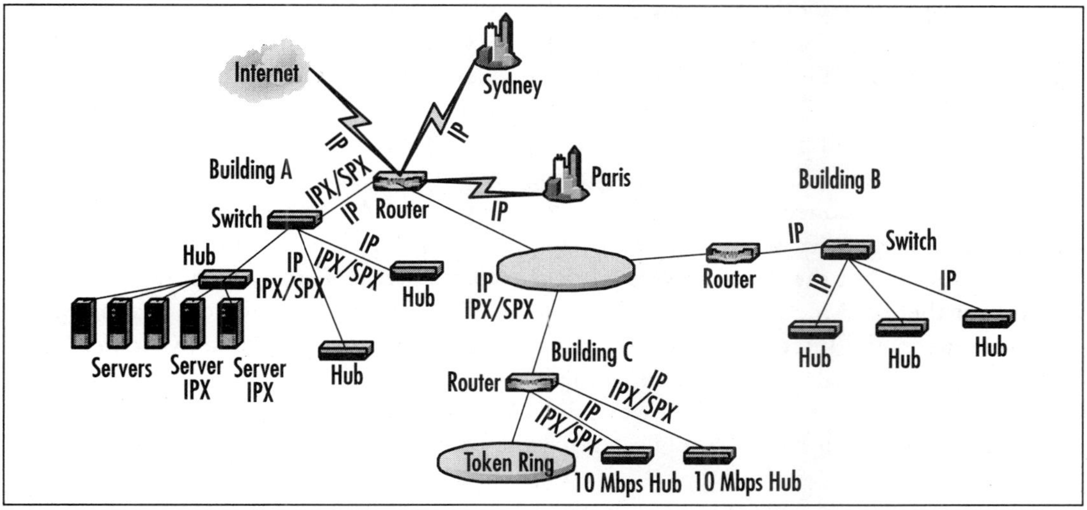

servers that use IPX/SPX to communicate with clients in Buildings A and C. No other protocols are used on the network. The protocol diagram appears as shown in Figure 2.6.

In addition to knowing the existing protocols, you should know the operating systems on servers that are currently used, their placement, and the services that run on them. Here we've touched on part of this information, but we really haven't explored it in detail. Servers are a source of data for clients on the network. This means that traffic tends to centralize around servers. Think of each server as the center of a wheel, with traffic creating logical spokes to all the clients. When you have multiple servers, you end up with multiple wheels overlapping each other. For this reason, you need to know where servers are located so that you can determine traffic patterns. The next step is to list the network operating systems and the services that are shared by those servers. Of particular importance are the servers that provide DNS services. These servers are required for Active Directory and may need to be reconfigured as a result of your Active Directory rollout. For this reason, when you list the DNS servers, you should also list the type of DNS software being used, the version, the zones provided by the DNS server, and whether the server is an Active Directory-integrated primary or a secondary zone server for each zone. A discussion of the DNS naming for the organization is also needed, since you might be changing or adding to the naming scheme.

In our ongoing example, the Munich location has two NetWare servers, 10 Windows NT 4.0 servers, and three Windows 2000 member servers. There is a single Windows NT 4.0 primary domain controller (PDC) in the company's single domain. There are also two backup domain controllers (BDCs) at the Munich location. In addition, both the Sydney location and the Paris location have a single BDC on site, which also run the local Dynamic Host Configuration Protocol (DHCP) server service. The NetWare servers provide file and print services. The Windows 2000 member servers and Windows NT 4.0 member servers also provide file and print services. Note that you will probably encounter servers that provide services to access a variety of peripherals on the network, such as faxes and printers. The peripheral equipment should be listed in addition to the server that provides that peripheral's services. The PDC is the sole DNS server and provides Windows Internet Naming Service (WINS) services. There is a single zone for the example.local domain. In addition to this type of diagram, you should list each server's hardware and software configuration on a separate sheet. This information might be needed for upgrades and compatibility.

Earlier we mentioned that the example company uses NAT to communicate across the Internet. This means that there is an Internet connection, which is in Munich, and that enables traffic to exit the company's network as well as enter it. This leads to the question of whether there is a method of remote access into the network. That remote access can take place across the Internet connection in the form of a virtual private network (VPN), or it can occur via dialup connections to the network, which in turn provides Internet access. You could choose to combine your description of servers and services with remote access and VPN. If you have a complicated remote access configuration, you should provide a separate diagram.

Finally, you should have an understanding of the clients in the network. First, you should know how many users work at each site. Next, you should have an understanding of the types of users who are on the network—whether they are power users or knowledge workers or if the focus of their jobs does not include much computer work, their hours of network usage, their applications, and the workstation operating systems. When planning for an Active Directory rollout, you need to know the users' IDs in order to ensure a successful upgrade or migration. In addition, you need to determine administrative areas and powers for users, so you should have an idea of what each user is responsible for and the administrative rights users require to perform their jobs.

TEST DAY TIP

Review the types of documents that will affect your Active Directory design: WAN map and traffic analysis, organization charts, and current domain design. You need to balance these against the organization's objectives, such as faster logons or streamlined trust relationships, when you answer scenario questions.

Creating a Checklist

Preparing for Active Directory is a lengthy process. Sometimes migrations necessitate a longer preparation period than an actual implementation phase. To keep on track during the preparation period, you should create a checklist of the items that you need to look at for each network location, each server, service, peripheral, workstation, and user. The more organized you are, the higher your success rate is likely to be. You might find that some things are required specifically for your own project, but the basic information that you should collect for each area can be seen in Table 2.1.

Table 2.1 Checklist for Active Directory Preparation Phase

Network Locations	
	Topology
	Transmission speed
	Number of segments
	Number of users at that location
	Servers at that location
	Number of workstations at that location
	Connectivity to other locations
	Protocols used
	IP addressing scheme, if any
Servers	
	Hardware configuration
	Network operating system
	Name
	IP address, if any
	Services provided
	DNS configuration, if any
	WINS configuration, if any
	Location
	Protocol configuration
Services	
	Windows NT 4.0 domain structure, if any
	Active Directory structure, if any
	DNS naming scheme
	WINS configuration
	DNS software and version, if not the server's native DNS service
Peripherals	
	Name
	Usage
	IP address, if any
	Server that provides the service for the peripheral
	Location

Continued

Table 2.1 Checklist for Active Directory Preparation Phase

Workstations	
	Operating system
	IP address, if any, or if using DHCP
	User(s) that use the workstation
	Location
Users	
	Name
	ID
	Location
	Administrative powers, if any

Expect the Unexpected

As stated in the beginning, most networks have grown over time. As a result, they are hybrids of various topologies. When you inventory each location, you are bound to run into some unique configurations. Perhaps you'll find someone using an archaic operating system on a server just to use a legacy application. For example, I once found a MUMPS server running a database application at a financial company. (MUMPS software is used in specific computational analysis. It is rare to find a MUMPS server, because they are generally created for a narrow set of uses.) In another situation, at a manufacturing company, I discovered a workstation that was running DOS because a DOS application was custom-written to move a mechanical arm and no one had the original code, nor did they have the specifications for the mechanical arm in order to write a new application. In another company, I found that the main DNS server was a UNIX version of BIND that wasn't compatible with Active Directory, but it was required for use with another application.

Regardless of what you discover in networks you work with, there is likely some way to overcome the challenge. In the MUMPS situation, the database application was migrated to a SQL server. In the DOS situation, the workstation was left unchanged. In the DNS situation, we created a subdomain structure for DNS just to incorporate Active Directory. Just make certain that you incorporate enough time in your project schedule as a cushion for handling the unexpected challenges that come your way.

EXAM 70-296 OBJECTIVE 6.2 6.2.1 6.2.2

Creating an Active Directory Hierarchy

Once you have a clear picture of your organization's current environment, you are ready to design your new Active Directory hierarchy. This hierarchy will contain, at a minimum, a forest with a root domain. Depending on your organization's needs, you might have child domains and multiple namespaces configured in several domain trees. The larger the organization and the more complex its needs, the more intricate the Active Directory forest will become.

Head of the Class...

Planning Your Active Directory Hierarchy

The Active Directory hierarchy of domains within a forest is a key component of the exam. You should expect to see questions that test your knowledge of when, why, and where to create new domains. In real life, design of an Active Directory forest and its domains is often based more on politics and preferences than on the design demands of the network environment. Keep in mind that the purist's viewpoint—based on actual requirements—is the way you should approach all Active Directory design scenarios. These are:

- Begin with a single forest.
- Create a single root domain using the DNS namespace at the smallest level for the organization. For example, if the company's name is Example Interiors Inc. and it has registered the domain name for eiinc.net, you should use eiinc.net as the root domain of the forest. (By contrast, in real life, you might not want your Web site's domain name to be integrated with your secure production Active Directory forest's root domain. In fact, you might want to use a subdomain of eiinc.net, such as corp.eiinc.net, as the forest's root domain, or you might prefer a different name altogether, such as eii.local.)
- When there is a physical discontinuity in the network, you should create a new domain as a subdomain of the root domain. For example, if you have a production plant in South America with intermittent network connectivity to the rest of the network, you should create a subdomain for that plant.
- When there is a need for a new security policy for a set of users, you should create a new domain. For example, the users on the network who work on government contracts will require a very strict security policy, whereas users who work on civilian contracts will not. Therefore, you should create two subdomains. (By contrast, in real life and depending on your government contracts, you might even be forced to create a different forest for such workers, or you might be able to apply that security policy via Group Policy settings to a specific organizational unit.)
- When a scenario has specific administrative requirements, you should pay attention to the clues in the question about whether the need is for separation or delegation. In the case of separation of administration, you should create a subdomain. In the case of delegation of administration, you should create an OU and delegate the administration.

Before You Start

Throughout the planning and preparation phases, you should make certain that you keep at hand all the information you have gathered. You will refer to this information during the design phase. In addition, it is helpful to have the contact information for administrators throughout the network.

At the start, you should know what a forest is, what a domain is, and how they will affect your design. The *forest* is the largest administrative boundary for users and computers in the network, and it logically groups one or more domains with each other. Even though most organizations require only a single forest, the first thing you should decide is how many forests you should have in your organization. The decision to have multiple forests should be limited to whether you need:

- Multiple schemas
- Administrative separation
- Organizational separation
- Connectivity issues

A *schema* lists and defines the types of objects and attributes that are included within the Active Directory database. The schema includes object types such as user accounts and attribute types such as password or phone number. When a new object is added to the Active Directory, it is created according to the "recipe" within the schema that defines what that object should be and which attributes it will include. When you add new types of objects and attributes to the Active Directory schema, you are said to be *extending the schema*. For example, when you install Microsoft Exchange Server 2000 or later, you will have new objects in the Active Directory database, such as mailbox information. Without extending the schema, the mailbox information is simply not available. If your organization needs a test domain for use in a lab and to test applications before installing them on the regular network, you should probably consider this a need for a separate schema and create a separate forest for a testing lab.

Test Day Tip

Review the reasons for having different forests and the reasons for having multiple domains. You should have the skill to make design and planning decisions for each level of an Active Directory hierarchy.

Administrative need for separation is sometimes a reason to have multiple forests. Keep in mind that multiple forests increase the overall administration of the organization, and the reason to create additional forests is usually caused by organizational politics more than actual need.

Another cause for multiple forests is organizational separation. In this scenario, more than one organization might share the network. A joint venture, for example, could have users that come from one or more businesses, and as a separate entity from each of the participating businesses, it would be a security strategy to provide a separate forest to the joint venture.

Finally, if you have a network that has physical discontinuity between network segments such that there is no connectivity, you will probably be forced to have separate forests at each separate site, or you should plan to put a connection in place. Physical discontinuity means that the domain controllers within the forest will not be able to replicate data, causing the various partitions—schema, configuration, domain, and global catalog—to fall out of synchronization, possibly leading to a future corruption. For example, let's imagine that our example company builds a large satellite office in the middle of South America in a location that has dialup lines with poor connectivity. This is a situation that might warrant a separate forest.

EXAM 70-296 OBJECTIVE 6.2.1

Forest Root

For each forest in your design, you should decide the name of the *forest root*. This is a critical decision because domain names are closely integrated with the DNS naming scheme. This means that the DNS naming scheme should be reviewed or planned at approximately the same time as the names of your domains.

The forest root domain provides its name to the entire forest. For example, let's say that you have a DNS naming scheme where example.com is used for the Web and you plan to use example.local for the internal organization. If you make the root domain example.local, the forest is named example.local. The forest is the largest administrative boundary in Active Directory. There are a few reasons to have multiple forests, such as the need for multiple schemas, the need for separate global catalogs so that the organization is logically separate, or connectivity problems that prevent communication between domain controllers.

At the creation of the forest root domain, the first domain controller takes on all operations master roles and the global catalog server role. The schema is created using default settings. It creates the NTDS.DIT file that holds the Active Directory domain information, along with the default objects within the domain. Default objects include (but are not limited to) predefined groups, such as the Enterprise Admins, Schema Admins, and Domain Admins, plus the Administrator user object, the first domain controller that was installed, the default site and site link, and OUs within the domain. The forest at its simplest is a single domain, but it can consist of more than one domain. The domains are typically organized in the structure of domain trees, formed by the contiguity of their namespaces. Exercise 2.02 explores the process of selecting a forest root domain name.

Exercise 2.02

Selecting a Forest Root Domain Name

Look at the DNS names that you will be using. In our example company, the company uses example.local for its internal DNS naming scheme. Given that the company wants to continue using this naming scheme, the forest root domain can be example.local. Keep in mind, however, that if the company wanted to have a separate DNS name for Active Directory, the company could use sub.example.local or anothername.local as the forest root domain name. In our example, though, we will use the example.local DNS name for the root, and the resulting design would resemble Figure 2.7.

Figure 2.7 The Forest Root Domain Is the Start of the Design and Planning of the Active Directory Hierarchy

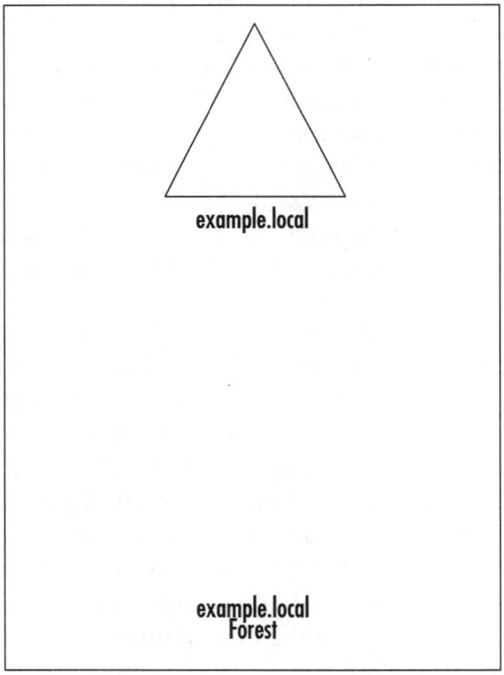

EXAM 70-296 OBJECTIVE 6.2.2

Child Domains

The next task in your plan is to determine whether to have child domains and then determine their placement and their names. The domain plan will follow the DNS namespace, which means that you should have a good idea of the namespace you intend to use. Although there is a trust relationship between the parent and the child domain, the administrator of the parent domain does not have automatic authority over the child domain, nor does the child domain's administrator have authority over the parent domain. Group Policy and administrative settings are also unique to each domain.

In our example company, the original scheme has a single Windows NT 4.0 domain. However, let's consider that both the Paris location and the Sydney location are requesting separate domains. Paris wants a separate domain for the research and development department that is designing a new e-commerce application requiring logon authentication by extranet users and wants to have that application in its own examplelocal.com domain that it will register with InterNIC. Sydney has had a significant growth rate and wants to establish its own domain for administrative purposes. The Sydney domain will then become part of the example.local namespace as a subdomain, which will be called sydney.example.local. Note that a child domain does not need to be in the same namespace in order to be a child of the forest root. However, any other domain is only a child domain of the upper levels of its own namespace, which means that examplelocal.com is not a child domain of sydney.example.local or vice versa. This design is shown in Figure 2.8.

Figure 2.8 This Forest Has Three Domains in Its Hierarchy

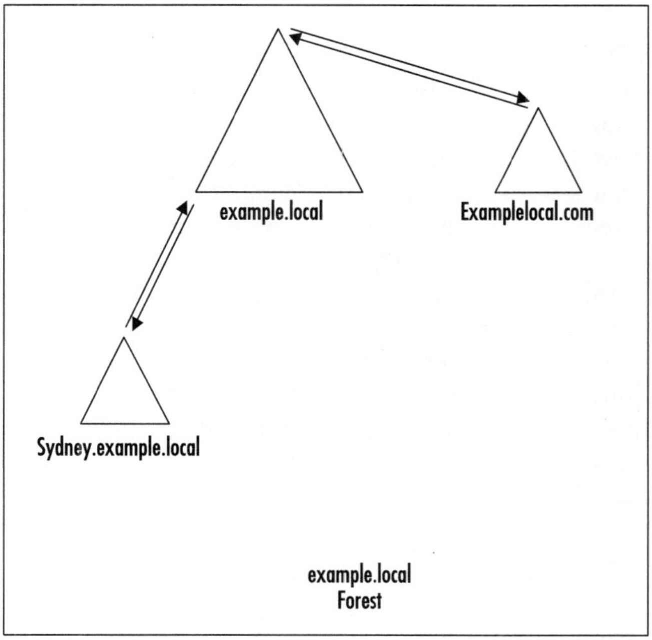

You should ensure that there is a need for each domain in each forest. In our example, the need for Sydney to have a separate domain is driven by its growth rate and need for administrative separation. By contrast, Paris's need for a separate domain is not for administration of all of Paris users but for an application. The design selected could have just as easily been handled as a separate forest for the Paris e-commerce application's domain, and Sydney's users could have been a part of the single domain just as they had been in the past Windows NT 4.0 domain. Remember that design decisions are not set in stone but rather based on the discretion of the designer as well as the needs expressed by users and administrators.

Child domains should be considered whenever you run into the following issues:

- A location communicates with the rest of the network via the Internet or dialup lines. The intermittent connectivity drives a need for a separate domain.
- A group within the organization requires its own domain wide security policies. Some group policy security-based settings can only be applied at the domain level.
- There is a need for administrative separation for a group or location. Delegation of administrative duties can overcome many of these claims, so it is not always necessary to create a separate domain. Often this is the need given when in fact the reason is political.

Whenever you decide to create additional domains, remember that each additional domain adds administrative overhead and increased replication traffic, and both of these can result in higher costs.

Domain Trees

A *domain tree* is simply a set of domains that forms a namespace set. For example, if you have four domains example.local, set1.example.local, set2.example.local, and second.set1.example.local, you have an entire domain tree. If you have another domain in the forest named example.com, it is located in another domain tree.

Child domains are used to either extend the forest root domain tree or to create new domain trees. Because a forest root domain does not need to have the same DNS namespace as the other domains in the forest, each namespace is considered a separate domain tree. In Windows Server 2003 Active Directory, you are able to establish separate domain trees even when using the same namespace. This is only a surface change, because the Kerberos trust relationships still provide the same infrastructure throughout the network. However, in cases in which physical discontinuity separates a domain from others in the same tree, you might consider establishing that domain as a separate domain tree to skip its being involved in trust resolution.

EXAM 70-296 OBJECTIVE 6.2.3 6.2.4 6.2.5 6.2.6

Configuring Active Directory

Before you configure Active Directory, you need to know which servers are going to become domain controllers and in which domain they will be placed. When installing, you must install at least one domain controller within the root domain before you can begin installing domain controllers in the child domains, working your way down each domain tree.

Once a domain controller has been installed, you can begin configuring the way that the database will function to meet your objectives. One of the things that you can configure is Active Directory application directory partitions. Keep in mind that Active Directory is a data store that contains the information about users, groups, computers, and other network services and resources. Each domain controller contains a copy of the Active Directory data store. There are four types of partitions of the Active Directory data store:

- **Domain** Contains information about the objects that are placed within a domain.
- **Configuration** Contains information about Active Directory's design, including the forest, domains, domain trees, domain controllers, and global catalog.
- **Schema** Contains description data about the types of objects that can exist within Active Directory.
- **Application** Contains specialized data to be connected with specific applications. This partition type is new to Active Directory and is intended for local access or limited replication. The application partition must be specially created and configured; it is not available by default.

The data itself is contained within a file named NTDS.DIT, which is contained on each domain controller. Unless the server is a Global Catalog server, a domain controller's NTDS.DIT file will only include the information for the domain controller's own domain, not any other domain.

EXAM 70-296 OBJECTIVE 6.2.3

Application Directory Partitions

Application directory partitions are new to Active Directory. When you configure an application directory partition, the data connected to a specific application's directory is stored for use by the local application and connected to Active Directory. Because many applications take advantage of simple directory data, this information can be stored and indexed with the Active Directory data. However, this application data is not needed for much of the administration of the network, nor is it always necessary for replication across the entire Active Directory network.

Exam Warning

Application directory partitions are new to Active Directory. To make certain that Windows 2000 Active Directory experts aren't skating through on the Windows Server 2003 Active Directory tests, new elements such as these are likely to be cleverly intertwined in scenario questions. To determine whether a question is asking about an application directory partition, look for phrases such as *locally interesting traffic* or *globally uninteresting traffic*.

For example, in our example, imagine that Sydney has implemented a SQL application that stores data within Active Directory. The only users who take advantage of the SQL application are located in Sydney, so it is not necessary to replicate that data to Munich or Paris. This is where the use of an application directory partition can ensure that the WAN link is not overwhelmed by unnecessary replication traffic.

The configuration principles are simple. Consider that Active Directory is a large database and that an application directory partition is a smaller database that can be indexed to Active Directory. If you have information that you want to keep locally, including extensions to the schema, you can place that information within an application directory partition.

In addition, any of these computers can contain multiple instances of application directory partitions. Exercise 2.03 walks through the process of installing a new application directory partition.

EXERCISE 2.03

INSTALLING A NEW APPLICATION DIRECTORY PARTITION

To install a new application directory partition, you can follow these instructions:

1. Click **Start | Run**.
2. Type **CMD** in the command line, and press **Enter** to open a command prompt window.
3. At the prompt, type **NTDSUTIL**.
4. A prompt for the NTDSUTIL tool appears. Type **DOMAIN MANAGEMENT**.
5. At the next prompt, type **CONNECTION**.
6. Next, type **CONNECT TO SERVER servername**, where *servername* is the DNS name of the domain controller that will contain the new partition.
7. Type **QUIT** to return to the domain management prompt.
8. Type **CREATE NC partitionname** *servername*, where *partitionname* is the name of the application directory partition in the format of *dc=newpart, dc=example, dc=local*, if you were creating a partition named newpart.example.local, and where *servername* is the fully qualified domain name (FQDN).

Managing Partitions

Application directory partitions are interconnected with Active Directory, which means that they can utilize the same management tools as Active Directory. As you can already see, application directory partitions are created using NTDSUTIL, an Active Directory utility. NTDSUTIL is also used to delete application directory partitions or to create replicas (copies) of the partition on another domain controller.

In addition, you can use the LDP.exe utility to manage the application directory partition using Lightweight Directory Access Protocol (LDAP) commands. Furthermore, you can use the Active Directory Services Interface (ADSI) Edit tool.

Naming Partitions

When you have multiple instances of application directory partitions running on a single computer, you need to have unique names for each, as well as different ports. The application directory partitions use an X.500 naming strategy. This means that although you will use an FQDN name for the names of domain controllers, you will only use an X.500 name for the application directory partition.

The X.500 name uses the following format for an application directory partition: *dc=partitionname, dc=domainname, dc=com*. Therefore, if you install an application directory partition on a domain controller named dc01.sub.example.local, and you want to name the application directory partition tapi01 because it will be used for a telephony application programming interface (TAPI) application, you will use the naming convention *dc=tapi01,dc=sub,dc=example,dc=local*. Make certain that you identify each subdomain and that the portions of the name are separated by commas.

Replication

As we stated earlier, each domain controller contains a set of partitions of Active Directory. Unless one is a Global Catalog server, domain controllers within the same domain contain replicas of the same partition. *Replication* is the process of ensuring that data is up to date across all replicas. Any data that has been changed, such as a new password for a user, must be copied to all other replicas of that same partition.

Active Directory uses a multimaster model for replication. Each domain controller is equal to all other domain controllers. This means that an administrator can add new objects, delete objects, or make changes to existing objects on any domain controller. Then, when replication takes place, that domain controller transmits the changes to its peers.

Sites are used for efficiency in replication. A site is considered a set of well-connected IP subnets, but it's manually configured by an administrator. *Well-connected* is a concept that usually depends on the network administrator's or designer's discretion. For example, in our example, we have three locations: Munich, Paris, and Sydney. Of these locations, Paris is fairly small and has a full E1 pipe to connect to Munich. Paris could be made its own site, or it could be placed within the Munich site. Sydney, with its size and growth rate, would probably be best as a separate site.

The Knowledge Consistency Checker (KCC) is a process that runs on each domain controller every 15 minutes to automatically create a replication topology, selecting which domain controllers to replicate with and when. This choice is based on the configuration that you specify when you specify the sites within the Active Directory Sites and Services console. When you manually specify certain items, such as a preferred bridgehead server, the KCC will not override your configuration.

Configuring & Implementing...

Configuring Replication of an Active Directory Application Directory Partition

Replication of Active Directory application directory partitions takes place between the domain controllers that hold the partition and its replicas. If there is a single partition, the data does not replicate. However, if there is no replica, that data will not be fault tolerant. In order to configure replication, you must simply create a replica of the partition referencing the partition by its distinguished name as it appears when X.500 naming is used. However, you reference the name of a domain controller by its FQDN as it appears in DNS naming.

The process for adding a replica of an application directory partition is:

1. Open a command prompt by clicking **Start | Run** and typing **CMD,** then pressing **Enter**.
2. Type **NTDSUTIL** at the command prompt and press **Enter**.
3. Type **DOMAIN MANAGEMENT** at the prompt and press **Enter**.
4. Type **CONNECTION** and press **Enter**.
5. Type **CONNECT TO SERVER domain_controller_name** and press **Enter**.
6. Type **QUIT** and press **Enter**.
7. Type **ADD NC REPLICA application_partition_name domain_controller_name** and press **Enter**.

EXAM 70-296 OBJECTIVE 6.2.4

Domain Controllers

DNS is integral to Active Directory. When DNS is not configured with the correct resource records for the new domain controller (or not configured with dynamic updates enabled for the future root domain's DNS zone), the Active Directory wizard will prompt you to properly configure an accessible DNS server before proceeding, allow it to install and configure DNS as a service on the new domain controller as part of the Active Directory installation process, or allow you to proceed with the installation of Active Directory and later configure DNS manually.

Once you have completed the installation of the first domain controller in the root domain of the forest, you have the following implementation tasks:

- Install the remaining domain controllers, if any, within the root domain.
- Create the child domains, if any, by installing the domain controllers for each of them.
- Implement application data partitions, if needed.
- Install and configure additional domain controllers as needed.
- Set the functional level of the domain(s).
- Establish trust relationships as needed.

When Windows Server 2003 installs on a new server, it automatically becomes a standalone server. It will be able to join a domain as a member server, share files, share printers, and provide applications. But for all that, you still don't have an Active Directory forest with a root domain.

By contrast, when you install Windows Server 2003 on an existing domain controller, it will upgrade the server's operating system and then automatically begin the Active Directory wizard. If the domain controller you are upgrading is a Windows 2000 server, the upgrade is automatic. If the domain controller is a Windows NT PDC or BDC, the Active Directory wizard begins so that you can promote the server to a domain controller and configure it anew.

NOTE

Before you install Active Directory, you should make certain that the file system you are using is NTFS. You can convert the file system using the command *convert volume /fs:ntfs*.

When you are ready to install Active Directory, you will use the Active Directory Promotion wizard to promote a standalone server to domain controller status. The first domain controller that you install is installed into the root domain of the forest. The Active Directory Promotion wizard is initiated by typing **DCPROMO** at the command prompt. You can also reach this wizard by following these steps:

1. In the Manage Your Server window, select **Add or Remove a Role**, as shown in Figure 2.9.

Figure 2.9 The Manage Your Server Console

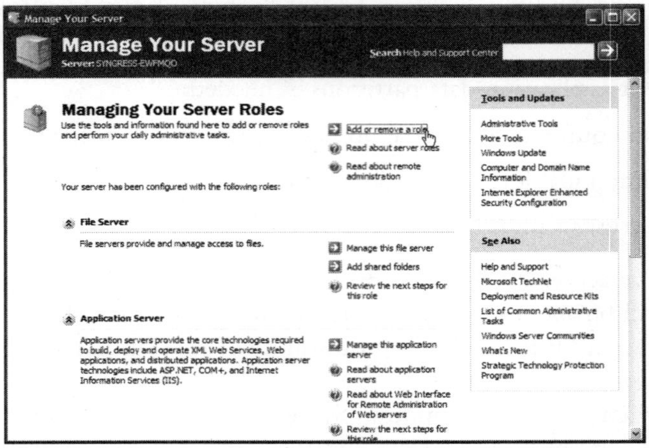

2. In the resulting dialog box, click **Next**.
3. The computer will locate the services that are currently configured and display those as well as the ones that are available to be configured. From this list, select **Domain Controller (Active Directory)**, as displayed in Figure 2.10, and click **Next**.
4. Click **Next** at the following screen. The DCPROMO wizard begins.

Figure 2.10 Selecting the Option to Initialize the Active Directory Wizard

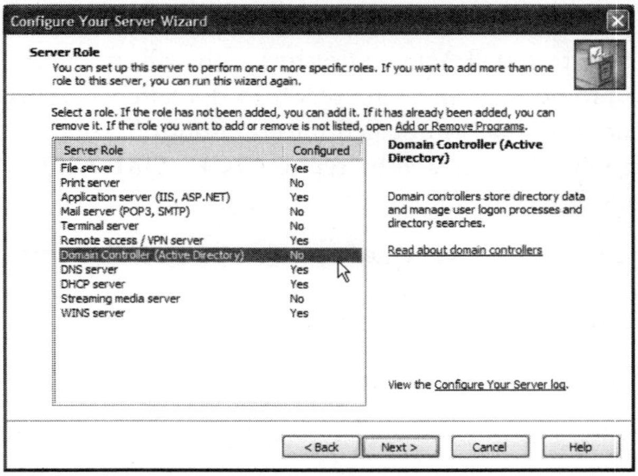

If you are currently using a Windows NT 4.0 network, you will recognize the benefits of using DCPROMO. In Windows 2000 and Windows Server 2003, you can promote a

standard server to a domain controller without having to reinstall the network operating system (NOS). This is also true of demotion. You can remove Active Directory from a domain controller and demote that domain controller to a standard file server without having to reinstall the NOS. Under Windows NT 4.0, the only way to change a server's role in the domain was to remove and reinstall the NOS.

Exam Warning

The installation of Active Directory via DCPROMO is little different from Windows 2000. The new version, however, has an improved DNS configuration option. In addition, there are compatibility warnings for older clients. Scenario questions may state a client workstation operating system (OS) version that is incompatible with Windows Server 2003. If given the option to upgrade the older client OSs, you should consider that a better answer than retaining the current configuration because the value of the new OSs plus the value of Windows Server 2003 Active Directory will be considered greater than the value of the status quo—especially when specific problems are mentioned regarding the current state of the network within the scenario.

There are several ways of configuring the domain controller. You first must know what domain the domain controller will belong to, and you should have DNS fully configured and functioning before you start. Given the extensive use of service resource records (SRV RRs) in DNS, the optimal configuration for DNS is to have dynamic DNS enabled so that the new domain controller will register its services in the DNS zone without requiring you to manually input them.

Before you begin a domain controller installation, gather the information that you will need for the server:

- Server name
- Domain name
- File system directory for placement of the Active Directory file
- File system directory for placement of the Active Directory logs
- File system directory for placement of the SYSVOL, which contains replicated data
- Domain Administrator's password
- Directory services restore mode password

Exercise 2.04 provides step-by-step instructions for installing a domain controller as the first domain controller in the forest.

Exercise 2.04

Installing the First Domain Controller in the Forest

The domain controller's installation is merely the first part toward configuration. After you have completed the Active Directory wizard, you will be ready to configure trust relationships, sites, user accounts, computer accounts, and Group Policy. To begin:

1. Click **Start | Run**. Type **DCPROMO** in the box, and press **Enter**.
2. You will see the Active Directory wizard's welcome screen. Click **Next**.
3. Click **Next** to bypass the warning about compatibility issues with Windows 95 and older Windows NT 4.0 clients.
4. Select a **Domain Controller for a new domain**. Click **Next**.
5. Select a **Domain in a new forest**, as shown in Figure 2.11. Click **Next**.

Figure 2.11 Selecting the Domain in a New Forest Option

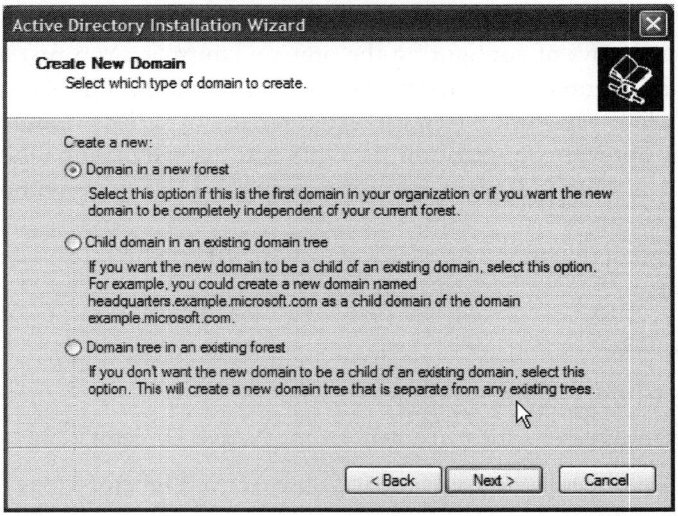

6. Type the DNS name for the root domain of your forest. Click **Next**.
7. Type the NetBIOS name of the domain and click **Next**, as shown in Figure 2.12. Do not name this domain the same as a Windows NT 4.0 domain on the network or you will have a conflict.

Figure 2.12 Selecting a NetBIOS Name for the New Domain

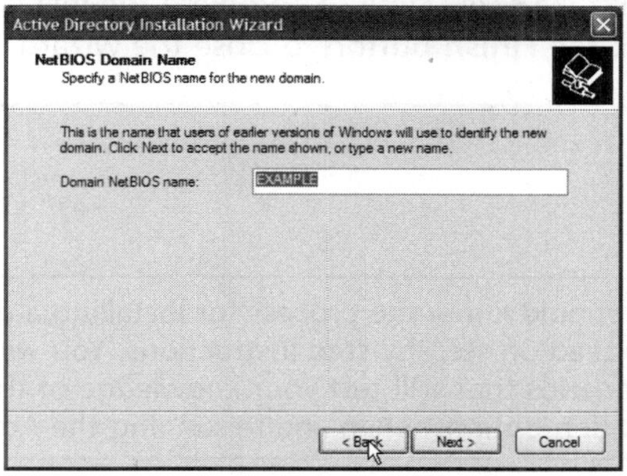

8. Verify the directory locations for Active Directory database and log files, and click **Next**.
9. Verify the location for the SYSVOL share. Click **Next**.
10. DNS will be tested as shown in the DNS Registration Diagnostics displayed in Figure 2.13. If it fails the test, you will be asked to select an option to configure DNS. Click **Next**.

Figure 2.13 The Improved Active Directory Wizard's DNS Registration Options

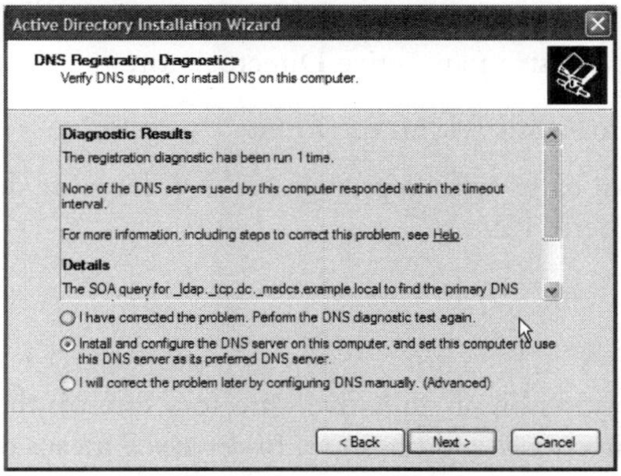

11. Select the permissions level for the domain controller. Click **Next**.
12. Type the password for restoring Active Directory services to this domain controller. Don't lose the password! Type in the password confirmation. Click **Next**.

13. Verify the summary screen options. Click **Next**. The Active Directory wizard will take some time to complete the installation. When it is finished, click the **Finish** button to close the wizard.

TEST DAY TIP

For the exam, you should know the process for installing a domain controller. But you will not be quizzed on step-by-step instructions. You will find questions leaning toward scenarios that will test your knowledge of the available Active Directory configuration options when you're running the Active Directory wizard.

EXAM 70-296 OBJECTIVE 6.2.6

Establishing Trusts

Trust relationships are necessary for an administrator to grant rights to the local resources to users from other domains, Kerberos realms, or entire forests. The way that a trust works is to simply enable the administrator to grant rights. Without a trust relationship in place, the rights cannot be granted at all. Even with a trust in place, if no rights have been granted to a resource, the resource cannot be accessed.

Types of Trusts

There are several types of trusts in an Active Directory forest:

- Implicit Kerberos trusts within the forest
- Explicit external trusts with Windows NT 4.0 domains, domains within other forests and Kerberos realms
- Forest trusts
- Shortcut trusts

The standard trust relationship in an Active Directory forest is the implicit Kerberos trust. This type of trust is bi-directional and transitive. *Bi-directional* means that when Domain A trusts Domain B, Domain B also trusts Domain A. *Transitive* means that when Domain A trusts Domain B and Domain B trusts Domain C, Domain A also trusts Domain C.

When there are Windows NT 4.0 domains, Kerberos realms, or multiple forests within an organization, the explicit external trust relationship can be used to facilitate the granting of rights. An explicit external trust relationship is unidirectional and nontransitive. This means that when Domain A trusts Domain B, Domain B does not have to trust Domain A in return. In addition, if Domain A trusts Domain B, and Domain B trusts Domain C, it does not follow that Domain A trusts Domain C. In fact, the explicit external trusts in Windows

Server 2003 Active Directory act exactly the same as the trust relationships between native Windows NT 4.0 domains. For example, an organization has two forests—one forest is the network's main forest and the other is a forest used for research and development. The main forest consists of a forest root domain and one child domain we will call the resource domain. Users in the lab must still access resources in the resource domain of the main forest, although they typically log on and access resources in the research and development forest daily. Therefore, an explicit trust between the users' domain and the resource domain in the main forest can be created. The resource domain in the main forest would have to trust the lab users' domain so that rights to the resources in the resource domain can be granted to the lab users. Because the trust relationship is unidirectional and nontransitive, the users will not be able to access resources in any other domain unless additional trusts are created.

Forest trust relationships are new to Active Directory under Windows Server 2003. Since forests can contain multiple domains containing both users and resources, a complex set of explicit external trust relationships was the only way to enable access to resources from the domains in one forest to the users in another forest. Imagine, for example, that an organization has two forests—one used for lab testing and the other used for standard business applications and resources. Users in the lab testing forest could not access mission-critical applications such as e-mail or files and printers without explicit trust relationships where the domains in the standard forest each trusted the domains in the lab testing forest. The forest trust relationship in the Windows Server 2003 Active Directory makes fairly simple the process of establishing trust relationships between the domains in one forest and those in another. Figure 2.14 displays a forest trust relationship.

Figure 2.14 The Forest Trust Is a Single Trust Relationship Between the Root Domains of Two Different Forests

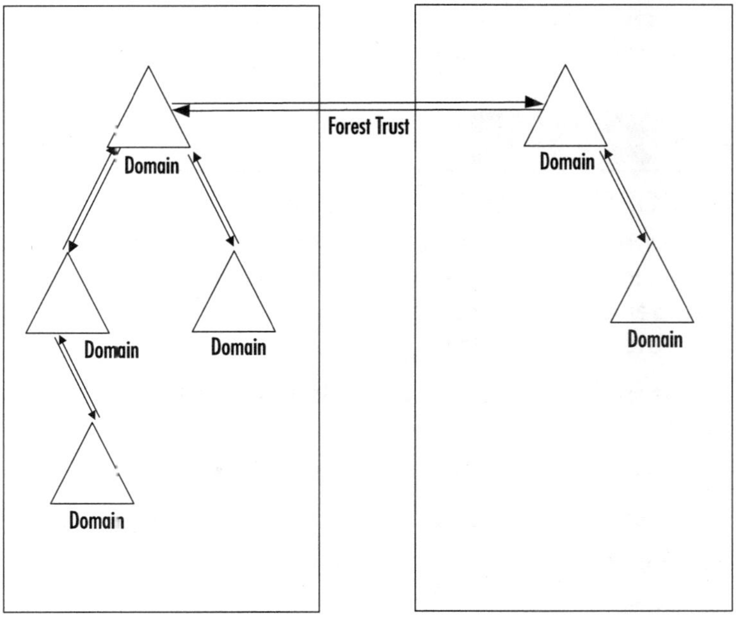

The forest trust is a unidirectional transitive relationship between the domains in one forest and the domains in a second forest, which is created through a single trust link between the root domains in each forest. When the trust is created such that Forest A trusts Forest B, the users in any domain within Forest B can be granted rights to access resources within any domain within Forest A. However, this trust will not work in the opposite direction. A separate trust would need to be created whereby Forest B trusts Forest A. The transitive nature of this type of trust is only applicable to domains—because any domain within the trusting forest would trust any domain within the trusted forest. However, the trust is not transitive between entire forests. For example, if Forest A trusts Forest B and Forest B trusts Forest C, Forest A does not trust Forest C. However, any domain within Forest A will trust any domain in Forest B because of the single trust relationship established between the root domain of Forest A and the root domain of Forest B.

Exam Warning

Keep an eye out for forest trust relationship questions. You should be familiar with the lack of transitivity of a forest to forest (to forest) trust, plus the ability to create both a one-way and two-way forest trust. The two-way trust is actually two one-way trusts in reverse directions.

The shortcut trust is created between two domains within a single forest. You might wonder why this is necessary, since there are Kerberos transitive trusts that connect all the domains within a forest. The need for a shortcut trust appears only in large, complex forests with multiple domains in multiple domain trees. The shortcut trust speeds up the resolution of the trust relationships between domains that exist deep within two different domain trees. Exercise 2.05 explains how to create a forest trust.

Exercise 2.05

Creating a Forest Trust Relationship

In order to create a forest trust relationship, you must have two forests whose root domains can communicate with each other. Both forests must be set to the Windows Server 2003 forest functional level, described in the following section. To create the forest trust:

1. Click **Start | Administrative Tools | Active Directory Domains and Trusts**.
2. In the left pane, navigate to the root domain of the forest.
3. Right-click the root domain and select **Properties** from the popup menu.
4. Click the **Trusts** tab.

5. Click **New Tru**st to start the Trust wizard.
6. Click **Next** at the welcome screen.
7. In the trust name, type the DNS name of the root domain of the other forest. Click **Next**.
8. Select the **Forest** trust in the trust type dialog box. Click **Next**.
9. Select whether the direction of this trust will be one-way (and if so, whether it is an incoming trust or outgoing trust) or two-way. Click **Next**.

New & Noteworthy...

Using a Forest Trust for a Lab Environment

One of the major changes in Active Directory was the addition of the forest trust. In Windows 2000 Active Directory, it appeared that Microsoft viewed a forest as a single entity that should stand alone and encompass an entire organization's internetwork. Real life, however, intruded on that vision. Organizations created multiple forests for a variety of reasons—not the least of which was the purpose of research and development.

Even when an organization created a single forest for its production users, the designers typically created a test forest for application development, deployment testing, and other research. The forest was usually much smaller in number of users, but it often mirrored the same number of domains and had a similar namespace. Given the many changes that a lab forest was often put through, users who were members of a lab forest found that they had to maintain two user accounts—one in the lab and one in the standard forest—in order to access resources such as files, e-mail, and business applications that existed within the production forest.

One of the ways that organizations attempted to make resource access easier for the lab forest users was to create explicit external trust relationships between all the domains within the production forest and the domains within the lab forest. If the lab forest underwent domain changes, new trust relationships had to be established.

Through the use of a forest trust relationship, it is a simple matter to create a single trust relationship between the production forest and the lab forest. Regardless of how the domains change within either forest, the trust relationship remains in place and provides the path for all lab users to access the business applications that they need without logging off one forest, then logging back onto the other.

Evaluating Connectivity

When you create a trust relationship of any sort, you must have connectivity between the domains and/or the realm involved or the trust relationship cannot be created. Ensuring that you can resolve the names of the domains involved via DNS is one of the first steps toward evaluating the connectivity. There is little need for much bandwidth to support a trust relationship, but to enable access to resources, you need to have available bandwidth.

When there is no connection between two domains, the trust cannot be created. The domain will not be recognized and you will be prompted for whether the DNS name you provided was a Kerberos realm.

EXAM 70-296 OBJECTIVE 6.2.5

Setting Functionality

A domain in a Windows 2000 Active Directory forest had two options: It could run in *mixed mode* (the default) or *native mode*. These modes have evolved into domain functional levels within Windows Server 2003 Active Directory. Furthermore, you can now achieve a set of forest functional levels. We look at both domain and forest functionality in this section. You must have certain information about the network environment available to you before you set a functional level for a domain or for the forest:

- Operating systems running on the domain controllers, both current and future
- Whether you plan to use Universal security groups
- Whether you plan to nest groups
- Whether you need security ID (SID) history
- If you intend to have a forest trust

This information will help you decide which domain and forest functional levels you should use.

Even if you have installed only Windows Server 2003 domain controllers, you should not raise your forest functional level to Windows Server 2003 if you plan to install or promote domain controllers with older operating systems in any of the forest's domains. After the forest functional level has been raised, you can't add any other domain controllers using Windows NT 4.0 or Windows 2000 throughout all domains in the forest.

Forest Functional Levels

There are three forest functional levels:

- Windows 2000
- Windows Server 2003 interim
- Windows Server 2003

TEST DAY TIP

Familiarize yourself with the features of the various forest and domain functional levels. Since these are new features in Windows Server 2003 Active Directory, you will be expected to know the abilities of the forest and domains at each functional level.

The Windows 2000 forest functional level provides the same services as a Windows 2000 forest. It can contain domains at any domain functional level, and it can contain domain controllers using Windows NT 4.0, Windows 2000, and Windows Server 2003 operating systems. The default forest functional level is Windows 2000. The Windows Server 2003 interim forest functional level is a special functional level used for forests that consist solely of Windows Server 2003 domain controllers and Windows NT 4.0 BDCs. The Windows Server 2003 forest functional level is the highest forest functional level and can only contain Windows Server 2003 domain controllers and domains that are at the Windows Server 2003 functional level.

You can follow Exercise 2.06 to raise the forest functional level. The Windows Server 2003 forest functional level provides the following capabilities:

- The ability to create a forest trust
- Domain renaming capability
- The *InetOrgPerson* object designated for Internet administration
- Improved global catalog and standard replication

EXERCISE 2.06

RAISING THE FOREST FUNCTIONAL LEVEL

Once you raise a forest functional level, you cannot change it back. In addition, you cannot add any domain controllers that are not of the Windows Server 2003 type. In order to raise the forest functional level:

1. Open the Active Directory Domains and Trusts console by clicking **Start | Administrative Tools | Active Directory Domains and Trusts**.
2. In the left pane, right-click the **top node**.
3. Select **Raise Forest Functional Level** from the popup menu.
4. A dialog box will display, allowing you to select the forest functional level.

Domain Functional Levels

Four domain functional levels are available within Windows Server 2003 Active Directory. These functional levels are:

- Windows 2000 mixed
- Windows 2000 native
- Windows 2003 interim
- Windows Server 2003

The Windows 2000 mixed domain functional level, the default for all new domains, is basically the same as a Windows 2000 mixed-mode domain under Windows 2000 Active Directory. This type of domain can have domain controllers using Windows NT 4.0, Windows 2000, and Windows Server 2003.

The Windows 2000 native domain functional level allows Windows 2000 and Windows Server 2003 domain controllers. This functional level offers the use of universal security groups, nesting groups, and SID history.

Exam Warning

You should know which operating systems can (and which cannot) be used in each of the domain functional levels. You will likely be faced with at least one scenario in which older domain controllers must be upgraded to achieve a higher domain or forest functional level. Always remember that you can run any operating system from Windows NT 4.0 SP3 or later on a member server, regardless of the functional level used.

The Windows Server 2003 interim domain functional level is intended only for use in upgrading a Windows NT 4.0 domain directly to Windows Server 2003. This functional level supports only Windows NT 4.0 and Windows Server 2003 domain controllers.

The Windows Server 2003 domain functional level can only be used when all domain controllers within the domain are of the Windows Server 2003 type. When the domain has been raised to Windows Server 2003, it will support domain controller renaming, converting groups, SID history, full group nesting, and universal groups as both security groups and distribution groups.

Exercise 2.07 reviews the process for raising a domain's functional level. To raise a domain's functional level, you begin in the Active Directory Domains and Trusts console.

EXERCISE 2.07

RAISING THE DOMAIN FUNCTIONAL LEVEL

1. Click **Start | Administrative Tools | Active Directory Domains and Trusts**.
2. In the left pane, click the domain that you want to raise the functional level.
3. Right-click that domain.
4. Select **Raise Domain Functional Level** from the popup menu.
5. In the resulting dialog box, click the drop-down arrow and select the new domain functional level.
6. Click **Raise**.

EXAM 70-296 OBJECTIVE 6.1 6.1.1 6.1.2

Global Catalog Servers

Each forest uses a single *global catalog* across all its domains. This global catalog acts as an index because it contains a small amount of information about the objects that exist across the entire Active Directory forest. Another task that is relegated to the global catalog is the duty of processing logons in order to allow querying of universal groups. (The logon and authentication process should be able to discover access rights through the querying of a user's universal group memberships.) Finally, the global catalog is instrumental during the process of a user (or application) querying the Active Directory to locate objects.

The global catalog is an index data store of the objects that exist across the entire forest. It contains a partial copy of objects within each domain so that users and applications can query objects regardless of their location within the forest. The global catalog stores only the attributes about each object that may be searchable, such as a printer's location or a user's telephone numbers. This ensures that the size of the global catalog remains manageable yet still provides a searchable database.

A *global catalog server* is a special domain controller that contains a copy of the global catalog in addition to a full copy of the Active Directory database partition for its domain. The first domain controller in the forest is automatically a global catalog server. The global catalog:

- Enables querying of objects
- Enables authentication of user principal names, which takes the form of user@domain.com
- Provides universal group membership information during logon

When you deploy Active Directory, you need to plan for the placement of the global catalog servers. In addition, when you determine that a global catalog server is not feasible for a location, you need to evaluate whether you should enable universal group caching so that users can log on when a global catalog server cannot be reached.

EXAM 70-296 OBJECTIVE 6.1

Planning a Global Catalog Implementation

The global catalog is integral to the logon process. Not only is it involved with any user principal name (UPN) logon, for which the user enters a UPN name in the form of user@domain.com, but when a global catalog server is not available to a user, the users' universal group memberships cannot be resolved and the user's actual permissions are not available. Global catalog servers are also accessed whenever a user or application queries Active Directory to search for objects such as printers. Because the global catalog is so intertwined with a user's Active Directory interaction, you should plan carefully where to place global catalog servers.

As with all planning activities, you must understand the environment, including the underlying network, the users, and an idea of how the future Active Directory will be designed. In order to gain this understanding, you should gather the following documents and information about the organization before you begin your planning and design:

- WAN and LAN maps
- Bandwidth consumption across slow links
- Current Windows NT 4.0 domain and Active Directory domain configuration
- User information including organizational charts, current IDs, and general information

The WAN and LAN maps will help you most during your planning process. With the global catalog so integral to logons, you might think that the easiest thing to do is to place a global catalog server at each location. However, doing so can increase your replication traffic as well as cost quite a bit of money if you have many small offices that don't really need local servers, domain controllers, or global catalogs. The tradeoff you must make is based on performance and need.

TEST DAY TIP

Global catalog server planning and placement are skills that are specifically explored on the exam. Make certain you understand the purpose of a global catalog server and the impact that placing one at a site will have on the underlying network links.

When you plan your global catalog server placement, you should review the load distribution across the network as well as the failure rate of your WAN links. For example, if you have two sites connected by a T3 line and there are hundreds of users at each site, you would likely place a global catalog server at each site. The T3 line can withstand the replication traffic. In addition, you would not want hundreds of users' logon and query traffic to be crossing a WAN link just to connect to the network. If you have a very small site on which you will have a domain controller, you might still not want to have global catalog replication traffic crossing the WAN if the WAN link is a small pipe or if it is heavily utilized.

You should consider the size of your global catalog database as well. For a global catalog with more than 500,000 objects, you will require at least 56Kbps to 128Kbps of available bandwidth for replication. For a network with a global catalog of that size, it is likely that there will be small offices with few users and a small WAN link that would not easily handle that type of bandwidth. In these cases, you should look at enabling universal group membership caching, which we review in the following section.

You should always remember these rules when you are planning your global catalog servers:

- The first domain controller that you install into the root domain of an Active Directory forest is a global catalog server.
- You can only have one global catalog data store in a forest. When you have multiple forests, you will not be able to combine their global catalog data. In addition, you need to know which users access which forests and plan placement of global catalog servers for each one of the forests.
- When users log on to the network or query Active Directory to search for a resource, traffic is generated to a global catalog server when universal group membership caching is enabled.
- In general, sites that have a domain controller can also maintain a global catalog server.
- The larger the forest in terms of objects, the larger the global catalog data store. This in turn increases the size of replication traffic.
- Logon and query traffic across a WAN link has a larger impact on the network than does replication traffic between sites.
- Users contact global catalog servers within their own site when logging on, browsing, or querying the network. If they cannot contact a global catalog server within their own sites, they will contact a global catalog server in a remote site.
- The larger the number of global catalog servers at sites on the WAN, means higher replication traffic, but less query and logon traffic across the WAN.

You should look at failure of WAN links and load distribution across the network in order to plan global catalog servers. Let's look at a star network that spans four cities: New York, Phoenix, Los Angeles, and Dallas. The headquarters for this company is in New York with 1600 users, and a large data center is in Phoenix with 433 users. The Los Angeles location is a sales office with nine users, and the Dallas site is a warehouse with 32 users. A T3 line connects New York and Phoenix. Frame Relay at 256Kbps connects the Dallas warehouse to New York, and a 56Kbps line connects the sales office to New York. Not only will knowing the size of the pipe be helpful but the usage is important. Using a network traffic-monitoring tool such as Performance Monitor, you would find that these links have at least 30 percent available bandwidth at all times. Given just this information, you can determine that the headquarters in New York, with 1600 users, will be a good place to have a global catalog server. In addition, the Phoenix data center, with 433 users, is another location that would be good for a global catalog server. The link between these two sites is at T3 speeds and has plenty of bandwidth available for replication between the global catalog servers.

Whether to place global catalog servers at the Los Angeles and Dallas locations is another question. Given that both of these sites have relatively few users, the need for a global catalog server is probably small. In the event that the WAN link went down, there is very little that logging onto the local network will provide unless there is a mission-critical application that requires network authentication. If the warehouse in Dallas had such an application, a global catalog server would be needed in Dallas just in case the WAN link failed.

For global catalogs with more than half a million objects, the bandwidth required for replication is between 56Kbps and 128Kbps available on the WAN link at all times. This is not available on the link between Dallas and New York; however, the global catalog will reach about 10,000 objects, considering that there is a couple thousand users, the same number of computers, plus mailboxes and other extraneous information.

The Los Angeles sales office is another matter entirely. With so few users and a small link, the users can log on across the WAN. Therefore, there is no need to place a global catalog server at that office. The WAN design of the network will help you place global catalog servers. However, sites in larger internetworks will also require additional global catalog servers. In order to decide the placement of multiple global catalog servers within a single site, you should look over the LAN information. You need to know the LAN topology as well as the number of users and their usage requirements.

When to Use a Global Catalog

You have very little choice about having a global catalog. A global catalog is automatically created when you install the first domain controller in the root domain of a new forest. When you have multiple domains in the forest, the global catalog provides users a way of finding the resources within other domains. The global catalog also provides universal group membership information in processing logons so that a user's credentials can be accurately determined.

You can, of course, choose how many global catalog servers you have. When a forest only has a single domain, the need for a global catalog server is extremely small. Domain controllers automatically contain the information for the entire domain, so there is no need for an index of those same objects in a global catalog data store.

The advantage of having a global catalog is realized when you have multiple domains in the forest because it ensures that users within any domain can query the network for resources, regardless of where those resources are located. The global catalog indexes information, which is configurable by the administrator so that only crucial data is included. When you have a global catalog server in a local site, logons and network queries are faster.

The disadvantages to having a global catalog lie in the additional traffic that is caused during replication, queries, browsing, and logons. You can overcome much of these traffic issues when you configure your sites and site links and select whether to use a global catalog server or to enable universal group caching on a domain controller.

EXAM 70-296 OBJECTIVE 6.1.1

Creating a Global Catalog Server

The process of creating a global catalog server is surprisingly simple. First, you must create the global catalog server on a domain controller. You cannot create it on a member server of the domain. If you have a member server that you want to reconfigure as a global catalog server, you first have to install Active Directory services using the Active Directory wizard. Exercise 2.08 provides the steps for creating a global catalog server.

Exercise 2.08

Creating a Global Catalog Server

1. Log on to the domain controller as a member of the Domain Admins or Enterprise Admins group.
2. Click **Start | Programs | Administrative Tools | Active Directory Sites and Services**.
3. Navigate to the site where the domain controller is located in the left pane. Expand the site, then expand the Servers container, and finally expand the server itself.
4. Right-click the **NTDS Settings** object below the server.
5. Select **Properties** from the popup menu.
6. Check the box marked **Global Catalog**, as shown in Figure 2.15.

Figure 2.15 Creating a Global Catalog Server

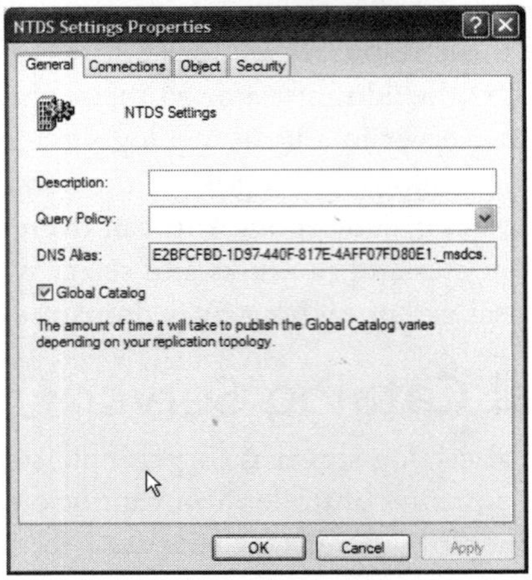

EXAM 70-296 BJECTIVE .1.2

Universal Group Membership Caching

Global catalog servers have a heavy impact on network traffic during replication. Allowing users to log on and query the network across WAN links can create even more load, so there is a tradeoff when you place global catalog servers at sites around the network. When users attempt to log on to the network, a global catalog server is contacted so that the user's membership within any universal groups can be resolved. This allows the logon attempt to determine the user's full rights and permissions. When the global catalog server is not available, the user's logon attempt is denied. However, Windows Server 2003 Active Directory allows you a way to have your cake and eat it, too. This new process, called *universal group membership caching,* is enabled on sites that contain domain controllers but do not have global catalog servers. When users log on to the network, the local domain controller contacts a global catalog server for that user's universal group memberships and then stores that information in cache for future logons. This process reduces the WAN traffic at logon.

When to Use Universal Group Membership Caching

Whether you decide to implement universal group membership caching or a global catalog server, you need a domain controller at the site. This means that you will have a certain amount of replication traffic across the WAN link, no matter what. So the main reason to do either is to localize the logon and query traffic.

Let's look at a specific situation in which it makes more sense to have universal group membership caching than a global catalog server. In this scenario, the forest is extensive, with multiple domains and over a half a million objects throughout. The actual site where universal group membership caching will be enabled is small, with 50 users and a domain controller. The users all belong to a domain with fewer than 10,000 objects in Active Directory. The WAN link is 56Kbps and heavily utilized. The impact of users logging onto the network is taking its toll—the users' traffic is traveling across the WAN in order to contact a global catalog server to resolve the universal group memberships—and the users complain of slow logons. To speed up the logons, you can either enable universal group membership caching or enable the global catalog on the local domain controller. Since the global catalog has over half a million objects, it requires between 56Kbps and 128Kbps in order for replication to take place, and the WAN link would not be able to carry that replication traffic. Therefore, this is the type of situation in which the best option is to enable universal group membership caching.

Another situation in which universal group membership caching works well is when the global catalog is so large that it taxes the resources of a domain controller. If this is the case, you can either upgrade hardware and enable the global catalog on the domain controller or you can enable universal group membership caching.

Exam Warning

Familiarize yourself with the differences between universal group membership caching and global catalog servers. Remember that universal group membership caching is enabled for an entire site, affecting all domain controllers within the site. By contrast, global catalog servers are enabled only for the domain controllers that you specify.

Configuring Universal Group Membership Caching

When you configure universal group membership caching, you do not specify individual domain controllers. Universal group membership caching is applicable to an entire site. If you have a site that includes a global catalog server, you do not need to enable universal group membership caching unless that site is split across WAN links. If you have a site that has no domain controllers, enabling universal group membership caching makes no difference to the traffic flow because a domain controller is required for storing the cache. Exercise 2.09 discusses the process of enabling universal group membership caching.

Exercise 2.09

Enabling Universal Group Membership Caching

In order to configure universal group membership caching, you enable it for the site rather than for a domain controller within the site. To do so:

1. Open the **Active Directory Sites and Services** console.

2. In the left pane, navigate to the site where universal group membership caching will be enabled.
3. Click the site.
4. In the right pane, right-click the **NTDS Site Settings** object.
5. Select **Properties** from the popup menu.
6. Check the box to **Enable Universal Group Membership Caching**, as shown in Figure 2.16.

Figure 2.16 Enabling Universal Group Membership Caching on a Domain Controller

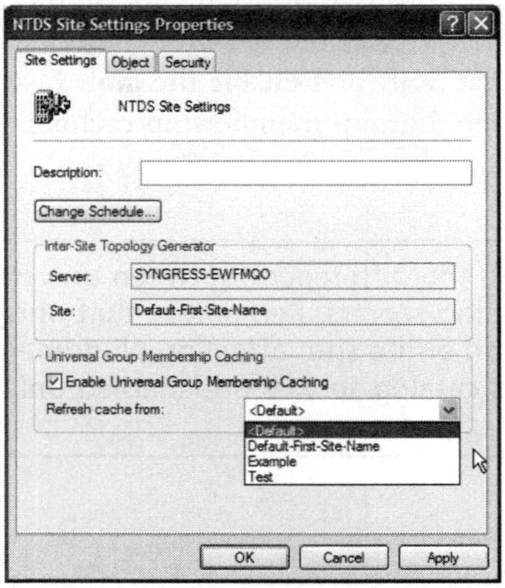

Adding Attributes to Customize the Global Catalog

Before you add attributes to the global catalog, keep in mind that doing so will have a negative impact on replication. Each new attribute increases the size of the global catalog, which increases the time it takes for replication to completely synchronize all the global catalog servers. You should only replicate attributes in the global catalog that must be indexed for queries or applications.

In order to add an attribute to the global catalog, you must use the Active Directory Schema snap-in, be logged in as a member of the Schema Admins group, and make the change on a domain controller that holds the Schema Master role. In the Active Directory Schema snap-in, you need to navigate to the attribute that you want to replicate and right-click it. Then select the **Properties** option from the popup menu, and check the box that states **Replicate this attribute to the Global Catalog**.

To open the Active Directory Schema snap-in, you must first register its DLL by typing **regsvr32.exe <systemroot>\system32\schmmgmt.dll** in the Run box or at a command prompt. Next, open a blank management console by typing **MMC** in the Run box or at a command prompt. In the MMC File menu, select **Add/Remove Snap-in**. Click **Add**, and select **Active Directory Schema**. Click **Add** again, and then click **Close** and click **OK**.

Effects on Replication

After you enable universal group membership caching on a domain controller, the domain controller will only replicate its own domain data with replication partners. There is a point at which, when a user first logs on, the domain controller contacts a global catalog server within another site to pull the user's universal group membership information. The domain controller then caches this information. Periodically thereafter, the domain controller refreshes that data. The default period for refreshing this data is every eight hours.

Security Considerations

The global catalog is built with security considerations in mind. When a user logs into the network, the global catalog is contacted for that person's universal group memberships to ensure that the user is granted the correct permissions to network resources. If a global catalog server cannot be located at the time of the user's logon, the user cannot access any network resources.

For a network that has few changes and is a low security risk, the global catalog is a reasonably secure system. Replication can cause a delay in updates reaching every site in the network—especially if replication will take place every few days. For example, imagine that you have a user who is accidentally added to a universal group that is a member of the Enterprise Admins group. This mistake is replicated across the network before you remove the user from the group. Even if you remove the user from the group in your site, the global catalog servers think that the user is a member of the Enterprise Admins group until replication takes place next. This leaves a temporary security hole. One way to overcome security concerns about universal group memberships is to force replication after you make any changes to group memberships.

Another security consideration is that involved with the universal group membership caching invoked on a site. The default caching period for a user's credentials tied to universal group memberships is eight hours. If you work in an environment that changes quite often, you will find that the eight-hour caching period might cause a security issue. In most environments, eight hours is a sufficient caching period. In a busy network, setting a more frequent period will address some of the security and administrative concerns.

Summary of Exam Objectives

The objectives for the exam focus on the design and implementation of an Active Directory forest. This means that you should have the skills to design a forest, including the root domain, additional domain trees, and child domains. These skills look at your ability to use the existing environment as well as the organization's goals and project objectives, then combine them with the Active Directory features and functions to come up with a resulting forest design that is optimized for the environment and meets business needs. In this process, you need to:

- Select and establish a forest root domain.
- Define the need and boundaries for child domains.
- Establish the namespaces and requirements for contiguities.
- Understand the implementation process for each domain controller.
- Know where to place global catalog servers throughout the network.

The exam objectives incorporate new features of forest design and implementation. These include (but are not limited to):

- Application directory partitions
- Forest trust relationships
- Forest and domain functional levels
- Universal group membership caching

The application directory partitions are intended for integration of the forest with applications that are implemented within certain locations in the network. The application directory partition would likely have the ability to integrate with the Active Directory, but because the application would only be required at a small number of sites, the replication impact of that data would be too high for it to be a part of a domain partition. Application directory partitions overcome this limitation by providing a locally implemented directory partition for the application that can be configured specifically to meet the needs of a set of users within the forest.

Forest trust relationships are added to the existing trusts—the implicit Kerberos trusts that exist between domains within a forest, the explicit external trusts that can be created with domains and Kerberos realms outside of the forest, and shortcut trusts that can be used to speed up resource access within a forest with numerous child domains or multiple domain trees. You should have a solid understanding of how each of these trust relationships work, their transitivity and direction, and when you should implement each type.

The new forest and domain functional levels extend the previous Windows 2000 concept of native and mixed-mode domains. You should have a good understanding of how the forest and domain functional levels affect the features that you are able to implement.

The ability to design a global catalog server placement among the sites you have designed is one of the critical skills for a forest since it will dictate how quickly users can log on, whether WAN outages will cause logon failures, and how much replication traffic will be transmitted across WAN links. In the Windows Server 2003 forest, you now have a new option to weigh against: whether to use a global catalog server or to enable universal group membership caching.

With the new features and functionality available in a Windows Server 2003 Active Directory forest, you need a solid foundation in understanding its value, benefits, and design. Furthermore, you should practice configuring each of these features and perform tests to see how users could be affected by their implementation.

Exam Objectives Fast Track

Designing Active Directory

- ☑ The forest root domain provides its name to the entire Active Directory forest.
- ☑ Design child domains in which you need specific separations, driven by network discontinuity, business requirements, or administrative separation.
- ☑ Gather information, such as network topology maps and organization charts, about the current environment before making your design decisions.

Configuring Active Directory

- ☑ You can add application directory partitions to Active Directory for use by local applications using the NTDSUTIL utility.
- ☑ There are four types of trusts: the implicit Kerberos trusts between domains within a forest, the explicit trusts between an Active Directory domain and an external domain or Kerberos realm, a shortcut trust between domains within a forest, and a forest trust between the root domains of two Windows Server 2003 forests.
- ☑ The forest has three functional levels: Windows 2000, Windows Server 2003 interim, and Windows Server 2003.
- ☑ Domains have four functional levels: Windows 2000 native, Windows 2000 mixed, Windows Server 2003 interim, and Windows Server 2003.

Global Catalog Servers

- ☑ The global catalog is a data store with a partial copy of objects that cross all the domains within a forest.
- ☑ Global catalog servers process logons in order to provide the universal group membership for a user and ensure that user has the appropriate credentials at logon.
- ☑ In the absence of a global catalog server and without universal group membership caching enabled for a site, a user's logon is denied.
- ☑ Universal group membership caching is enabled for an entire site, whereas global catalog servers are enabled on individual domain controllers.

Exam Objectives Frequently Asked Questions

The following Frequently Asked Questions, answered by the authors of this book, are designed to both measure your understanding of the Exam Objectives presented in this chapter, and to assist you with real-life implementation of these concepts. You will also gain access to thousands of other FAQs at ITFAQnet.com.

Q: When you design the forest root domain, why is it such a big deal to select the right name?

A: The forest root domain will become the name of the forest. If you use a name that will be accessible via the Internet, you will have security issues. If you use a name that is not going to be recognized in your DNS scheme, your users will not be able to log on. If you misspell the name during installation, you will have to rename the domain and forest, either using the domain renaming tool (allowed only at the forest functional level of Windows Server 2003) or by reinstalling. If you upgrade an existing domain and make a serious naming error, you will have to recover your original domain and start from the beginning.

Q: In designing domains for a real network, people bring up a whole lot of other reasons for having more child domains than seem to be in the design rules. Why is that?

A: Politics are a major driver for creating additional separations within a business or organization. The reality is that you can design a single domain and probably achieve everyone's business requirements simply through a good OU and administrative delegation system. However, there is a sense of security when you have your "own domain," and many people will think up a variety of reasons to make that happen for themselves.

Q: Why do you need an organizational chart when you design your domain hierarchy?

A: The organizational chart will give you an idea of the political separations within the organization. Even though you might be able to design a single domain, you could need the org chart later, for OU design within the domain.

Q: When would anyone need an application directory partition? There aren't really applications that use it yet.

A: True. Application directory partitions are new, which means that no one really uses them—yet. However, TAPI applications have been developed to use the application directory partition. In addition, this type of partition offers developers a new way to utilize directory service data without directly impacting the main Active Directory partitions.

Q: The forest trust could make things very easy to manage, but we already have a complex set of external trusts between domains in our Windows 2000 Active Directory forests. Should we change over when we upgrade?

A: That all depends on your organization's needs. You should review which resources users need to access and what type of security you need to have in place. From there, you can compare whether a forest trust will meet your needs or if you should continue with external trusts.

Q: What's the point of having so many domain and forest functional levels?

A: The domain and forest functional levels are a way to unlock the native capabilities of the Windows Server 2003 Active Directory. If you decide to leave everything at the default levels even though your domain controllers have all been upgraded, the Active Directory will not be able to take advantage of the new features that could be available, such as a forest trust relationship.

Q: Why does the global catalog appear to have more importance than before?

A: There are two reasons. First, the global catalog is an absolute requirement if you have multiple domains in your forest. Planning for the global catalog is critical to ensuring that users can log on to the network. Second, a new feature, universal group membership caching, can be implemented in place of the global catalog, so you need to know the differences between the two and when to use each.

Q: How do you go about creating a global catalog server?

A: You use the Active Directory Sites and Services console, and locate the domain controller that you are going to turn into a global catalog server. Then you right-click the NTDS Settings of the domain controller to access the NTDS Settings Properties dialog and check the box for global catalog server.

Q: What do I do if I want to change a global catalog server into a universal group membership caching server?

A: First, you can remove the global catalog server by unchecking the box in the server's NTDS Settings Properties dialog box. But when you enable universal group membership caching, you will not be doing so for an individual server; you will be enabling it for the entire site of which the domain controller is a member. This is performed in the NTDS Site Settings Properties dialog box of the site.

Self Test

1. Your network currently uses a single Windows NT 4.0 domain named EXAMPLE, which is used by 2000 people at 12 different offices. The company has registered the name exampleinc.com for e-mail purposes. You have a PDC and seven BDCs. You discover that none of your domain controllers can support Windows Server 2003. You decide to install a new domain for Windows Server 2003 Active Directory using all new equipment, then migrate users, computers and data after the new domain is established. Which of the following names should you select for your root domain?

   A. example.local

   B. exampleinc.com

   C. sub.example.local

   D. sub.exampleinc.com

2. You have a Windows 2000 Active Directory forest with 14 domains. The company has undergone some changes, many of which have streamlined administrative duties. Instead of several different administrative groups heading up their own divisions, the company now has a central administrative unit with three subunits that handle help desk and password changes, deskside support and computer account management, and installations and deployments, respectively. The company has decided to restructure the domains so that the forest root domain is empty except for forest management. You are now designing the child domains. How many should you design?

   A. 0

   B. 1

   C. 3

   D. 13

3. You have been hired as a consultant to review an Active Directory design for Example Inc. The company hands you its WAN map, an organizational chart, and its Active Directory design. Headquarters for Example Inc. are in Boston. You immediately notice that the WAN map has a Boston location, a New York location, and a Philadelphia location. In addition, you discover that the Active Directory root name is intended to be NY.example.com. The child domains are intended to be named Boston.example.com and philly.example.com. What is wrong with this design?

   A. The names of cities cannot be the same as a site, which you assume they will use.

   B. Boston.example.com should be the root of the forest, since it is the headquarters.

   C. The root domain namespace and the child domains are at the same level.

   D. The name example.com was not registered.

4. You are an administrator for an automotive parts company. Your manufacturing plant is located in Flint, Michigan, and you have a large office in Detroit, Michigan. You have small offices on site at your main business partner, an automotive company. Your headquarters is in Paris, France. You have three names registered with InterNIC: autoparts.net, autoparts.fr, and autoparts.co.uk. The autoparts.fr and autoparts.co.uk names are used on the Web to sell automotive parts to European and Pacific Rim countries and for research and development, respectively. The autoparts.net name is not used. Which of the following names will you select for the forest root domain?

   A. autoparts.fr

   B. autoparts.co.uk

   C. autoparts.local

   D. autoparts.net

5. Your help desk staff have decided to implement a new TAPI application that will integrate with Active Directory. The application will only be used at the help desk location in Atlanta. They require fault tolerance for the application. You have seven other branches and do not want any excess traffic on your WAN links to them. How do you assist the help desk staff with their request?

   A. Deny the request for the application. It will overwhelm the WAN links.

   B. Implement the TAPI application with extensions to the schema and new objects to be replicated across the network.

   C. Create an application directory partition on an Atlanta domain controller.

   D. Create one application directory partition and two replicas on three separate Atlanta domain controllers.

6. You have a Windows NT 4.0 network with three domains that you will be migrating to an Active Directory Windows Server 2003 forest. You will also create a mirrored Windows Server 2003 lab forest for research and development. You want to allow users in the lab forest to have access to the production forest's resources. How do you enable this ability?

   A. Create a one-way forest trust in which the production forest trusts the lab forest.

   B. Create an explicit external trust relationship in which the lab forest root domain trusts the production forest root domain.

   C. Create a two-way forest trust between the production and lab forests.

   D. Create a one-way explicit trust in which the production forest root trusts the lab forest root.

7. You have a Windows NT 4.0 network with three domains that you will be migrating to a Windows Server 2003 Active Directory forest. Your domain controllers are not able to support the Windows Server 2003 operating system. You create a new forest and migrate users and computers to the new forest. During the migration, you create a trust relationship so that users who are in the new forest can access resources on member servers of the old domains. What type of trust relationships will you need to create?

   A. A forest trust relationship

   B. Explicit external trust relationships

   C. Implicit Kerberos trust relationships

   D. Shortcut trust relationships

8. Your Windows 2000 Active Directory forest has just been upgraded to Windows Server 2003. You have added seven new domains because you are merging with another company. Users in your sub.child.trunk.root.local domain are having lengthy access times for resources in the new.child.trunk.other.co.local domain, whose resources are in the same building as the users trying to access them. How can you speed up access?

   A. Move the users to a new building.

   B. Create an explicit external trust relationship between the domains.

   C. Raise the domain functional level to Windows Server 2003.

   D. Create a shortcut trust relationship.

9. You are designing an Active Directory network. There will be two forests in the final design. Forest A will trust Forest B in the final configuration. You will have several member servers that will run Windows NT 4.0 and several that will run Windows Server 2000. Which forest functional level should you select?

   A. None; you cannot configure this forest

   B. Windows 2000

   C. Windows Server 2003 interim

   D. Windows Server 2003

10. You have an Active Directory network with three domains. Domain 1 is at the domain functional level of Windows 2000 native. Domain 2 is at the domain functional level of Windows Server 2003 interim. Domain 3 is at Windows Server 2003. What is the highest level you can have for the forest functional level?

    A. Windows 2000

    B. Windows Server 2003 interim

    C. Windows Server 2003

    D. None; this forest cannot be configured

11. You are upgrading a Windows NT 4.0 domain and a Windows 2000 Active Directory forest with two domains to Windows Server 2003. In your final forest configuration, you will have domain controllers with either Windows 2000 server or Windows Server 2003 operating systems. Which domain functional levels are the highest you can reach?

    A. Windows 2000 mixed

    B. Windows 2000 native

    C. Windows Server 2003 interim

    D. Windows Server 2003

12. You have a network with four locations: NY, PHX, LA, SEA. You have three domains that contain both users and network resources. You install a new printer in the SEA location. The printer is in the root domain, which has most of its other resources in the NY location. Several users in a child domain at the SEA location complain that it takes a long time to access the printer. What steps can you take to speed up access to the printer?

    A. Create a shortcut trust to the root domain from the child domain.

    B. Add a global catalog server to the NY location.

    C. Add a global catalog server to the SEA location.

D. Enable universal group membership caching at SEA.

13. You have a network with five locations. You have configured four sites, one of which combines the offices at two locations and is named COMBO. There is one global catalog server at each site and domain controllers at all five locations. At COMBO's Office A, users are periodically complaining that they cannot log on. However, at COMBO's Office B, there have been no problems. In what two ways can you fix this problem? (Select two answers.)

    A. Install another domain controller at COMBO's Office A.

    B. Enable a global catalog server at COMBO's Office A.

    C. Enable a global catalog server at COMBO's Office B.

    D. Enable universal group membership caching for the entire COMBO site.

14. You have two forests. Each of these forests is used across your five office locations. You have users who access resources in both forests. You have explicit external trust relationships between certain domains to allow access. These users often complain that they cannot query for resources in one of the forests in the same window that they browse the other forest. What can you do to fix this problem?

    A. Add a global catalog server.

    B. Enable universal group membership caching.

    C. Create a new trust.

    D. Nothing.

15. You are designing a Windows Server 2003 forest. You will have a single domain in the forest. You will have three sites with over 400 users each. You will not be using UPN names. How many global catalog servers should you plan for?

    A. 0

    B. 1

    C. 2

    D. 3

Self Test Quick Answer Key

For complete questions, answers, and explanations to the Self Test questions in this chapter as well as the other chapters in this book, see the Self Test Appendix.

1. **B**
2. **B**
3. **C**
4. **D**
5. **D**
6. **A**
7. **B**
8. **D**
9. **D**
10. **A**
11. **B**
12. **C**
13. **B**, **D**
14. **D**
15. **B**

Chapter 3

MCSA/MCSE 70-296

Managing and Maintaining an Active Directory Infrastructure

Exam Objectives in this Chapter:

- 7.1 Manage an Active Directory forest and domain structure.
- 7.1.1 Manage trust relationships.
- 7.1.2 Manage schema modifications.
- 7.1.3 Add or remove a UPN suffix.
- 7.2 Restore Active Directory directory services.
- 7.2.1 Perform an authoritative restore operation.
- 7.2.2 Perform a nonauthoritative restore operation.

- ☑ Summary of Exam Objectives
- ☑ Exam Objectives Fast Track
- ☑ Exam Objectives Frequently Asked Questions
- ☑ Self Test
- ☑ Self Test Quick Answer Key

Introduction

To pass the 70-296 exam, you not only need to know how to plan and configure an Active Directory structure—you also have to know how to manage it once it is in place. Unfortunately, Active Directory is not something that can be implemented and then walked away from. In your role as a networking professional, you will experience times when you must make some minor changes to your structure as well as some major changes.

There might come a time in your environment when you will add or remove domains from your Active Directory structure. Events such as company mergers, branch closures, and other business-oriented events can trigger a need to reconfigure your structure to accommodate change. In these types of events, you might need to add or remove trusts between domains, add OUs, or perform other administrative tasks that can have a huge impact on your structure. In this chapter, you will learn how to manage your Active Directory structure, including handling tools at your disposal for these management tasks.

Along with these changes to your Active Directory structure, there might come a time when you realize a change that you made to your structure was incorrect. Unfortunately, there is no Undo command in the Active Directory tools. However, as it was with Windows 2000, Active Directory restore tools are your best friends when these types of problems occur. In this chapter, you will learn the Active Directory restore types and how to properly restore Active Directory.

Let's begin this chapter with a discussion of the different ways that you can manage your Active Directory structure.

Choosing a Management Method

Microsoft has provided a number of tools to help you manage Active Directory. You can administer your Active Directory installation using Windows graphical user interface (GUI) tools, various command-line utilities, and more advanced scripting functions. Each method has certain advantages, so as we perform the many exercises in this chapter we'll discuss both GUI and command-line procedures to accomplish each task. You'll notice that we focus primarily on the GUI interface, since this will likely be your tool of choice in your day-to-day operations (not to mention on the 70-296 exam!).

Using a Graphical User Interface

The most common means of administering your Active Directory infrastructure is through the built-in GUI utilities that are added during the Active Directory installation process (dcpromo.exe). The Microsoft Management Console (MMC) centralizes the graphical tools that you will use to administer your Active Directory installation as well as most other Windows Server 2003 components into a single management console that can be run from an administrative workstation or the server itself. Similar to Windows 2000, the MMC provides a common interface and presentation for Microsoft utilities as well as an increasing number of third-party management tools. You'll use a number of snap-ins to the MMC to manage your Windows Server 2003 Active Directory implementation.

The greatest advantage to using the GUI utilities to administer your network is one of simplicity: Microsoft has distilled the most common tasks into an easy-to-follow Wizard format, in which you are prompted for information at each step.

Trust relationships, a major component of this chapter, are managed using the Active Directory Domains and Trusts tool. This console is located in the Administrative Tools folder on your domain controller, or you can load the administrative tools onto your local workstation. Administration of Active Directory objects such as users, groups, and OUs can be accomplished with the Active Directory Users and Computers tool, and tasks associated with the physical layout of your Active Directory infrastructure can be completed using the Active Directory Sites and Services tool. In addition to the built-in utilities discussed here, there are any number of free and commercial GUI tools available from the Microsoft Web site and other third-party vendors. Figures 3.1–3.3 illustrate each of the built-in tools we've just mentioned; we discuss these extensively throughout this chapter and the rest of the book.

Figure 3.1 Active Directory Domains and Trusts

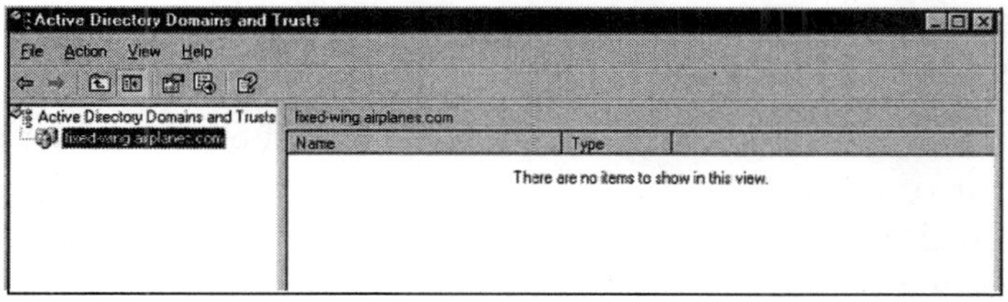

Figure 3.2 Active Directory Sites and Services

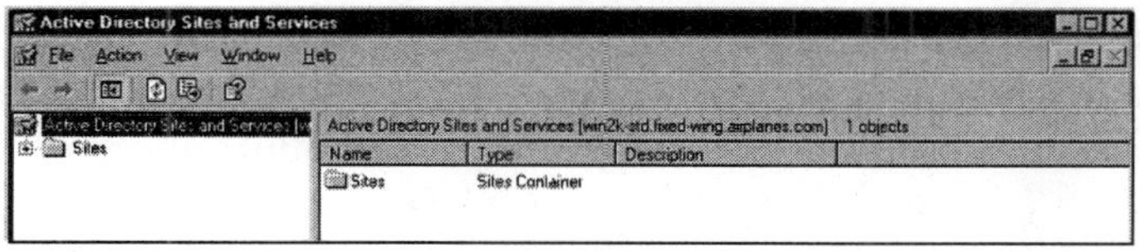

Figure 3.3 Active Directory Users and Computers

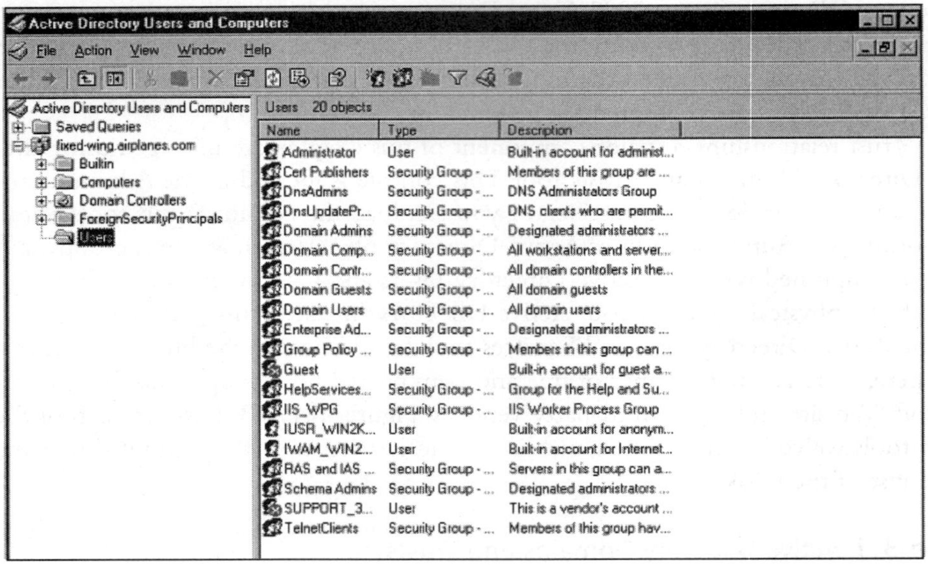

Using the Command-line

For more granular control of administrative functions, you should consider using Microsoft's array of utilities that you can run from the command-line interface (CLI) to manage your Windows Server 2003 environment. You can choose from preinstalled utilities included in the Windows operating system as well as additional tools that you can install from the ~\Support\Tools folder of the server source media.

Command-line utilities can help streamline the administrative process in cases where you find yourself issuing the same command or making the same configuration change on a regular basis. As we discuss in the "Using Scripting" section that follows, CLI utilities can be integrated into batch files, login scripts, and other automated scripting functions in order to speed the administrative process. Some command-line utilities also do not have an equivalent within the GUI environment, such as the *CSVDE* utility that allows you to import information from a comma-separated (.CSV) text file directly into the Active Directory database. If you have large amounts of information to enter into Active Directory, the command-line utilities discussed here can make your administrative tasks far more efficient.

Defining Commands

In Table 3.1, we've included a partial list of the command-line utilities available to Windows Server 2003 administrators. You can find a complete listing on the Microsoft Developer Network site at http://msdn.microsoft.com. You can see the syntax and optional parameters of most of these commands by typing **utility /?** at the Windows command prompt—for example, the *ntdsutil /?* command lists all possible parameters for the *ntdsutil* utility.

Table 3.1 Windows Server 2003 Command-Line Utilities

Utility Name	Description
CSVDE	Allows information to be imported to and exported from Active Directory using a .CSV format.
DSADD	Creates users, groups, computers, contacts, and OUs within the Active Directory database.
DSMOD	Modifies the attributes of an existing object within Active Directory. DSMOD can modify users, groups, computers, servers, contacts, and OUs.
DSRM	Deletes objects from Active Directory.
DSMOVE	Working from a single domain controller, DSMOVE either renames an object without moving it or moves it from its current location in the directory to a new location within the Active Directory tree. (To move objects between domains, you'll need to use the Movetree command-line tool.)
DSQUERY	Allows you to find a list of objects in Active Directory using specified criteria. You can use this utility to search for computers, contacts, subnets, groups, OUs, sites, servers, and user objects.
DSGET	Displays specific attributes of object types within Active Directory. You can view attributes of any of the following object types: computers, contacts, subnets, groups, OUs, servers, sites, and users.
LDIFDE	Creates, modifies, and deletes directory objects. You can also use LDIFDE to extend the Active Directory schema, export user and group information to other applications or services, and populate Active Directory with data from other directory services.
NETDOM	Installed from the ~\Support\Tools directory on the Windows Server 2003 CD, this tool is used primarily in creating, verifying, and removing trust relationships on a Windows network. You'll see this tool mentioned several times in the "Managing Trusts" section of this chapter.
NTDSUTIL	This is the "Swiss Army knife" of Active Directory management tools. Among other things, *ntdsutil* can perform database maintenance of Active Directory, manage single operation masters, and remove meta-data left behind by domain controllers that were removed from the network without being properly uninstalled.

Using Scripting

You can extend the usefulness of Windows Server 2003 command-line utilities even further by including them in various scripting utilities. The applications that you can use to apply scripting to your network administration tools are virtually endless, but two of the more readily available are *Windows Scripting Host* and the *Active Directory Services Interface (ADSI)*. ADSI provides an interface for most common scripting languages to query for and manipulate directory service objects, allowing you to automate such tasks as creating users and resetting passwords.

Just like individual command-line utilities, scripting allows you to increase the efficiency of your administrative tasks even further by allowing you to automate processes that would otherwise be tedious and time-consuming. For example, a university administrator might create a batch file to automatically create new user accounts for each semester's batch of incoming students, which would prove much more efficient than manually entering each object's information into the MMC GUI. The flexibility of the command-line utilities allows you to integrate them into any number of scripting applications, including VBScript, Perl, and Windows logon scripts. These scripts can be launched manually, scheduled to run at regular intervals, or integrated into a Web or intranet application to be run on demand—for example, by a user needing to reset her password. Although an in-depth discussion of Windows scripting is beyond the scope of this book, you can find a wide variety of information and reference material on the MSDN site at http://msdn.microsoft.com.

EXAM 70-296 OBJECTIVE 7.1 7.1.1 7.1.2 7.1.3

Managing Forests and Domains

As an MCSE, you'll be expected to have the skills necessary to manage forests and domains with your Active Directory infrastructure. You'll need to be familiar with performing such familiar tasks as creating new forests, domains, and child domains, as well as with the new functionality offered by Windows Server 2003. In this section we cover the tasks associated with managing Active Directory at the domain and forest levels.

EXAM 70-296 OBJECTIVE 7.1

Managing Domains

Active Directory domains are the cornerstone of a well-formed Active Directory implementation; they provide the most common framework for managing your Active Directory environment. You'll perform some of the tasks described in this section only when your network environment changes—for example, creating a new domain tree or a child domain after creating a new department or merging with another company. Other tasks, including creating and managing organizational units, managing domain controllers, and assigning and managing permissions on Active Directory objects, will be a part of your daily life. The following pages detail the steps necessary to perform a wide array of domain management functions. Knowing how to perform these tasks will not only help you on the 70-296 exam but also in the real world of network administration.

Remember from your Windows 2000 studies that Active Directory *domains* are used to organize objects within Windows Server 2003, whereas Active Directory *sites* map to the physical layout of your network infrastructure. You can have a single domain that includes multiple sites, or you can have a single site that contains many domains. Domains allow you to manage your Active Directory environment in the way that best meets your needs without locking you into matching your administrative layout to your company's physical structure. Windows Server 2003 domains can contain any combination of Active Directory objects, including servers, OUs, users, groups, and other resources. Windows Server 2003 computers can function as standalone servers that house shared resources as well as domain controllers that handle user authentication and authorization functions.

Creating a New Child Domain

Active Directory is designed to remain flexible enough to meet the changing and growing needs of a company's organizational structure. For example, let's say that you administer the airplanes.com Active Directory domain. As the company has grown, the board of directors has decided to subdivide the production team into two halves, fixed-wing.airplanes.com and biplanes.airplanes.com, both of which will ultimately report to the main airplanes.com management office. As the IT manager, you decide to create a child domain for each production subdivision. This will allow you to subdivide network resources between the two new divisions as well as delegate IT management functions of each child domain while still maintaining overall administrative authority on the airplanes.com network. Your new domain structure will resemble the one shown in Figure 3.4. Exercise 3.01 goes through the steps needed to create a new child domain.

Figure 3.4 Parent and Child Domains

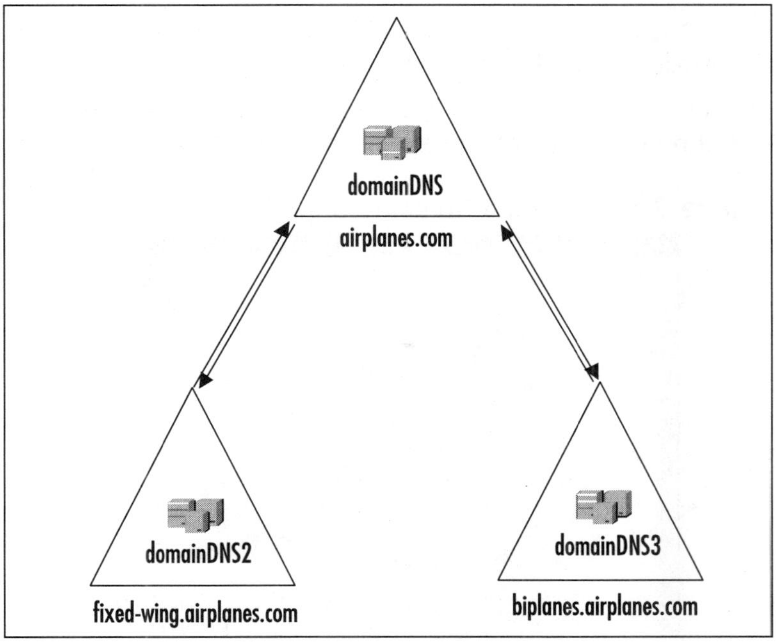

Test Day Tip

When you create a child domain, a two-way transitive trust is automatically created between the parent and child domains. Remember the transitive property from your high school mathematics class: If A equals B and B equals C, A must therefore equal C. It works the same way in a trust relationship: If Domain A trusts Domain B and Domain B trusts Domain C, Domain A automatically trusts Domain C. (This is different from the NT 4.0 trust environment in which you would have needed to manually create another trust between Domain A and Domain C.)

Exercise 3.01

Creating a Child Domain

1. From a Windows Server 2003 machine, click **Start | Run**, then type **dcpromo** to launch the Active Directory Installation Wizard.
2. If the Operating System Compatibility page appears, read the information presented and click **Next**.
3. On the Domain Controller Type screen, shown in Figure 3.5, select **Domain controller for a new domain**. Click **Next** to continue.

Figure 3.5 Creating a Domain Controller

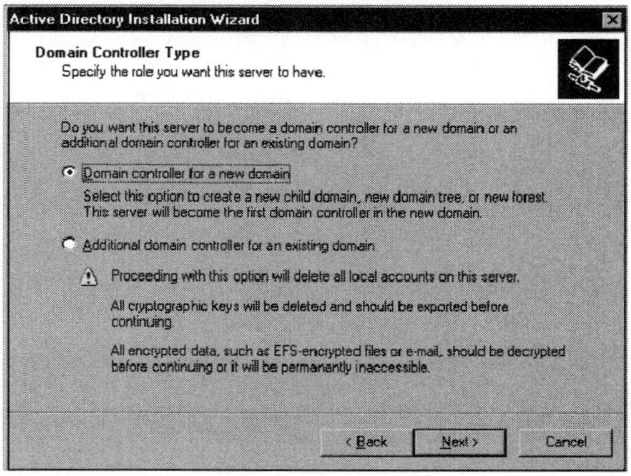

4. On the Create New Domain page, select **Child domain in an existing domain tree**, and then click **Next**.

5. The next screen, shown in Figure 3.6, prompts you for the username, password, and domain of the user account with the necessary rights to create a child domain. Enter the appropriate information and click **Next**.

Figure 3.6 Creating a Child Domain

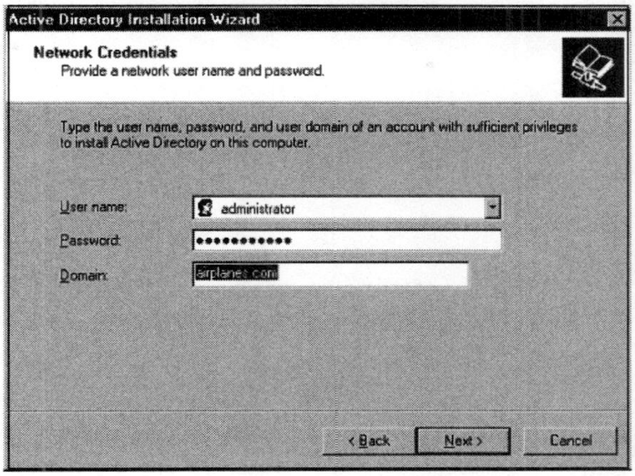

Exam Warning

In order to create a child domain in a Windows Server 2003 network, you must be a member of the Enterprise Admins group in the parent domain. The Enterprise Admins group exists only in the root domain of the forest; by default members of this group have administrative authority to every domain within a Windows Server 2003 forest.

6. On the Child Domain Installation screen, verify the name of the parent domain and enter the new child domain name, in this case **fixed-wing.airplanes.com**. Click **Next** to continue.
7. The NetBIOS Domain Name page, shown in Figure 3.7, will suggest a default NetBIOS name that down-level clients will use to connect to this domain. Accept the suggested default or type in a NetBIOS domain name of your choosing, then click **Next**.
8. On the Database and Log Folders screen, shown in Figure 3.8, enter the location in which you want to install the database and log folders, or else click **Browse** to navigate to the location using Windows Explorer. Click **Next** when you're ready to continue.

Figure 3.7 Specifying the NetBIOS Domain Name

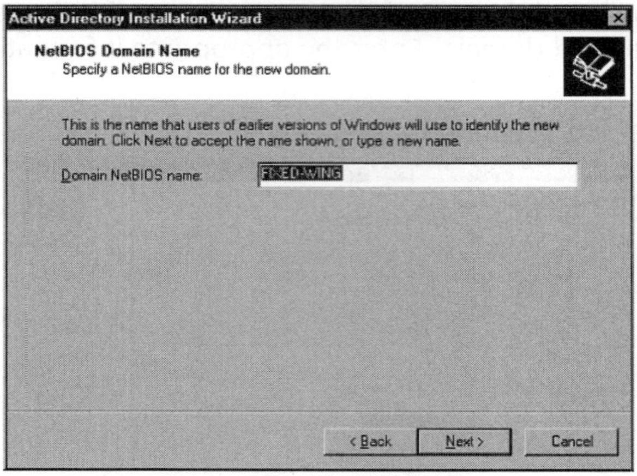

Figure 3.8 Database and Log Folder Locations

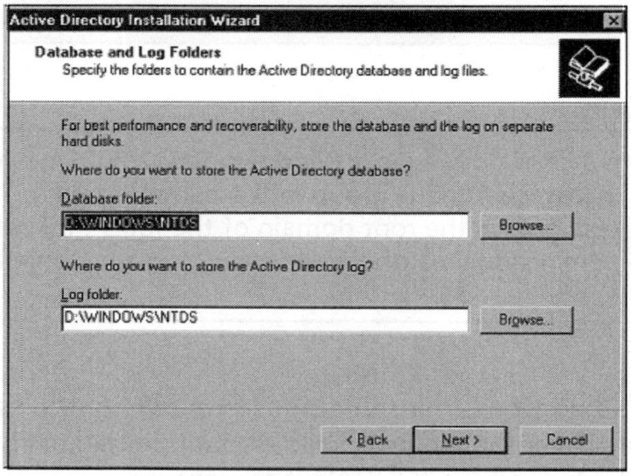

9. From the Shared System Volume page, type or browse to the location where you want to install the SYSVOL folder and then click **Next**.
10. The DNS Registration Diagnostics screen will prompt you to verify that the computer's DNS configuration settings are accurate. Click **Next** to move to the next step.
11. From the Permissions screen, select one of the following options:
    - Select **Permissions compatible with pre-Windows 2000 server operating systems** if your network still contains Windows NT 4.0 domain controllers.

- Choose **Permissions compatible only with Windows 2000 or Windows .NET server operating systems** if your domain controllers are running exclusively Windows 2000 or later.

12. The **Directory Services Restore Mode Administrator Password** screen will prompt you to enter the password that you want to use if you ever need to start the computer in Directory Services Restore Mode. Click **Next** when you've entered and confirmed the password.
13. Review the Summary page. If you are satisfied with your selections, click **Next** to begin the Active Directory installation. The installation will take several minutes and will require you to reboot the machine when you're finished. This server will be the first domain controller in the new child domain.

EXAM WARNING

Windows Server 2003 Web Edition cannot run Active Directory. It can participate on a Windows network as a member server only. Your Windows Server 2003 domain controller must be running Standard Edition, Enterprise Edition, or Datacenter Edition.

Managing a Different Domain

If you have administrative rights to multiple Windows Server 2003 domains, you can manage all of them from a single desktop. For example, if you are the administrator for the airplanes.com domain, you can perform administrative functions for the fixed-wing.airplanes.com domain to cover for someone who is on vacation or on sick leave. You can also use the steps described in this section to manage any Windows 2000 domains that still exist within your Active Directory forest.

To manage a different domain in Active Directory Users and Computers, for example, right-click the current domain name and click **Connect to Domain**. You'll see the dialog box shown in Figure 3.9, where you can specify a new domain name and optionally set this as the default domain name for the current console. You can use this functionality to create customized Management Consoles that will allow you to quickly access all the Windows Server 2003 domains that you administer.

Figure 3.9 Connecting to a Different Domain

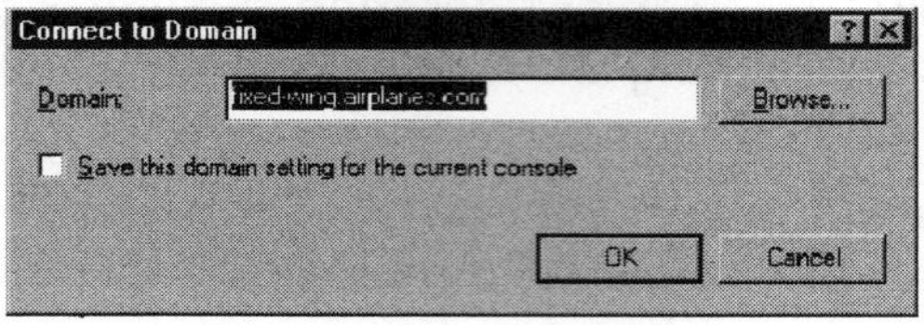

Removing a Domain

In a number of situations, you might need to remove an Active Directory domain: You might be restructuring your Active Directory environment, or reorganizing departments or locations within your company's business structure. The process of removing an Active Directory domain is relatively straightforward; however, there are a number of considerations to keep in mind before you do so. First and most obvious, removing an Active Directory domain will permanently destroy any user, group, and computer accounts stored within that domain. Additionally, if you are removing the last domain in a forest, removing the domain will also automatically delete the entire forest. If you are certain that you are ready to remove an Active Directory domain, it's also important to remember the following points:

- If the domain in question has any child domains, the domain cannot be deleted. You must delete all child domains before proceeding. If you attempt to delete a domain that has a child domain, the procedure described in this section will fail.
- In a multidomain environment, be certain that the domain controllers in the domain being removed do not hold the Domain Naming Master or Schema Master operations roles. These are operations master roles (See "Understanding Operations Masters" later in this section) that exist on only one machine in each forest. Therefore, if the controller in question is performing one of these functions, you'll need to use the *ntdsutil* command to transfer these roles to another domain controller in another domain before continuing, in order to allow your Windows Server 2003 forest to continue to function properly.

You'll need to follow this procedure for every domain controller associated with the domain you want to remove:

1. Click **Start | Run**, then type **dcpromo**. Click **Next** from the opening screen of the Active Directory Installation wizard.
2. On the Remove Active Directory screen shown in Figure 3.10, place a check mark next to **This server is the last domain controller in the domain** and click **Next** to continue.
3. Follow the prompts until the wizard begins the removal process. The process will take several minutes, after which you'll be prompted to reboot.

Figure 3.10 Removing Active Directory

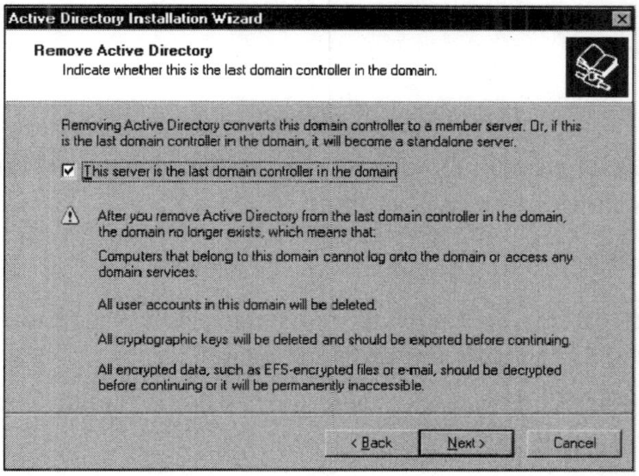

Deleting Extinct Domain Metadata

If one of your Windows Server 2003 domain controllers suffers a catastrophic failure and you are unable to remove it from the domain in a graceful manner, you can use the following steps to delete the Active Directory metadata associated with that domain controller. *Metadata* here refers to information within Active Directory that keeps track of the information that is housed on each one of your domain controllers. If a DC fails before you can remove it from the domain, its configuration information will still exist within the Active Directory database. This out-of-date information can cause data corruption or troubleshooting issues if it is not removed from Active Directory. It's important that you only follow these steps to remove the metadata of a domain controller that could not be cleanly decommissioned; do not delete the metadata of any domain controllers that are still functioning on your Windows Server 2003 network. In order to delete the metadata associated with a failed Active Directory controller, you'll use the *ntdsutil* command-line utility:

1. Click **Start | Programs | Accessories | Command Prompt**.
2. Type **ntdsutil** and press **Enter**. You'll see the following prompt:

   ```
   ntdsutil:
   ```

3. At the *ntdsutil* prompt, type **metadata cleanup** and press **Enter**. You'll see the following:

   ```
   metadata cleanup:
   ```

4. From this prompt, type **connection** and press **Enter** to go to the connection prompt:

   ```
   connection:
   ```

5. Type **connect to server *Server***, where *Server* is the name of a functioning controller in your domain. Press **Enter**, then type **quit** to return to the *metadata cleanup* prompt.

```
metadata cleanup:
```

6. At the metadata cleanup command, type **select operation target** and press **Enter** to go to the associated prompt:

```
select operation target:
```

7. From **select operation target**, type **list sites** and press **Enter**. You'll see a list of available sites, each with a number next to it.
8. Type **select site *SiteNumber***, where *SiteNumber* is the number next to the site in question.
9. Again from the *select operation target* prompt, type **list domains in site**. Repeat the process from Step 8 by typing **select domain *DomainNumber*** and selecting the appropriate domain number from the list of domains in the site you selected.
10. Type **list servers in site**. Select the number of the server whose metadata you want to remove, then type **select server *ServerNumber*** and press **Enter**.
11. Once you have selected the appropriate site, domain, and server, type **quit** to return to the following prompt:

```
metadata cleanup:
```

12. Type **remove selected server** and press **Enter** to begin the metadata cleanup process.

Raising the Domain Functional Level

You probably recall that in Windows 2000, you were able to configure your Active Directory domains in either mixed mode or native mode. Mixed-mode operation provided backward compatibility for any remaining NT 4.0 BDCs still existing on your network. Mixed-mode domains could contain Windows NT 4.0 BDCs and were unable to take advantage of such advanced Windows 2000 features as universal security groups, group nesting, and security ID (SID) history capabilities. When you set your domain to native mode, these advanced functions became available for your use.

Windows Server 2003 takes this concept of domain functionality to a new level, allowing you to establish four different levels of *domain functionality* with differing feature sets available, depending on your network environment. The four domain functional levels available in the new release of Windows Server are as follows:

- Windows 2000 mixed
- Windows 2000 native
- Windows Server 2003 interim
- Windows Server 2003

The default domain functional level is still Windows 2000, mixed mode, to allow you time to upgrade your domain controllers from Windows NT 4.0 and Windows 2000 to Windows Server 2003. Just as in the previous release of Windows, however, when you raise the functional level, advanced domainwide Active Directory features become available. Just as NT 4.0 controllers were not able to take advantage of the features available in Windows 2000 native mode, Windows 2000 domain controllers will not be aware of the features provided by the Windows Server 2003 level of domain and forest functionality.

In Table 3.2, you can see the four levels of domain functionality available in Windows Server 2003 and the types of domain controllers that are supported by each.

Table 3.2 Domain Functional Levels within Windows Server 2003

Domain Functional Level	Domain Controllers Supported
Windows 2000 mixed (default)	Windows Server 2003 family
	Windows 2000
	Windows NT 4.0
Windows 2000 native	Windows Server 2003 family
	Windows 2000
Windows Server 2003 interim	Windows Server 2003 family
	Windows NT 4.0
Windows Server 2003	Windows Server 2003

Test Day Tip

The Windows Server 2003 interim domain functional level is a special level that's available if you're upgrading a Windows NT 4.0 PDC to become the first domain controller in a new Windows Server 2003 domain.

When you upgrade the domain functional level of your Windows Server 2003 domain, new administrative and security features will be available for your use. Similarly to setting Windows 2000 to either mixed or native mode, specifying the domain functional level is a one-way operation; it cannot be undone. Therefore, if you still have domain controllers that are running Windows NT 4.0 or earlier, you shouldn't raise the domain functional level to Windows 2000 native. Likewise, if you haven't finished migrating your Windows 2000 domain controllers to Windows Server 2003, you should leave the domain functional level lower than Windows Server 2003.

To raise the functional level of your Windows Server 2003 domain, use the steps that follow:

1. Open **Active Directory Domains and Trusts**.
2. Right-click the domain that you want to manage and select **Raise Domain Functional Level**. On the screen shown in Figure 3.11, you'll see the current functional level of your domain as well as the following two options to choose from:

   - To raise the domain functional level to Windows 2000 native, select **Windows 2000 native** and then click **Raise**.
   - For Windows Server 2003, select the appropriate option and then click **Raise** to complete the operation.

Figure 3.11 Raising the Domain Functional Level

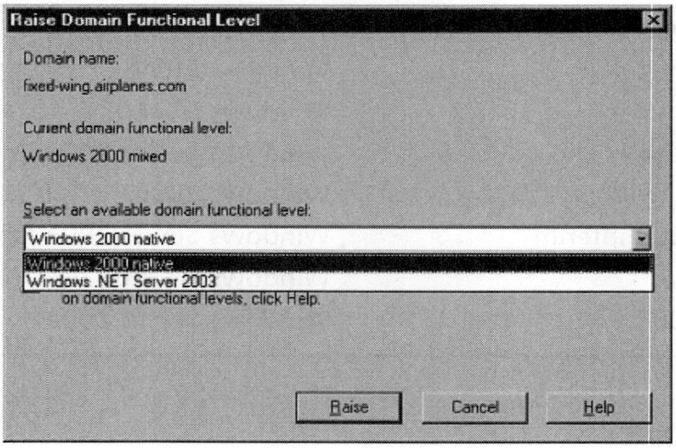

Managing Organizational Units

OUs in Windows Server 2003 are basically identical to their function in Windows 2000: They serve as Active Directory containers that you can use to organize resources within a single domain. You can use OUs to organize users, groups, printers, computers, and other objects as long as they are within the same domain. (OUs cannot contain objects located in other domains.) You can use OUs to delegate administrative control over a specific group of users and resources without needing to grant administrative access to the rest of the objects within the domain. Using OUs in this manner will allow you to create a distributed administrative model for your network, at the same time minimizing the number of domains needed.

Delegating administration tasks allows you to assign a range of responsibilities to specific users and groups while still maintaining control over domain- and forestwide administrative functions on your network. For example, you can create an OU containing all user and computer accounts within the airplanes.com accounting department and then assign a power user within the department the ability to reset user passwords for accounting department users only. Another potential use is to allow an administrative assistant the ability to edit user information to update telephone and fax information for the users he supports.

If your administrative model is a decentralized one, delegating control will allow users to take more responsibility for their local network resources. Delegation of authority also creates added security for your network by minimizing the number of user accounts that you need to add to the powerful Domain Admin and Enterprise Admin users groups. You can delegate a wide range of tasks within Windows Server 2003, including the following:

- Create, delete, and manage user accounts
- Reset user passwords
- Create, delete, and manage groups
- Read user account information
- Modify group memberships
- View and edit Group Policy information

In Exercise 3.02 we'll create a new OU within a Windows Server 2003 domain, then delegate the ability to manage user accounts to a user within the OU.

EXERCISE 3.02

CREATING AN ORGANIZATIONAL UNIT AND DELEGATING CONTROL TO A LOCAL ADMINISTRATOR

1. Open **Active Directory Users and Computers.**
2. Right-click the domain, then select **New | Organizational Unit**. Enter a descriptive name for the OU and click **OK**.
3. From the MMC console, right-click the OU that you just created. (Press **F5** to refresh the console if you don't see the new OU listed.)
4. Click **Delegate Control** to start the Delegation of Control Wizard.
5. Click **Next** to bypass the introduction screen.
6. On the Users or Groups screen, click **Add** to specify the users who should have the administrative rights you specify for this OU. Click **Next** when you're ready to continue.

7. In the Tasks to Delegate screen, shown in Figure 3.12, you can either select one or more preconfigured tasks to delegate or create a custom task. In this example, we delegate the ability to create, delete, and manage user accounts. Make the appropriate selection and click **Next** to continue.

Figure 3.12 Using the Delegation of Control Wizard

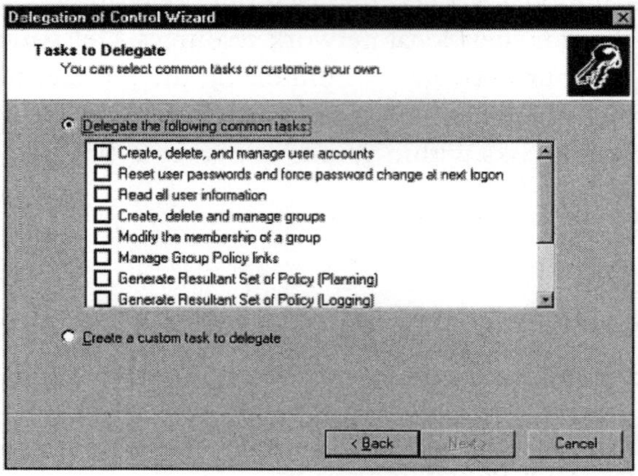

8. On the Summary screen, review the selections you've made and click **Finish** to complete the delegation process.

Assigning, Changing, or Removing Permissions on Active Directory Objects or Attributes

Your life as an administrator becomes much simpler when you can assign permissions to groups or OUs rather than to individual objects. For example, if Andrew from the marketing department needs to manage the printers in his department, you can set the necessary permissions on the individual printers in the Marketing OU or on the Marketing OU itself. In the case of the former, you'll need to manually specify Andrew's permissions every time you add a new printer to the Marketing OU. However, if you give Andrew rights at the OU level, any new printer objects created within the Marketing OU will automatically be assigned the same rights as the existing printers.

Along with using the Delegation of Control wizard discussed in the previous section, you can manually assign permissions to any object within the Active Directory database, including users, groups, printers, and OUs. You'll assign these permissions using the Active Directory Users and Computers interface, as shown in the following steps:

1. Open **Active Directory Users and Computers**. Within the console window, click **View | Advanced Features** to access the Security property page for the Active Directory objects within your domain.
2. Right-click the object that you want to assign permissions to (in this case, the **Human Resources OU**), click **Properties** and select the **Security** tab. You'll see the screen shown in Figure 3.13.

Figure 3.13 Assigning Permissions to Active Directory Objects

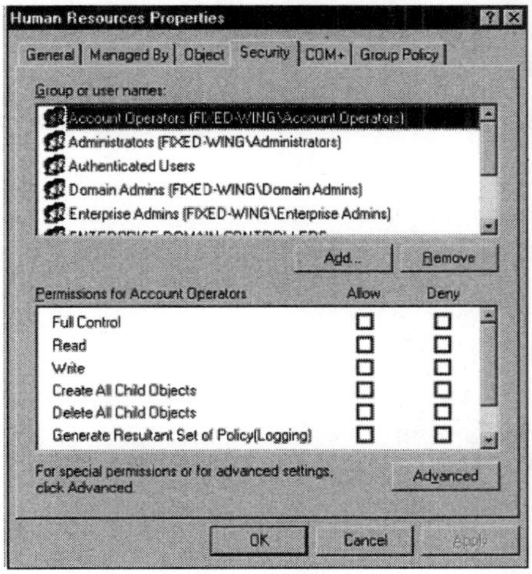

3. Click **Add** to create a new entry in the object's access control list (ACL), or click **Remove** to delete an existing permission assignment. Select the user or group that you want to grant permissions to, then click **OK**.
4. You can grant or deny any of the basic permissions listed in the bottom half of Figure 3.10, or click the **Advanced** button, select the user you want to modify permissions for, and click **Edit** for a detailed list of other assignable permissions.
5. Click **OK** when you're done. Repeat Steps 3 and 4 for each additional user or group to which you want to assign permissions.

Managing Domain Controllers

Windows Server 2003 has introduced a simplified mechanism to rename a domain controller if you need to restructure your network's organizational or business needs. This new functionality, available only if the domain functional level is Windows Server 2003, works to ensure that your clients will suffer no interruptions in their ability to authenticate against the renamed domain controller or locate any resources hosted on it. When you rename a domain controller, its new name is automatically updated within Active Directory as well as distributed to the dynamically updatable DNS servers on your network and Active Directory.

The amount of time it will take for this propagation to take place will depend on the specific configuration of your network. Replication over a WAN link will be significantly slower than over a LAN, for example. During any latency in replication, your clients might not be able to access the newly renamed domain controller; however, this should not pose a barrier to client authentication since there should be other domain controllers available.

Renaming a Domain Controller

To rename a domain controller on your Windows Server 2003 network, use the following steps:

1. Open a command prompt.
2. Type **netdom computername CurrentComputerName /add:NewComputerName**.
3. Ensure that the computer account updates and DNS registrations are completed, then type **netdom computername** ***CurrentComputerName*** **/makeprimary:***NewComputerName*.
4. Restart the computer.
5. From the command prompt, type **netdom computername** ***NewComputerName*** **/remove:***OldComputerName*.

EXAM WARNING

Both *NewComputerName* and *OldComputerName* need to be in FQDN format, such as *controller2.airplanes.com* rather than just *controller2*.

Understanding Operations Masters

Windows Server 2003, like its predecessor, supports multimaster replication to share directory data between all domain controllers in the domain, thus ensuring that all domain controllers within a domain are essentially peers; the concept of the PDC and the BDC are long gone. However, some domain and forest changes need to be performed from a single machine to ensure consistency of the Active Directory database. As an administrator, you'll designate a single domain controller, called an *operations master*, to perform these changes.

The number and description of operations masters in a Windows Server 2003 domain are identical to those that existed under Windows 2000. Each Windows Server 2003 forest must contain one and only one of the following:

- The *schema master,* which controls all updates and modifications to the Windows Server 2003 Active Directory schema
- The *domain naming master,* which controls the addition and removal of domains within a Windows Server 2003 forest

Likewise, each Windows Server 2003 domain must contain one of each of the following operations masters:

- The *relative ID (RID) master* allocates a sequence of unique relative ID numbers to each domain controller to allow for the creation of objects (such as users, groups, and computers) with unique SIDs. The RID master also assists with the movement of these types of objects bewtween domains.
- The *primary domain controller (PDC) emulator master* provides logon services to any down-level Windows clients, mimicking the role of an NT 4.0 PDC. If any NT 4.0 BDCs remain on the network, the PDC emulator will replicate directory information to the BDCs as well.
- The *infrastructure master* coordinates references to any objects from other domains within the forest.

Responding to Operations Master Failures

If a Windows Server 2003 server domain controller that holds an operations master role suffers a hardware or software failure, you have the option of forcibly *seizing* the role and assigning it to another domain controller. In most cases, this is a drastic step that shouldn't be undertaken if the cause of the failure is a simple network or hardware issue that can be resolved in a relatively short time. We discuss the potential impact of seizing the various operations roles in this section.

The following operations master roles should not be seized unless you are completely unable to return the original holder of these roles to the Windows network:

- Schema master
- RID master
- Domain naming master

A temporary loss of any of these three roles will not affect the operations of your users or the availability of your network under most circumstances. (If the schema master has failed, you will not be able to install a new application that is needed to extend the schema, for example.) A domain controller whose schema master, RID master, or domain naming master role has been seized must *never* be brought back online. The domain controller in question must be reformatted and reinstalled before returning to the network or your Active Directory database will become completely corrupted. If this happened, you would be forced to restore the entire Active Directory structure from backup rather than simply rebuilding a single server.

The loss of the infrastructure master will not be visible to your network users, either, and will only affect administration of your network if you need to move or rename a large number of domain accounts. Unlike the three roles discussed in the previous paragraph, though, you can return the original infrastructure master to production without reinstalling the operating system, making the prospect of seizing the infrastructure master a slightly less daunting proposal.

The only one of the five operations masters whose loss will be immediately noticeable to your end users is the PDC emulator, especially if you are supporting clients who rely on that role for authentication. For that reason, you might want to immediately seize the PDC emulator role if the original master suffers any sort of failure. Like the infrastructure master, you can return the original PDC emulator to the network without reformatting or reinstalling the OS.

Seizing an Operations Master Role

To transfer an operations master role to a different server, follow the steps listed in this section:

1. Open a command prompt and type **ntdsutil**.
2. At the *ntdsutil* command prompt, type **roles**.
3. At the *fsmo maintenance* command prompt, type **connections**.
4. At the *server connections* command prompt, type **connect to server *DomainController***, where *DomainController* is the FQDN of the domain controller that you want to assign the operations master role to.
5. At the *server connections* prompt, type **quit**.
6. At the *fsmo maintenance* command prompt, enter any of the following:
   - **seize schema master**
   - **seize domain naming master**
   - **seize infrastructure master**
   - **seize RID master**
   - **seize PDC emulator**
7. After you specify which role you want to seize and press **Enter**, you'll be prompted to confirm the operation. Click **Yes** to continue or **No** to cancel.

EXAM 70-296 OBJECTIVE 7.1 7.1.2

Managing Forests

Many of the tasks associated with managing forests in your Active Directory environment should not be undertaken without significant planning and testing, because they will have a broad effect on the entirety of your network infrastructure. Many of the functions discussed in this section revolve around features that are new to Windows Server 2003. Application directory partitions allow Active Directory-aware software to store their application data in multiple locations within your Active Directory infrastructure, allowing for fault tolerance and improved performance because clients will be able to access application data from multiple locations. If all the domain controllers in a forest are running Windows Server 2003, you now have the option to raise the functional level of the forest to introduce new security features across the entire forest. We'll also cover the steps needed to access the schema, the repository within Active Directory where all directory objects are defined and managed.

Creating a New Domain Tree

Like Windows 2000, a Windows Server 2003 Active Directory forest can contain one or more domain trees. You'll create a new domain tree when you need to create a domain whose DNS namespace is not related to the other domains in the forest but whose schema, security boundaries, and configuration need to be at least somewhat centrally managed. A good example of this is the acquisition of a company whose IT management functions will be taken over by the new parent company. In this case, the DNS name of the acquisition's domain (and any of its child domains) does not need to contain the full name of the parent domain. For example, if airplanes.com purchased a competing airplane manufacturer that already had an established Web presence under www.customairplanes.com, you could create a separate domain tree for the customairplanes.com company and its user base. Figure 3.14 provides a graphical example of this scenario.

Figure 3.14 Multiple Domain Environments

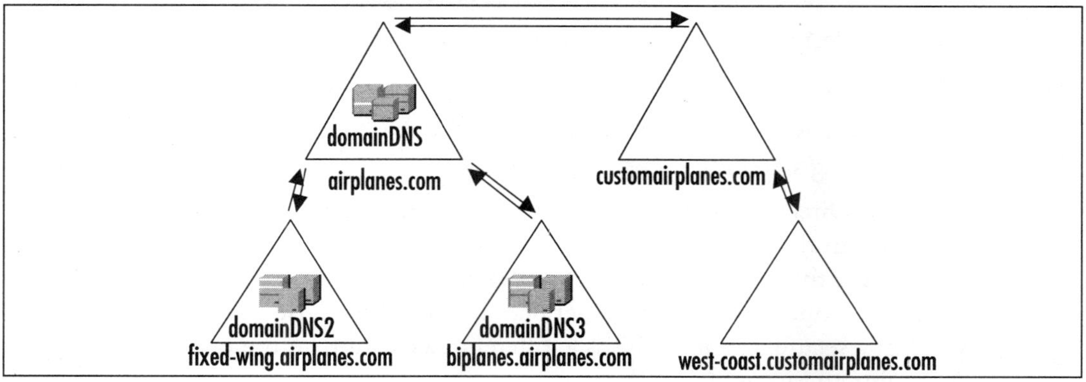

To create a new domain tree, use the procedure that follows:

1. From the Run line or a command prompt, type **dcpromo** to begin the Active Directory Installation Wizard.
2. Read the information presented on the Operating System Compatibility page and click **Next** to continue.
3. On the Domain Controller Type page, select click **Domain controller for a new domain** and click **Next**.

4. On the Create New Domain page, select **Domain tree in an existing forest**.
5. On the Network Credentials page, you'll be prompted to enter the username, password, and domain of a user account with the appropriate security to create a new domain tree. Click **Next** when you're ready to proceed. (As with most domain and forest management functions, the user account that you're using must be a member of the Enterprise Admins group to succeed.)
6. On the New Domain Tree page, enter the full DNS name of the new domain and click **Next**.
7. Verify or change the NetBIOS name suggested by the Installation wizard for backward compatibility. Click **Next** to continue.
8. On the Database and Log Folders screen, specify the drive letter and directory that will house the database and log folders and then click **Next**. (You can also use the **Browse** button to select the directory that you want.)
9. The next screen you'll see will be the Shared System Volume page. From here, manually type or browse to the directory where you want the Sysvol to be installed. Click **Next** to continue.
10. The DNS Registration Diagnostics screen will prompt you to choose an existing DNS server for name resolution, configure DNS after Active Directory installation, or install and configure the DNS Server Service on the local machine as *part* of the Active Directory installation. Click **Next** once you've made your selection.
11. From the Permissions page, select one of the following:
    - Permissions compatible with pre-Windows 2000 server operating systems
    - Permissions compatible only with Windows 2000 or Windows Server 2003 operating systems
12. From the Directory Services Restore Mode Administrator Password screen, enter and confirm the password that you want to assign to the local Administrator account for this server, and then click **Next**. You'll need this password in order to start the computer in Directory Services Restore Mode. Be sure to store this password in a secure location. This is a different password than the one for the domain Administrator account.
13. The Summary screen will allow you to review any changes and settings that you've specified. Click **Back** to make any changes, or click **Next** to begin installing Active Directory on this machine. The installation process will take several minutes, after which you'll be prompted to restart the computer.
14. Once the machine has restarted, this will be the first domain controller in the new domain tree. Windows Server 2003 will automatically create a two-way transitive trust relationship between the new domain and the root domain of the Active Directory forest.

Raising the Forest Functional Level

Similar to the domain functional level, Windows Server 2003 has created differing forest functional levels that can enable new Active Directory features that will apply to every domain within an Active Directory forest. When you first create a Windows Server 2003 Active Directory forest, its forest functionality level will be set to Windows 2000. Depending on your environment, you can consider raising the forest functional level to Windows Server 2003; however, just like the domain functional level, changing the forest functional level is a one-way operation that cannot be undone. As such, if any of your domain controllers are still running Windows NT 4.0 or Windows 2000, you shouldn't raise your forest functional level to Windows Server 2003 until your existing domain controllers have been upgraded. Table 3.3 details the types of domain controllers that are supported by each of the forest functional levels.

Table 3.3 Controllers Supported by Different Forest Functional Levels

Forest Functional Level	Domain Controllers Supported
Windows 2000 (default)	Windows NT 4.0 Windows 2000 Windows Server 2003 family
Windows Server 2003 interim	Windows NT 4.0 Windows Server 2003 family
Windows Server 2003	Windows Server 2003 family

Raising the Forest Functional Level

To raise the functional level of your Windows Server 2003 forest, follow the steps included here:

1. Open Active Directory Domains and Trusts.
2. Right-click the **Active Directory Domains and Trusts** node and select **Raise Forest Functional Level**.
3. From Select an available forest functional level, select **Windows Server 2003** and then click **Raise**.
4. If there are domain controllers or domains in your forest that cannot be upgraded to the new forest functional level, click **Save As** in the Raise Forest Functional Level dialog box to create a log file that will specify which of your domain controllers need to be upgraded or domains need to have their functional level raised.

New & Noteworthy...

Windows Server 2003 Domain and Forest Functionality

When you raise the domain and/or forest functionality level within your Active Directory environment, certain advanced features will be available for your use. At the domain level, the Windows Server 2003 functional level will provide the following advantages that are not available in either Windows 2000 mixed or native mode. You can enable these features on a domain-by-domain basis:

- **Domain controller rename tool** This Resource Kit utility allows you to rename a domain controller if your business or organizational structure changes.
- **Converting groups** Enables the ability to convert a security group to a distribution group and vice versa.
- **InetOrg Person** Objects ease the migration from other LDAP-enabled directory applications to Active Directory.
- **The lastLogonTimestamp attribute** Keeps track of the last logon time for either a user or a computer account, providing the administrator with the ability to track the account's history.

Raising the forest functional level creates the following features that you can implement throughout your Windows Server 2003 forest:

- **Domain rename** Allows you to rename an entire Active Directory domain.
- **Forest trusts** Enables one and two-way transitive trusts between separate Windows Server 2003 forests.
- **InetOrg Person objects** Can now be made available throughout your entire Windows Server 2003 forest.
- You can now reuse the object identifier, the *ldapDisplayName*, and the *schemaIdGUID* that are associated with a defunct schema object, whether a class or an attribute.
- **Linked value replication** Allows individual values of a schema attribute to be replicated separately. In Windows 2000, if an administrator or application made a change to a member of a group, for example, the entire group needed to be replicated. With linked value replication, only the group member that has changed is replicated, greatly improving replication efficiency and speed in larger environments.

Continued

- **Dynamic auxiliary classes** Allow you to link auxiliary schema classes to an individual object rather than entire classes of objects. This also serves to improve replication under Windows Server 2003.
- **Global catalog replication** This feature has also been improved by propagating only partial changes when possible.

Managing Application Directory Partitions

Windows Server 2003 has introduced the concept of *application directory partitions*, which allow Active Directory-aware applications to store information specific to the operation of their application in multiple locations within a Windows Server 2003 domain. This system provides fault tolerance and load balancing in case one server that houses an application partition fails or is taken offline. You can configure this application-specific data to replicate to one or more domain controllers located anywhere within your Windows Server 2003 forest.

TEST DAY TIP

Application directory partitions differ from domain directory partitions in that with the former, you can select which domain controllers should receive copies of the replicated data, whereas in a domain directory partition, data is replicated to *all* domain controllers within that domain. Storing application data in this manner can help reduce replication traffic on your network, since the application partition data will only be replicated to the domain controllers that you specify, allowing you to replicate data only to those servers to which it would be useful.

Application directory partitions follow the same DNS-based naming structure as the rest of your Windows Server 2003 domain and can exist in any of the following locations:

- As a child of a domain directory partition
- As a child of an application directory partition
- As a new tree in the Active Directory forest

For example, you can create an application directory partition for an Active Directory-aware database application as a child of the airplanes.com domain. If you named the application directory partition *databaseapp*, the DNS name of the application directory partition would then become *databaseapp.airplanes.com*. The LDAP distinguished name of the application directory partition would be *dc=databaseapp, dc=airplanes, dc=com*. You could then create an application directory partition called *databaseapp2* as a child of databaseapp.airplanes.com, and the DNS name of the application directory partition would be *databaseapp2.databaseapp.airplanes.com* and the distinguished name would be *dc=databaseapp2, dc=databaseapp dc=*

airplanes, dc=com. In the final example, if the domain airplanes.com was the root of the only domain tree in your forest and you created an application directory partition with the DNS name of *databaseapp* (with the distinguished name of *dc=databaseapp*), this application directory partition would not exist on the same tree as the airplanes.com domain. It would instead become the root of a new tree in the Windows Server 2003 forest.

Application directory partitions are almost always created by the applications that will use them to store and replicate data within the domain structure; however, Enterprise Admins can manually create and manage application directory partitions when testing and troubleshooting is necessary. You can use any of the following tools to create and manage application directory partitions:

- Third-party tools from the vendor that provided the application
- The *ntdsutil* command-line tool
- ADSI

In this section, we focus on using the *ntdsutil* utility to create and manage application directory partitions.

Creating or Deleting an Application Directory Partition

In this section, we discuss the steps necessary to manage Application Directory partitions.

1. From the command prompt, type **ntdsutil**.
2. Enter the following commands at the *ntdsutil* menu prompts:

```
C:\ntdsutil
ntdsutil>domain management
domain management>connection
connection>connect to server servername
connection>quit
```

3. To create an application directory partition, enter the following at the *Domain Management* prompt:

```
domain Management> create nc ApplicationDirectoryPartition
DomainController
```

4. To delete an application directory partition, enter the following at the *Domain Management* prompt:

```
domain Management> delete nc ApplicationDirectoryPartition
```

Use Table 3.4 to determine the values of the *servername, ApplicationDirectoryPartition,* and *DomainController* variables.

Table 3.4 NTDSUTIL Parameter Definitions

Variable Name	Definition
ServerName	The full DNS name of the domain controller to which you want to connect—for example, controller1.airplanes.com.
ApplicationDirectoryPartition	The distinguished name of the application directory partition that you want to create or delete. For example, the distinguished name of the application directory databaseapp.airplanes.com is dc=databaseapp,dc=airplanes,dc=com.
DomainController	The full DNS name of the domain controller on which you want to create or delete the application directory partition. If you want to create or delete the partition on the domain controller that you already specified with the *Servername* variable, you can type *NULL* for this value.

For example, to create an application directory partition called *application1* as a child of the domain *biplanes.airplane.com* on the domain controller called *controller1.biplanes.airplanes.com,* you would enter the following in Step 3 of this procedure:

```
create nc dc=application1,dc=biplanes,dc=airplanes,dc=com
controller1.biplanes.airplanes.com
```

If you later decide that you want to delete this partition, you can follow the same procedure using the following syntax:

```
delete nc dc=application1,dc=biplanes,dc=airplanes,dc=com
```

EXAM 70-296 OBJECTIVE 7.1.2

Managing the Schema

Similarly to the previous release of the operating system, the Windows Server 2003 Active Directory schema contains the definitions for all objects within Active Directory. Whenever you create a new directory object such as a user or group, the new object is validated against the schema to determine which attributes the object should possess. (A printer object should have very different attributes than a user object for example.) In this way, Active Directory validates every new object that you create against the appropriate definition within the schema before it records the new object in the Active Directory database. Each forest can contain only one schema, which is replicated along with the rest of the Active Directory database to every domain controller within the forest. If your implementation or security needs require you to maintain different schemas for different business units, you need to create a separate forest for each individual schema that you need to maintain. For example, you may create a separate forest for application testing so that any test changes to the schema will not replicate throughout your entire Active Directory forest.

The Windows Server 2003 schema comes preloaded with an extensive array of object classes and attributes that will meet the needs of most organizations; however, some applications extend the schema by adding their own information to it. Exchange 2000 and 2003 are good examples of this. In order to manage the schema directly, you'll need to install the Active Directory Schema snap-in. Due to the delicate nature of schema management operations, this utility is not installed on a Windows Server 2003 server by default. Listing all the schema classes and attributes within Active Directory would require a book unto itself; if you are interested, a comprehensive reference is available on the MSDN Web site.

Installing the Active Directory Schema Snap-in

This section walks you through the steps needed to install the Active Directory Schema snap-in:

1. From a command prompt, type the following to register the necessary .DLL file on your computer: **regsvr32 schmmgmt.dll**.
2. To access the Active Directory Schema snap-in, you'll need to add it to the Microsoft Management Console. Click **Start** | **Run**, then type **mmc /a** and click **OK**. You'll see a blank MMC console.
3. Click **File** | **Add/Remove Snap-in** | **Add**.
4. Browse to **Active Directory Schema** within the Snap-In menu, shown in Figure 3.15. Click **Add** and then click **Close** to add the snap-in to the MMC console.

Figure 3.15 Adding the Schema Management Snap-In

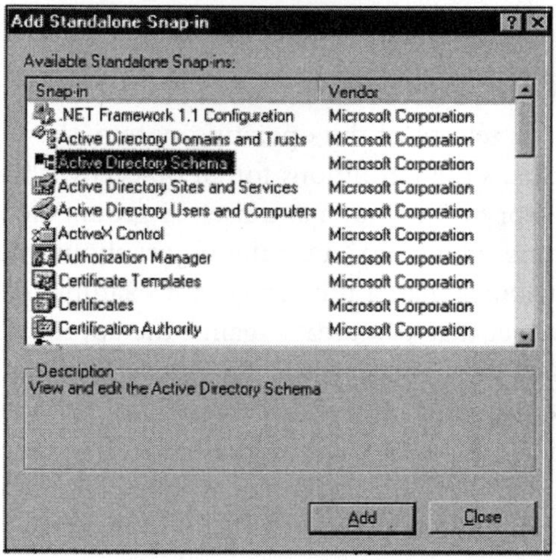

5. Save the console in the system32 directory as **schmmgmt.msc**. (You can add a shortcut to this tool in the Documents and Settings\All Users\Programs\Administrative Tools folder if you wish.)

Securing the Schema

You can protect the Active Directory schema from unauthorized changes by using ACLs to determine who can make alterations to the schema. When you first install Windows Server 2003, the only users who have write access to the schema are members of the Schema Admins group, and the only default member of this group is the Administrator account in the root domain of the forest. You should restrict membership in the Schema Admins group as much as possible, since careless or malicious alterations to the schema can render your network inoperable. To modify the permissions assigned to your Active Directory schema, follow these steps:

1. Open the Active Directory Schema snap-in.
2. Right-click **Active Directory Schema** and then click **Permissions**.
3. Click the **Security tab**. In the Group or user names section, select the **group whose permissions you want to change**.
4. Under Permissions for Administrators, select **Allow** or **Deny** for the permissions you want to change. Click **OK** when you're done.

Adding an Attribute to the Global Catalog

By default, the global catalog stores a partial set of object attributes so that users can search for information within Active Directory. Although the most common attributes are already included in the global catalog, you can speed up search queries across a domain for an attribute that is not included by default by adding it to the global catalog.

Keep in mind that this sort of change will affect all domains in your forest and will cause a full synchronization of all object attributes that are stored in the global catalog if your forest functional level is not set to Windows Server 2003. This can cause a noticeable spike in network traffic; for that reason, you should carefully consider and test any additions to the global catalog before implementing them in a production environment.

To add an attribute to the global catalog:

1. Open the Active Directory Schema snap-in.
2. In the console tree, click **Attributes**, and right-click the name of the attribute that you want to add to the global catalog.
3. Select **Properties**. You'll see the screen shown in Figure 3.16.

Figure 3.16 Replicating an Attribute to the Global Catalog

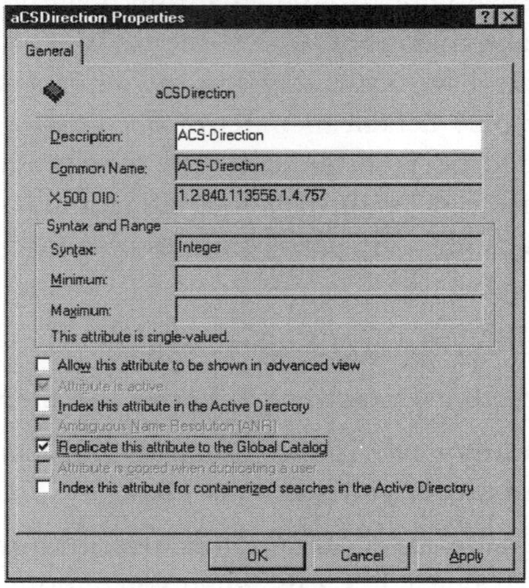

4. Place a check mark next to **Replicate this attribute to the Global Catalog**, and then click **OK**.

EXAM 70-296 OBJECTIVE 7.1.1

Managing Trusts

As in previous versions of the Windows server operating system, Windows Server 2003 *trusts* allow network administrators to establish relationships between domains and forests so that users from Domain A can access resources in Domain B. Unlike previous releases of Windows, however, Windows 2000 and Server 2003 allow for the creation of transitive trusts. This means that if Domain A trusts Domain B, and if Domain B trusts Domain C, Domain A automatically trusts Domain C as well. (You might remember the days of Windows NT 4.0, when the number of trust relationships you needed to create in a large environment became staggeringly large: A network with 10 domains would require the administrator to manually create *90* trust relationships to allow for the kind of trust relationships that Windows 2000 and Server 2003 create automatically.) In this section, we cover the various types of trust relationships that you can create to allow your users to quickly and easily access the resources they require.

Head of the Class...

Trusted and Trusting Domains

When you create a new domain in Windows Server 2003, a two-way transitive trust is automatically created between it and any existing domains in the Windows Server 2003 forest. However, for security reasons you might want to create a trust relationship that only operates in one direction. In this case, you will have a trusted domain that contains the user resources that require access and the trusting domain that contains the resources being accessed. Diagrammatically, this concept would be represented using an arrow pointing toward the trusted domain.

It's sometimes tough to remember which domain is the *trusted* domain and which the *trusting* domain and which way the arrow was supposed to point. Here's a good way to help you remember: Think of the last two letters in *trust-ED* as talking about a guy named Ed. The *trust-ED* domain is the one that contains users, since Ed is there. The *trust-ING* domain contains the *thing* that your users are trying to access. It's the *trust-ING* domain because that's where the *things* are. Using this memory aid, when you're looking at a diagram of a one-way trust relationship on the 70-296 exam, you'll remember that the arrow is pointing to Ed. Take a look at the diagram in Figure 3.17.

Figure 3.17 Trusted and Trusting Domains

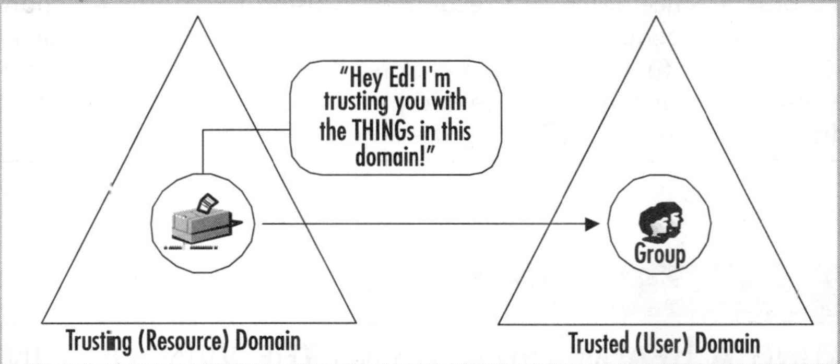

Try to find other humorous anecdotes like this one as you're preparing for the exam. Rote memorization will only stay with you for so long; personalizing a concept in this way makes it more real for you (and hence easier to remember).

Creating a Realm Trust

Windows Server 2003 allows you to create a trust relationship with an external Kerberos realm, allowing cross-platform interoperability with other Kerberos services such as UNIX and MIT-based implementations. You can establish a *realm trust* between your Windows Server 2003 domain and any non-Windows Kerberos v5 realm. This trust relationship will allow pass-through authentication, in which a trusting domain (the domain containing the resources to be accessed) honors the logon authentications of a trusted domain (the domain containing the user accounts). You can grant rights and permissions in the trusting domain to user accounts and global groups in the trusted domain, even though the accounts or groups don't exist in the trusting domain's directory. Realm trusts can also be either one-way or two-way.

You can create a realm trust using the Active Directory Domains and Trusts GUI or the *netdom* command-line utility. To perform this procedure, you must be a member of the Domain Admins or Enterprise Admins group or you must have been delegated the appropriate authority by a member of one of these groups. (We discussed delegation of authority in the "Managing Organizational Units" and the "Assigning, Changing, or Removing Permissions on Active Directory Objects or Attributes" sections.) To manage trust relationships, you'll need the Full Control permission.

Test Day Tip

As a best practice, Microsoft recommends using the *RunAs* function to perform most trust procedures. You can configure Active Directory Domains and Trusts to use the *RunAs* function by right-clicking the shortcut and selecting **RunAs**. You'll be prompted for the username and password that you want to use to access the administrative utility; by leaving the logon information blank.

Exercise 3.04

Creating a Realm Trust Using the Windows Interface

1. Click **Start | Programs | Administrative Tools | Active Directory Domains and Trusts**. Enter the appropriate username and password to access the utility.
2. Right-click the domain that you want to administer, and select **Properties**.
3. Click the **Trusts** tab, click **New Trust**, and then click **Next**. You'll see the window shown in Figure 3.18.

Figure 3.18 Specifying the Name of the Target Domain

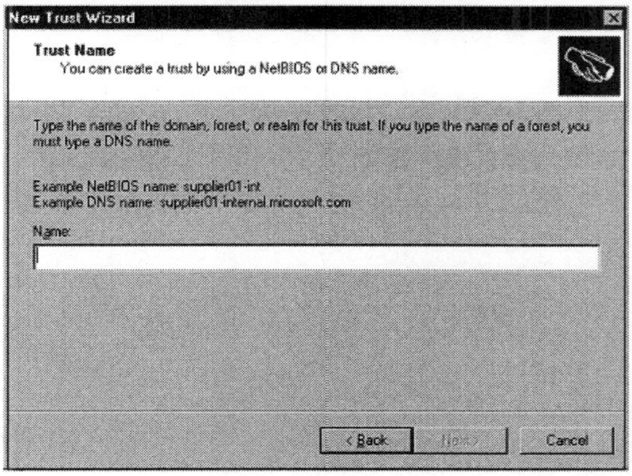

4. On the Trust Name page, type the name of the Kerberos realm that you want to establish a trust relation ship with, and then click **Next**.
5. On the Trust Type page, select the **Realm Trust** option, and then click **Next**.
6. You'll be taken to the screen shown in Figure 3.19. From the Transitivity of Trust page, you have the following options:

Figure 3.19 Transitivity of Trust

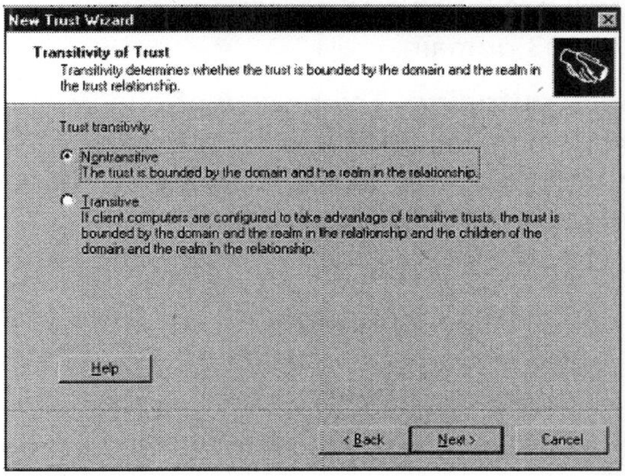

- To form a trust relationship between your Windows Server 2003 domain and *only* the realm specified in the Trust Wizard, click **Nontransitive** and then click **Next**.
- To form a trust relationship between the Windows Server 2003 domain, the specified realm, and *all other trusted realms*, click **Transitive** and then **Next**.

7. On the Direction of Trust page, select one of the following options from the screen shown in Figure 3.20.

Figure 3.20 Specifying the Direction of the Trust Relationship

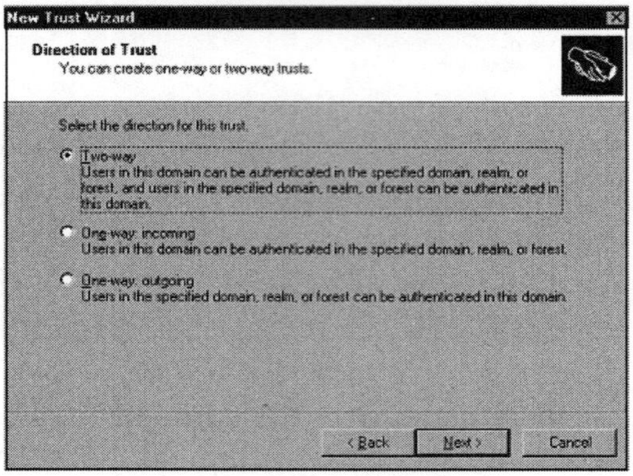

- **Two-way** This will create a two-way realm trust, where users in your domain and the specified external realm will be able to access resources in either domain or realm.
- **One-way incoming** Users in your Windows Server 2003 domain will be able to access resources in the external realm, but external users will not be able to access any resources in your Windows Server 2003 domain.
- **One-way outgoing** The reverse of one-way: incoming. Users in the external realm will be able to access files within your domain, but your Windows Server 2003 users will not be able to access any resources in the external realm.

8. Finally, you'll need to enter the password that will be used to establish the trust relationship. This password will need to be entered by the administrator of the Kerberos realm as well. Enter the trust password on the screen shown in Figure 3.21.
9. Click **Next** and then **Finish** to complete the creation of the new realm trust.

Figure 3.21 Creating a Trust Password

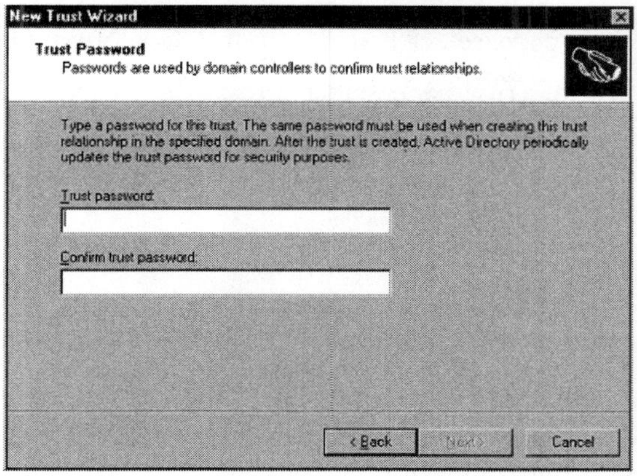

Managing Forest Trusts

Windows Server 2003 has introduced a new feature that will allow administrators to easily establish trusts between domains in different forests. Creating a *forest trust* will form implied trust relationships between every domain in both forests. You must manually establish a forest trust, unlike other types of trusts that are automatically created, such as the trust relationship between a parent and a child domain within the same forest. You can only create this type of trust between the forest root domains between two Windows Server 2003 forests.

Forest trusts are transitive and can be one-way or two-way. A one-way trust will allow members of the trusted forest to access files, applications, and resources that are located in the trusting forest. However, as the name implies, the trust operates in only one direction; if you establish a one-way forest trust between Forest A (the trusted forest) and Forest B (the trusting forest), members of Forest A can access resources located in Forest B but not the other way around. In this example, for users in Forest B to access resources in Forest A, you would instead need to create a two-way forest trust. This would allow users and groups from either forest to utilize resources located in the other forest. Each domain within Forest A will also trust all domains in Forest B, and vice versa.

To create a forest trust in your Windows Server 2003 forest root domain, follow these steps:

1. Click **Start | Programs | Administrative Tools | Active Directory Domains and Trusts**. If you are using the *RunAs* function, enter the administrative username and password when prompted.
2. Right-click the forest root domain and select **Properties**.
3. On the **Trusts** tab, click **New Trust** and then click **Next**.

4. On the Trust Name page, type the DNS name of the target forest and click **Next** to continue.
5. On the Trust Type page, select **Forest trust**. Click **Next** to continue.
6. On the Direction of Trust page, select one of the following options:

   - **Two-way forest trust** Users in the local and remote forest will be able to access resources in either forest.
   - **One-way: incoming** Users in the remote forest will be able to access resources within the forest specified in Step 2, but users in this forest will not be able to access any resources in the remote forest.
   - **One-way: outgoing** The reverse of the previous bullet point. Users in the forest specified in Step 2 will be able to access resources in the remote forest but not the other way around.

Creating a Shortcut Trust

Authentication requests between two domains must travel a *trust path*. By default this path is comprised of the default trusts between the parent and child domains that extend from the authentication domain to the domain that is being accessed for its resources. In a complex forest, these default paths can be quite long, which can slow down access times. You can reduce delays through the use of *shortcut trusts*. Shortcut trusts are one-way or two-way transitive trusts that you can use to optimize the authentication process if many of your users from one domain need to log onto another domain in the forest structure. As illustrated in Figure 3.22, the shortcut trust between Domain A and Domain F shortens the path traveled for User1's resource request between the two domains. In the figure, User A must access the printer in Domain F by referring to the trust relationship between Domain A and Domain B, then between Domain B and Domain C, and so forth until reaching Domain F. The shortcut trust creates a trust relationship directly between Domain A and Domain F, which greatly shortens the authentication process in an enterprise domain with a large series of forest trust relationships.

Use these steps to create a shortcut trust using the GUI interface:

1. Click **Start | Programs | Administrative Tools | Active Directory Domains and Trusts**.
2. Right-click your domain name and select **Properties**.
3. From the **Trusts** tab, click **New Trust** and then **Next**.
4. On the Trust Name screen, enter the DNS name of the target domain. Click **Next** when you're ready to continue.

Figure 3.22 Shortcut Trusts

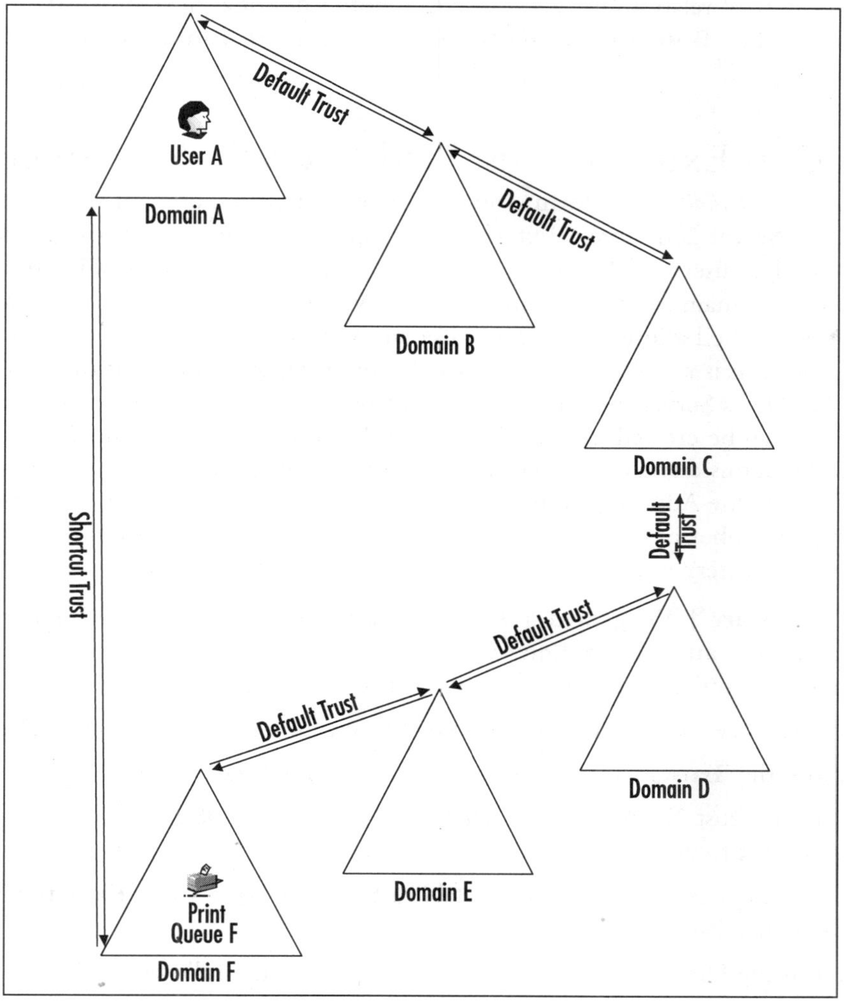

5. From the Direction of Trust page, select one of the following options:
   - **Two-way** Creates a two-way shortcut trust so that the login process will be optimized in both directions.
   - **One-way incoming** Hastens the login process for users in an external domain to access the domain you administer. If users in your domain need to authenticate to the target domain, they must traverse the usual trust path between the two.
   - **One-way outgoing** Accomplishes the reverse: User logins from your domain to the target domain will be able to use this shortcut trust, but incoming login requests will not.

6. If you have Domain Admin or Enterprise Admin access to each domain involved in the trust relationship, you can create both sides of a shortcut trust at the same time. Click **Both this domain and the specified domain** on the Sides of Trust page.

Creating an External Trust With the Windows Interface

You'll create an *external trust* to form a nontransitive trust with a domain that exists outside your Windows Server 2003 forest. External trusts can be one-way or two-way and should be employed when users need access to resources located in a Windows NT 4.0 domain or in an individual domain located within a separate Windows 2000 or 2003 forest with which you haven't established a forest trust. You'll use an external trust instead of a forest trust if the trusting domain is running Windows NT 4.0 or 2000, or if you want to restrict access to another Windows Server 2003 forest simply to resources within a single domain. External trusts can be created using either the GUI interface or the command line. As with most of the functions discussed in this chapter, you must be a member of the Domain Admins or Enterprise Admins group or you must have been delegated the appropriate authority by a member of one of these groups in order to perform these procedures. Here's how to create an external trust:

1. Click **Start | Programs | Administrative Tools | Active Directory Domains and Trusts**. Enter the appropriate username and password to run the utility if you've configured the shortcut to use *RunAs*.
2. Right-click the domain that you want to create a trust for, and click **Properties**.
3. From the **Trusts** tab, click **New Trust** and then **Next**.
4. On the Trust Name screen, enter the DNS or NetBIOS name of the domain that you want to establish a trust with, then click **Next**.
5. The next screen allows you to establish the Trust Type. Click **External Trust**, then click **Next** to continue.
6. From the Direction of Trust screen, select one of the following:
   - **Two-way** Establishes a two-way external trust. Users in your domain and the users in the specified domain will be able to access resources in either domain.
   - **One-way incoming** Users in your Windows Server 2003 domain will be able to access resources in the trusting domain that you specify, but the trusting domain will not be able to access any resources in the Windows Server 2003 domain.
   - **One-way outgoing** The reverse of one-way incoming: Users in the external domain can access resources in your domain, but your users will not be able to connect to resources in the external domain.

7. Click **Next** when you've determined the direction of the trust you're creating. On the Outgoing Trust Properties sheet, you can choose one of the following options:
   - To allow users from the external domain to access all resources in your Windows Server 2003 domain, select **Allow authentication for all resources in the local domain**. (You'll most commonly select this option if both domains are part of the same company or organization.)
   - In order to restrict users in the external domain from obtaining access to any of the resources in your domain, click **Allow authentication only for selected resources in the local domain.** This option should be used when each domain belongs to a separate organization. Once you've made your selection, click **Next** to continue.
8. If you have Domain Admin or Enterprise Admin access to each domain involved in the trust relationship, you can create both sides of an external trust at the same time. Click **Both this domain and the specified domain** on the Sides of Trust page.

Selecting the Scope of Authentication for Users

Once you've created a trust relationship between two separate forests, you'll need to indicate the scope of authentication for users from the trusted domain. You can either allow users in the trusted forest to be treated as members of the Authenticated Users group in the local forest or you can specify that users from the other forest must be granted explicit permission to authenticate to local resources. (You'll hear the latter option referred to as an *authentication firewall.*) If users from the trusted domain are not treated as members of the Authenticated Users group in the trusting domain, they will only be able to access any resources for which they have been granted specific permissions. This is a more restrictive means of granting access and should be used when the trusting domain contains extremely sensitive or compartmentalized data. Specify the scope of authentication for any trusts you've created using the following steps:

1. Click **Start | Programs | Administrative Tools | Active Directory Domains and Trusts**.
2. Right-click the domain that you want to administer, and select **Properties**.
3. On the **Trusts** tab, select the trust that you want to administer under **Domains trusted by this domain (outgoing trusts)** or **Domains that trust this domain (incoming trusts)** and do one of the following:

   - To select the scope of authentication for users who authenticate through an *external* trust, select the external trust that you want to administer and then click **Properties**. On the **Authentication** tab, click either **Domain-wide** or **Selective authentication**. If you select **Selective authentication**, you need to manually enable permissions on the local domain and on the resource to which you want users in the external domain to have access. Otherwise, the users from the trusted domain will automatically be added to the Authenticated Users group in the trusting domain.

- To select the scope of authentication for users authenticating through a *forest* trust, click the forest trust that you want to administer, and then click **Properties**. On the **Authentication** tab, click either **Forest-wide** or **Selective authentication**. If you select **Selective authentication**, you need to manually enable permissions on each domain and resource in the local forest that users in the second forest should be able to access.

Exam Warning

Selective authentication is available only with external and forest trusts. It cannot be used with a realm trust.

Verifying a Trust

Once you have created a trust relationship, you might need to verify that the trust has been created properly if the users in either domain are not able to access the resources that you think they should. You can perform this troubleshooting technique using the following steps:

1. Click **Start | Programs | Administrative Tools | Active Directory Domains and Trusts**.
2. Right-click the domain you want to administer and click **Properties**.
3. From the **Trusts** tab, click the trust that you want to verify, and select **Properties**.
4. Click **Validate** to confirm that the trust relationship is functioning properly. Select from one of the following options:

   - If you select **No, do not validate the incoming trust**, Microsoft recommends that you repeat the procedure on the remote domain to ensure that it is fully functional.
   - If you choose **Yes, validate the incoming trust**, you'll be prompted for a username and password with administrative rights to the remote domain.

Test Day Tip

You can verify trusts for shortcut, external, and forest trusts but not realm trusts.

Removing a Trust

If you need to delete a trust relationship between two domains, you can do so in one of two ways. From the command line, you can use the *netdom* Support Tools utility with the following syntax:

```
netdom trust TrustingDomainName /d:TrustedDomainName /remove /UserD:User
/PasswordD:*
```

UserD and *PasswordD* refer to a username and password, respectively, with administrative credentials for the domain that you're administering.

To remove a trust using the Windows interface, follow these steps:

1. Click **Start | Programs | Administrative Tools | Active Directory Domains and Trusts**.
2. Right-click your domain name and select **Properties**.
3. On the **Trusts** tab, select the trust that you want to remove, either under **Domains trusted by this domain (outgoing trusts)** or **Domains that trust this domain (incoming trusts)**, and click **Remove**.
4. Choose whether you want to remove the trust relationship on the local domain *only* or on both the local and the other domain. If you choose **Yes, remove the trust from both the local domain and the other domain**, you'll need to have access to a user account and password that has administrative rights in the remote domain. Otherwise, choose **No, remove the trust from the local domain only** and have an administrative user with the appropriate credentials repeat the procedure on a domain controller in the remote domain.

Configuring & Implementing...

Managing Trust Relationships at the Command Line

Although the Windows GUI certainly makes creating and managing trust relationships a snap, at times you might want or need to do so from the command line—you could be working in a test environment or other scenario in which your domain structures change frequently, which would make the command line a more efficient option for managing your network. In this case, you can turn to the *netdom* utility that's found in the \Support directory of the Windows Server CD. The basic syntax of the utility is as follows:

```
netdom trust TrustingDomainName /d:TrustedDomainName /add UserD:
administrator /PasswordD: password
```

TrustingDomainName specifies the DNS name of the target domain in the trust relationship that you're creating; *TrustedDomainName* specifies the trusted or account domain. (When using the command line, you're supplying the *UserID* and password within the command-line syntax itself. As such, you don't need to use the *RunAs* function described for use with the Active Directory Domains and Trusts

Continued

utility.) You can also use *netdom* to specify the password that you'll use to connect to one or both domains and to establish the trust as one-way or two-way. For example, to create a two-way trust between DomainA and DomainB, you would type the following at the command prompt:

```
netdom trust DomainA /d:DomainB /add /twoway
```

You can use this syntax with the *netdom* utility whether you are creating a forest, a shortcut, or an external trust. To establish a realm trust from the command line, you'll use a slightly different syntax:

```
netdom trust TrustingDomainName /d:TrustedDomainName /add /realm
/PasswordT:NewRealmTrustPassword
```

As before, *TrustingDomainName* specifies the DNS name of the trusting domain in the new realm trust, and *TrustedDomainName* refers to the DNS name of the trusted domain in the new realm trust. *NewRealmTrustPassword* is the password that will be used to create the new realm trust. The password that you specify needs to match the one used to create the other half of the trust in the external Kerberos realm, or the creation of the trust relationship will fail.

Finally, you can use *netdom* to verify a trust relationship as follows:

```
netdom trust TrustingDomainName /d:TrustedDomainName /verify
```

The *netdom* command has numerous other optional command-line parameters that you can view by entering **netdom trust | more** at the Windows command prompt.

EXAM 70-296 OBJECTIVE 7.1.3

Managing UPN Suffixes

Within the Active Directory database, each user account possesses a logon name, a pre-Windows 2000 user logon name (this is the equivalent to the NT 4.0 Security Account Manager, or SAM, account name), and a UPN suffix The UPN suffix refers to the portion of the username to the right of the @ character. In a Windows 2000 or Server 2003 domain, the default UPN suffix for a user account is the DNS domain name of the domain that contains the user account. For example, the UPN suffix of fakeuser@syngress.com is syngress.com.

You can add alternative UPN suffixes in order to simplify network administration and streamline the user logon process by creating a single UPN suffix for all users. Consider an Active Directory forest that consists of two discontinuous domain names as the result of a corporate merger: mikesairplanes.com and joesairplanes.com. Rather than forcing the users from each domain to remember which UPN they need to specify when logging onto the different domain systems, you can create an alternative UPN suffix so that all user accounts can be addressed as *username*@thebigairplanecompany.com, allowing users from each domain to use a consistent naming syntax when logging onto systems from the two separate domains. Take another real-world example: Let's say that your company uses a deep domain structure, which could create long domain names that become difficult for your users to remember. You can use an alternative UPN suffix to allow users to remember user@airplane rather than user@sales.denver.westcoast.usa.airplane.com.

TEST DAY TIP

Since the UPN suffix is only used within the Active Directory forest, it does not need to be a valid DNS domain name; you can create a UPN suffix of thebigairplanecompany.com even if that isn't a registered domain name. However, UPN suffixes should still conform to DNS naming conventions for valid characters and syntax; avoid using underscores and other illegal characters.

To add a new UPN suffix to a Windows Server 2003 domain:

1. Open **Active Directory Domains and Trusts**.
2. Right-click the **Active Directory Domains and Trusts** icon and select **Properties**.
3. On the **UPN Suffixes** tab, enter an alternative UPN suffix for the forest, and click **Add**.
4. If you want to add any more UPN suffixes, repeat Step 3 until you're finished. Click **OK** when you're done.

EXAM 70-296 OBJECTIVE 7.2

Restoring Active Directory

Similarly to Windows 2000, Windows Server 2003 allows you to restore your Active Directory data in case of a system hardware failure, data corruption, or accidental deletion of critical data. Active Directory restores can only be performed from the local Windows Server 2003 domain controller; you cannot restore the Active Directory directory to a remote computer without the aid of a third-party utility. In order to restore this data on a domain controller, you must first restart the domain controller in Directory Services Restore Mode using the password that you specified during the installation of Active Directory on the server. This allows you to restore Active Directory directory service information as well as the SYSVOL directory itself. To access Directory Services Restore Mode, press **F8** during startup and select that choice from the list of startup options. Windows Server 2003 includes the option to perform authoritative and nonauthoritative restores of Active Directory information. The new release also includes a third option called a *primary restore* that was not available in previous versions of Active Directory. We discuss all three of these options in this section.

EXAM 70-296 OBJECTIVE 7.2.2

Performing a Nonauthoritative Restore

When restoring objects to the Active Directory database, you can perform either an *authoritative* or a *nonauthoritative* restore. The *nonauthoritative restore* is the default restore type for Active Directory; it allows restored objects to be updated with any changes held on other domain controllers in the domain after the restore has completed. For example, let's say that on a Wednesday you restore user *jsmith's* Windows user object from the Monday backup file. Between Monday and Wednesday, *jsmith's* Department attribute was changed from *Marketing* to *Human Resources*. In this scenario, the *jsmith* object from the Monday backup tape will still possess the old *Marketing* Department attribute. However, this information will be updated to *Human Resources* at the next replication event, since the other domain controllers will update the restored controller with their newer information. Using this default restore method, any changes made subsequent to the backup being restored will be automatically replicated from the other Windows Server 2003 domain controllers.

Just as in Windows 2000, you must first boot into Directory Services Restore Mode in order to restore the System State data on a domain controller. Use the **F8** key to access the Startup options menu during the Windows Server 2003 bootup process, then scroll to **Directory Services Restore Mode** and press **Enter**. This startup mode allows you to restore the SYSVOL directory and Active Directory, as discussed in the next exercise.

Exam Warning

Remember that you'll be prompted for the Directory Services Restore Mode password that you created during the installation of Active Directory on the server. This will likely not be the same as your current administrative password. For this reason, it is generally a best practice to keep such critical but seldom-used passwords in a safe-deposit box or other secure location so that you can access them easily during a recovery situation.

Exercise 3.05

Performing a Nonauthoritative Restore

1. Once you have booted into Directory Services Restore Mode, open the Windows Backup utility by clicking **Start | All Programs | Accessories | System Tools | Backup**.
2. Click **Next** to bypass the Welcome screen. Then select **Restore Wizard** to begin the restore process, as shown in Figure 3.23.

Figure 3.23 Beginning the Restore Process

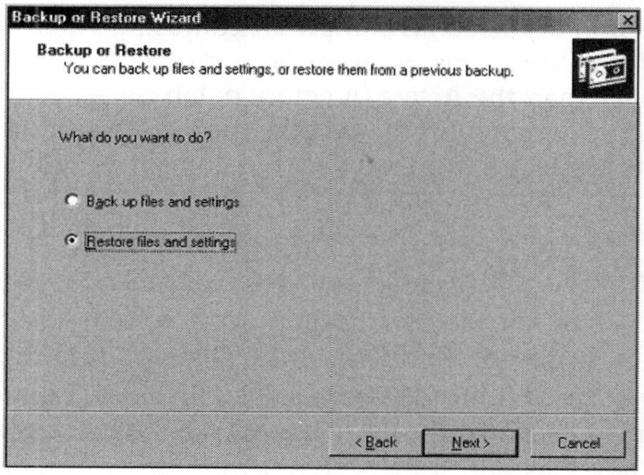

3. On the screen shown in Figure 3.23, select the radio button next to **Restore files and settings**, then click **Next** to continue to Figure 3.24.

Figure 3.24 Selecting the Files and Information to Restore

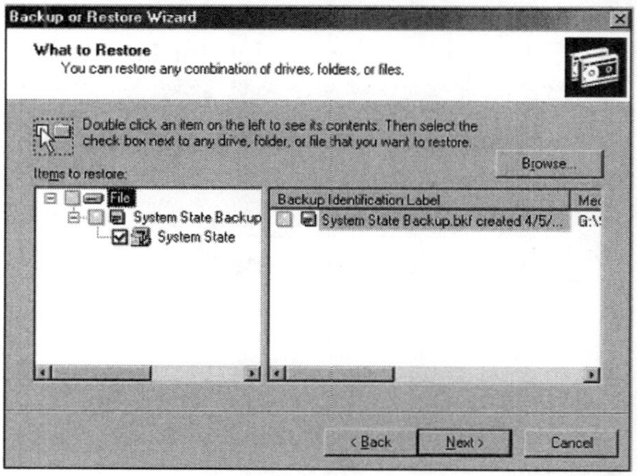

4. Place a check mark next to the files and data that you want to restore. (In this case, the backup only contains the System State data, so that will be the only check mark necessary.) Click **Next** when you've finished making your selections.
5. Once you've completed the previous steps, you'll see a Summary screen that displays the information that will be restored and the options that will be used during the restore. Simply clicking **Finish** will launch the restore process using the following default options: files will be restored to their original locations, and existing files will not be replaced. Instead of clicking on **Finish**, click on **Advanced** and proceed to Step 6.

Test Day Tip

The text in the Summary screen is somewhat confusing when you're restoring the System State information. "Existing files: Do not replace" only applies to any files or directories *other* than the Active Directory database, as you will see in the following Advanced screens. Using the default options, the Active Directory database *will* overwrite the existing information on the domain controller being restored.

6. In the Where to Restore screen (see Figure 3.25), you will select the location to which the files, folders, and System State information should be restored. If you want the System State to automatically overwrite any existing information, select **Original location**. Otherwise, you can choose one of the other two options: **Alternate location** will restore any files and folders to another directory or drive while maintaining the existing directory structures. **Single folder** will restore all files into a single directory, regardless of the folders or subfolders present in the backup file. Click **Next** when you've made your selection. You'll see the screen shown in Figure 3.26.

Figure 3.25 Selecting a Destination for Restored Files

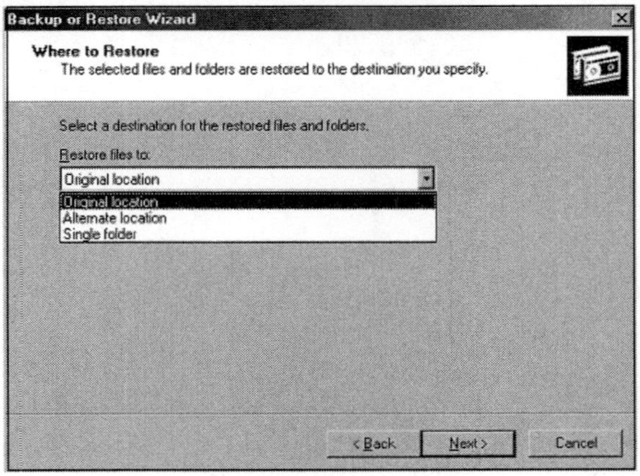

7. From this screen you will instruct the Restore wizard to leave any existing files intact, to replace them if they are older than the files that exist on the backup media, or to overwrite existing files en masse. You must make this decision globally, unlike when performing a Windows Explorer file copy, in which you are prompted to overwrite on each individual file. (As stated in the previous Warning, remember that this *only* applies to user files or folders that you are restoring in addition to the Active Directory database.) Click **Next** to continue to Figure 3.27.

Figure 3.26 Choosing How to Restore Existing Files

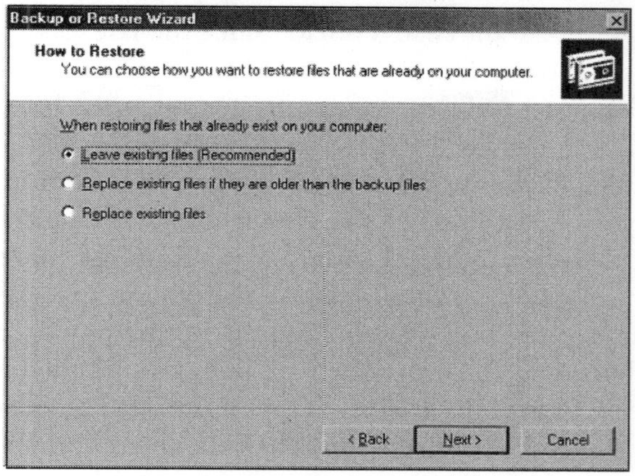

Figure 3.27 Selecting Advanced Restore Options

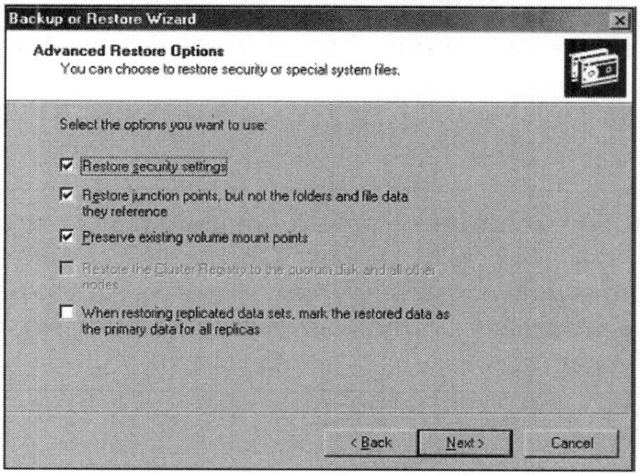

8. Use this screen to change any final security settings, if necessary. Click **Next** and then click **Finish** to launch the restore process. You'll see a progress window to indicate that the restore is under way.
9. Since you have restored Active Directory data during this process, you'll be prompted to reboot when the restore has completed. After rebooting, check the Event Viewer for any error messages, and verify that the desired information has been restored properly.

EXAM 70-296 OBJECTIVE 7.2.1

Performing an Authoritative Restore

In some cases, you might not want changes made since the last backup operation to be replicated to your restored Active Directory data. In these instances, you will want all domain controller replicas to possess the same information as the backed-up data that you are restoring. To accomplish this goal, you'll need to perform an *authoritative restore*. This is especially useful if you inadvertently delete users, groups, or OUs from the Active Directory directory service and you want to restore the system so that the deleted objects are recovered and replicated. (Otherwise, the replication updates from the more up-to-date domain controllers will simply "re-delete" the information that you just worked so hard to restore.)

When you mark information as authoritative, the restore process changes the objects' update sequence numbers (USNs) so that they are higher—and therefore considered newer—than any other USNs in the domain. This ensures that any data that you restore is properly replicated to your other domain controllers. In an authoritative restore, the objects in the restored directory replace all existing copies of those objects, rather than the restored items receiving updates through the usual replication process. To perform an authoritative restore of Active Directory data, you need to run the *ntdsutil* utility after you have restored the System State data but before you reboot the server at the end of the restore process. The following exercise covers the steps in using *ntdsutil* to mark Active Directory objects for an authoritative restore.

Test Day Tip

If you are performing a restore because a single domain controller's system disk has failed or its Active Directory database has become corrupted, you can typically perform a nonauthoritative restore without the need for the *ntdsutil* utility, since the other domain controllers within your domain still possess intact copies of the Active Directory database.

Exercise 3.06

Performing an Authoriatative Restore

1. Follow the steps listed in Exercise 3.05 to perform a nonauthoritative restore. When the restore process completes and you are prompted to reboot the domain controller, select **No**. From a command prompt, type **ntdsutil** and press **Enter**.
2. Type **authoritative restore** and press **Enter**.

3. To authoritatively restore the entire Active Directory database from your backup media, type **restore database** and press **Enter**. Click **Yes** to confirm. You will see the progress window shown in Figure 3.28.

Figure 3.28 Performing an Authoritative Restore

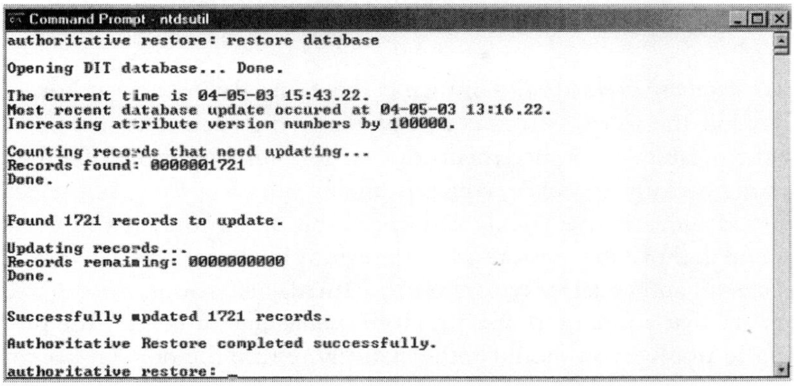

4. Type **quit** until you return to the main command prompt, then reboot the domain controller. Check the Event Viewer and the Active Directory management utilities to confirm that the restore completed successfully.

Understanding NTDSUTIL Restore Options

Ntdsutil.exe provides a number of optional parameters in performing an authoritative restore of the Active Directory database. In the previous exercise, you simply used the *restore database* syntax to authoritatively restore the entire Active Directory structure. However, you can exert much more granular control over the Active Directory restore using the command-line syntax discussed here. (You can always type **ntdsutil /?** for a listing of all available options.)

The complete list of available restore options within *ntdsutil* is as follows:

```
{restore database|restore database verinc %d|restore subtree %s|restore
subtree %s verinc %d|restore objext %s |restore object %s verinc %d}
```

These individual parameters perform the following tasks:

- ***restore database*** Marks the entire database as authoritative. All other domain controllers will accept replication data from the restored server as the most current information.

EXAM WARNING

The schema cannot be authoritatively restored. If the Active Directory schema has become corrupted, you must use a *primary restore* from backup media created before the offending schema modifications were performed. We discuss primary restores in the next section.

- ***restore database verinc %d*** This marks the entire database as authoritative and increments the version number by *%d*. Referring back to Figure 3.28, you can see that the default syntax increments the version number by 100000 for every day since the backup was made, which is usually sufficient to mark the database restore as authoritative. You'll need to use this option only if you need to perform a second authoritative restore over a previous incorrect one. For example, if you perform an authoritative restore using a Tuesday afternoon backup and discover afterward that you require the Tuesday *morning* tape to correct the problem you're trying to resolve, you should authoritatively restore the domain backup using a higher version number, such as 200000. This will ensure that the other controllers in your domain will regard the second restore operation as authoritative.
- ***restore subtree %s*** Use this syntax to restore a specific subtree (and all children of that subtree) as being authoritative. The subtree is defined using the fully distinguished name (FDN) of the object.
- ***restore subtree %s verinc %d*** This performs the same function as *restore database verinc %d* for a single subtree.

Performing a Primary Restore

You'll perform a primary restore when the server you are trying to restore contains the only existing copy of any replicated data—in this case the SYSVOL directory and the Active Directory data. Using a primary restore allows you to return the first replica set to your network; do not use this option if you've already restored other copies of the data being restored. Typically, you'll perform a primary restore only when you have lost all the domain controllers in your domain and are rebuilding the entire Active Directory structure from your backup media. You'll perform a primary restore very similarly to a nonauthoritative restore, but in the final Advanced Options screen (again, looking at Figure 3.28 in Exercise 3.06), place a check mark next to **When restoring replicated data sets, mark the restored data as the primary data for all replicas**.

Summary of Exam Objectives

The subjects discussed in this chapter addressed a number of topics on the 70-296 exam relating to creating and managing trust relationships. Like its predecessor, Windows Server 2003 automatically creates trust relationships between all domains within a single forest, freeing you from the need to create and maintain them manually. New to Windows Server 2003 is the ability to create transitive trust relationships between separate Active Directory forests as well as establishing a trust relationship with a UNIX-based MIT Kerberos domain. You can also create shortcut trusts within an Active Directory forest to speed resource access between multiple domains as well as external trusts with existing Windows 2000 and NT 4.0 domains on your network.

Once you've implemented your Active Directory infrastructure, you'll need to perform a number of ongoing tasks to maintain it in top working order. To help you reach this goal, exercises in this chapter cover the steps needed to create a forest root domain or child domains as your organization grows or changes. You can also raise the Active Directory domain functional level and forest functional level of your Active Directory infrastructure in order to leverage the new Windows Server 2003-specific features discussed in this chapter. We also discussed the necessary steps in creating, managing, and delegating control of OUs to better organize your network resources. In addition, we discussed the best way to manually view and modify the Active Directory schema as a troubleshooting task.

The final topic we discussed in this chapter was the process of performing both authoritative and nonauthoritative restores of the Active Directory database. In the event of any sort of hardware or software failure on your network, both of these restores will help you recover your Active Directory installation as painlessly as possible. Nonauthoritative restores recover a domain controller or specific objects within Active Directory that will be brought up to date by other domain controllers on the network. Authoritative restores mark any restored data as the most recent copy of information, useful in the case of recovering deleted or corrupted items without having the deletion or corruption return through the normal replication process. It's critical to have a firm grasp of the Active Directory restoration process, since the things than *can* go wrong inevitably *do.*

Exam Objectives Fast Track

Choosing a Management Method

☑ The most common administrative tools are the graphical user interface (GUI) utilities that are automatically installed when you run *dcpromo* to install Active Directory. The three most common of these are Active Directory Users and Computers, Active Directory Domains and Trusts, and Active Directory Sites and Services.

☑ Windows Server 2003 offers an array of command-line utilities that can add, delete, and remove Active Directory objects, create and delete trust relationships, manage domain controllers, and much more.

☑ Combine command-line utilities with Microsoft or third-party scripting tools such as VBScript, Windows Scripting Host, and the like to create powerful utilities to streamline repetitive administrative tasks.

Managing Forests and Domains

☑ Base your decision to create multiple domains within a single forest on whether you need to maintain a separate security boundary or Active Directory schema for either organization or business units. Use multiple domains or OUs to delegate some administrative responsibility while still maintaining a centrally administered network. If you need to maintain two discrete entities in terms of security and network management, multiple forests are the way to go.

☑ Raising the domain or forest functional level allows you to implement security and administrative improvements, but it will not allow any Windows NT 4.0 or 2000 domain controllers to participate in the domain. You'll need to either upgrade all down-level domain controllers on your network or demote them to standalone server status.

☑ You can create all necessary trust relationships—forest, shortcut, realm, or explicit—using either the Active Directory Domains and Trusts GUI or the *netdom* command-line utility.

Restoring Active Directory

☑ You can restore Active Directory or System State using the native Windows Server 2003 Backup utility or a tool from a third-party vendor.

☑ The default Active Directory restore type is *nonauthoritative*, whereby any restored objects will be updated by any other domain controllers within the replication topology to bring the restored objects up to date.

☑ To prevent the restored copy of an object or objects from receiving updates, use the *ntdsutil* command-line utility to mark the restored data as *authoritative*. All other domain controllers take the restored copy of the object as the definitive copy and will update their own information accordingly.

Exam Objectives Frequently Asked Questions

The following Frequently Asked Questions, answered by the authors of this book, are designed to both measure your understanding of the Exam Objectives presented in this chapter, and to assist you with real-life implementation of these concepts. You will also gain access to thousands of other FAQs at ITFAQnet.com.

Q: How do I decide between implementing a separate domain versus an organizational unit?

A: You'll want to create a domain if the resources you're attempting to group together have different security requirements than the rest of the existing network. Certain security settings, especially account policies, can only be implemented at the domain level, not at the OU level.

Q: I have a third-party utility that accesses my Active Directory data via LDAP; however, it cannot read signed or encrypted LDAP data. How can I disable this feature?

A: In the HKEY_LOCAL_MACHINE\SOFTWARE\Microsoft\Windows\CurrentVersion\AdminDebug key, create a DWORD value called *AdsOpenObjectFlags* according to the information in Table 3.5. Change the value of the key to any of the following, depending on your needs. (Remember that editing the Registry can be a risky proposition and that you should have a viable backup on hand in case anything goes awry.)

Table 3.5 Registry Values to Disable Signed and/or Encrypted LDAP Traffic

Value	Disables
1	Signing
2	Encrypting
3	Signing and encrypting

Q: What happens to Windows NT 4.0 trust relationships when you upgrade to Windows Server 2003?

A: When you upgrade a Windows NT 4.0 domain to a Windows Server 2003 domain, all your existing Windows NT 4.0 trusts are preserved as is. Remember that trust relationships between Windows Server 2003 domains and Windows NT 4.0 domains are nontransitive.

Self Test

1. Your Windows Server 2003 Active Directory structure contains multiple domains and child domains, as shown in the following illustration. Many of your users need to work from different locations at various points throughout the week, and they are having difficulty remembering the information that they need to enter when logging onto different domains within the network. What is the most efficient way for you to make the login process simpler for your users when they are logging onto the network from different domains?

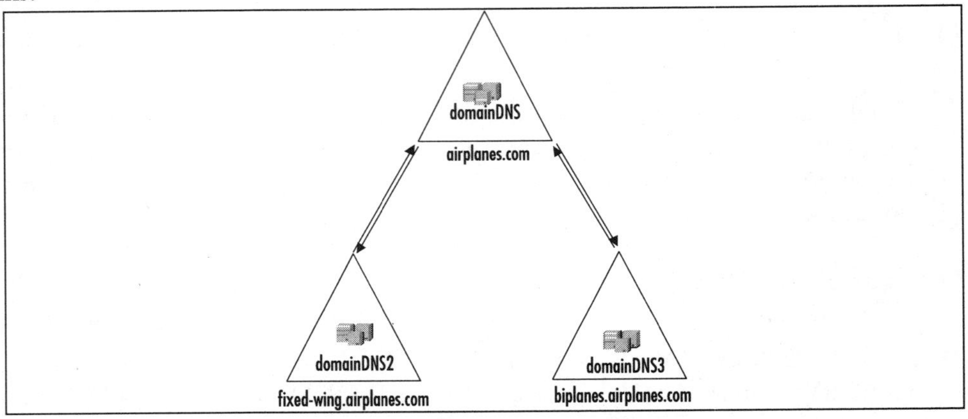

   A. Create local accounts in each domain from which roaming users need to log in.

   B. Create two-way transitive trusts between all domains within your Active Directory forest.

   C. Create a single common UPN suffix so that users can log in simply by entering their usernames, regardless of where on the network they attempt to log in from.

   D. Implement a RADIUS database to handle login requests from multiple domains.

2. Your organization includes a large sales department, with many representatives who only come into the corporate headquarters a few times a month. For this reason, many of them forget their network passwords. You would like Jane, a power user in the sales department, to be able to reset passwords for the members of her department. What is the *best* way to implement this solution without allowing Jane any more administrative access than necessary?

   A. Make Jane a member of the Domain Admins group.

   B. Install a domain controller in the sales department and run *dcpromo* to create a new domain in your organization's Active Directory forest.

   C. Create a separate OU for the sales department and delegate the authority to reset passwords to Jane's user account.

   D. For each user account in the sales department, grant Jane's account the Change Password right.

3. You are the administrator of the fixed-wing.airplanes.com Windows Server 2003 domain. You are installing an Active Directory-aware database application that has created an application partition directory called a*pplication25* on the dc1.fixed-wing.airplanes.com domain controller as a child domain of the fixed-wing.airplanes.com domain. If there are no other application partition directories within your domain, what is the fully qualified DNS name of this partition directory?

   A. application25.dc1.fixed-wing.airplanes.com

   B. application25.airplanes.com

   C. application25.fixed-wing.airplanes.com

   D. application25.com

4. You are attempting to raise the functional level of your domain to Windows Server 2003 in order to take advantage of the advanced Active Directory features that it offers. You are able to authenticate and browse the network, and you access Active Directory Domains and Trusts using the login credentials of your user account in the Enterprise Admins group. When you attempt to raise the forest functional level, you receive an error message, and the functional level is not raised to Windows Server 2003. Of the following, which is the most likely cause of this failure?

   A. Your forest still contains Windows NT4 and/or Windows 2000 domain controllers.

   B. TCP/IP is not running on your network.

   C. Your user account is not a member of the Schema Admins group.

   D. Your workstation has a failed NIC.

5. You need to make some alterations to the schema in your Active Directory forest. You've used the *regsvr32* utility to register schmmgmt.dll on your administrative workstation. However, when you open the Administrative tools folder, the Active Directory Schema snap-in does not appear. What do you need to do in order to manage the Active Directory schema from your workstation?

   A. You cannot manage the schema from your workstation. You need to log onto the server that holds the schema master operational role.

   B. Open a blank Microsoft Management Console and add the Active Directory Schema snap-in.

   C. Run schmmgmt.exe from your workstation command prompt.

   D. Use the ADSI Editor in the Windows Server 2003 Resource Kit.

6. Your forest is structured according to the following illustration. You have a group of developers in the east.fixed-wing.airplanes.com domain who need to access files in the development.central.biplanes.airplanes.com domain on a regular basis. The users are complaining that accessing the files in the development domain is taking an unacceptably long time. What can you do to improve their response time?

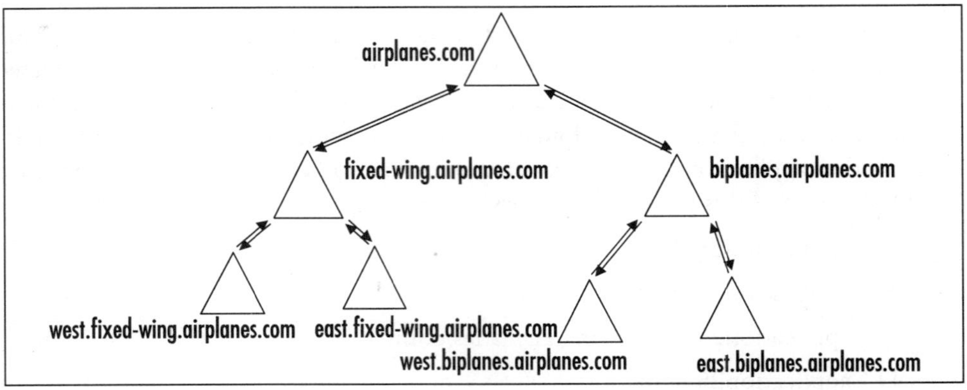

A. Create a domain local group in the development domain and add the developers' user accounts to it.

B. Create a shortcut trust between the east.fixed-wing.airplanes.com domain and the development.central.biplanes.airplanes.com domain.

C. Place the resources in the development domain into an OU. Use the Delegation of Control wizard to grant the users in the east.fixed-wing.airplanes.com domain the appropriate permissions.

D. Create an external trust between the fixed-wing.airplanes.com domain and the biplanes.airplanes.com domain.

7. You need to perform an authoritative restore on a domain controller on your network. From the Windows Server 2003 Windows Advanced Options menu, you select the option for Directory Services Restore Mode. When prompted, you enter the username and password of your individual account that is a member of the Domain Admins and Enterprise Admins groups. You are unable to log onto the server. What is the cause of the login failure?

   A. You need to log onto the server using the local administrator account and the Directory Services Restore Mode password that you specified when you ran the Active Directory Installation wizard.

   B. Your account does not meet the password complexity requirements of the local system policy.

   C. Your account has been locked out.

   D. Your account needs to be a member of the Schema Admins group.

8. You are the administrator of the network shown in the following figure. You have just installed an Active Directory-aware enterprise resource planning (ERP) application on your network, which has created an application directory partition on dc1.biplanes.airplanes.com. You perform nightly backups of the data contained in this partition, but you are still concerned that a server failure will leave your mission-critical ERP application unavailable to your network users for an unacceptable length of time. What is the most efficient way to increase the fault tolerance of this application?

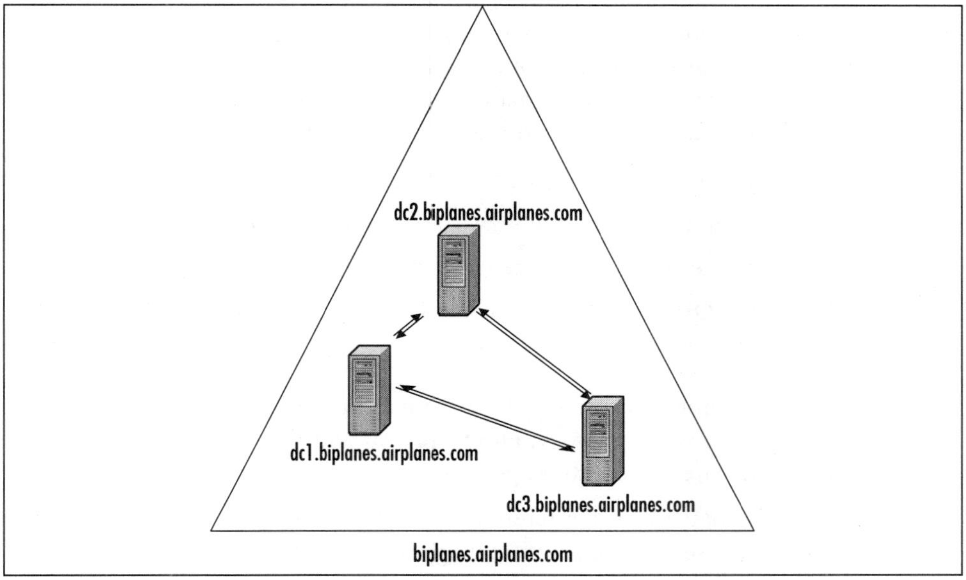

A. Increase the frequency of your backups.

B. Configure a second application directory partition on dc2.biplanes.airplanes.com, and configure the partition directory on dc1 to replicate its information to the new partition directory.

C. Store a local copy of the application's data on each user's workstation so that they can work from the local copy in case the server goes down.

D. Create a duplicate installation of the ERP application on a test server and restore the previous evening's production backups to the test server on a daily basis.

9. You are the administrator of a Windows Server 2003 network with three domain controllers; a portion of the network is shown in the following illustration. You perform a full backup of Active Directory on a nightly basis. On Monday afternoon, a member of your help desk inadvertently deletes the Human Resources OU. What is the best way to restore this information while losing as little information as possible?

   A. Manually recreate the OU and its contents. Any permissions associated with deleted user groups will automatically transfer over to the recreated OU.

   B. Perform a primary restore of the entire Active Directory database.

   C. Perform a nonauthoritative restore of the deleted OU so that it will receive any updates that had been performed since the OU was deleted.

   D. Perform an authoritative restore of the deleted OU so that it will not be deleted again at the next Active Directory replication.

10. The domain controller on your network that held the domain naming master operations role suffered a failed power supply. Since you needed to create new domains

because of a recent corporate merger, you immediately seized the domain naming role to another domain controller. Your hardware technicians have replaced the power supply on the original domain naming master. What do you need to do before you return the original domain controller to the network?

A. Use *ntdsutil* to seize the domain naming role back to the original domain controller.

B. Nothing. Simply return the server to production as normal.

C. Reformat the machine and reinstall the operating system.

D. Use Active Directory Domains and Trusts to reassign the domain naming master back to the original domain controller.

11. You have a comma-separated text file containing updated account information for existing users on your network. How can you add this information to your Active Directory database as quickly as possible?

A. Using the text file as a reference, update the user accounts using the Active Directory Users and Groups management console.

B. Use the LDIFDE command-line utility to import the .CSV information directly into Active Directory.

C. Purchase a third-party add-on utility to import the information into Active Directory.

D. Delegate control over the Users container and have a help desk associate enter the information using Active Directory Sites and Services.

12. You have two user accounts on your Windows Server 2003 network: one account that belongs to the Domain Admins and Enterprise Admins group that you use to perform sensitive administrative tasks, and one nonadministrative user that you use for everyday logins and activities. What is the most efficient and secure way to access the Windows Server 2003 Administrative Tools using your "superuser" account?

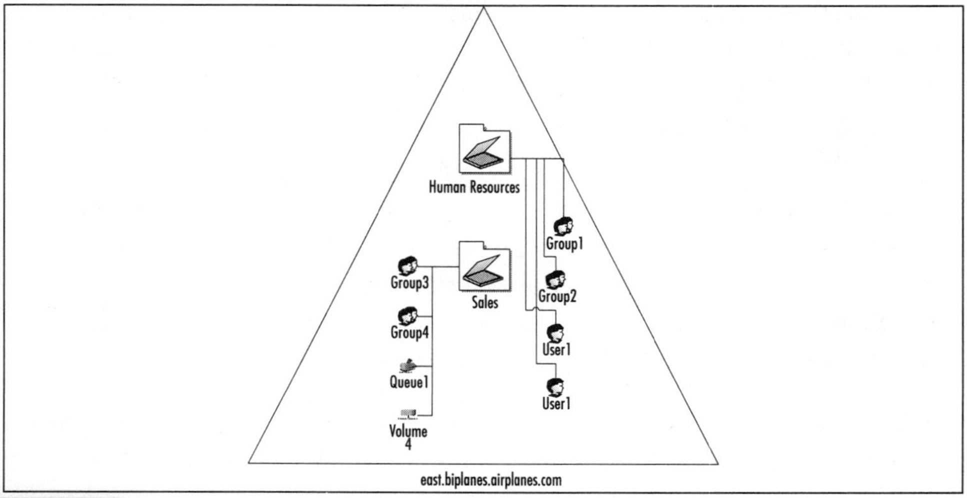

A. Use the *RunAs* function to launch the Administrator Tools using your administrator account's login information.

B. Log out of your workstation and log back in with your administrator account whenever you need to perform a management task.

C. Walk over to a server to access the administrative tools.

D. Log onto your workstation using your administrator account at all times; you shouldn't maintain two user accounts within your domain.

13. You have just created a child domain on your Windows Server 2003 network. What type of trust relationship exists by default between the parent and child domains?

A. One-way: outgoing from the parent domain to the child domain

B. Two-way transitive

C. One-way: incoming from the parent domain to the child domain

D. One-way: outgoing from the child domain to the parent domain

E. One-way: incoming from the child domain to the parent domain

14. You have just been informed that your company's training department, whose resources are currently housed in their own domain called *training.mycompany.com*, is changing its department name to Staff Development. The vice president of the department would like their Active Directory domain renamed to staffdevelopment.mycompany.com. All domain controllers are running Windows Server 2003. How can you meet the vice president's request? (Choose all that apply.)

A. Rename the training.mycompany.com domain using Active Directory Domains and Trusts.

B. Raise the domain functional level of the training.mycompany.com domain to Windows Server 2003.

C. Use the *DomainRename* Resource Kit utility to rename training.mycompany.com to staffdevelopment.mycompany.com.

D. Raise the forest functional level of your Active Directory forest to Windows Server 2003.

15. You have five domain controllers in your Windows Server 2003 domain, each of which maintains an operations master role. Your domain is operating at the Windows Server 2003 domain functional level. PDC1.AIRPLANES.COM, the machine that hosts the PDC emulator role, fails. Your hardware technicians estimate that it will be out of service for 48 hours. Your Windows NT 4.0 Workstation clients report that they cannot log onto the network. How can you resolve this situation as quickly as possible?

A. Wait for your hardware technicians to repair the PDC emulator.

B. Upgrade a Windows NT 4.0 member server to Windows Server 2003 and assign it the PDC emulator role.

C. Install a Windows NT 4.0 domain controller to handle down-level client authentication until the PDC emulator is repaired.

D. Use *ntdsutil* to seize the PDC emulator role and assign it to another domain controller.

Self Test Quick Answer Key

For complete questions, answers, and explanations to the Self Test questions in this chapter as well as the other chapters in this book, see the Self Test Appendix.

1. **C**
2. **C**
3. **C**
4. **A**
5. **B**
6. **B**
7. **A**.
8. **B**
9. **D**
10. **C**.
11. **B**
12. **A**
13. **B**
14. **B**, **C**
15. **D**

Chapter 4

MCSA/MCSE 70-296

Implementing PKI in a Windows Server 2003 Network

Exam Objectives in this Chapter:

- 5.1 Configure Active Directory directory services for certificate publication.
- 5.2 Plan a public key infrastructure (PKI) that uses Certificate Services.
- 5.2.1 Identify the appropriate type of certificate authority to support certificate issuance requirements.
- 5.2.2 Plan the enrollment and distribution of certificates.
- 5.2.3 Plan for the use of smart cards for authentication.

☑ Summary of Exam Objectives

☑ Exam Objectives Fast Track

☑ Exam Objectives Frequently Asked Questions

☑ Self Test

☑ Self Test Quick Answer Key

Introduction

In this connected world, failing to provide confidentiality and integrity for data communications can be a costly mistake. Due to the vastness of the Internet and the growing number of users joining the Internet each day, it is becoming more and more difficult to identify and validate the identities of Internet users and connected businesses. If the Internet is to thrive as a legitimate form of communications, a system had to be developed for validating the identity of users and businesses. Not only did there have to be a validation system, there had to be a way to manage and secure the identities once they have been verified. The solution to this problem was the development of the *public key infrastructure (PKI)*.

Microsoft, realizing the impact that PKI has had and will continue to have on data communications, has continued to interweave PKI technology with its own Active Directory and Windows technology. However, getting PKI integrated into your Active Directory structure is not an easy task; but is it not impossible. As with the creation of your Active Directory structure, taking the time to properly plan and implement PKI into your environment can be the difference between a smooth integration and a configuration nightmare.

As a Windows Server 2003 MCSE candidate, you are expected to understand the concepts behind PKI, its components, and how to plan and integrate it into your Windows Server 2003 Active Directory structure. By the end of this chapter, you should have a clear understanding of how this process is completed. Let's begin our discussion of PKI with a general overview of cryptology and PKI.

An Overview of Public Key Infrastructure

With the incredible growth of the Internet, there is an increasing need for entities (people, computers, or companies) to prove their identities. The problem is, anyone can be sitting behind a keyboard at the other end of a transaction or communication, so who is responsible for verifying that person's credentials?

PKI was developed to solve this very problem. The PKI identification process is based on the use of unique identifiers known as *keys*. Each person using PKI is assigned two different keys—a *public key* and a *private key*—which are mathematically related. The public key is openly available to the public, whereas only the person the keys were created for knows the private key. Through the use of these keys, messages can be *encrypted* and *decrypted* so that parties can transfer messages in confidence.

PKI has become such an integrated part of Internet communications that most users are unaware that they use it every time they access the World Wide Web. PKI is not limited to the Web; applications such as Pretty Good Privacy (PGP) also use a form of PKI. The logical place to begin our discussion is to start at the heart of PKI, which is a method securing data transmission known as *cryptology*.

Understanding Cryptology

For as long as people have been writing down information, we have needed to keep some information secret, either by hiding its existence or changing its meaning—a practice known as *cryptography*. *Cryptology* is the study of the science of cryptography. *Encryption*, a type of cryptography, refers to the process of scrambling information so that the casual observer cannot read it. These methodologies use algorithms and keys. An *algorithm* is a set of instructions for mixing and rearranging an original message, called *plaintext*, with a message key to create a scrambled message, referred to as *ciphertext*. Similarly, a cryptographic *key* is a piece of data used to encrypt plaintext to ciphertext, ciphertext to plaintext, or both (depending on the type of encryption).

What does the word *crypto* mean? It has its origins in the Greek word *kruptos*, which means *hidden*. Thus the objective of cryptography is to hide information so that only the intended recipient(s) can "unhide" it. In crypto terms, the hiding of information is called *encryption*, and when the information is unhidden, that process is called *decryption*. A *cipher* is used to accomplish the encryption and decryption. *Merriam-Webster's Collegiate Dictionary* defines *cipher* as "a method of transforming a text in order to conceal its meaning." The information that is being hidden is called *plaintext*; once it has been encrypted, it is called *ciphertext*. The ciphertext is transported, secure from prying eyes, to the intended recipient(s), where it is decrypted back into plaintext.

Finally, there are two different subclasses of algorithms: block ciphers and stream ciphers. *Block ciphers* work on "blocks," or chunks of text in a series. Just as a letter is composed of many sentences, plaintext is composed of many blocks, which are typically variable lengths of bits. In contrast, a *stream cipher* operates on each individual unit (either letters or bits) of a message.

Encryption

Encryption is a form of cryptography that "scrambles" plaintext into unintelligible ciphertext. Encryption is the foundation of such security measures as digital signatures, digital certificates, and the PKI that uses these technologies to make computer transactions more secure. Computer-based encryption techniques use keys to encrypt and decrypt data. A *key* is a variable (sometimes represented as a password) that is a large binary number—the larger, the better. Key length is measured in bits, and the more bits in a key, the more difficult the key is to "crack."

The key is only one component in the encryption process. It must be used in conjunction with an encryption *algorithm* (a process or calculation) to produce the ciphertext. Encryption methods are usually categorized as either symmetric or asymmetric, depending on the number of keys that are used. We discuss these two basic types of encryption technology in the following sections.

Symmetric Encryption Algorithms

The most widely used type of encryption is *symmetric encryption*, which is aptly named because it uses one key for both the encryption and decryption processes. Symmetric encryption is also commonly referred to as *secret-key encryption* and *shared-secret encryption*, but all terms refer to the same class of algorithms.

The reasons that symmetric encryption systems are abundant are their speed and simplicity. The strength of symmetric algorithms lies primarily in the size of the keys used in the algorithm as well as the number of cycles each algorithm employs. The cardinal rule is "fewer is faster."

By definition, all symmetric algorithms are theoretically vulnerable to *brute-force attacks*, which are exhaustive searches of all possible keys. Brute-force attacks involve methodically guessing the key to a message. Given that all symmetric algorithms have a fixed key length, a large number of possible keys can unlock a message. Brute-force attacks methodically attempt to check each key until the key that decrypts the message is found. However, brute-force attacks are often impractical because the amount of time necessary to search the keys is greater than the useful life expectancy of the hidden information. No algorithm is truly *unbreakable*, but a strong algorithm takes so long to crack that the likelihood of cracking an algorithm is very improbable. Because brute-force attacks originate from computers, and because computers are continually improving in efficiency, an algorithm that is resistant to a brute-force attack performed by a computer today will not necessarily be resistant to attacks by computers 5 to 10 years in the future.

Asymmetric Encryption Algorithms

The most recent developments in cryptography are the discovery of *asymmetric algorithms*, which are characterized by the use of two different keys to encrypt and decrypt information. Asymmetric encryption is commonly referred to as *public key cryptography* because the encryption key can be freely distributed. Similarly, the decryption key is called the *private key* and must be held in strict confidence. Although these keys are generated together and generally exhibit a mathematical relationship, the private key cannot be derived from the public key.

Instead of relying on the techniques of substitution and transposition, which symmetric key cryptography uses, asymmetric algorithms rely on the use of large-integer mathematics problems. Many of these problems are simple to do in one direction but difficult to do in the opposite direction. For example, it is easy to multiply two numbers together, but it is more difficult to factor them back into the original numbers, especially if the integers used contain hundreds of digits. Thus, in general, the security of asymmetric algorithms is dependent not upon the feasibility of brute-force attacks but the feasibility of performing difficult mathematical inverse operations and advances in mathematical theory that may propose new "shortcut" techniques.

Asymmetric cryptography is much slower than symmetric cryptography, for several reasons. First, asymmetric cryptography relies on exponentiation of both a secret and a public exponent, as well as generation of a modulus. Computationally, exponentiation is a processor-intensive operation. Second, the keys used by asymmetric algorithms are generally larger than those used by symmetric algorithms, because the most common asymmetric attack (factoring) is more efficient than the most common symmetric attack (brute force).

For these reasons, asymmetric algorithms are typically used only for encrypting small amounts of information.

TEST DAY TIP

Remember that public key cryptography is based on asymmetric encryption algorithms.

Hashing Algorithms

Hashing is a technique in which an algorithm (also called a *hash function*) is applied to a portion of data to create a unique digital "fingerprint" that is a fixed-size variable. If anyone changes the data by so much as one binary digit, the hash function will produce a different output (called the *hash value*) and the recipient will know that the data has been changed. Hashing can ensure integrity and provide authentication as well. The hash function cannot be "reverse-engineered"; that is, you can't use the hash value to discover the original data that was hashed. Thus hashing algorithms are referred to as *one-way hashes*. A good hash function will not return the same result from two different inputs (called a *collision*); each result should be unique. All of the encryption algorithms we've studied so far, both symmetric and asymmetric, are reversible—in other words, they can be converted from cleartext to ciphertext and back again, provided that the appropriate keys are used. However, there is no reversible function for hashing algorithms, so original material cannot be recovered. For this reason, hashing algorithms are commonly referred to as *one-way hashing functions*. However, irreversible encryption techniques are useful for determining data integrity and authentication.

Sometimes it is not necessary or even desirable to encrypt a complete set of data. Suppose someone wants to transmit a large amount of data, such as a CD image. If the data on the CD is not sensitive, the sender might not care that it is openly transmitted, but when the transfer is complete, he or she will want to make sure that the image received is identical to the original image. The easiest way to make this comparison is to calculate a hash value on both images and compare results. If there is a discrepancy of even a single bit, the hash values of the two will be radically different. Provided they are using a suitable hashing function, no two inputs will result in an identical output, or *collision*. The hashes created, usually referred to as *digital fingerprints*, are usually of a small, easily readable, fixed size. Sometimes these hashes are referred to as *secure checksums* because they perform similar functions as normal checksums but are inherently more resistant to tampering.

Encrypted passwords are often stored as hashes. When a password is set for a system, it is generally passed through a hashing function, and only the encrypted hash is stored. When a person later attempts to authenticate, the password is hashed and that hash is compared to the stored hash. If these are the same, they are authenticated; otherwise, access is rejected. In theory, if someone were to obtain a password list for a system, it would be useless since by definition it is impossible to recover the original information from its hashed value. However, attackers can use dictionary and brute-force attacks by methodically comparing the output hash of a known input string to the stolen hash. If they match, the password has been *cracked*. Thus proper password length and selection are highly desirable.

Benefits of Public Key Infrastructure

PKI is made up of several different components. The centerpiece of PKI is the *certificate authority (CA)*. A CA functions as the management center for *digital certificates*. Digital certificates are collections of predefined information that is related to a public key. Some PKI implementations use a *registration authority (RA)*. An RA is used to take some of the burden off the CA by handling verification prior to certificates being issued.

Since many PKI implementations become very large, a system must be in place to manage the issuance, revocation, and general management of certificates. PKI, being a *public key* infrastructure, must also be able to store certificates and public keys in a directory that is publicly accessible. A user can create their public and private keys using another application and make the public key available to the CA. Or, a CA can create the private and public keys of a keypair at the same time, using a predetermined algorithm. In this case, the private key is given to the person, computer, or company that is attempting to establish its credentials. In both instances, the public key is then stored in a directory that is readily accessible by any party that wants to verify the credentials of the certificate holder. For example, if Ben wants to establish secure communications with Jerry, he can obtain Jerry's public key from the CA and encrypt a message to him using his (Jerry's) public key. When Jerry receives the message, he validates Ben's public key with the CA. Assuming the CA responds that the certificate is valid, Jerry then decrypts the message with his (Jerry's) private key (see Figure 4.1).

Figure 4.1 The PKI Key Exchange

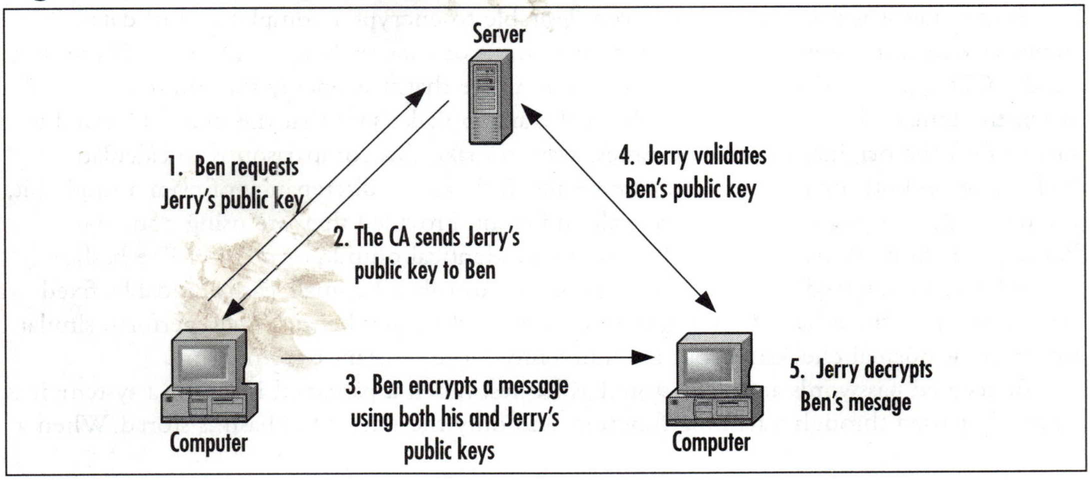

An RA acts as a proxy between the user and the CA. When a user makes a request to the CA, the RA receives the request, authenticates it, and forwards it to the CA. The CA returns a response to the RA, and the RA forwards the response back to the original user. RAs are most often found in *standalone* or *hierarchical* models, where the workload of the CA might need to be offloaded to other servers.

Let's look at PKI from a nontechnical perspective. Let's say that in anticipation of the big raise you are going to receive once you pass the 70-296 exam, you decide to go to the local electronics store and purchase a new television set. You decide to purchase it with a personal check. You give your check and driver's license to the clerk to process the transaction. The clerk verifies the check by comparing the information on the check with the information on your license.

What happened here? How does this transaction relate to PKI?

1. You decided which television you wanted to purchase and brought it to the clerk. You *initiated* the transaction with the clerk.
2. The clerk asked for your driver's license. At this point the clerk requested a *digital certificate* from a *trusted authority*.
3. The clerk verifies the check by validating the information on your license, which has been issued by a trusted authority (the Department of Motor Vehicles). At this point the clerk *validates your certificate*.
4. After validating your information, the clerk trusts you and completes the transaction. The clerk gives you the new television.

Obviously, PKI is a little more technically involved than the example we just ran through, but this is a great foundation for discussing how PKI works. In our example, the sales clerk mitigates the risks associated with a check purchase by following store procedure for "trusting" the customer and accepting his or her check. PKI makes it possible for one entity to trust another by providing *privacy, authentication, nonrepudiation,* and *integrity.*

Privacy

The use of PKI provides for the privacy, or *confidentiality,* of communications between two entities over a network. A user can be confident that the data that he or she is sending (or receiving) will not be intercepted and read by a third party that could be listening to network traffic. Even if a hacker or other third party intercepts a data packet, it will be useable by this person, since only the sender and receiver hold the "keys" to unlock the encrypted data.

Authentication

When communicating with another entity, PKI provides verification that the other party is whom it claims to be. In other words, by communicating through a public key infrastructure, you have a high level of assurance that the person you expect to be on the other side of the wire is indeed that person.

Nonrepudiation

Because PKI provides for a level of authentication that a person is whom he or she claims to be, it also offers *nonrepudiation*. Nonrepudiation means that a person cannot deny the authenticity or origin of the data they are transmitting to another party in a PKI. *Digital signatures* are used to ensure that data has been electronically *signed* by a particular person or entity and that this same person or entity cannot later deny that he, she, or it had sent it.

Integrity

The *American Heritage Dictionary* definition of *integrity* reads, "The state of being unimpaired; soundness." In a PKI, having integrity means that data has not been modified during the transmission from one entity to another. Without data integrity, data could be modified during transfer, providing the recipient of the data with incorrect information.

Components of Public Key Infrastructure

Several components make up a typical PKI. Each component plays an important role in the implementation of PKI, and each component must be properly designed and managed to maintain the integrity of your implementation. The components, which we briefly discuss before moving onto the topic of planning a Windows Server 2003 PKI, are:

- Digital certificates
- Certificate authorities
- Certificate policy and practice statements
- Publication points
- Certificate revocation lists
- Certificate trust lists
- Key archival and recovery
- Standards

Let's begin this section with a discussion of digital certificates, which are users' passport to a public key infrastructure.

Digital Certificates

In our example with the sales associate, we compared a digital certificate to a driver's license (see Figure 4.2). A *digital certificate* is the tool used for binding a public key with a particular owner. Let's continue our analogy. The information listed on a driver's license is:

- Name
- Address

- Date of birth
- Photograph
- Signature
- Social Security number (or another unique number)
- Expiration date
- Signature/certification by an authority (in this case, the seal of the Commonwealth of Massachusetts)

Figure 4.2 A Sample Driver's License

Why is this information important? Because it provides crucial information about the *certificate owner.* The signature from a state official suggests that the information provided by the certificate owner has been verified and is legitimate. Digital certificates work in almost exactly the same manner, using unique characteristics to determine the identification of a certificate owner. The information contained in the certificate is part of the X.509 certificate standard, which is discussed in the following section.

X.509

Before discussing X.509, it is important to know that it was developed from the X.500 standard. X.500 is a directory service standard that was ratified by the International Telecommunications Union (ITU-T) in 1988 and modified in 1993 and 1997. It was intended to provide a means of developing an easy-to-use electronic directory of people that would be available to all Internet users.

The X.500 directory standard specifies a common root of a hierarchical tree. Contrary to its name, the root of the tree is depicted at the top level, and all other containers (which are used to create "branches") are below it. There are several types of containers, with a specific naming convention. In this naming convention, each portion of a name is specified by the abbreviation of the object type or container it represents. A CN= before a username represents it is a *common name,* a C= precedes a *country*, and an O= precedes an *organization.*

Compared to Internet Protocol (IP) domain names (for example, host.subdomain.domain), the X.500 version of CN=host/C=US/O=Org appears excessively complicated.

Each X.500 local directory is considered a *directory system agent (DSA)*. The DSA can represent either single or multiple organizations. Each DSA connects to the others through a *directory information tree (DIT)*, which is a hierarchical naming scheme that provides the naming context for objects within a directory.

X.509 is the standard used to define a digital certificate. Section 11.2 of X.509 describes a certificate as allowing an association between a user's distinguished name (DN) and the user's public key. (You can read more about X.509 at www.mcg.org.br/cert.htm#1.1.) The DN is specified by a naming authority (NA) and used as a unique name by the CA that will create the certificate. A common X.509 certificate includes the following information (see Figures 4.3 and 4.4):

- **Serial number** A unique identifier.
- **Subject** The name of the person or company that is being identified.
- **Signature algorithm** The algorithm used to create the signature.
- **Issuer** The trusted source that verified the information and generated the certificate.
- **Valid from** The date the certificate was activated.
- **Valid to** The last day the certificate can be used.
- **Public key** The public key that corresponds to the private key.
- **Thumbprint algorithm** The algorithm used to create the unique value (thumbprint) of a certificate.
- **Thumbprint** A unique value which positively identifies the certificate. If there is ever a question about the authenticity of a certificate, check this value with the issuer.

Figure 4.3 The General Tab of a Certificate

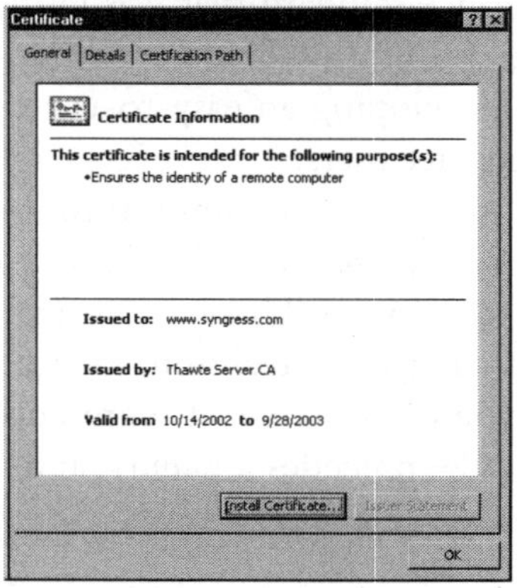

Figure 4.4 The Details Tab of a Certificate

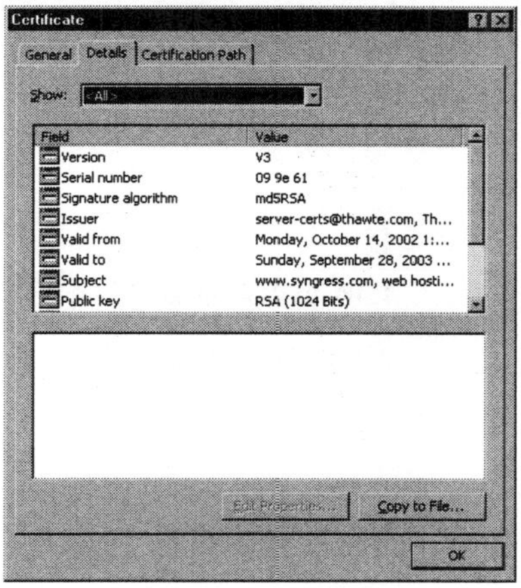

Certificate Authorities

A certificate authority, or CA, is a trusted server (or company such as VeriSign or Thawte) that is responsible for issuing digital certificates. CAs can exist in several different fashions, or *trust models*. For example, when multiple CAs are used, they are known as a *hierarchical model*. CA servers that stand alone and do not communicate with other CA servers are said to function in the *single CA model*. There is also a third type of trust model, known as a *Web-of-trust* or *chain-of-trust model*. But before looking at trust models in depth, let's look at the word *trust* itself. The idea behind a trust is that Party A places a set of expectations on Party B. Assuming that the *trusted* party (B) meets the expectations of the *trusting* party (A), a *one-way trust relationship* is formed. Likewise, if Party A also meets the expectations of Party B, a *two-way trust relationship* is formed. In a marriage, a husband and wife expect each other to act in a certain way. They have formed a *two-way trust relationship* (see Figure 4.5).

Figure 4.5 A Two-Way Trust Relationship

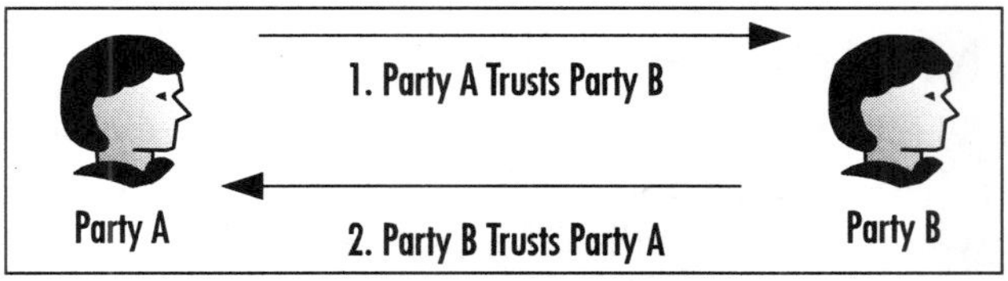

In a two-way trust, you simply trust someone (or something) to whom you are directly related. This trust is said to be based on the *locality* of the parties. When you are closer to a person or object, you are more likely to have a higher confidence in them. For example, Tim's wife, Amanda, wants to have a party at their house. Amanda wants to invite her best friend, Kate, whom Tim has met on several occasions and with whom he has some comfort level. Kate asks if she can bring her boyfriend, Mike. Although Tim does not know Kate's boyfriend, he still has a level of confidence in Mike because of the *chain of trust* established first through his wife, then Kate, and lastly Kate's boyfriend. This type of trust relationship is known as a *transitive trust* (see Figure 4.6).

Figure 4.6 A Chain of Trust

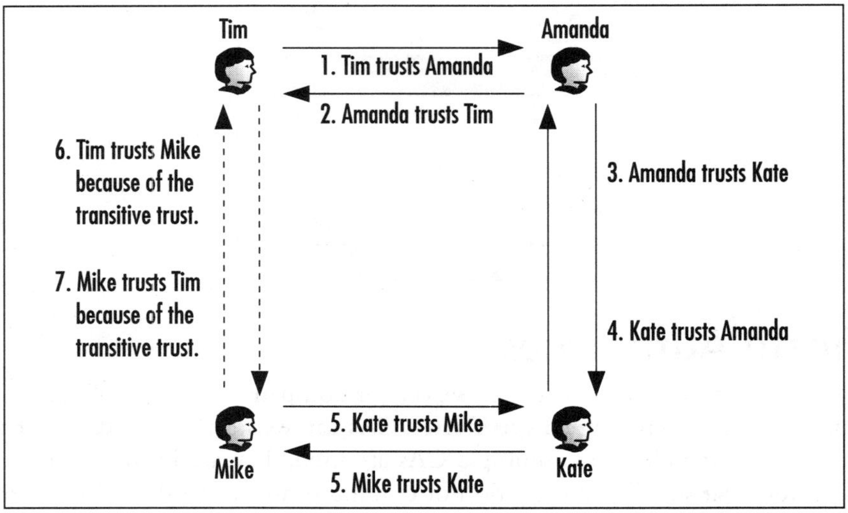

Single CA Models

Single CA models (see Figure 4.7) are very simplistic. Only one CA is used within a PKI. Anyone who needs to use the CA is given the public key for the CA, often using an out-of-band method. *Out-of-band* means that the key is not transmitted through the media that the end user intends to use with the certificate. In a single CA model, an RA can be used to verify the identity of a subscriber as well as set up the preliminary trust relationship between the CA and the end user.

Hierarchical Models

In a hierarchical model, a *root CA* functions as a top-level authority over CAs beneath it, called *subordinate CAs.* The root CA also functions as a *trust anchor* to the CAs beneath it. A *trust anchor* is an entity known to be sufficiently trusted and therefore can be used to trust anything connected to it. Going back to the example of Tim, his wife would be the trust anchor, since Tim has sufficient trust in her. In terms of PKI, the root CA is the most trusted.

Since there is nothing above the root CA, it must create a *self-signed* certificate. With a self-signed certificate, the certificate issuer and the certificate subject are exactly the same. As the trust anchor, the root CA must make its own certificate available to all the users (including subordinate CAs) that will ultimately be using the root CA.

Figure 4.7 A Single CA Model

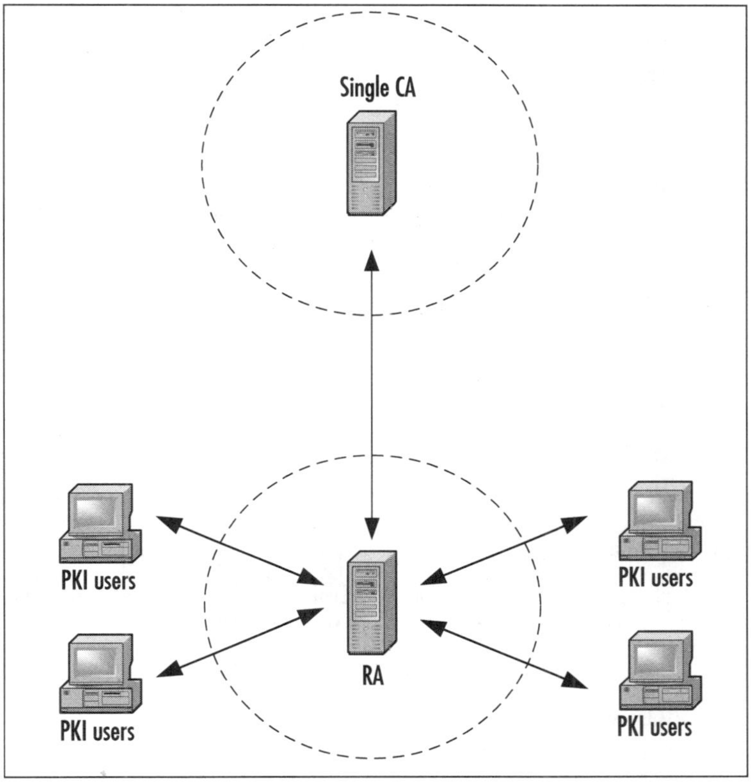

Configuring & Implementing...

A Compromised Root CA

Keeping a root CAs keys secure should be priority number one in PKI security. The work that goes into revoking and replacing a compromised root CA key is tremendous. Not only does the root CA have to be revoked and recreated, but so do any certificates created by a subordinate CA now suspect of being compromised. The saving grace of root CAs is that, typically, they are infrequently used except to certify subordinate CAs. Therefore, you have the ability to take your root CA offline in most network environments. By taking the root CA offline, you are eliminating any network access to the CA, preventing attackers from communicating directly with the CA server. However, you still need to maintain physical security to your root CA. In other words, don't disconnect your CA server from your network and keep it in your office or any other unsecured area. It's best to keep your root CA server in a locked server room or even a locked closet, where physical access to the server is limited to a select number of people.

After the root CA comes the *intermediate CA*. In most hierarchies, there is more than one intermediate CA. The intermediate CA is a subordinate CA, responsible for issuing certificates to the subordinate CAs below it, known as *leaf CAs*. Leaf CAs are responsible for issuing certificates to end users, servers, and other entities that use certificates. The hierarchical model, the most popular model used today, is shown in Figure 4.8.

Figure 4.8 A Hierarchical Model

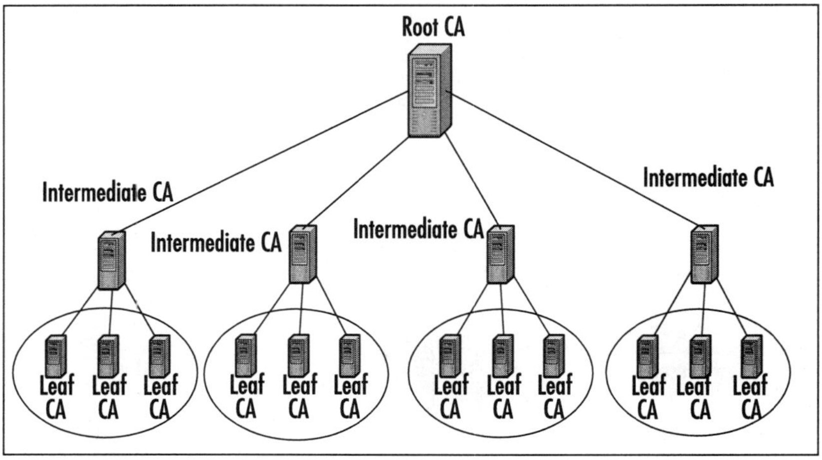

Hierarchical models work well in larger hierarchical environments, such as large government organizations or corporate environments. In situations in which different organizations are trying to develop a hierarchical model together (such as companies that have merged or formed partnerships), creating a hierarchical model can be nightmarish for the simple reason that it can be difficult to get all parties to agree on one single trust anchor.

Web-of-Trust Models

In the Web-of-trust or mesh model (see Figure 4.9), key holders sign each other's keys, thereby validating the keys based on their own knowledge of the key's owner. The encryption program, PGP, which encrypts and decrypts information such as files and e-mail, is based on the Web-of-trust model. Keys are individually held so that if one person certifies someone of a questionable nature, not everyone in the Web of trust will do so as well. Whereas a hierarchical model works well in larger enterprises, a peer-to-peer model works well with smaller groups that have established a relationship. Using this model Joe can sign Jane's key and pass it along to Peter. Peter will see that Joe has signed the key. If he believes Joe is reputable, it allows him to make a judgement about whether or not to trust Jane's key.

Figure 4.9 A Web-of-Trust Model

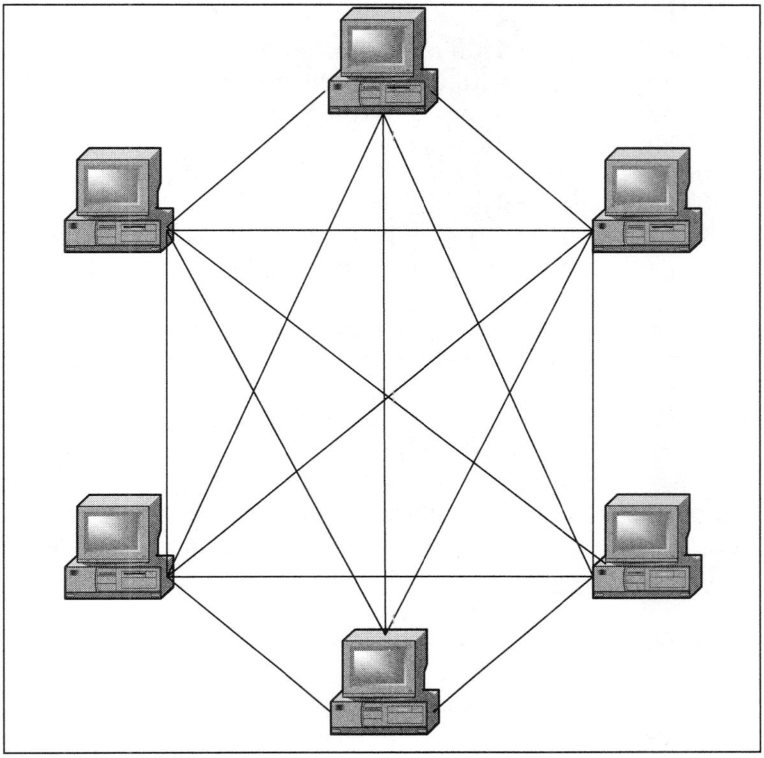

Certificate Policy and Practice Statements

Now that you know what a digital certificate is and what it comprises, you might be wondering what exactly a digital certificate can be issued for. A CA can issue a certificate for a number of different reasons, but it must indicate exactly what the certificate will be used for. The set of rules that indicates exactly how a certificate may be used is called a *certificate policy*. The X.509 standard defines certificate policies as "a named set of rules that indicates the applicability of a certificate to a particular community and/or class of application with common security requirements."

Different entities have different security requirements. For example, users want a digital certificate for securing e-mail, Syngress wants a digital certificate for its online store, and the Department of Defense (DoD) wants a digital certificate it can use to protect secret information regarding nuclear submarines. All three want to secure their information, but the requirements of the DoD are most likely more restrictive than those of the users, and certificate owners use the policy information to determine if they want to accept a certificate. The certificate policy is a plaintext document that is assigned a unique *object identifier (OID)* so that that anyone can reference it.

Configuring & Implementing...

Multiple Policies

Often a certificate is issued under a number of different policies. Some policies are of a technical nature, some refer to the procedures used to create and manage certificates, and others are policies the certificate user has determined are important, such as application access, system sign-on, and digitally signing documents. In some cases, such as government certificates, it is important that a certificate fall under multiple policies. In dealing with security systems, it is important to make sure the CA has a policy covering each item required. By not associating a certificate with a policy, you can put the validity and credibility of your CA server in question.

Another important aspect of managing certificate policies—whether single policies or multiple policies—is deciding the actual policy to be associated with a CA certificate. As with most decisions of this magnitude, it's better not to go it alone. It's always a good idea to involve other decision makers from your organization as resources permit. For example, the legal department and company executives might have more insight into some of the business needs of certificates within your organization and could feel it's necessary that a certificate serve only a single purpose. In general, make sure you cover all your bases before making decisions on certificate polices.

It is important to have a policy in place to state what is going to be done, but it is equally important to explain exactly how to implement those policies. This is where the *certificate practice statement (CPS)* comes in. A CPS describes how the CA plans to manage the certificates it issues. If a CA does not have a CPS available, users should consider finding another CA.

Exam Warning

Make sure you understand how a certificate policy differs from a CPS.

Publication Points

For PKI to work, it requires a location where certificates can be both stored and published to individuals requesting them. Different PKI implementations use different types of key management. The hierarchical model, for example, uses *centralized* key management. The key management in the hierarchical model is centralized because all the public keys are held within one central location. This location is the central point of distribution, which can be a folder on the CA server, or in a directory service like Active Directory. We discuss certificate stores and publication later in this chapter.

Certificate Revocation Lists

A certificate is revoked when the information contained in the certificate is no longer considered valid or trusted. This happens when a company changes its Internet service provider (ISP) or moves to a new physical address or the contact listed on the certificate has changed. In an organization that has implemented its own PKI, a certificate owner can have his or her certificate revoked upon terminating employment. The most important reason to revoke a certificate is if the private key has been compromised in any way. If a key has been compromised, it should be revoked immediately.

Along with notifying the CA of the need to revoke a certificate, it is equally important to notify all certificate users of the date that the certificate will no longer be valid. After notifying users and the CA, the CA is responsible for changing the status of the certificate and notifying users that it has been revoked. If a certificate is revoked because of key compromise, you must publish the date the certificate was revoked as well as the last date that communications were considered trustworthy. When a certificate revocation request is sent to a CA, the CA must be able to authenticate the request with the certificate owner. Once the CA has authenticated the request, the certificate is revoked and notification is sent out.

Certificate owners are not the only ones who can revoke a certificate. A PKI administrator can revoke a certificate, but without authenticating the request with the certificate owner. A good example of this is a corporate PKI. If Mary, an employee of SomeCompany Inc., leaves the company unexpectedly, the administrator will want to revoke her certificate. Since Mary is gone, she is not available to authenticate the request. Therefore, the administrator of the PKI is granted the ability to revoke the certificate.

The X.509 standard requires that CAs publish certificate revocation lists (CRLs). In their simplest form, CRLs are published forms listing the revocation status of certificates that the CA manages. Revocation can take several forms. Following are descriptions of two of them: simple CRLs and delta CRLs.

Simple CRLs

A *simple CRL* is a container that holds a list of revoked certificates with the name of the CA, the time the CRL was published, and when the next CRL will be published. A simple CRL is a single file that continues to grow over time. The fact that only information about the certificate is included, and not the certificate itself, controls the size of a simple CRL container.

Delta CRLs

Delta CRLs handle the issues that simple CRLs cannot—size and distribution. Although a simple CRL only contains certain information about a revoked certificate, it can still become a large file. The issue here is, how do you continually distribute a large file to all parties that need to see the CRL? The answer is delta CRLs. In a delta CRL configuration, a *base* CRL is sent to all end parties to initialize their copies of the CRL. After the base

CRL is sent, updates known as *deltas* are sent out on a periodic basis to inform the end parties of any changes.

Another method of verifying the state of a certificate is called the Online Certificate Status Protocol (OCSP).

Online Certificate Status Protocol

The OCSP was defined to help PKI certificate revocation bypass the limitations of CRL schemes. OCSP returns information relating only to certain certificates that have been revoked. With OCSP, there is no need for the large files used in a CRL to be transmitted. A query is sent to a CA regarding a particular certificate over transport protocols such as Hypertext Transfer Protocol (HTTP). Once the CA receives and processes the query, an *OCSP responder* replies to the originator with the status of the certificate as well as information regarding the response. A OCSP response consists of:

- The status of the certificate (good, revoked, or unknown)
- The last update on the status of the certificate
- The next time the status will be updated
- The time that the response was sent back to the requestor

One of the most glaring weaknesses of OCSP is that it can return information on only a single certificate and does not attempt to validate the certificate for the CA that issued it.

Certificate Trust Lists

A *certificate trust list,* or *CTL*, is a list of root CAs that are considered to be trustworthy. By maintaining a CTL, you can automatically verify a certificate against a your list of trusted certificate authorities. Windows Server 2003 comes with a predefined CTL that you can use as a default or that you can add to and remove CAs from as needed. We discuss the Windows CTL in more depth later in this chapter, when we discuss configuring PKI within Active Directory (Objective 5.1).

Key Archival and Recovery

Different PKI implementations use different types of key management. The hierarchical model, for example, uses *centralized* key management. The key management in the hierarchical model is centralized because all the public keys are held within one central location. Older implementations of PGP used *decentralized* key management, since the keys are contained in a PGP users' key ring and no one entity is superior over another.

Whether to use centralized or decentralized key management depends on the size of the organization. Under older versions of PGP, you would typically only hold the keys of those PGP users that you trusted. This works great for PGP, since most people have a manageable number of keys on their key ring. However, for a large organization of 10,000 that requires all its employees to use digital signatures when communicating, managing PGP keys would be impossible.

Whether you use centralized management or decentralized management for keys, you must design a secure method of storing those keys. Imagine what would happen if a person left a wallet on a counter in a department store and someone took it. The wallet's owner would have to call her credit card companies to close her accounts, go to the DMV to get a duplicate driver's license, change her bank account numbers, and so forth.

Now imagine what would happen if Company X put all its private keys into a publicly accessible File Transfer Protocol (FTP) site. Basically, once hackers discovered that they could obtain the private keys, they could very easily listen to communications between the company and clients and decrypt and encrypt messages being passed.

Taking this a step further, imagine what could happen if a root CA key was not stored in a secure place; all the keys that the CA had generated would have to be invalidated and regenerated.

So, how can we store private keys in a manner that guarantees their security? Not storing them in a publicly accessible FTP folder is a start. There are also several options for key storage, most falling under either the *software storage* category or the *hardware storage* category.

Hardware Key Storage versus Software Key Storage

A private key can be stored on an operating system (OS) by creating a directory on a server (for example, Windows 2000) and using permissions (NTFS in Windows 2000) to lock access to the directory. The issue is that storing private keys using software relies on the security of the OS and the network environment itself.

Say that you are the senior administrator for a company. You have a higher access level than all the other administrators, engineers, and operators in your company. You create a directory on one of the servers and restrict access to the directory to you and the chief information officer (CIO). However, Joe, an IT staffer, is responsible for backups and restores on all the servers. Joe is the curious type and decides to look at the contents that are backed up each night onto tape. Joe notices the new directory you created and wants to see what is in there. Joe can restore the directory to another location, view the contents within the directory, and obtain a copy of the private keys. As the security administrator, you can handle this problem two different ways. First, you can enable auditing for the network OS. Auditing file access, additions, deletions, and modifications, you can track this type of activity within the network. Likewise, permissions for the backup operator can be limited to backup only and require another party (such as the network administrator) to perform restores.

There is another risk involved with the software storage of private keys. You granted access to yourself and the company CIO, Phil. Phil has a bad habit of leaving his computer without logging out or locking the screen via a screen saver. Dave, the mail clerk, can easily walk into Phil's office and look at all the files and directories that Phil has access to, thereby accessing the directory where the private keys are stored. Because it often occurs while a user is at lunch and away from his desk, this type of attack is known as a *lunchtime attack*. The best fix for lunchtime attacks is user education. Teaching users to properly secure their workstations when not in use prevents many types of security breaches, including lunchtime attacks.

It is generally accepted that software storage is not a reliable means of storing private keys. To overcome the issues of software storage, *hardware storage modules (HSMs)* were created. HSMs, such as smart cards, PCMCIA cards, and other hardware devices, store private keys and handle all encryption and decryption of messages so that the keys do not have to be transmitted to the computer. Using magnetic media for hardware storage works but can become unreliable after a period of time. Keeping the keys off the computer prevents information about the keys from being discovered if the system is compromised.

Smart cards are the most reliable method of storing private keys using the hardware storage method. Since smart cards are normally about the size of a credit card, they are easily stored and can resist a high level of physical stress. Smart cards can also get very expensive. Unlike a credit card that has a magnetic strip, smart cards store information using microprocessors, memory, and contact pads for passing information (see Figure 4.10).

Figure 4.10 A DSS Smart Card

Standards

Without standards and protocols, a juggernaut like PKI would become unmanageable. For a real-life example, look at the U.S. railroad system in its earlier days. Different railroad companies were using rails of differing sizes and different widths between the rails. This made it impossible for a train to make it across the country and, in some cases, across regions. In the end, it cost millions of dollars to standardize on a particular type of track.

To avoid this type of disaster, a set of standards was developed early on for PKI. The Public Key Cryptography Standards (PKCS) are standard protocols used for securing the exchange of information through PKI. The list of PKCS standards was created by RSA laboratories, the same group that developed the original RSA encryption standard, along with a consortium of corporations, including Microsoft, Sun, and Apple. The list of active PKCS standards is as follows:

- **PKCS #1: RSA Cryptography Standard** Outlines the encryption of data using the RSA algorithm. The purpose of the RSA Cryptography Standard is the development of digital signatures and digital envelopes. PKCS #1 also describes a syntax for RSA public keys and private keys. The public key syntax is used for certificates; the private key syntax is used for encrypting private keys.
- **PKCS #3: Diffie-Hellman Key Agreement Standard** Outlines the use of the Diffie-Hellman Key Agreement, a method of sharing a secret key between two parties. The secret key is used to encrypt ongoing data transfer between the two parties. Whitfield Diffie and Martin Hellman developed the Diffie-Hellman algorithm in the 1970s as the first asymmetric cryptographic system. Diffie-Hellman overcomes the issues of symmetric key systems because management of the keys is less difficult.
- **PKCS #5: Password-Based Cryptography Standard** Outlines a method for encrypting a string with a secret key that is derived from a password. The result of the method is an octet (eight-character) string.
- **PKCS #6: Extended-Certificate Syntax Standard** Deals with extended certificates. Extended certificates are made up of the X.509 certificate plus additional attributes. The additional attributes and the X.509 certificate can be verified using a single public key operation. The issuer that signs the extended certificate is the same as the one that signs the X.509 certificate.
- **PKCS #7: Cryptographic Message Syntax Standard** The foundation for the Secure/Multipurpose Internet Mail Extensions (S/MIME) standard. It is compatible with Privacy-Enhanced Mail (PEM) and can be used in several different architectures of key management.
- **PKCS #8: Private Key Information Syntax Standard** Describes a method of communication for private key information that includes the use of public key algorithms and additional attributes (similar to PKCS #6). In this case, the attributes can be a distinguished name or a root CA's public key.
- **PKCS #9: Selected Attribute Types** Defines the types of attributes for use in extended certificates (PKCS #6), digitally signed messages (PKCS #7), and private key information (PKCS #8).
- **PKCS #10: Certification Request Syntax Standard** Describes a syntax for certification requests. A certification request consists of a distinguished name, a public key, and additional attributes. Certification requests are sent to a CA, which then issues the certificate.
- **PKCS #11: Cryptographic Token Interface Standard** Specifies an application program interface (API) for token devices that hold encrypted information and perform cryptographic functions, such as smart cards and Universal Serial Bus (USB) pigtails.

- **PKCS #12: Personal Information Exchange Syntax Standard** Specifies a portable format for storing or transporting a user's private keys and certificates. Ties into both PKCS #8 (communication of private key information) and PKCS #11 (Cryptographic Token Interface Standard). Portable formats include diskettes, smart cards, and Personal Computer Memory Card International Association (PCMCIA) cards.

PKI standards and protocols are living documents, meaning that they are always changing and evolving. Additional standards are proposed every day, but before they are accepted as standards they are put through rigorous testing and scrutiny.

Windows PKI Components

As you can see, there are several components that make up a PKI. Each component has a purpose, and each one plays a key role in the PKI. The Microsoft Windows PKI has four fundamental components. Each of these components serves a separate function within the PKI configuration. Some components you will manage directly, and some are more "behind the scenes." You will not interact with the latter components on a day-to-day basis unless you also develop applications requiring PKI functionality. The four fundamental components of the Windows PKI are:

- Microsoft Certificate Services
- Active Directory
- CyptoAPI
- CAPICOM

Microsoft Certificate Services

The Windows Server 2003 certificate services allow you to issue, store, publish, and manage certificates. This component is the centerpiece of the Windows Server 2003 PKI because it provides a centralized tool for managing the certificates as well as the policies associated with issuing, managing, and revoking certificates. One of the biggest benefits to implementing a Windows Server 2003 PKI for your organization is cost. External certificate authorities such as VeriSign and Thawte provide an excellent service, but their services are not cost effective, since each entity that requires a certificate must purchase that certificate from the vendor. In an organization that requires hundreds of certificates, this cost is unacceptable. Microsoft understood this requirement and the cost associated with the need and has provided a solution that is cost effective but also adheres to industry standards and provides for ease of management.

Active Directory

As we mentioned previously, Windows PKI has the ability to use Active Directory for storing certificates and CRLs and to publish root CA certificates and cross-certificates. Active Directory also allows for the mapping of certificates to user accounts for the authentication of clients and controlling access to network resources. Using Active Directory for the storage of PKI components, further reduces the need for additional management utilities within your environment.

One way that Active Directory provides for centralized management is through the use of *public key Group Policy*, which is used to control which CAs are to be trusted, as well as autoenrollment and renewal of certificates that have been issued by Microsoft certificate services. By creating a public key Group Policy, you can specify PKI requirements for the computers that will be using your Windows PKI implementation.

CryptoAPI

An application program interface, or API, is the method by which one application can make requests of an operating system or other application. Through the use of *CryptoAPI,* programmers can develop software applications than can communicate with the operating system or other applications through encrypted means. This also means that your PKI infrastructure can communicate via a standard interface with third-party cryptographic service providers, or CSPs. CSPs are used to enhance the interoperability of the Windows PKI with third-party PKIs. Due to this CryptoAPI and standard interface with CSPs, Windows Server 2003 PKI has the ability to use smart card technology. Later in this chapter, when we cover objective 5.2.3 (using smart cards), we discuss how Windows Server 2003 PKI can use smart cards to further secure your environment.

CAPICOM

Microsoft describes CAPICOM as a new COM client that uses CryptoAPI and PKI to perform cryptographic operations such assigning data, verifying digital signatures, encrypting data for specific receivers, and managing digital certificates. In case you're unfamiliar with COM concepts, Component Object Model (COM) is a framework for providing interoperability in developing program component objects. COM provides a set of interfaces that allow clients and servers to communicate within the same physical computer. Distributed Component Object Model (DCOM) is another framework based on COM that can be used for requesting services from other computers on a network. Finally, CAPICOM is designed to work with CryptoAPI functions to enable programmers to integrate digital signatures and data encryption features into their applications. You can learn more about the CAPICOM client at http://msdn.microsoft.com/library/default.asp?url=/library/en-us/security/security/capicom_reference.asp.

EXAM 70-296 OBJECTIVE 5.2

Planning the Windows Server 2003 Public Key Infrastructure

The key to any successful project or implementation is proper planning prior to implementation. When designing a Windows Server 2003 PKI, you need to examine several areas prior to implementation. Anyone who has ever implemented a new technology can tell you that it is much easier to fix a problem prior to rollout than it is to go back later and try to rectify the problem. In this section, we discuss several areas in which you need to make decisions based on your organization and your need for a PKI. Before we begin discussing the items you need to take into consideration prior to rollout, let's take a minute to discuss some of the new PKI features available in Windows Server 2003.

Microsoft has added functionality to the PKI functionality available in Windows 2000. Windows Server 2003 contains several new features and upgrades for you to use within your PKI, specifically revolving around certificate services:

- Certificate Templates MMC snap-in
- Certificate autoenrollment and autorenewal for all subjects
- Delta CRLs
- Role-based administration
- Key archival and recovery
- Event auditing
- Qualified subordination

Each of these new or updated features provides for simplification of the PKI as well as ease of management. Let's take a few moments before we begin planning the PKI to briefly discuss each of these new features, starting with the Certificate Templates MMC snap-in and editable certificate templates.

The Certificate Templates MMC Snap-in

In a Windows 2000 PKI, certificate templates existed but could not be modified. In Windows Server 2003, Microsoft has granted administrators the ability to modify certificate templates for various purposes. Having the ability to modify a security template gives you the ability to:

- Supersede templates
- Configure a certificate template for key archival and recovery
- Configure a certificate template for client autoenrollment
- Modify enrollment policy

- Make certificate or application policy critical
- Change key usage
- Change basic constraints

Each of these features is made available through the Certificate Templates MMC, which allows for the modification of existing templates but also provides for duplication or renaming of templates, establishing and applying enrollment policies as well as application policies, autoenrollment for certificates, and setting access control on a template for enrollment by a user or computer. We'll touch on some of these features later in the chapter, when we discuss Objective 5.2.2, certificate enrollment and distribution.

Certificate Autoenrollment and Autorenewal for All Subjects

If you used PKI in Windows 2000, you might remember that it was possible to autoenroll for computer certificates but not for user certificates. In Windows Server 2003, Microsoft has made it possible to configure your environment for user autoenrollment. As a member of the Enterprise Admins group in a Windows Server 2003 domain, you can specify the types of certificates that a user can automatically be issued. Autoenrollment is controlled by setting security permissions on certificate templates through the Certificate Templates management tool. A client can then access the template in Active Directory and automatically enroll for a certificate that he or she has rights to request. Likewise, autorenewal is used to control who can autorenew their certificates. Every certificate in the certificate store that has a template extension can potentially be autorenewed by the system, reducing the amount of administrative work that you need to perform for the renewal of certificates.

Delta CRLs

In today's unsecured world, it is becoming more and more important to stay aware of any changes in the status quo as they relate to our network security. To aid in this, Microsoft has provided for the use of delta CRLs for a Windows Server 2003 PKI, which is available in Windows Server 2003 Standard Edition, Windows Server 2003 Enterprise Edition, and Windows Server 2003 Datacenter Edition. As we discussed when we examined the components of PKI, delta CRLs are CRLs that contain the list of changes in revocation status since the issuance of the full CRL. Delta CRLs are a small subset of data compared to the full CRL and generate significantly less network traffic, which is priceless when you're communicating over slow bandwidth connections.

Role-Based Administration

As your organization continues to grow, you might find the need to delegate certain administrative roles to various people in your organization. Microsoft has provided for such functionality in Windows Server 2003, giving you the capability to separate roles for the management and maintenance of a CA. You can use role-based administration to organize your administrators into predefined roles, each with its own level of administrative ability and assigned tasks. Roles available in Windows Server 2003 are:

- CA Administrator (overall administration)
- Certificate Manager (issues and manages certificates and their permissions)
- Auditor (manages auditing and security log permissions)
- Backup Operator (similar to the OS group Backup Operations)
- Enrollees (users of the PKI)

Key Archival and Recovery

One of the scariest things that can happen to you as a PKI administrator is a complete failure of a CA server that results in the loss of private keys and the key database. In Windows Server 2003, you can configure your CA server to archive the keys that are associated with the certificates that it issues. In addition, if the need should ever arise, you can perform a recovery of the keys and the key database.

Event Auditing

One of the keys of providing a secure infrastructure is to have a system of checks and balances within that infrastructure, including the ability to log and review events that have occurred on the system. Using event auditing in a Windows Server 2003 PKI provides the ability to log most events that occur on a server running certificate services. Auditing is recommended when there is a need to track administrative functions such as issuance of certificates, certificate template modification, and changes in administrative roles.

Qualified Subordination

Qualified subordination in a Windows Server 2003 PKI adds additional configuration and administrative functionality over standard CA subordination configurations, including the ability to specify the namespaces for which a subordinate CA will issue certificates, defining how certificates issued by the qualified subordinate can be used, and enabling cross-certification, where certificates can be used in separate certification hierarchies.

The Process for Designing a PKI

The planning and implementing of a PKI within your environment is not something that you should take lightly, nor should it be implemented haphazardly. As with any enterprisewide implementation, bringing all potential issues and concerns to the table prior to rollout is important for a sound and smooth implementation. Several issues involving the organization layout can affect a PKI rollout. These issues include:

- Office locations
- Link speeds
- Organizational security requirements
- Client OS compatibility
- Outside influences (for instance, government regulations)
- Resources (both physical and administrative)

Office placement and link speeds can determine how your *certification authority infrastructure* might look if CAs and RAs are required in various offices. Organizational security requirements will certainly affect how you design your PKI. In some environments, only certain departments might need PKI. For example, a pharmaceutical company that needs to protect R&D secrets might require the additional security provided by PKI, whereas other departments within the company might not. Client operating systems could become an issue in some organizations. For example, a company could still be using older Windows operating systems and would require an upgrade to a newer OS in order to support PKI. You certainly would not want to roll out PKI as an organizational requirement if certain users would not be able to perform their job functions because of it.

Outside influences can also play a major role in the design of your PKI. For example, many government organizations require not only encryption via PKI but a certain level of encryption known as FIPS, which is often required for doing business with the federal government. You will want to know up front if there are any outside influences that could play a role in the PKI design.

Lastly, resources are almost always an issue in an IT shop. For example, if your office location and link speeds dictate that you should have a CA in each remote office, you need the servers to support this system. That said, Microsoft recommends five steps for designing your PKI:

1. Define the certificate requirements.
2. Create a certification authority infrastructure.
3. Extend the certification authority infrastructure.
4. Configure certificates.
5. Create a management plan.

Defining Certificate Requirements

The first thing that needs to be thought out prior to implementation is to define your business requirements for the addition of a PKI. Is PKI being implemented to substantiate an overall business security policy, or does this involve a specific application need, user need, or business function? This would be the time when you need to look at the location of the user base that needs to use PKI, specifically relating to link speed and IT resources. It also brings up a valid question that should be answered at this stage: Does PKI meet the minimum requirements for the business requirement? If it does not meet the minimum requirements, there is no point in going forward at this point.

At this stage, you should also begin creating your certificate policies and practice statements. It's always easiest to keep running documentation during the design and implementation phase of a project rather than trying to go back later and remember all the things you did prior to rollout. The documentation you are developing will become your *certificate practice statement*, or CPS. When developing your CPS, it's important to get the input of all entities that might have a stake in the PKI implementation as well as the policy statement. When applicable, you should involve not only the relevant IT staff but also company executives, human resources personnel, and legal counsel. Microsoft offers several recommendations for information that you might want to include within your policy statement:

- How users are authenticated to the CA
- Legal issues, such as liability, that might arise if the CA becomes compromised or is used for something other than its intended purpose
- The intended purpose of the certificate
- Private key management requirements, such as storage on smart cards or other hardware devices
- Whether the private key can be exported or archived
- Requirements for users of the certificates, including what users must do in the event that their private keys are lost or compromised
- Requirements for certificate enrollment and renewal
- Minimum length for the public key and private key pairs

As we mentioned earlier, a CPS describes how the CA plans to manage the certificates it issues. The CPS details how a certificate policy is to be carried out based on your company's architecture and operating procedures. Microsoft recommends the following be included in the CPS:

- Identification of the CA (including CA name, server name, and DNS address)
- The certificate policies that are implemented by the CA and the certificate types that are issued
- The policies, procedures, and processes for issuing, renewing, and recovering certificates
- Cryptographic algorithms, CSPs, and key length used for the CA certificate
- Physical, network, and procedural security for the CA
- The certificate lifetime of each certificate issued by the CA

- Policies for revoking certificates, including conditions for certificate revocation, such as employee termination and misuse of security privileges
- Policies for CRLs, including where to locate CRL distribution points and how often CRLs are published
- A policy for renewing the CAs certificate before its expiration

Now that you have laid out your plan for your PKI and have begun your documentation of the PKI, you can begin creating the CA infrastructure.

Creating a Certification Authority Infrastructure

At this stage, you are essentially charting the information from the requirements phase into what will ultimately be your infrastructure. This is where you must begin appropriating equipment to serve as a CA or RA, planning for CA trusts, and determining if your CA infrastructure will be integrated with Active Directory.

As an example, let's say that Wally's Tugboats Inc. has a home office in Florida and a manufacturing and storage facility in Oregon. The research and development office for Wally's Tugboats is in Jacksonville, Florida, and the main office is located in Orlando. Based on what you discovered during the design phase, you decide that you will host the root CA server and an intermediate CA server in the Orlando office, with a leaf CA server in the Jacksonville and Oregon offices. These servers will follow a hierarchy that originates with the root CA server in the Orlando office. The CA servers for Wally's Tugboats will also be integrated in Active Directory. Key questions to think about when planning your infrastructure are:

- Where will the root CA reside?
- Will you use internal CAs or external (vendor) CAs?
- Are there any requirements for scalability or performance?
- Will your CAs integrate with Active Directory? If they will, where in the forest will you put them?
- Who will manage the CAs, both locally and remotely?
- What roles will the CAs play?
- How many CAs will your organization require?

Extending the CA Infrastructure

What if Wally's needed to provide for secure communications via PKI with its suppliers or raw goods? You would need to be able to extend the infrastructure for compatibility with CAs outside your organization. You would need to plan for issues such as cross-certification. *Cross-certification* occurs when two CAs agree to trust each other's public keys as though they had issued the keys themselves. The two CAs essentially exchange cross-certificates, enabling the users in their respective PKIs to interact securely. If Wally's needed to securely communicate with RawMetals Inc. for its supply of raw metals to build its ships, a cross-certification would need to be developed so that the two infrastructures could trust one another. In our example, we will not be using cross-certifications within our PKI.

Configuring Certificates

During this stage of the design process, you need to begin making decisions about the characteristics of the certificates you will be issuing. The considerations relating to certificate configuration might include:

- What will be the strength of the encryption key?
- How long will certificates be valid?
- Will you allow certificates to be renewals?
- Will certificates be used with smart cards?

Creating a Certificate Management Plan

This stage of the design process revolves around the management of certificates and CAs for post-implementation. Specifically, you need to decide how you will manage requests for certificates, how certificates are issued to end users (via Web site, e-mail, secured folders, diskette, etc.), how certificate revocation lists are to be managed, and how you will handle key recovery. Some questions you need to answer prior to implementation are:

- Will you allow users to request their own certificates?
- Will you use autoenrollment?
- Will you use Web enrollment?
- What types of certificates do you want your CA servers to serve to users?
- If you choose to manually distribute certificates, how will you distribute them?

Test Day Tip

Many Microsoft scenario-based questions give you the answer to certain questions right in the text, so make sure to read the test scenarios carefully. If you get a question relating to certificate management plans, you could find the information you need right in the scenario.

At this stage, you are almost ready to begin your PKI implementation. However, we need to discuss some of these points in a little more depth. First, let's take a more in-depth look at the types of Windows CAs you can use within your organization.

EXAM 70-296 OBJECTIVE 5.2.1

Types of Certificate Authorities

As a Windows 2000 MCSE, you are familiar with the types of CA available on the Windows operating system. There are four base types of CA:

- Enterprise root
- Enterprise subordinate
- Standalone root
- Standalone subordinate

In this section, we review the various types of certificate authorities and the reasons you might want to choose a particular CA over another based on your organizational needs. Before we look at the actual CA types, we need to review the concept of online and offline CAs.

Online versus Offline Certificate Authorities

In some organizations, it might be necessary to design a PKI strategy by which the root CA is not physically connected to your organization's network. Based on your company's security guidelines, you might need an isolated, offline root CA in order to protect it from possible attacks by intruders via the network. Obviously, if the root CA is not physically connected to your network, the only way that a would-be attacker could compromise your root CA would be through physical access at the console.

Root versus Subordinate Certificate Authorities

At the beginning of the chapter, we discussed how CAs are used to develop a certification hierarchy. In a certification hierarchy, a root CA is the most trusted type of CA within the PKI. Protection of the root CA is critical, since a compromise of the root CA impacts the security of the entire organization. As we just discussed, taking a root CA offline is one way to secure it from a compromise. In organizations in which the root CA is left online, it typically is used only to issue certificates to subordinate CAs, not to users or other entities.

A subordinate CA is a second-tier (or lower) CA within the certification hierarchy. Subordinate CAs are used to issue certificates for specific uses, such as e-mail, digital signatures, and Web security. Subordinate CAs can also issue certificates to other, more subordinate CAs. There is essentially no limit to the number of subordinate CAs you can have within your environment; the only issue revolving around subordinate CAs is the relationship between the number of subordinate CAs and the amount of administration required. As with any type of server, the more you add, the more work it will become for you. Going back to the example of Wally's Tugboats, it's a good idea to have an intermediate subordinate CA in each of the offices, but to have subordinate leaf CAs in each of the offices would not be necessary based on Wally's needs and would merely create an administrative burden to the user. It's also worth noting in the Wally's tugboat example that we not only placed the root CA in the Orlando headquarters; , we also placed an intermediate subordinate CA there. As we just discussed, the root CA should not be used to supply general-use certificates, so the subordinate CA in the Orlando office will be used instead of the root CA for day-to-day certificate management.

Enterprise CA versus Standalone CAs

There are many similarities between enterprise and standalone CAs. For instance, both can issue certificates for S/MIME (e-mail), SSL (Web servers), and digital signatures. The key difference between an enterprise CA and a standalone CA is the ability to integrate your certificates with Active Directory. Enterprise CAs also provide for the use of *certificate templates*, which specify the format and content of certificates based on how the certificates will be used. When a user requests a certificate from an enterprise CA, the user has the option of selecting from among several types of certificates that are based on these certificate templates. Certificate templates provide for:

- Security permissions that determine whether a user or group requesting a certificate is authorized to receive the type of certificate that they are requesting
- Certificate extensions, which reduce the amount of information a user requesting a certificate needs to supply about the certificate and its intended use, in turn saving users from making technical decisions about the type of certificate that they need

We discuss certificate templates in more depth a little later in this chapter, when we discuss managing certificates. Now, with all this talk about the benefits of enterprise CAs, don't assume that standalone CAs are inferior or obsolete. In fact, standalone CAs still serve important functions within a PKI. For example, if Wally's Tugboats wanted to offer certificates to its customers, partners, or vendors, having a standalone CA would be the ideal choice because standalone CAs do not automatically issue certificates, since the credentials of the certificate requestor cannot be automatically validated, as they can with an enterprise CA. Since Wally's customers, partners, and vendors are not likely to have an account in the wallystugboats.com Active Directory, the PKI administrator needs to (and should) validate an identity prior to issuing a certificate. Certificates that are requested by a standalone CA are put into a *pending* status until the administrator manually issues them. Microsoft recommends that standalone CAs be primarily used as trusted offline root CAs or when public networks (such as the Internet) are involved.

Exam Warning

If you have a question about standalone CA servers and certificate issuance, remember that certificate requests are placed into a pending state and require manual intervention by the administrator.

Another area that we need to discuss is enrollment and distribution of certificates. Regardless of the type of CA (enterprise or standalone) you choose, you have the ability to offer your users Web enrollment to request certificates. However, by using enterprise CAs in Windows Server 2003, you have the ability to further reduce user interaction and administrative work by using *autoenrollment*.

Let's move on now to discuss the enrollment and distribution of certificates in a Windows Server 2003 PKI.

EXAM 70-296 OBJECTIVE 5.2.2

Enrollment and Distribution

Once you have decided on a PKI design and CA hierarchy, you must decide how you will enroll and distribute certificates to users within your organization. Windows Server 2003 certificate services provides three means of enrolling and distributing certificates: Web enrollment, autoenrollment, and, of course, manual enrollment. For purposes of this exam, we are not going to discuss manual enrollment; instead, we focus on the Web enrollment and autoenrollment functions.

Web Enrollment

Web enrollment is simply a set of Web pages (see Figure 4.11) that are created when you install Certificate Services in Windows Server 2003. Web enrollment works in conjuction with the Internet Information Server (IIS) service. The Web enrollment interface provides an easy means for users to perform many of the common CA services, including:

- Requesting a new certificate
- Requesting a CA's certificate revocation list (CRL)
- Requesting a CA's own certificate
- Smart card certificate enrollment
- Checking the status of a pending certificate request

Figure 4.11 The Web Enrollment Welcome Page

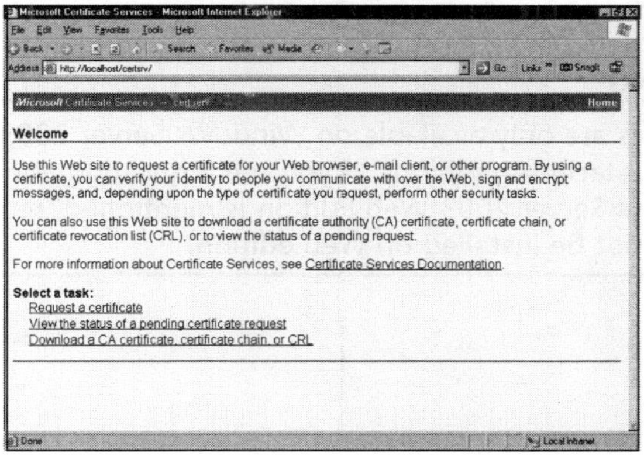

Web enrollment is a great tool to reduce the amount of administration necessary for an organization's PKI. If, for some reason, Web enrollment is a feature that you do not want or need, you can quite easily disable it by using the IIS management console. For example, if Wally's Tugboats wanted to keep the requesting and issuance of certificates limited to IT administrative staff, they could shut off the Web enrollment site and handle all requests manually through the Certification Authority snap-in (see Figure 4.12).

Test Day Tip

Remember that the Web enrollment service is the user interface for certificate management, whereas the Certification Authority snap-in is used as the administrator's interface.

Figure 4.12 The Certification Authority Snap-in

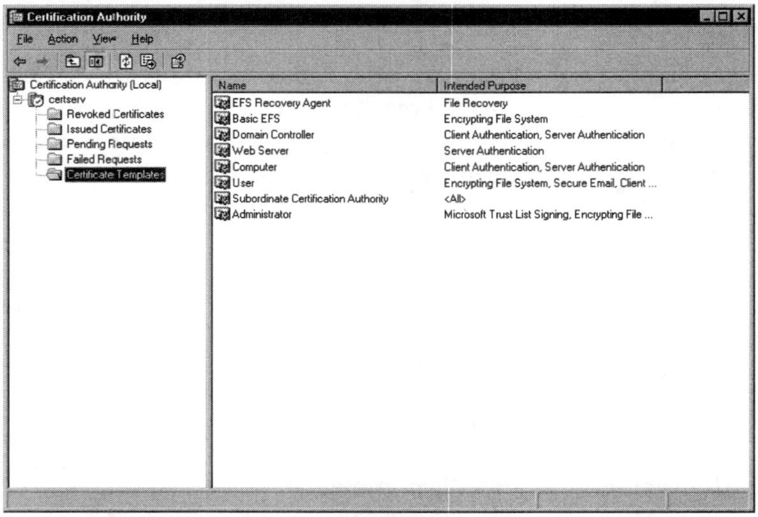

Exam Warning

Certificate services are only available on Windows Server 2003 Standard, Enterprise, and Datacenter editions. If you see a question about certificate services in which Windows Server 2003 Web Edition is mentioned, remember that certificate services cannot be installed on Web edition.

Head of the Class...

Separating Web Enrollment from the CA Server

In some environments, it could be beneficial to separate the Web enrollment server from the CA server. For example, you might not want to have the IIS service running on a domain controller that is also functioning as a CA server for security purposes—specifically that Active Server Pages (ASP) must be enabled on the IIS server in order for Web enrollment to function.

For this reason, a separate Windows Server 2003 server can be configured to function as the front-end Web enrollment server for the PKI. If you should choose to install the Web enrollment pages on a separate computer from the CA, the computer account must be trusted for delegation within Active Directory. For more information on delegation, see www.microsoft.com/technet/treeview/default.asp?url=/technet/prodtechnol/windowsserver2003/proddocs/entserver/538.asp. For more information on using a separate server for Web enrollment services, go to www.microsoft.com/technet/treeview/default.asp?url=/technet/prodtechnol/windowsserver2003/proddocs/standard/sag_CSprocsInstallWebClient.asp.

Autoenrollment

The Microsoft marketing platform for Windows Server 2003 is: "The Windows Server 2003 family helps organizations do more with less." One of the ways that Windows Server 2003 helps you do more with less is through the use of certificate autoenrollment, which is defined as "a process for obtaining, storing, and updating the certificates for subjects without administrator or user intervention." Certificate autoenrollment allows clients to automatically submit certificate requests and retrieve and store certificates. Autoenrollment is managed by the administrator (or other staff members who have been delegated authority) through the use of certificate templates so that certificates are obtained by the appropriate target and for the appropriate purpose. Autoenrollment also provides for automated renewal of certificates, allowing the entire certificate management process to remain in the background from the perspective of the user.

Exam Warning

Windows Server 2003 Enterprise Edition or Windows Server 2003 Datacenter Edition is required to configure certificate templates for autoenrollment requests.

From a planning perspective, you will want to decide if autoenrollment is right for your organization and which users or groups should be configured to use autoenrollment. Say that Wally's Tugboats has a roaming sales force that needs access to network resources while on the road. Typically, these sales associates are novice computer users who have no interest in learning about functions such as Web enrollment; their sole purpose is to sell tugboats. Through autoenrollment, the administrator of Wally's Tugboats can specify that members of the SalesTeam group in Active Directory have the ability to autoenroll for a certificate. We walk through the process of setting up autoenrollment later in this chapter, when we discuss objective 5.1, configuring PKI within Active Directory.

EXAM WARNING

Remember that autoenrollment is used for the automatic enrollment of *users*, not *computers*.

EXAM 70-296 OBJECTIVE 5.2.3

Using Smart Cards

In our discussion of the different types of CAs, we mentioned that the key difference between enterprise CAs and standalone CAs is that enterprise CAs tie into the Active Directory directory services. Another benefit that comes from the use of enterprise CAs with Active Directory is the use of smart cards for logging into a Windows Server 2003 domain. Although smart cards are covered in much more depth in Chapter 5 of this book, we wanted to take a few moments here to discuss the planning process for using smart cards with PKI.

Unlike Windows 2000, which used smart cards primarily for user logon, Windows Server 2003 uses smart cards for a variety of functions. As the system administrator, you need to work with your IT group to plan for the use of smart cards. Specifically, you will want to discuss:

- Business needs for smart cards
- Smart card usage
- Smart card enrollment

Defining a Business Need

Defining a business need for smart cards in today's environment is much easier than it was even just a few years ago. With the increase in information theft and the reduction in cost of security tools such as smart cards, many organizations are willing to examine their own security practices for areas of improvement. Let's say that Wally's Tugboats operates a 24/7 sales center, which is staffed almost exclusively by temporary employees. Turnover and lack of proper temporary employee screening is a huge issue within the sales center. As the administrator, you can easily justify the need for a smart card implementation in the sales center for purposes of authentication and nonrepudiation.

Smart Card Usage

As we mentioned, Microsoft has taken smart card usage a bit further than was previously available in Windows 2000. The additional ways that smart cards can be used in Windows

Server 2003 include storing administrative credentials and mapping network shares. Part of the planning process for the deployment of smart cards is to determine exactly what the smart cards will be used for. In our business need example, it was pretty clear that we needed the smart cards for user authentication. However, you could find that you can extend the smart card offering beyond simple user authentication.

Smart Card Certificate Enrollment

By default, users are not allowed to enroll for a smart card logon certificate. In order for a user to enroll for a smart card logon certificate, a system administrator must grant the user (or a group of which the user is a member) access rights to the smart card certificate template. Microsoft recommends that users enrolling for smart card certificates use smart card enrollment stations that have been integrated with certificate services. Enterprise CAs have smart card enrollment stations installed by default, allowing an administrator to handle requests for and installation of smart card certificates on behalf of the user. By having an administrator handle the entire smart card enrollment process, there is no need to grant users access rights to the smart card certificate template.

As part of the planning process, you need to decide where smart card enrollment stations will be placed. Since enrollment stations are configured by default on CAs, you will want to make sure that the enrollment stations are stored in a secure location. Smart cards should be treated the same as any other type of security token (ID badges, access cards, etc.) and kept secure from general users and outside parties.

EXAM WARNING

You could get a question relating to the types of smart cards available for use with Windows Server 2003. The following types of smart cards are the *only* ones that can be used with Windows Server 2003:

- Gemplus GemSAFE 4k
- Gemplus GemSAFE 8k,Infineon SICRYPT v2
- Schlumberger Cryptoflex 4k,
- Schlumberger Cryptoflex 8k
- Schlumberger Cyberflex Access 16k

EXAM 70-296 OBJECTIVE 5.1

Configuring Public Key Infrastructure within Active Directory

In this section, we apply the information we've previously discussed and implement PKI into an Active Directory-enabled Windows Server 2003 network. Using the Wally's Tugboats Inc. example, let's walk through each step necessary to creating a functional and fluid PKI. The good news is, most of the real grunt work is done; we have gone over the components of a PKI, considered the decisions necessary to plan the PKI, and thought about the features that Windows Server 2003 brings to a PKI. Now we get to turn all the paperwork and thought processes into a functional PKI.

Throughout this section, we discuss each step of the implementation and configuration process and perform several exercises that correspond to each step. The most logical first step is to review the methods that we can use to install certificate services onto our Windows Server 2003 machine. Keep in mind that the purpose of this section is to configure PKI *within* AD, which makes the assumption that you have already installed Active Directory onto your server. In order to perform these next few steps, you need to have access to the cabinet files for Windows Server 2003 (on CD, a local folder on your hard drive, or on a network share).

Although we could come up with several variations of installing certificate services onto a Windows Server, there are essentially two main ways to accomplish this task:

- Insert the Windows Server 2003 CD into your CD-ROM drive and click **Install optional Windows components** (see Figure 4.13).

Figure 4.13 The Windows Server 2003 Autorun Splash Screen

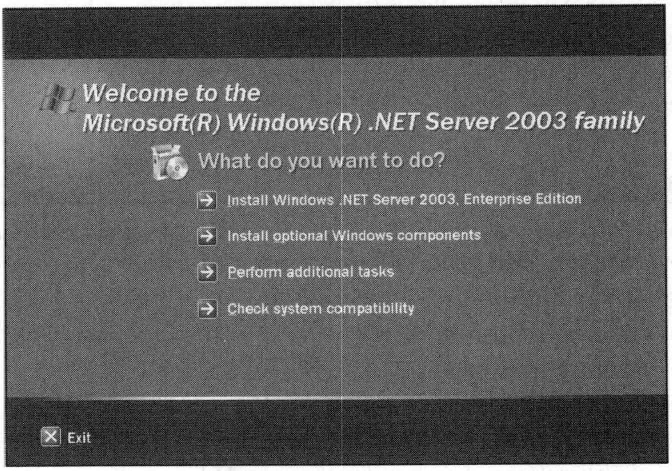

- Or click **Start | Control Panel | Add or Remove Programs** and click **Add/Remove Windows Components**.

In Exercise 4.01, we begin installing the certificate services. You can choose either installation method as long as you are running the installation on a server that exists within a Windows Server 2003 Active Directory domain.

Exercise 4.01

Installing Windows Server 2003 Certificate Services

For our example, let's install an online enterprise root CA on one of the domain controllers within the wallystugboats.com domain. You need to have IIS installed on the server before beginning this exercise. Let's begin by inserting the CD into the server's CD-ROM drive:

1. Insert the Windows Server 2003 CD into your CD-ROM drive and click **Install optional Windows components**.
2. When the Wizard Components window opens, place a check mark in the **Certificate Services** box. Notice the warning message that appears, informing you that once you install certificate services, you will not be able to rename the server (see Figure 4.14). Click **Yes** to clear the warning message, and click **Next** to continue.

Figure 4.14 Certificate Services Warning Message

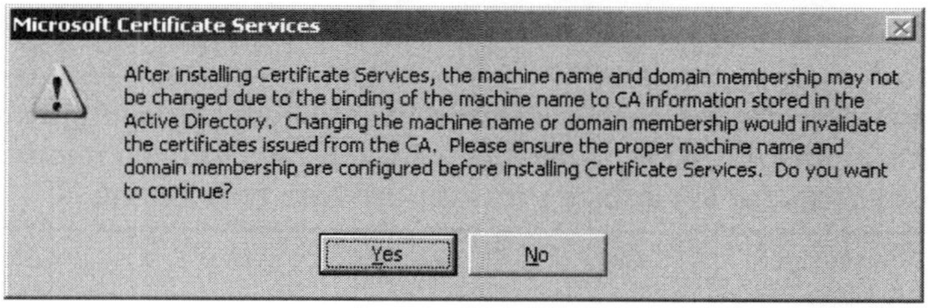

3. As we mentioned at the beginning of the exercise, we're going to be configuring this CA as the enterprise root CA for the wallystugboats.com domain. Select **Enterprise Root CA** from the CA Type window, as shown in Figure 4.15, and click **Next**.

Figure 4.15 Certificate Services CA Type Selection Window

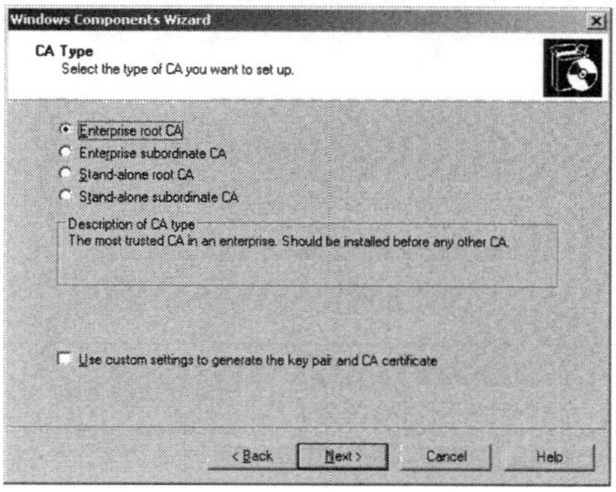

4. Enter a common name for your certificate authority. This is the name by which the CA will be known within your enterprise as well as in Active Directory. In our example, we use **certserv** as our common name. Next, adjust the validity period so that the certificates issued by this CA are valid for **3 years** instead of 5 years. Notice that the expiration date is now exactly three years from when you changed this setting. Click **Next** to continue.

NOTE

At this stage, the key pair is being generated.

5. Accept the defaults for the database file and database log locations and click **Next**. Windows will begin configuring the CA components. Windows will need to stop the IIS services in order to complete the certificate services installation.

NOTE

If you are warned about Internet Information Services not being installed and Web enrollment support not being available, click **Cancel**. You will need to install IIS prior to installing your CA in order to support Web enrollment.

6. Web enrollment will also require that ASP be enabled. Note the warning about the potential security vulnerabilities by enabling ASP, as shown in Figure 4.16, and click **Yes**.

Figure 4.16 ASP Warning Message

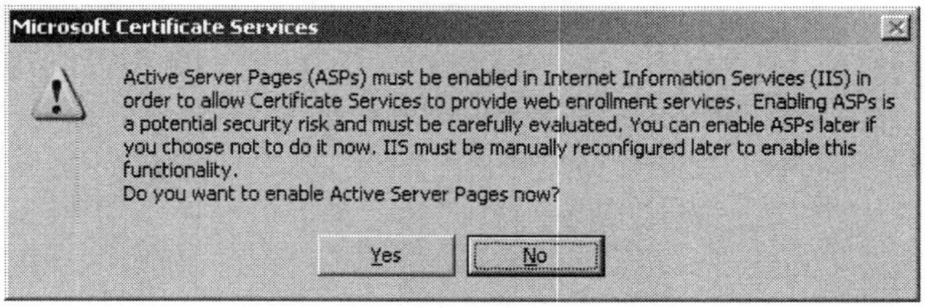

7. Click **Finish** when the installation has completed.

Web Enrollment Support

If you received the warning message about IIS not being installed, you probably noticed that Web enrollment support was not enabled. Web enrollment relies on the IIS service for the publication of the Web enrollment Web pages and components. IIS provides the user with the front-end interface that serves for the automatic back-end certificate creation. In Exercise 4.02, we use the Web enrollment services to request a certificate.

Test Day Tip

If you are faced with a question on the exam that involves Web enrollment not being accessible, read through the scenario again to see if there is any mention of IIS being installed on the server. If IIS is not installed, you know that Web enrollment will not work.

Exercise 4.02

Using Web Enrollment to Request a Certificate

In this exercise, we create a request for a Web server certificate. In order to perform this exercise, you need to have a server running Windows Server 2003 with certificate services installed. You can perform the exercise from either the server itself or another client with network connectivity to the server. Let's begin the exercise by opening a Web browser window:

1. In the Address window of your Web browser, type **http://localhost/certsrv** and press **Enter** if you are doing this exercise from the server. If you are attempting the exercise from another machine, enter the name of the machine in place of *localhost* (for example, **http://myCAserver/certsrv** or **http://mycaserver.mycompany.com/certsrv**).
2. On the Microsoft Certification Services Welcome page, shown in Figure 4.17, click **Request a certificate**.
3. On the Request a Certificate page, click **advanced certificate request**.
4. On the Advanced Certificate Request page, click **Create and submit a request to this CA**.
5. Since we are going to be requesting a Web server certificate, click the drop-down list under Certificate Template and select **Web Server**.

Figure 4.17 The Microsoft Certification Services Welcome Page

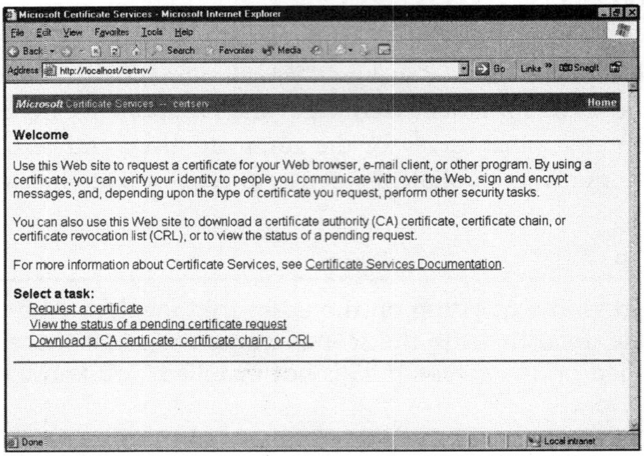

6. Next, enter the information for the offline template. This is the subject information that will be associated with the certificate, as illustrated in Figure 4.18.

Figure 4.18 Entering the Certificate Information

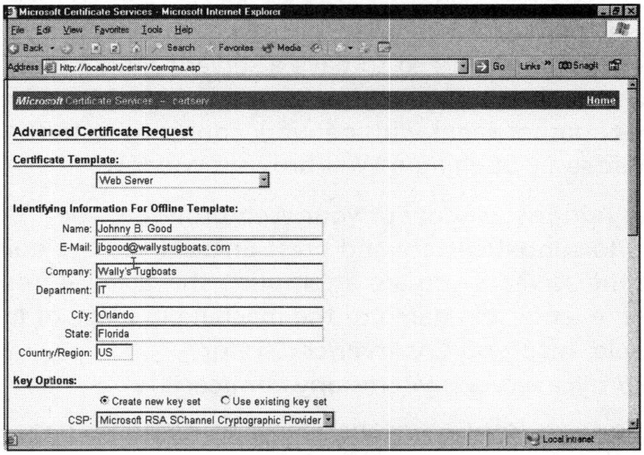

7. For purposes of this exercise, you can leave the rest of the information as it is. Next, scroll to the bottom of the page and click the **Submit** button. If you receive a warning about a potential scripting violation, click **Yes** to continue.

8. The server will process the certificate and present you with an option to install the new certificate. At this stage, you could install the certificate on the appropriate Web server. The enrollment process is complete.

Creating an Issuer Policy Statement

We are discussing issuer policy statements as part of the installation process, but technically they need to be configured *before* certificate services is installed. By configuring your CA to present its policy statement, users can see the policy statement by viewing the CA's certificate and clicking **Issuer Statement**. However, for the policy statement to appear, the file CAPolicy.inf must be properly configured and placed in the systemroot directory (typically, C:\WINDOWS). Before you implement your issuer policy statement, it's always a good idea to run it by upper management and legal staff as permitted, since the policy statement gives legal and other pertinent information about the CA and its issuing policies, as well as limitations of liability. For more information on issuer policy statements, visit www.microsoft.com/technet/treeview/default.asp?url=/technet/prodtechnol/windowsserver2003/proddocs/datacenter/sag_CS_Setup.asp. Figure 4.19 shows the issuer policy statement for www.verisign.com, an Internet CA.

Figure 4.19 The Issuer Policy Statement for VeriSign

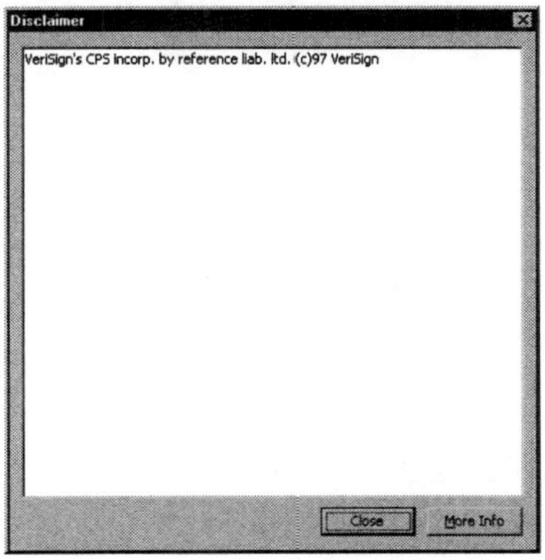

The following code shows a sample CAPolicy.inf file:

```
[Version]
Signature="$Windows NT$"

[CAPolicy]
Policies=UsagePolicy


[UsagePolicy]
OID=1.1
Notice="Certificates issued from this certification authority (CA)
```

```
are intended for the sole usage of user authentication of Wally's
Tugboats employees. Any misuse of this system may be punishable
by law."
```

EXAM WARNING

For the exam, you need to remember the name of the issuer policy statement file, where the file is stored, and when in the CA installation process it should be created and placed in the directory.

Managing Certificates

Once you have configured your CA server, you'll want to examine some of the various ways that you can manage your certificates. One of the biggest advantages of Windows Server 2003 is the range of management tools you have at your disposal. In this section, we take a look at four different aspects of managing certificates:

- Managing certificate templates
- Using autoenrollment
- Importing and exporting certificates
- Revoking certificates

Managing Certificate Templates

In a Windows PKI, certificate templates are used to assign certificates based on their intended use. When requesting a certificate from a Windows CA, a user is able to select from a variety of certificate types that are based on certificate templates. Templates take the decision-making process out of users' hands and automate it based on the configuration of the template as defined by the systems administrator. Now, in Windows Server 2003, you also have the ability to modify and create certificate templates as needed. In Exercise 4.03, we duplicate an existing certificate template for use with autoenrollment. Before we move onto the exercise, let's quickly recap the subject of certificate autoenrollment.

Using Autoenrollment

As we've discussed, autoenrollment is an excellent tool that Microsoft developed for PKI management in Windows Server 2003. Although it does reduce overall PKI management, autoenrollment can be a little tricky to configure. First, your Windows Server 2003 domain controller must also be configured as a root CA or an enterprise subordinate CA. In Exercise 4.03, we walk through the steps of configuring autoenrollment in your organization.

NOTE

Windows Server 2003 Enterprise Edition or Datacenter Edition is required to configure certificate templates for autoenrollment requests.

EXERCISE 4.03

CONFIGURING AUTOENROLLMENT

As we mentioned, you first need to configure your domain controller as a root CA or an enterprise subordinate CA. If you have not yet done this, you can refer back to Exercise 4.01 and install certificate services on your domain controller. Let's begin configuring our CA for autoenrollment:

1. Click **Start | Administrative Tools | Certification Authority**. When the Certification Authority management tool opens, right-click **Certificate Templates** and click **Manage** (see Figure 4.20). The certificate templates management tool will open.

Figure 4.20 The Certification Authority Tool

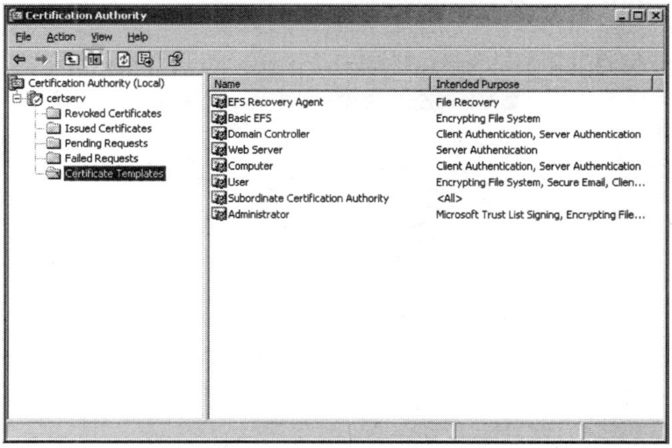

2. Next we need to create a template for autoenrolled users. You can either create a new template or duplicate an existing template. For our example, we duplicate the User template by right-clicking the **User template** and selecting **Duplicate Template**.
3. In the Properties of the New Template window (see Figure 4.21), enter **User Autoenrollment** in the Template Display Name window.

Figure 4.21 Properties of New Template Window

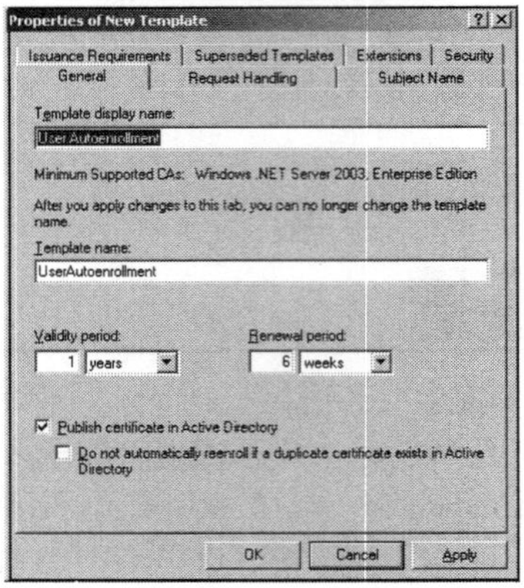

4. Click the **Security** tab to adjust the permissions assigned to this template. This is where you can designate groups to have the ability to autoenroll for a certificate. For our example, we're going to allow all domain users to autoenroll. In the **Group or user names** field, click **Domain Users**. In the **Permissions for Domain Users** list, check **Autoenroll** in the Allow column and ensure that **Enroll** is also allowed (see Figure 4.22).

Figure 4.22 The Security Tab of the New Template

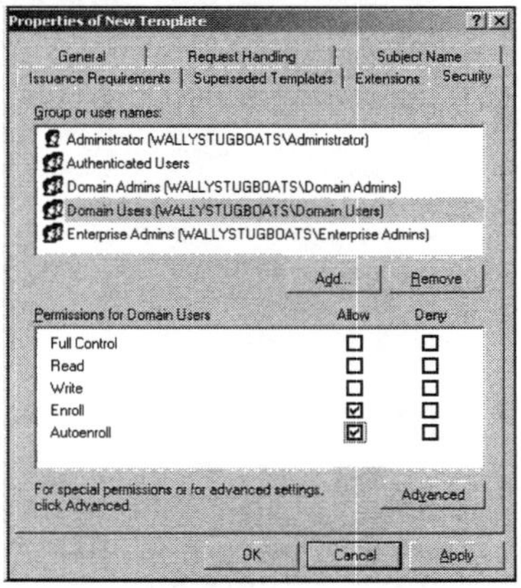

5. Click **OK** to save the new template. You can now close the certificate templates management tool.

   Next we need to authorize our CA to issue autoenrollment certificates. Essentially, without having a CA enabled to issue certificates to our User Autoenrollment template group, it's simply a dormant template.

6. Maximize your Certification Authority management tool, and right-click **Certificate Templates**. Select **New | Certificate Template to Issue** from the context menu.
7. Select **User Autoenrollment** from the list of templates and click **OK** (see Figure 4.23).

Figure 4.23 Selecting the User Autoenrollment Template

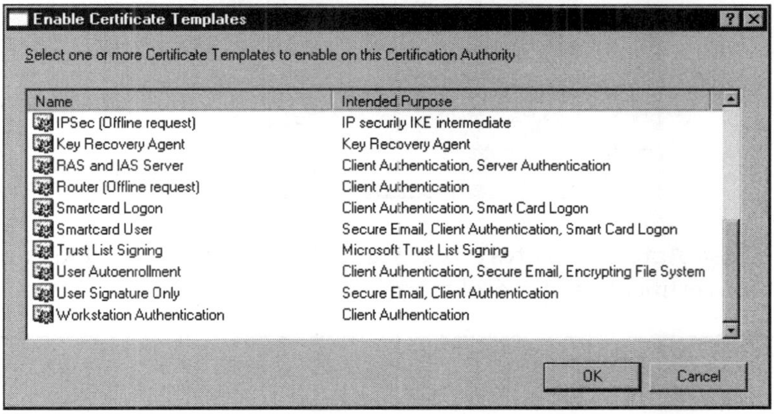

8. Next we need to adjust the Group Policy to allow for users in the GPO to autoenroll for certificates. Click **Start | Administrative Tools | Active Directory Users and Computers**.
9. Right-click the domain name (in our example, **wallystugboats.com**), and click **Properties**.
10. Click the **Group Policy** tab of the domain properties, and then click the **Edit** button.
11. In the console tree, click **User Configuration | Windows Settings | Security Settings | Public Key Policies**.
12. In the details pane, double-click **Autoenrollment Settings**.
13. In the Autoenrollment Settings Properties window (see Figure 4.24), check the box next to **Renew expired certificates, update pending certificates, and remove revoked certificates** as well as **Update certificates that use certificate templates** and click **OK**.

Figure 4.24 The Autoenrollment Settings Properties Window

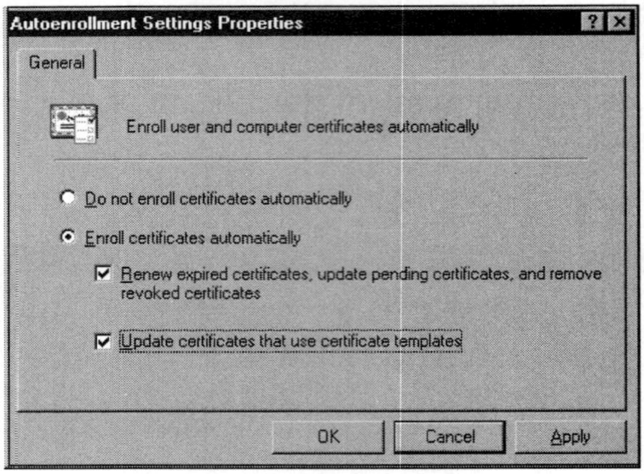

14. Close **Active Directory Users and Computers**. Your PKI is now ready for certificate autoenrollment.

Importing and Exporting Certificates

There could come a time when you need to import a certificate for a computer, user, or service account to use. For instance, you might be installing a certificate that was sent in a file by another CA or restoring a lost certificate from a system backup. Likewise, you might need to export a certificate for backup or to copy it. Windows Server 2003 allows you to import certificates from a standard format and place them within your certificate store. The reverse is true of exporting certificates; certificates are extracted from the certificate store and placed in a file that uses a standard certificate storage format.

Test Day Tip

Remember that Active Directory can be used in a Windows Server 2003 PKI as a certificate store.

Certificate imports are handled through the Certificates snap-in and can be accomplished quite easily by right-clicking the logical store where you want to import the certificate, selecting **All Tasks | Import** from the contect menu (see Figure 4.25), and following the on-screen instructions. Likewise, you can export a certificate by right-clicking the individual certificate and selecting **Export** from the context menu.

Figure 4.25 Importing a Certificate

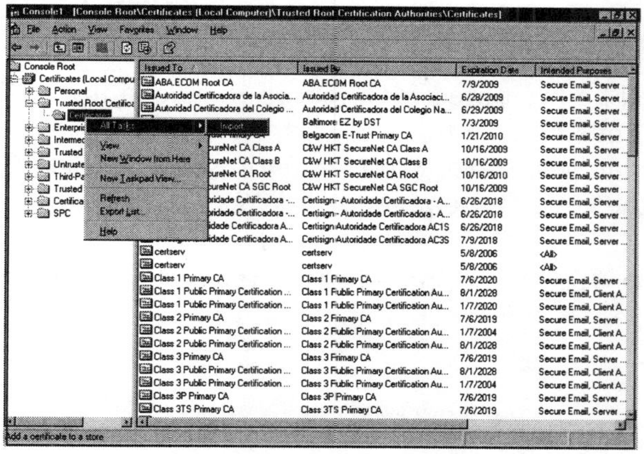

Revoking Certificates

As we mentioned earlier, revocation of a certificate invalidates a certificate as a trusted security credential prior to the original expiration of the certificate. A certificate can be revoked for a number of reasons:

- Compromise or suspected compromise of the certificate subject's private key
- Compromise or suspected compromise of a CA's private key
- Discovery that a certificate was obtained fraudulently
- Change in the status of the certificate subject as a trusted entity
- Change in the name of the certificate subject

Through the Windows interface, Microsoft has simplified the process of revoking certificates. In Exercise 4.04, we walk through the steps of revoking a certificate.

EXERCISE 4.04

REVOKING A CERTIFICATE

In this exercise, we walk through the steps necessary to revoke a certificate that has been issued by a Windows Server 2003 CA. In our exercise, we use the Web server certificate that we created using Web enrollment.

1. Open the Certification Authority management tool by clicking **Start | Administrative Tools | Certification Authority**.
2. Click **Issued Certificates**.

3. In the details pane, right-click the Web server certificate for Wally's Tugboats. From the context menu, click **All Tasks** and then click **Revoke Certificate**.
4. You will be prompted for a reason to revoke the certificate (see Figure 4.26). Let's assume that our certificate is being revoked, because this particular Web server is no longer in service. Select **Cease of Operation** from the context menu, and click **Yes**.

Figure 4.26 Choosing a Reason for Certificate Revocation

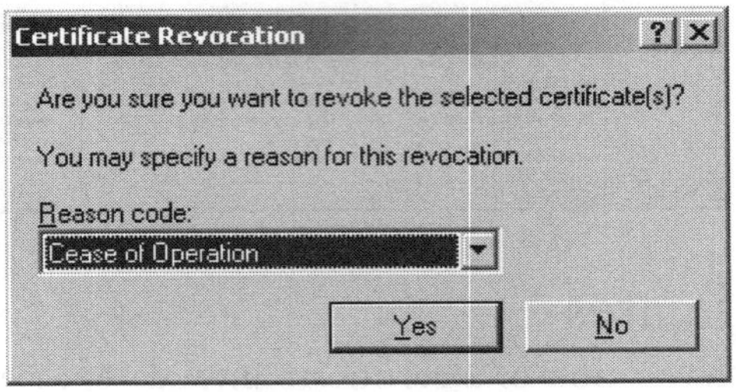

5. Your certificate has been revoked.

Configuring Public Key Group Policy

In Windows 2000, you learned about the advantages of using Group Policy to administer your Windows 2000 network. One area that you might not be aware of in terms of Group Policy functionality is its tie-in with PKI. Although it is not necessary for you to use PKI Group Policy settings in your organization, they give you additional flexibility and control of CA trusts and certificate issuance. Three areas that we will discuss relation to Group Policy are :

- Automatic Certificate Request
- Certificate Trust Lists (CTLs)
- Common Root Certificate Authorities

Automatic Certificate Request

As we discussed earlier, you can have users automatically enroll for certificates within a Windows Server 2003 network. You also have the ability to force computers to automatically request and install certificates from a CA. As with user autoenrollment, this feature is helpful in reducing the amount of administrative effort in ensuring that computers have the appropriate certificates to perform cryptographic operations within your environment.

Automatic certificate enrollment allows computers within a Group Policy object (GPO) to automatically request the certificates from the CAs designated within the Group Policy. The actual certificate request occurs the first time that a computer associated with a specific GPO boots up on the network and authenicates with Active Directory.

EXAM WARNING

Remember, this topic is different from autoenrollment. These certificates stay with the computer and are assigned the first time that the computer signs into the network after it has been assigned a Group Policy.

Managing Certificate Trust Lists

Another feature of Group Policy interaction with PKI is the ability to create and distribute a certificate trust list (CTL). A *certificate trust list* is a list of root CA certificates that are considered trustworthy for particular purposes. In other words, Certificate Authority A might be trustworthy for client authentication but not for IPSec. Certificate Authority B might be trustworthy for secure e-mail but not for client authentication. It is also possible to have multiple CTLs within an organization, allowing you to separate CTLs based on use and assign particular CTLs to particular GPOs, which can then in turn be assigned to specific domains, sites, or OUs.

Common Root Certificate Authorities

Lastly, you can establish common trusted root CAs. Some organizations might decide that it is not in their best interests to host CAs within their domains. In other cases, they could use a combination of internal and external CAs for their PKI. Whatever the case, you can use Group Policy to make computers and users aware of common root CAs that exist outside your domain.

EXAM WARNING

Remember that this discussion applies only to CAs that exist *outside* your organization. Users and computers will already be aware of CAs that are part of your Windows Server 2003 environment and will trust them by default.

Publishing the CRL

On several occasions throughout this chapter, we have alluded to the fact that the CRL must be published in order for CAs and certificate users to be aware of certificates that have been revoked, regardless of the reason they have been revoked. In Windows Server 2003, there are two methods for publishing the CRL:

- Scheduled publication
- Manual publication

Scheduled Publication

One of the features of certificate services is that every CA automatically publishes an updated CRL after an interval of time specified by the CA's administrator. This interval of time is known as the CRL *publish period*. After the initial setup of a CA, the CRL publish period is set to one week (based on the local computer's time, starting from the date when the CA is first installed).

EXAM WARNING

Don't confuse a CRL publish period and the validity period of a CRL. The validity period of a CRL is the period of time that the CRL is considered authoritative by a verifier of a certificate.

Manual Publication

You can also publish a CRL on demand at any time, such as when a valuable certificate becomes compromised. Choosing to publish a CRL outside the established schedule resets the scheduled publication period to begin at that time. In other words, if you manually publish a CRL in the middle of a scheduled publish period, the CRL publish period is restarted.

It is important to realize that clients that have a cached copy of the previously published CRL will continue using it until its validity period has expired, even though a new CRL has been published. Manually publishing a CRL does not affect cached copies of CRLs that are still valid; it only makes a new CRL available for systems that do not have a cached copy of a valid CRL.

Backup and Restoring Certificate Services

As important as it is to back up a file server or domain controller in your Windows Server 2003 network, it is just as important to back up a CA in a Windows Server 2003 PKI. As with any other type of server, a CA is vulnerable to accidental loss due to hardware or storage media failure. Microsoft provides basic backup functionality in Windows Server

2003, which you can use to back up the system state data for the server. If you do not want to use Microsoft's Backup program(although this would be the best method), you can also use the Certification Authority snap-in to back up private key information, the certificate that the CA uses for digital signatures, and the certificate database itself. In Exercise 4.05, we walk through the steps of using the Certification Authority management tool.

EXERCISE 4.05

CERTIFICATION AUTHORITY BACKUP AND RECOVERY

In this example, we use one of our CA servers in the Wally's Tugboats domain to back up and restore the CA's private key, CA certificate, certification database, and database log:

1. Open the Certification Authority management tool by clicking **Start | Administrative Tools | Certification Authority**.
2. Right-click the name of the CA. In our example, we use the **certserv** CA server. From the context menu, select **All Tasks**, and then choose **Back up CA**.
3. Click **Next** at the Welcome screen.
4. Next we need to select the items we want to back up and the location to store them. In the Items to Back Up window (see Figure 4.27), check **Private key and CA certificate** and **Certification database and certification database log.** In addition, select a location where you want to store your backup files. For our example, we'll store them in a directory on our hard drive. If this were a real scenario, you would likely want to store the backup on another server. Click **Next** to continue.

Figure 4.27 The Items to Back Up Window

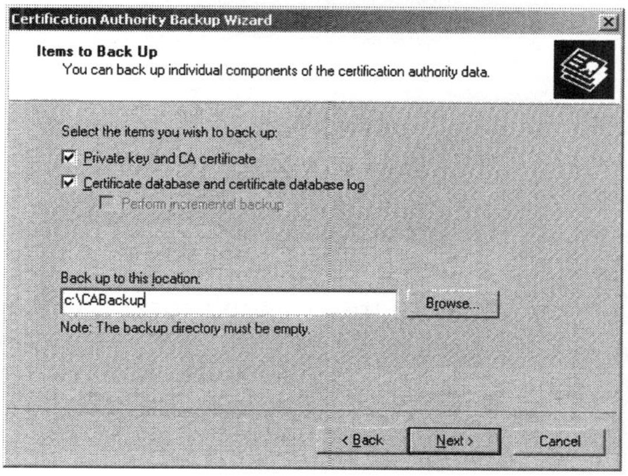

6. Next you need to select a password to gain access to the private key and certification file. You should choose a password that is difficult to figure out but one that you will also be able to remember. In our example, we use **tugb0atz**. Enter the password and re-enter it in the password confirmation box, and click **Next**.
7. Click **Finish** to complete the backup process.

Next let's revoke a certificate within our CA database. If you're unsure how to revoke a certificate, follow the steps in Exercise 4.04. Once the certificate has been revoked, we're going to restore our CA database in order to recover the certificate.

8. Open the Certification Authority management tool by clicking **Start | Administrative Tools | Certification Authority**.
9. Right-click the name of the CA. In our example, we use the **certserv** CA server. From the drop-down menu, select **All Tasks** and then select **Restore CA**.
10. You will be prompted to stop the certificate services. Click **OK** to stop it.
11. Click **Next** at the Welcome screen.
12. For our example, we'll restore only the database and the database log. In the Items to Restore window (see Figure 4.28), check **Certificate database and certificate database log**. You also need to enter the location of the stored data. Click **Next** to continue.

Figure 4.28 Items to Restore Window

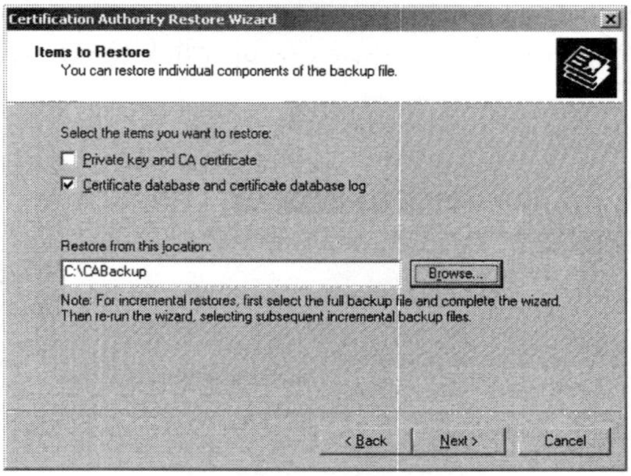

13. Click **Finish** to complete the restore process. Once the restore is complete, you will be prompted to start certificate services. Click **Yes** to restart the service.

14. Take a look at your issued certificates. You should see the certificate that you revoked.

New & Noteworthy...

More Work to Be Done

After you have restored your CA to a functional state, your work is still not done. You need to check the IIS services on the CA. If the IIS metabase is damaged or missing, IIS will not start, which will cause the certificate services Web pages to fail as well. You can use the IIS snap-in to back up and restore the IIS metabase. If you cannot restore a clean copy of the metabase, you can also recreate it. Once you have recreated the metabase, you need to use the command-line tool *certutil* to reconfigure the IIS server to support the CA Web pages. For more information on backup and restore of the IIS metabase, visit www.microsoft.com/technet/treeview/default.asp?url=/technet/prodtechnol/windowsserver2003/proddocs/datacenter/mb_rely_backuprestore.asp. You can also learn more about the *certutil* command-line tool at www.microsoft.com/technet/treeview/default.asp?url=/technet/prodtechnol/windowsserver2003/proddocs/standard/sag_cs_certutil8.asp.

Summary of Exam Objectives

We began this chapter with an overview of the core components and concepts behind a public key infrastructure, or PKI. Although this discussion might seem elementary to some of you, it's important to take a step back and review the basics before moving forward with new concepts—like learning to walk before you run. We discussed the makeup of a digital certificate and the information needed by a certificate authority (CA) to produce a certificate. We also discussed the different types of CA models: standalone, chain-of-trust, and hierarchical. Each of the CA models has its own pros and cons and serves a purpose based on what you are trying to accomplish with your PKI. Since this is a Microsoft exam, we also covered the core components that make up a Windows Server 2003 PKI and the role each component plays.

Next we discussed the decision-making process behind the planning of a Windows Server 2003 PKI. Each step in the decision-making process requires some additional resources and some in-depth thought prior to moving forward. As we saw, each decision is subjective in that there is no clear-cut answer to each step and the answers will vary based on the organization.

Last, we stepped through implementing PKI into Active Directory, walking through several of the features that you have at your disposal for managing your PKI. Understanding each of these features is important not only for passing the exam but also for day-to-day management of a Windows Server 2003 PKI.

Exam Objectives Fast Track

Overview of Public Key Infrastructure

- ☑ *Encryption* is the foundation of such security measures as digital signatures, digital certificates, and the public key infrastructure that uses these technologies to make computer transactions more secure. Computer-based encryption techniques use keys to encrypt and decrypt data.
- ☑ PKI makes it possible for one entity to trust another by providing *privacy, authentication, nonrepudiation,* and *integrity.*
- ☑ Asymmetric encryption is commonly referred to as *public key cryptography* because different keys are used to encrypt and decrypt the data.
- ☑ The most widely used type of encryption is *symmetric encryption,* which is aptly named because it uses one key for both the encryption and decryption processes.
- ☑ Symmetric encryption is also commonly referred to as *secret key encryption* and *shared-secret encryption;* all three terms refer to the same class of algorithm.

Components of Public Key Infrastructure

☑ In a hierarchical model, a *root CA* functions as a top-level authority over CAs beneath it, called *subordinate CAs*. The root CA also functions as a *trust anchor* to the CAs beneath it. A *trust anchor* is an entity known to be sufficiently trusted and therefore can be used to trust anything connected to it.

☑ X.509 is the standard used to define a digital certificate. Section 11.2 of X.509 describes a certificate as allowing an association between a user's distinguished name (DN) and the user's public key. The DN is specified by a naming authority (NA) and used as a unique name by the CA, which will create the certificate.

☑ Microsoft Windows PKI has four fundamental components. Each of these components serves a separate function within the PKI configuration. Some components you will manage directly, and some are more "behind the scenes"; you will not interact with the latter on a day-to-day basis unless you also develop applications requiring PKI functionality. The four fundamental components of the Windows PKI are Microsoft Certificate Services, Active Directory, CyptoAPI, and CAPICOM.

Planning the Windows Server 2003 Public Key Infrastructure

☑ There are five recommended steps for designing a Windows PKI: define the certificate requirements, create a CA infrastructure, extend the CA infrastructure, configure certificates, and create a management plan.

☑ In a certification hierarchy, a root CA is the most trusted type of CA within the PKI. Protection of the root CA is critical since a compromise of the root CA impacts the security of the entire organization.

☑ The Web enrollment interface provides for an easy means for users to perform many of the common CA services, including requesting a new certificate, requesting a CA's certificate revocation list (CRL), requesting a CA's own certificate, enrolling smart card certificates, and checking the status of a pending certificate requests.

☑ By default, users are not allowed to enroll for a smart card logon certificate. In order for a user to enroll for a smart card logon certificate, a system administrator must grant the user (or a group in which the user is a member) access rights to the smart card certificate template.

☑ Certificate autoenrollment allows clients to automatically submit certificate requests, retrieve, and store certificates. Autoenrollment also provides for automated renewal of certificates, allowing the entire certificate management process to remain in the background from the perspective of the user.

Configuring Public Key Infrastructure within Active Directory

- ☑ In a Windows PKI, certificate templates are used to assign certificates based on their intended use. When requesting a certificate from a Windows CA, a user is able to select from a variety of certificate types that are based on certificate templates. A template takes the decision-making process out of the hands of users and automates it based on the configuration of the template as defined by the system administrator.
- ☑ For a policy statement to appear on a Windows Server 2003 CA, the file CAPolicy.inf must be properly configured and placed in the system root directory (typically, C:\WINDOWS).
- ☑ A certificate can be revoked for a number of reasons, including: compromise or suspected compromise of the certificate subject's private key; compromise or suspected compromise of a CA's private key; discovery that a certificate was obtained fraudulently; change in the status of the certificate subject as a trusted entity; or change in the name of the certificate subject.

Exam Objectives Frequently Asked Questions

The following Frequently Asked Questions, answered by the authors of this book, are designed to both measure your understanding of the Exam Objectives presented in this chapter, and to assist you with real-life implementation of these concepts. You will also gain access to thousands of other FAQs at ITFAQnet.com.

Q: When should autoenrollment be used?

A: This is at the discretion of the administrator. For example, autoenrollment might be used in an environment with a high turnover rate, such as a telemarketing company. Rather than occupying an IT staff's time creating certificates, the process can be automated when the user signs on for the first time.

Q: The recommended steps for designing a PKI are discussed in the chapter, but they're kind of vague. Can you expand on some of the steps?

A: The fact is, the steps seem vague because the answers are very subjective based on individual environments. For example, creating a management plan is based on the culture of the organization. In other words, Company ABC might feel that that publishing certificates on a diskette is a secure and reasonable distribution method. However, Company XYZ could feel that certificates should be distributed and stored on a smart card.

Q: Why would I want to use the backup and restore method offered in the Certificate Services management tool and not just use my third-party backup software?

A: The answer here is speed. Typically, it's much faster to restore the CA components from a separate drive, network share, or removable media than it is to search a tape backup medium such as a DAT.

Q: Smart cards sound like the way to go for securing digital certificates. Is there any downside to using smart cards?

A: From a technology standpoint, no. However, depending on your organization, you could find that smart card implementations are out of reach financially due to the price of the cards and readers. However, this situation has changed and will continue to change over time.

Self Test

1. You have installed certificate services on a Windows Server 2003 server named CA101.somecompany.com. Your boss has decided that he wants to change all the servers to a naming convention that is more descriptive to the organization. He wants to rename CA101.somecompany.com to certserver.somecompany.com. You explain to your boss that renaming a server with certificate services is not a good idea. Which of the following answers *best* describes the reason that you should not rename the server?

   A. Once a server has joined an Active Directory domain, you cannot change the name without reloading the server.

   B. The server name is bound to the CA information in Active Directory, and changing the name would invalidate certificates that have been issued by the server.

   C. DNS will not allow for the renaming of a CA server.

   D. You can change the name of the CA server, as long as you use the certutil.exe –*R* option prior to the server rename, so that all the clients and subordinate servers are aware of the name change.

   E. None of the above.

2. You have installed certificate services on a Windows Server 2003 server, but after installation you are unable to open the Web enrollment Web site. What must you do in order to run Web enrollment on the server?

A. You must stop and restart certificate services or restart the computer before Web enrollment will work.

B. You must run certutil.exe *–w [servername]* to activate Web enrollment.

C. Prior to installing certificate services, you must install IIS on the server.

D. You must open the Certificate Services management tool, right-click the server-name, open the **Properties** for the server, and check off **Web enrollment** on the **General** tab.

E. Web Enrollment is a Windows 2000 feature and was not carried over to Windows Server 2003.

3. You want to create an issuer policy statement for your Windows Server 2003 certification authority. What file must you place in the %systemroot% directory prior to the certificate services install?

A. The name of the server with a file extension of .inf—for example, certserv.inf

B. IssuerPolicy.inf

C. CAPolicy.txt

D. CAPolicy.inf

E. None of the above

4. You want to back up your CA information using the Certificate Services management tool. Which items can you backup using this method? (Choose four answers.)

A. Private key

B. Group policies

C. CA certificate

D. Certificate database

E. System state

F. Certificate database log

5. A Microsoft Windows PKI has four fundamental components. Each of these components serves a separate function within the PKI configuration. What are the four fundamental components of the Windows PKI? (Choose four answers.)

A. Microsoft Certificate Services

B. Web enrollment

C. CryptoAPI

D. CAPICOM

E. DCOM

F. Active Directory

6. There are several differences and similarities between standalone CA servers and enterprise CA servers. However, there is one key difference between the two as well. What is this difference?

   A. Web enrollment

   B. Issuer policies

   C. Active Directory integration with certificates for standalone CA servers

   D. Active Directory integration with certificates for enterprise CA servers

7. In Windows Server 2003, you can separate the front end of the Web enrollment services from the back-end Certificate Services server. What must you do in order to use Web enrollment on a server separate from the CA server?

   A. You must configure the computer account for the front-end server to be trusted for delegation within Active Directory.

   B. You must configure the computer account for the front-end server to be trusted for delegation within the Certificate Services management tool.

   C. You must configure the computer account for the back-end server to be trusted for delegation within Active Directory.

   D. You must configure the computer account for the back-end server to be trusted for delegation within the Certificate Services management tool.

   E. None of the above; the Web enrollment services cannot be on a separate machine.

8. David is mapping out his CA servers for his PKI. David decides that he will need one root CA, four intermediate CAs, and three leaf CAs beneath each of the four intermediate CAs. Based on this configuration, which is depicted in the following figure, what type of CA model has David designed?

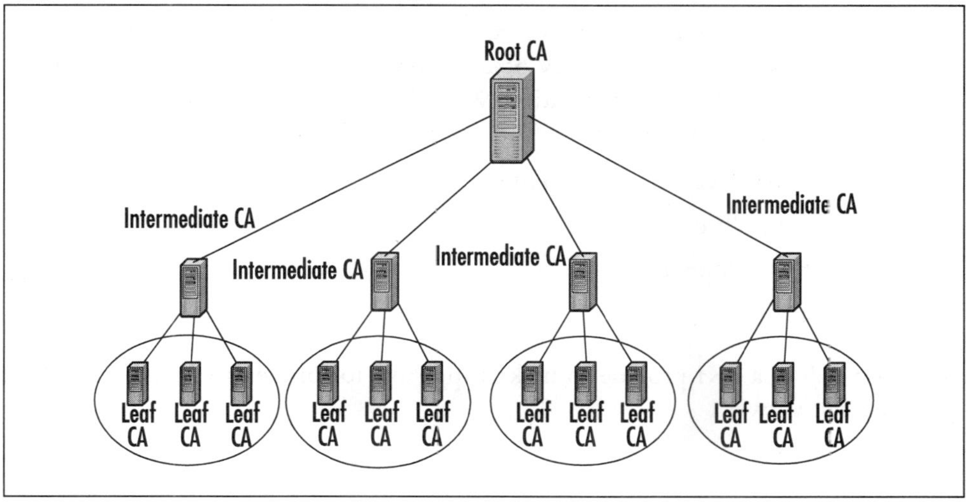

A. Standalone CA

B. Chain of trust

C. CA hierarchy

D. CA tree

9. Denise, an employee in XYZ Corporation, is returning from her honeymoon and has decided to take her husband's last name. Denise works in the accounting department for XYZ, which requires the use of smart cards to store certificates for department employees. You explain to Denise that you need to revoke her old certificate and create a new one for her. Why do you need to revoke her old certificate and create a new one?

   A. You do not have to revoke the certificate and create a new one; you can just change her name on the certificate and the CA server.

   B. Denise's account was deactivated while she was on her honeymoon, which requires the creation of a new certification.

   C. There has been a change in the name of the public key subject.

   D. There has been a change in the name of the certificate subject.

10. What feature of a Windows Server 2003 PKI can programmers use to develop software to communicate with other applications using encryption?

   A. Certificate services

   B. CryptoAPI

   C. Active Directory

   D. CAPICOM

11. Jeff wants to simplify the process for user enrollment into his company's PKI by allowing users to automatically obtain, store, and update their certificates without administrator or user intervention. What feature of Windows Server 2003 PKI can Jeff use to accomplish this task?

   A. Automatic certificate enrollment

   B. Autoenrollment

   C. Web enrollment

   D. CAPICOM

12. What does a PKI provide to make it possible for one entity to trust another? (Select the *best* answer.)

   A. Privacy

   B. Integrity

C. Authentication

D. Nonrepudiation

E. All of the above

F. None of the above

13. Matthew is explaining certificate revocation lists (CRLs) to his coworker Jenna. Jenna asks Matthew how a CRL can be distributed within a Windows Server 2003 PKI. What options are available in a Windows Server 2003 PKI for distribution of CRLs?

    A. Manual distribution

    B. Automatic distribution

    C. Scheduled distribution

    D. Forced distribution

    E. Answers A and C

    F. Answers B and D

    G. None of the above

14. Brittany has been tasked by her supervisor to develop a process plan for the development of her public key infrastructure. What five steps does Microsoft recommend for designing a PKI? (Choose all correct answers.)

    A. Define the certificate requirements

    B. Install certificate services

    C. Install Active Directory

    D. Create a certification authority infrastructure

    E. Extend the certification authority infrastructure

    F. Configure sites and services

    G. Configure certificates

    H. Create a management plan

15. You are the network administrator for International Tea Leaves Inc. and have been tasked with creating a PKI for the company. Tea Leaves Inc. has offices in several locations across the globe. You are trying to determine where CAs should be placed within your infrastructure. Which of the following answers will most likely affect your decision?

    A. WAN link speed

    B. Internet connectivity

    C. Server processor speed

    D. Number of users in an office

Self Test Quick Answer Key

For complete questions, answers, and explanations to the Self Test questions in this chapter as well as the other chapters in this book, see the Self Test Appendix.

1. **B**
2. **C**
3. **D**
4. **A, C, D, F**
5. **A, C, D, F**
6. **D**
7. **A**
8. **C**
9. **D**
10. **B**
11. **B**
12. **E**
13. **E**
14. **A, D, E, G, H**
15. **A**

Chapter 5

MCSA/MCSE 70-296

Managing User Authentication

Exam Objectives in this Chapter:

Introduction

In today's connected world, proof of your identity is often required to ensure that someone else is not trying to use your identity. It used to be that a username and password were sufficient information to authenticate someone to a network. However, password authentication is only the first step in true authentication of a user's identity in today's environment. You must have a well-defined password policy, which includes account lockout, password rotation, and other options to ensure limited access to your network. In this chapter, we develop a password policy for your Windows Server 2003 network. However, sometimes passwords and password policies are not enough, and we have to take authentication to the next plateau.

Tools such as biometric devices, token devices, voice identification, and smart cards are becoming much more mainstream for user authentication as the price continues to drop and acceptance continues to rise. If you have ever seen a large data center, you have probably seen biometric tools such as thumbprint scanners or palm scanners at entryways for employees to gain access. Other sites use smart card readers for access to public computer kiosks. For example, Sun Microsystems requires the use of smart cards for students to sign into class each day. Each student is assigned a smart card and a four-digit personal identification number (PIN) that they must use to sign in each day before class begins.

In Windows 2000 XP, and Server 2003 Microsoft has implemented smart card technology into the operating system as well as Active Directory to provide you with enhanced authentication abilities in order to add security to your network. As a Windows Server 2003 MCSE, you are required to understand how to implement smart card technologies and manage resources through the use of smart cards.

Let's begin with a discussion of password policies.

EXAM 70-296 OBJECTIVE 8.1.2

Password Policies

Since they are largely created and managed by end users, passwords have the potential to be the weakest link in any network security implementation. You can install all the high-powered firewall hardware and VPN clients you like, but if your vice president of sales uses the name of her pet St. Bernard as her password for the customer database system, all your preventative measures might be rendered useless. Since passwords are the "keys to the kingdom" of any computer system, the database that Windows Server 2003 uses to store password information will be a common attack vector for anyone attempting to hack your network. Luckily, Windows Server 2003 offers several means to secure passwords on your network. A combination of technical measures, along with a healthy dose of user training and awareness, will go a long way toward protecting the security of your network systems.

Creating an Extensive Defense Model

In modern computer security, a system administrator needs to create a security plan that uses many different mechanisms to protect your networks from unauthorized access. Rather than relying solely on a hardware firewall and nothing else, *defense in depth* would also utilize strong passwords as well as other security mechanisms on local client PCs in the event that the firewall is compromised. The idea here is to create a series of security mechanisms so that if one of them is circumvented, other systems and procedures are already in place to help impede an attacker. Microsoft refers to this practice as an *extensive defense model*. The key points of this model are the following:

- A viable security plan needs to begin and end with user awareness, since a technical mechanism is only as effective as the extent to which the users on your network adhere to it. As an administrator, you need to educate your users about how to best protect their accounts from unauthorized attacks. This can include advice about not sharing passwords, not writing them down or leaving them otherwise accessible, and making sure to lock a workstation if the user needs to leave it unattended for any length of time. You can spread security awareness information via e-mail, posters in employee break areas, printed memos, or any other medium that will get your users' attention.
- Use the system key utility (*syskey*) on all critical machines on your network. This utility, discussed later in this chapter, encrypts the password information that is stored in the Security Accounts Manager (SAM) database. At a minimum, you should secure the SAM database on the domain controllers in your environment; you should consider protecting the local user database on your workstations in this manner as well.
- Educate your users about the potential hazards of selecting the Save My Password feature or any similar feature on mission-critical applications such as remote access or VPN clients. Make sure that users understand that the convenience of saving passwords on a local workstation is far outweighed by the potential security risk if a user's workstation becomes compromised.
- If you need to create one or more service accounts for applications to use to interface with the operating system, make sure that these accounts have different passwords. Otherwise, compromise of one such account will leave multiple network applications open to attack.
- If you suspect that a user account has been compromised, change the password immediately. If possible, consider renaming the account entirely, since it is now a known attack vector.
- Create a password policy and/or account lockout policy that is appropriate to your organization's needs. (Both these policies are discussed more fully later in this chapter.) It's important to strike a balance between security and usability in designing these types of account policies: A 23-character minimum password length might seem like a good security measure on paper, for example, but any security offered by such a decision will be rendered worthless when your users leave their impossible-to-remember 23-character passwords written down on sticky notes on their monitors for all the world to see.

Strong Passwords

In discussing security awareness with your user community, one of the most critical issues to consider is that of password strength. A weak password will provide potential attackers with easy access to your users computers, and consequently the rest of your company's network; well-formed passwords will be significantly more difficult to decipher. Even though password-cracking utilities used by attackers continue to evolve and improve, educating your users to the importance of strong passwords will provide additional security for your network's computing resources.

According to Microsoft, a weak password is one that contains any portion of your name, your company's name, or your network login ID. So, if my username on a network system were *hunterle*, and my network password were *hunter12!@!*, that would be considered a weak password. A password that contains any complete dictionary word—*password, thunder, protocol*—is also considered weak. (It should go without saying that blank passwords are weak as well.) By comparison, a strong password (in addition to not employing any of the previously described weak characteristics) will not contain any reference to your username, company name, or any word found in the dictionary. Strong passwords should also be at least seven characters long and contain characters from each of the following groups:

- **Uppercase letters** A, B, C ...
- **Lowercase letters** z, y, x ...
- **Numeric digits** 0, 1, 2, 3, 4, 5, 6, 7, 8, or 9
- **Nonalphanumeric characters** !, *, $, }, etc.

Each strong password should be appreciably different from any previous passwords that the user has created: P!234abc, Q!234abc, and R!234abc, although each meeting the described password criteria, would not be considered strong passwords when viewed as a whole. To further complicate matters, an individual password can still be weak even though it meets the criteria. For example, IloveU123! would be a fairly simple password to crack, even though it possesses the length and character complexity requirements of a strong password.

System Key Utility

Most password-cracking software used in attacking computer networks attempts to target the SAM database or the Windows directory services in order to access passwords for user accounts. To secure your Windows Server 2003 password information, you should use the System Key Utility (the syskey.exe file itself is located in the ~\System32 directory by default) on every critical machine that you administer. This utility encrypts password information in either location, providing an extra line of defense against would-be attackers. To use this utility on a workstation or member server, you must be a member of the local Administrators group on the machine in question. (If the machine is a member of a domain, remember that the Domain Admins group is added to the local Administrators group by default.) On a domain controller, you need to be a member of the Domain Admins or Enterprise Admins group.

Test Day Tip

On workstations and member servers, password information is stored within the computer's Registry. Domain controllers integrate password information into the directory services database that is replicated between domain controllers.

In the Exercise 5.01, we go through the steps in enabling the System Key Utility on a Windows Server 2003 server.

EXERCISE 5.01

Creating a System Key

1. From the Windows Server 2003 server desktop, click **Start | Run**, then type **syskey** and click **OK**. You'll see the screen shown in Figure 5.1.

Figure 5.1 Enabling *syskey* Encryption

2. As shown in Figure 5.1, select **Encryption Enabled**, then click **Update**.
3. Choose from the security options shown in Figure 5.2. The various options available to you are as follows:

- **Password Startup, administrator-generated password** This choice encrypts the account password information and stores the associated key on the local computer. In this case, however, you will select a password that will be used to further protect the key. You'll need to enter this password during the computer's bootup sequence. This is a more secure option than storing the startup key locally as described in the following point, since the password used to secure the system key isn't stored anywhere on the local computer. The drawback to this method is that an administrator must be present to enter the *syskey* password

Figure 5.2 Selecting *syskey* Encryption Options

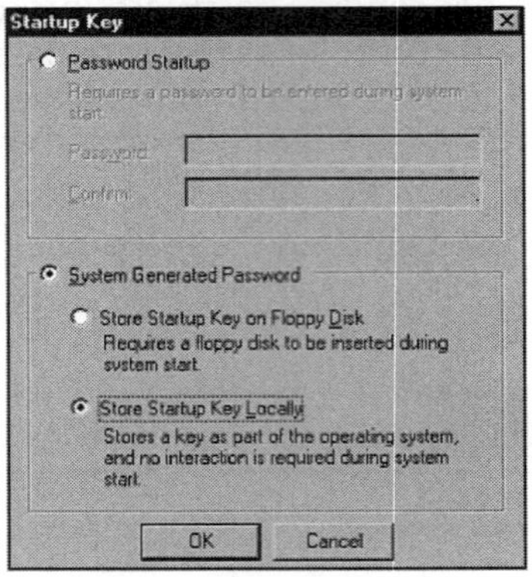

whenever the machine is rebooted, which might make this a less attractive option for a remote machine that requires frequent reboots.

- **System Generated Password, Store Startup Key on Floppy Disk** This option stores the system key on a separate diskette, which must be inserted during the system startup. This is the most secure of the three possible options, since the system key itself is not stored anywhere on the local computer and the machine will not be able to boot without the diskette that contains the system key.
- **System Generated Password, Store Startup Key Locally** This choice encrypts the SAM or directory services information using a random key that's stored on the local computer. You can reboot the machine without being prompted for a password or a diskette; however, if the physical machine is compromised, the system key can be modified or destroyed. Of the three possible options when using *syskey*, this is the least secure.

Exam Warning

If you lose the diskette or forget the password that you created when you ran *syskey*, you won't be able to boot the computer in question without restoring the Registry or the Active Directory database from a point before you implemented *syskey*.

4. Once you have selected the option that you want, click **OK** to finish encrypting the account information. You'll see the confirmation message shown in Figure 5.3.

Figure 5.3 Confirmation of *syskey* Success

Defining a Password Policy

Using Active Directory, you can create a policy to enforce consistent password standards across your entire organization. Among the criteria that you can specify are how often passwords must be changed, how many unique passwords a user must utilize when changing his or her password, and the complexity level of passwords that are acceptable on your network. Additionally, you can specify an account lockout policy that will prevent users from logging in after a certain number of incorrect login attempts. In this section, we discuss the specific steps necessary to enforce password and account lockout policies on a Windows Server 2003 network.

TEST DAY TIP

To create or edit a password policy or an account lockout policy, you must be logged on as a member of the Domain Admins or Enterprise Admins group. You can use the *RunAs* function for increased security.

Applying a Password Policy

In Exercise 5.02, we discuss how to establish a password policy for your Windows Server 2003 domain.

EXERCISE 5.02

CREATING A DOMAIN PASSWORD POLICY

1. From the Windows Server 2003 desktop, open **Active Directory Users and Computers**. Right-click the domain that you want to set a password policy for, and select **Properties**.

2. Click the **Group Policy** tab, as shown in Figure 5.4. You can edit the default domain policy, or click **New** to create a new policy. In this case, click **Edit** to apply changes to the default policy.

Figure 5.4 The Group Policy Tab

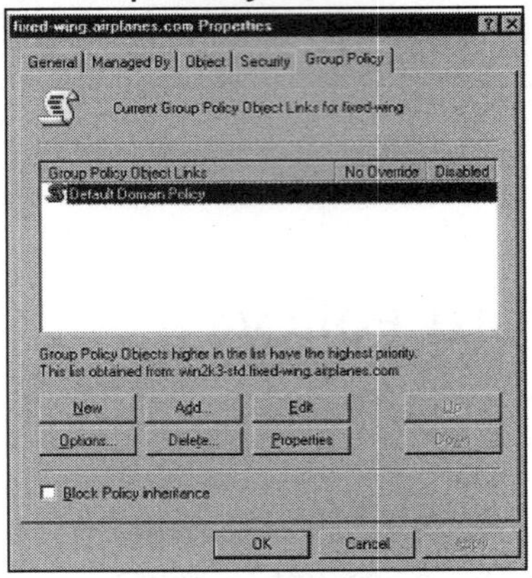

3. Navigate to the Password Policy Node by clicking **Computer Configuration | Windows Settings | Security Settings | Account Policies | Password Policy**. You'll see the screen shown in Figure 5.5.

Figure 5.5 Configuring Password Policy Settings

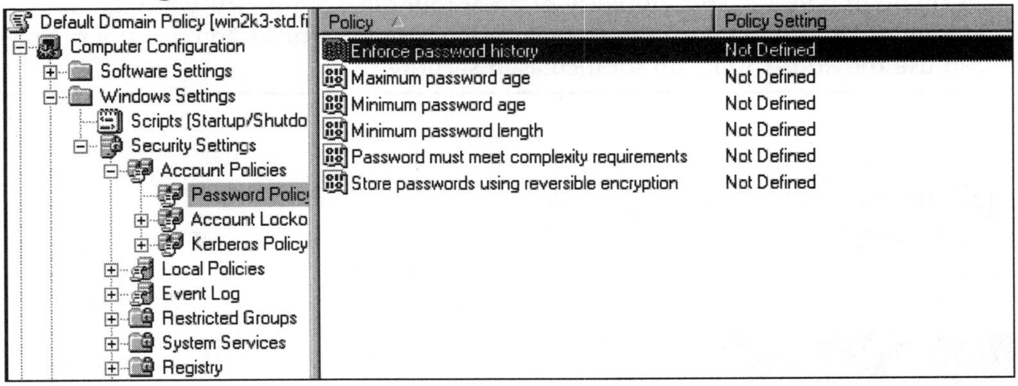

4. For each item that you want to configure, right-click the item and select **Properties**. In this case, let's enforce a password history of three passwords. In the screen shown in Figure 5.6, place a check mark next to **Define this policy setting**, and then enter the appropriate value. Using password policies, you can configure any of the following settings:

Figure 5.6 Defining the Password History Policy

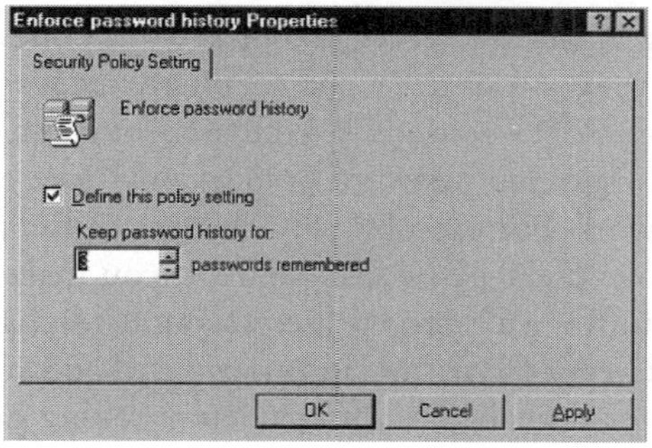

- **Enforce password history** This option allows you to define the number of unique passwords that Windows will retain. This prevents users from using the same passwords again when their passwords expire. Setting this number to at least three or four prevents users from alternating repeatedly between two passwords whenever they're prompted to change their passwords.
- **Maximum password age** This defines how frequently Windows will prompt your users to change their passwords.
- **Minimum password age** This ensures that passwords cannot be changed until they are more than a certain number of days old. This works in conjunction with the first two settings by preventing users from repeatedly changing their passwords to circumvent the "Enforce password history" policy.
- **Minimum password length** This option dictates the shortest allowable length that a user password can be, since longer passwords are typically stronger than shorter ones. Enabling this setting also prevents users from setting a blank password.
- **Password must meet complexity requirements** This policy setting, when activated, forces any new passwords created on your network to meet the following requirements: minimum of six characters in length, containing three of the following four character groups: uppercase letters, lowercase letters, numeric digits, and nonalphanumeric characters such as %, !, and [.
- **Store passwords using reversible encryption** This option stores a copy of the user's password within the Active Directory database using reversible encryption. This is required for certain message digest functions to work properly. This policy is disabled by default and should be enabled only if you are certain that your environment requires it.

Modifying a Password Policy

You can modify an existing Windows Server 2003 password policy by navigating to the policy section listed in the previous exercise and making whatever changes you desire. Unlike other types of Group Policy settings in which client settings refresh themselves every 30 minutes, new and modified password policies only take effect on any *new* passwords created on your network. For example, any changes to the password policies might take effect the next time your users' passwords expire. If you make a radical change to your password policy, you need to force all desired user accounts to change their passwords in order for the change to take effect. For this reason, you should carefully plan your password policy so that you can create all necessary settings before rolling out Active Directory to your clients.

Applying an Account Lockout Policy

In addition to setting password policies, you can configure your network so that user accounts will be locked out after a certain number of incorrect logon attempts. This can be a *soft lockout*, in which the account will be re-enabled after 30 minutes, for example. You also have the option of configuring a *hard lockout*, in which user accounts will only be re-enabled by the manual intervention of an administrator. Before implementing an account lockout policy, you need to understand the potential implications for your network. An account lockout policy will increase the likelihood of deterring a potential attack against your network, but you also run the risk of locking out authorized users. You need to set the lockout threshold high enough that authorized users will not be locked out of their accounts due to simple human error of mistyping their passwords before they've had their morning coffee; three to five is a common threshold. You should also remember that if a user changes his or her password on Computer A while already logged onto Computer B, the session on Computer B will continue to attempt to log into the Active Directory database by using the old (now incorrect) password, which will eventually lock out the user account. This can be a common occurrence in the case of service accounts and administrative accounts. Exercise 5.03 details the necessary steps in configuring account lockout policy settings for your domain.

EXAM WARNING

The issue of password synchronization described in the previous paragraph is not an issue for organizations that are only running Windows Server 2003 operating systems.

Exercise 5.03

Creating an Account Lockout Policy

1. From the Windows Server 2003 desktop, click **Start | Programs | Administrative Tools | Active Directory Users and Computers**.
2. Right-click the domain you want to administer, then select **Properties**.
3. Click **New** to create a new Group Policy, or select **Edit** to modify the default domain policy.
4. Navigate to the account lockout policy by clicking **Computer Configuration | Windows Settings | Security Settings | Account Policies | Account Lockout Policy**. You'll see the screen shown in Figure 5.7.

Figure 5.7 Account Lockout Policy Objects

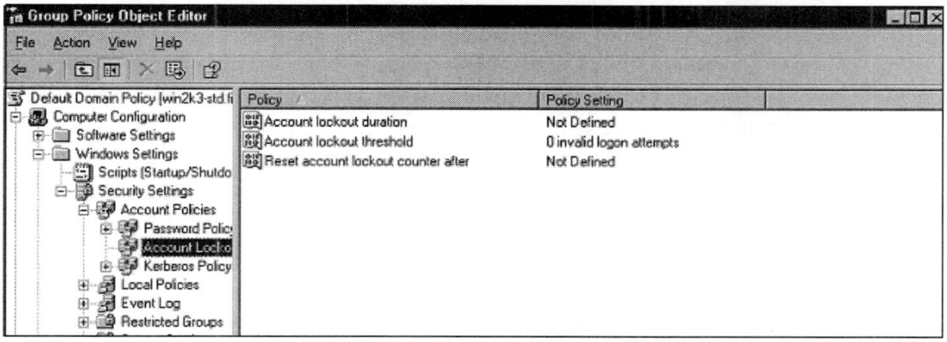

5. For each item that you want to configure, right-click the item and select **Properties**. To illustrate, let's create an account lockout threshold of three invalid logon attempts. From the screen shown in Figure 5.8, place a check mark next to **Define this policy setting**, and then enter the appropriate value. Using account lockout policies, you can customize the following configuration settings:
   - **Account lockout duration** This option determines the amount of time that a locked-out account will remain inaccessible. Setting this option to 0 means that the account will remain locked out until an administrator manually unlocks it. Select a lockout duration that will deter intruders without crippling your authorized users; 30 to 60 minutes is sufficient for most environments.

Figure 5.8 Configuring the Account Lockout Threshold

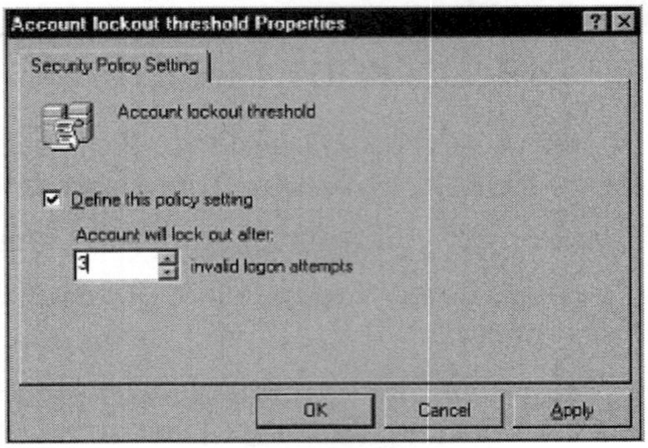

- **Account lockout threshold** This option determines the number of invalid login attempts that can occur before an account will be locked out. Setting this option to 0 means that accounts on your network will never be locked out.
- **Reset account lockout counter after** This option defines the amount of time in minutes after a bad login attempt that the "counter" will reset. If this value is set to 45 minutes, and if user *jsmith* types his password incorrectly two times before logging on successfully, his running tally of failed login attempts will reset to 0 after 45 minutes have elapsed. Be careful not to set this option too high, or your users could lock themselves out through simple typographical errors.

Modifying an Account Lockout Policy

You can modify an existing account lockout policy by navigating to the policy section listed in the previous section and making any necessary changes. Users will not need to change their passwords in order for new or modified account lockout policies to take effect.

Password Reset Disks

A potential disadvantage to enabling strong passwords on your network is that your users will likely forget their passwords more frequently. It's only to be expected, since *Y!sgf($q* is a far more difficult password to remember than ,say, *goflyers.* In previous releases of Windows, if a user forgot her local user account password, the only recourse was for an administrator to manually reset it. If you do this in Windows XP or Server 2003, the user will lose any

Internet passwords that were saved on her local computer, as well as any encrypted files or e-mail encrypted with the user's public key. Because of this, Windows Server 2003 and Windows XP provide a better solution for forgotten passwords. In the newest release of Windows, your users can create password reset disks for their local user accounts so that they won't lose any of their valuable data in the event that they forget their passwords.

When you create a password reset disk, Windows creates a *public and private key pair*. The private key is stored on the password reset disk itself; the public key is used to encrypt the user's local account password. In case the user forgets the password, he or she can use the private key that's stored on the reset disk to decrypt and retrieve the current password. When you use the password reset disk, you'll be prompted to immediately change the password for your local user account, which will then be encrypted with the same public and private key pair. Your users will not lose any data in this scenario because they are only changing their passwords rather than requiring an administrator to reset them.

EXAM WARNING

If you implement password reset disks on your network, it is vital that you store them in a secure location, because they can allow unauthorized access to your network if they fall into the wrong hands.

Creating a Password Reset Disk

To create a password reset disk:

1. Press **Ctrl+Alt+Del**, and click **Change Password**.
2. In the **User name** field, enter the logon of the account for which you're creating the password reset disk.
3. In the **Log on to** field, make sure that the Local Computer Name is specified, rather than any domain that the computer is configured to log into.
4. Once you've entered the appropriate username, click **Backup** to begin the Forgotten Password wizard.
5. Click **Next** to bypass the Welcome screen of the Forgotten Password wizard. You'll be prompted to insert a blank, formatted diskette into your A:\ drive. Insert the diskette.
6. Click **Next** again to create the password reset disk.
7. Once you've finished creating the password reset diskette, be sure to store it in a secure location.

EXAM WARNING

You can only create password reset disks for local computer accounts. You cannot create a reset disk for a domain account or from a domain controller.

Resetting a Local Account

If a user has forgotten the password to his local user account and has not previously created a password reset disk, your only alternative is to reset his local account password. Remember that doing so will cause the user in question to lose the following information:

- Any e-mail encrypted with the user's public key
- Internet passwords that are saved on the local computer
- Local files that the user has encrypted

In Exercise 5.04, we cover the steps required to reset a local user account if you do not have a password reset disk available.

EXERCISE 5.04

RESETTING A LOCAL USER ACCOUNT

Follow these steps to reset a local user account:

1. Log onto the workstation using the local administrator account or an account that is a member of the Domain Admins group on your Windows domain.
2. Open the Computer Management MMC console by clicking **Start | All Programs | Administrative Tools | Computer Management**.
3. In the left-hand pane of the Computer Management console, click **Computer Management | System Tools | Local Users and Groups | Users**. You'll see the screen shown in Figure 5.9.

Figure 5.9 Administering Local Users

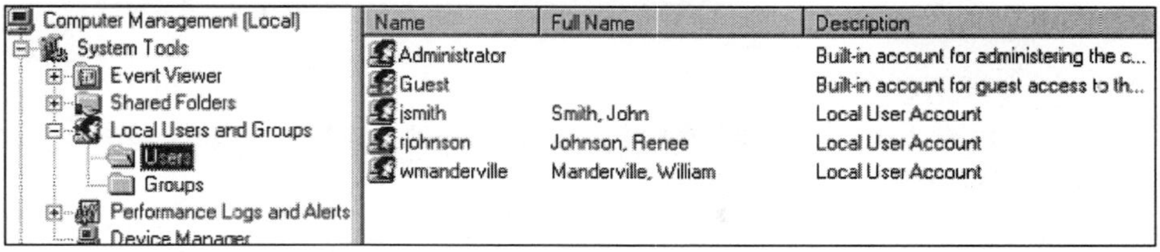

4. Right-click the user account whose password you need to reset, and then click **Set Password**. You'll see the warning message shown in Figure 5.10.

Figure 5.10 Warning of Potential Data Loss When Resetting a

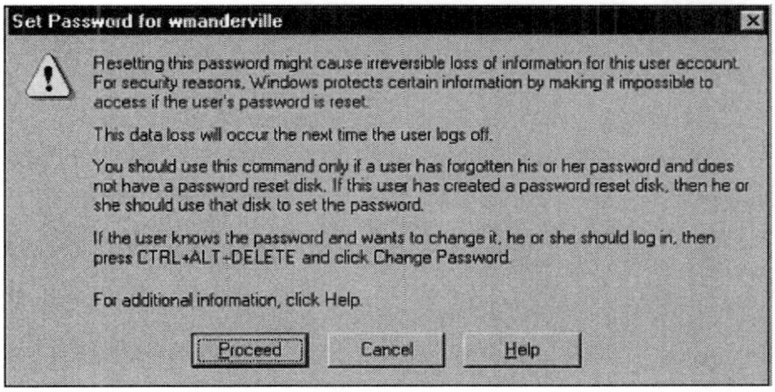

Click **Proceed** to reset the user's password. You'll see the screen shown in Figure 5.11, which will give you one last warning regarding the potential data loss associated with resetting a local user account password. Enter a new password that meets the complexity requirements of your domain password policy, then click **OK**. (Since this is a local password, the complexity requirements of your domain password policy will not be automatically enforced. However, you should nonetheless create a strong password for the local account on your workstation.) A popup window will indicate that the password was set successfully. Click **OK** again to return to the Computer Management Console.

Figure 5.11 Resetting the Local User Password

5. If you would like the user to change his password at his first login, right-click the user object and select **Properties**. Place a check mark next to **User Must Change Password at Next Logon**, then click **OK**.
6. Log out of the workstation and allow the user to log in with his newly reset password.

EXAM 70-296 OBJECTIVE 8.1

User Authentication

Any well-formed security model needs to address the following three topics: authentication, authorization, and accounting (you'll sometimes see the last one referred to as *auditing*). Put simply, authentication deals with *who* a person is, authorization centers around *what* an authenticated user is permitted to do, and accounting/auditing is concerned with tracking *who did what* to a network file, service, or other resource. Windows Server 2003 addresses all three facets of this security model, beginning with the user authentication strategies that we discuss in this chapter.

Regardless of which protocol or technical mechanism is used, all authentication schemes need to meet the same basic requirement of verifying that a user or other network object is in fact who it claims to be. This can include verifying a digital signature on a file or hard drive or verifying the identity of a user or computer that is attempting to access a computer or network resource. Windows Server 2003 offers several protocols and mechanisms to perform this verification, including (but not limited to) the following:

- Kerberos
- NT LAN Manager (NTLM)
- Secure Sockets Layer/Transport Security Layer (SSL/TLS)
- Digest authentication
- Smart cards
- Virtual private networking (VPN)

In the following sections, we'll describe the particulars of each authentication mechanism available with Windows Server 2003 and the appropriate use for each. The most common authentication mechanism that dates back to the mainframe days is *password authentication*. This occurs when the user supplies a password to a server or host computer and the server compares the supplied password with the information that it has stored in association with the username in question. If the two items match, the system permits the user to log on. Concerns regarding password authentication have largely been connected with ensuring that user passwords are not transmitted via cleartext over a network connection. In fact, many modern password authentication schemes such as NTLM and Kerberos never transmit the actual user password at all.

Another concern that is more difficult to address is that of user education. Even after years of reminding users of the importance of choosing strong passwords and protecting their login information, many still use their children's names as passwords. In a world of increasingly connected computing systems, the importance of creating strong password policies as part of your network's security plan cannot be overstated. To assist in this task, Windows Server 2003 allows you to establish password policies to mandate the use of strong, complex passwords, as we discussed earlier in the chapter. You can also mandate that your users log in using smart cards, a topic that we cover in depth in a later section.

Need for Authentication

User authentication is a necessary first step within any network security infrastructure because it establishes the identity of the user. Without this key piece of information, Windows Server 2003 access control and auditing capabilities would not be able to function. Once you understand how the various authentication systems function, you'll be able to use this information to create an effective user authentication strategy for your network. The location of your users, whether they are connected to the LAN via a high-speed network connection or a simple dialup line, and the client and server operating systems in use throughout your organization will dictate the appropriate authentication strategy for your users. Keep in mind as we go along that a fully functional authentication strategy will almost certainly involve a combination of the strategies and protocols described in this chapter, because a single solution will not meet the needs of an enterprise organization. Your goal as a network administrator is to create an authentication strategy that provides the optimum security for your users while allowing you to administer the network as efficiently as possible.

Single Sign-on

A key feature of Windows Server 2003 is support for single sign-on, an authentication mechanism that allows your domain users to authenticate against any computer in a domain while only needing to provide their login credentials one time. This system allows network administrators to manage a single account for each user, rather than dealing with the administrative overhead of maintaining multiple user accounts across different domains. It also provides greatly enhanced convenience for network users, since needing to maintain only a single password or smart card makes the network login process much simpler. (This also diminishes network support calls, reducing even further the support required to maintain a network.)

Whether your network authentication relies on single sign-on or not, any authentication scheme is a two-step process. First the user must perform an *interactive logon* in order to access her local computer. Once the user has accessed the local workstation, *network authentication* allows her to access needed network services or resources. In this section, we examine both of these processes in detail.

Interactive Logon

A network user performs an interactive logon when he presents his network credentials to the operating system of the physical computer that he is attempting to log into—usually his desktop workstation. The logon name and password can either be a local user account or a domain account. When logging on using a local computer account, the user presents credentials that are stored in the SAM database stored on the local machine. Any workstation or member server can store local SAM-based accounts, but those accounts can be used only for access to that specific computer. When using a domain account, the user's domain information is authenticated against the Active Directory database. This allows the user to gain access to not only the local workstation but to the Windows Server 2003 domain and any trusting domains. In this case, the user's domain account bypasses the workstation's SAM database, authenticating to the local workstation using the information stored in Active Directory. Figure 5.12 provides an illustration of these two processes.

Figure 5.12 Interactive Logons Using Local and Domain Accounts

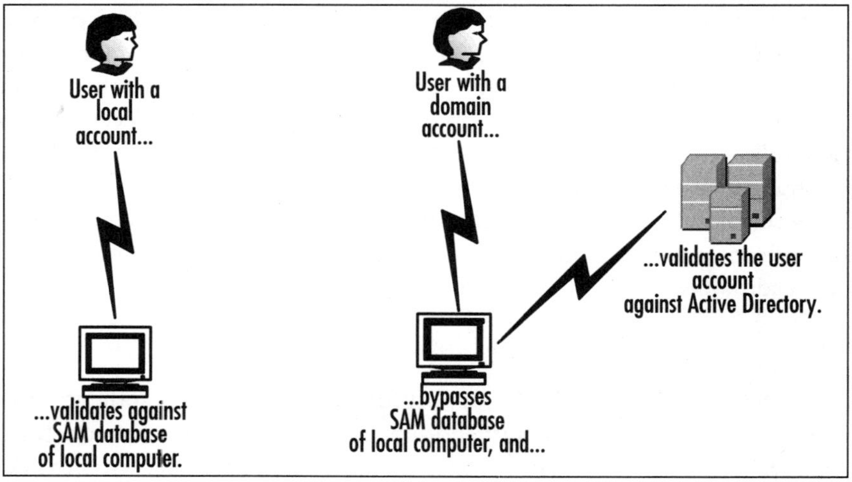

Network Authentication

Once a user has gained access to a physical workstation, it's almost inevitable that the user will require access to files, applications, or services hosted by other machines on the LAN or WAN. *Network authentication* is the mechanism that confirms the user's identity to whatever network resource that the user attempts to access. Windows Server 2003 provides several mechanisms to enable this type of authentication, including Kerberos, SSL/TLS, and NTLM to provide backward compatibility with Windows NT 4.0 systems.

Using the previous description of interactive logons, users who log on using a local computer account must provide logon credentials again every time they attempt to access a network resource, since the local computer account only exists within the individual workstation or member server's SAM database rather than a centrally managed directory service like Active Directory. If the user logs on using a domain account, on the other hand, the user's credentials are automatically passed to any network services that they need to access. For this reason, the network authentication process is transparent to users in an Active Directory environment; the network operating system handles everything behind the scenes without the need for user intervention. This feature provides the foundations for single sign-on in a Windows Server 2003 environment by allowing users to access resources in their own domains as well as other trusted domains.

EXAM DAY TIP

Network authentication using a domain account can be accomplished via a username and password or with a smart card device.

Authentication Types

Windows Server 2003 offers several different authentication types to meet the needs of a diverse user base. The default authentication protocol for a homogeneous Windows Server 2003 environment is Kerberos version 5. This protocol relies on a system of tickets to verify the identity of network users, services, and devices. For Web applications and users, you can rely on the standards-based encryption offered by the SSL/TLS security protocols as well as Microsoft Digest. To provide backward compatibility for earlier versions of Microsoft operating systems, Windows Server 2003 still provides support for the NTLM protocol as well. In this section, we examine the various authentication options available to you as a Windows administrator.

Kerberos

Within a Windows Server 2003 domain, the primary authentication protocol is Kerberos version 5. Kerberos provides thorough authentication by verifying not only the identity of network users but also the validity of the network services themselves. This latter feature was designed to prevent users from attaching to "dummy" services created by malicious network attackers to trick users into revealing their passwords or other sensitive information. The process of verifying both the user *and* the service that the user is attempting to use is referred to as *mutual authentication*. Only network clients and servers that are running the Windows 2000, Windows Server 2003, or Windows XP Professional operating systems will be able to use the Kerberos authentication protocol; any down-level clients that attempt to use a "Kerberized" resource will use NTLM authentication instead. (We discuss NTLM more fully in a later section.) All 2000/2003/XP Professional machines that belong to a Windows Server 2003 or Windows 2000 domain will use the Kerberos protocol enabled as the default mechanism for network authentication for domain resources.

The Kerberos authentication mechanism relies on a key distribution center (KDC) to issue *tickets* that allow client access to network resources. Each domain controller in a Windows Server 2003 domain functions as a KDC, allowing for fault tolerance in the event that one domain controller becomes unavailable. Network clients use DNS to locate the nearest available KDC to acquire a ticket and provide network authentication. Kerberos tickets contain an encrypted password that confirms the user's identity to the requested service. These tickets remain resident in memory on the client computer system for a specific amount of time, usually 8 or 10 hours. The longevity of these tickets allows Kerberos to provide single sign-on capabilities so that the authentication process as a whole becomes transparent to users once they've initially entered their logon credentials.

Understanding the Kerberos Authentication Process

When a user enters his or her network credentials on a Kerberos-enabled system, the following steps take place. These transactions occur entirely behind the scenes; the user is only aware that he or she has entered the password or PIN number as part of a normal logon process. Here is a simplified single domain Kerebos exchange:

1. Using a smart card or a username/password combination, a user authenticates to the KDC. The KDC issues a *ticket-granting ticket (TGT)* to the client system. The client retains this TGT in memory until needed.
2. When the client attempts to access a network resource, it presents its TGT to the *ticket-granting service (TGS)* on the nearest available Windows Server 2003 KDC.
3. If the user is authorized to access the service that it is requesting, the TGS issues a *service ticket* to the client.
4. The client presents the service ticket to the requested network service. Through mutual authentication, the service ticket proves the identity of the user as well as the identity of the service.

EXAM WARNING

Kerberos authentication relies on timestamps to function properly. As such, all clients that are running the Kerberos client must synchronize their time settings with a common time server. If the time on a network client is more than 5 minutes slow or fast compared with the KDC, Kerberos authentication will fail.

The Windows Server 2003 Kerberos authentication system can also interact with non-Microsoft Kerberos implementations such as MIT and UNIX-based Kerberos systems. This new "realm trust" feature, covered in Chapter 3, allows a client in a Kerberos realm to authenticate against Active Directory to access resources, as well as vice versa. This interoperability allows Windows Server 2003 domain controllers to provide authentication for client systems running UNIX/MIT Kerberos, including clients that might be running operating systems other than Windows XP Professional or Windows 2000. Conversely, it also allows Windows-based clients to access resources within a UNIX-based Kerberos realm.

Secure Sockets Layer/Transport Layer Security

Any time that you visit a Web site that uses an https:// prefix instead of http://, you're seeing Secure Sockets Layer (SSL) encryption in action. The SSL protocol operates at the network layer of the OSI model, providing encryption for protocols such as HTTP, LDAP, and IMAP operating at the higher layers of the protocol stack. SSL provides three major functions in encrypting TCP/IP-based traffic:

- **Server authentication** Allows a user to confirm that an Internet server is really the machine that it is claiming to be. It's difficult to think of anyone who wouldn't like the assurance of knowing that they're looking at the genuine Amazon.com site and not a duplicate created by a hacker before entering their credit card information.
- **Client authentication** Allows a server to confirm a client's identity. This is important for a bank that needs to transmit sensitive financial information to a server belonging to a subsidiary office, for example. Combining server and client authentication provides a means of mutual authentication similar to that offered by the Kerberos protocol.
- **Encrypted connections** Allows all data that is sent between a client and server to be encrypted and decrypted, allowing for a high degree of confidentiality. This function also allows both parties to confirm that the data was not altered during transmission.

The Transport Layer Security (TLS) protocol is currently under development by the Internet Engineering Task Force (IETF). It will eventually replace SSL as a standard for securing Internet traffic while remaining backward compatible with earlier versions of SSL. RFC 2712 describes the way to add Kerberos functionality to the TLS suite, which will potentially allow Microsoft and other vendors to extend its use beyond LAN/WAN authentication to use on the Internet as a whole.

SSL and TLS can use a wide range of ciphers to allow connections with a diverse client base. However, you can edit the Registry on the Windows Server 2003 server hosting your Web presence to restrict these to specific ciphers only. Within the Registry editor on the server, browse to the following key: HKEY_LOCAL_MACHINE\SYSTEM\CurrentControlSet\Control\SecurityProviders\SCHANNEL\Ciphers, as shown in Figure 5.13. Each available cipher has two potential values:

- **0xffffffff** (enabled)
- **0x0** (disabled)

Figure 5.13 Editing SSL/TLS Ciphers

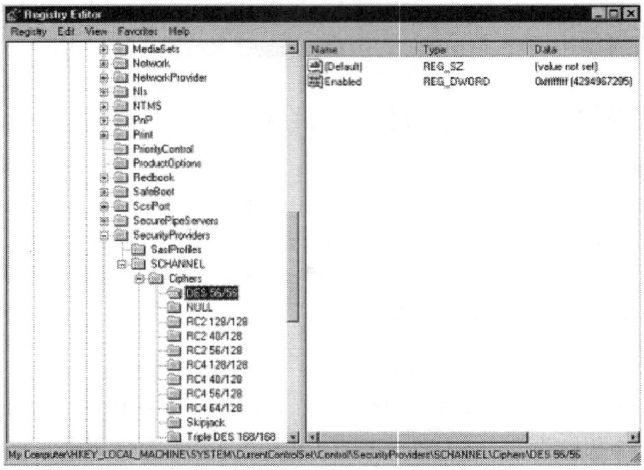

NT LAN Manager

Versions of Windows earlier than Windows 2000 used NTLM to provide network authentication. In a Windows Server 2003 environment, NTLM is used to communicate between two computers when one or both of them is running NT 4.0 or earlier. For example, NTLM authentication would be used in the following communications:

- Workstations or standalone servers that are participating in a workgroup instead of a domain used NTLM for authentication
- Windows 2000 or Windows XP Professional computers logging onto an NT 4.0 PDC or BDC
- A Windows NT 4.0 Workstation client authenticating to an NT 4.0, Windows 2000, or Windows Server 2003 domain controller
- Users in a Windows NT 4.0 domain that has a trust relationship with a Windows 2000 or Windows Server 2003 domain or forest

NTLM encrypts user logon information by applying a mathematical function (or *hash*) to the user's password. The NT 4.0 SAM database doesn't store the user's password; rather, it stores the value of the hash that is created when NTLM encrypts the password. In addition, the client machine actually applies the hash to the user's password *before* transmitting it to the domain controller; in this way, the user's password is never actually transmitted across the network. (And the transmission of the hash value itself is transmitted in an encrypted form, increasing the protocol's security even further.)

Using simple numbers for the sake of example, let's say that the NTLM hash multiplies the value of the password by 2. Let's say further that user *JSmith* has a password of 3. The conversation between *JSmith*, *JSmith's* workstation, and the domain controller will go something like this:

JSmith: My password is 3.

JSmith's workstation: Hey, Domain Controller! *JSmith* wants to log in.

Domain controller: Send me the hash value of *JSmith's* password.

JSmith's workstation: The hash value of her password is 6.

Domain controller: Okay, the number 6 matches the value that I have stored in the SAM database for the hash of *JSmith's* password. I'll let her log in.

The NTLM hash function only exists in Windows Server 2003 for backward compatibility with earlier operating systems; if your network environment is running exclusively Windows 2000 or later, you should implement a stronger form of authentication such as Kerberos. Using NTLM is preferable to sending authentication information using no encryption whatsoever, but NTLM has several known vulnerabilities that do not make it the best choice for network authentication if your operating system supports more advanced schemes.

Digest Authentication

Microsoft provides *digest authentication* as a means of authenticating Web applications that are running on IIS. Digest authentication uses the *Digest Access Protocol*, which is a simple challenge-response mechanism for applications that are using HTTP or Simple Authentication Security Layer (SASL)-based communications. When Microsoft Digest authenticates a client, it creates a *session key* that is stored on the Web server and used to authenticate subsequent authentication requests without needing to contact a domain controller for each individual authentication request. Similar to NTLM, digest authentication sends user credentials across the network as an encrypted hash so that the actual password information cannot be extracted in case a malicious attacker is attempting to "sniff" the network connection. (A *sniffer* is a device or software application that monitors network traffic for sensitive information, similar to a wiretap on a telephone.)

NOTE

SASL is a protocol developed by Carnegie Mellon University to provide application security for client/server applications.

Before implementing digest authentication on your IIS server, you need to make sure that the following requirements have been met:

- Clients who need to access a resource or application that's secured with digest authentication need to be using Internet Explorer 5 or later.

- The user attempting to log on to the IIS server as well as the IIS server itself need to be members of the same domain or need to belong to domains that are connected by a trust relationship.
- The authenticating users need a valid account stored in Active Directory on the domain controller.
- The domain that the IIS server belongs to must contain a domain controller running Windows 2000 or 2003. The IIS server itself also needs to be running Windows 2000 or later.
- Digest authentication requires user passwords to be stored in a reversibly encrypted format within Active Directory. You can establish this setting from the Account tab of the user's Properties sheet in Active Directory Users and Computers, or use a Group Policy to enable this feature for a large number of users. After changing this setting, your users need to change their passwords so that a reversibly encrypted hash can be created; the process is not retroactive.

Passport Authentication

If you've ever logged onto the MCP Secure Site at www.microsoft.com, you've probably already seen *Passport authentication* in action. Any business that wants to provide the convenience of single sign-on to its customers can license and use Passport authentication on its site. Passport authentication enables your company or client to deliver a convenient means for customers to access and transact business on a given site. Sites that rely on Passport authentication use a centralized Passport server to authenticate users, rather than hosting and maintaining their own proprietary authentication systems. Companies can also use Passport authentication to map sign-in names to information in a sales or customer database, which can offer Passport customers a more personalized Web experience through the use of targeted ads, content, and promotional information. Using .NET Passport can help your business increase its sales and advertising revenues through improved customer loyalty. As Microsoft Passport has gained acceptance, the Passport sign-on logo (shown in Figures 5.14 and 5.15) has begun to appear on more and more corporate and e-commerce Web sites.

Figure 5.14 Passport Sign-On Through www.ebay.com

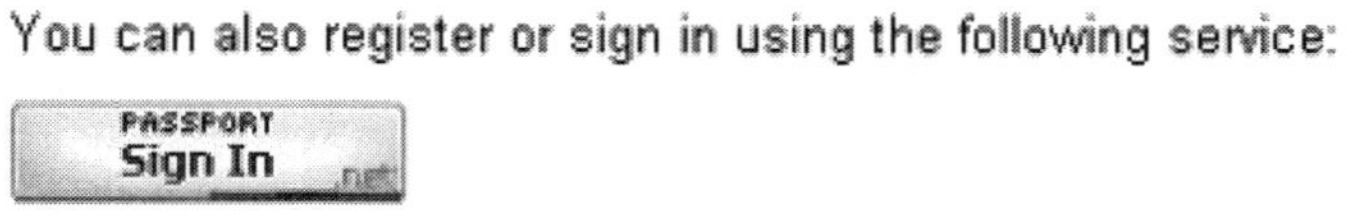

Figure 5.15 Passport Sign-On Through www.expedia.com

From a technical perspective, Passport authentication relies on standards-based Web technologies, including SSL encryptions, HTTP redirects, cookies, and symmetric key encryption. Because the technology utilized by Passport authentication is not proprietary, it is compatible with both Microsoft Internet Explorer *and* Netscape Navigator as well as some flavors of UNIX systems and browsers. The single sign-on service is similar to forms-based authentication that is common throughout the Internet; it simply extends the functionality of the sign-on features to work across a distributed set of participating sites.

Exam Warning

Both the Internet Explorer and Netscape Navigator browsers need to be at version 4 or higher in order to access sites using Passport authentication.

Head of the Class...

Passport's Advantages for Businesses

Microsoft introduced the .NET Passport service in 1999, and since then the system has become responsible for authenticating more than 200 million accounts. Many prominent businesses, including McAfee, eBay, NASDAQ, and Starbucks, have integrated .NET Passport into their Web authentication schemes. If you are considering integrating Passport authentication into your Web authentication strategy, here are some of the advantages:

- **Single sign-in** Allows your users to sign onto the Passport site once to access information from any participating Web site. This alleviates the frustration of registering at dozens of different sites and maintaining any number of different sets of logon credentials. The Passport service allows more than 200 million Passport users quick and easy access to your site.
- **The Kids Passport service** Provides tools that help your business comply with the legal provisions of the U.S. Children's Online Privacy Protection Act (COPPA). Your company can use the Passport service to conform with the legal aspects of collecting and using children's personal information and to customize your Web site to provide age-appropriate content.
- **Maintain control of your data** Since the Passport service is simply an authentication service, your customer information and data will still be

Continued

controlled in-house and are not shared with the Passport servers unless you configure your Web site to do so.

At the time of this writing, there are two fees for the use of Passport authentication: a US$10,000 fee paid by your company on an annual basis, and a periodic testing fee of US$1,500 per URL. The $10,000 is not URL specific and covers all URLs controlled by a single company. Payment of these fees entitles your company to unlimited use of the Passport authentication service for as many URLs as you have registered for periodic testing.

Understanding Passport Authentication Security

Microsoft has created several key features within Passport authentication to ensure that the security and privacy of your customers and users can be maintained at the highest possible level. Some of the security features employed by Passport authentication are as follows:

- The Web pages used to control the sign-in, sign-out, and registration functions are centrally hosted, rather than relying on the security mechanisms of each individual member site.
- All centrally hosted pages that are used to exchange usernames, passwords, or other credential information always use SSL encryption to transmit information.
- Passport authentication-enabled sites use encrypted cookies to allow customers to access several different sites without retyping their login information. However, an individual site can still opt to require users to return to the Passport sign-in screen when accessing their site for the first time.
- All cookie files related to Passport authentication use strong encryption. When you set up your site to use Passport, you receive a unique encryption key to ensure the privacy of your users' personal information.
- The central Passport servers transmit sign-in and profile information to your site in an encrypted fashion. You can then use this information to create local cookies, avoiding any further client redirection to the Passport servers.
- A Web site that participates in Passport authentication will never actually receive a member's password. Authentication information is transmitted via a cookie that contains encrypted timestamps that are created when the member first signs onto Passport. The Microsoft Passport sign-out function allows users to delete any Passport-related cookies that were created on their local machines during the time that they were logged onto Microsoft Passport.

- A participating Web site only communicates directly with the central Passport server to retrieve configuration files, which are then cached locally by the individual member server. All information that is exchanged between clients and the Passport servers takes places using HTTP redirects, cookies, and encrypted queries.

Internet Authentication Service

Beginning as early as the Option Pack add-on for NT 4.0, Microsoft has offered the Internet Authentication Service (IAS) as a Remote Authentication Dial-In User Service (RADIUS) server. The release of IAS offered with Windows Server 2003 expands and improves the existing IAS functionality and includes connection options for wireless clients and proxying to remote RADIUS servers. IAS is available in the Standard, Enterprise, and Datacenter Editions of Windows Server 2003 but not the Web Edition. Since it functions with a wide range of wireless, remote access, and VPN equipment, IAS can be used for everything from the smallest corporate remote access solution to managing the user base of a major ISP. The IAS can manage all aspects of the login process: directing the user authentication process, verifying a user's authorization to access various network resources, and collecting logging information to provide accountability for each user's logins and activity.

EXAM WARNING

Windows Server 2003 Standard Edition can only support a maximum of 50 RADIUS clients and two RADIUS server groupings. The Enterprise and Datacenter Editions of Windows Server 2003 allow you to configure an unlimited number of RADIUS clients and server groups.

IAS supports a variety of authentication methods that can meet the needs of most modern client platforms. In addition, you can add custom authentication methods to meet any specialized requirements of your network security policy. The default authentication methods supported by IAS are the password-based Point-to-Point Protocol (PPP) and the Extensible Authentication Protocol (EAP). By default, IAS supports two EAP protocols: EAP-MD5 and EAP-TLS. Supported PPP protocols include:

- Password Authentication Protocol (PAP)
- Challenge Handshake Authentication Protocol (CHAP)
- Microsoft Challenge Handshake Authentication Protocol (MS-CHAP)
- MS-CHAP version 2

Once a user has been authenticated, IAS can use a number of methods to verify that the authenticated user is authorized to access the service to which he or she is attempting to connect. As with authentication methods, you can use the software development kit

(SDK) to create custom authorization methods to meet your business needs. Authorization methods supported by IAS include the following:

- **Dialed Number Identification Service (DNIS)** DNIS bases its authorization decision on the phone number that the caller is using. As a cost-saving measure, for example, you might want to authorize only users within a local calling area to use a particular number.
- **Automatic Number Identification/Calling Line Identification (ANI/CLI)** ANI/CLI is the opposite of DNIS; it authorizes access based on the number that a user is calling *from*.
- **Guest authorization** Guest authorization allows access to an access point or dialup number without a username and password. This is becoming more common in airplane terminals, coffee shops, and other venues that provide a wireless access point to their clientele. To protect the access point in question, users connecting with guest authorization typically have a severely curtailed set of operations that they can perform—Web browsing only, for example.
- **Remote access policies** These are the most effective way to set authorization for Active Directory user accounts. Remote access policies can authorize network access based on any number of conditions such as group membership, time of day, or access number being used. Once a user has been authorized, you can also use remote access policies to mandate the level of encryption that remote access clients need to use in order to connect to your network resources, as well as setting any maximum time limits for a remote connection or inactivity timeout values. Packet filters can also control exactly which IP addresses, hosts, and/or port numbers the remote user is permitted to access while connected to your network.

New & Noteworthy...

New Features in Internet Authentication Service

IAS has been around in various incarnations since Windows NT 4.0, but it has several new features under Windows Server 2003 that make it an ideal solution for enterprise environments. Some of these new features are as follows:

- **RADIUS proxy** In addition to providing its own RADIUS authentication services, you can configure IAS to forward authentication requests to one or more external RADIUS servers. The external RADIUS server does not need to be another IAS server; as long as it is running an RFC-compliant RADIUS installation, the external server can be running any type of platform and operating system. IAS can forward these requests according to username, the IP address of the target RADIUS server, and other conditions as necessary. In a large, heterogeneous environment, IAS can be configured to differentiate between the RADIUS requests

Continued

that it should handle by itself and those that should be forwarded to external servers for processing.

- **Remote-RADIUS-to-Windows-User mapping** This new feature allows you to further segregate the authentication and authorization processes between two separate servers. For example, a user from another company can be authenticated on the RADIUS server belonging to his or her separate company while he or she will receive authorization to access your network through this policy setting on your IAS server.
- **Wireless access points** Support for Wireless APs to allow authentication and authorization for users with IEEE 802.1*x*-compliant wireless network hardware. IAS can authenticate wireless users through the Protected Extensible Authentication Protocol (PEAP), which offers security improvements over EAP.
- **SQL database support** IAS can log auditing information for better centralized data collection and reporting.
- **Network access quarantine control** This allows you to severely restrict the network access of remote clients until you can verify that they comply with any corporate security policies, such as mandatory antivirus protection or service pack installations. Once you have verified the compliance of these remote machines, you can remove them from quarantine and allow them access in accordance with your network's remote access policy.
- **Authenticated switching support** A network switch provides filtering and management of the physical packets transmitted over a LAN or WAN. To prevent unauthorized access to the network infrastructure, many newer switches require users to provide authentication before being allowed physical access to the network. Under Windows Server 2003, IAS can act as a RADIUS server to process the login requests from these advanced pieces of network hardware.

Using IAS for Dialup and VPN

The RADIUS protocol provided by the IAS service is a popular means of administering remote user access to a corporate network. For example, you can have your users dial a local telephone number for a regional ISP, then authenticate against your IAS server using a VPN client. If the remote user is in the same local calling area as your corporate network, you can integrate IAS with the familiar Routing and Remote Access feature to allow them to dial directly into a modem attached to the IAS server. IAS then uses RADIUS to forward the authentication and authorization request to the appropriate Active Directory domain.

In this section we cover the necessary steps to allow dialup access to your corporate network. For the sake of the exercises in this section, we assume that your users are dialing directly into a remote access server that is running IAS. In Exercise 5.05, we cover the necessary steps to install and configure IAS on a domain controller in your Windows Server 2003 domain.

Exam Warning

Microsoft recommends that you configure at least two IAS servers within your Active Directory environment to provide fault tolerance for your dialup and VPN authentication needs. If you have only one server configured and the machine hosting IAS becomes unavailable, dialup and VPN clients will not be able to connect until you return the machine to service. By using two servers, you can configure your remote access clients with the information for both, allowing them to automatically fail over to the secondary IAS server if the primary one fails.

Exercise 5.05

Configuring IAS on a Domain Controller

1. From the Windows Server 2003 desktop, open the Control Panel by clicking **Start | Programs | Control Panel**. Double-click **Add/Remove Programs**.
2. Click **Add/Remove Windows Components**. When the Windows Components Wizard appears, click **Networking Services**, and then click **Details**. You'll see the screen shown in Figure 5.16.

Figure 5.16 Installing the Internet Authorization Service

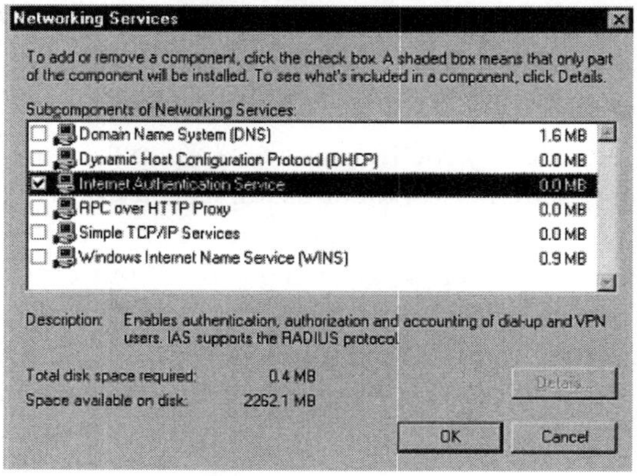

3. Place a check mark next to **Internet Authentication Service** and then click **OK**.
4. Click **Next** to begin the installation. Insert the Windows Server 2003 CD if prompted. Click **Finish** and **Close** when the installation is complete.

   Now that you've installed the Internet Authorization Service, you need to register the IAS server within Active Directory. (This process is similar to authorizing a newly created DHCP server.) Registering the IAS server allows it to access the user accounts within the Active Directory domain.
5. Click **Start | Programs | Administrative Tools | Internet Authentication Service**. You'll see the screen shown in Figure 5.17.

Figure 5.17 The IAS Administrative Console

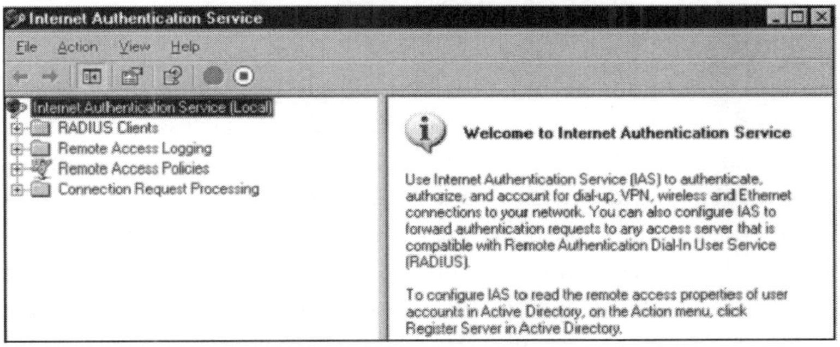

6. Right-click the **Internet Authentication Service** icon and click **Register Server in Active Directory**.
7. Click **OK** at the next screen, shown in Figure 5.18. This step allows IAS to read the dial-in properties for the users in your domain.

Figure 5.18 Configuring Permissions for IAS

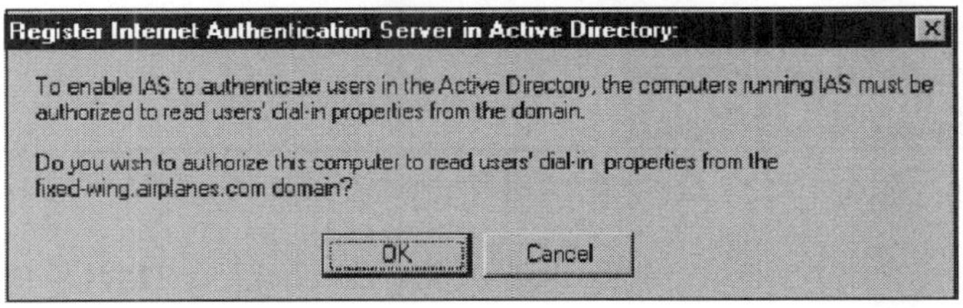

Test Day Tip

You can also register an IAS server using the *netsh* command-line utility. To add an IAS server with the DNS name of dc1.airplanes.com, use the following syntax: *netsh ras add registeredserver dc1.airplanes.com.*

Once you've installed and authorized an IAS server, you can use the Internet Authentication Service icon in the Administrative Tools folder to configure logging as well as to specify which UDP port that IAS will use to transmit logging information. To administer the IAS server, click **Start** | **Programs** | **Administrative Tools** | **Internet Authentication Service**. Next you need to create remote access policies to enable your Active Directory users to access your network through the IAS server.

Creating Remote Access Policies

Similarly to using Windows 2000, you can control remote access capabilities of users and groups via a remote access policy. You can have multiple policies associated with various users and groups, and each policy can allow or deny remote access to the network based on a number of factors such as date and time, Active Directory group membership, connection type (modem versus VPN), and the like. Your goal as an administrator is to create remote access policies that reflect the usage needs of your company or clients. If your remote access capabilities are limited to three dialup modem connections, for example, you might want to restrict the use of these modems during the day to those users who have a specific need for it. For example, you might have a small number of regional sales directors who work from various locations and need to access reporting data during the day.

In Exercise 5.06, we create a remote access policy that limits remote access connections on your network to members of the SalesVP group between the hours of 8:00 A.M. and 5:00 P.M., Monday through Friday. Creating this policy will allow your company's sales vice presidents to access the information they need rather than allowing extraneous remote access connections to tie up your limited resources. To perform this exercise you should create a security group named SalesVP prior to starting.

Exercise 5.06

Creating a Remote Access Policy

1. Open the IAS administration utility by clicking **Start** | **Programs** | **Administrative Tools** | **Internet Authentication Service**.
2. Right-click **Remote Access Policies** and select **New Remote Access Policy**. Click **Next** to bypass the initial screen in the wizard. You'll see the screen shown in Figure 5.19. Click **Use the wizard to set up a typ-**

Figure 5.19 Creating a Remote Access Policy

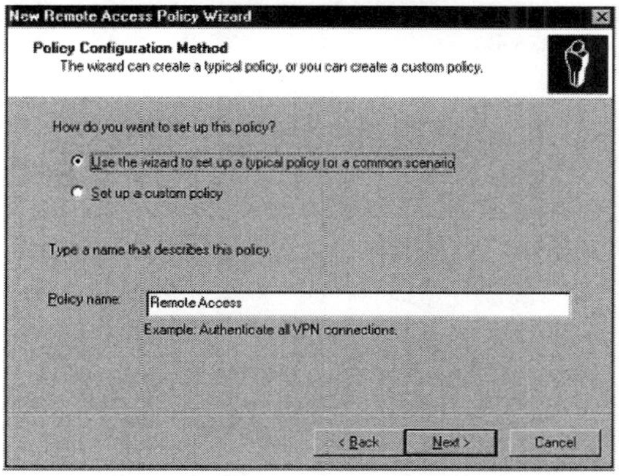

ical policy for a common scenario, enter a name to describe the policy, and then click **Next**.

3. From the **Access method** screen, select the access method that this policy will apply to. You can select one of the following methods:
    - VPN access
    - Dialup access
    - Wireless access
    - Ethernet
4. For the purpose of this example, select **Dial-Up Access**, then click **Next**.
5. Decide whether to grant remote access permission on a user or group level. Using groups provides easier and more efficient administration because you can group users with common remote access needs and add or remove users from the group as necessary. Select **Group**, and then select the **SalesVP** group. Click **Next** to continue.
6. On the screen shown in Figure 5.20, select the authentication method that this remote access policy will use. If your clients are using software that can handle the higher encryption levels, you can disable weaker encryption schemes such as CHAP to prevent users from connecting with a lower level of encryption.
7. Click **Next** to continue. On the next screen, select the levels of encryption that your users can employ to connect to the IAS server. You can select an encryption level of 40-, 56-, or 128-bit encryption or choose not to mandate encryption at all. Click **Next** and then click **Finish** to set these standard policy settings.

Figure 5.20 Remote Access Authentication Methods

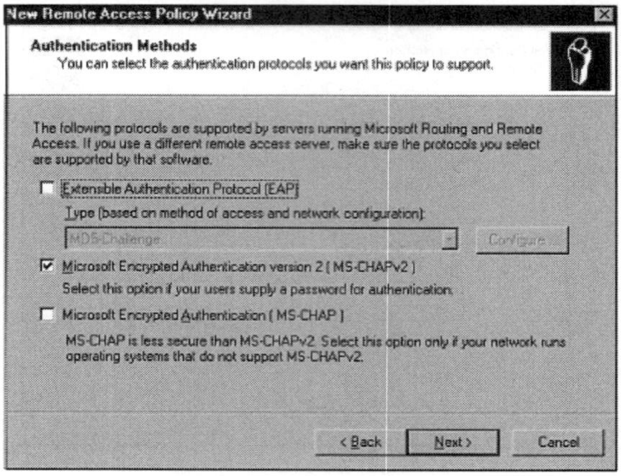

8. Next you'll want to further modify the remote policy so that users can only connect to your dialup modems between 8:00 A.M. and 5:00 P.M., Monday through Friday. Right-click the remote access policy that you just created, and select **Properties**.
9. Click **Add** to include another condition to this policy, adding new conditions one at a time. Figure 5.21 illustrates the various conditions that you can use to grant or deny remote access to your clients.

Figure 5.21 Remote Access Policy Conditions

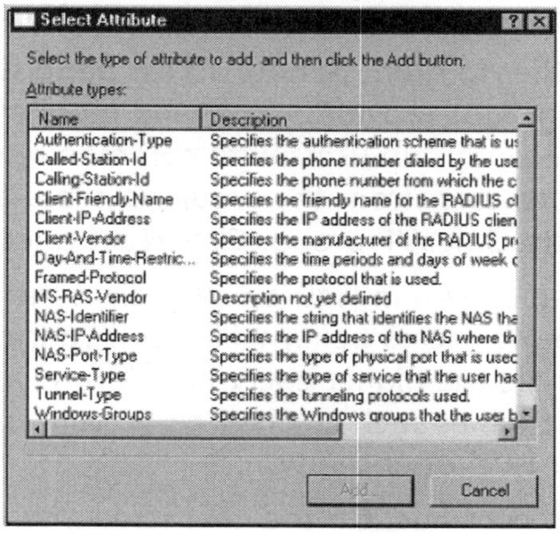

The final step in enabling remote access via IAS is to configure your Active Directory users or groups to use the remote access policy that you just created. To configure the SalesVP group to use the remote access policy, follow these steps:

10. In Active Directory Users and Computers, right-click the **SalesVP** group, and select **Properties**.

11. Click the **Remote Access** tab, and select **Click on Control Access Through Remote Access Policy**. Click **OK**, repeating this step for any other users or groups who require the remote access policy.

Using IAS for Wireless Access

Windows Server 2003 has made it a relatively straightforward matter to enable a Wireless AP to interact with IAS. Wireless clients can authenticate against an IAS server using smart cards, certificates, or a username/password combination. The actual sequence of events when a wireless device requests access to your wired network will proceed in this manner:

1. When a wireless client comes within range of a Wireless AP, the Wireless AP requests authentication information from the client.
2. The client sends its authentication information to the Wireless AP, which forwards the login request to the RADIUS server (in this case, IAS).
3. If the login information is valid, IAS transmits an encrypted authentication key to the Wireless AP.
4. The Wireless AP uses this encrypted key to establish an authenticated session with the wireless client.

To allow wireless clients to access your network, you need to perform two steps: create a remote access policy that allows wireless connectivity, and add your Wireless APs as RADIUS clients on the IAS server so that they can forward login information to IAS for processing. (You'll configure your Wireless AP as a RADIUS client according to the instructions provided by the Wireless AP manufacturer.) A remote access policy for wireless users should contain the following information:

- **Access method** Wireless access
- **User or group** Group, specifying the WirelessUsers group, for example
- **Authentication methods** Smart card or other certificate
- **Policy encryption level** Strongest encryption; disable all other possible encryption levels
- **Permission** Grant remote access permission

Other Uses for IAS

You can use IAS in many different situations to provide various types of remote access for your network users. Besides the uses we've already covered, you can also configure IAS to handle the following:

- **Authenticating switches** You can use remote access policies to allow IAS to act as a RADIUS server for Ethernet switches that have the ability to authenticate to a central server. You can enforce this type of authentication through the use of remote access policies to ensure that no "rogue" or unauthorized switches are brought online within your network infrastructure.
- **Outsourcing remote access connections** IAS allows an organization to outsource its remote access infrastructure to a third-party ISP. In this situation, a user connects to an ISP's dialup, but the user's login credentials are forwarded to your corporate IAS server for processing; your IAS server will also handle all logging and usage tracking for your remote users. This system can provide a great deal of cost savings for an organization because it can utilize the ISP's existing network infrastructure, rather than creating its own network of routers, access points, and WAN links. IAS can also provide a similar service for outsourcing wireless access, in which a third party vendor's Wireless AP forwards the user's authentication information to your IAS server for processing.

Creating a User Authorization Strategy

Windows Server 2003 offers a wide array of options for user authentication and authorization, allowing you to design a strategy to meet all your end users' needs. Rather than being locked into a single technology or protocol, you can mix and match the solutions presented in this section to best meet the needs of your users and organization. When creating a user authorization strategy, you need to keep a few key points in mind:

1. ***Who* are your users?** More specifically, what type of computing platforms are they using? If you are using Windows Server 2003 operating systems and the latest Microsoft clients for across your entire enterprise, you can mandate the highest levels of Kerberos v5 encryption. At that point you can increase the security level of your network by disabling all earlier forms of encryption, since they won't be in use on your network. If, however, you are supporting down-level clients such as Windows NT 4.0 Server or Workstation, you need to make allowances for these users to transmit their information using NTLM or NTLMv2 encryption.
2. ***Where* are your users located?** If your company operates only in a single location, you can use firewall technologies to render your network resources inaccessible to the outside world. In all likelihood, however, you'll need to provide some mechanism for remote access, either for traveling users or for customers connecting via a Web browser. In this case you'll want to select the highest level of encryption that

can be handled by your remote users and clients. This is a simpler matter for remote users because you can mandate a corporate software policy dictating that everyone uses the most recent version of Internet Explorer. Allowing for customer access creates a more complex environment, since you obviously cannot control which browsers or platforms your clients will be using. Implementing an authentication method such as digest authentication requires all users to have Internet Explorer 5 or better, but most modern Web browsers, regardless of software vendor, provide support for other technologies such as SSL encryption.

Educating Users

The more highly publicized network security incidents always center on a technical flaw—an overlooked patch that led to a global DoS attack, a flaw that led to the worldwide propagation of an e-mail virus, or the like—but many network intrusions are caused by a lack of knowledge among corporate employees. For this reason, user education is a critical component of any security plan. Make sure that your users understand the potential dangers of sharing their login credentials with anyone else or leaving that information in a location where others could take note of it—the famed "password on a sticky note" cautionary tale in action. Your users will be far more likely to cooperate and comply with corporate security standards if they understand the reasons behind them and the damage that they could cause by ignoring security measures.

Security education should not only be thorough, it should also be repetitive. It is not enough to simply provide security information at a new-employee orientation and never mention it again. As a network administrator, you should take steps to make sure that security awareness remains a part of your users' daily lives. You can promote this awareness through the simplest of measures: including a paragraph in an employee newsletter, sending bulletins to the user base when a new virus is becoming a threat, and the like. (At the same time, though, you should avoid sending out so much information that your users become overwhelmed by it; a security bulletin that no one reads is no more useful than one that you don't send at all.) By combining user education with technical measures such as password policies and strong network authentication, you will be well on your way to creating multiple layers of protection for your network and the data it contains.

EXAM 70-296 OBJECTIVE 8.1.1

Using Smart Cards

Smart cards provide a portable method of providing security on a network for such tasks as client authentication and securing user data. In this section, we provide an overview of smart card technology as well as the steps involved in utilizing smart cards on your Windows Server 2003 network. Smart card implementations rely in part on the Certification Authority service, so we'll spend some time discussing the use of certificates within Windows Server 2003 as well.

Support for smart cards is a key feature within the Windows Server 2003 family. Smart cards provide tamper-resistant, safe storage for protecting your users' private keys, which are used to encrypt and decrypt data, as well as other forms of your users' personal information. Smart cards also isolate security processes from the rest of the computer, providing heightened security because authentication operations are performed on the smart card, which is not always present at the computer. Finally, smart cards provide your users with a portable means of transmitting their logon credentials and other private information, regardless of their location.

Configuring & Implementing...

Smart Cards in Action

The use of smart cards for authentication and data encryption is a new but growing trend within enterprise networks. Not only can the cards themselves be used for network authentication; they can be imprinted with employee information so that they can also serve as identification badges. A good illustration of this type of implementation is the RSA SecurID Card from www.rsasecurity.com, shown in Figure 5.22.The RSA devices use an internal clock to generate a new PIN every 60 seconds, creating a highly secure authentication method that is as portable and convenient as a common credit card or automated teller machine (ATM) card.

Figure 5.22 RSA SecurID Card

In some cases, smart card technology can also be integrated into an existing employee identification system by imprinting employee information onto a smart card. Obviously, special care needs to be taken in such implementations so that the smart card components do not become damaged through everyday use. The advantage to this type of smart card rollout is that users do not have to remember to carry five different pieces of ID with them; the ID card that gets them in the office door is the same one that logs them onto their computers. You'll also see smart cards that are configured as smaller "fobs," or tags, that can be stored on a keychain, and some vendors have even integrated smart card technology into handheld devices and cell phones. The smart card readers themselves can be standalone readers, or else a smart card "fob" can be inserted directly into a workstation's USB port.

Using a smart card for network logons provides extremely strong authentication because it requires two authentication factors: something the user *knows* (the PIN) along with something the user *has* (the smart card itself). This system provides stronger authentication than a password alone, since a malicious user would need to have access to both the smart card and the PIN in order to impersonate a legitimate user. It's also difficult for an attacker to perform a smart card attack undetected, because the user would notice that his or her smart card was physically missing.

When to Use Smart Cards

Smart cards can provide security solutions for a number of business and technical processes within your organization. When deciding whether or not to add smart cards to a given system, you'll need to weigh the security benefits against the costs of deployment, both in terms of hardware costs and ongoing support. Smart cards can secure any of the following processes within your business:

- Using a smart card for *interactive user logons* provides security and encryption for all logon credentials. Relying on smart cards instead of passwords means that you will not need to worry about the quality and strength of user passwords.
- Requiring smart cards for *remote access logons* prevents attackers from using dialup or Internet connections to compromise your network, even if they gain physical access to a remote laptop or home computer.
- *Administrator logons* are ideal candidates for smart card authentication, since they have the potential to wreak far more havoc on a network installation than an account belonging to a less powerful network user. By requiring your administrators to use smart cards, you can greatly reduce the possibility that an attacker can gain administrative access to your network. However, keep in mind that some administrative tasks are not suited for smart card logons; as such, your administrators should have the option of logging on with a username/password combination when necessary.
- *Digital signing and encryption* of private user information such as e-mail and other confidential files are enabled with smart cards.

Implementing Smart Cards

Utilizing smart cards on your network involves a number of preparatory steps that we discuss in this section. First we look at the steps involved in establishing a CA on your network, as well as discussing the related concepts and terminology. Next we examine the process of establishing security permissions for users and administrators to request certificates to use with their smart card and smart card readers. Finally we walk step by step through the process of setting up a smart card enrollment station to issue certificates to your end users as well as the actual procedure to issue a smart card certificate to a user on your network. We end this section with some best practices for providing technical support for the smart card users on your network.

PKI and Certificate Authorities

Smart card authentication relies on *certificates* to control which users can access the network using their smart cards. As you learned in Chapter 4, certificates are digitally signed statements that verify the identity of a person, device, or service. Certificates can be used for a wide variety of functions, including Web authentication, securing e-mail, verifying application code validity, and allowing for smart card authentication. The machine that issues certificates is referred to as a *certificate authority*, and the person or device that receives the certificate is referred to as the *subject* of the certificate. Certificates typically contain the following information:

- The subject's public key value
- Any identifying information, such as the username or e-mail address
- The length of time that the certificate will be considered valid
- Identifier information for the company/server that issued the certificate
- The digital signature of the issuer, which attests to the validity of the subject's public key and their identifying information

Every certificate also contains *valid from* and *valid to* dates to prevent potential misuse stemming from employee turnover and the like. Once a certificate has expired, the user needs to obtain a new certificate in order to continue to access the associated network resources. Certificate authorities also maintain a certificate revocation list that can be used in case a certificate needs to be cancelled before its regular expiration date.

Certificates are perhaps most useful to establish *mutual authentication* between two entities—users, computers, devices, and so on—who need to authenticate to one another and exchange information with a high level of confidence that each entity is who or what it claims to be. Because of this need, many companies install their own certificate authorities and issue certificates to their internal users and devices in order to heighten the security of their network environment. This provides the assurance not only that the user is who they say they are, but it assures the user that his or her session is not being misdirected to a "phony" server being used to intercept sensitive information.

Support for smart cards is a key feature of the PKI that's included with Windows Server 2003. You need to take several steps in order to prepare your Windows Server 2003 network to allow your company to use smart card devices. The first step is to install Certificate Services on at least one of your Windows Server 2003 servers. Refer to Chapter 4 for details and instructions on installing Certificate Services.

Once you've established your server as a certificate authority, you need to create three types of *certificate templates* to allow for smart card use on your network. Just like a document template in business application software such as Microsoft Word, a certificate template allows multiple certificates to be created using the same basic settings. Templates are critical for this purpose because they ensure that all certificates issued will contain the same security information. The security templates that you need to create are:

- **Enrollment Agent Certificate** Allows a Windows Server 2003 machine to act as an enrollment station, creating certificates on behalf of smart card users who need to access the network.
- The **Smart Card Logon Certificate** Allows your users to authenticate to the network using a smart card inserted into a smart card reader.
- **Smart Card User Certificates** Not covered extensively in this section; provide the capability to secure e-mail once a user has been authenticated.

You'll be prompted to create these certificate templates automatically the first time that you open the Certificate Template MMC console. Click **Start | Run**, then type **certtmpl.msc** and click **OK**. When you're prompted to install new certificate templates, click **OK**. This step also upgrades any existing templates on your server if the machine was functioning as a CA under a previous version of Windows.

Setting Security Permissions

In order to implement PKI certificates, administrators and users need the appropriate permissions for the certificate templates that are installed on the certificate authority. You can grant, edit, or remove these permissions in the Certificate Templates MMC snap-in. In order to edit these permissions, you need to be a member of the Enterprise Admins group or the Domain Admins group in the forest root domain. To manage permissions on your security templates, do the following:

1. Open the Certificate Templates MMC console by clicking **Start | Run**, then typing **certtmpl.msc** and clicking **OK**. You'll see the screen shown in Figure 5.23.

Figure 5.23 Managing Certificate Templates

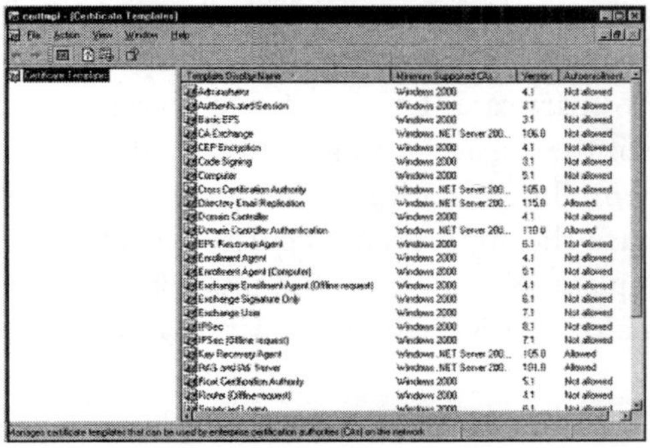

2. Right-click the certificate template whose permissions you need to change, and select **Properties**.
3. On the **Security** tab shown in Figure 5.24, add the users and groups who will need to request certificates based on this template. Under the **Allow** column, place a check mark next to the **Read** and **Enroll** permissions. Click **OK** when you've set the appropriate permissions for all necessary users and groups.

Figure 5.24 Setting Permissions for Certificate Templates

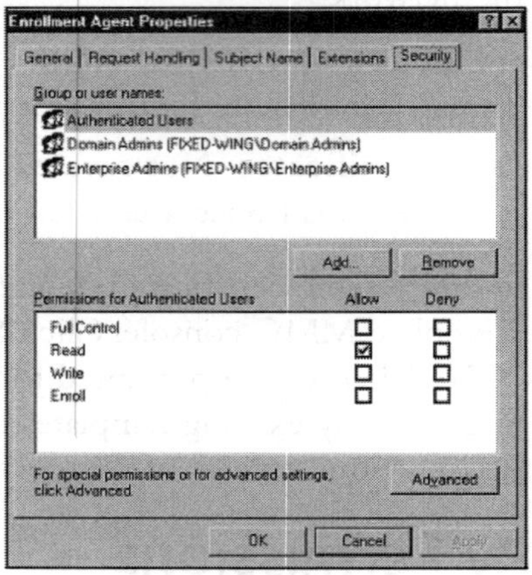

Test Day Tip

If you want your users to be able to retrieve and renew their certificates without any intervention on their part, you'll also need to allow the Autoenroll permission within the Certificate Templates console.

Enrollment Stations

To distribute certificates and keys to your users, the certificate server that's included with Windows Server 2003 includes a *smart card enrollment station*. The enrollment station allows an administrator to request a smart card certificate on a user's behalf so that it can be preinstalled onto the user's smart card. The certificate server signs the certificate request that's generated on behalf of the smart card user. Before your users can request certificates, you need to prepare the enrollment station to generate certificates for their use. A smart card administrator must have the appropriate security permissions to administer the Enrollment Agent certificate template, as detailed in the preceding section. Any machine running Windows XP or Windows Server 2003 can act as an enrollment station.

Issuing Enrollment Agent certificates

To prepare your certification authority to issue smart card certificates, you'll first need to prepare the Enrollment Agent certificate. Before you begin, make sure that your user account has been granted the **Read** and **Enroll** permissions, as discussed in the preceding section. To create an Enrollment Agent certificate, follow the steps included here.

1. Open the Certificate Authority snap-in by clicking **Start | Programs | Administrative Tools | Certification Authority**.
2. In the console tree, navigate to **Certificate Authority |** ***ComputerName*** **| Certificate Templates**.
3. From the **Action** menu, click **New | Certificate to Issue**. You'll see the screen shown in Figure 5.25.

Figure 5.25 Issuing a Certificate Template

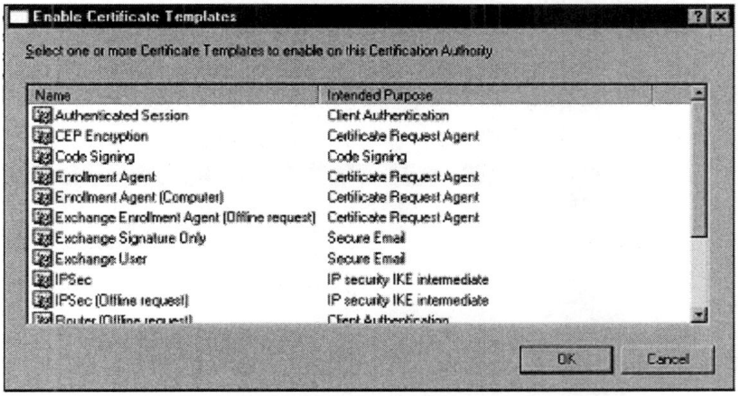

4. Select the **Enrollment Agent** template, and click **OK**.
5. Return to the **Action** menu, and select **New | Certificate to Issue**. Select one of the following options:

   - To create certificates that will only be valid for user authorization, select the **Smart Card Logon** certificate template, and click **OK**.
   - For certificates that can be used both for logon and to encrypt user information such as e-mail, click the **Smart Card User** certificate template, then click **OK**.

Once you've created the Enrollment Agent certificate, anyone with access to that certificate can generate a smart card on behalf of all users in your organization. The resulting smart card could then be used to log on to the network and impersonate the real user. Because of the capabilities of this certificate, you need to maintain strict controls over who has access to them.

Requesting an Enrollment Agent Certificate

In Exercise 5.07, we prepare a Windows Server 2003 machine to act as a smart cart enrollment station. Be sure that the user account you're using to log on has been granted the Read and Enroll permissions for the Enrollment Agent certificate template.

EXERCISE 5.07

CREATING A SMART CARD CERTIFICATE ENROLLMENT STATION

1. Log onto the machine as the user who will be installing the certificates.
2. Create a blank MMC console by clicking **Start | Run**, then type **mmc** and click **OK**.
3. From the console window, click **File | Add/Remove Snap-in**, then select **Add**.
4. Double-click the **Certificates** snap-in. Click **Close** and then click **OK**. You'll see the Certificates snap-in shown in Figure 5.26.

Figure 5.26 The Certificates Management Console

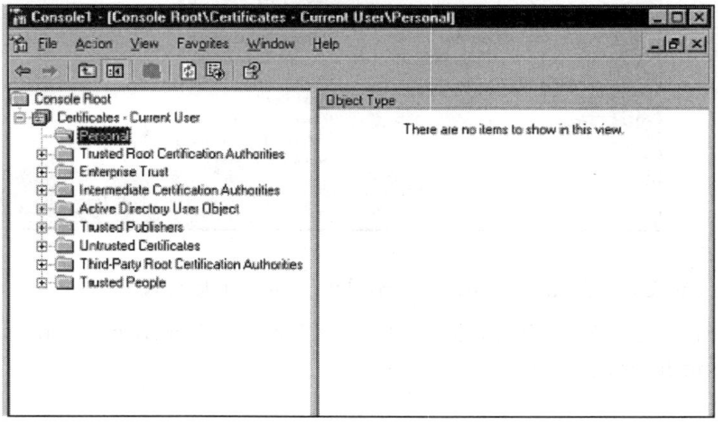

5. In the right-hand pane, click **Certificates | Current User | Personal**.
6. Click **Action | All Tasks**, and then select Request New Certificate. Click **Next** to bypass the Welcome screen.
7. Select the Enrollment Agent certificate template and enter a description for the certificate, in this case **Smart Card Enrollment** Certificate. Click **Next** to continue.
8. Click **Finish** to complete the installation of the enrollment agent.

Enrolling Users

The process of setting up your company's employees to use smart cards includes hardware, software, and administrative considerations. On the hardware side, you need to purchase and install smart card readers for all your users' workstations. Assuming that the readers are Plug-and-Play compatible, the hardware installation process should be fairly uncomplicated. Once the necessary hardware is in place, you'll then use the Enrollment Station to install smart card logon or user certificates for each user's smart card as well as setting initial PINs for them to use. Along with these technical issues, you will also be required to create and document policies regarding identification requirements to receive a smart card or reset a forgotten PIN. Finally, you'll need to train your users on the new procedure to log onto a smart card-protected workstation, since the familiar **Ctrl + Alt + Del** key sequence will be a thing of the past.

Installing a Smart Card Reader

Most smart card readers are Plug-and-Play compatible under the Windows Server 2003 software family, so their actual installation is relatively straightforward. If you're using a reader that is not Plug-and-Play compatible or that has not been tested by Microsoft, you need to obtain installation instructions from the card reader's manufacturer. As of this writing, the smart card readers listed in Table 5.1 are supported by Windows XP and Windows Server 2003. The corresponding device drivers will be installed on the workstation or server when the card reader has been detected by the operating system.

Table 5.1 Supported Smart Card Readers Under Windows Server 2003

Brand	Smart Card Reader	Interface	Device Driver
American Express	GCR435	USB	Grclass.sys
Bull	SmarTLP3	Serial	Bulltlp3.sys
Compaq	Serial reader	Serial	grserial.sys
Gemplus	GCR410P	Serial	Grserial.sys
Gemplus	GPR400	PCMCIA	Gpr400.sys
Gemplus	GemPC430	USB	Grclass.sys
Hewlett-Packard	ProtectTools	Serial	Scr111.sys
Litronic	220P	Serial	Lit220p.sys
Schlumberger	Reflex 20	PCMCIA	Pscr.sys
Schlumberger	Reflex 72	Serial	Scmstcs.sys
Schlumberger	Reflex Lite	Serial	Scr111.sys
SCM Microsystems	SCR111	Serial	Scr111.sys
SCM Microsystems	SCR200	Serial	Scmstcs.sys
SCM Microsystems	SCR120	PCMCIA	Pscr.sys

Continued

Table 5.1 Supported Smart Card Readers Under Windows Server 2003

Brand	Smart Card Reader	Interface	Device Driver
SCM Microsystems	SCR300	USB	Stcusb.sys
Systemneeds	External	Serial	Scr111.sys
Omnikey AG	2010	Serial	Sccmn50m.sys
Omnikey AG	2020	USB	Sccmusbm.sys
Omnikey AG	4000	PCMCIA	Cmbp0wdm.sys

To install a smart card reader on your computer, simply attach the reader to an available port, either serial or USB, or insert the reader into an available PCMCIA slot on a laptop. If the driver for the reader is preinstalled in Windows Server 2003, the installation will take place automatically. Otherwise, the Add Hardware wizard will prompt you for the installation disk from the card reader manufacturer.

EXAM WARNING

If a smart card reader is attached to a serial port, you need to reboot the machine before Windows will detect the device and install the appropriate driver.

Issuing Smart Card Certificates

Once you've established the appropriate security for the certificate templates and installed smart card readers on your users' workstations, you can begin the process of issuing the smart card certificates that your users need to access the network. This enrollment process must be a controlled procedure. In much the same way that employee access cards are monitored to ensure that unidentified persons do not gain physical access to your facility, smart card certificates need to be monitored to ensure that only authorized users can view network resources. In Exercise 5.08, we use the Web enrollment application to set up a smart card with a logon certificate.

EXERCISE 5.08

SETTING UP A SMART CARD FOR USER LOGON

1. Log onto your workstation with a user account that has rights to the Enrollment Agent Certificate template in the domain where the user's account is located.
2. Open **Internet Explorer**, and browse to **http://servername/certsrv**, where *servername* is the name of the CA on your network.

3. Click **Request a certificate**, then click **Advanced Certificate Request**. You need to choose one of the following options:
   - A **Smart Card Logon** certificate if you want to issue a certificate that will only be valid for authenticating to the Windows domain
   - A **Smart Card User** certificate will allow the user to secure e-mail and personal information as well as logging onto the Windows Server 2003 domain
4. Under **Certificate Authority**, select the name of the CA for your domain. If there are multiple CAs in your domain, click the one that you want to issue the smart card certificate.
5. For **Cryptographic Service Provider**, select the CSP of the smart card's manufacturer. This choice is specific to the smart card hardware; consult the manufacturer's documentation if you are uncertain.
6. In **Administrator Signing Certificate**, select the Enrollment Agent certificate that will sign the certificate enrollment request. Click **Next** to continue.
7. On the User to Enroll screen, click **Select User** to browse to the user account for which you are creating the smart card certificate. Click **Enroll** to create a certificate for this user.
8. You'll be prompted to insert the user's smart card into the reader on your system. When you click **OK** to proceed, you'll be prompted to set an initial PIN for the card.
9. If another user has previously used the smart card that you're preparing, a message will appear indicating that another certificate already exists on the card. Click **Yes** to replace the existing certificate with the one you just created.
10. On the final screen, you have the option to either view the certificate you just created or begin a new certificate request.
11. Close your browser when you've finished creating certificate requests so that no extraneous certificates can be created if you walk away from the enrollment station.

Assigning Smart Cards

Once you've preconfigured your users' smart cards, you need to establish guidelines defining how cards are assigned to users who require them. This part of your smart card deployment plan is more procedural than technical, because you need to determine acceptable policies and service-level agreements for your smart cards and smart card readers. For example, what type of identification will you require in order for a user to obtain a smart card? Even if yours is a small enough organization that you recognize all your users on sight, you should still record information from a driver's license or another piece of photo identification for auditing purposes.

Another set of issues revolves around your users' PINs. How many unsuccessful logon attempts will you allow before locking out a smart card? Although this number will vary according to your individual business requirements, three or four PIN entry attempts are usually more than sufficient. Next you need to decide whether you will allow users to reset their own PINs or if they'll need to provide personal information to security or help desk personnel to have them reset by the IT staff. The former option is more convenient for your user base, but that convenience will come at the expense of potential security liabilities. If user PINs need to be reset by the IT staff, decide what type of information users need to present in order to verify their identities. Document all applicable security policies and distribute them to your administration and security personnel, and make sure that your users are aware of these policies *before* they take possession of their smart cards.

Logon Procedures

To log on to a computer using a smart card, your users no longer need to enter the **Ctrl + Alt + Del** key combination. Rather, they simply insert the smart card into the smart card reader, at which point they'll be prompted to enter their PINs. Once the PIN is accepted, the user has access to all local and network resources to which the user's Active Directory user account has been granted permissions.

TEST DAY TIP

When using Microsoft's built-in software, smart card logons only work on computers that are attached to a domain. A machine that uses a standalone or workgroup configuration cannot use smart cards for authentication.

Revoking Smart Cards

Along with creating policies for issuing and configuring smart cards, you should consider how your organization will handle revoking the smart card of an employee who resigns or is terminated. To be successful, this decision should be viewed as a joint effort between your company's administrative staff, such as payroll and human resources, and the IT department.

Just as an employee needs to return ID badges and keys as part of the exit process, they should also be required to return their smart cards to the company. Whether the employee exits the company in a graceful manner or not, you should add the employee's smart card certificate(s) to your CA's CRL at the same time that you disable or delete the employee's other logon IDs and credentials. Depending on the manufacturer of the smart card, you might have an option to physically disable the smart card itself on the basis of a serial number or other unique identifier.

Planning for Smart Card Support

Like any device or technology used to enhance network security, smart cards require you to make plans to educate your users on how to use them as well as providing administrative tools to support their ongoing use. First, make sure that your users understand the purpose of deploying smart cards; you'll receive a much better response if they comprehend the importance of the added security, rather than if they're simply handed a smart card and told to use it. Emphasize that the smart card is a valuable resource to protect the company and its assets, rather than simply another corporate procedure designed to annoy employees or waste their time. They should know whom they should call for help and technical support if this is different from their usual support contacts, as well as what to do if their card is lost or stolen. Maintain a printed version of this information, and distribute it to your users when they receive their smart cards. You can also publish this information on your corporate intranet, if you have one. When orienting your users to the use of smart cards, make sure that you cover the following key points:

- **Protect the external smart card chip** If the chip itself becomes scratched, dented, or otherwise damaged, the smart card reader might not be able to read the data on the chip. (This is similar to the magnetic strip on a credit card or an ATM card.)
- **Do not bend the card** Bending the card can destroy the card's internal components. This can extend to something as simple as a user putting the smart card in a back pocket, because they might sit on the card and break its internal components.
- **Avoid exposing the card to extreme temperatures** Leaving a smart card on the dashboard of a car on a hot day can melt or warp the card; extremes of cold can make the card brittle and cause it to break.
- **Keep the smart card away from magnetic sources** Avoid magnetic sources such as credit cards and scanners at retail stores.
- **Keep the smart card away from young children and pets** Smart cards present a potential swallowing or choking hazard.

Along with user education, there are several settings within Active Directory Group Policy that can simplify the administration of smart cards on your network. Some of these, such as account lockout policies and restricted login times, will impact users by default if they rely on their smart cards for domain logons. Other policy settings are specific to managing smart cards on your network. Within Group Policy, you can enable the following settings:

- **Smart card required for interactive logon** This setting prevents a user account from logging onto the local computer by presenting a username/password combination; the user will only be able to authenticate by using a smart card. This provides strict security for your users; however, you should plan an alternate means of authentication in case your smart card implementation becomes unavailable for any reason. This policy is not appropriate for users who need to perform administrative tasks such as installing Active Directory on a server or joining computers to a Windows Server 2003 domain.

Exam Warning

This policy only applies to interactive and network logons. Remote access logons are managed by separate policies on the remote access server, as described in a previous section.

- **On smart card removal** Allows you to mandate that when a user removes his smart card from the reader, his session is either logged off or locked to prevent him from leaving an active session running when he walks away. User education is critical if you select the forced logoff option, because users need to make sure that they've saved changes to any of their documents and files before they remove their smart cards.
- **Do not allow smart card device redirection** Prevents your users from using smart cards to log onto a Terminal Services session. Set this policy if you're concerned about conserving network resources associated with your Terminal Server environment.
- **Account lockout threshold** Although this setting is not specific to smart cards, smart card PINs are more susceptible to password attacks, so your lockout threshold settings should be adjusted accordingly.

From an administrative standpoint, there are several other important considerations in creating a support structure for smart card use. You need to identify the people within your organization who will be able to perform security-related tasks such as resetting PINs or distributing temporary cards to replace those that are lost or forgotten. You also need to decide how you'll handle personnel changes such as name and employment status as well as any special procedures for high-level employees, traveling users, and support personnel.

Summary of Exam Objectives

This chapter has addressed several key skills that are measured by Microsoft Exam 70-296: Planning, Implementing, and Maintaining a Microsoft Windows Server 2003 Environment for an MCSE Certified on Windows 2000. You should be well versed in the concepts presented in this chapter as well as the exercises designed to give you hands-on experience with some of the new functions and features of Windows Server 2003.

Planning a user authentication strategy involves a firm understanding of the various authentication protocols offered by Windows Server 2003. The default authentication protocol for LAN communication is Kerberos v5, though NTLM is still supported to allow communication with any down-level machines that are still running Windows NT 4.0. Digest authentication, along with SSL/TLS, can provide secure access for users accessing your company's resources via the World Wide Web. Finally, there are a number of available technologies for your users who require remote access via a VPN, including IPSec and EAP-TLS, which can also be used for wireless authentication. You can implement one or more of these technologies in constructing an authentication scheme for your network users.

In a Windows Server 2003 environment, you can use smart cards to implement a strong means of authentication for your network users. Smart cards rely on Certificate Services (discussed in Chapter 4) to create enrollment certificates to configure smart cards, as well as logon certificates to enable your users to authenticate and access network resources using their smart cards. This section concluded with best practices for managing smart cards on your network, including preparing, issuing, maintaining, and revoking smart cards for the users on your network.

User passwords are often the weakest link in any network security scheme. To help combat this tendency, Windows Server 2003 allows you to configure password and account lockout policies for all user accounts within a domain. You can configure passwords to expire after a number of days as well as mandating a minimum length and how many unique passwords will be stored in Active Directory before a user can reuse an old password. Mandating password complexity forces your users to create passwords that contain multiple types of characters: uppercase, lowercase, alpha-, and nonalphanumeric. In addition, you can enforce an account lockout policy that will disable a user account after a certain number of incorrect logon attempts.

Exam Objectives Fast Track

Password Policies

☑ According to Microsoft, complex passwords consist of at least seven characters, including three of the following four character types: uppercase letters, lowercase letters, numeric digits, and nonalphanumeric characters such as & $ * and !.

- ☑ Password policies, including password length and complexity as well as account lockout policies, are set at the domain level. If you have a subset of your user base that requires a different set of account policies and other security settings, you should create a separate domain to meet their requirements.
- ☑ Be sure that you understand the implications of an account lockout policy before you enable one in a production environment.

User Authentication

- ☑ Kerberos v5 is the default communication method between two machines that are both running Windows 2000 or later. For pre-Windows 2000 clients and servers, NTLM authentication is used.
- ☑ Internet Authentication Service can be used for a variety of applications: as a RADIUS server or proxy, to authenticate network hardware such as switches, and to provide remote access and VPN authentication.
- ☑ To provide authentication for Web applications, you can implement either SSL/TLS for standards-based encryption, which is recognized by a wide range of browsers and platforms, or Microsoft Digest, which is specific to Internet Explorer version 5 or later.

Using Smart Cards

- ☑ Microsoft Windows Server 2003 relies on its public key infrastructure (PKI) and Certificate Services to facilitate smart card authentication.
- ☑ Smart card certificates are based on the following three certificate templates: the Enrollment Agent certificate used to create certificates for smart card users, the smart card Logon certificate that provides user authentication only, and the smart card User certificate that allows for both authentication and data encryption.
- ☑ Several Group Policy settings are specific to smart card implementations; other account policy settings will also affect smart card users.

Exam Objectives Frequently Asked Questions

The following Frequently Asked Questions, answered by the authors of this book, are designed to both measure your understanding of the Exam Objectives presented in this chapter, and to assist you with real-life implementation of these concepts. You will also gain access to thousands of other FAQs at ITFAQnet.com.

Q: How can I configure a smart card user to be able to temporarily log onto the network if the user has forgotten her card?

A: In the user's **Properties** sheet within **Active Directory Users and Computers**, make the following changes on the **Account** tab:

1. Clear the check mark next to Smart Card is Required for Interactive Logon.
2. Place a check mark next to User Must Change Password at Next Logon.

Finally, right-click the user object and select **Reset Password**. Inform the user of her new password and that she needs to change it the first time she logs on.

Q: What weaknesses does the Kerberos authentication protocol possess?

A: The largest concern to be aware of when using Kerberos authentication centers is the physical security of your KDCs as well as your local workstations. Since Kerberos attempts to provide single sign-on capabilities for your users, an attacker who gains access to your workstation console will be able to access the same resources that you are able to access yourself. Kerberos also does not protect against stolen passwords; if a malicious user obtains a legitimate password, he or she will be able to impersonate a legitimate user on your network.

Q: What are the advantages of implementing a "soft lockout" policy versus a "hard lockout" within the account lockout policies?

A: A hard lockout policy refers to an account lockout that must be manually cleared by an administrator. This setting provides the highest level of security but carries with it the risk that legitimate users will be unable to access network resources; you can effectively create a DoS attack against your own network. A soft lockout that expires after a set amount of time helps avert password attacks against your network while still allowing legitimate users a reasonable chance to get their jobs done. For example, if your account lockout policy specifies that accounts should be locked out for one hour after two bad logon attempts, this setting renders even an automated password-guessing utility so slow as to be nearly ineffective.

Q: My organization is in the planning stages of a smart card rollout. What are the security considerations involved in setting up a smart card enrollment station?

A: Since a smart card enrollment station allows you to create certificates on behalf of any user within your Windows Server 2003 domain, you should secure these machines heavily in terms of both physical location and software patches. Imagine the damage that could be wrought if a malicious user were able to create a smart card logon certificate for a member of the Domain Admins group and use it to log onto your network at will.

Q: How can I convince my users that the company's new smart card rollout is something that is protecting them, rather than simply "yet another stupid rule to follow"?

A: One of the most critical components of any network security policy is securing "buy-in" from your users: A security mechanism that is not followed is not much more useful than not having one to begin with. Try to explain the value of smart card authentication from the end user's perspective. If you work in a sales organization, ask your sales force how they would feel if their client contacts, price quotes, and contracts fell into the hands of their main competitor. In a situation like this, providing a good answer to "What's in it for me?" can mean the difference between a successful security structure and a failed one.

Self Test

1. You have created an e-commerce Web application that allows your customers to purchase your company's products via the Internet. Management is concerned that customers will not feel comfortable providing their credit card information over the Internet. What is the most important step to secure this application so that your customers will feel confident that they are transmitting their information securely and to the correct Web site?

   A. Use IP restrictions so that only your customers' specific IP addresses can connect to the e-commerce application.

   B. Issue each of your customers a smart card that they can use to authenticate to your e-commerce Web site.

   C. Place your company's Web server behind a firewall to prevent unauthorized access to customer information.

   D. Install a Secure Sockets Layer (SSL) certificate on your Web server.

2. What is a potential drawback of creating a password policy on your network that requires user passwords to be 25 characters long?

A. Users will be more likely to write down a password that is so difficult to remember.

B. User passwords should be at least 30 characters long to guard against brute-force password attacks.

C. There are no drawbacks; this solution creates network passwords that will be impossible for an unauthorized user to penetrate.

D. Windows Server 2003 will not allow a password of more than eight characters.

3. Your network configuration includes a Terminal Server designed to allow users at remote branches to access network applications. The Terminal Server often becomes overloaded with client requests, and you have received several complaints regarding response times during peak hours. You have recently issued smart cards for the users located at your corporate headquarters and would like to prevent those users from using their smart cards to access the Terminal Server. How can you accomplish this goal in the most efficient manner possible?

   A. Enable auditing of logon/logoff events on your network to determine which smart card users are accessing the Terminal Server, then speak to their supervisors individually.

   B. Create a separate OU for your Terminal Server. Create a global group containing all smart card users, and restrict the logon hours of this group for the Terminal Servers OU.

   C. Enable the "Do not allow smart card device redirection" policy within Group Policy.

   D. Create a global group containing all smart card users, and deny this group the "Log on locally" right to the computers on your network.

4. You have recently begun a new position as a network administrator for a Windows Server 2003 network. Shortly before he left the company, your predecessor used the *syskey* utility on one of your domain controllers to create a password that needed to be entered when the machine is booted. You reboot the controller, only to discover that the password that the previous administrator recorded is incorrect, and he cannot be reached to determine the correct password. How can you return this controller to service as quickly as possible?

   A. Reformat the system drive on the server and reinstall Windows Server 2003.

   B. Boot the server into Directory Services Restore Mode and restore the controller's Registry from a point before the previous administrator ran the *syskey* utility.

   C. Boot the server into Safe Mode and run *syskey* again to change the password.

   D. Use *ntdsutil* to seize the PDC emulator role and transfer it to another controller.

5. Your Active Directory domain contains a mixture of Windows Server 2003, Windows 2000 Server, and Windows NT 4.0 domain controllers. Your clients are similarly heterogeneous, consisting of Windows XP and Windows 2000 Professional along with NT 4.0 Workstation. What is the most secure network authentication method available to you in this environment?

   A. Password Authentication Protocol (PAP)

   B. NTLM

   C. NTLMv2

   D. Kerberos version 5

6. According to Microsoft, which of the following would be considered weak passwords for a user account named *jronick*? (Choose all that apply.)

   A. S#n$lUsN7

   B. soprano

   C. ronickrj

   D. Oo!dIx2

   E. new

7. You are the network administrator for the Windows Server 2003 domain diagrammed in the following illustration. Your boss has been reading about Kerberos authentication and is concerned that your KDC represents a single point of failure for your company's network authentication. How should you respond to this concern?

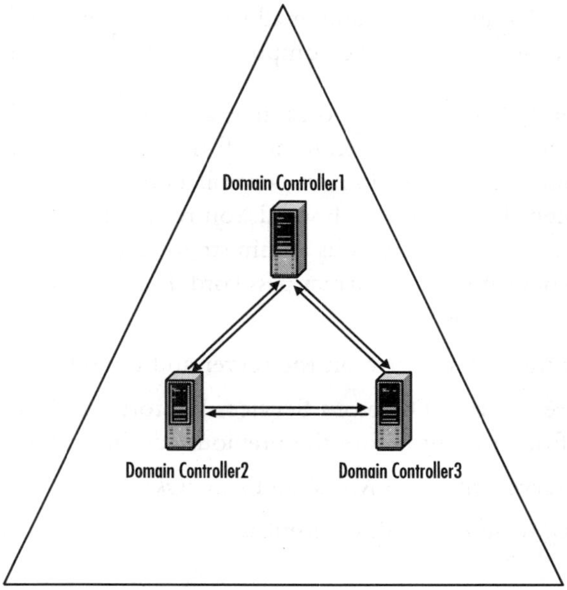

A. Every Windows Server 2003 domain controller acts as a KDC. If your DC1 controller fails, DC2 and DC3 will still perform the KDC functions.

B. Your network requires only one KDC to function since you are only using a single domain.

C. The KDC function is a single master operations role. If the machine that houses the KDC role fails, you can use *ntdsutil* to assign the role to another server.

D. If the KDC fails, your network clients will use DNS for authentication.

8. You have implemented a password policy that requires your users to change their passwords every 30 days and retains their last three passwords in memory. While sitting in the lunch room, you hear someone advise his coworker that all she needs to do to get around that rule is to change her password four times so that she can go back to using the password that she is used to. What is the best way to modify your domain password policy to avoid this potential security liability?

   A. Increase the maximum password age from 30 days to 60 days.

   B. Enforce password complexity requirements for your domain users' passwords.

   C. Increase the minimum password age to seven days.

   D. Increase the minimum password length of your users' passwords.

9. You have created a Web application that relies on digest authentication. You check the account properties of one of the user accounts and see the following screen. What is the most likely reason that your users cannot authenticate?

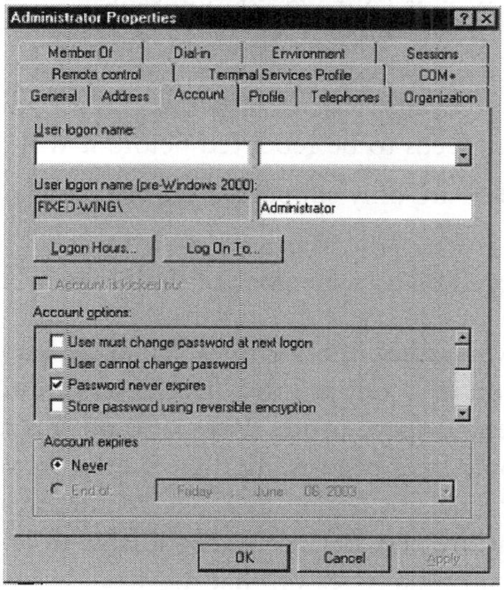

A. When you log on using digest authentication, the Windows username is case-sensitive.

B. To use digest authentication, users must be running Internet Explorer version 6.

C. Your users' passwords are set to expire every 60 days, which is causing digest authentication to fail.

D. You must enforce the "Store passwords using reversible encryption" setting for all users who need to authenticate using digest authentication.

10. A developer on your network uses a workstation that is not attached to the corporate domain. He phones the help desk to report that he has forgotten the password to his local user account. If he has not previously created a password reset disk, what information will he lose when the password for his local account is reset? (Choose all that apply.)

A. Local files that the user has encrypted

B. E-mail encrypted with his public key

C. His Internet Explorer favorites and links

D. The entries in the Recent Documents dialog box

11. You have attached a smart card reader to your Windows XP Professional workstation's serial port. The reader is not detected when you plug it in and is not recognized when you scan for new hardware within Device Manager. The smart card reader is listed on the Microsoft Web site as a supported device, and you have verified that all cables are connected properly. Why is your workstation refusing to recognize the smart card reader?

A. You need to run the manufacturer-specific installation routine.

B. The workstation needs to be rebooted before it will recognize the card reader.

C. Smart card readers are only supported on machines running Windows Server 2003.

D. You are not logged on as a member of the Domain Admins group.

12. You are a new network administrator for a Windows Server 2003 domain. In making user support calls, you have noticed that many users are relying on simplistic passwords such as their children's or pets' names. Passwords on this network are set to never expire, so some people have been using these weak passwords for months or even years. You change the default Group Policy to require strong passwords. Several weeks later, you notice that the network users are still able to log on using their weak passwords. What is the most likely reason that the weak passwords are still in effect?

A. You must force the users to change their passwords before the strong password settings will take effect.

B. The Group Policy settings have not replicated throughout the network yet.

C. Password policies need to be set at the OU level, not the domain level.

D. The users reverted back to their passwords the next time that they were prompted to change their passwords.

13. You were walking through your server room when you noticed that a contractor had plugged his laptop directly into one of your network switches and was using your company bandwidth to download pirated software onto his hard drive. You have recently upgraded your network switches and routers to the most up-to-date hardware available. What is the best way to prevent this sort of illegitimate access to your network in the future?

    A. Install smart card readers on all your users' desktops.

    B. Implement the Internet Authentication Service's ability to authenticate Ethernet switches on your network.

    C. Do not allow outside contractors to bring any hardware into your building.

    D. Disable the Guest account within Active Directory.

14. You have recently deployed smart cards to your users for network authentication. You configured the smart card Logon certificates to expire every six months. One of your smart card users has left the company without returning her smart card. You have disabled this user's logon account and smart card, but management is concerned that she will still be able to use the smart card to access network resources. How can you be sure that the information stored on the former employee's smart card cannot be used to continue to access network resources?

    A. Monitor the security logs to ensure that the former employee is not attempting to access network resources.

    B. Use the smart card enrollment station to delete the user's smart card Logon certificate.

    C. Deny the Autoenroll permission to the user's account on the smart card Logon Certificate template.

    D. Add the user's certificate to the CRL on your company's CA.

15. The account lockout policy on your Windows Server 2003 domain is set up as shown in the following illustration. You come into work on a Monday morning and are informed that many of your users' accounts were locked out over the weekend. Your company's help desk staff have unlocked the user accounts in question, but they are now reporting that your Exchange server and Microsoft SQL databases are not accessible by anyone in the company. Network utilization is at normal levels. What is the most likely reason that these applications are not responding?

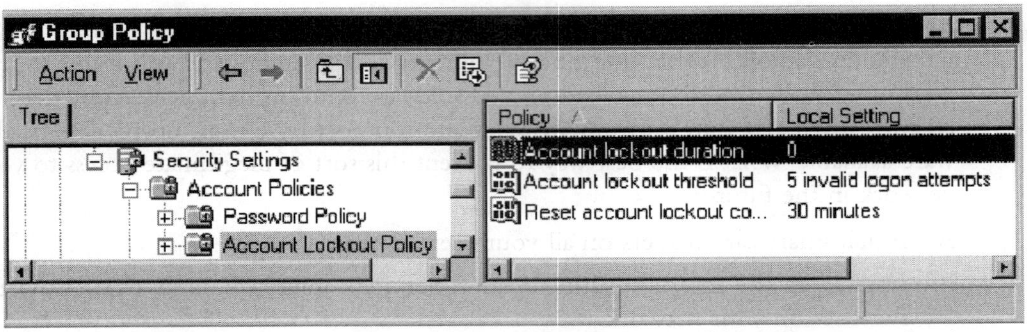

A. An attacker has deleted the Exchange and SQL executables on your production servers.

B. The accounts that Exchange and SQL use to start or connect to the network have been locked out and need to be manually unlocked.

C. The users whose accounts were unlocked by the help desk need to reboot their workstations to access these applications.

D. An attacker is perpetrating a DOS attack against your network.

Self Test Quick Answer Key

For complete questions, answers, and explanations to the Self Test questions in this chapter as well as the other chapters in this book, see the Self Test Appendix.

1. **D**
2. **A**
3. **C**
4. **B**
5. **C**
6. **B, C, E**
7. **A**
8. **C**
9. **D**
10. **A, B**
11. **B**
12. **A**
13. **B**
14. **D**
15. **B**

Chapter 6

MCSA/MCSE 70-296

Developing and Implementing a Group Policy Strategy

Exam Objectives in this Chapter:

9.1	Plan a Group Policy strategy.
9.1.1	Plan a Group Policy Strategy using Resultant Set of Policy (RSoP) Planning mode.
9.1.2	Plan a strategy for configuring the user environment using Group Policy.
9.1.3	Plan a strategy for configuring the computer environment using Group Policy.
9.2	Configure the user environment using Group Policy.
9.2.1	Distribute software using Group Policy.
9.2.2	Automatically enroll user certifications using Group Policy.
9.2.3	Redirect folders using Group Policy.
9.2.4	Configure user security settings using Group Policy.

- ☑ Summary of Exam Objectives
- ☑ Exam Objectives Fast Track
- ☑ Exam Objectives Frequently Asked Questions
- ☑ Self Test
- ☑ Self Test Quick Answer Key

Introduction

One of the most powerful tools that you have at your disposal in a Windows Server 2003 environment is Group Policy. As with Windows 2000, you can use Group Policy to control users, computers, and groups of users from a centralized location. Through the use of Group Policy, you can control users' desktops to create a standardized environment, making management and administration that much easier for the IT staff that must support it.

Group Policy also offers the ability to distribute software based on a particular Group Policy resource designation. Being able to offer your users software for their job functions without having to physically travel to or remotely connect to their computers reduces the amount of time you need to spend playing PC support technician. However, making sure that software doesn't get into the wrong hands is also critical. You wouldn't want a temporary employee in data entry to be able to install your accounting department's bookkeeping software, would you? Using Group Policy, you can distribute the software while limiting the audience that has access to particular packages.

In this chapter, we plan and create a Group Policy strategy in Windows Server 2003, discussing the tools we have at our disposal for Group Policy. We then configure the user environment through the Group Policy tools and plans that we discussed. Let's begin with a discussion of planning Group Policy through the use of Resultant Set of Policy (RSoP).

EXAM 70-296 OBJECTIVE 9.1

Developing a Group Policy Strategy

Group Policy is one of the administrative strengths of Active Directory. By simply invoking a Group Policy object (GPO) and configuring its contents, an administrator can lock down security for an entire domain, establish a consistent desktop environment, establish a roaming-friendly network, and distribute software. Under Windows 2000, the main tool for managing Group Policies was the Group Policy Editor. In fact, it took time, attention, and a little detective work to ferret out conflicts or plan the best application of a set of Group Policies. In Windows Server 2003 Active Directory, an administrator has the ability to use RSoP in addition to Group Policy Editor to help in both planning and troubleshooting Group Policies.

When you are developing a Group Policy strategy, you should keep in mind that you always start with a blank slate. All policy settings are, by default, not configured. You can either enable a setting, which might also require you to provide specific configuration information, or you can disable it. Each GPO has two nodes:

- User Configuration
- Computer Configuration

User objects inherit the User Configuration policies, and computer objects inherit the Computer Configuration policies. Both the user configuration and computer configuration nodes contain software settings, which are used to distribute software (and are most easily configured if the software uses Windows Installer).

Problems and conflicts can occur with multiple GPOs, in which one GPO ends up overriding the settings of other GPOs. In addition, some Group Policies do not directly conflict but can cause the same result as a conflict. For example, if you disable the Windows Installer and Control Panel for a user in one GPO, the user will not be able to install any software that you publish in any other GPO.

TEST DAY TIP

Review the Group Policy inheritance pattern. Given a basic configuration, you should be able to identify which Group Policies would be inherited and which would not.

In the following section, we look at Group Policy planning. This includes planning the environment for user objects as well as the environment for computer objects. One of the first things we review is how to use the new RSoP to develop a strategy for Group Policy.

EXAM 70-296 OBJECTIVE 9.1.1

Planning Group Policy with RSoP

The Resultant Set of Policy Wizard is a tool that helps you make sense of the myriad options available when you apply Group Policy. The tool is basically a query wizard for polling your existing Group Policies. In gathering the Group Policies that are attached to the site, the domain, and each of the OUs that eventually reach the user and/or computer object involved, RSoP is able to give you a clear picture of which Group Policies are applied, at which level, and which Group Policies are blocked from being applied.

Even when you use RSoP to help plan Group Policies, you should have a clear understanding of how Group Policies function. In the following sections we discuss Group Policy and traditional Group Policy planning processes, followed by the integration of RSoP into the Group Policy planning process and conducting RSoP queries in Planning mode.

Group Policy Overview

The power of administration with Active Directory lies in Group Policy, when it is effectively structured. The goal of using Group Policy for administration is to establish an environment that user objects and computer objects will maintain even if users attempt to make changes to their systems. Keep in mind that Group Policies:

- Take advantage of the Active Directory domain, site, and OU structure
- Can be secured, blocked, and enforced
- Contain separate user environment and computer environment configurations

- Can be used to enforce software distribution and installation
- Establish domain password and account policies
- Can lock down an environment for one set of users but free it for another set

Group Policies can be applied at any level of the Active Directory hierarchy. Once a Group Policy is applied, the next level inherits it until it finally reaches the target user or computer object. The order of inheritance starts at the Local Group Policy, which exists on the computer itself. Following that, site level Group Policy is applied, followed by the domain level Group Policy and then the OU level Group Policy starting at the top of the OU hierarchy and working its way to the OU where the user is located. Figure 6.1 shows how this process works.

Figure 6.1 Group Policy Is Inherited in a Structured Fashion

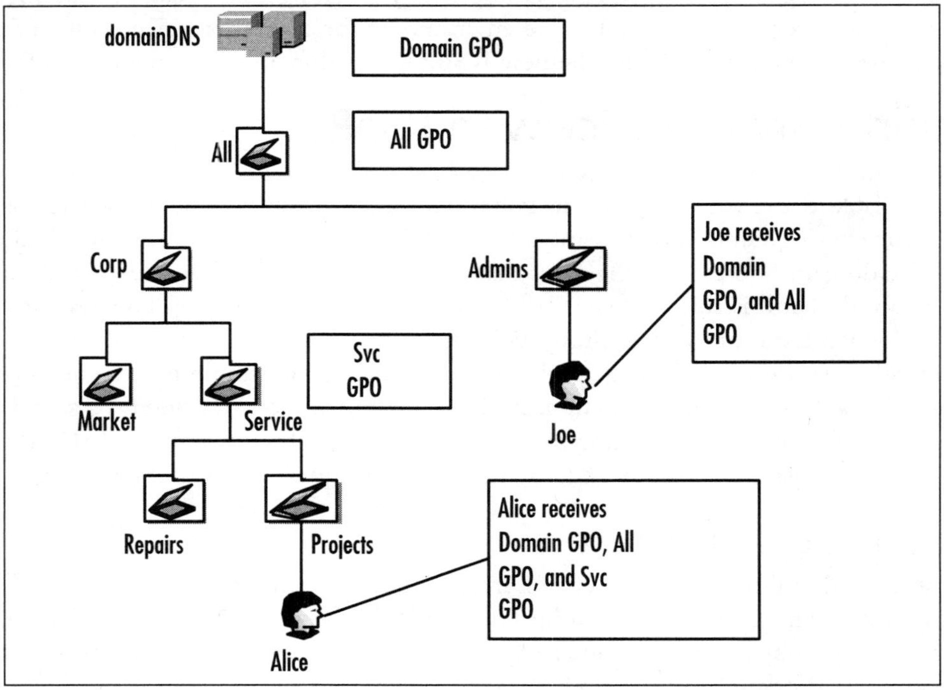

In some situations, a Group Policy can be established at a higher level but is not desired at a lower level. For example, a network administrator might decide to enforce a desktop configuration across the entire network, and given a case in which there are many top-level OUs, the best way to do so is to establish a domainwide group policy. However, if the network administrator wants administrators to be able to change their desktop configurations at any time, the policy should not be applied to the administrators' OU. In these cases, you can block the Group Policy from being inherited. Blocking inheritance might be necessary for certain situations, but it can become cumbersome if it becomes a practice. Blocked and enforced inheritance can cause unexpected results, especially if others don't know that a Group Policy has been blocked or enforced. For this reason, it is better to design an OU structure that works in concert with Group Policy, rather than one that works against the inheritance flow. Figure 6.2 shows how a policy can be blocked from inheritance.

Figure 6.2 Group Policy Inheritance Can Be Blocked

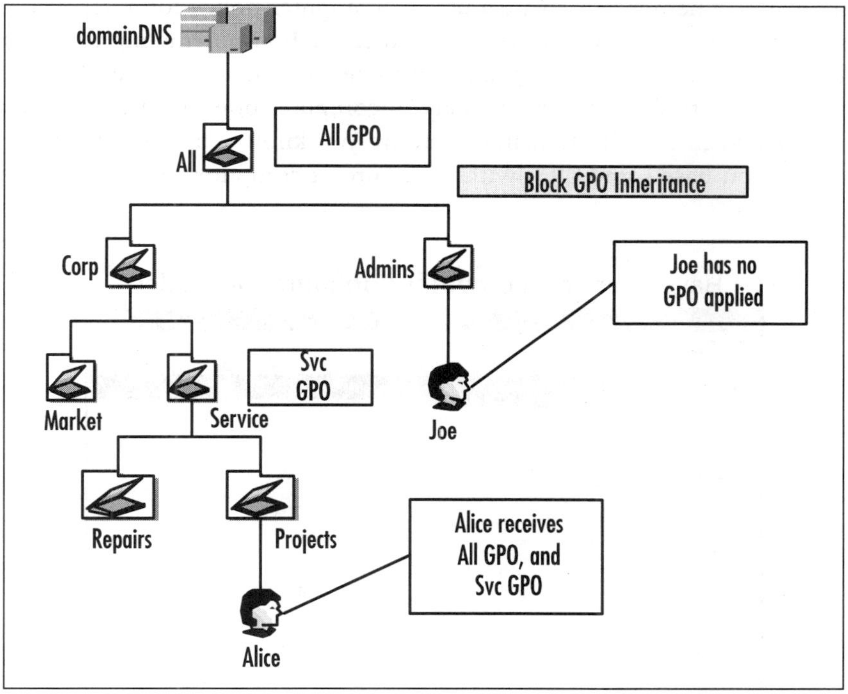

Test Day Tip

Review how blocking inheritance and enforcing inheritance will affect the pattern of Group Policy inheritance. Remember that blocking inheritance should be done only when there are no other options that will suffice. It is better to reorganize OUs, objects, and GPOs than to block inheritance, except in special circumstances.

In Figure 6.3, you will see a picture of the Group Policy editor displaying a single GPO. In the GPO are two top-level folders, or *nodes*. One is the user configuration node; the other is the computer configuration node. As you can probably guess, the user configuration node establishes the environment for a user and follows that user around the network. The computer configuration node establishes the environment for a computer and stays with that computer regardless of which users are logging onto it. This concept can be confusing if you create a GPO with computer configuration information and apply it to an OU that contains only user objects. For example, if you have two OUs named Users and Computers containing user and computer objects, respectively, you can create a GPO with the computer configuration information configured in it. If you apply that GPO to the Users OU, it will not affect any computers, because they are in the Computers OU.

To make GPO application less confusing, you can follow the rule of keeping user objects from a certain department with their own computer objects in the same OU. That way it won't matter whether you create a user or computer policy for a department—it will always be applied to the correct object. Another method of handling this situation is to make a rule to always keep user objects and computer objects in separate OUs and create GPOs that apply only to user objects or solely to computer objects. (It helps to use the word *user* or *computer* in the GPO's name to ensure you know which is which.) It usually gets confusing if you have some OUs with a mixture of computers and users and some that are separated.

Figure 6.3 GPOs Have User and Computer Configuration Nodes

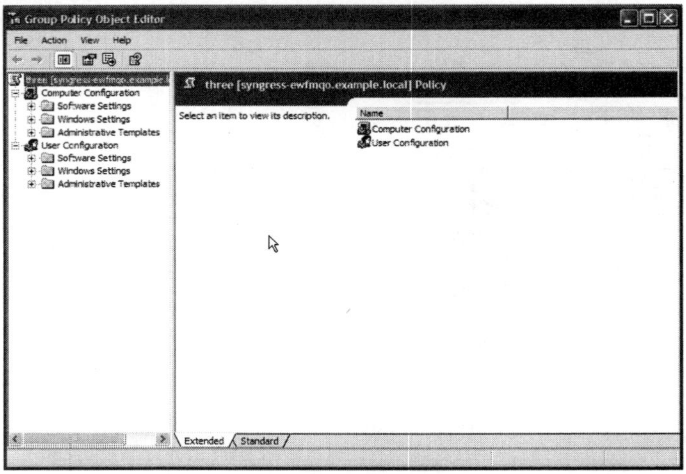

Among the headaches of managing a network are making certain that users receive the correct software applications or that computers have the right software applications available on them. Group Policies lessen this challenge by making it easy to distribute software to any user or computer as well as to apply patches or remove or replace software. One of the reasons that Group Policies work so well in this area is that they can use the Windows Installer service. You have the option of either publishing or assigning software. When you publish software, the installation becomes available in the Add/Remove Programs icon of the Control Panel. When you assign software, it is installed. You can distribute software to either a computer object or a user object. When you distribute the software to a computer object, the software is available upon computer start up. When you distribute the software to a user object, the software is available only after the user logs on. (Assigning software to users slows logons due to the time it takes to install.)

Exam Warning

GPOs and Group Policy are two different things. When you see *GPO* mentioned on the exam, it is referring to a single, whole set of policies that you set for a user or computer. When you see the term *Group Policy* mentioned, it could be referring either to the Group Policy capability within Active Directory, or it could be referring to a single option within a GPO.

Another issue with managing a network is maintaining security. Group Policies are used to establish different types of security for users. The default domain policy is used for establishing the Password Policy and Account Lockout Policy for domain users when they log on to any computer in the network. This is one of the few features that are established solely on a domainwide basis.

The ability to lock down an environment is highly desirable for computers that are placed for public use. For example, many organizations maintain public kiosks that must be managed remotely from a configuration standpoint. Let's take an example of an imaginary pharmaceutical company that places a kiosk at each one of its pharmacies to display information about medication and provide information about the completion of a prescription. With Group Policy, each kiosk can be configured to:

- Log on to the network automatically.
- Distribute, update, or even remove existing software (without the need to be present at the machine).
- Change the computer's environment to be the software application (rather than Windows Explorer) so that people are prevented from accessing anything other than the application.
- Prevent access to any desktop, Control Panel, file path, or network resources.
- Prevent the rebooting of the computer or the user logging off.
- Prevent the installation of any software applications, other than those that have been assigned.

Within the same domain, the pharmaceutical company administrator can also provide different applications to workstations at each of the pharmacies, allow users to have access to resources and be able to logoff as they need to, and even provide different configurations to users at other offices. By organizing users and computers into an OU structure that matches the organization's needs, an administrator can use Group Policy to make network administration an easier task than it would otherwise be.

EXAM WARNING

When you are shown a specific Group Policy setting, remember that the description of the Group Policy is very important to the results you will get when you enable or disable that Group Policy. A Group Policy setting that is described as "Disable ..." is only disabled when the setting is enabled. It's tricky but a little easier to remember if you think of the option to enable a policy setting as *turning it on* and disabling it as *turning it off*.

The Planning Process

When you plan your Group Policies, you first must know your organization's requirements. If you deploy restrictions that are not necessary, users will protest. If you do not deploy restrictions when they are necessary, problems will persist.

You should be aware of whom needs to access which resources at which times. Try to design your OU structure to match these needs, with the users and computers that have the least restrictions at the top of the OU tree and the users and computers requiring the most restrictions at the bottom of the tree. This technique lets you deploy Group Policy in a layered fashion.

It is best to use a test OU structure to test user and computer objects and try out Group Policies prior to deploying them across the network. In all cases, you should not edit the default domain policy except to establish your password and account policies for the domain.

When you create a test OU with test user and computer objects, you can use RSoP to help simulate the Group Policies and use them to establish new ones in the actual OUs. For example, let's assume that you have a user who has the exact environment that you want everyone in a certain group to use. This user's environment is entirely created through Group Policies applied to both the user and computer configuration nodes in several OUs. In order to determine which Group Policies are being applied, you can use RSoP to discover which Group Policies have "won" and are applied. RSoP displays only the Group Policies that have been configured. Anything that has not been enabled or disabled will not appear in your results. If you want to see what the users in that group already have applied to their user and computer configurations, you can run another RSoP query and then look for the differences that need to be resolved. In fact, by running a series of RSoP Planning mode queries, you can see how users are affected if they are moved to another OU, added to a different security group, or provided a computer whose object is in a different OU.

When you have completed your planning process, you should know the pieces of information outlined in Table 6.1.

Table 6.1 Required Information for the Planning Process

Required Information	Itemized lists
The types of policies that you need to apply	Domain level policies that affect all domain users, including password policies and account lockout policies. User configurations, including: ■ Security settings for software restrictions and file restrictions ■ Folder redirection ■ Administrative template restrictions, such as Control Panel and desktop restrictions or specific registry keys ■ Software distribution for specific groups of users ■ Smart card authentication, as applicable ■ Logon and logoff scripts Computer configurations, including: ■ Local security settings (for computers that are offline from the network) ■ Software distribution for specific sets of computers ■ Windows settings directing how the operating system will act and appear ■ Administrative template restrictions ■ Startup and shutdown scripts
The locations where each policy should be applied	Which policies should be applied to all domain users. Which policies should be applied to all users or computers at a site, regardless of their domain affiliation. Which policies should be applied to each of the OUs.
The users or computers that should not be affected by certain Group Policies	Whether to block inheritance for certain policies. Whether to prevent administrators from being affected by certain policies.
How rights and permissions will affect Group Policy application	Which security groups will prevent certain Group Policies from being applied. What rights must be granted so that users can read or apply Group Policies.

Continued

Table 6.1 Required Information for the Planning Process

Required Information	Itemized lists
	What rights should not be granted to filter out a Group Policy for a certain security group. Who should have the rights to make changes or apply new Group Policies in the future, after your configuration is set.
What your RSoP results will be for each set of users	Test your Group Policy selections: ■ Use a test set of OUs that mirrors your actual set of OUs (this will not have a negative impact on your network). ■ Create a test user object. ■ Move a test computer object into the OU. ■ Apply the Group Policy settings as you have planned them. ■ Include any policy inheritance blocks or enforcements that you plan. Validate your results: ■ Logon in the test OU as the test user on the test computer. ■ Document your results. ■ Use RSoP queries to produce Group Policy settings results.

Using RSoP

As a query engine, RSoP provides a unique way to investigate your Group Policy application and ensure that implementation matches your intended results. You have two modes available in an RSoP query:

- Planning mode
- Logging mode

Planning mode allows you to query and test policy settings in order to simulate the effects on computers and users. You can look at the Group Policy settings that are applied at an OU level, even if that OU contains no user or computer objects. *Logging mode* tells you the policy settings for an existing computer or user who is currently logged onto the network.

You can use the RSoP wizard for either Planning or Logging mode queries. This is an MMC snap-in that you can add just as you would any other MMC snap-in. (We'll go over the specific steps in the next section.) After you run the RSoP wizard, you can generate results for a query and view them in the MMC window (you can see this screen later in the chapter, in Figure 6.9). If you want to compare users or other views, you can add the RSoP snap-in multiple times to a single window and have them all available in a tree structure for easy access and comparison.

One of the unique capabilities RSoP provides is *loopback processing*. When you use loopback processing, you can simulate the application of a different set of user policies for use on a specific computer. For example, if you had a set of computers for public use in a library or a classroom, you might want the user policy modified regardless of which user is logging on. This is useful in any situation in which a person who has a certain set of rights available at his personal workstation will be limited because the computer is provided only for special uses.

The RSoP Snap-in

RSoP uses a snap-in module for the MMC. You need to add this module manually in order to begin using the program. You can access the wizard by right-clicking on a user or computer object in Active Directory Users and Computers and selecting **All Tasks | Resultant Set of Policy (Logging)** or **Resultant Set of Policy (Planning)**.

To open the Resultant Set of Policy wizard, do the following:

1. Click **Start | Run** and type **mmc**, then click **OK**.
2. From the Microsoft Management Console, select the **File** menu and then click **Add/Remove snap-in**.
3. Click the **Add** button.
4. Select **Resultant Set of Policy** from the list, and click the **Add** button.
5. Click the **Close** button to return to the console.

New & Noteworthy...

RSoP Is Command-Line Worthy

You can start the RSoP snap-in by typing **rsop.msc** at a command prompt. This command opens RSoP in Logging mode for the currently logged-in user, rather than giving you the RSoP Wizard. If you are addicted to the command line and want to show the Logging mode results for a specified target computer, you can use the command:

rsop.msc /RsopNamespace:namespace /RsopTargetComp:computername.

The nice thing about being able to use the command line for RSoP is that you can develop scripts to help in troubleshooting. For example, you could create a script that prompts you for the namespace and computer name. Then that script could generate the RSoP results to appear graphically on whatever computer at which you happen to be seated. As an administrator, if you are at a user's desk, having a script available can save you both time and trouble.

You can also start the RSoP snap-in by typing **rsop.msc** at a command prompt. This command opens RSoP in Logging mode for the currently logged-in user, rather than presenting you with the RSoP wizard.

Viewing Policy Settings

Before you are able to view policy settings in RSoP, you must conduct a query. With the RSoP snap-in added to an MMC, click the **Action** menu and select **Generate RSoP Data**. The RSoP wizard begins with the Welcome screen. After clicking **Next**, you will be able to select the mode to use, as shown in Figure 6.4.

Figure 6.4 Selecting Planning or Logging Mode in the RSoP Wizard

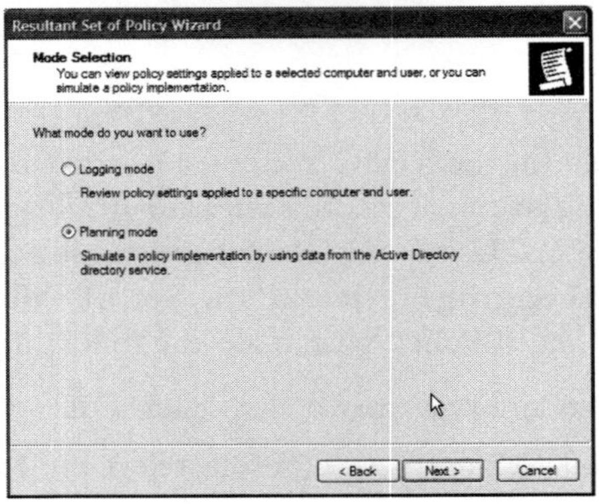

In order to perform a simulation, you need to select **Planning mode**. Logging mode only looks at existing policies, whereas Planning mode allows you to test "what if?" scenarios through various simulations. After you select the Planning mode option, click **Next**. The following dialog screen, shown in Figure 6.5, lets you select the OUs containing the user and computer objects that you want to test.

Figure 6.5 Selecting the Containers for the User and Computer Objects to Simulate

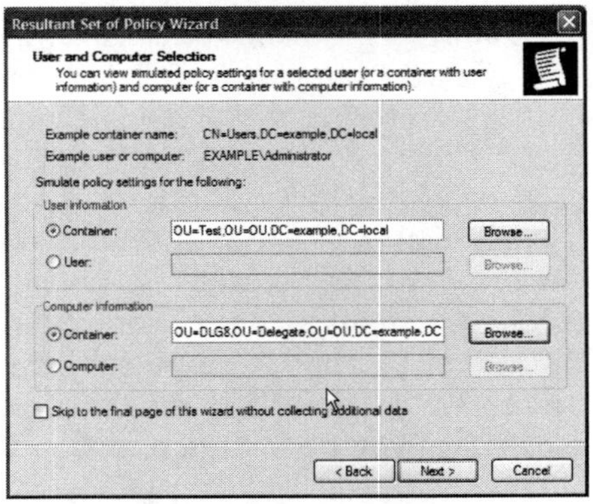

The next set of options, displayed in Figure 6.6, are Advanced Simulation options. First you are given the ability to select the simulation for a slow network link or for loopback processing. When you select the option for a slow network link, you can get an idea of how Group Policy settings will affect users across slow WAN links or those who use remote node computing across dialup lines. Whenever you deploy a Group Policy that distributes software, you should test it with RSoP and select the option for a slow network link so you will know how users will be affected by the software distribution Group Policy setting. When you select loopback processing, you are telling RSoP to replace or merge the user's normal Group Policies with the settings selected for the computer. This action is useful when you have a public computer.

Figure 6.6 Simulating a Slow Link or Using Loopback Processing

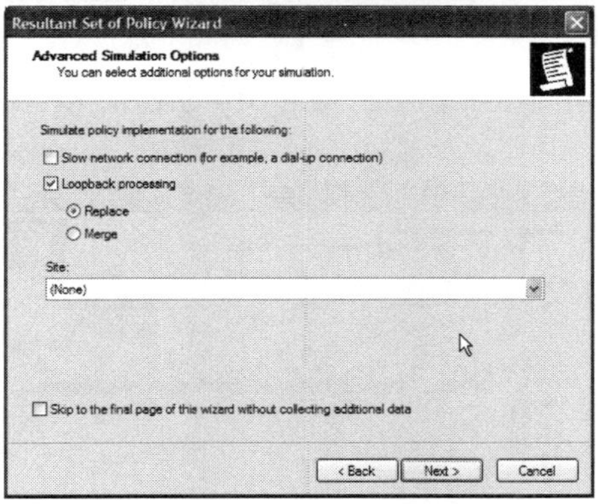

Test Day Tip

Look over the RSoP query dialogs in Planning mode. Remember that you can simulate slow network connections, being connected to different sites, using merged or replaced user configuration settings, linked WMI filters, and security groups in Planning mode but not Logging mode.

The next two screens have further advanced simulation options. You can look at the Windows Management Instrumentation (WMI) filters to see how they will affect Group Policies, as shown in Figure 6.7. WMI is a component of Windows systems that provides management information about various components, such as services and devices. A WMI filter sifts through the information that is available in order to display or transmit only that information that is required. WMI filters are configurable by an administrator, and there are no default WMI filters. If you have no WMI filters, you do not need to select this option. You can simulate the effect security group memberships will have on Group Policies, which is shown in Figure 6.8.

Figure 6.7 RSoP Planning Mode Allows You to Simulate the Effect of WMI Filters

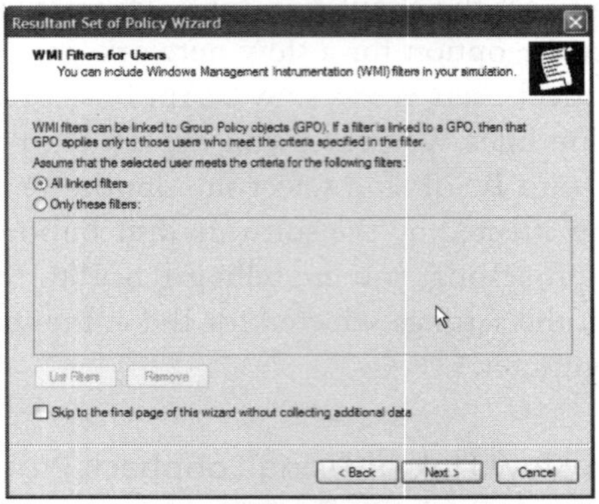

Figure 6.8 The Option of Integrating Security Group Membership in RSoP Simulations

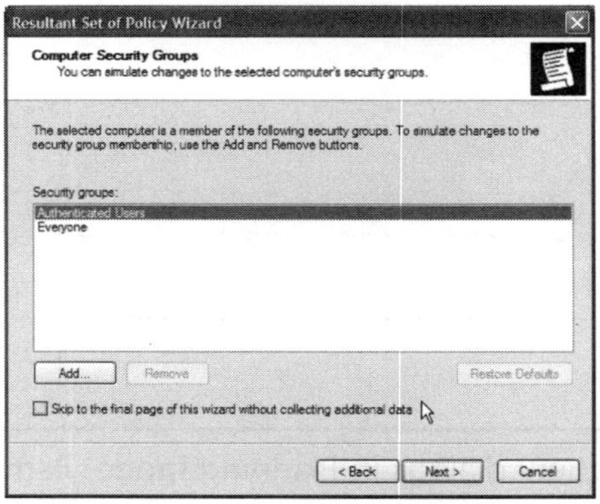

At any point during the RSoP process, you can select the check box to skip to the final screen. For example, you can decide to test a user's results with a slow network link, which means that you would not need to configure any other RSoP options. To avoid paging through each of the following dialog screens, you can simply check the box to **Skip to the final page of the wizard** and receive your RSoP results. At the final screen you will process the information that you input into the RSoP wizard by clicking the **Finish** button. Then you will view the results of the policy settings. When you first see the RSoP results, you will notice that they appear to be similar to what you might see in the Group Policy Editor. However, you will also notice that the RSoP results only display the Group Policies that have been configured and inherited. Anything that is not included will not appear in the window. RSoP results are shown in Figure 6.9.

Figure 6.9 RSoP Results Appear in the Same Tree Structure as Group Policies in the Group Policy Editor

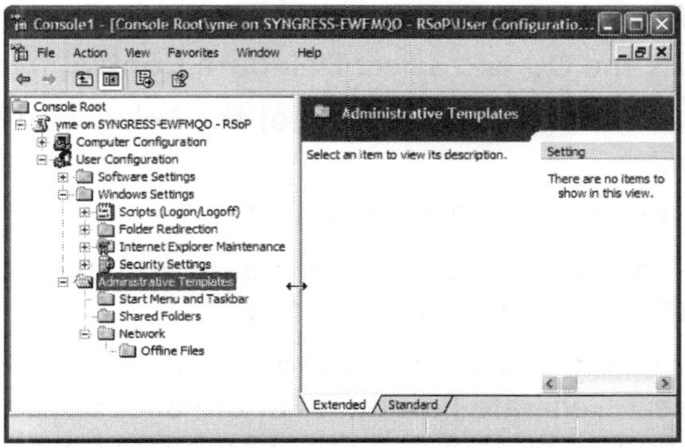

In the RSoP results window, you can drill down into each Group Policy setting and view the settings that have been applied. For software distribution, you will see the results in the Software Settings container in the RSoP results window. You will see the name of each deployed package, the software version, whether the application is published or assigned, the source location, and the name of the GPO that deployed the software. (This information is very helpful because multiple GPOs can deploy the same application.) You can view Group Policy settings for everything from Administrative Templates to Security Settings.

Delegating Control

You can delegate control of the RSoP wizard to users who should have the ability to generate RSoP results for either planning or troubleshooting purposes. For example, you might have a power user who has control over Group Policy for her department's OU. In that case, you should also delegate RSoP for that OU to the user so that she can test Group Policies before applying them to her department. In this case, you might also want to create a test OU and delegate the test OU so that the user is not testing Group Policies after applying them to her department's users and computers. Exercise 6.01 discusses how to delegate control of RSoP so that a user can generate RSoP queries.

EXERCISE 6.01

DELEGATION OF RSOP QUERY CONTROL

In order to delegate control:

1. Click **Start | Administrative Tools | Active Directory Users and Computers** console.

2. Navigate in the directory tree to the OU where you will be delegating control so that the users you select will be able to run RSoP on this OU and below.
3. Right-click the OU and select **Delegate Control** from the context menu.
4. You will see the welcome screen of the Delegation of Control Wizard. Click **Next**.
5. The first dialog box is the Users or Groups page. Click **Add**.
6. Add the name(s) of the users or groups who will be able to run RSoP on this OU. Click **OK**. Then click **Next**.
7. The next dialog box allows you to select the tasks that you will delegate. Select Generate Resultant Set of Policy option(s) for Planning and/or Logging by checking the appropriate boxes. Click **Next**.
8. In the summary page, verify that the information is correct, and then click **Finish**.

Queries

As a query engine, the Resultant Set of Policy Wizard simply guides you to query the Group Policies in Active Directory. You have the option of running queries on a variety of containers and objects within a domain hierarchy.

Exam Warning

RSoP queries can be generated through three methods: command-line invocation of the RSoP console in Logging mode, right-clicking an object within Active Directory Users and Computers, and adding the RSoP snap-in to the MMC and then Generating RSoP Data for a selected location.

- **Running queries on a computer account** In order to run a query on a computer object, you can use the Active Directory Users and Computers console. Select the computer you want to see the policies for by browsing for it and right-clicking it. Point to the **All Tasks** option and select **Resultant Set of Policy (Planning)** or **Resultant Set of Policy (Logging)** on the menu. You can then view the query data in the RSoP window.
- **Running queries on a user account** You can run a query on a user account from within the Active Directory Users and Computers console in addition to running the query from within the RSoP snap-in. In the Active Directory Users

and Computers console, navigate to the user object that you want to query. Right-click the user account. Select the **All Tasks** option from the popup menu. Click **Resultant Set of Policy (Planning)** or **Resultant Set of Policy (Logging)**.

- **Running queries on a domain** To run an RSoP query on a domain, you can right-click the domain node in the Active Directory Users and Computers console. Select **All Tasks** from the popup menu, and then select **Resultant Set of Policy (Planning)**.
- **Running queries on an OU** Organizational units are shown in the Active Directory Users and Computers console. You can right-click the OU that you want to query and select the **All Tasks** option from the popup menu. From there, you can select **Resultant Set of Policy (Planning)** to generate the query.
- **Running queries on a site** To generate a query on a site, you must begin in the Active Directory Sites and Services console. Within this console, navigate to the **Sites** container, and expand it to display all the sites. Right-click the site, select **All Tasks**, and then click **Resultant Set of Policy (Planning)**.
- **Running queries on a local computer** When you are looking at the policies that have been applied to the local computer, you can run the Resultant Set of Policy Wizard on them. Open a blank MMC, add the RSoP snap-in to the MMC, and then select **Generate RSoP Data** from the **Action** menu. Click **Next** at the Welcome screen. Select **Logging Mode**, click **Next**, and then select **This Computer** to generate the local computer query. Planning mode is not available for local computer queries.

Head of the Class...

Running Queries with RSoP: Logging or Planning?

The nice thing about being able to query user, computer, OU, site, and domain objects from within either the Active Directory Users and Computers or Active Directory Sites and Services console is that the task is so easy to perform. You simply navigate to your target object, right-click, select **All Tasks**, and point to **Resultant Set of Policy**.

Some of the objects allow you to select between Planning and Logging mode; others are either strictly planning or strictly logging. Remember that when you are planning, you never have to use a specific user or computer object. You can simulate the Group Policies for a completely empty OU. When you are troubleshooting, however, you will log each Group Policy as it is applied. To perform that task, you require a user object or a computer object. For this reason, the Local Computer query is available in Logging mode only.

Logging mode does not provide you with the additional simulation options for a slow network link, loopback processing, WMI filter links, and security group

Continued

testing. You can obtain these options only through Planning mode. These are all "what if?" options, such as: What if you had a slow link? What if you had a security group membership that denied access to a GPO?

EXAM 70-296 OBJECTIVE 9.1.2

Planning the User Environment

Planning a user environment through Group Policy requires you to focus on the options available within the user configuration node of Group Policy. You will see three top-level folders (and many subfolders of options) within the user configuration node, as shown in Figure 6.10. These folders are:

- Software
- Windows Settings
- Administrative Templates

Figure 6.10 User Configuration Node

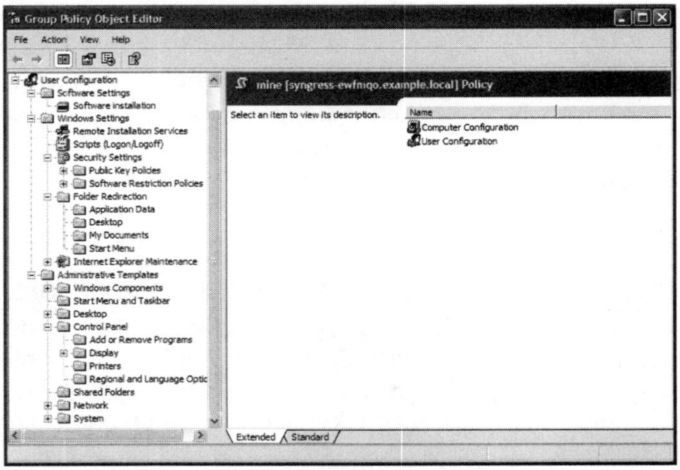

When you plan the software for a user environment, you need to first decide whether to distribute software to a set of users so that they will have the same software regardless of where the users log on, or whether you need to distribute software to a set of computers so that the computers have the software permanently available regardless of which user logs on. You probably have several applications that must be distributed to users, as well as several applications that must be distributed to computers.

Exam Warning

There are too many Group Policy settings to memorize them all. However, you should be able to identify the types of Group Policies by sight. Not only should you be able to navigate to the correct location to apply Group Policies such as password policies, but you should be able to identify the dialog screens for software distribution, Password Policy, Account Lockout Policy, Certificate Autoenrollment, and Folder Redirection.

Within the Windows Settings of the user configuration node, you can establish Group Policies for several different features of Windows. Not only is this the folder where you establish logon and logoff scripts, but you can autoenroll certificates for users in the security settings. Logon and logoff scripts execute in sequence for each GPO that includes a script unless you enable them to run synchronously. Windows Settings contains the Group Policies for redirecting folders. You can redirect Application Data, a user's desktop, the My Documents folder, and the Start menu. In doing this, a user will have his or her most frequently used private data available on any computer that is connected to the network. Windows Settings also allow you to customize the Internet Explorer interface.

Administrative Templates includes hundreds of very specific configuration settings that will edit the Registry settings on a computer for the user who logs on. Within the Administrative Templates section you will find that Windows Components such as NetMeeting, Windows Installer, and so on can be managed. For example, you can set a Group Policy that says a user does not have the ability to change the history settings on a computer. The Start Menu and Taskbar Group Policy settings allow you to configure how the Start menu works, such as whether users will see the Favorites or the Search menu item. The Desktop section allows you to hide or disable icons on the desktop or remove the Properties option from the popup menu for the standard desktop icons. When you have computers that are used by multiple users, you will probably select the **Don't Save Settings** option for the Desktop so that users who make changes will not affect other users who log on afterward. Another item within the Desktop setting is desktop wallpaper. By establishing a unique desktop wallpaper for each GPO, you can make testing fairly easy because you will have immediate visual clues as to which GPO was the last one that was processed. The Control Panel option within Group Policy enables you to lock down the Control Panel and its icons from curious users. Under Network, you can configure how users can interact with offline files and whether they are allowed to make changes to network connections.

You should investigate each Group Policy setting that is available within a GPO and consider which groups of users in your organization need those settings. Most corporate organizations consist of clearly defined departments, such as accounting, sales, and so forth. People within those groups usually require identical configurations and security options. In an Accounting group, you might decide that the users are savvy enough to have access to all their desktop, Start menu, and Control Panel. You might also decide that the users rarely move to other computers, so there is no need to redirect their folders to a network location. However, in comparison, a sales department might use computers that are accessible by the public and might require a more controlled desktop, Start menu, and Control Panel. In addition, a sales department might share computers and would benefit from Folder Redirection.

Not only should you list the clearly defined groups, but you should also consider people who cross multiple groups. You might include *everyone* as one of the groups, and *everyone but administrators* as another group. Furthermore, you might find *managers* as a cross-functional team, or *power users.* As you develop these types of groups, you could find that they need additional software, additional rights, or different options than you might select for the rest of the people within their departmental group. These are the groups for which you can either create an OU structure to organize them or create security groups. If you choose the former, you can use policy inheritance blocking or enforcement to ensure that the proper GPOs are applied. If you choose the latter, you can filter the GPO application based on security group membership.

EXAM 70-296 OBJECTIVE 9.1.3

Planning the Computer Environment

The Computer Configuration node of a Group Policy is used for establishing the computer environment. The computer environment is usually easier to plan because there are usually only a small number of types of computers in an organization. These types typically fall into the following categories:

- **Publicly accessible** These computers should be fully locked down and automated to prevent errors, reduce deskside management costs, and prevent security breaches.
- **Organizationally accessible** These computers are usually assigned to individual users but are in locations that any user could easily access and use, such as a cubicle.
- **Management or traveler** These computers are usually assigned to a manager or a person who has significant security rights in the organization. Often, these are mobile systems (laptops or tablet PCs) that move about the network. Even so, these computers are usually kept within offices or locked rooms when onsite. Although these computers appear to be restricted, a user could probably access them without too much trouble. These machines require mobile security and offline files. They need local security settings so that the data on the computer is secured, even when a person logs on when not connected to the network. These

machines usually need to have extra software installed. Finally, the computer needs to be able to fit into multiple network settings. It is not often feasible to lock down the desktop on a mobile computer or a management computer.

- **Secured** These computers usually have data held locally, or an application, that is considered mission-critical at some level. They are often kept in locked rooms and require similar security as that you would apply to a member server. Locking down the desktops on these computers is usually not an option for the users who are supposed to have access to them. (However, it is usually okay to lock down the desktop for users who shouldn't have access to them.)

When you plan your computer environment, you should divide your computers into similarly used groups. Then look at the options for the computer configuration node, which is shown in Figure 6.11, at the time you organize your Group Policies. Notice that the Computer Configuration node contains policies similar to the User Configuration node, with the addition of others.

Within the Computer configuration node you have three top-level folders :

Figure 6.11 The Computer Configuration Node

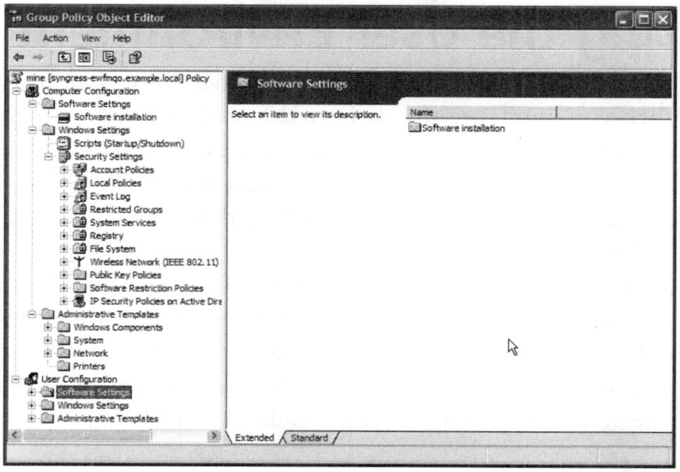

- Security Settings
- Software
- Administrative Templates

Within Security Settings, you will see that you have the ability to set the Account Policies, including both the Password Policy and Account Lockout Policy for computers. Keep in mind that the only time that Account Policies apply to computers that are actually connected to your network is when they are linked at the domain level. If you attempt to set these Group Policy settings in a GPO that is attached to an OU, they will have no effect on the computer when it is connected to the network.

EXAM WARNING

If on the exam you are provided the option to set a Password Policy and apply it to an OU, remember that it would only be considered a distraction from the way that a computer would function on the network. Password policies are applicable only to the entire domain. If you are told that two groups in a network need two different password policies, the network should have two domains.

The Administrative Templates within the computer configuration node offer different options from the user configuration Administrative Templates. These Group Policies allow you to configure the way that the computer functions during logon, whether the computer will use disk quotas, and how computers will implement Group Policy. You can also configure offline files, printer sharing, network configuration settings, and so on.

Configuring the User Environment

EXAM 70-296 OBJECTIVE 9.2

In this section, we look at how to configure the user environment through the use of Group Policies. When you configure the user environment, you create new GPOs at each level within the domain, site, and OUs until you reach the container for the user that you are configuring. You should have a plan listing the users who have similar configuration needs, plus an OU structure that will help you (rather than hinder you) in creating an inheritance flow of Group Policies.

Creating GPOs is done within the Group Policy Object Editor. You can access this console by adding it to the MMC as a snap-in, but we recommend that you use the Active Directory Users and Computers console to then go into the Group Policy Object Editor, because that way you will automatically link the GPO at the correct domain or OU container. When you create a GPO for a site, you should use the Active Directory Sites and Services console.

EXERCISE 6.02

CREATING A NEW GROUP POLICY OBJECT

In order to start the Group Policy Object Editor, you should:

1. Open the **Active Directory Users and Computers** console.
2. Navigate in the left pane to the OU where you will be creating a new GPO.

3. Right-click the OU.
4. Select **Properties** from the popup menu.
5. Click the **Group Policy** tab, which is shown in Figure 6.12.

Figure 6.12 The Group Policy Tab Is Available on the Properties Menu of a Domain, Site, or OU Object

6. Click the **New** button.
7. Type a name for the new GPO.
8. Click the **Edit** button, and the Group Policy Editor will start, as shown in Figure 6.13.

Figure 6.13 The Group Policy Editor Contains the Unconfigured Settings for All User and Configuration Node Group Policies

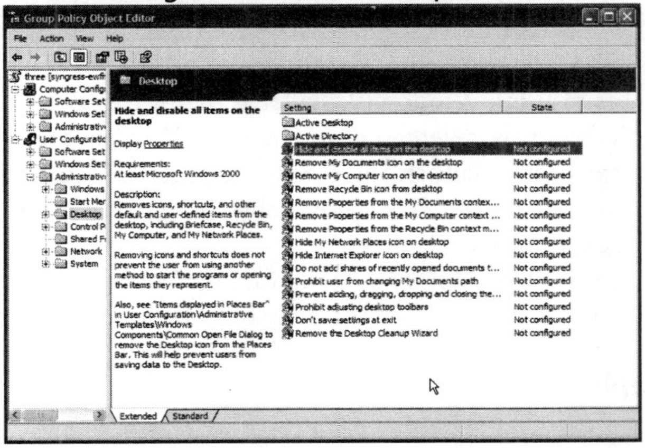

EXAM 70-296 OBJECTIVE 9.2.1

Distributing Software

In order to distribute software to a user, you use the Software Settings in a Group Policy. When you use this capability, you are able to use any software that uses the Windows Installer natively. For all other applications that use a different installation method, you need to create a .ZAP file. A .ZAP file is simply a text file that states how to run the setup executable for an application.

Configuring & Implementing...

Watch Your .ZAPs and .TXTs

Many organizations use applications that are "homegrown" and do not conform to the Windows Installer specification. Manufacturers don't necessarily conform to the Windows Installer specification, either. This makes the .ZAP file method of distributing software via Group Policy a quite possible option.

The .ZAP file is fairly simple to create. It is identical in structure to .INI files. In these, there is a heading in square brackets, which is then followed by options and their parameters. In the .ZAP file format, the first heading (which is required) is [Application]. This is followed by options such as FriendlyName=, SetupCommand=, and so on. FriendlyName= is followed by a name for the application. SetupCommand= is followed by the Universal Naming Convention (UNC) name of the path to the setup file. You can also have a second heading in the .ZAP file, which is [Ext] and can be used for extension information. This second heading is purely optional.

When you create a .ZAP file, you will most likely use a text editor. The problem with this is that many text editors automatically save any file with a .TXT extension. Further complicating this matter is the fact that Windows Explorer is commonly configured to hide the extension from the user, so a file that has a .TXT extension actually appears to have a .ZAP extension. Since a .ZAP file requires the .ZAP extension, any software that is distributed with an incorrectly named .ZAP.TXT file will not install correctly until the file is renamed without the .TXT.

One of the benefits of using Windows Installer is that it carries the ability to repair an application. If a user accidentally deletes a core file, the self-repair capability comes into play. When the user next tries to launch the damaged application, the computer checks the .MSI file and transform to see if the files are available. If a critical file is missing, the file is copied and the application can then launch.

From the standpoint of deploying patches and fixes, the use of Windows Installer reduces an administrator's time and effort considerably. The administrator simply runs the patch against the .MSI file and locates the GPO that originally deployed the software, then selects **Redeploy application**.

Group Policy allows you to create an upgrade relationship between two applications that are not related by either vendor or version. In doing so, the Group Policy setting can be configured to direct each user with the old version of the software to immediately remove and replace that software with the new version. Since the two software applications do not need to be related, this functionality allows an administrator to cancel all versions of one type of application (such as a graphics application) with something entirely different (such as a data-modeling application). In all likelihood, you will be able to use this method for replacing one virus software with another, or perhaps one word processing application with another, without fear of loss of functionality or accidental software license violations.

When you distribute software, you should consider the options to enable or disable when it comes to the Windows Installer and Control Panel. If, for example, you disable the Add/Remove Programs icon in Control Panel, any user who has had software published to him will not be able to access the installation for that software through this utility. If you disable Windows Installer for a user, you will not be able to distribute any software using the Windows Installer method. (You can, however, disable Windows Installer for nonmanaged applications only, which allows you to enable your Group Policy distributed software and prevents a user from installing anything else that uses the Windows Installer.)

In order to configure a software application for distribution:

1. Navigate to and right-click the **User Configuration Software Installation** node Group Policy, as shown in Figure 6.14.

Figure 6.14 The Software Installation node Group Policy for Distributing Software to Users Is in the User Configuration Node

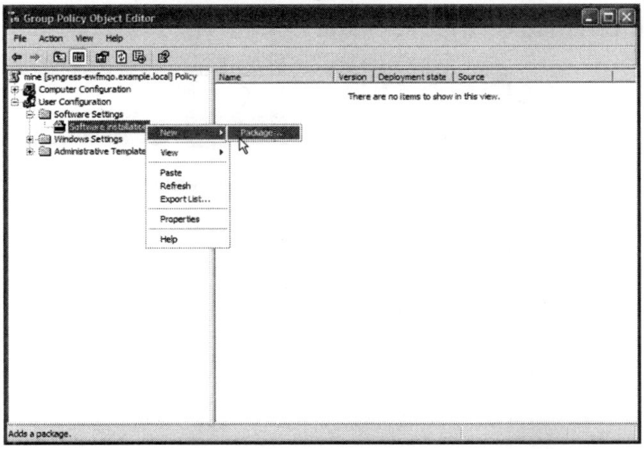

2. Select **New | Package** from the popup menu.
3. You are now allowed to browse for the .MSI or .ZAP file from the dialog screen. After you select the appropriate software installation package, you are presented with the dialog box shown in Figure 6.15.

Figure 6.15 You Can Publish, Assign, or Further Configure Each Software Package

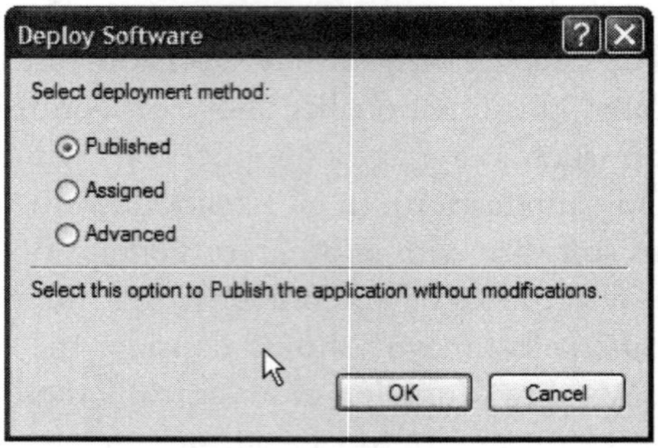

4. Here you will select whether to publish or assign the software. You only need to use the Advanced option if you will be making other configuration changes to the installation. For the purpose of our exercise, we have selected the **Published** option.
5. After you finalize your software distribution package, it will appear within the Software Installation node. You can then right-click the package, reconfigure it, redeploy it, publish it rather than assign it (or vice versa), or remove the software. Some of these tasks are shown in Figure 6.16.

Figure 6.16 Once Software Is Distributed, You Can Perform Ongoing Maintenance of that Package

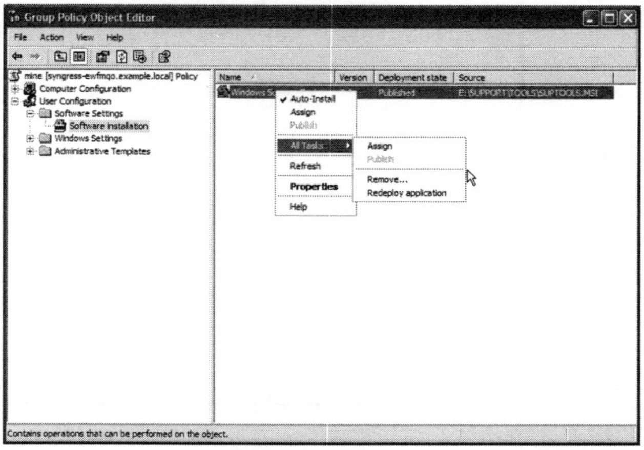

Test Day Tip

Know the difference between using Windows Installer packages and .ZAP text files. In addition, be able to explain when it is better to assign software than to publish it, and vice versa.

EXAM 70-296 OBJECTIVE 9.2.2

Autoenrolling User Certificates

User certificates are distributed by certification authority (CA) servers. When you plan for autoenrollment of certificates, you can reduce errors made by users who do not know when to accept certificates on their computer. This option can be configured so that there is no user interaction at all. Autoenrollment makes management of the network a bit easier.

When you configure autoenrollment, you can configure the certificate templates through the CA server under Windows Server 2003 in addition to configuring the autoenrollment in Group Policy. Since your clients may receive certificates from other types of CAs, you should always configure Group Policy settings when you want certificates to automatically be accepted by users. To do this:

1. Navigate to and double-click the **Autenrollment Settings** Group Policy setting, as shown in Figure 6.17.

Figure 6.17 Configuring Certificate Autoenrollment for Users in Group Policy

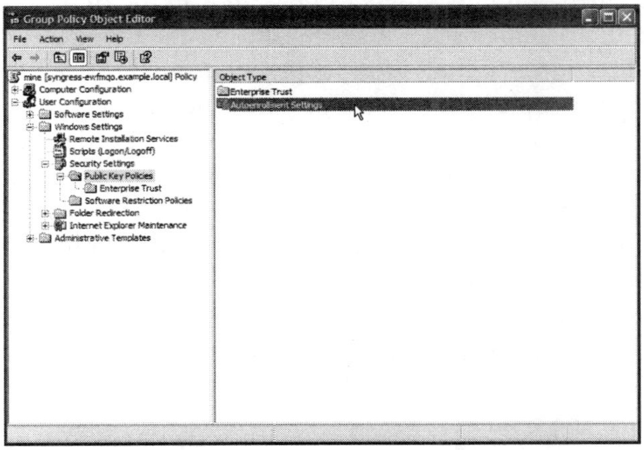

2. The Autoenrollement Settings Properties dialog box shown in Figure 6.18 should appear. Select the radio button and check boxes that best represent the behavior that you want to be carried out. You can enable certificate autoenrollment with either little or no user involvement. These options are also shown in Figure 6.18.

Figure 6.18 Autoenrollment Options Provide Little or No Interaction Between Users and Certificates

3. When the process is complete, click **OK** to finish.

EXAM 70-296 OBJECTIVE 9.2.3

Redirecting Folders

Folder Redirection is a user configuration option that allows you to configure the Desktop, Start menu, Application Data settings, and My Documents folder so that the identical contents appear regardless of which computer a user logs onto on the network. When you configure Folder Redirection so that different groups have different locations for their folders, be very careful when you move users to new OUs in the Active Directory tree, because they could lose their "information luggage" during the move!

Folder Redirection is valuable for people who wander around a network using different workstations or for people who receive or exchange their equipment on a regular basis. If your organization has users or groups of users who exhibit this behavior as part of their jobs, Folder Redirection is exactly what the doctor ordered. For example, if you have a group of teachers who move from classroom to classroom during the day, redirecting their folders to a network location would make each workstation that they move to appear with the exact same documents, Start menu items, and desktop data that the teachers expect to see. A teacher could save a document to the desktop in Classroom A and not have to go back to Classroom A to find that document later on. Instead, the document will show up on the desktops of the computers in Classrooms B and C and so forth, always with the latest changes that the teacher made.

Folder Redirection might not be right for people whose mobile computers are used offline. In these cases, a user could seem to "lose" documents or Start menu items and the like every time the user disconnects from the network. Imagine getting a phone call from an irate executive who lost his PowerPoint presentation because he saved it to the desktop while connected to the network but couldn't find it when he was ready to give the presentation after he disconnected from the network. Folder Redirection is useful for a specific set of people. If you choose to use Folder Redirection with mobile users, you should also consider configuring offline files in a way that synchronizes the redirected folders with the folders that users will use when disconnected from the network.

Test Day Tip

Be able to identify the folders that can be redirected and what those folders are used for.

When you redirect folders, you have four types that you can configure: Application Data, My Documents, Desktop, and Start Menu. These types are detailed in Table 6.2.

Table 6.2 Folder Types That Can Be Redirected

Folder Name	Usage	When to Redirect
Application Data	Applications use this folder to store data specific to . the user.	Redirect when you want applications to function the same way for a user without requiring reconfiguration each time the user moves to a new system.
My Documents	This is the default storage container for a user's data files.	Redirect when you want a user to access the same documents from any location in the network. It's preferable to redirect this folder when users do not have portable computers.
Desktop	The data files saved to the desktop are available wherever the user logs on.	Redirect when users save data files to the desktop. Do not use this option when you prevent users from making changes to the desktop.
Start Menu	The icons and data files placed in the Start menu are redirected so that they are available wherever a user logs on.	Redirect when you have consistent software installations throughout the network, when users save data files to icons on the Start menu, and when you want the user to have access to the Favorites and Printers and Faxes that the user typically uses.

In order to redirect folders, you need to perform the following steps:

1. Navigate in the GPO User Configuration node to **Windows Settings** and then to the **Folder Redirection** node.
2. Right-click the folder that you will be redirecting.

3. Select **Properties** from the popup menu. You will see the dialog box showing that the Folder Redirection for that folder is Not Configured, as displayed in Figure 6.19.

Figure 6.19 The Initial Setting for Folder Redirection Is Not Configured

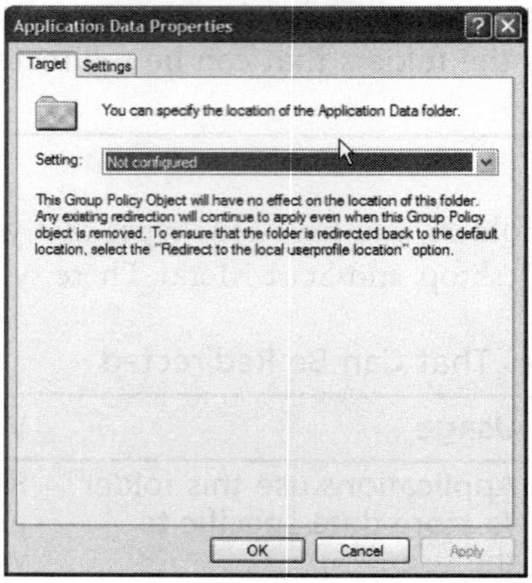

4. Click the **down arrow** on the **Setting** box to select either a Basic or Advanced Group Policy setting, as shown in Figure 6.20.

Figure 6.20 Selecting Either Basic or Advanced Settings

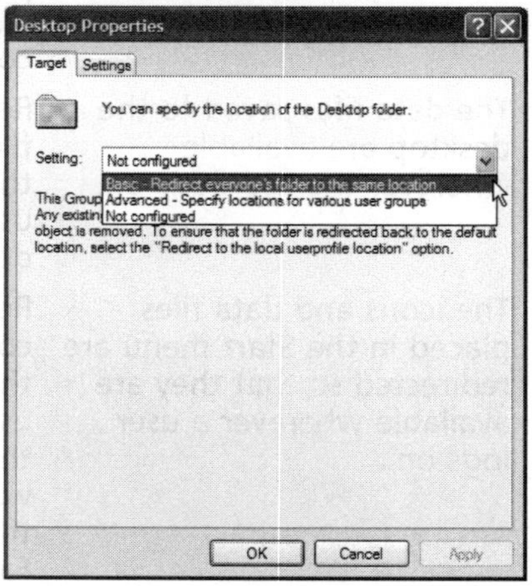

5. When you select the Basic option, which applies to all users, you are provided further configuration options, as shown in Figure 6.21.

Figure 6.21 Selecting Where the Folders Are Redirected in Further Options

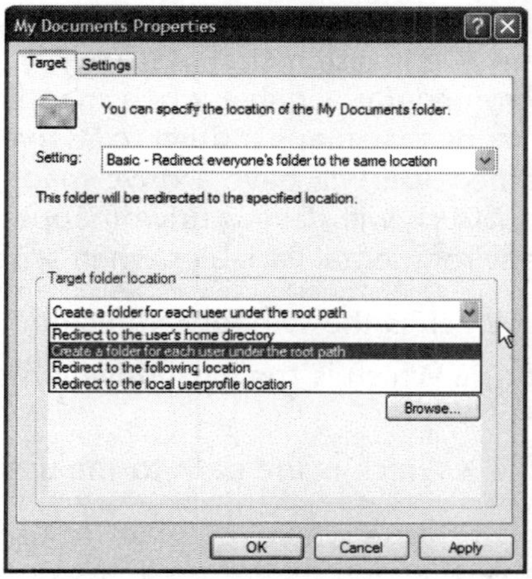

6. If you select the **Advanced** setting, you can add groups and configure the location for each group's redirected folders, as shown in Figure 6.22.

Figure 6.22 Advanced Settings Allow Redirection of Folders Based on a User's Security Group Membership

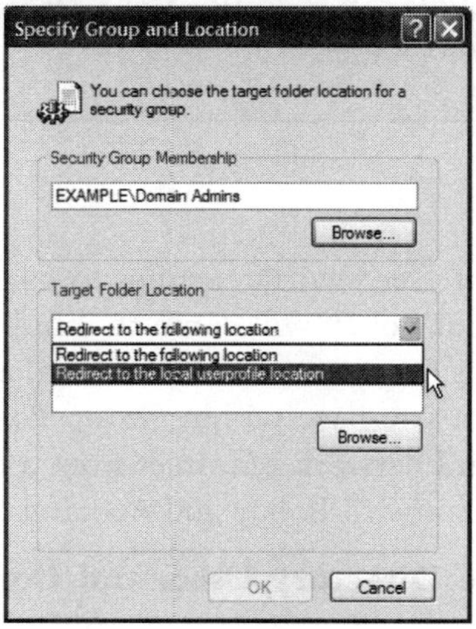

7. When you are finished making changes, click **OK** until all dialog boxes are closed.

Configuring & Implementing...

Redirecting Folders Without Environmental Variables

The Group Policy for folder redirection allows you to create a new folder for each individual user within the location that you specify, which is similar to using the %USERNAME% environmental variable when mapping drive letters. For example, you could create a script that maps a drive to \\server\share\path\%username%. In doing so, a user named *JOE* will have a drive mapped to \\server\share\path\JOE, while a user named *MARY* will have a drive mapped to \\server\share\path\MARY. You can use many environmental variables when scripting. These include:

- %windir% Which is the Windows directory location
- %systemroot% Which is the local drive where Windows has been installed
- %userprofile% Which is the path to the user's profile

However, problems arise when you want to use %USERNAME% or any other environmental variable that you might use in a script in the folder redirection path of Group Policy. In fact, you will not be very successful with any Group Policy setting that you configure with an environmental variable. This is due to the fact that the Group Policy takes effect before environmental variables are set.

Given the way that the folder redirection Group Policy functions, if you plan to use folder redirection, use a network share along with the option to create a folder for each user under the root path. Then, if you need to access the redirected folder during a script, you can then use the %USERNAME% variable along with the UNC name of the shared folder.

EXAM 70-296 OBJECTIVE 9.2.4

User Security

There are different types of user security settings to configure in Group Policies. Usually, a password or account lockout policy will come to mind. However, these are actually computer configuration settings that you would set for an entire domain at the domain level. The remaining options that you have within Group Policy for securing a user's resources, or even securing computer and network resources from a user, are considerable.

To edit the domain's Password Policy and Account Lockout Policy, do the following:

1. Open the **Active Directory Users and Computers** console.
2. Navigate to and right-click the correct domain node.
3. Select **Properties** from the popup menu.
4. Click the **Group Policy** tab.
5. Select **Default Domain Policy** and click the **Edit** button.

6. Navigate to the **Computer Configuration** node through **Windows Settings | Security Settings**.
7. To edit the Password Policy, the Account Lockout Policy, or the Kerberos Policy, double-click **Account Policies** and then make the configuration changes to the policy settings in question.
8. To edit further security options, drill into Local Computer Policy settings. The Default Domain Policy affects the users who are logging onto the domain. The Local Computer Policy settings in the **Computer Configuration node | Windows Settings | Security Settings** affect users who log on to the machine locally.

    When you use mobile computers, you can establish a security setting that will take place offline so that the machine is less vulnerable when it is away from the office.

When you establish user security, you should consider the types of action that a user should and should not be able to perform. If a certain task is considered outside the scope of a user's capabilities or job requirements, you might want to secure that action. For example, a user who installs additional software on an organization's computer would cause an unlicensed software problem for the organization. This is something that can be controlled through a variety of Group Policy settings.

You can restrict desktop and Control Panel settings through the Administrative Templates. These are individual Group Policy settings that you can enable or disable. For example, you can disable the user's access to the Control Panel or prevent the user from shutting down the computer.

Within the User Configuration node, you can configure software restriction policies to prevent users from installing software. These policies also allow you to restrict users from accessing files within the Windows and Windows\System32 folders. To create a software restriction policy:

1. Within the Group Policy Editor, navigate to the **User Configuration** node.
2. Open **Windows Settings**.
3. Open **Security Settings**.
4. Find and right-click **Software Restriction Policies** in the left pane and select **New Software Restriction Policies** from the popup menu. Two new subfolders and three new policy setting options will appear in the Software Restriction Policies folder.
5. To select which users to apply software restrictions to, edit the **Enforcement policy** setting.
6. To prevent a user from running any software, double-click **Security levels**. Edit the **Disallowed** policy.
7. To prevent a user from accessing Registry keys, click **additional rules**. Edit the policies for the paths that you do not want users to access.

Summary of Exam Objectives

Active Directory Group Policy is an intricate and complex tool that can be used to manage the environment of both users and computers across the network. In any Active Directory implementation, if you intend to take advantage of Group Policy, you need to develop a Group Policy strategy that takes advantage of the structure of your OU hierarchy.

Group Policies are applied in the order in which they are layered, one after the other, to create a final set of Group Policy settings. When multiple GPOs are applied that have the same setting configured, only the last GPO that is processed will "win" and provide the final setting to the user or computer object. The order that GPOs are applied is as follows:

1. Local policy
2. Site policy
3. Domain policy
4. Organizational Unit policy, beginning at the top of the OU tree and working toward the OU containing the user or computer object

You can block inheritance or enforce the inheritance of a Group Policy. If you block inheritance of Group Policies or use an enforced Group Policy, there could be an unexpected result.

Resultant Set of Policy (RSoP) is a new tool provided with the Windows Server 2003 Active Directory for both planning and troubleshooting Group Policy problems. RSoP can be used to simulate Group Policies, view the effects of security group membership, and provide you with a clear set of applied Group Policies when users in one location log on to computers in a different location.

Once Group Policy has been planned; you can then begin configuring the environment. You can configure the Default Domain Policy to establish both password policies and account lockout policies. In addition, you can configure a user's environment so that the user receives software delivered automatically through Group Policy, user certificates are automatically received and enrolled, and the user's data is provided to the user regardless of which computer the user logs onto.

Exam Objectives Fast Track

Developing a Group Policy Strategy

☑ Resultant Set of Policy (RSoP) is a Group Policy tool for both planning and troubleshooting Group Policy settings.

- ☑ Group Policies are inherited beginning with the local policy, followed by the site, domain, and then each nested OU that contains the user and computer objects affected.
- ☑ RSoP can be invoked in Logging mode from within Active Directory Users and Computers console by right-clicking a container, user, or computer object and selecting **All Tasks**, then choosing **Resultant Set of Policy (Logging)** from the context menu.
- ☑ When RSoP provides its results, it only displays those settings that are configured, ignoring any Group Policies that remained unconfigured throughout the successive application of GPOs.
- ☑ Each GPO contains both a user configuration node and a computer configuration node. The user configuration node applies to user objects; the computer configuration node applies to computer objects.

Configuring the User Environment

- ☑ Users can automatically receive software distributed through Group Policy. When software is assigned to a user, that user automatically has the software installed on any computer he or she logs onto. When software is published to a user, the software installation will be available within the Control Panel's Add/Remove Programs icon.
- ☑ Distributed software that uses the Windows Installer method can be redeployed, removed, and patched through Group Policy.
- ☑ Administrators can autoenroll users' certificates and require no interaction between the certificate and the user by configuring the autoenrollment policy.
- ☑ Folder redirection can be performed for the Application Data, Desktop, Start Menu, and My Documents folders.
- ☑ When applying user security through Group Policy, you must configure a domain level GPO in order to apply Password and Account Lockout Policies that affect domain users.

Exam Objectives Frequently Asked Questions

The following Frequently Asked Questions, answered by the authors of this book, are designed to both measure your understanding of the Exam Objectives presented in this chapter, and to assist you with real-life implementation of these concepts. You will also gain access to thousands of other FAQs at ITFAQnet.com.

Q: How can you use RSoP to plan if you can only look at one user's or computer's policies at a time?

A: You can add multiple instances of RSoP to a single MMC window. In each of these instances, you can generate RSoP data for different computers or different users, or a combination of the two, and then be able to navigate through the various RSoP instances to compare and contrast the data you discover through your queries.

Q: How does enforced inheritance work?

A: Enforcing the inheritance of a Group Policy is simply saying that the Group Policy that you are enforcing will be moved to the last GPO in line. Let's say that you have a domain policy for distributing the Office XP software. When you deploy this policy, you find that some OUs have blocked policy inheritance. When you enforce the GPO that you have configured, it will be moved to the end of the line and be processed last. As the last GPO processed, the GPO will "win" and be applied to the users.

Q: Why are you only allowed to run a planning query on a container, but you can execute either a planning or a logging query on a user or a computer object?

A: Planning mode is intended for simulations. If you move a user from one container to another, you will likely be planning for that move by generating a query. However, when you execute an RSoP query on a user or computer object, you might be troubleshooting that particular user's or computer's Group Policies, which means that you would need to log exactly what that particular object is experiencing, including that user's security group memberships.

Q: How can you configure folder redirection for a mobile user?

A: If you have mobile users and still want to use folder redirection for them, you should make certain that the mobile users have access to their files when they are off the network. To do so, you need to configure the Group Policy for Offline Files and synchronize the local folders to the redirected folders on the network. You should make certain that users synchronize their files at the time that they logoff the network.

Q: What is the benefit to assigning software rather than publishing it?

A: With publishing, some users will not be aware that the software application they are seeking is available for installation within the Control Panel's Add/Remove Programs utility. For these people, assigning a software application to the computer makes it instantly available when the user logs on. In other cases, even if it is assigned to them and available right on their desktop, you may have a problem with people uninstalling software applications. Assigning the software to their computers can help to ensure that the application keeps being reinstalled, no matter what uninstalling mischief your users are up to. The main disadvantage to assigning software to a computer is that the time to start the machine will be longer the first time after the software is assigned or at any other time in which reinstallation becomes necessary.

Self Test

A Quick Answer Key follows the Self Test questions. For complete questions, answers, and explanations to the Self Test questions in this chapter as well as the other chapters in this book, see the Self Test Appendix.

1. You are the network administrator for Vinca Jams. The company is a large food manufacturing and distribution corporation with locations all over the world. As a result, you have over 36 sites configured. You have three domains in Active Directory: vincajams.com, corp.vincajams.com, and food.vincajams.com. In each domain you have identical sets of 10 OUs, beginning with All, followed by Exec, Mgmt, Admins, and Standard. Within Standard, you have Finance, Accounting, Sales, Production, and Maintenance. You are developing a Group Policy strategy for user passwords. What will be the maximum number of different policies that you can configure for users who log on to the domain?

   A. 1

   B. 3

   C. 10

   D. 36

2. Your network has a single domain named saddlebags.org, with two sites, named Boston and NY, and four OUs. A single top OU named Corp contains three OUs named Admins, Mgmt, and Org, which are all configured as peers. You have created a GPO named POL1 that distributes Office XP to computer objects. You have also created a GPO named POL2 that redirects the My Documents folders to a network share. You want to make certain that Office XP is deployed to every user in the network. You want to make sure that folder redirection is performed for management and the rest of the organization, but not for administrators. To which of the following should POL1 be applied?

   A. Saddlebags.org

   B. Boston

   C. Mgmt

   D. Admins

3. You have a single domain with a single site. You are in the process of planning Group Policy for your network. During your testing phase, you have finally created the perfect desktop, Password Policy, redirected folders, and secured computer and user objects. You have made so many changes, blocked and enforced a variety of policies, and have applied so many GPOs in your test OU structure that you are not certain which Group Policies have been finalized. Which of the following actions can you take to make certain that the user object's Group Policies are documented and can be recreated in the production portion of the OU tree?

   A. In Active Directory Sites and Services, right-click the site and select **All Tasks | Resultant Set of Policy (Planning)**.

   B. In Active Directory Users and Computers, right-click the test OU at the top of the OU hierarchy and select **All Tasks | Resultant Set of Policy (Planning)**.

   C. In Active Directory Domains and Trusts, right-click the domain and select **All Tasks | Resultant Set of Policy (Logging)**.

   D. In Active Directory Users and Computers, right-click the user object and select **All Tasks | Resultant Set of Policy (Planning)**.

4. You have deployed a set of several Group Policies to the domain, the site, and the OU hierarchy. The various Group Policies consist of folder redirection, Password Policies, and locking down the desktop and Control Panel. Password Policy is applied to the domain. Desktop lockdown is applied to the Upgrade OU. Control Panel lockdown is applied to the Corp OU. Folder redirection is applied to the Clerical OU. You perform an RSoP query on a user and computer object that are both in the OU tree of All\Corp\Mgmt\LA\Upgrade. Which Group Policies will you not see in this query?

   A. Password Policy

   B. Desktop lockdown

   C. Control Panel lockdown

   D. Folder redirection

5. You are the network administrator of a domain with a complex OU hierarchy. About a dozen users have been moved out of the marketing department into sales. You move the user accounts into the new OU. You provide the users with new computers that are members of their new Sales OU. The marketing department and the sales department have different configurations for folder redirection, software applications that are distributed to users and computers, Control Panel lockdown, and autoenrollment of certificates. When you move the user objects from the Marketing to the Sales OU, which should you follow up with further configuration?

   A. Folder redirection

   B. Software distribution

   C. Control Panel lockdown

   D. Autoenrolled certificates

6. You are the network administrator for a large forest. You have recently hired on an assistant. You decide to grant your new assistant the rights to perform RSoP queries in the test OU structure of the domain. Which of the following wizards will you need to use to provide your assistant with the correct rights?

   A. Resultant Set of Policy Wizard

   B. Delegation of Control Wizard

   C. Active Directory Installation Wizard

   D. Group Policy Editor Wizard

7. Users in the Corp OU have the need for a software application named FINANCE. However, you discover that all users who are in the Corp\General OU should not receive FINANCE. Which *two* of the following actions should you take?

   A. Assign FINANCE to Corp users

   B. Assign FINANCE to Corp\General computers

   C. Block inheritance to Corp

   D. Block inheritance to Corp\General

8. You have a set of Group Policies that function well in your test lab. You want to see how these policies will work for users who log on using remote access through dialup or VPN across the Internet. Which of the following RSoP options should you select?

   A. Loopback processing

   B. Linked WMI filters

   C. Slow network connection

   D. Logging mode

9. You are planning the computer environment for a set of kiosks that you will place at pharmacies. You require that each of the kiosks is locked down and prevented from accessing any network resources other than the application that you are making available to the public. Each kiosk should be identical to the others. There are 10 kiosks, one for each pharmacy site. The pharmacies each have one to five other networked computers onsite. Each pharmacy has its own OU that is below the Pharm OU. Where should you place the kiosk computer objects?

   A. In an OU that is analogous to the site the kiosk is in

   B. In the pharmacy OU where it is located

   C. In the Pharm OU

   D. In a Kiosks OU below the Pharm OU

10. You are the network administrator for an Active Directory forest. You have three domains and seven sites. Each site contains users from each domain. Users in the Atlanta site require an application called PROJ. Users in the root domain, vincajax.com, require a strict Password Policy. Users in the JOBs OU within the corp.vincajax.com domain require folders to be redirected to a network share. To which of the following locations will you apply the GPO that distributes PROJ?

    A. Vincajax.com

    B. Corp.vincajax.com

    C. Atlanta

    D. JOBs

11. The manager of your company's service department has just invested in a new software application that she asks you to deploy to all 234 service department members. This application does not use Windows Installer. Currently the service department members are located in an OU that they share with the maintenance and file room departments. These departments do not require the new software application. Users in the service department often use computers belonging to the sales and file room departments. Which of the following actions should you take in deploying this application? (Select all that apply.)

    A. Install each service department computer separately.

    B. Create a .ZAP file for the application and deploy it by publishing it to users.

    C. Move all service department users into an OU that is nested within their current OU.

    D. Create a transform for the application and deploy it by publishing it to computers.

12. You have three groups of users in your company. Administrators have full access to everything within their computer and have no Group Policies aside from the domain's Password and Account Policies. The second group is power users, who have partial access to their computers and are able to configure desktop, Start menu, and printers. Power users are not allowed to install any software that is not approved. The third group is regular users. Regular users do not have access to any Control Panel or desktop configuration options. No one in the network should have to wait to log on to a computer because it impacts productivity, but users typically turn their computers on in the morning and then grab a cup of coffee. If you deploy a software application to all users, which of the following is the best method if you use Group Policy?

    A. Assign the application to users.

    B. Assign the application to computers.

    C. Publish the application to users.

    D. Publish the application to computers.

13. You have configured a GPO for the folder redirection of the Start menu. A user calls up and claims that his Favorites menu items keep appearing and then disappearing from his Start menu. What could be the problem?

    A. The user has accidentally received someone else's Group Policy.

    B. The Group Policy is refreshing on a periodic basis.

    C. The user's computer is periodically disconnecting from the network.

    D. The user has accidentally deleted the Favorites option from the Start menu.

14. You are the network administrator for Vinca Ink, a small company. In your network, you have created the following OU structure. The Corp OU is at the top of the hierarchy. Within Corp, you have the Admins OU and the General OU. Members of the production department, who are members of a security group that receives full access to the PROD server, want to have their My Documents folders redirected to the \\PROD\DESKTOP share. Which options do you select to configure this setting without affecting the other users in the General OU?

    A. Not configured

    B. Basic: Redirect everyone's folder to the same location

    C. Advanced: Specify locations for various user groups

    D. Cannot be done

15. You are configuring the Password Policy for the users within All Corp OU (which is the top of the OU tree) in the vincajax.com domain. There is only one site in Atlanta. To which of the following locations will you configure this policy?

    A. All Corp OU and create a new GPO for Password Policies

    B. The Domain Controllers OU, editing the Default Domain Controllers Policy

    C. The vincajax.com domain, editing the Default Domain Policy

    D. The Atlanta site, creating a new GPO for Password Policies

Self Test Quick Answer Key

For complete questions, answers, and explanations to the Self Test questions in this chapter as well as the other chapters in this book, see the Self Test Appendix.

1. **B**
2. **A**
3. **D**
4. **D**
5. **A**
6. **B**
7. **A**, **D**
8. **C**
9. **D**
10. **C**
11. **B**, **C**
12. **B**
13. **C**
14. **C**
15. **C**

Chapter 7

MCSA/MCSE 70-296

Managing Group Policy in Windows Server 2003

Exam Objectives in this Chapter:

10.1 Troubleshoot issues related to Group Policy application deployments. Tools might include RSoP and the *gpresult* command.

10.2 Troubleshoot the application of Group Policy security settings. Tools might include RSoP and the *gpresult* command.

- ☑ Summary of Exam Objectives
- ☑ Exam Objectives Fast Track
- ☑ Exam Objectives Frequently Asked Questions
- ☑ Self Test
- ☑ Self Test Quick Answer Key

Introduction

Group Policy in Windows Server 2003 is a very useful tool. As with Active Directory, we must be able to manage Group Policies and troubleshoot them when problems arise. Distributing applications through Group Policy is a wonderful feature and cuts down on the amount of time you will have to spend at an end user's desk; however, it isn't always the easiest thing to implement. Likewise with security settings that are implemented through Group Policy—they are a helpful feature but can cause unexpected side effects when they are rolled out to the user community.

In Chapter 6, you learned to how plan and configure a Group Policy strategy. You used tools such as the Resultant Set of Policy (RSoP) to plan and create your Group Policies. In this chapter, we use the RSoP tool and others to manage these policies once they have been put into place. You will learn how to manage these Group Policies for changes, but you will also learn how to troubleshoot a Group Policy that is ineffective or is not working properly once deployed.

Let's begin the topic of Group Policy management with a discussion of how you, the administrator, can change and build on Group Policies that have already been implemented.

Managing Applications

As we discussed in Chapter 6, you can use Group Policy to manage the distribution, installation, and maintenance of Active Directory-aware applications on your corporate network. The scope of these management functions can extend from the initial deployment of an application through the installation of any upgrades, patches, or fixes. You can use the Software Installation function of Group Policy to maintain consistent versions of an application, replace a deployed application with a new version, and remove the application from a workstation or server. You can associate these Group Policy settings with a specific computer so that the program will be available for anyone who logs onto a shared workstation or to allow roaming users' applications to "follow" them from workstation to workstation.

In order to install an application via Group Policy, you need to obtain a Microsoft Software Installer (MSI) package to automate the installation process. Many newer applications are Active Directory-aware, released from their manufacturers with preconfigured MSI files for your use. If the program that you want to deploy does not have an associated MSI package, you can use a third-party application such as WinINSTALL (www.wininstall.com), InstallShield's AdminStudio (www.installshield.com), or Wise Packaging Studio (www.wise.com) to create a customized installer for your use. In the case of legacy applications for which you cannot obtain or create an MSI package, you can create a text-based .ZAP file containing instructions for deployment.

When deploying an application, you have a choice of either *publishing* it or *assigning* it to a user or assigning it to a computer. If you assign an application to a user, the user will see a shortcut to the application on any workstation that the user logs into. The software will be automatically installed on the workstation the first time that the user double-clicks the associated icon. Assigning an application to a computer causes the program to be installed when the machine is first powered up, regardless of which user logs on.

If you want an application to be optionally available for users to install, you can publish it instead of assigning it. A published application will appear in the Add/Remove Programs applet in the Windows Control Panel. A published application will also be installed if a user attempts to launch a file that is associated with the application. Double-clicking on a Word document would launch the Microsoft Word installer if it hadn't already been installed on the system, for example. You can publish applications for user accounts but not computers.

TEST DAY TIP

.ZAP files typically require user intervention during the installation process; therefore, these applications can only be *published*, not *assigned*.

In Exercise 7.01, we publish a simple MSI installer package to the members of the Domain Admins group of a Windows Server 2003 domain.

EXERCISE 7.01

ASSIGNING AN MSI PACKAGE

1. Open Active Directory Users and Computers by clicking **Start | Programs | Administrative Tools | Active Directory Users and Computers**.
2. Right-click the domain node and select **Properties**.
3. On the Group Policy tab, click **New** to create a new Group Policy object (GPO). Name this GPO **Domain Admins GPMC Installation**.
4. Highlight the GPO you just created and select **Edit**. Navigate to **User Configuration | Software Settings | Software Installation**.
5. Right-click **Software Installation** and click **New | Package**.
6. Browse to the .MSI package that you want to distribute. Be sure that the installer is located on a network share that all users who need it can access. Click **Open** when you're ready to continue. You'll see the screen shown in Figure 7.1.

Figure 7.1 Deploying an Application via Group Policy

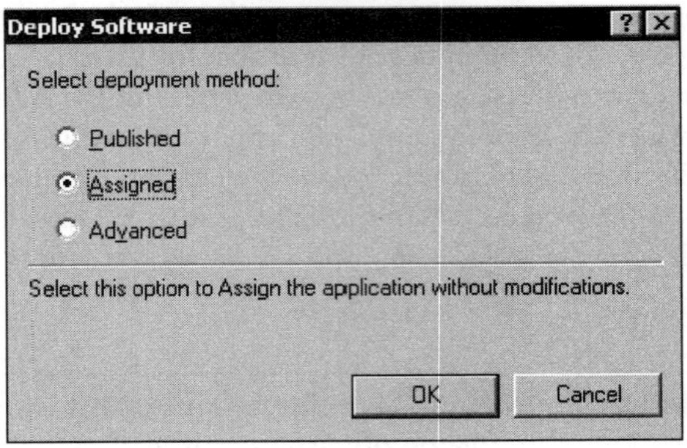

7. Since we want this application to be available to all Domain Admins regardless of which machine they log onto, we will assign this application. Click the appropriate radio button (**Assigned**) and click **OK**.
8. To further customize the behavior of this .MSI package, right-click the package name and select **Properties**. From the **Deployment** tab shown in Figure 7.2, you specify various options to modify the installation parameters.

Figure 7.2 GPO Deployment Options

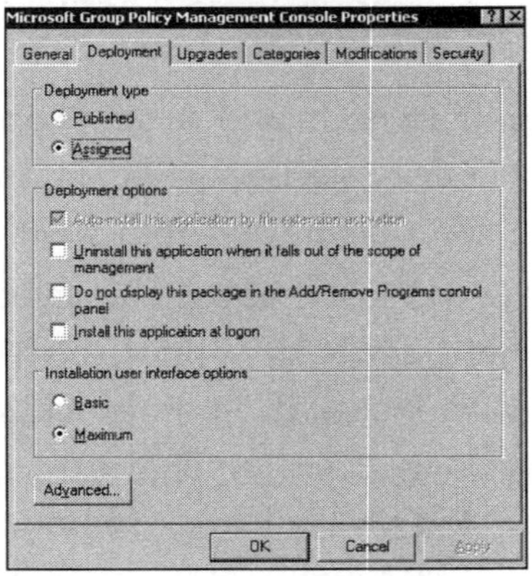

9. Since we only want this GPO to be applied to Domain Admins, we need to edit the permissions assigned to the object. Right-click the top-most node in the Group Policy Object Editor and select **Properties**.
10. Click the **Security** tab. You'll see the screen shown in Figure 7.3.

Figure 7.3 Setting Security on Group Policy Objects

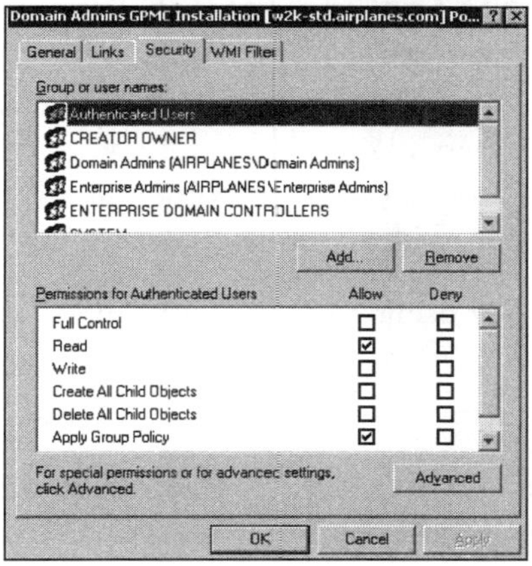

11. Remove the check mark next to **Apply Group Policy** for the Authenticated Users group. This will prevent users who are not members of the Domain Admins group from having the GPMC package installed when they log on.
12. Click the **Domain Admins** security group and add a check mark next to the **Apply Group Policy** permission. This will allow the GPMC package to install whenever a member of the Domain Admins group logs onto a network workstation.
13. Close the Group Policy Editor when you have assigned the appropriate permissions to the Group Policy you've created.

If you decide that you need to remove an application that you've deployed via Group Policy, simply right-click the package in the Group Policy Object Editor and select **All Tasks | Remove**. You'll see the screen shown in Figure 7.4. Just as in Windows 2000, you'll have the option to either immediately uninstall the deployed software or to allow existing users to continue to use the software and simply prevent any new installations.

Figure 7.4 Software Removal Options

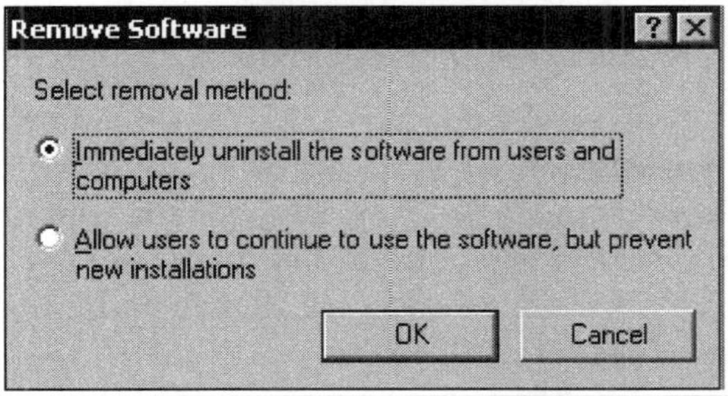

Managing Security Policies

Security settings and policies are rules that are configured on a computer or multiple computers for protecting resources on a computer or network. Security settings can control the way users can authenticate to a network or computer, the resources a user or group can access, and the user or group's actions that are recorded in a system's event logs. You can change the security configuration within Active Directory in two ways:

- Create a security policy using Security Templates, and then import it into a Group Policy object.
- Directly edit the Security Settings section of a GPO.

You can create a full range of system security parameters for your network using the Security Templates MMC snap-in, and importing a template into Group Policy can ease administration by allowing you to configure security settings for an entire domain simultaneously. You can use security templates to define any setting present within a GPO, including:

- Account, password, and account lockout policies
- Kerberos policies
- User rights assignments
- File system permissions

Template information is stored as a text-based file, allowing you to copy and paste or import and export the entire template or just a portion of its values. Like Windows 2000 before it, Windows Server 2003 comes with several preconfigured security templates that you can use to apply varying degrees of security to your servers and workstations, although these templates should not be applied to production systems without testing them first. The preconfigured templates available for your use are:

- **Default security (setup security.inf)** This template is used to reapply the default security settings to a machine if its security settings become corrupted or otherwise unusable.
- **Domain controller default security (DC security.inf)** This represents the security settings that are in place when you first promote a Windows Server 2003 server to domain controller status. As with the setupsecurity.inf file, you can use this template to roll back to a working template if a DC's security settings become unusable.
- **Compatible workstation (compatws.inf)** This creates a more relaxed security environment for occasions when your users require administrative privileges to run legacy or proprietary applications. You should not apply this template to domain controllers, because it relaxes the default permissions assigned to the Users and Domain Users groups.

- **Secure (securedc.inf, securews.inf)** A secure template defines more rigorous security settings, including strong password and lockout settings. It also configures servers to use only NTLMv2 authentication instead of LM or NTLM when servicing clients. Applying the Secure template to a server causes the server to reject any connection attempts that do not use NTLM or NTLMv2.
- **Highly Secure (hisecdc.inf, hisecws.inf)** A highly secure template assigns all the security settings present in the Secure template and then even further restricts the types of network traffic that servers and workstations will accept. A highly secure domain controller will reject not only LM packets but also NTLM. Hisecdc.inf also requires SMB packet signing and encryption.
- **System Root Security (rootsec.inf)** This template is used to reapply security settings to the systemroot directory of the main system drive.

Head of the Class...

Test First, and Ask Questions First, Too

Security templates make it comparatively simple to roll out security settings to a domain, but the importance of testing any new settings before applying them to a production environment cannot be overemphasized. Although you might logically want to apply the highest security settings possible, you must be sure that your domain environment can still function after the template has been applied. For example, if you apply the Highly Secure template, you should ensure that all domain controllers in your environment are running Windows 2000 or later, or they will lose their ability to communicate within the domain. This is the kind of thing that you will be much better off discovering in a test lab, rather than your help desk receiving "I can't log in!" phone calls at 8:00 A.M. on a Monday.

If you choose to directly edit your network's security settings, you can use the utilities discussed in this and the previous chapter to implement, manage, and troubleshoot your Group Policy security settings. You can also directly edit a GPO in order to fine-tune settings that you applied using a security template. Either method allows you to centrally manage security settings for an entire Active Directory forest or domain.

Head of the Class...

Recovering the Default Domain Group Policy Objects

When an Active Directory domain is created using dcpromo.exe, two default GPOs are automatically installed:

- The Default Domain Policy
- The Default Domain Controllers Policy

If the settings in these default GPOs are incorrectly configured or otherwise become corrupted, you could experience problems with client authentication, Active Directory replication, and other network functions. If the default policies become so badly damaged that you cannot simply restore network functions by resetting a setting or three back to their original values, you need to restore the default GPOs.

In a Windows Server 2003 domain, you can accomplish this task using the dcgpofix.exe that is included with the operating systems. This tool restores these default GPOs to their original settings, although any settings that have been added or modified will be lost. For more information, see *dcgpofix* in Help and Support Center for Windows Server 2003. The syntax of the *dcgpofix* command is as follows:

```
Syntax

dcgpofix [/ignoreschema][/target: {domain | dc | both}]


Parameters

/ignoreschema will ignore the Active Directory schema version number.
This is an optional switch.

/target: {domain | dc | both} specifies the target domain, domain
controller, or both. If you do not specify the /target, dcgpofix will
use both by default. This switch is also optional.
```

There is no tool for automatically repairing the default policies in Windows 2000 domains.

EXAM 70-296 OBJECTIVE 10.1

Troubleshooting Group Policies

Especially in an environment with many different OUs and policies applied at varying levels of the Active Directory hierarchy, Group Policies can sometimes behave in unexpected ways, either applying settings that you were not expecting or not affecting workstations that need to be controlled in some way. Along with factors specific to Group Policy that can cause issues, you might also need to look at underlying operating system and network connectivity issues to determine why a specific GPO isn't functioning properly.

Windows Server 2003 includes several utilities to assist you in troubleshooting misbehaving GPOs that we discuss in detail in this section. Most of these utilities are equally useful in troubleshooting security policies and application deployment; we'll point out any specific "gotchas" as we examine the various troubleshooting options available to you. Some of the utilities we look at are:

- GPResult
- GPOTool
- WinPolicies
- GPUpdate

We begin this section by examining various steps that you can take to troubleshoot Group Policy, including issues not specific to Group-Policy that can cause GPOs to fail or behave unexpectedly. Then we take a look at issues that are more particular to GPO functions such as the deployments of Software Installation and Security Settings. We conclude this section by looking at several utilities available to assist you in troubleshooting, including the ones in the preceding list.

Troubleshooting the Group Policy Infrastructure

GPOs can sometimes fail because of underlying issues with network connectivity or the Windows operating system. In order for Group Policy to be processed at the client, there needs to be functional network connectivity between the client workstation and at least one domain controller. When you're troubleshooting connectivity issues, be sure that you address the following possibilities:

- Group Policy requires TCP/IP to function properly. Even if you use another protocol on your network, GPOs will not be transmitted to your clients unless you also install TCP/IP.
- If a user is logging onto a workstation with cached credentials and is using offline files, they might not notice any connectivity issues. Be sure to use troubleshooting tools such as *ping* and *netstat* to verify that a workstation is actually communicating with the rest of the network.
- Network clients should be using some form of time synchronization such as the Windows Time Service. If the workstation's clock is not in sync with the rest of the network, it can create a myriad of otherwise untraceable problems, including authentication difficulties. When you're troubleshooting a situation in which a user is unable to access system resources such as the GPO, compare the time and date on the client with that of the domain controller and other network clients.
- GPOs use the Internet Control Message Protocol (ICMP) to detect slow network links. If your network configuration involves any hardware- or software-based firewall solutions, you need to enable ICMP packets between your domain controllers and clients.

Once you have eliminated network connectivity as a source of the problem, you should examine other potential causes within the Windows Server 2003 operating system itself, including the following:

- You should ensure that the DNS service is functioning and properly configured on one or more domain controllers in your environment. Active Directory clients use DNS, not NetBIOS, to locate a domain controller and access any applicable GPOs. Also, if a GPO entry (such as Folder Redirection) points a client to another network location such as a file server, the client will use DNS to locate *that* resource as well.
- Network clients require access to the SYSVOL share on all domain controllers in order to access Group Policy templates. Difficulty in accessing SYSVOL can result from incorrect network permissions or a problem with network replication.
- Be sure that the user or computer is a member of the appropriate site, domain, or OU to receive GPO settings. Remember that GPOs are not applied on the basis of group membership; group membership is used solely for setting permissions on Active Directory objects.
- Use tools such as *replmon* to ensure that Active Directory and file system replication are taking place correctly. If replication is malfunctioning, network clients might be using outdated versions of GPOs.
- To use the Groupl Policy Management Console (GPMC) and administer GPOs, you need to have the necessary privileges to create GPOs and/or manage links from a specific site, domain, or OU. You have the option of delegating control of existing GPOs to specific users or groups, so it is possible for someone to be able to use the GPMC to *view* GPOs without being able to modify, delete, or link them.

Configuring & Implementing...

Group Policy Behavior Over Slow Links

We'd all like to live in a world where our clients and servers are all connected by reliable, high-speed connectivity, but in some cases this simply isn't possible. To address the special needs of users connecting to a Windows Server 2003 network via a network link that is operating at 500Kbps or slower, Microsoft has altered the default behavior of Group Policy over a slow link such as a dialup modem or Integrated Services Digital Network (ISDN) line. When troubleshooting Group Policy settings via a slow link, keep the following points in mind:

- When a computer connects to an Active Directory-enabled Windows network over a slow link, Security Settings and Administrative Template settings are always applied, regardless of the connection speed.
- Software Installation, Startup and Logon scripts, and Folder Redirection settings are not applied over a slow link by default.

Continued

Even if you configure your Group Policy settings to run scripts over slow links, the scripts might run so slowly that they time out, creating an error on the client when the script fails to complete.

- Group Policy settings are not processed if the user connects to the network using cached credentials. To ensure that Group Policy is applied when users connect over a slow link, you must educate your users to select the **Logon using dialup connection** check box while logging onto their workstations.

Troubleshooting Software Installation

You must be aware of a number of issues specific to software installation settings when troubleshooting Group Policy. One of the most common issues centers on how logon scripts and policies are processed at the client. *Synchronous processing* means that Group Policy settings are applied one after the other. One must complete before the next will start. Additionally, a user will not receive a logon prompt until all computer related GPOs have been processed, or a desktop until all user related GPOs have been fully processed. With *asynchronous processing* a user may receive a logon prompt and have their interface appear ready before all GPOs have been applied. In this mode GPOs can run as a background task after startup and logon have completed. Software installation may need to occur at startup, so depending on how a client is handling GPO processing, it could take more than one logon or reboot for a software installation setting to be applied. Table 7.1 lists the default processing options for Active Directory-aware Windows operating systems; these behaviors can be modified through a Group Policy setting.

Table 7.1 GPO Processing Options

Operating System	Startup GPO Processing	Logon GPO Processing	GPO Refresh Processing
Windows 2000	Synchronous	Synchronous	Asynchronous
Windows XP Professional	Asynchronous	Asynchronous	Asynchronous
Windows Server 2003	Synchronous	Synchronous	Asynchronous

Test Day Tip

If Software Installation settings are applied through the Computer Configuration settings, installation will take place when the computer boots up.

File system rights can also affect software installation by rendering a client workstation incapable of accessing the necessary MSI packages. You need to be sure that your user accounts have the necessary NTFS and share permissions to access the network location where any MSI packages are being stored, as well as ensuring that share and directory names have been entered correctly into the GPO. You should also be aware of the following issues:

- MSI packages require that the logged-on user have the necessary privileges to install the package on his or her workstation; they do not support elevated privileges or the *RunAs* function.
- Be aware of the **Uninstall this application when it falls out of the scope of management** setting, especially if a user has changed security groups or OUs recently.
- If you've packaged a software installer into a .ZAP file, it cannot be removed via Group Policy and must be uninstalled manually.
- You cannot use Group Policy to install software that needs to be available on a Terminal Server. You need to install it locally as an administrator on the server itself.
- If double-clicking a file launches a different application than you were expecting, be sure that there aren't any locally installed applications that could have *hijacked* the file extension.

Troubleshooting Policy Inheritance

Especially in a complex environment, Group Policy inheritance can create unexpected results at the client level. You need to have a firm understanding of policy inheritance processing and rules when deploying and troubleshooting Group Policy behavior. For example, child containers inherit settings deployed by GPOs that are linked to higher containers within your Active Directory structure. These inherited settings combine with any settings deployed in GPOs linked directly to the child containers. If multiple policy objects lead to conflicting values for a given setting, the GPO with the highest precedence will prevail. GPOs are processed at the client level in the following order:

1. The local GPO is applied first
2. Site
3. Domain
4. OU; if a user is a member of a nested OU, GPOs associated with parent OUs are processed before those associated with child OUs

EXAM WARNING

Group Policy is processed in a *last write wins* model. GPOs that are later in processing order will take precedence over GPOs that are processed earlier.

When troubleshooting Group Policy inheritance, keep the following tips in mind:

- Conflict resolution applies to individual GPO settings, not to the entire GPO. Therefore, you can have a single setting in a GPO encounter a conflict that needs to be resolved while other settings in the same GPO are applied without issue.
- Child OUs inherit Group Policy settings from parent OUs by default, but child *domains* do not inherit Group Policy settings from their parent domains.
- Certain Group Policy settings, particularly password policies and account lockout policies, can only be applied at the domain level.
- The Enforce setting forces a GPO to apply to all Active Directory objects within a given site, domain, or OU, regardless of what settings are applied later. If multiple GPOs are applied with the Enforce option, the setting that is enforced *first* will win. This is the *reverse* of the usual GPO processing rules.
- Block Inheritance applies to an entire site, domain, or OU and prevents any GPO settings from being applied unless the GPO has the Enforce setting enabled.
- Be aware of Enforce and Block Inheritance settings, since they will cause the usual inheritance and processing rules to no longer apply.

Using RSoP

The Resultant Set of Policy (RSoP) function is a new feature of Group Policy management that simplifies the implementation and troubleshooting of GPOs. RSoP can query existing policies that have been applied against a site, domain, OU, or individual computer so that the results of that query can be analyzed by an administrator. RSoP can provide information regarding all possible policy settings that have been configured by an administrator, including:

- Administrative Templates
- Folder Redirection
- Internet Explorer Maintenance
- Security Settings
- Scripts
- Group Policy Software Installation

When multiple GPOs have been applied throughout the Active Directory structure, RSoP can assist you in determining which settings have taken precedence and have ultimately been applied against the user or computer in question.

You can use the RSoP function in two different modes: planning mode and logging mode. *Planning mode* allows you to simulate the potential effects of a new policy or policy setting before you actually implement it on your network. *Logging mode*, conversely, assists in examining existing policy settings that currently apply to a computer or user object. Planning mode allows you to examine "what-if?" scenarios regarding group membership and other factors; logging mode simply provides information regarding the existing policy settings for a given user/computer combination.

Using RSoP in Logging Mode

When used in logging mode, RSoP can assist you in troubleshooting both security settings and software installations. This is especially useful in determining how security group memberships and individual security settings will affect Group Policies as well as examining exactly which settings have been applied (or not applied) to a specific computer or user.

You'll use the Resultant Set of Policy Wizard to create an RSoP query in logging mode. You can access this wizard from a blank Microsoft Management Console (MMC), Active Directory Users and Computers, Active Directory Sites and Services or the Group Policy Management Console that you installed in Exercise 7.01. When the wizard has completed, it displays its results in the RSoP snap-in within the MMC. You can then save, change, or refresh the information used to generate the query. In Exercise 7.02, we examine the steps in running an RSoP query against a single computer.

Test Day Tip

In order to create multiple queries, you need to add multiple Resultant Set of Policy snap-ins to the MMC one at a time.

Exercise 7.02

Running an RSOP Query

1. Open a blank MMC console by clicking **Start | Run**, typing **mmc** and clicking **OK**.
2. Click **File | Add/Remove Snap-in**. Select the **Standalone tab**, click **Add**, then browse to **Resultant Set of Policy**. Click **Add** again and then **Close**.

3. Click **OK** to return to the Microsoft Management Console.
4. Right-click the **Resultant Set of Policy** node and select **Generate RSoP Data**, as shown in Figure 7.5.

Figure 7.5 Generating RSoP Data

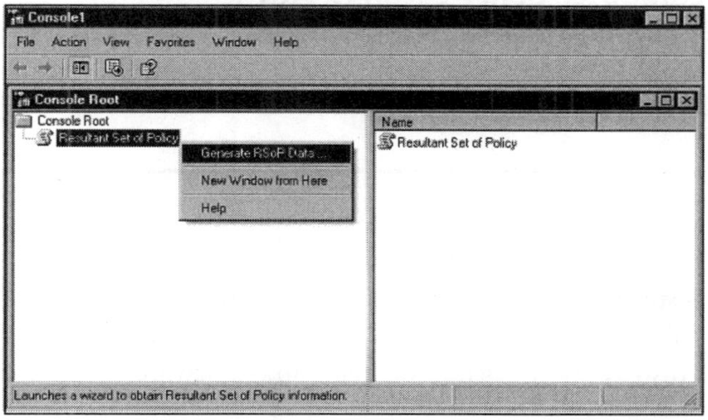

5. Click **Next** to bypass the initial Welcome screen.
6. On the **Mode Selection** page, click **Logging mode**, and then click **Next**.
7. The Computer Selection screen (shown in Figure 7.6) gives you the option to generate data about the computer on which you're running the RSoP snap-in or to select another computer on the network. You can also place a check mark next to **Do not display policy settings for the selected computer in the results (display user policy settings only)** to restrict the output of the query. Click **Next** when you're ready to continue.

Figure 7.6 Computer Selection in the RSoP Query Wizard

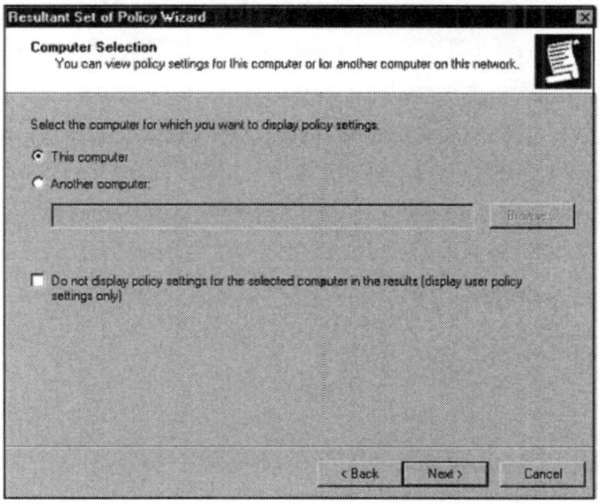

8. The next screen is the User Selection screen. Similarly to the screen in the previous step, you can generate the RSoP query based on the currently logged-on user or select another user in the Active Directory database. You can also restrict the results of the query by selecting **Do not display policy settings for the selected user in the results (display computer policy settings only)**.
9. The final screen will display a summary of the choices you've made. Click **Next** to begin the RSoP query. Click **Finish** when the query has completed.

After you run the Resultant Set of Policy wizard, the RSoP console will be populated with data from the results of the query. The specific results for Software Settings, and Windows Settings, will appear in the right-hand side of the MMC console window. For example, RSoP will display the information regarding software installation settings as listed in Table 7.2.

Table 7.2 Software Installation Information Generated by RSoP

Name	Lists the name of the deployed package.
Version	Lists the software version of the deployed package.
Deployment state	Indicates whether the package is assigned or published.
Source	Specifies the source location of the deployed package.
Origin	Lists the name of the Group Policy object that deployed the package.

Security Settings information appears the same as for Group Policy with one exception: When you double-click a policy setting, the Security Policy Settings tab will not be available, and you'll see a Source GPO column instead. The Source GPO column indicates which Group Policy objects affect a policy setting, as illustrated in Figure 7.7.

Now that we've covered the steps in running an RSoP query to examine production data on a given workstation, we'll turn to its other function on your network: planning. Exercise7.03 walks you through the process of creating a Group Policy simulation using RSoP in planning mode.

Figure 7.7 Results of RSoP Query

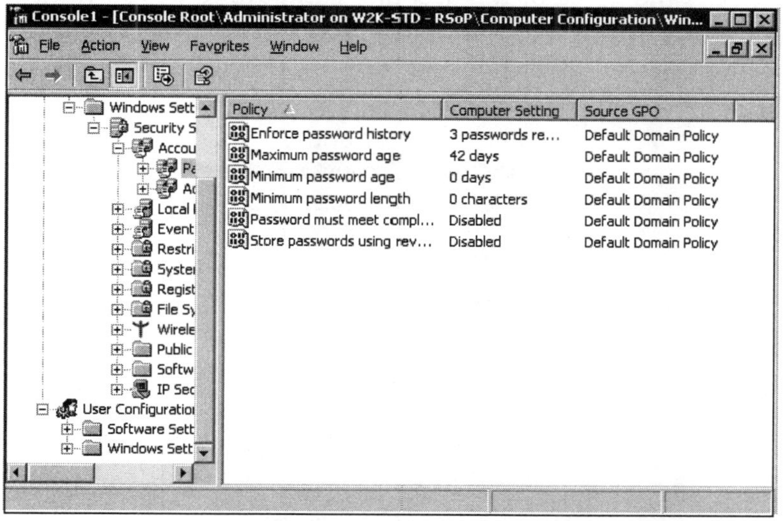

EXERCISE 7.03

USING RESULTANT SET OF POLICY IN PLANNING MODE

1. From an MMC console with the RSoP snap-in loaded, right-click **Resultant Set of Policy**, and then click **Generate RSoP Data**. Click **Next** to bypass the initial Welcome screen.
2. On the **Mode Selection** page shown in Figure 7.8, select **Planning mode** and then click **Next**.

Figure 7.8 Selecting the RSoP Report Mode

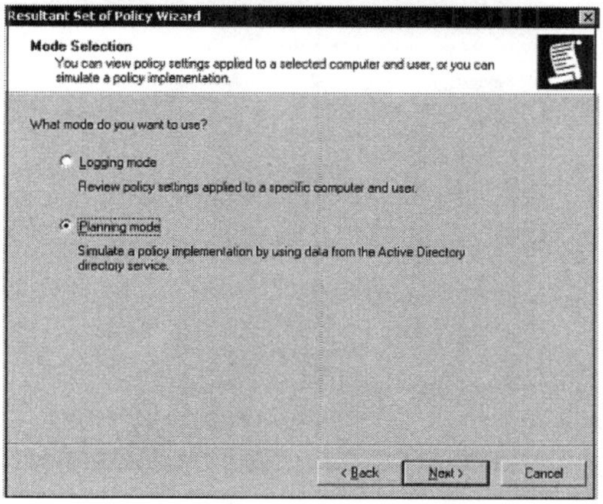

3. On the **User and Computer Selection** page shown in Figure 7.9, specify the name of the user and computer that you want to analyze, and then click **Next**. Alternately, you can select an entire user and/or computer container to analyze.

Figure 7.9 Specifying the User and Computer Information

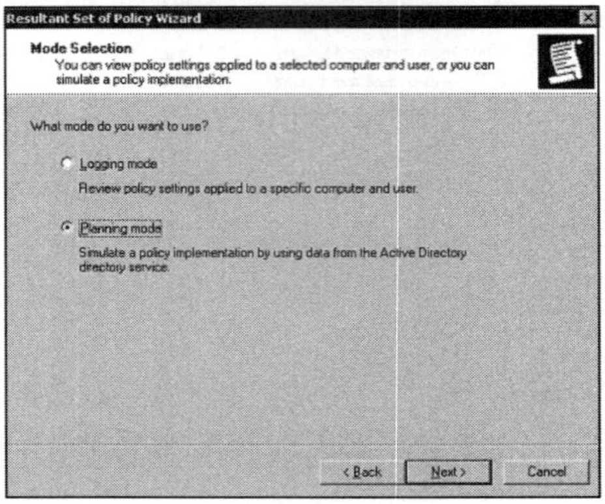

4. From the **Advanced Simulation Options** screen shown in Figure 7.10, you can choose to modify the report results as though a slow network connection and/or loopback processing were being used by placing check marks in the appropriate boxes. If you want to simulate loopback processing, you need to select either **Replace**, to simulate Group Policy settings based only on GPOs applied to the computer, or the **Merge** option, to simulate GPO settings based on both the computer and the user. Click **Next** when you're ready to continue.

Figure 7.10 Advanced Simulation Options

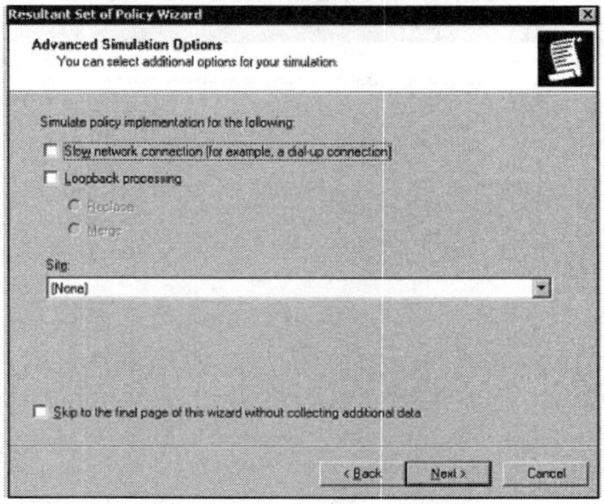

5. Next you'll see the security groups that the specified user is a member of on the User Security Groups screen, as shown in Figure 7.11. You can use the **Add** or **Remove** buttons to specify different security group memberships to simulate. (If you make a mistake, you can click **Restore Defaults** to start over.) Click **Next** when you're ready to continue.

Figure 7.11 Simulating User Security Group Membership

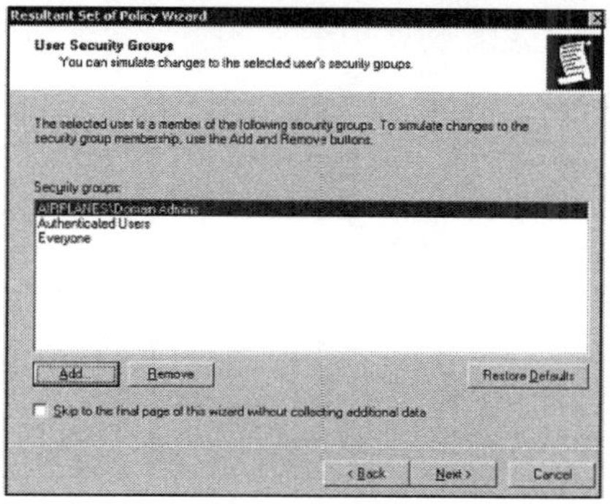

6. The following screen lists the security groups that the specified *computer* is a member of. Just as in Step 5, you can use the **Add** or **Remove** buttons to change the contents of the RSoP report. Click **Next** to continue.

7. By default, the report includes all possible WMI filters, as shown in Figure 7.12. If you've created any WMI filters that would cause the computer you've specified to *not* be subject to Group Policy, you should remove them by clicking **Only these filters** and selecting **Remove**. Click **Next** to repeat the process for any computer-specific WMI filters.

Figure 7.12 Selecting WMI Filters

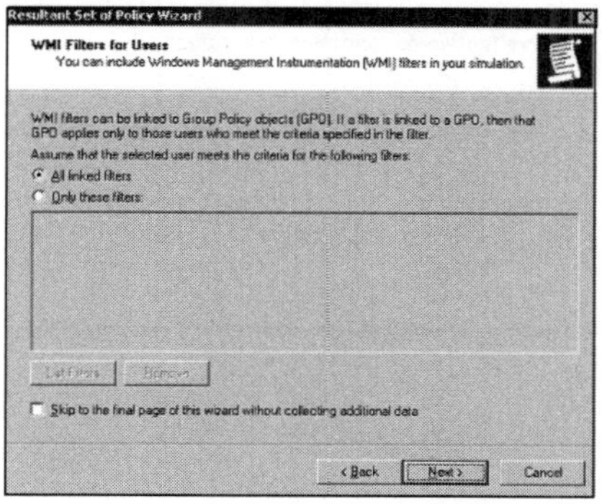

8. Click **Next** again. You'll see the Summary screen shown in Figure 7.13. If you are satisfied with the selections you've made, click **Next** again to run the simulation. It could take several minutes to complete.

Figure 7.13 RSoP Summary Screen

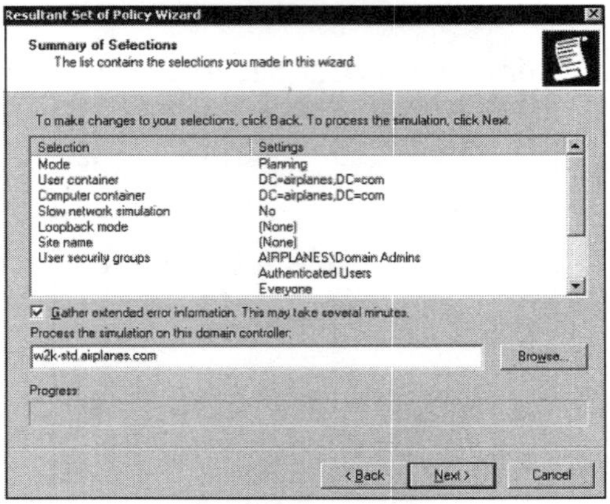

9. When the simulation has completed, click **Finish**. In the console tree, click the RSoP query to view the data. You'll see a screen similar to the one shown in Figure 7.14.

Figure 7.14 A Completed RSoP Simulation

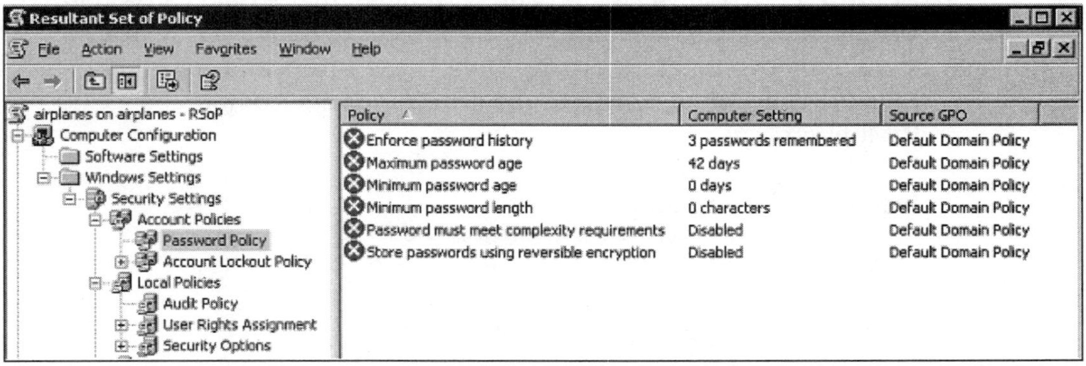

Using RSoP to Troubleshoot Security Settings

The RSoP function can assist you in troubleshooting security settings in the following three areas:

- Security templates
- Group Policy filtering
- Individual security settings

As you know, security templates allow you to easily create and assign a full configuration of security settings for one or more computers on your network. You can apply templates to a local computer or import them into a GPO within Active Directory, at which point Group Policy will process the security template and propagate the appropriate changes to those users and computers that are affected by the GPO in question. RSoP can help you verify that security templates have been applied properly and can point out any settings that might have been overwritten due to conflicting policy settings. This will help you identify and correct any potential security breaches caused by an improperly implemented security template.

You can use security group membership to refine the list of computers and users that are affected by a given GPO using security filtering. The RSoP snap-in takes security groups into consideration when creating its reports and "what-if?" scenarios, allowing you to see how security group memberships are affecting the application of Group Policy settings on your network. RSoP also takes into account any individual security settings that have been applied locally to a specific user or computer.

Using GPResult.exe

GPResult.exe is a command-line utility available with Windows 2000 and Windows Server 2003 that gathers and reports RSoP data for machines similar to what you'd see in a Group Policy Results report in the GPMC. The syntax and parameters for gpresult.exe are as follows:

```
gpresult [/s Computer [/u Domain\User /p Password]] [/user TargetUserName] [/scope
{user|computer}] [/v] [/z]
```

- **/s *Computer*** Specifies the DNS name or IP address of the remote computer you want to analyze. (Do not use a UNC name such as \\SERVER.) If you do not specify this parameter, GPResult will analyze the local computer.
- **/u *Domain\User*** Provides the logon credentials under which GPResult runs (similar to the *RunAs* function). By default, GPResult uses the security context of the user who is logged onto the computer that issues the command.
- **/p *Password*** Specifies the password of the user account that is specified in the */u* parameter.

- **/user** ***TargetUserName*** Specifies the username of the user you want GPResult to analyze.
- **/scope {user | computer}** Allows you to restrict the GPResult analysis to display only user or computer results. If you do not use this parameter, GPResult displays both user and computer settings.
- **/v** Displays verbose policy information.
- **/z** Displays all available information about Group Policy, producing even more complete information than the **/v** parameter. You should pipe the output of this command to a text file when you use this parameter by specifying the following: **gpresult /z >policy.txt**.

Here are some examples of properly formatted GPResult queries. The following query analyzes the RSoP for user *jsmith* on workstation \\jsmith-ws:

```
gpresult /user jsmith /s jsmith-ws
```

The following syntax analyzes the RSoP for user *acctmgr* on the machine \\DC1. It will return only the User Configuration section of the RSoP data and will access DC1 using the specified logon credentials:

```
gpresult /s DC1 /u AIRPLANES\supervisor /p p@ssW23 /user acctmgr /scope USER
```

The following syntax analyzes RSoP for user *emanderville* on computer DC1. It returns all possible information using the */z* switch and copies the returned information to the file policy.txt:

```
gpresult /s DC1 /u AIRPLANES\supervisor /p p@ssW23 /user emanderville /z >
policy.txt
```

You can see a sample output for the *GPResult* command here:

```
==============================================================
  User Group Policy results for:

  CN=Smith\, Joanne, CN=Users,DC=biplanes,DC=airplanes,DC=com
  Domain Name:                BIPLANES
  Domain Type:                Windows 2003
  Site Name:                  Default-First-Site-Name
  Roaming profile:       (None)
  Local profile:          C:\Documents and Settings\Smith
  The user is a member of the following security groups:
     BIPLANES\Domain Users
     BIPLANES\Domain Admins
     BIPLANES\Enterprise Admins
```

```
###############################################################
Last time Group Policy was applied: Monday, June 02, 2003 at 11:04:31 AM
Group Policy was applied from: dc1.biplanes.airplanes.com
===============================================================
The user received "Registry" settings from these GPOs:
     Default Domain Policy
###############################################################
Last time Group Policy was applied: Monday, June 02, 2003 at 11:14:58 AM
Group Policy was applied from: dc1.biplanes.airplanes.com

===============================================================
```

Other Troubleshooting Techniques

The Windows Server 2003 Resource Kit provides additional tools to assist you in troubleshooting Group Policy and underlying infrastructure and replication issues. You can view the full syntax of each command by running them from the command line using the */?* switch. Some of the available tools are listed here:

- **GPMonitor.exe** The Windows Server 2003 Resource Kit includes a tool that collects information every time there is an update or a refresh to Group Policies, then forwards that information to a central location that you can query.
- **GPOTool.exe** A command-line utility that monitors replication between controllers within a Windows Server 2003 domain. It examines each controller within a domain and inspects the consistency between the Group Policy stored in the Active Directory database and the Group Policy template information stored in the SYSVOL directory. The tool also determines if all GPOs are consistent between controllers and displays detailed information about replicated data. The output of GPOTOOL resembles the following:

```
Validating DCs...
Available DCs:
dc1.airplanes.com
dc2.airplanes.com
dc3.airplanes.com
Searching for policies...
Found 3 policies
============================================================
Policy {13290349-FE7A-4DB9-9D94-48A203146E87}
Policy OK
```

```
===========================================================
Policy {1E401EB6-301E-4A35-A377-DDF5150DCC68}
Policy OK
===========================================================
Policy {31B2F340-016D-11D2-945F-00C04FB984F9}
Policy OK
===========================================================

Policies OK
```

- **WinPolicies.exe** A Windows Server 2003 Resource Kit Utility that allows you to investigate detailed Group Policy and Registry log information. You can see some of the troubleshooting options available with WinPolicies in Figure 7.15.

- **GPUpdate.exe** Refreshes the Group Policy settings on a client, replacing

Figure 7.15 WinPolicies Resource Kit Utility

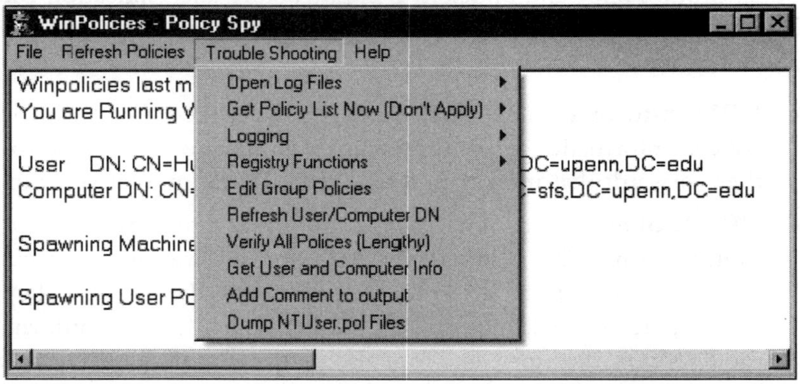

the *secedit /refresh_policy* command that you used in Windows 2000. You can use this utility if you suspect that GPO refresh is not functioning or if you've made a change that you want to see applied immediately. The syntax for *gpupdate* is as follows:

```
GPUpdate [/Target:{Computer | User}] [/Force] [/Wait:<value>] [/Logoff]
[/Boot] [/Sync]
```

- ***/Target :{ Computer | User}*** Allows you to specify that only User or Computer policy settings should be refreshed. By default, both User and Computer policy settings are refreshed.

- ***/Force*** Prompts GPUpdate to reapply all policy settings. By default, it will only reapply those settings that have changed since the last Group Policy refresh.
- **/Wait:{value}** Causes GPUpdate to wait a certain number of seconds for all policy processing to finish. The default value if this parameter is not specified is 600 seconds. The value 0 means not to wait; -1 causes GPUpdate to wait indefinitely. If the time limit is exceeded, the command prompt returns while policy processing continues.
- **/Logoff** Forces the user to log off the computer after the Group Policy settings have been refreshed. This is required for those Group Policy settings that are only processed when a user logs on, including Software Installation and Folder Redirection. This option has no effect if no extensions are called that require a logoff.
- **/Boot** Causes a reboot after the Group Policy settings are refreshed. This is required for those Group Policy settings that are only processed on computer startup, especially computer-targeted Software Installation. Like the */Logoff* option, this option has no effect if no extensions are called that require a reboot.
- ***/Sync*** Causes the next policy application to occur synchronously on startup or logon. You can specify this for the user, computer, or both using the */Target* parameter. The */Force* and */Wait* parameters are ignored if the */Sync* option is specified.

Using the Group Policy Management Console

Before the release of Windows Server 2003, network administrators needed to use several different applications and utilities to manage Group Policy settings on their networks. Depending on the specific function, you might have needed to use Active Directory Users and Computers, Active Directory Sites and Services, or the RSoP snap-in to access the various pieces of Group Policy functionality. The Group Policy Management Console (GPMC) brings together existing Group Policy functions into a single management console as well as offering several new capabilities. The GPMC allows you to control multiple domains and forests, enabling you to easily manage Group Policy settings across an entire enterprise. You can customize a GPMC console to display all domains and forests within your administrative control or restrict it to only a subset of the network, allowing you to delegate administrative functions to multiple administrators within the enterprise.

You can run the GPMC from any machine running either Windows Server 2003 or Windows XP Professional with Service Pack 1. If you are going to install the GPMC on your XP Professional workstation, you also need to install a hotfix from Microsoft to upgrade the

GPEDIT.DLL file. (This hotfix will be included in Windows XP Service Pack 2.) The GPMC is available as a free download from the Microsoft Web site; you can install it by simply double-clicking the **gpmc.msi** file once you've downloaded it to your workstation.

New & Noteworthy...

Group Policy Management Console Features

In an attempt to make the lives of network administrators somewhat simpler, Windows Server 2003 has introduced the GPMC as the new means of managing Group Policies across an enterprise network. The GPMC comprises an MMC as well as a collection of automated scripts that can be run from the command line as well as integrated into batch files or other applications to streamline administration. Additionally, the GPMC provides the following improvements over the Windows 2000 Group Policy Object Editor:

- The ability to back up and restore individual GPOs
- Easier administration of Group Policy security settings
- Import/export and copy/paste functions that allow you to transfer GPO settings between domains and OUs
- On-demand reports of GPO settings and RSoP data in HTML format
- Simplified user interface and preloaded scripts to automate GPMC-related tasks

The default scripts that are included with the GPMC installation allow you to quickly do the following:

- List all GPOs in a domain
- List disabled GPOs
- List GPO information
- List GPOs at a backup location
- List GPOs by policy extension
- List GPOs by security group
- List GPOs orphaned in SYSVOL
- List GPOs with duplicate names
- List GPOs without security filtering
- List Scope of Management (SOM) information
- List SOM with links to GPOs in external domains
- List unlinked GPOs in a domain
- Print the SOM policy tree

Key Features and Benefits

The GPMC provides one-stop shopping to view all GPOs, sites, domains, and OUs across your enterprise. This utility can be used to manage domains running any combination of Windows 2000 and Windows Server 2003. The GPMC also offers a number of new features to streamline and improve Group Policy management on your network, including Windows Management Interface (WMI) filtering and over 200 new configurable settings within the Windows Server 2003 Administrative Templates. These new settings allow for even more granular control over components of the Windows environment, including the Control Panel, Terminal Services, Remote Assistance, networking and dial-up settings, network logon functions, roaming profiles, client DNS settings, and more.

WMI filtering is another new feature offered by Group Policy under Windows Server 2003. You can now filter the effects of a GPO dynamically using selected attributes of target computers. For example, you can create a WMI filter to include any machines with more than 250MB of free disk space or all Windows XP Professional workstations running Service Pack 1. For readers who are familiar with Microsoft Systems Management Server (SMS), this is a similar function to that offered by creating groups of computers to manage within SMS. Windows Server 2003 now allows you to leverage this function without purchasing additional software. Additionally, the Group Policy Modeling function includes an option to use WMI to perform a "what-if?" analysis based on specific WMI properties; effectively allowing you to ask: "If I base this GPO on the following WMI filter, which machines will and will not be affected?"

Once you've installed the GPMC, the Group Policy tab in Active Directory Users and computers and Active Directory Sites and Services will only contain a button that allows you to open the GPMC. It will not contain the other information or buttons you are used to finding there. The necessary steps to perform common Group Policy tasks within GPMC have changed only slightly; we discuss each of them in this section. When you first open the GPMC by clicking **Start | Administrative Tasks | Group Policy Management**, you'll see the screen shown in Figure 7.16. By default, the GPMC will attempt to access the forest that the currently logged-on user has access to. You can right-click the topmost Group Policy Management node and select **Add Forest** to access another Windows 2000 or 2003 forest.

Figure 7.16 Group Policy Management Console

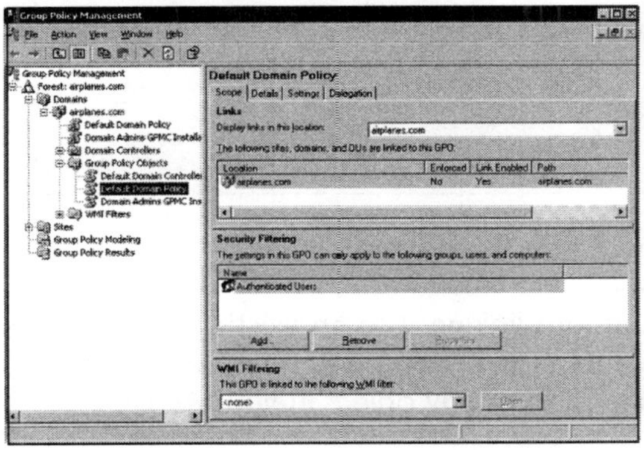

GPMC allows you to create a new GPO and link it to a site, domain, or OU in a single step. From the GPMC console, right-click the relevant domain, site, or OU, and select **Create and link a GPO here**. Enter a name for the new GPO and click **OK**. This will create a blank GPO that is linked to the location you selected. You will see a shortcut to the new GPO by expanding the [+] sign next to the icon, as shown in Figure 7.17.

Figure 7.17 Create and Link a New GPO

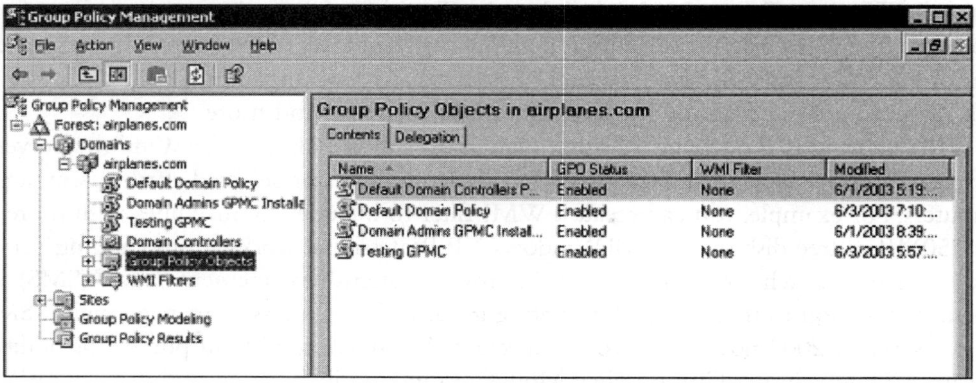

You can link an existing GPO to a site, domain, or OU by right-clicking the object in question and selecting **Link an Existing GPO Here**. From the screen shown in Figure 7.18, you can select an existing GPO to apply to an Active Directory container.

Figure 7.18 Linking an Existing GPO

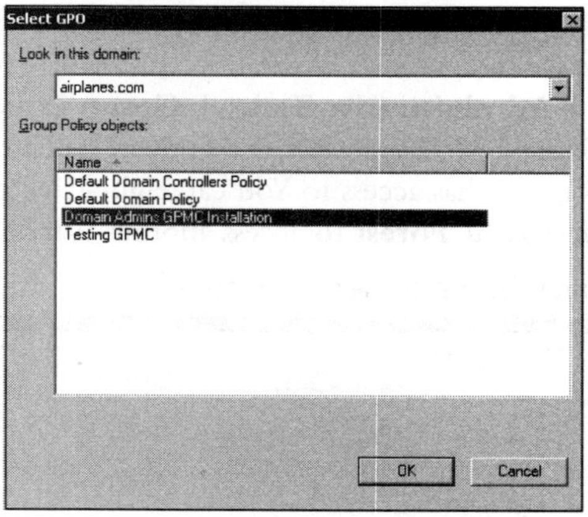

Test Day Tip

To create a GPO without linking it to an existing site, domain, or OU, right-click **Group Policy Objects** in the GPMC and select **New**. This allows you to configure the GPO before linking it to any object in your Active Directory infrastructure.

You'll still use the Group Policy Object Editor snap-in to edit any GPOs in your environment; however, you'll now launch this snap-in by right-clicking the GPO, such as the one under the Group Policy Objects section in the GPMC, and selecting **Edit**, as illustrated in Figure 7.19.

Figure 7.19 Launching the GPO Editor Snap-in from GPMC

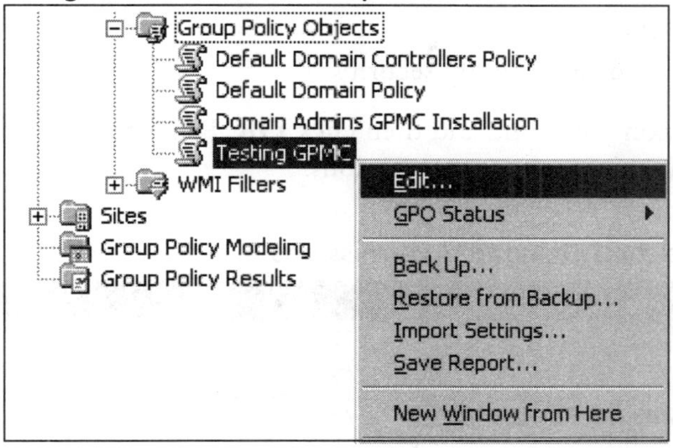

Delegating Control of a GPO via GPMC

You can also delegate permissions on a specific GPO to distribute administration of your Active Directory database by selecting a GPO and clicking the **Delegation** tab, as shown in Figure 7.20.

Figure 7.20 Delegating Authority Using GPMC

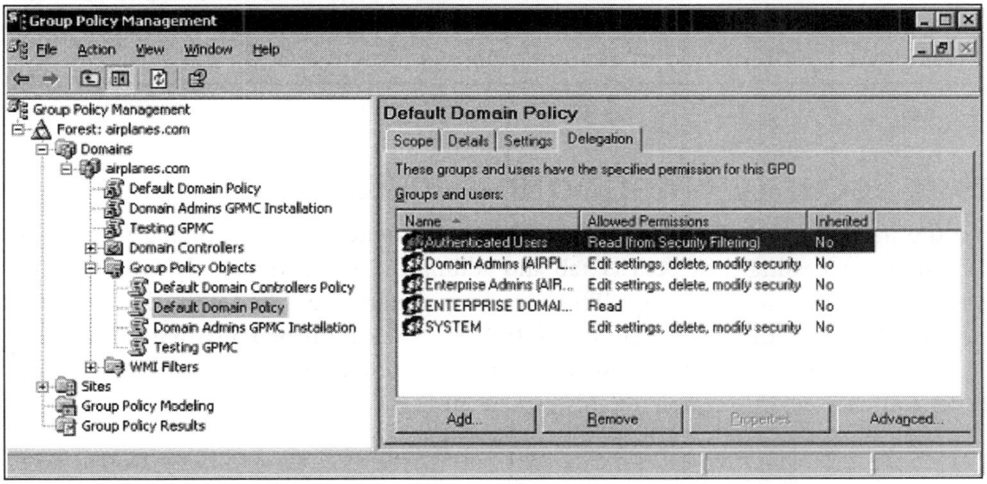

To delegate permissions over this GPO, click the **Add** button. Manually enter or browse to the name of the user or group who needs authority delegated delegated, and click **OK**. You'll see the screen shown in Figure 7.21. You can choose from the following preconfigured permissions:

- Read
- Edit settings
- Edit settings, delete, modify security

Make the selection you want, and then click **OK**. Repeat this process for each user or group to which you need to assign permissions.

Figure 7.21 Selecting Delegated Permissions

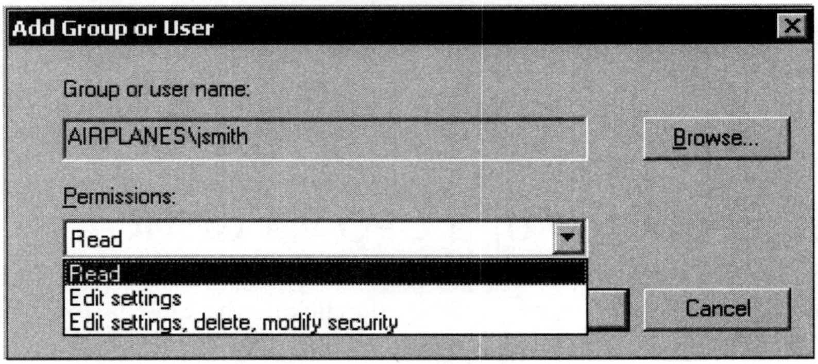

EXAM WARNING

You can select the Advanced button from the Delegation tab to use the previous (Windows 2000) method of assigning permissions to a GPO.

Using Security Filtering in GPMC

Before the introduction of the Group Policy Management console, applying security to a GPO involved accessing the Security tab and adding the Read and Apply Group Policy permissions for any relevant groups. This process is greatly simplified with the introduction of the GPMC. Select the **Scope** tab of a GPO, and click **Add** or **Remove** in the Security Filtering section to control which users, groups, and computers that a given GPO will apply to. You can see an example of this process in Figure 7.22.

Figure 7.22 Security Filtering Using GPMC

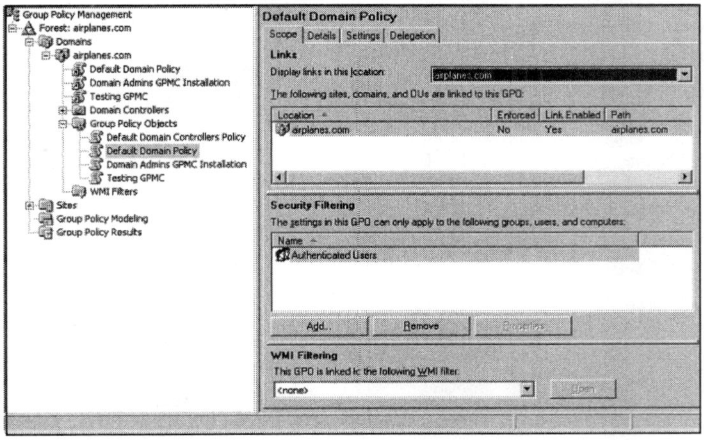

Using GPMC as a Troubleshooting Tool

GPMC can greatly assist you in troubleshooting GPO behavior on your network, because it provides a well-organized view of all GPOs present on your network and how they are linked to the sites, domains, and OUs within Active Directory. You can also easily determine which GPO links are enabled or disabled for a container, as well as viewing the properties and settings of a specific GPO.

Group Policy Results reports are similar to using RSoP in logging mode; they gather information from a network client to show which policies and settings are in effect, along with client event-logging information. You can generate this report by right-clicking **Group Policy Results** and selecting the **Group Policy Results Wizard**. The wizard itself is identical to the one illustrated in Exercise 7.02, Running an RSOP Query.

As you can see in Figure 7.23, the Group Policy Results report includes a list of GPOs that have been applied as well as those that have not. From the **Settings** tab you can determine which settings have been applied and which GPOs supplied the value for the settings. (We've only included a small portion of the available information; the entire report is quite extensive.)

Exam Warning

Because Group Policy Results reports use functionality that was introduced with Windows XP and Windows Server 2003, you can only generate these reports for machines running one of these operating systems.

Figure 7.23 GPMC Group Policy Results

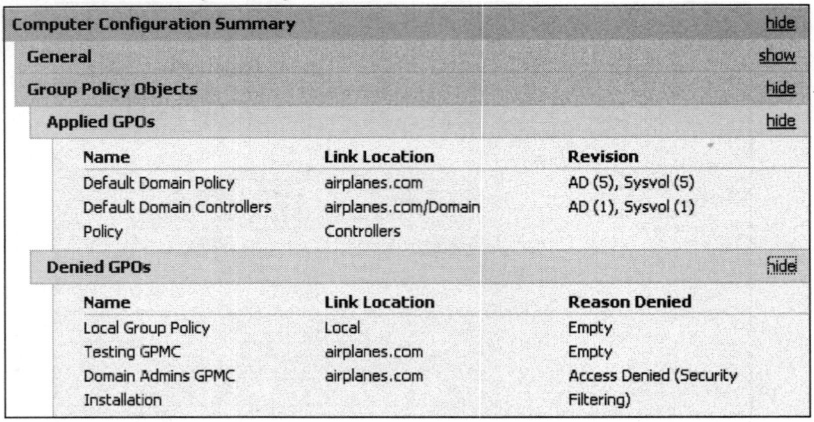

You can combine the data in the Applied GPOs and Denied GPOs sections with the information on the Settings tab to troubleshoot the reason a given GPO setting has not been applied at a client level. Use the information in Table 7.3 as a starting point to organize the troubleshooting process for your network clients.

Table 7.3 Potential Causes for GPO Settings Not Being Applied Correctly

GPO Listed Under Applied GPOs, Denied GPOs, or Not at All	Setting Listed on the Settings Tab?	Some Potential Reasons for the Failure
Applied	Yes	GPO inheritance Replication Group Policy refresh Asynchronous processing Client-side extensions Loopback processing
Applied	No	Replication Group Policy refresh Operating system support Slow link
Denied	No	Security filtering Disabled GPO Inaccessible data Empty GPO WMI filter

Continued

Table 7.3 Potential Causes for GPO Settings Not Being Applied Correctly

GPO Listed Under Applied GPOs, Denied GPOs, or Not at All	Setting Listed on the Settings Tab?	Some Potential Reasons for the Failure
Not listed	No	Scope of management Replication Group Policy refresh Network connectivity

For example, let's say that you have created a GPO called Folder Settings that was linked to the Sales OU and configured to redirect the My Documents folder to a location on a central file server, but the Folder Redirection setting is not being enforced for the users in the Sales OU. When you run a GPMC Group Policy Results report, you see that the Folder Settings GPO is included in the list of Applied GPOs, but the Folder Redirection information does not appear on the Settings tab. Using the information in this table, you can see that some likely causes for failure are:

- Replication
- Group Policy refresh
- Operating system support
- Slow links

This information gives you an organized plan of attack to determine why a particular GPO or GPO setting is not being applied as you think it should be.

Creating a Group Policy Modeling Report

Like the Group Policy Results report discussed in the previous section, the GPMC Modeling function uses the steps that you used to generate this report via the RSoP snap-in. Simply right-click the **Group Policy Modeling** node and select **Group Policy Modeling Wizard**. Specify the computer or computer/user combination you want to investigate, just as you did in Exercise 7.03, Using Resultant Set of Policy in Planning Mode. The report that appears in your details pane will look similar to the one shown in Figure 7.24.

Figure 7.24 GPMC Modeling Report

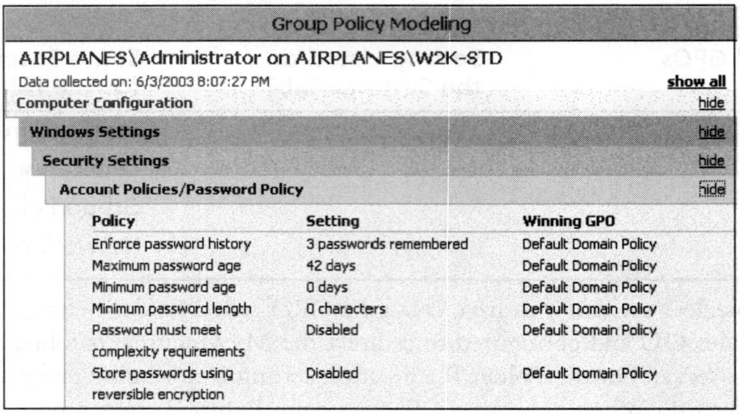

Managing Windows 2000 Domains

You can use the GPMC to manage Windows domains that contain any combination of Windows Server 2003 and Windows 2000—even domains that are only comprised of Windows 2000 servers. However, remember that the GPMC console itself does not run on the Windows 2000 operating system; you'll need to install it on a machine running Windows XP Professional or Windows Server 2003 member server. In addition, the GPMC functions such as WMI filters and Group Policy modeling that do not exist in Windows 2000 environments are not available when you access a Windows 2000 domain with the GPMC.

Summary of Exam Objectives

Windows Server 2003 provides a number of tools and utilities to manage the Group Policy objects (GPOs) that you've created. Individual GPOs can be managed using commands within the Active Directory Users & Computers utility that you're quite familiar with, as well as Active Directory Sites and Services. Since GPOs can be linked to a site, domain, or OU, you can manage Group Policy settings in either of these utilities, depending on the *scope* of the GPO.

You can use a number of utilities to monitor and troubleshoot Group Policy settings; some of these are included in the Windows Server 2003 operating system, and others are freely available via the Windows Server 2003 Resource Kit. GPUpdate is an update to the *secedit* utility in Windows 2000; you'll use it to force a client or server to update its Group Policy settings after you make a critical change. You'll use GPResult, GPMonitor, and other Resource Kit utilities to monitor and troubleshoot Group Policy behavior from the command line, whereas WinPolicies provides a graphical interface to view monitoring and logging information.

The Resultant Set of Policies (RSoP) MMC snap-in allows you to analyze a specific user/computer combination to determine exactly which GPOs and settings are being applied to a given client. This information is invaluable in troubleshooting an environment with multiple (and potentially conflicting) GPOs that have been applied to various points within Active Directory. When you work with a Windows Server 2003 domain, RSoP also allows you to simulate changes to a given GPO to determine how client settings might change before applying a new policy to a production environment.

Finally, the Group Policy Management Console (GPMC) is a new feature of Windows Server 2003 that provides a unified reporting and troubleshooting interface for Group Policy settings across one or more Windows domains. You can use GPMC to manage multiple Windows 2000 and Windows Server 2003 forests across your enterprise. GPMC provides easy access to all GPOs and GPO links on your network and can provide functions similar to those of the RSoP snap-in using improved HTML-formatted reporting. GPMC also installs with many preconfigured command-line scripts to assist you in automating the maintenance of Group Policy operations.

Exam Objectives Fast Track

Managing Applications

☑ Software Installation settings are only applied during startup (if applied to the Computer Configuration section of a GPO. If Group Policy is being applied asynchronously, this might require multiple logons or reboots for a new software package to be properly applied.

☑ Programs installed using .ZAP packages cannot be managed, upgraded, or uninstalled via Group Policy; they need to be maintained manually.

- ☑ You can use GPUpdate with the */Logoff* or */Boot* switch to force a client to log off or reboot after refreshing a GPO to which you've made Software Installation settings changes.
- ☑ Be sure that any MSI packages and other relevant files are stored on a network share that is accessible to all users who need to have it installed.

Managing Security Policies

- ☑ Account policies, password policies, and account lockout policies can only be applied at the domain level. If a group of your users have different security requirements from the remainder of the network, consider creating a a separate domain for them in the forest.
- ☑ GPResult allows you to create a text file detailing exactly which security settings have been applied to a specific client and which GPOs applied those settings.
- ☑ Unlike Software Installation settings that are only applied on startup or logon, security settings are updated whenever the GPO refreshes, which occurs every 90 minutes by default.

Troubleshooting Group Policies

- ☑ If Uninstall this application if the user falls out of the scope of management is applied, the application may uninstall if the user's group memberships change or the user's computer object is moved to another OU, domain, or site..
- ☑ Security templates allow you to quickly import a wide range of security settings into a GPO.
- ☑ Use Enforce and Block Inheritance with care because they will change the default behavior of Group Policy inheritance within your Active Directory structure.

Using the Group Policy Management Console

- ☑ The GPMC can run from any Windows Server 2003 or Windows XP computer and can manage any combination of Windows 2000 and Windows Server 2003 domains.
- ☑ The GPMC allows you to simplify the process of assigning permissions and delegating responsibility to GPOs on your network.

☑ The Group Policy Results wizard creates an HTML-formatted report that organizes GPO settings in an easy-to-read format for reporting and troubleshooting.

Exam Objectives Frequently Asked Questions

The following Frequently Asked Questions, answered by the authors of this book, are designed to both measure your understanding of the Exam Objectives presented in this chapter, and to assist you with real-life implementation of these concepts. You will also gain access to thousands of other FAQs at ITFAQnet.com.

Q: I am administering a network for a government office that requires unified and stringent security standards for all user desktops. What is the easiest way to accomplish this task?

A: Use the Security Configurations and Analysis snap-in to apply and test the HISECWS.INF template on a representative workstation in your environment and make any necessary modifications. When you are satisfied that the template will still allow your users to perform their tasks, import the .INF file into a GPO and apply it to a site, domain, or OU.

Q: Can I apply a different password policy to an individual OU than the one I've applied to the rest of my network?

A: Password policies need to be implemented at the domain level. If you have a specific subset of users who require different security settings from the rest of your network, consider creating a separate domain in the forest to accommodate their needs.

Q: Why are Software Installation policies only applied at system startup or user logon?

A: This restriction exists by design and is intended to prevent a situation in which a GPO might attempt to install, upgrade, or uninstall a given application while a user is using it, which would create confusion, increased support calls, and the potential for data corruption and end-user downtime.

Q: I have a user who connects to the corporate network using a VPN client from her home PC running Windows XP Professional. I have created a GPO to mandate security settings for remote users, but the policy is never applied. What is happening?

A: In this situation, the GPO settings never reach the remote user because she has already logged onto her workstation before connecting to the VPN client. You can provide normal GPO processing by having the user connect to the corporate network via the initial Ctrl+Alt+Del logon prompt.

Q: Can I export information generated by the Group Policy Results or Group Policy Modeling reports to create a central reporting database?

A: GPMC data can be exported to HTML or XML format, making it easily portable to other formats and applications.

Q: Can I use the Group Policy Management Console to replace Active Directory Users and Computers?

A: No. The GPMC supplements Active Directory Users & Computers as well as Active Directory Sites & Services, it but does not replace either. The GPMC is strictly designed to handle Group Policy administration tasks, whereas the other two utilities are still necessary to perform tasks such as creating user and computer objects, managing sites and site links, and the like.

Self Test

A Quick Answer Key follows the Self Test questions. For complete questions, answers, and explanations to the Self Test questions in this chapter as well as the other chapters in this book, see the Self Test Appendix.

1. You have created and linked a single GPO to your Windows Server 2003 domain to apply various security settings to your client workstations, as well as redirecting the contents of each user's C:\Documents and Settings\%username%\My Documents folder to a central server location of \\FILESERVER1\DOCS\%username%\My Documents. This server share is backed up every night; no client systems are included in the backups. You have several users in a remote branch office that is connected to the corporate headquarters via a 128Kbps ISDN line. One of your branch users calls the help desk needing a file in his My Documents folder restored from backup after he deleted it accidentally. You are dismayed to find that his information does not exist on the FILESERVER1 share. Most other GPO settings have been applied to the client workstation, including event log auditing and account lockout settings. What is the most likely reason that the branch user's files have not been redirected to the central file server?

   A. Folder Redirection settings are not applied by default when a user logs onto the network using a slow link.

   B. The branch users do not have the Apply Group Policy permission assigned to them for the GPO.

   C. You need to link the GPO to the OU that the user objects belong to, not just the domain.

   D. The GPO is being applied synchronously when the branch users log onto their workstations.

2. You have created an MSI installer package to distribute GPMC to your help desk. You have added the package information to the User Configuration | Software Settings section of the Default Domain GPO, and you have enabled the Apply Group Policy permission to the HelpDesk global group. You've saved the GPMC.MSI file to the E:\PACKAGES directory of the W2K-STD Windows Server 2003 file server, as shown in the following figure. Your help desk staff is reporting that the GPMC software has not been installed on their workstations, despite several reboots. Each help desk staffer is a local administrator on his or her workstation and is able to access shared directories on this and other Windows Server 2003 file servers. From the information shown in the figure, what is the most likely reason that the MSI package is not being distributed?

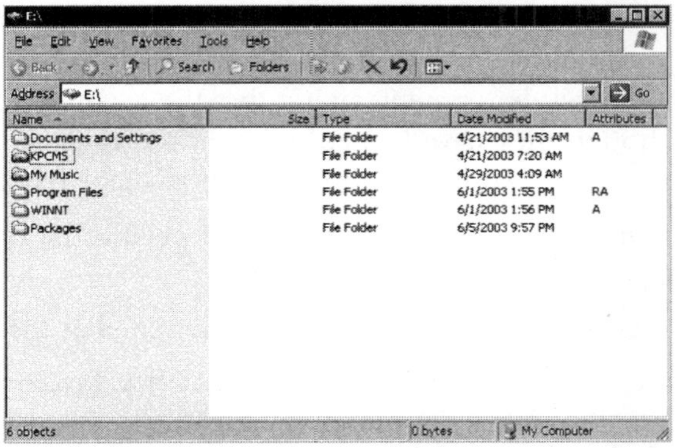

A. The Apply Group Policy permission can only be applied to individual user accounts, not to groups.

B. You need to create a share for the E:\packages directory so that the help desk staff can access the MSI package over the network.

C. MSI packages must be stored in the SYSVOL share on a domain controller.

D. Software Installation settings need to be applied to the Computer Configuration section of a GPO, not the User Configuration section.

3. You have a test lab consisting of four Windows XP Professional workstations that you use to investigate new software packages and security settings before rolling them out to a production environment. This lab exists in a separate TEST domain with its own domain controller, DC1.TEST.AIRPLANES.COM. You are making many changes to security settings on the Default Domain Policy on DC1 and would like to test the results immediately so that you can implement the security setting on your production network as quickly as possible. What is the most efficient way to accomplish this goal?

A. Use GPOMonitor to indicate when the Group Policy objects perform a background refresh.

B. Update the GPO to force Group Policies to refresh every 60 seconds.

C. Reboot the test lab workstations after each change that you want to test.

D. Run GPUpdate.exe from the command line on the test workstations after each change that you want to test.

4. You have a new accounting software package that you would like to install for the Payroll OU of your Windows Server 2003 domain. You would like this software to be available to any user who logs onto each Windows XP Professional workstation in the payroll department. You create a new GPO and assign the MSI package to the Computer Configuration section, and then link the new GPO to the Payroll OU with the appropriate security filtering permissions. You send an e-mail to the payroll department staff instructing them to log off their workstations and log back in to prompt the software installation to begin. Your help desk begins to receive calls from the users in the payroll department, saying that the accounting package has not been installed, even though they have logged off and onto their workstations several times. What is the most likely reason that the software package has not been installed?

   A. The workstations in the payroll department need to be rebooted before the software package will be installed.

   B. Software Installation packages can only be assigned at the domain level.

   C. The software can be installed using the Add New Programs section of the Add/Remove Programs Control Panel applet.

   D. Logon scripts are running asynchronously; they must be reconfigured to run synchronously.

5. You are the network administrator for a Windows Server 2003 network that has a corporate headquarters and several remote sales offices, each connected to the main office via 56K dialup modems. After a recent bout of attempted hacker attacks at the remote sites, your firewall administrator has decided to block NetBIOS, ICMP, and IGMP traffic from entering or leaving any remote site. Shortly after this solution is implemented, you receive several complaints from users at the remote sites that the logon times to their Windows XP Professional workstations have increased dramatically, often timing out and forcing them to reboot their machines. What is the most likely reason that this is occurring?

   A. Each remote site should have its own domain controller to handle logon processing.

   B. Group Policy does not function in environments that include firewalls.

   C. Windows XP Professional requires NetBIOS to connect to a Windows Server 2003 domain controller.

   D. Group Policy is no longer able to detect slow network links.

6. You are a network administrator for an accounting firm with 200 employees that has been contracted to perform an audit of data stored in a proprietary 16-bit data entry application that was never upgraded to a 32-bit format. The application will only be used for the duration of this contract and does not have any option for a network or Terminal Services installation. How can you install this application on each workstation most efficiently?

   A. Use a ZAP file published via a GPO to automate the installation process.

   B. Contract a software developer to upgrade the application to an Active Directory-aware platform such as Visual Basic.

   C. Send a broadcast e-mail with installation instructions and the location of the setup files to all users who require the software.

   D. Install the software once on the domain controller and create a link to the program on each user's desktop.

7. You have recently begun a new position as a network administrator for a Windows Server 2003 domain. Your predecessor created a number of GPOs, and it seems as if each network user has different policy settings applied to his or her account. You would like to simplify the GPO implementation on your network, and you want to begin by creating a baseline report of exactly which GPOs are in effect for the various users on the network. What is the most efficient means of accomplishing this goal?

   A. Use the Resultant Set of Policy snap-in to view the GPO settings for each user/computer combination on the network.

   B. Use the Group Policy Results report in the GPMC to export the GPO settings of each user/computer combination to a single XML file for analysis.

   C. Use the GPResults.exe command-line utility to generate a report for all users on the domain.

   D. Export the Event Viewer Security logs from each workstation and collate the results for analysis.

8. You are the network administrator for a Windows Server 2003 domain with network resources from each department grouped into separate OUs: Finance, IT, Sales, Development, and Public Relations. You have assigned the MSI package shown in the following figure to the Development OU. User *EMandervile* is a telecommuting user who is transferring from development to public relations. What is the most efficient way to remove this application from *EMandervile's* workstation?

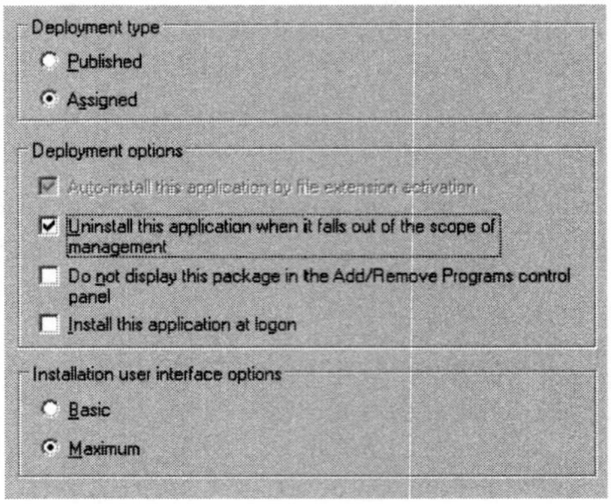

A. Visit *EMandervile's* home office and manually uninstall the application from his home workstation.

B. Redeploy the MSI package to the Development OU after moving *EMandervile's* user account.

C. Email *EMandervile* instructions to uninstall the application from his home office workstation.

D. Since "Uninstall this application when it falls out of the scope of management" is selected, the application will automatically be uninstalled after you move *EMandervile's* account from the Development OU to the Public Relations OU.

9. You have been reading about the new features offered by the GPMC and would like to use it to manage your Windows environment, shown in the following figure. Your administrative workstation is located in Domain A, and you have administrative control over Domain A, Domain B, and Domain C. Which of the following would allow you to use GPMC from your present location? (Choose all that apply.)

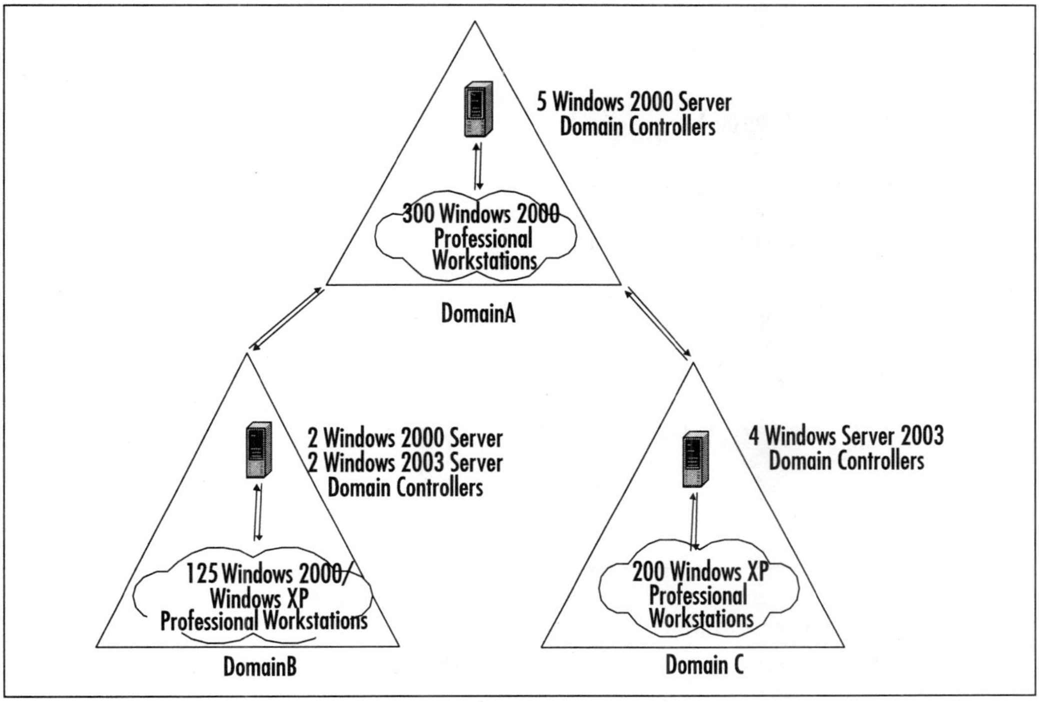

A. Install the GPMC on your existing Windows 2000 Professional workstation.

B. Upgrade your administrative workstation to Windows XP Professional, SP1, and install the necessary hotfix from Microsoft before installing the GPMC.

C. Install a Windows Server 2003 member server in Domain A, and install the GPMC on the member server.

D. Install the GPMC onto a Windows 2000 Server in Domain A, and use the GPMC from the server console.

10. Your Active Directory domain is configured like the one shown in the following figure. Which GPO settings would be applied to a computer located in the Marketing OU? (Choose all that apply.)

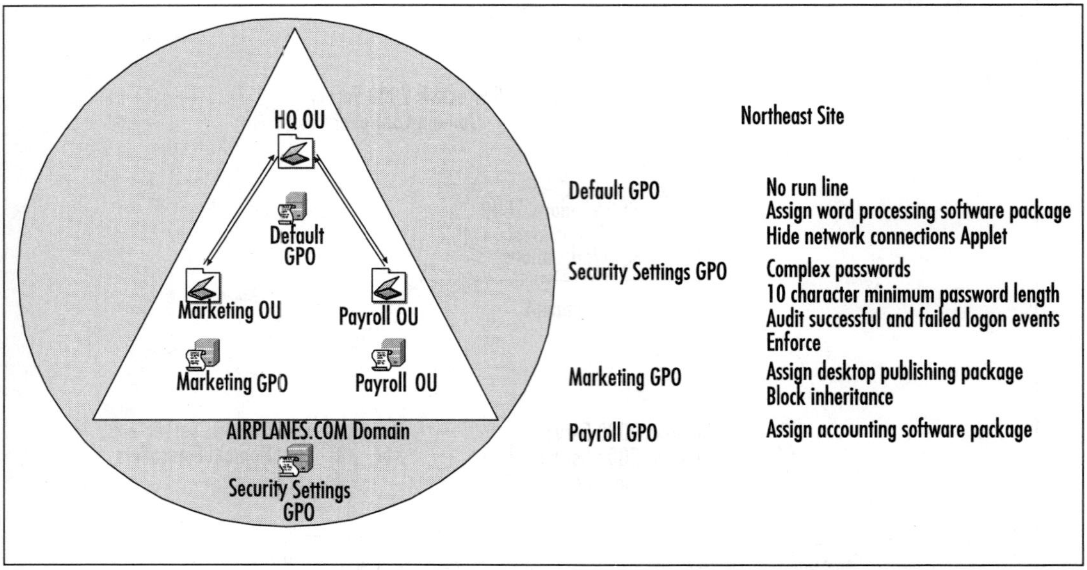

A. The Network Connections applet will be hidden.

B. Successful and failed logon events will be recorded to the event log.

C. A desktop publishing software package will be assigned.

D. The Run line will not be visible.

11. You are the network administrator of the Windows Server 2003 forest shown in the following figure. Which of the following Password Policy values will be in effect for clients in the sales.north.biplanes.airplanes.com domain?

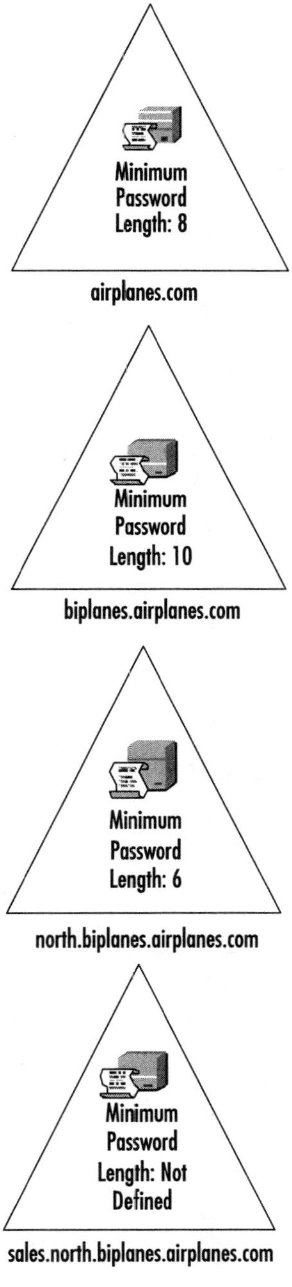

A. Six characters

B. Eight characters

C. Ten characters

D. Not defined

12. By default, how does Windows Server 2003 process GPO settings at startup and at logon?

    A. Startup: Synchronous

    B. Startup: Asynchronous

    C. Logon: Asynchronous

    D. Logon: Synchronous

13. Your Active Directory environment is configured as shown in the following figure, with two conflicting Enforces. Which setting(s) will be applied to a client in the Collections OU? (Choose all that apply.)

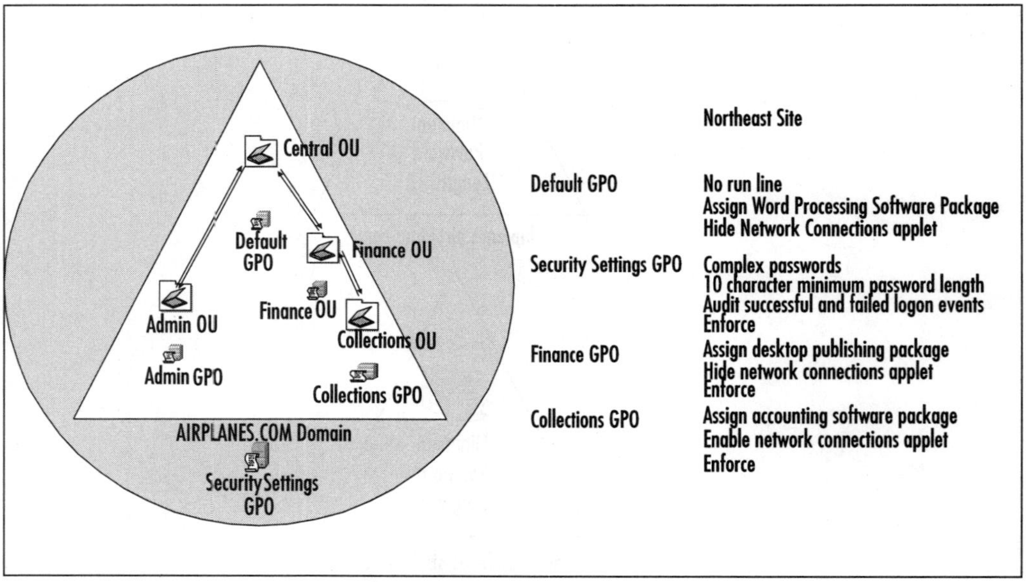

    A. The desktop publishing package will be assigned.

    B. The Network Connections applet will be hidden.

    C. The Network Connections applet will be visible.

    D. The Run line will be hidden.

Self Test Quick Answer Key

For complete questions, answers, and explanations to the Self Test questions in this chapter as well as the other chapters in this book, see the Self Test Appendix.

1. **A**
2. **B**
3. **D**
4. **A**
5. **D**
6. **A**
7. **C**

8 **D**

9. **B**, **C**

10 **B**, **C**

11. **D**

12 **B**, **C**

13. **A**, **B**, **D**

Chapter 8

MCSA/MCSE 70-296

Securing a Windows Server 2003 Network

Exam Objectives in this Chapter:

1.1	Configure security for servers that are assigned specific roles.
1.2	Plan security for servers that are assigned specific roles. Roles might include domain controllers, Web servers, and mail servers.
1.2.1	Deploy the security configuration for servers that are assigned specific roles.
1.2.2	Create custom security templates based on server roles.
4.3	Plan security for data transmission.
4.3.1	Secure data transmission between client computers to meet security requirements.
4.3.2	Secure data transmission by using IPSec.
5.3	Plan a framework for planning and implementing security.
5.3.1	Plan for security monitoring.
5.3.2	Plan a change and configuration management framework for security.
5.4	Plan a security update infrastructure. Tools might include Microsoft Baseline Security Analyzer and Microsoft Software Update Services.

Introduction

It probably goes without saying that IT security is currently a hot topic and will continue to be important for some time to come. Most network and security administrators have discovered that security isn't a static condition but rather is constantly flowing and morphing in scope. At this juncture, it is not unusual to find that new security vulnerabilities are identified and patches for those vulnerabilities are released on what might seem a daily basis. A fix that you applied two weeks ago might not cover 10 or 15 issues that have come up since that day.

Although you will never have a 100 percent secure environment, that doesn't mean that you can't take steps to protect yourself from would-be intruders. Working with IT security, it becomes obvious that security can't be a "one size fits all" strategy. Different operating systems have different security vulnerabilities, and the roles that servers play have an impact on the type of security they need. For example, an internal print server has different security requirements than an e-mail server, which might be accessible via the Internet. To get even more granular, an internal DNS server might need to be more secure than an external DNS server. To pass the 70-296 exam, you need to understand the different roles that a Windows Server 2003 server can be configured to perform and how to secure those servers based on their roles.

Even with your servers properly identified and secured according to their role definitions, you must also be able to secure the data as it is being transmitted to the host from a client (or another host). Developing a plan for secure data transmission and using tools such as IPSec to secure transmissions are key components for offering a secure, end-to-end solution in your environment. In this chapter, we also discuss planning for secure data transmission as well as how IPSec works and how it is integrated into Windows Server 2003. Let's begin the chapter with an explanation of the various server roles in Windows Server 2003.

TEST DAY TIP

Each of the server roles examined in this chapter is fair game for exam questions. An understanding of security principles and the newly defined security levels for the various roles is required to pass the exam. Best practices and base security configurations, along with application of those configurations in the enterprise, all constitute knowledge you are expected to have in order to do well on this exam.

Understanding Server Roles

Windows Server 2003 has the capability to provide a much-expanded set of services to your organization. In past versions of the Windows Server platform, many default configurations have been created during install that were not needed in every environment in which they were installed. For instance, IIS 5.0 was a default component of Windows 2000 server installs and often was unneeded and in fact contributed to security vulnerabilities due to the default installation, if left in that state. Additionally, many other services and features were installed that simply proved to be unnecessary to the operation of the server in the mode in which it was used. Windows Server 2003 has been delivered with a much different base installation than previous versions and security that is delivered locked-down to begin with, instead of being delivered in a loose security configuration. Many of the services formerly installed by default are now left to the administrator to install as appropriate to the server's operation and the organization's needs. Furthermore, installation into a workgroup environment instead of a domain environment reduces the subset of installed applications. In this section, we look at the various roles that you can configure for Windows Server 2003 and what is added to the base server setup as you add these roles. A new utility, Managing Your Server, is provided in the Administrative Tools folder to work with server roles. We also note those roles that are not available if you are using Windows Server 2003 Web Edition, which is limited in scope and usage.

File Servers

The file server role is one of the most used roles in setting up our servers using Windows Server 2003 and is not available in Windows Server 2003 Web Edition. This role is similar to what you as an administrator have understood as a file server from past Windows versions. Access control for Active Directory domain accounts and publication of resources in Active Directory require that the machine be a member of the domain. If that authentication process is unneeded, the machine can operate in the file server role without becoming a member of the domain. Configuration of the file server role allows sharing of resources such as files and folders with network users when necessary. The file server role, when set up according to recommendations, uses all the capabilities of NTFS to protect files from unauthorized access. The file server role setup allows sharing of resources and the use of NTFS benefits such as disk quotas, file compression, Encrypting File System (EFS), and the Indexing Service. The file server role can also allow varying degrees of offline file usage, dependent on the needs of your organization. No services are added to the server in this configuration, but we explore the security recommendations and needs later in the chapter.

Print Servers

The print server role allows the administrator to configure the server to operate and control printing on the network. This role is not available in Windows Server 2003 Web Edition. Windows Server 2003 installations may be configured with the print server role to provide services to multiple client types and to control access to print services. If you need to publish the printers in Active Directory or the administrator wants to control access to printers based on Active Directory accounts, the machine must be made a member of the domain. If not, it can operate as a print server as a standalone machine. As with previous Windows editions, the print server can be used to control access to print devices, hours of operation, and priority of operation levels. Servers being considered for use as print servers should have the standard installation levels in place and should use NTFS. It is possible to use EFS to encrypt spooled documents, thus protecting your data and information at a higher level than was normally configured in the past.

EXAM WARNING

Be sure that you are comfortable with each of the roles that can be configured in Windows Server 2003. The new division of duties and security configurations and recommendations for the various roles lend themselves to a large variety of scenario-based questions. Study and learn the differences, particularly the differences that exist between the basic application server role and an actual installation of a full Web server. Additionally, common roles such as file server, DHCP server, and DNS server will be covered during the examination.

Application Servers

The addition of the application server role to your server requires installing additional capabilities to the base server. During this configuration, Internet Information Services 6.0, an Application Server console, COM+, and a Distributed Transaction Coordinator (DTC) component are added. IIS 6.0, like its predecessors, is a full-featured Web server. It is used to provide the infrastructure for the .NET platform and to provide existing Web-based applications and services. COM+ is an extension of the Component Object Model (COM), allowing more flexibility to programmers developing content. DTC operates in much the same fashion as the same components in IIS 5.0, coordinating the operations of COM+ objects, so little change will be detected. A new Application Server console is created, allowing you to have a central location to manage Web applications. The IIS 6.0 installation process installs as highly secure and by default does not allow the use of such components as ActiveX controls. The administrator must configure the use of the server as appropriate for the organization's or clients' needs. Additionally, decisions must be made about the use of ASP.NET features if your organization is going to utilize the advanced programming features of the new platform. We look at the security specifics of this default locked down state later in the chapter.

Mail Servers

Windows Server 2003 includes a new feature with the addition of POP3 services capability to the basic server platform. The installation of the mail server role requires installing a portion of the application server role's functionality because the SMTP service and POP3 service installation requires IIS 6.0 features for its operation. This server role allows the administrator to provide a POP3 presence for users, as well as SMTP for outgoing mail. This service does not provide the functionality of products such as MS Exchange Server (such as IMAP mail services), but it does allow the administrator to provide e-mail services to end users. As with the other server functions, it is highly recommended that the server administrator utilize the benefits of NTFS for the creation of disk quotas and security of files and information as appropriate. A number of additional security concerns exist in this configuration; we explore these issues in depth later in the chapter.

New & Noteworthy...

IIS 6.0 Installed with the Application Servers Role

IIS 6.0 is not installed with the default installation of Windows Server 2003. Instead, it is added when you create an application server role and is initially installed in a tightly locked-down security condition. It is important that the administrator review the condition of the IIS 6.0 installation to assure compatibility with hosted applications and Web services from clients and users. You will find that the base install of IIS 6.0 in the application server role does not include all the functionality that was previously installed in IIS 5.0 on Windows 2000 machines. For instance, you'll find that the virtual SMTP service and default FTP site are not automatically installed when IIS 6.0 is installed in this configuration.

New & Noteworthy...

POP3 and SMTP Server Capabilities Have Been Added to Windows Server 2003

Windows Server 2003 includes a new capability to provide services to your users with the addition of a POP3 mail server role and expanded capabilities of the previous limited SMTP server functionality. This will allow configuration of e-mail services for many smaller environments, allowing greater capability for your operations. This server does not provide the feature set of a product such as Exchange 2000, but does provide basic e-mail services for clients. Although the role is more secure than many implementations, e-mail security concerns that exist for other platforms require the attention of the administrator to properly secure the services and to prevent unauthorized relaying of e-mail through the system.

Terminal Servers

The terminal server role is used in some environments in which multiple users need or desire access to a common work platform utilizing the same consistent applications throughout. For example, an organization that wants to have a centralized installation of the Microsoft Office suite could utilize the capabilities of Terminal Services by installing the Office applications on the terminal server with appropriate licensing, and they'd have better control over the use and maintenance of the component applications.

A change that has occurred in the terminal server role is that it is no longer necessary to install Terminal Services to provide remote administration of a server. Instead, Remote Desktop functionality is utilized for this option, thus not requiring that this role be used for administrative connections. Configuration of a terminal server role requires that the administrator evaluate the current hardware on the machine hosting Terminal Services, because additional 11MB to 21MB of RAM is recommended per client connection utilized on the server. Additionally, as in past versions, a Terminal Services licensing server must be installed (and the licensing server should be installed on a different server, not the Terminal Services server), or the terminal server will stop accepting unlicensed connections 120 days after the first client connection. A new version of the Remote Desktop Client is available and should be installed for clients accessing the Windows Server 2003 terminal server. As with all the server roles, NTFS is recommended to control resources and access levels to the information stored on and accessible through the Terminal Services session.

Remote Access and VPN Servers

The role of the remote access server contains a group of potential services that have not been combined in one place in previous versions of Windows. The Windows Server 2003 implementation includes the capability within the Routing and Remote Access Services (RRAS) server to provide VPN connectivity. It should be noted that although the Web edition supports VPN connections, it is limited to one connection and has limited functionality. The standard server edition can support a maximum of 1000 VPN connections, and other versions are unlimited. Additionally, the RRAS server provides the capability to perform NAT operations, assign DHCP addresses to RRAS clients, and control access through the VPN, either locally or through configuration to use a RADIUS server, to perform the authentication prior to allowing the connection. As with previous versions, the RRAS server has the ability to provide connection services via modem or network interfaces. More than one network interface (may be a modem interface) must be present for the RRAS server to be configured. RRAS server installations install Routing and Remote Access features to the base configuration that are not present in the default installation and require other security precautions to protect the resources on the internal network from unauthorized access and attack. We'll discuss securing these servers later in the chapter.

TEST DAY TIP

While preparing in and studying the area of server roles, pay particular attention to the domain controller role. If you have experience with Windows 2000 Active Directory, many of the tools used to administer and plan for the security of the domain controller role will seem familiar. However, Windows Server 2003 Active Directory adds further functionality to the schema, and it is important to review the new capabilities regarding cross-forest trusts (now transitive) and other new features provided in the new role. Many of the recommendations for provision of security are similar to previous versions, but you should know and understand the ramifications of some of the new capabilities prior to taking the test.

Domain Controllers

Domain controller (DC) functionality is not supported in Windows Server 2003 Web Edition but is available in all other versions. The domain controller role is provided to support the Active Directory structure developed within your organization, and the individual DC can be configured in various configurations, depending on your needs. The domain controller role is used to provide authentication services for the domain through the implementation of Active Directory in Windows Server 2003. The installation of Active Directory in this version is performed in much the same fashion as in Windows 2000 Active Directory installations. The process can be performed from the command line or through the Manage Your Computer interface that allows configuration of the various server roles. The installation uses DCPromo, as with the Windows 2000 DC setup process. A number of security changes are implemented during this process of installation of Active Directory on the machine. An important issue arises during this process: Since the process removes the local accounts database and the existing cryptographic keys from the base installation, access to encrypted documents, including e-mail, is removed.

NOTE

In the case of Windows Server 2003, any documents (including encrypted e-mail) that are encrypted prior to promotion as a DC are *deleted* during the installation of Active Directory. This is important, so we look at the topic in more detail in our discussion about securing DCs later in the chapter.

Operations Masters

Operations masters roles are created by default on specific instances of the installation of domain controllers. The operations masters include the following, which are installed by default as indicated:

- PDC emulator role, to provide PDC services to down-level clients. One per domain; default install is on the first DC installed in the domain.
- RID master, to assign Active Directory Relative Identifier numbering. One per domain; default install is on the first DC in the domain.
- Infrastructure master, to provide location awareness for the domain. One per domain; default install is on the first DC in the domain.
- Schema master, to control the writable copy of the schema. One per forest; installed on the first DC in the forest.
- Domain naming master, to approve or control the naming of domains in the forest. Installed by default on the first DC in the forest.

These roles are installed in the same default locations as were used in Windows 2000 Active Directory and may be transferred to other DCs to distribute the load and provide fault tolerance to Active Directory operations. One change of note: In Windows Server 2003 Active Directory configurations, the Domain Naming Master no longer needs to be located on a Global Catalog Server, as we review next.

Global Catalog Servers

Global Catalog (GC) servers may be installed on a DC as needed throughout the Active Directory structure. By default, the first server in the forest promoted to a DC is also the only GC server created. As the administrator adds sites to the Active Directory configuration and as more DCs are added for other replication and authentication reasons, it might be appropriate to add more GC servers to existing DCs to distribute the GC load over more of the network. The GC servers contain information about other domains and the objects they contain, along with a subset of information that might be commonly requested about Active Directory objects. Additionally, the GC stores the information about Universal Group members in a native mode domain and must be present for logon authentication of users who belong to universal groups. The security of the GC servers is incumbent upon the settings that are configured on the DC on which they are operating.

EXAM WARNING

While studying for the exam, remember that some server roles produce much more vulnerability than others. Although Windows Server 2003 includes templates and settings that are far more secure than earlier versions, the considerations about physical and virtual location of the servers and methods to appropriately control access are important to your understanding of how configuration and security of the various roles are interrelated. You should have a firm grasp of the relative risk factors and be able to describe base- and role-specific security needs for the various roles, both for the exam and for your use in designing and implementing Windows Server 2003 in your operations.

DNS Servers

The DNS server role can be created on any of the Windows Server 2003 platforms, including Web Edition. The DNS server role is used to provide DNS name resolution services to clients needing resolution of FQDNs to IP addresses for connection purposes. Creation of the DNS server role requires that the administrator have knowledge of the domain name space requirements for the network design and have available the necessary information to configure the server appropriately. Addition of the DNS server role also requires a good understanding of the security risks that are assumed with the installation and how to appropriately configure security of the information that is accumulated and held in the DNS zone information files. General DNS functionality was covered in Chapter 1, but we discuss the security ramifications and configuration of the DNS server role later in this chapter.

DHCP Servers

DHCP server roles can be created on any Windows Server 2003 platform. The requirements for establishing a DHCP server role are primarily the same as existed in the Windows 2000 installation platform. In an Active Directory domain, the DHCP server must be authorized in Active Directory before its service will start and grant address leases to clients. A standalone DHCP server running either Windows 2000 or Windows Server 2003 will not grant addresses to clients if it detects that Active Directory in its reachable network. A number of services can be detailed to the client through the use of Scope options, and functionality has been added to the service on the DHCP server to help with security of the process and blocking of rogue DHCP servers to keep system disruption at as low a level as possible. DHCP servers have the potential to become a security weakness and require some planning and configuration, in addition to Windows Server 2003 base configurations, to maintain the integrity and security of the process. We discuss the security concerns and setup of the role later in the chapter.

WINS Servers

Although Windows 2000 Active Directory and Windows Server 2003 Active Directory domains do not require WINS for name resolution, the administrator might need WINS for name resolution in the event that down-level clients still exist that utilize WINS and NetBIOS communication for that purpose. Windows Server 2003 includes a server role for the WINS server that can be configured to provide that resolution service as needed. Security concerns that have been evident in past configurations of WINS still exist, and the administrator must follow configuration procedures and utilize appropriate security measures to mitigate the risks involved.

Streaming Media Servers

The streaming media services server role can be configured on both the Server and Enterprise platforms, but it is unavailable on the 64-bit versions of Windows Server 2003 and Web Edition. The streaming media server role allows a network administrator to provide media services such as streaming video and audio to users on the Internet or intranet using Windows Media Services. Streaming media services deliver content using multicast services in the Class D network space, and the service is highly configurable to utilize available resources and bandwidth effectively and efficiently.

In Table 8.1, you'll find a short list of the potential server roles and where they may be used.

Table 8.1 Detailing Windows Server 2003 Roles

Potential Server Role	Supported in Web Edition?	Supported in Server and Enterprise Editions?
Application server	Yes	Yes
DHCP server	Yes	Yes
DNS server	Yes	Yes
Domain controller	No	Yes
File server	No *	Yes
Global Catalog server	No	Yes
Mail server	Yes	Yes
Operations master	No	Yes
Print server	No **	Yes
Remote access server	Yes ***	Yes
Streaming media server	No	Yes
Terminal server	No	Yes
WINS server	Yes	Yes

Notes: * File sharing is available, but file and print services for Macintosh are not available.
** Printer and fax sharing is not available, thus blocking this use in this role.
*** Supports a single VPN connection capability but not full remote access functionality.

Test Day Tip

Practice the various methods for configuring roles. In this chapter, we review the use of the new Manage Your Computer utility, but remember that this is not the only way to create a server role. For instance, recall that you can use the **Start | Control Panel Add/Remove Programs | Add Windows Components** tools to define and refine the particular installation that you are creating. It is a good practice, however, to review the information found in the Manage Your Computer utility to review and check off the various tasks needed to keep the role secure.

Exercise 8.01

Create and Configure a Server Role

Exercise 8.01 assumes that you have installed Windows Server 2003 in either the Server or Enterprise Edition base install. The procedure is identical in either platform. Note that the Manage Your Computer console is not included in the Web Server Edition. We install the file server role for purposes of our illustration in this exercise.

WARNING

For these exercises, role configuration should not be performed on production machines in your network.

1. If the Manage Your Computer wizard does not start at logon, you can open it by navigating to **Start | Administrative Tools | Manage Your Server**. With the Manage Your Server console open, you'll see the screen shown in Figure 8.1. Select **Add or remove a role**.

Figure 8.1 The Manage Your Server Console

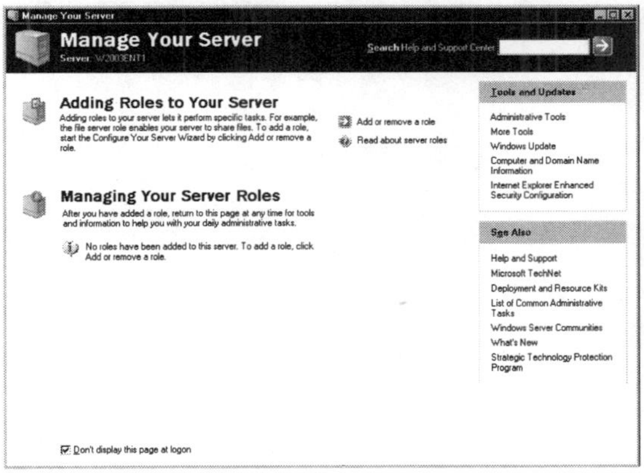

2. Review the information shown in the Configure Your Server Wizard screen, shown in Figure 8.2, and then click **Next**. You'll see the Network Detection screen, as shown in Figure 8.3.
3. The next screen, shown in Figure 8.4, details the roles that can be configured on this server. Select **File server**, and click **Next**.

Figure 8.2 The Configure Your Server Wizard Information Screen

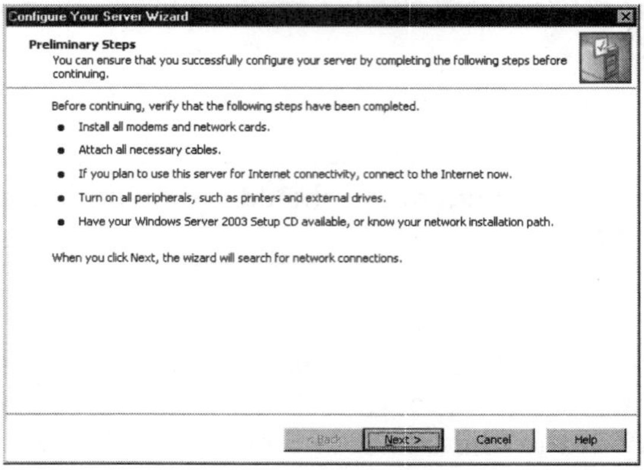

Figure 8.3 The Network Detection Screen

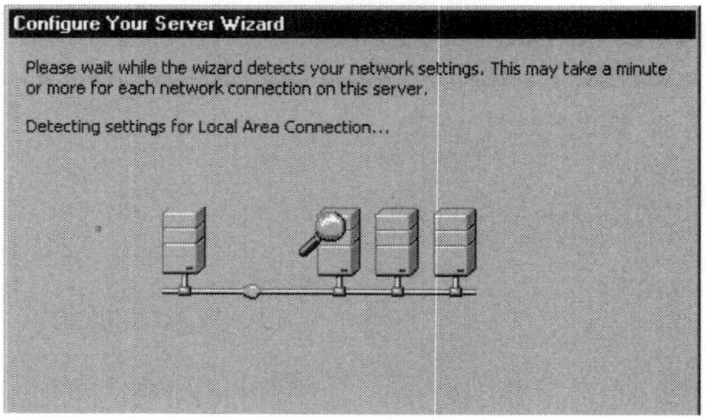

Figure 8.4 The Server Role Selection Options Page

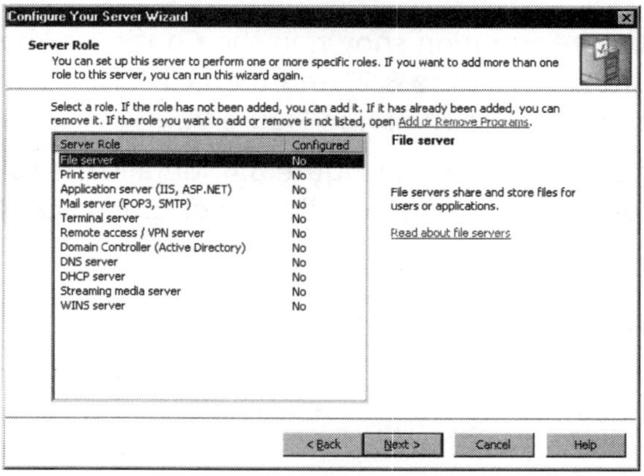

4. The next step in the process is to make a decision about whether or not to establish disk quotas that are generally applied or specific quotas for users. This can't be performed on drives not formatted with NTFS. Figure 8.5 shows the File ServerDisk Quotas setup screen. For this exercise, accept the defaults, and click **Next**.

Figure 8.5 The File Server Disk Quotas Setup Screen

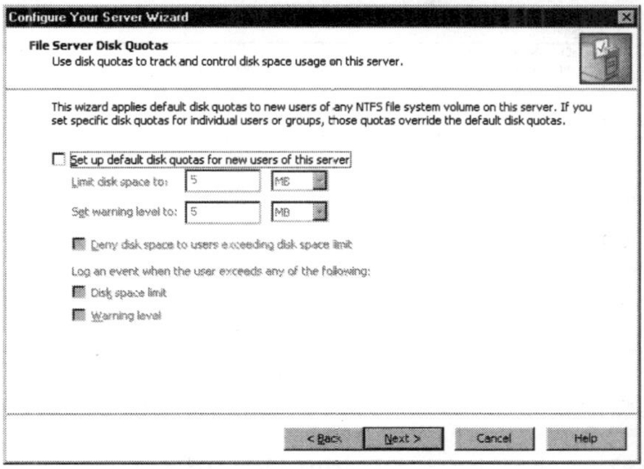

5. Following decisions on disk quotas, you will be asked to make a choice about whether or not to use the File Server Indexing Service, as shown in Figure 8.6. If your operation requires the use of the File Server Indexing Service for searching, activate it here. Read the notes about performance, and then, for our exercise, accept the defaults by clicking **Next**.

Figure 8.6 The File Server Indexing Service Screen

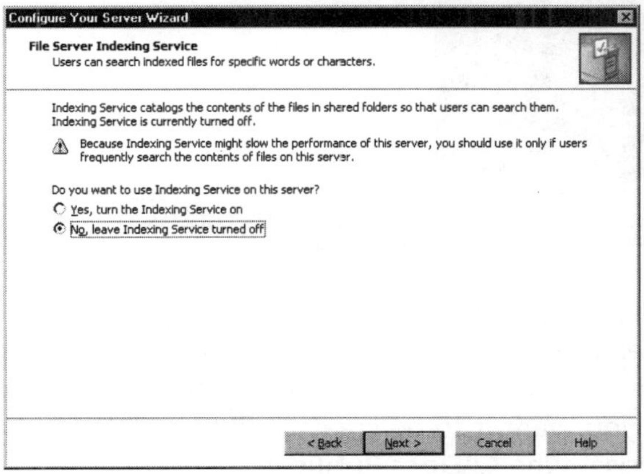

6. The next screen provides a review screen of the settings you have chosen, as shown in Figure 8.7. Click **Next**, and proceed to the Share a Folder Wizard screen.

Figure 8.7 The Summary of Selections Screen

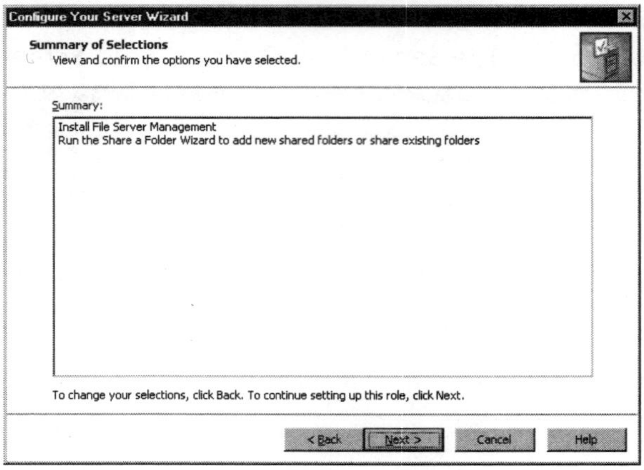

7. Click **Next** at the Share a Folder Wizard screen, shown in Figure 8.8.

Figure 8.8 The Share a Folder Wizard Screen

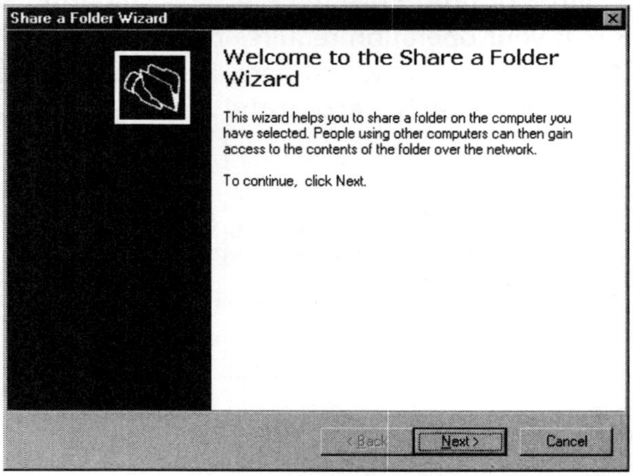

8. Figure 8.9 depicts the Folder Path screen you use in the wizard to select the folder you want to share. You can browse to an existing folder or simply enter a pathname. If the folder has not been created, you will be asked if you want it to be created after you click Next. For purposes of the exercise, type **C:\Docs\Public** in the Folder path line, as illustrated, and click **Next**. Select **Yes** when you are asked if you want to create the folder.

Figure 8.9 The Folder Path Selection Screen

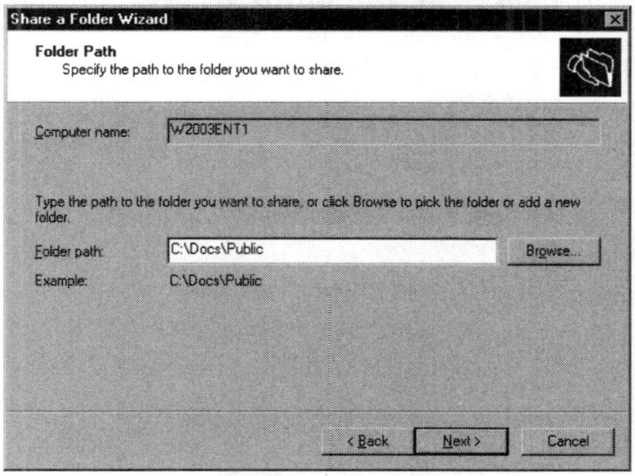

9. The next step in the Share a Folder wizard is to select the name for the shared resource. Here you can name the folder in a manner that is appropriate for your organization. Try to use intuitive names for shared resources to assist users in locating available resources. Type a name (here we use **Public**, as shown in Figure 8.10) for the shared folder in the Share Name box and a description for the resource, if you like. Additionally, this screen allows for configuration of offline file availability. For this exercise, accept the default and select **Next**.

Figure 8.10 The Name, Description, and Settings Screen

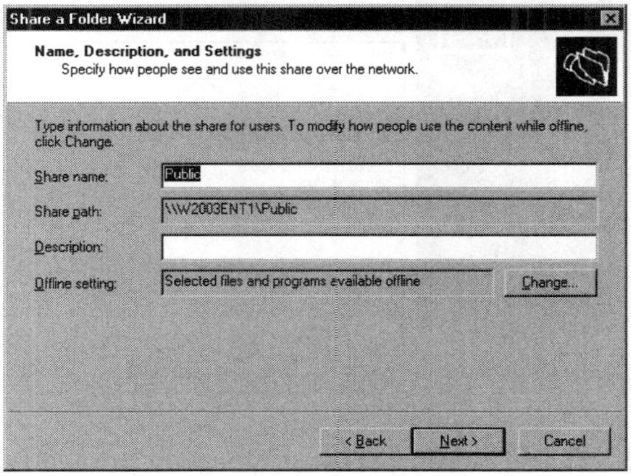

10. Of course, establishment of a shared resource would not be complete without making decisions about the level of access that is to be permitted from the network. Figure 8.11 shows the choices available. For

purposes of this exercise, select **Administrators have full access; other users have read and write access**, and then click **Finish**.

Figure 8.11 The Permissions Setting Screen

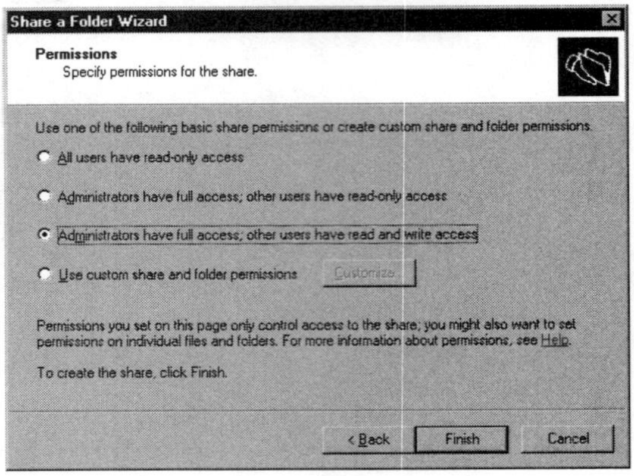

11. Following the setting of permissions, the wizard indicates the success of the sharing operation and allows you to configure further sharing during this process if you want to do so. Figure 8.12 shows this screen. Click **Close** to exit this wizard.

Figure 8.12 The Sharing Was Successful Screen

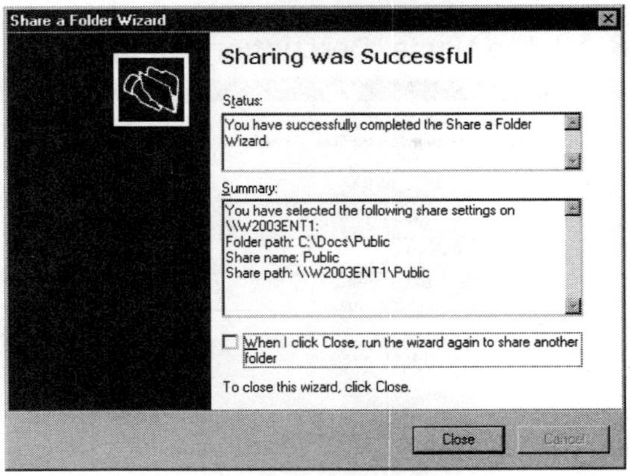

12. After closing the sharing wizard, you will proceed to the screen shown in Figure 8.13. At this point, the server role has been defined, but your work is not totally finished. You should proceed through the **View the next steps for this role** information to verify NTFS permissions and other necessary settings for the file server's security. For purposes of this exercise, click **Finish**.

Figure 8.13 The Configuration Confirmation Screen

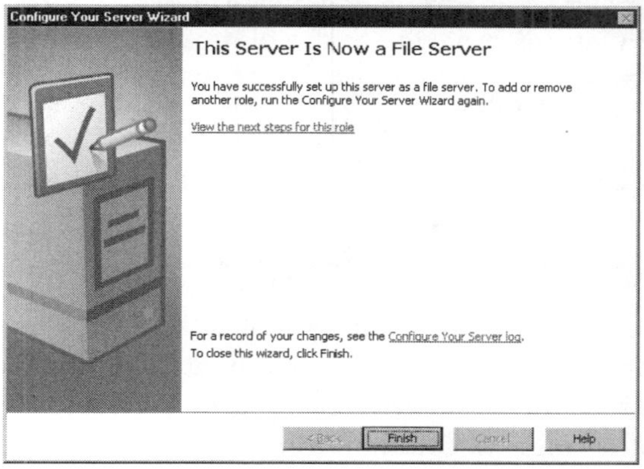

Configuring & Implementing...

Be Sure It's Secure!

As you begin to secure and configure your server using Windows Server 2003, remember not to be complacent in your work to secure the machine from unauthorized access and to provide the most secure machine possible while still allowing the functionality that is necessary for its use in your particular operation. It has been demonstrated repeatedly that improperly understood security settings or improperly configured servers provide gaping holes in security plans and implementations. For instance, many administrators did not realize that unpatched IIS 5.0 implementations could cause their networks and machines to be subject to breach. These administrators failed to patch because they weren't hosting a Web site or other IIS 5.0 operation such as FTP and therefore didn't regard the patch notices as being applicable to them. In fact, IIS 5.0 was installed with a default installation of the Windows 2000 operating system and was not secure. That type of configuration mistake very often leads to an extreme financial loss, the loss of client and customer confidence, and exposure to great risk factors that can devastate an organization.

While you are performing your installation tasks, verify visually and physically that services that are not needed in the current configuration are in fact stopped or disabled. Windows Server 2003 incorporates a number of security changes that assist you in this process, but it still is the administrator's responsibility to check for and correct deficiencies or problems that exist. For instance, the default in Windows Server 2003 disables the Telnet server, which in Windows 2000 was defaulted to manual start. This does enhance security, but you must still verify the condition of the service because other administrators might have enabled the service and left it on.

Since you are working with the materials in this book, it is obvious that you want to know about the system. Be sure to continue to expand your knowledge of

Continued

the changes in settings and operation as well as growing your understanding of the new and enhanced features provided in the platform. Never assume that a feature is required or not a potential source of breach without studying and identifying each of them.

EXAM 70-296 OBJECTIVE 1.1 1.2 1.2.1

Securing Servers by Roles

Now that we've had a chance to look at the various roles that are available in Windows Server 2003, we need to begin discussing the appropriate security configurations that should be used in each role when you are creating it or providing combinations of roles on the server. A number of settings are common to all server roles; these settings are needed to assure the security of the server, regardless of the platform you are running or the server role you are configuring. To save redundancy, let's look at the conditions that you should configure for any of the roles and that should be present before that configuration is begun. Table 8.2 discusses the common configuration items that you should have in place before configuring a role.

Table 8.2 Common Configuration Items Recommended for All Server Roles

Configuration Item	Reason
NTFS file system	Provides local and network file access permissions, file compression, and encryption capabilities.
Strong passwords: Password is at least seven characters long. Does not contain your username, real name, or company name. Does not contain a complete dictionary complexity requirement. Is significantly different from previous passwords. Passwords that increment (Password1, Password2, Password3 ...) are not strong. Contains characters from each of the following four groups: ■ Uppercase letters A, B, C ... ■ Lowercase letters a, b, c ... ■ Numerals 0, 1, 2, 3, 4, 5, 6, 7, 8, 9	Weak passwords provide means and opportunity for attackers to enter your system. *Note: When creating an enabled account or changing a password, Windows Server 2003 notifies you if the administrator password does not meet complexity requirements.*

Continued

Table 8.2 Common Configuration Items Recommended for All Server Roles

<table>
<tr><th>Configuration Item</th><th>Reason</th></tr>
<tr><td>■ Symbols found on the keyboard (all keyboard characters not defined as letters or numerals) ` ~! @ # $ % ^ & * ( ) _ + - = { } | [ ] \ : " ; ' < > ? , . /</td><td></td></tr>
<tr><td>Network connectivity</td><td>Needed in all server roles.</td></tr>
<tr><td>Users and groups planned and/or created</td><td>Appropriate use of users and groups allows the configuration of security using the principle of least privilege. This configuration allows users to have a level of access appropriate to the tasks they are responsible for performing but no more than is absolutely needed. This should be planned and implemented before any role is assigned to a server.</td></tr>
<tr><td>All known and applicable hotfixes, patches, or updates applied to the system</td><td>Security vulnerabilities have been taken into consideration in the design and creation of Windows Server 2003 servers. However, it is the administrator's responsibility to verify the condition of the install prior to connecting the server to the Internet or a production network.</td></tr>
<tr><td>Virus-scanning software</td><td>Virus-scanning software should be platform appropriate and must be up to date and configured for maximum protection of resources.</td></tr>
</table>

After verifying that these conditions exist, it is also wise to check to make sure that the default service settings have been left intact. Table 8.3 details the service configurations that exist in a default clean install of the Windows Server 2003 platform.

NOTE

These settings will not be configured on an upgrade installation. Instead, the previous system's settings will be maintained. If you desire to have the same configuration as a clean install, follow the settings in Table 8.3.

Table 8.3 Default Service Settings for a Windows Server 2003 Installation

Service Name	Standard Edition	Enterprise Edition	Datacenter Edition	Web Edition
Key: D = Disabled M = Manual M/S = Manual/Started A = Automatic/Started (sm) = Will also start in some selections in safe mode * New status in Windows Server 2003				
Alerter *	D	D	D	D
Application Layer Gateway Service	M	M	M	M
Application Management	M	M	M	M
Automatic Updates	A	A	A	A
Background Intelligent Transfer Service	M	M	M	M
Clipbook *	D	D	D	D
COM+ Event System	M/S	M/S	M/S	M/S
COM+ System Application	M	M	M	M
Computer Browser (sm)	A	A	A	A
Cryptographic Services	A	A	A	A
DHCP Client (sm)	A	A	A	A
Distributed File System	A	A	A	A
Distributed Link Tracking Client	A	A	A	A
Distributed Link Tracking Server*	D	D	D	D
Distributed Transaction Coordinator	A	A	A	A
DNS Client (sm)	A	A	A	A

Continued

Table 8.3 Default Service Settings for a Windows Server 2003 Installation

Service Name	Standard Edition	Enterprise Edition	Datacenter Edition	Web Edition
Error Reporting Service	A	A	A	A
Event Log (sm)	A	A	A	A
File Replication	M	M	M	M
Help and Support (sm)	A	A	A	A
HTTP SSL	M	M	M	M/S
Human Interface Device Access	D	D	D	D
IAS Jet Database Access	NA	M (64 Bit only)	M (64 Bit only)	NA
IIS Admin	NA	NA	NA	A
IMAPI-CD-Burning COM Service *	D	D	D	D
Indexing Service	M	M	M	M
Internet Connection Firewall/Internet Connection Sharing	D	D	NA	NA
Intersite Messaging	D	D	D	D
IPSec Services	A	A	A	A
Kerberos Key Distribution Center	D	D	D	D
License Logging	A	A	A	A
Logical Disk Manager	A	A	A	A
Logical Disk Manager Administrative Service	M	M	M	M
Messenger * (sm)	D	D	D	D
Microsoft Software Shadow Copy Provider (only on Web Server by default)	NA	NA	NA	M
MSSQL$UDDI	Not installed by default in any version			
MSSQLServerADHelper	Not installed by default in any version			
.NET Framework Support Service	Not installed by default in any version			

Continued

Table 8.3 Default Service Settings for a Windows Server 2003 Installation

Service Name	Standard Edition	Enterprise Edition	Datacenter Edition	Web Edition
Net Logon (changes to A if member of domain)	M	M	M	M
NetMeeting Remote Desktop Sharing *	D	D	D	D
Network Connections	M/S	M/S	M/S	M/S
Network DDE *	D	D	D	D
Network DDE DSDM *	D	D	D	D
Network Location Awareness	M/S	M/S	M/S	M/S
NT LM Security Support Provider	M	M	M	M
Performance Logs and Alerts	M	M	M	M
Plug and Play (sm)	A	A	A	A
Portable Media Serial Number (n/a on 64 bit)	M	M	M	M
Print Spooler	A	A	A	A
Protected Storage	A	A	A	A
Remote Access Auto Connection Manager	M	M	M	M
Remote Access Connection Manager	M	M	M	M
Remote Administration Service	NA	NA	NA	A
Remote Desktop Help Session Manager	M	M	M	M
Remote Procedure Call (RPC) (sm)	M	M	M	M
Remote Registry	A	A	A	A
Remote Server Manager	NA	NA	NA	A
Removable Storage	M	M	M	M
Resultant Set of Policy Provider	M	M	M	M
Routing and Remote Access *	D	D	D	D

Continued

Table 8.3 Default Service Settings for a Windows Server 2003 Installation

Service Name	Standard Edition	Enterprise Edition	Datacenter Edition	Web Edition
Secondary Logon	A	A	A	A
Security Accounts Manager	A	A	A	A
Server	A	A	A	A
Shell Hardware Detection	A	A	A	A
Simple Mail Transfer Protocol (SMTP)	Installed by default only on Web Edition			A
Smart Card	M	M	M	M
Special Administration Console Helper	M	M	M	M
SQLAGENT$UDDI	Not installed in typical installation			
System Event Notification	A	A	A	A
Task Scheduler	A	A	A	A
TCP/IP NetBIOS Helper	A	A	A	A
Telephony	M	M	M	M
Telnet *	D	D	D	D
Terminal Services	M/S	M/S	M/S	M/S
Terminal Services Session Directory *	D	D	D	D
Themes *	D	D	D	D
Uninterruptible Power Supply	D	D	D	D
Upload Manager *	D	D	D	D
Virtual Disk Service	M	M	M	M
Volume Shadow Copy	M	M	M	M
WebClient *	D	D	D	D
Web Element Manager	NA	NA	NA	A
Windows Audio	A	D	D	D
Windows Image) Acquisition (WIA	D	D	D	D
Windows Installer	M/S	M/S	M/S	M/S

Continued

Table 8.3 Default Service Settings for a Windows Server 2003 Installation

Service Name	Standard Edition	Enterprise Edition	Datacenter Edition	Web Edition
Windows Management Instrumentation (WMI)	A	A	A	A
Windows Management Instrumentation Driver Extensions	M	M	M	M
Windows Media Services	Not installed by default in any version			
Windows Time	A	A	A	A
WinHTTP Web Proxy Auto-Discovery Service	M	M	M	M
Wireless Configuration	A	A	A	M
WMI Performance Adapter	M	M	M	M
Workstation	A	A	A	A
World Wide Web Publishing	NA	NA	NA	A

After verification of these base settings and the normal configuration settings detailed in Table 8.2, we're ready to begin looking at securing the different server roles that we have configured.

Securing File Servers

File servers fulfill a very important function within organizations. Aside from today's dependence on e-mail services, the file server is the repository of our most critical asset: data. The storage of information can be performed on many different classes of machines and certainly can be handled on many platforms within the organization. However, if we are to utilize the full capability of Windows Server 2003 for protecting our data and make it universally available to appropriate users, we must act to secure the file server to provide that service. To provide that security, we begin with the basic settings detailed earlier in this section and follow up with more security-related checks and configuration changes to better provide for the security of this role. A number of additional tasks can and should be performed on these servers. Consider the following tasks as being necessary to provide a more complete security solution:

- Create an access policy that provides for the principle of least privilege. Grant access based on individual user need rather than general, vague groupings that have been used in the past. Use NTFS permissions to lock down the access allowed on files and folders.

- Utilize Encrypting File System to further protect critical information. Encrypt folders prior to moving documents, rather than encrypting a folder that contains documents. This provides an added benefit of encrypting temporary files that are created during work in an application along with the originals.
- Create a reasonable audit policy for monitoring access to file and folder objects on the server. Make sure that the created log files are adequately reviewed for access violations that might have occurred.
- Analyze the types of data being stored on the server to determine if it is appropriate to further protect the data and the transmission of data on the network to or from the file server with the creation of IPSec policies or other encryption methods to protect the data on the wire. For instance, if confidential proprietary information, financial records, employee records, or other sensitive information are stored on this equipment, your analysis and consultation with management team members could dictate a particular course of protection be designed.
- Assure that virus protection programs are adequate and updated regularly to provide protection from attack or compromise of the system.

EXAM WARNING

Each of the roles that is discussed for security configuration can also be configured through the use of the Control Panel's Add/Remove Programs feature in the Add/Remove Windows Components section. You are advised to explore this area to discover the services and components that are installed in different default combinations than were used in Windows 2000. For instance, the defaults for IIS 6.0 installation are far different than they were for IIS 5.0 in Windows 2000.

Securing Print Servers

Print servers provide a different level of need than other roles because they must provide for the protection of the printing process. The print server configuration on a Windows Server 2003 machine can be accomplished through use of the Manage Your Computers utility. Additionally, the creation of a local printer that is shared for network use causes the Print Server role to be created automatically. In configuring the print server, a number of further configuration modifications will help provide good service and security for document printing. Consider the following as you secure the print server (in addition to following the best practices that we discussed earlier):

- Establish and implement good guidelines for the delegation of permission to manage or control printer objects. Use appropriate group assignments and built-in groups appropriately to delegate permission to work with the printer object.
- Verify the security of the spool folder on the print server to assure that it is not accessible by unauthorized printer objects or users. Furthermore, assure that it is of sufficient size to handle the spooling of anticipated print jobs and loads.
- Control the publication of the print server to Active Directory in a domain environment. This is accomplished on the Sharing tab of the printer's Properties page, where you can select or deselect the option to publish the printer.
- Audit access to and use of the printer object to assure appropriate usage and access are as designed and implemented.
- Locate print devices for confidential print jobs in physically secure locations.

Securing Application Servers

Installation or creation of the application server role in Windows Server 2003 installs IIS 6.0 on the server in its default security configuration. In the case of IIS 6.0, this means that it is installed in a much tighter configuration than was provided with IIS 5.0. IIS 6.0 is not part of the default installation of Windows Server 2003 except in the Web Edition. Due to the fact that we are installing Web Services with this role configuration, we must be very cognizant of the changes that occur and work to secure the platform and the content at a different level than with other services. The IIS 6.0 installation creates a number of changes and includes options to add Front Page Server Extensions and ASP.NET extensions to the service (ASP.NET is Microsoft's platform for development of Web services and integration). These changes include:

- Folders
  - Inetpub, with an Admin Scripts and WWW Root folder established
  - WM Pub folder
- User, machine, and group accounts
  - **IUSR_*computername*** Anonymous access account
  - **IWAM_computername** Launch IIS Process Account
  - **OWS_numbers_admin** Sharepoint admin role account
  - **ASPNET machine account** to run ASP.Net worker processes (if configured for ASP.NET)
  - **IIS_WPG** IIS worker process group account
  - **Network Services** Built-in group for control of IIS worker processes

- New Services
  - **IIS Admin Service** To start and stop the IIS service
  - **World Wide Web Publishing Service** To run the Web site operation

NOTE

It is notable that the installation of the application server mode, although including IIS 6.0 base functionality for Web services, does not install SMTP, NNTP, FTP, Remote Administration tools, or other services without explicitly adding these functions. The *worker processes* referred to in the preceding listing are a new refinement in IIS 6.0 that allows processes to be called from multiple accounts and used as needed, while isolating the processes from each other to eliminate the possibility of interactions between applications interfering with each other. These worker processes run at a lower priority and under lower-level credentials than they would have in IIS 5.0. To accommodate the new levels, new security accounts and groups have been added (*ASPNET* machine account and the *IIS_WPG* and *Network Services* groups). This topic is revisited in the Web Servers section later in the chapter.

These changes, coupled with the fact that you now have configured a limited Web server, require some additional configuration by the administrator to maintain a secure server. In addition to those detailed for all roles, these include the following recommendations:

- Verify NTFS permissions and access controls for the installed folders.
- Verify the membership and function of the newly created groups.
- Implement a firewall if one is not currently configured. Windows Server 2003 includes a stateful firewall product called Internet Connection Firewall that can be used if you do not have a previously installed firewall application or device in place.
- Implement IPSec for protection of network data.
- Implement SSL and appropriate encryption and authentication protocols.

Web Servers

Be sure to spend the time necessary to research and learn about IIS 6.0 defaults and the appropriate methods of configuration of IIS 6.0 as you begin to implement Web Services. You can find considerable information in the Windows Server 2003 Help and Support Center and on the Microsoft site at www.microsoft.com/windowsserver2003/proddoc/default.mspx. The application server role we looked at provides a slightly different set of services in its basic configuration than is provided through installation of a Web Edition server or a complete Web Server install. For instance, the default Web Edition installation, in addition to the items detailed previously in the application server role discussion, adds SMTP services and remote browser-based administration capabilities to the installation. This also occurs if you elect to install the capability to host Web Services in application server mode.

Default Configuration

The default installation provides a certain level of security but prohibits the use of active content, server-side includes, WebDAV, and FrontPage Server extensions as Web server content unless explicitly configured to be allowed by the administrator. Control of these features is provided through a new wizard in the Internet Information Server IIS Management Console, shown in Figure 8.14. (Active Server Pages are not allowed by default but have been allowed on the pictured server to allow remote administration tools to operate.)

Figure 8.14 Showing Web Service Extensions Disabled by Default

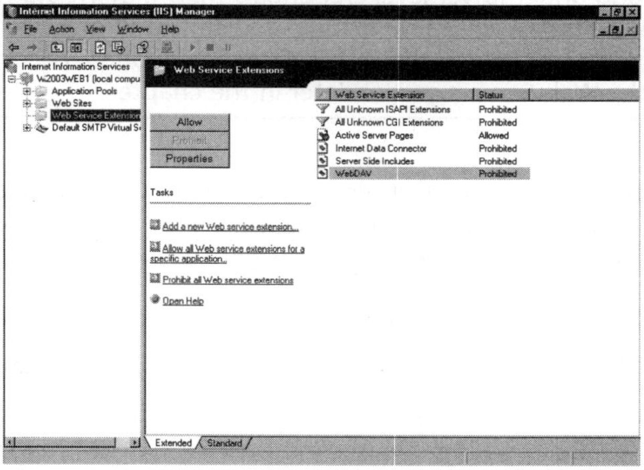

Security Features

Additionally, security concerns in regard to IIS processes and other problems that existed in IIS 5.0 default installations have been disabled by default in IIS 6.0. If you intend to use IIS 6.0 functions, you need to spend some time learning about and correctly configuring the settings according to your operation's needs. The way IIS 6.0 operates within the system has changed, including the level of privilege IIS 6.0 uses. IIS 6.0 isolates application operations into *worker processes*, which run individually if they fail don't affect the server. These worker processes run as a low-privileged account by default and are controlled under the settings of a Network Service account, which is a new built-in account with seven allowed privileges:

- Adjust memory quotas for a process
- Generate security audits
- Logon as a service

- Replace a process-level token
- Impersonate a client after authentication
- Allow logon locally
- Access this computer from the network

These enhancements improve the overall security of Web services installations by not creating immediate security problems with installation. The tightened security and lower authority levels utilized by IIS 6.0 provide much more protection than is present in previous Windows versions.

Test Day Tip

Review the server roles and their security settings prior to test day. If at all possible, practice and test the various configurations so that you are comfortable with the MMC tools and locations. This allows for a fuller and more rewarding testing experience because you can relax and concentrate on the topics at hand instead of having to concentrate on the location of things that you need to work with.

Securing Mail Servers

Windows Server 2003 mail server roles provide the capability to offer POP3 mail services for organizations that do not need the expanded capabilities of products such as Exchange to handle mail volumes and added functionality. Installation of the mail server role adds the following items to the server during setup of the POP3 functionality:

- **POP3 Users group** Members can access mailboxes but may not log on to the server
- **IIS Admin Service** Provides for administration of SMTP service
- **SMTP Service**
- **Mailroot folder and subfolders below the Inetpub root folder** For storage and transfer of mail

The configuration of the mail server role starts the Microsoft POP3 service (pop3.exe) automatically at boot. Like IIS 6.0, the POP3 service runs under the NetworkService account credentials, which were detailed earlier in the discussion of application and Web server roles. As with all mail server configurations, security settings and configuration are necessary for proper operation and to prevent mail relay from spammers. After performing the normal security checks, including verifying NTFS permissions on *mailroot* and subfolders, you also need to configure SMTP. To perform this task, use the Management Console. Figure 8.15 shows the first of the configuration screens you'll see after you open the base console. (If you want to compare the POP3 features of Windows Server 2003 and Exchange Server 2003, you can find the information at www.microsoft.com/technet/prodtechnol/exchange/Exchange2003/POP3EXWN.asp?frame=true.)

Figure 8.15 The Internet Information Services Manager MMC

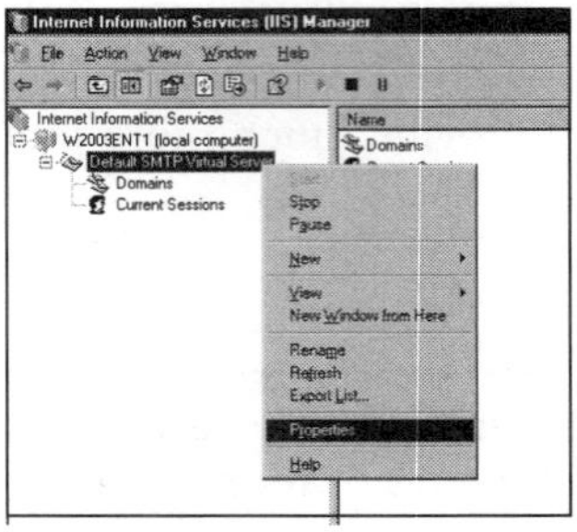

After selecting the view the properties of the SMTP server, a screen like the one shown in Figure 8.16 will appear, showing the properties and available configuration pages for the SMTP server operation.

Figure 8.16 The Default SMTP Virtual Server Properties Screen

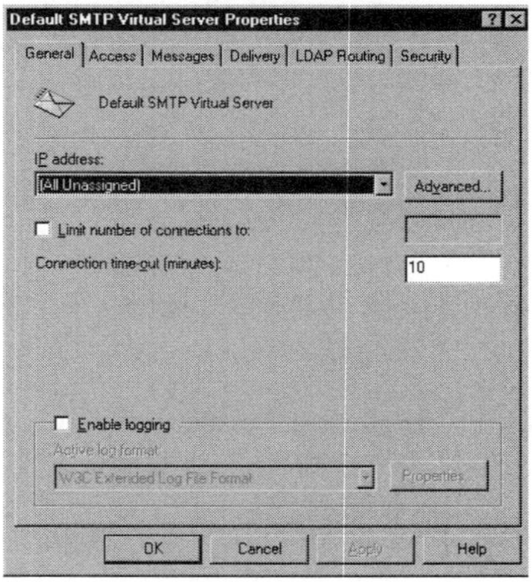

After selecting the **Access** tab, you have the ability to choose the mail server's authentication method (anonymous, Basic, or Integrated Windows Authentication) by choosing the **Authentication** button, establish secure communications requirements by clicking the **Certificate** button, or perform Connection Control (allow or deny domains, IP address blocks, and so on) by selecting the **Connection** button. This is also the page where we can set and enforce relay restrictions to stop or limit spamming operations. If you click the **Relay** button, as in Figure 8.17, you will reach that settings page, shown in Figure 8.18.

Figure 8.17 The SMTP Properties Page Access Tab

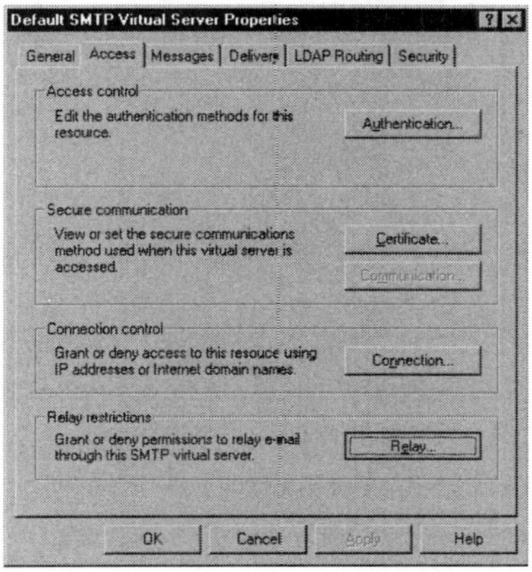

Figure 8.18 shows the Relay Restrictions page, where we can allow or deny access to send mail through this server. If the check box is checked at the bottom in a domain, the SMTP server will allow outbound mail from all machines authenticated in the domain, without further configuration by the administrator.

Figure 8.18 Relay Restrictions Configuration

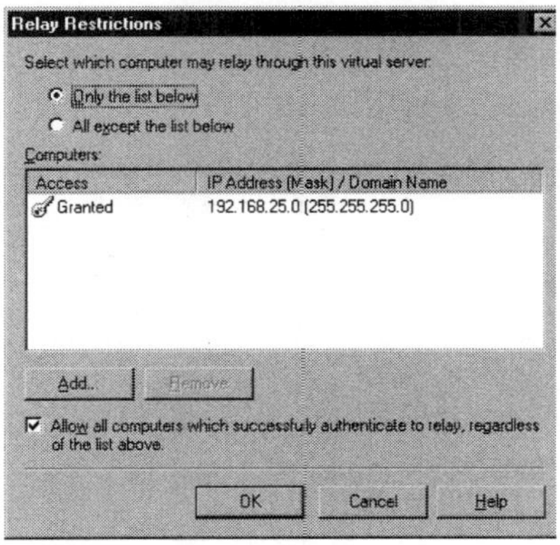

Finally, we need to verify the settings on the Security tab of the SMTP Virtual Server Properties page, as shown in Figure 8.19. This setting confirms the accounts that are allowed to act as operators for the mail server. Like IIS configurations, this should be limited to those who must work directly on the configuration of the server itself.

Figure 8.19 The SMTP Security Tab

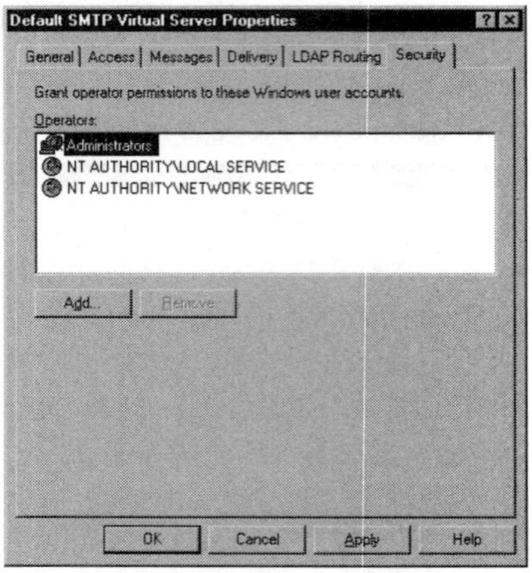

Secure Password Authentication

Secure password authentication adds an extra layer of security to users' retrieval of mail and verifies their identities as they connect to the server. Normal POP3 authentication transmits the username and password in cleartext to the mail server; secure password authentication (SPA) protects that information while it's being used for authentication. SPA is configurable within the POP3 service MMC. If SPA is required, the username for login to the mailbox changes from *username@domain.com* to *username*. A password is entered in either case. Figure 8.20 shows the POP3 Service MMC server properties page, which allows the choice of requirement for SPA.

Figure 8.20 Selecting Secure Password Authentication for the POP3 Server

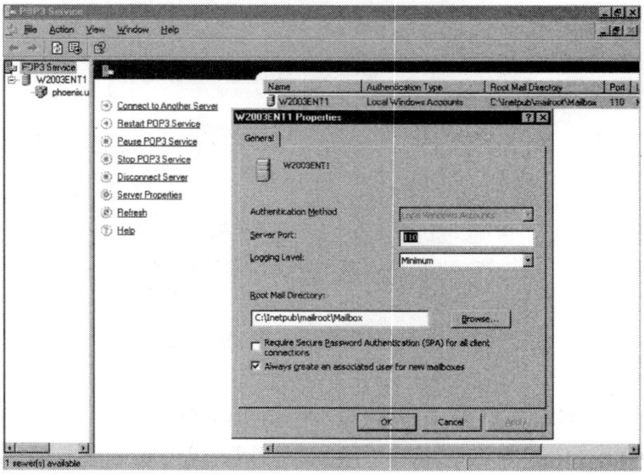

NOTE

The creation of mailboxes on the POP3 server can be configured to always create an associated user for new mailboxes, as depicted in Figure 8.20. This process places the user in the POP3 Users group, which has access only to the mailbox for which it is created. This user account does not have access to other resources on the server.

Securing Terminal Servers

Terminal servers, by their very definition and method of use, require special consideration as we begin to secure this role. As mentioned earlier, the machine need not be configured for Terminal Services if the only need is to connect for remote administration, because this feature can now be handled through the use of Remote Desktop connections.

In configuring the terminal server for use, the basic considerations in regard to the application of appropriate service packs and up-to-date patch application are the same as for other roles. Of course, it is also important to consider patching and updating any known vulnerability that might exist in the installed application base that could potentially cause a breach of security on the terminal server. You should be aware that there are two security modes in which terminal server can operate. In the first mode, *full security*, applications are written to run in the context of the ordinary user. This mode is the default for Windows Server 2003, as it was in Windows 2000. It is possible to run in the second mode, *relaxed security*. This mode allows users to change files and Registry settings in places not normally allowed in the full security mode. The administrator can use this mode to allow operation of legacy applications, but then planning for auditing and control of the remote user must proceed with much more care and caution to protect the terminal server and its data. In either case, applications should be installed and tested prior to allowing user access to the terminal server. We also must consider the methods we will use to protect the applications that have been installed on the server.

Additionally, we need to consider protection of the connections that are being used to the terminal server and the users' shared applications and information that reside on the terminal server. The administrator must make a decision about the level of encryption that should be utilized for the network connections using RDP. There are four levels of encryption that are possible for Terminal Services communications. These are:

- **Low** This level uses 56-bit encryption to protect the transmission.
- **Client Compatible** This level uses the maximum key strength that is supported on the client.
- **High** This level uses the highest key strength supported by the server, up to Strong 128-bit encryption, and clients that cannot support that configuration cannot connect.

- **FIPS Compliant** Data transmission is protected using Federal Information Processing Standard (FIPS) 140-1 validated encryption methods.

This setting is configured in **Terminal Services Configuration | Connections | RDPTcp Properties**, as shown in Figure 8.21.

Figure 8.21 Setting the Encryption Level for Terminal Services Communications

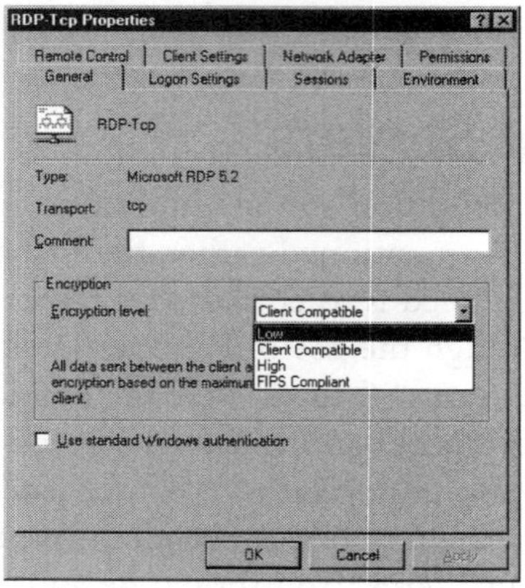

Further configuration for the access levels of the terminal server users will also be required. All users of the terminal server must have user accounts added to the Remote Desktop Users group. Access can be defined to allow Full Control (Administrators) or User Access (Remote Desktop Users). Only users or groups that the administrator adds to the Remote Desktop Users group will have access.

Securing Remote Access and VPN Servers

Remote access servers allow access to internal networks through an outside interface. This access point may be through an unprotected or hostile network or a dialup connection. This process is controlled and configured through the Routing and Remote Access management console provided in the Administrative Tools folder. The remote access server can present some particularly challenging conditions to the administrator who is attempting to secure the role. This is because the server has the potential to be configured in countless ways to provide functionality in a number of areas. For instance, the Routing and Remote Access configuration allows for configuration as a LAN router, a VPN server, a VPN server with NAT, the use of DNS and DHCP implementations in the internal network, and configurations for any combination of these service types through customization. Some security checks are common to all these potential configurations, and we look at these areas of concern as we continue in this section. First, there is a common set of configuration checks that we must perform in addition to the base settings for all servers we discussed earlier. These are:

- Access type for the VPN or RAS connection must be configured.
- Remote access policies must be created and operational.
- Static packet filters may be applied.
- Services and ports available to VPN or RAS clients must be defined.
- Logging of protocols should be established and enabled.
- VPN ports can be added, removed, or edited as needed.

After these tasks are performed, we could decide to increase the level of security for RRAS and VPN connections by requiring the use of secure tunnel capabilities such as L2TP and IPSec to further protect our networks. Additionally, the following areas should be considered in configuring the overall security of the RRAS/VPN configuration:

- Define the types of clients to be supported. It is preferable from a security standpoint to utilize the security capabilities of Windows 2000, Windows XP, and Windows Server 2003 rather than older down-level clients because authentication then uses Kerberos with a higher level of protection than is available on the older clients such as Windows 98 using NTLM or NTLMv2. Additionally, IPSec and L2TP capabilities are not supported with Windows NT 4.0, Windows 98, Windows Me, or other down-level client packages.
- Consider the authentication methods to be supported. For higher security, utilize MSChapv2 or EAP instead of the older PAP, SPAP, or CHAP authentication methods.
- Consider data encryption.
- Consider the use of RADIUS to centralize the application of authentication methods to multiple RRAS servers. In addition, consider whether to support Windows Authentication or RADIUS in your operation.
- In configuring the VPN server, allow the assignment of DHCP information from the VPN server or a DHCP server.
- Require the use of L2TP/IPSec rather than the weaker PPTP. This can be accomplished with down-level clients by using upgraded client software available from the Microsoft download site.

Test Day Tip

Remote access/VPN server roles also must be configured appropriately for the authentication methods that will be used. Before testing, be sure to refresh your understanding not only of the concepts that are related to the physical security of the server role but also why and where RADIUS would be used in the enterprise environment to provide assistance to the authentication process.

Securing Domain Controllers

The domain controller role introduces some security concerns that are not present in other roles. With other roles, much of the security configuration that we perform has to do with securing file systems and defining appropriate methods of authentication, followed by changes limiting local access to resources. These resources, of course, can be such things as files and folders, printers, and other resources we might choose to make available to the users from our organization or to the public, customers, or partners as appropriate to our particular needs and business. When we begin to look at securing the domain controller role, we must also consider what would happen if we were not successful or complete in the work we did to secure this role. Potential problems include exposure of our entire infrastructure and all its resources to attack, theft, or damage. This is because the DC is the role that provides the authentication piece for the security of all the other roles. If an attacker is successful in breaching our defenses on a machine configured with this role, there exists a real chance that we have lost control of all our assets and information. Therefore, we'll spend a bit of time on this role and discuss the best practices that should be employed as we work to secure this role.

The discussion about the appropriate file system format to be used with a DC should never arise. Protection of the DC's data can only be accomplished if the server is formatted and protected using the base settings we've looked at previously. Additionally, more than possibly any other role, it is imperative that this server be located in a part of the facility that is physically secure and where physical access control is present and enforced. The promotion of the server to the domain controller role produces special conditions and configurations. To begin with, the DC promotion applies a new security template to the machine that increases its local security and defines far different conditions in regard to the users who may log on interactively and perform any system function on the DC. This is followed with the transformation of the local SAM database to the protected Active Directory service. *As mentioned in the initial discussion of DC promotion, any encrypted documents stored locally on the server (including encrypted e-mail) at the time of the conversion to domain controller will be deleted.* This is due to the fact that the encryption keys used to protect those documents will no longer be valid, and thus the data will be unrecoverable after the conversion. Obviously, it is important to decrypt and move those files prior to the conversion.

The creation of the DC also creates the entire Active Directory structure and installs the domain-based administration tools. As was the case in Windows 2000, a number of new groups are created for domain use. A number of these groups could be of concern to administrators who have worked with Windows 2000 Active Directory. For instance, in Windows Server 2003 Active Directory, new groups exist with much more limited scope than was true in Windows 2000. There is a new Terminal Service License Servers group, a TelnetClient group (used to allow access and logon locally rights to Telnet users), and others that have lower access permissions defined than existed in Windows 2000. Additional security considerations in securing the Windows Server 2003 DC include these:

- The DC server must be physically secure and access controlled.
- Membership in Domain Administrators and Enterprise Administrators groups must be restricted.
- Consideration should be given to the use of *syskey* to protect the Active Directory database. (The *syskey* utility provides varying levels of protection and strong encryption of passwords stored in Active Directory.)
- Delegation of control over DC configurations should be closely monitored.
- Evaluation of higher security templates should be performed to determine if a need exists to tighten the security parameters of the system.

Securing DNS Servers

DNS servers provide FQDN and IP address resolution for client machines. Additionally, in a Windows 2000 or Windows Server 2003 domain structure, DNS provides the referrals through LDAP to clients searching for DCs and other domain resources through the maintenance of SRV records within the DNS zone records. These DNS zone records contain FQDN or hostname-to-address mappings for our networks, and with the addition of dynamic DNS capabilities in the last few years, they contain a wealth of information that could be of great interest to attackers. The records themselves are also subject to compromise from other network operations, so there are a significant number of issues to deal with in making sure that this particular role is well secured. We've discussed the basic configurations of security all through this section, and those apply to this role as well. Let's take a look at some of the things that contribute to security problems with the role as well as recommendations for keeping your DNS server role protected.

Security issues from past DNS implementations are also of concern today in Windows Server 2003 DNS implementations, along with some that are new:

- Zone transfers should always be directed to specific DNS servers rather than being allowed to any server. This prevents disclosure of the zone records to other servers. This is very important, since these records detail the machine names and addresses of the entire zone. Additionally, in an Active Directory domain implementation, the SRV records detailing the name of servers providing Active Directory services are detailed in the zone record.
- Multihomed machines configure the DNS server to respond to requests only on the internal interface. DNS should not respond to requests from unprotected or unauthorized networks.
- Consider using only secure dynamic update if you are allowing dynamic update. This prevents spoofing of DNS records by unauthorized machines or users, because the machine or user must be authenticated before the update will be processed.
- Use Active Directory Integrated zones if utilizing Active Directory to protect the zone files from outside interception.

Securing DHCP Servers

Incorrectly configured and protected DHCP servers present a very real and potentially serious access point to your internal network and all the resources that are available within. At the least, the potential exists that network communications could be disrupted. DHCP servers respond to all requests for service from clients that they "hear" on their network segment or that are relayed from other subnets through routers that support such relaying, and they do not block requests or refuse distribution of addressing information under normal circumstances. In a Windows 2000 or Windows Server 2003 domain structure, this is partly controlled if the server is a member of a domain, but rogue servers installed in the network running other operating systems can still provide addressing information to client machines.

DHCP servers in the Windows Server 2003 domain network must be authorized in Active Directory by a member of the Enterprise Admins security group. Once the server is authorized and initializes on the network, it broadcasts a DHCPINFORM packet that requests responses from other DHCP servers on its network. Other DHCP servers hearing this broadcast respond with the location of a DC, and the DHCP server checks to find out if it is authorized. If authorization is present, the DHCP server begins servicing requests from client machines. If not, it logs an event to the log and does not service client requests. This verification process occurs approximately once per hour of operation. Windows Server 2003 servers with DHCP installed that are not members of a domain will react to the response of any DC they can reach exactly like members of a domain. In other words, any Windows Server 2003 server that detects that authorization for its DHCP service is not present will not respond to service requests from clients.

Known Security Issues

A number of known security issues are present with DHCP implementations. Generic security concerns include the problem of rogue DHCP servers in the network space. The authorization process designed into Windows 2000 and Windows Server 2003 is intended to minimize the effects (or possibility) of these servers granting address information within the network. The requirement for Enterprise Admins to authorize the server in Active Directory is part of that process to stop unintended disruptions through unauthorized installations of DHCP. However, DHCP servers that operate on other platforms do not fall under these rules and still present a risk. In addition to the rogue DHCP issue, these issues require your consideration as you prepare your DHCP security plan:

- DHCP is not an authenticated protocol. Users and machines requesting service are not required to authenticate before being granted a lease. Therefore anyone with physical access to the network through unprotected access ports can obtain addressing information. These clients can also obtain addressing options such as WINS, DNS, and other service and class information from the scopes, which could give insight into the construction of your network. Clients who want to perform malicious acts can request multiple leases and attempt to disrupt the assignment of addresses to valid client machines.

- With dynamic DNS updating available in Windows Server 2003 and Windows 2000 networks, it is possible for the DHCP server to be used as a part of a DoS attack against the DNS server by requesting large numbers of leases from the DHCP server and having the information be updated in the DNS zone records.

Securing the DHCP service requires the use of the base security settings discussed previously. You must also assure that physical access to your network is restricted and that the number of persons allowed to administer DHCP is limited. Auditing and review of the DHCP logs at *%windir%*\System32\DHCP is highly recommended to detect unusual lease request activity or updating of information to the DNS server.

Securing WINS Servers

WINS is used for NetBIOS name resolution services. As was true with the Windows 2000 WINS capabilities, it is anticipated that eventually the need for WINS will disappear as down-level clients are phased out. Basic server configuration considerations apply as to all Windows Server 2003 deployments. We also must be concerned about eliminating unnecessary services and correctly configuring local network firewalls and routers to limit access to the WINS server to the internal network, because connection to the WINS server or improper configuration can lead to an attacker being able to quickly enumerate the network service information and use it to breach your network.

Now that we've completed our discussion of the methods and recommendations for securing the various server roles, let's proceed to an exercise to utilize the appropriate tools and practice securing the file server role.

Exercise 8.02

Securing a File Server Role

Note

In this exercise, we utilize the file server role that we configured in Exercise 8.01. If you removed the role, go ahead and create the base file server outlined in the previous exercise.

Exercise 8.02 is illustrated using a standalone server configuration and therefore uses local users and groups in defining access and share permissions. The procedure for creating and securing the file server in a domain environment is similar. To demonstrate the processes used to secure a file server role, we work to implement some of the best practices for securing the file server role. These include:

- Set appropriate permissions on shared resources.
- Define groups and membership.
- Secure data.
- Audit access to sensitive data.

Now do the following:

1. Create these new folders and subfolders: **C:\Sales, C:\Sales\Cost Information, C:\Sales\Pricing Information, C:\Human Resources, C:\Human Resources\Employee Benefits Information, C:\Human Resources\Confidential, C:\Human Resources\Employee Reviews and C:\Administration, C:\Administration\Financial Reports,** and **C:\Administration\Proprietary**.
2. Create the following security groups using the appropriate tools (**Start Administrative Tools | Computer Management | Local Users and Groups**): **Sales Managers, Sales Staff; HR Managers, HR Staff, Senior Management**.
3. Create the following users and group memberships: **Sales Manager 1 (Sales Managers), Sales Staff 1 (Sales Staff), HR Manager 1 (HR Managers), HR Staff 1 (HR Staff), VP 1, President 1 (Senior Management).**
4. Using Windows Explorer, access the Properties sheet for each of the folders and use the Sharing and Security tabs to implement the following levels of access for the resources you've created:
   - **Administration Folder** The Senior Management group should have full control access to the Administration folder and subfolders. No other user group (including Administrators) should have any access to the resource.
   - **Human Resources Folder** All users should have full control share access to the Human Resources folder. HR staff should have full control of employee benefits information, but only HR managers and senior management should have access to confidential and employee reviews folders. All users should have read and execute permissions for the Employee Benefits folder.
   - **Sales Folder** Senior management, sales staff, and sales managers should have full control share access to the Sales folder. Senior management, sales staff, and sales managers should have full control of the Pricing folder, and all others should not have access to this folder. Sales managers and senior management should have full control access to the Cost folder.

5. Using Local Security Policy, shown for reference in Figures 8.22 and 8.23, configure auditing to include object access success and failure on the folders you created that contain sensitive or restricted data. You can assign auditing through the folder's Properties sheet using the **Advanced** button on the Security tab and then selecting **Auditing**. (*Hint:* When auditing for this type of access, configure auditing for the Everyone group to include all access success and failures.)

Figure 8.22 Local Security Policy MMC Showing Audit Object Access Selection

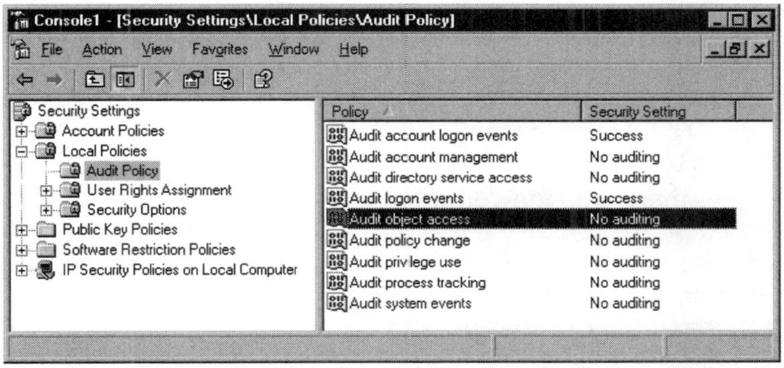

Figure 8.23 Configuring Audit Object Access Success and Failure

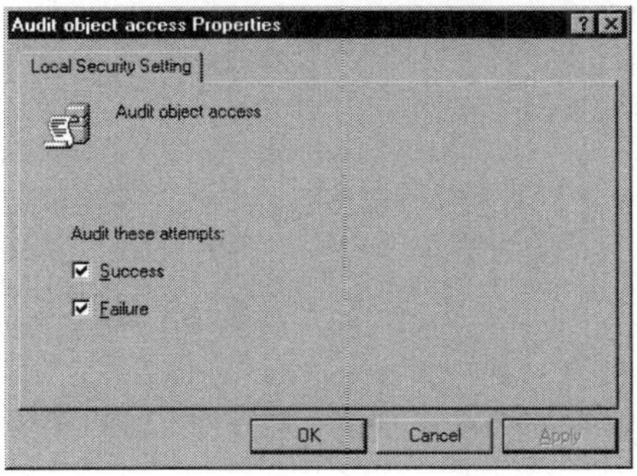

6. Log in using the various users you have created, and verify that the access levels are correctly enforced. You can test full control by creating a document, saving it, and deleting it from a folder. If you have properly applied the permissions as indicated, no user (including the administrator) should be able to access the restricted folders unless he or she has membership in the defined group. View the Security log in Event Viewer to check the access success or failure on the resources you configured in Step 5.

NOTE

In the case of a production system, we would also implement EFS to protect confidential information. In Windows Server 2003, it is possible to have multiple user access EFS-protected documents through creation of appropriate certificates from a Certification Authority and importing those certificates to the machine that hosts the resource to be protected. This is a significant change from the single-user restriction for EFS that was present in Windows 2000.

Head of the Class...

Why, Oh Why, Are There So Many Different Configurations for Security?

As we have seen, there are many different considerations for the configurations of our servers based on the roles we have chosen for them. Often, a server fulfills more than a single role, and we are forced to modify the configuration of the server's security to accommodate the new use. Couldn't it be simpler to configure all this? Unfortunately, the answer to that question is no.

Each of the roles that we configure exposes a different set of problems and areas that we must be concerned about as we move to protect the data or resource that we are providing. These data and resources could be for the use of the public, our own users, partner connections, or customers. Different methods of access, including dialup connections, remote access via unprotected networks, and extranet connections, along with other types of entry points, complicate the configurations we must make and add to the number of possible things that we must be aware of as we provide the security for our operations.

How, then, can we be sure that we've done everything that is possible to secure the data and still allow those who need access to have it reliably and when they need it? We accomplish this goal through constant vigilance, training, and utilization of best practices whenever possible to provide the most secure environment for each platform and service that we configure in our systems. This begins with the universal requirements in Windows Server 2003 server configurations to:

- Perform clean installations if at all possible to avoid inheritance of weak security settings from upgrades.
- Use strong passwords, as previously defined.
- Use NTFS formatted disks on all drives.
- Enforce the principle of least privilege; assign access only on an as-needed basis.

Continued

- Be aware of and apply fixes, patches, service packs, and updates in a timely manner.
- Install and maintain an appropriate antivirus package and update it regularly.
- Install and configure appropriate firewall configurations to isolate and protect the internal network.
- Regularly evaluate and update security configurations and settings to reflect needs in your system.
- *Audit access*, and read the logs!

Follow these recommendations, and you will go a long way towards making your overall individual configurations easier and more secure. Windows Server 2003 has the tools for you to keep things secure; you simply have to use them to create the effective security that you need.

EXAM 70-296 OBJECTIVE 1.2.2

Security Templates

Security templates contain the settings that are applied to our workstations and servers based on the level of security that we determine is needed in our particular situation. During a clean installation of Windows Server 2003, a base template and security configuration are applied. This initial template defines the level of user access, basic security, and permissions settings on the roots of drives and special folders. The default configuration also establishes the settings for such things as password policy, password complexity, logon rights, and actions that users or groups may be permitted to do or may be restricted from doing. As the initial templates are applied, they define the default security level for the server. Microsoft supplies a number of preconfigured templates that apply various settings for servers and workstations with different jobs. For instance, as the role of DC is established, a template for a machine configured as a DC is applied. This template and role have much different security needs and configuration settings than a machine configured as a base server. In this section of the chapter, we take a close look at the concepts and practices that will lead to understanding and developing the capability to analyze current levels of security. Once we have established an analysis methodology, we continue by taking you through the process of modifying or customizing these settings, allowing you to make them appropriate for use in your own network and providing the protection that your environment requires.

EXERCISE 8.03

PERFORMING AN INITIAL SECURITY ANALYSIS WITH SECURITY CONFIGURATION AND ANALYSIS TOOLS

Before we go too much further in our discussion of creating security templates, it is important to take a look at just exactly what it is that we are trying to accomplish with our template work. To that end, this exercise walks you through performing an initial security analysis so that you understand what we're about to work on and why this configuration is important to the security of your operations and systems. Now do the following:

1. To start, open a blank MMC. For this step, simply type **MMC** at the run command. When the window is open, select **File | Add/Remove Snap-in**, as shown in Figure 8.24.

Figure 8.24 The Initial MMC Console Screen

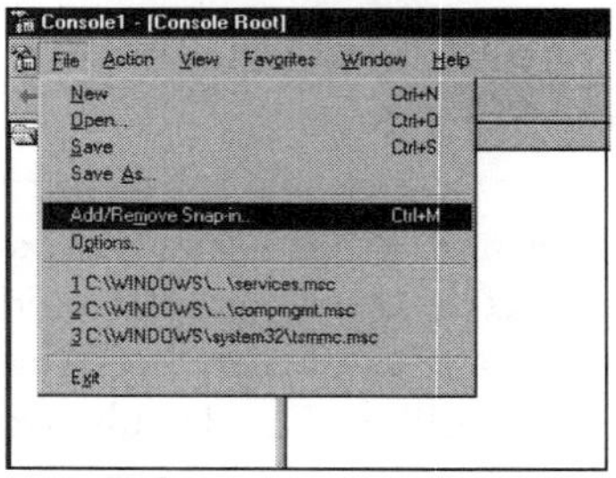

2. After opening the original console, select to **Add** the **Security Configuration and Analysis** and **Security Templates** snap-ins, and then click **Close** on the Add Standalone Snap-in window, as shown in Figure 8.25.
3. Click **OK** in the Add/Remove Snap-in window, as shown in Figure 8.26.
4. Select **Security Configuration and Analysis**, and you will reach the screen shown in Figure 8.27. Create a new database by selecting **Security Configuration and Analysis**, then right-click and select **Open Database**.

Figure 8.25 Adding Standalone Snap-ins to the MMC

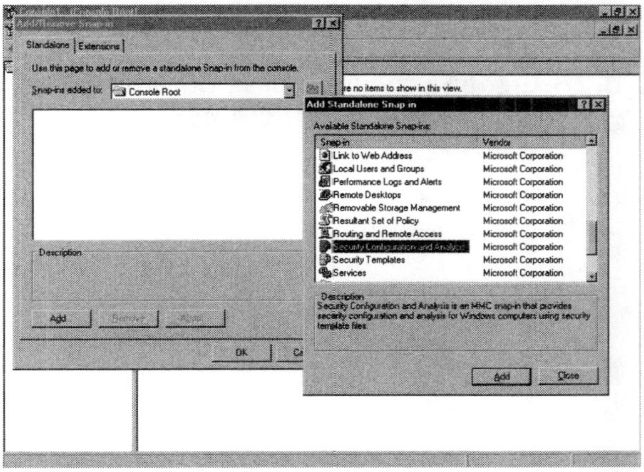

Figure 8.26 The Add/Remove Snap-in Window

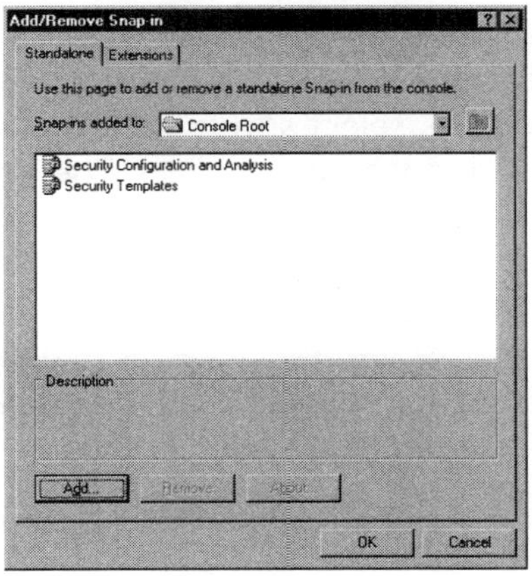

Figure 8.27 The Security Configuration and Analysis Console

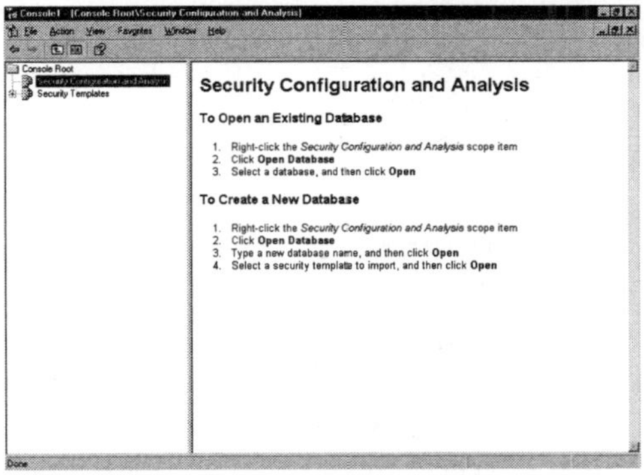

5. When asked to name the database, type **base template** in the name box, and select **Open**. This process is shown in Figure 8.28.

Figure 8.28 Creating the New Base Database File for Comparison

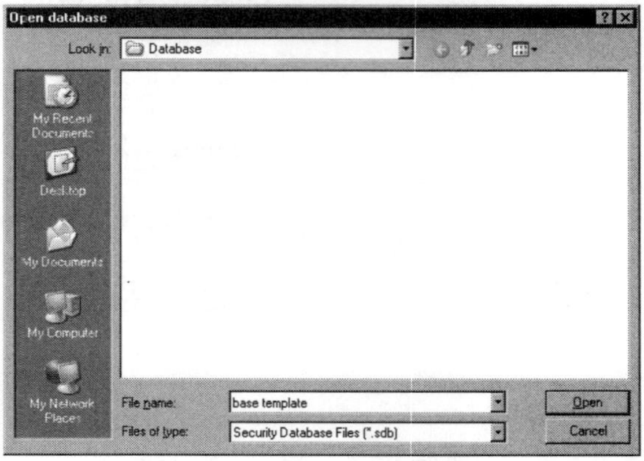

6. After you have named the template, you will be asked to select a template to import. This process allows us to begin the comparison process. For the exercise, select **setup security.inf** and we'll proceed to use that template to perform our analysis. The Import Template screen is shown in Figure 8.29.

Figure 8.29 Selecting the Template to Import for Analysis

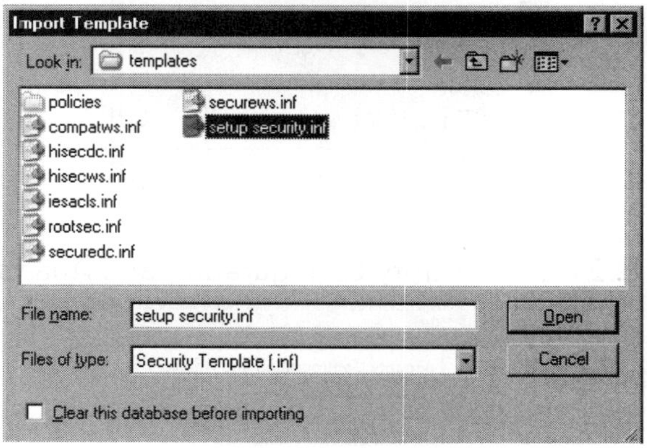

7. When you are returned to the main console window, notice that there is now a definition of the template file we are working with. Right-click **Security Configuration and Analysis**, and select **Analyze Computer Now,** as shown in Figure 8.30. As the process is working, the Analyzing System Security screen will show you that the process is going through a number of steps to accomplish its tasks. Figure 8.31 shows that screen.

Figure 8.30 Beginning the Analysis Comparison

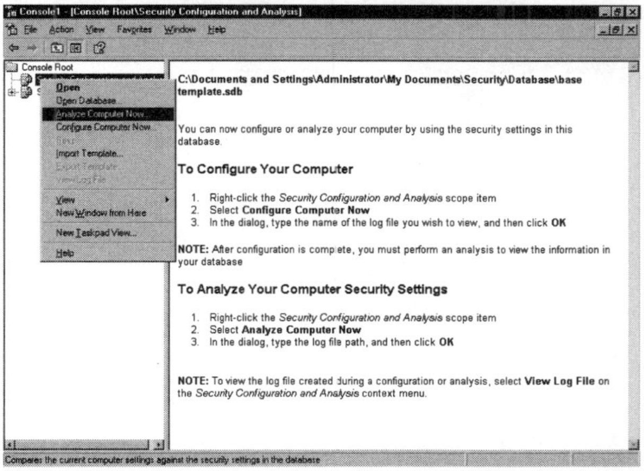

Figure 8.31 The Analyzing System Security Progress Screen

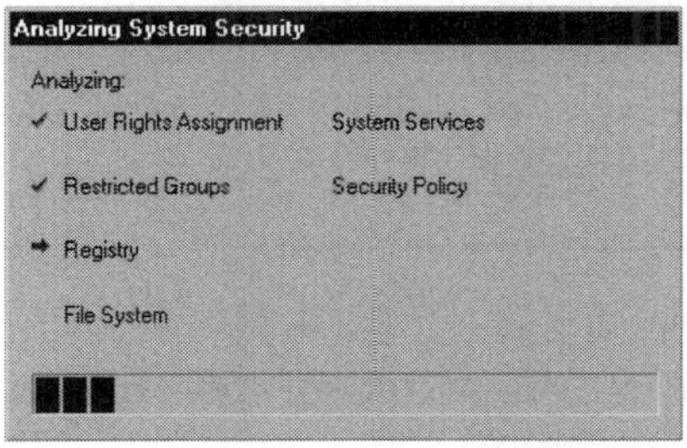

8. After the analysis process has concluded, the right pane of the MMC will contain the results of the analysis. At this time, we are performing the analysis merely to determine if there are differences between the existing machine configuration and the template to which we are comparing it. Figure 8.32 shows the template after the analysis is complete.

9. Having reached this point, we can now review the results of the analysis. Take a few minutes (or more if you like) to look through all the various settings and conditions that exist. In Figure 8.33, the User Rights Assignment section is expanded, providing a view of the database settings compared to the settings that are currently implemented on the machine. This examination shows that some settings do not comply with the settings in the template used for examination (the template that we imported earlier). Icons with an *x* indicate that the settings do not match the template.

Figure 8.32 The MMC After Performing the Security Analysis

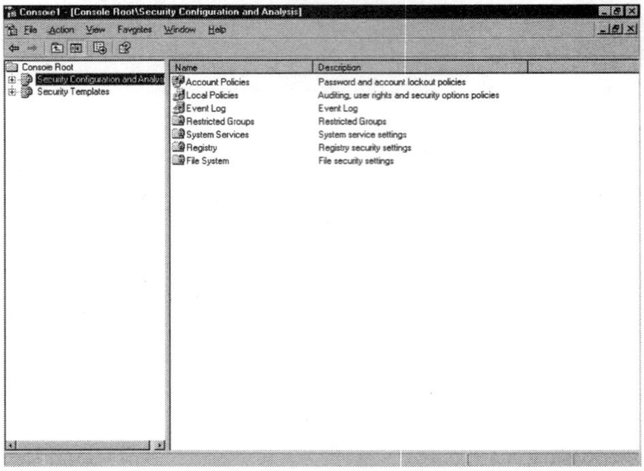

NOTE

The template we imported is the template that reflects the security created by a clean base install. Some settings were modified for illustration purposes, and they show up as not matching. If you performed this operation with the indicated template on a machine with no modifications, the expected result would be that all conditions would match.

Figure 8.33 Viewing the Results of the Analysis Comparison

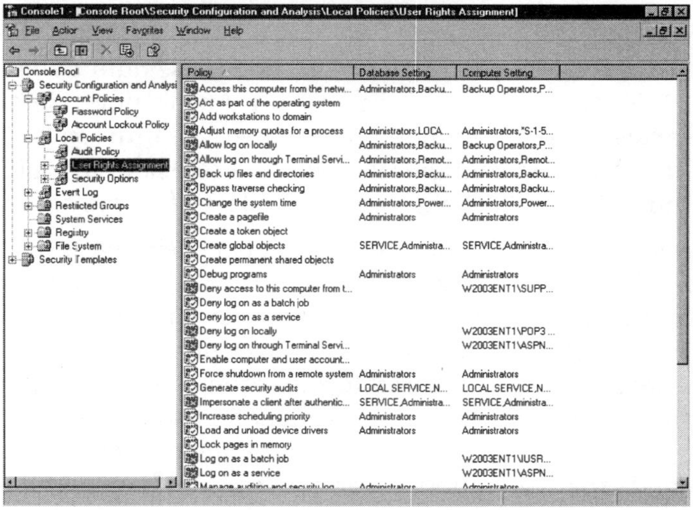

The process that you have just examined can be used to compare existing machine configurations against any template. This allows the administrator and planning team to make decisions about whether an existing template is providing the level of security that is needed for the operation or if a modification should be made to create a different degree of protection.

10. Before finishing this exercise, *save* the MMC console as **Security Configuration.** We'll use this MMC again in a later exercise.

EXAM WARNING

Because security has become such a necessity in the day-to-day operation of our networks, exam content that tests the ability to perform functionally is emphasized more heavily than rote memorization of statistics. It is imperative that you use and understand the various configuration tools and situations in which it is appropriate to use each of the tools to maintain the integrity of your systems. It is no longer sufficient to know only where to locate the resources; you also need to understand the how and why of their operation. Be sure to use the tools and practice with them to make sure you understand the material before you begin to test.

Creating Security Templates

Creating security templates allows the administrator and planning team to uniquely define the scope of security and methods of securing the server roles as needed for operations and security. The security template creation process can start with an existing template (discussed later in this section), or a template can be created from a blank template, allowing for absolute definition of all settings by the design team. While working on Exercise 8.03, you had the opportunity to view the wealth of settings that are configurable. When that analysis is complete, a configuration that is manually configured or changed by the administrator on a machine starting from the base template created during the installation process can be saved as a template through an export process, or portions of another security template that contains elements that are desired can be copied into a new, unconfigured template. The process can create an unlimited number of configurations. This allows for later application or reapplying of the template as well as the ability to distribute the template to other machines as needed, through either local application or Group Policy application in Active Directory.

Best Practices

You should consider and plan security template creation and application prior to actually completing the creation of the template. Planning allows you to design the templates to provide the most effective method of distribution. In the following list, the best practices that should be incorporated into the creation of templates are discussed (adapted from Windows Server 2003 Help):

- Never apply templates to computers or networks without testing to ensure that security is correctly configured. This includes predefined and custom templates.
- Do not directly edit the predefined templates. Instead, create new templates and copy appropriate sections into the new template. This method maintains the integrity of the base templates.
- Do not edit the Setup security.inf template. This is the base setting for all installs.
- Do not apply the Setup security.inf template via Group Policy. This template is intended for local application via the appropriate tools, such as *Secedit* from the command line or the Security Configuration and Analysis MMC.
- Do not apply the Compatible template to DCs. Security configurations in this template severely weaken security levels and should not be used for domain controllers.

Modifying Existing Templates

Modifying existing templates is not recommended if the template is a predefined template. However, it is a normal practice to modify existing templates after creation to further enhance or modify the security conditions being enforced through that particular template. The simplest method of modifying templates is to open them in an MMC using the Security Templates snap-in. This provides the ability to change and save any settings that are necessary to accomplish the configuration you have decided to implement.

Following the modification process, it is wise to analyze the new settings with the Security Configuration and Analysis snap-in or through use of the *Secedit* command at the command line.

Applying Templates

Once created, templates can be applied utilizing a number of different tools. On a local machine, the template can be applied through the use of the Security Configuration and Analysis snap-in, the *Secedit* command from the command line, or scripting. The templates can also be distributed to machines through the use of GPOs in an Active Directory domain. Exercise 8.04 provides you with the opportunity to both modify and apply security templates.

EXERCISE 8.04

CREATING AND APPLYING MODIFIED OR CUSTOM SECURITY TEMPLATES

In this exercise, we build on the original tasks that were completed in the previous exercise utilizing the MMC console tools to analyze the security of the local computer. This exercise provides you with the opportunity to create a custom security template, and to apply it and verify the configuration changes that occur as you apply the new configuration.

NOTE

Please *do not perform this exercise on a production machine*. This exercise is in no way intended to provide a secure environment and is for illustrative purposes only.

1. To begin the exercise, return to the MMC that you saved in Exercise 8.03. If you didn't save it, you can create another MMC for this exercise by following the steps in Exercise 8.03 to get the base management console with the Security Configuration and Analysis and Security Templates snap-ins in place and ready to use.
2. Expand **Security Templates**, highlight the folder, right-click, and select **New Template**. This sequence produces the screen shown in Figure 8.34. Type **New Base Server Configuration** and a description in the boxes, and then click **OK**.

Figure 8.34 Creating a New Template

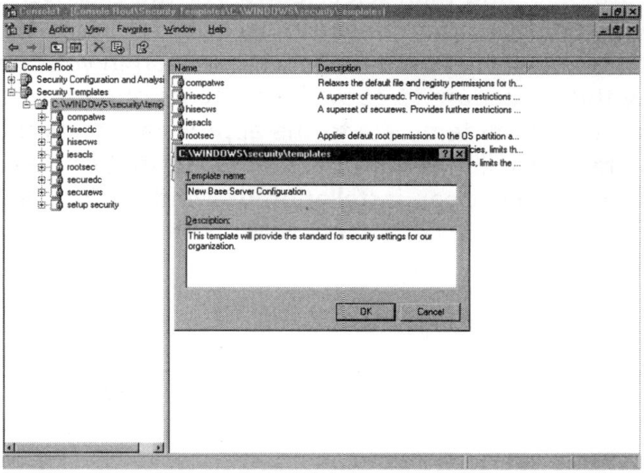

3. Expand your new template, and **Password Policy** page, as shown in Figure 8.35. Notice that no configurations have been defined. Take a tour through your newly created template and you will find that this is the case throughout. This template allows you to start from scratch in your construction of the new security template.

Figure 8.35 The Contents of a Newly Created Blank Template

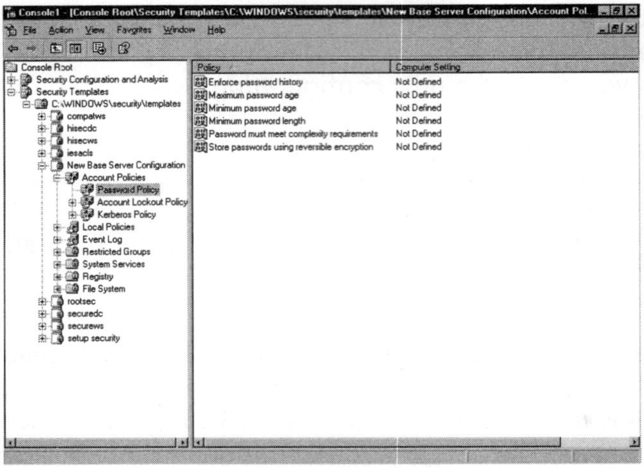

4. In most cases, it is not desirable to try to construct all the parameters securing your systems from a totally blank template. Fortunately, there is great flexibility in this process, and we are free to import portions of other templates into our template to give us a base construction to modify for our needs. To perform this task, we must expand and highlight an area from another policy that we want to utilize, as is shown in Figure 8.36, and then select **Copy**. For the exercise, **Copy** the **Account Policies** from the **setup security** template, and then **paste** the contents to the **Account Policies** section in your new template. Follow this procedure to copy the contents of each of the sections of the setup security template to the appropriate section of your new template. This will give us a new template that contains the settings from the normal, clean installation of Windows Server 2003.

Figure 8.36 Copying the Contents of a Section of Another Template to the New Template

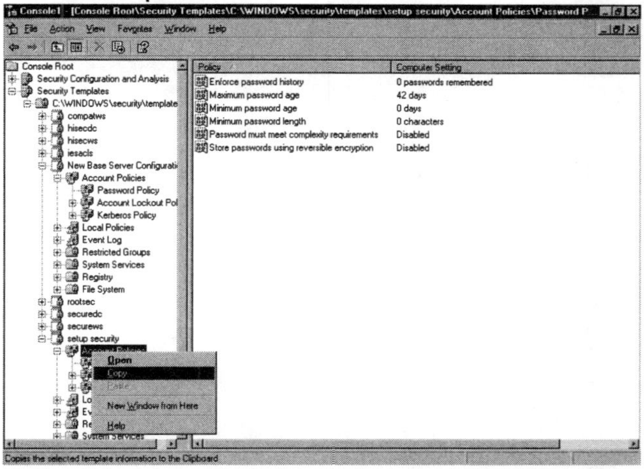

5. After you have completed Step 4, save the template's changes, as shown in Figure 8.37 by clicking on **New Base Server Configurations | Save**.

Figure 8.37 Saving the Newly Modified Template

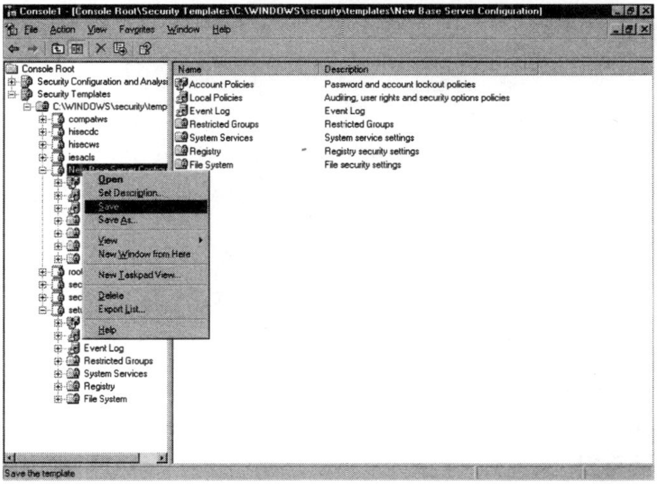

6. After you save the template, it is time to begin the process of modification to suit the needs of the organization. To begin with, select **Enforce password history policy** in Password Policy, then right-click and select **Properties**, as shown in Figure 8.38.

Figure 8.38 Selecting the Properties Sheet to Begin Modification of the Template

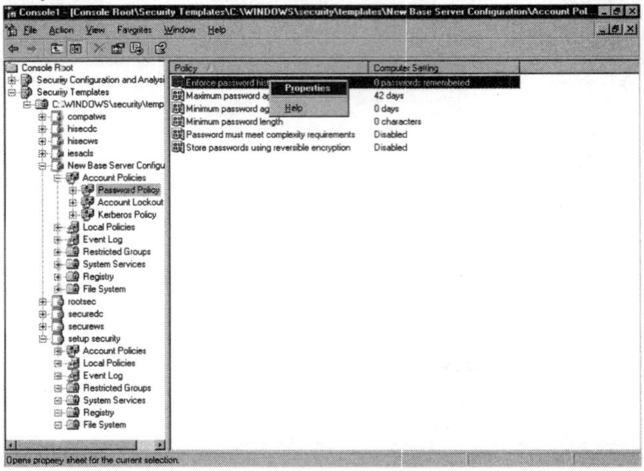

7. The Properties sheet, shown in Figure 8.39, allows us to modify the settings for the template. For this exercise, modify the template to **18** passwords.

Figure 8.39 The Enforce Password History Properties Page

8. Next, modify the maximum password age settings to **35** days following the same procedure to get to the Properties sheet, as shown in Figure 8.40.

FFigure 8.40 The Maximum Password Age Properties Sheet

9. Following successful completion of the modifications, save the modifications to the template, as shown in Figure 8.41.

Figure 8.41 Saving the Modified Template

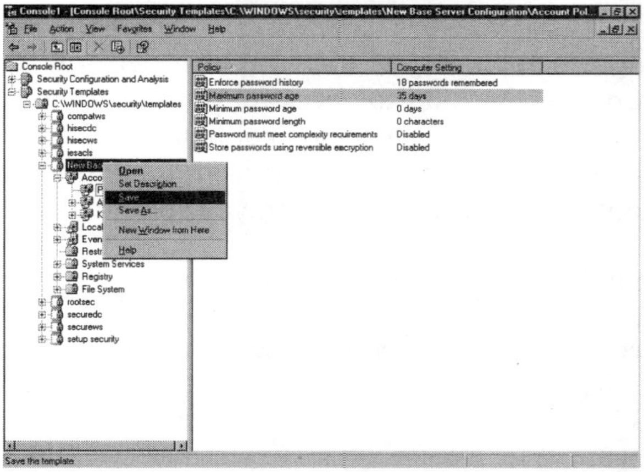

10. Next, following the procedures outlined in Exercise 8.03, import the newly created template into your database. You might find that it is more effective to select the check box that clears the old settings from the template or templates. (If you are going to do that on a previous database, you might want to save the content to use again, since this procedure will remove the settings currently stored in your database.) Import the **New Base Server Configuration** template that you just created. Your screen should be similar to Figure 8.42.

Figure 8.42 Importing the Newly Created Template for Analysis

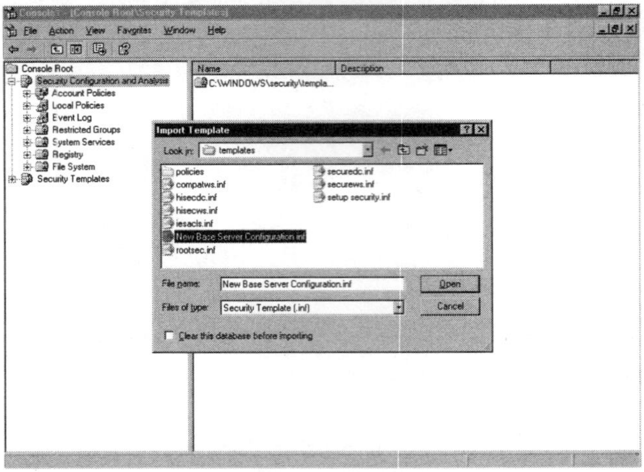

11. Following the importing of the template, perform the security analysis tasks from Exercise 8.03 to check for differences in the policy you've created and the current machine configuration. Figure 8.43 shows the analysis results that were returned from the analysis. (Your results might look different depending on your original configuration.)

Figure 8.43 Showing the Results of the Security Analysis with the New Template

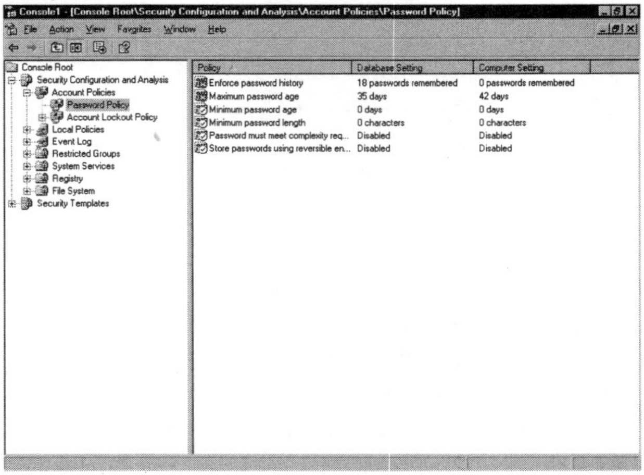

12. Following the analysis and verification that the settings are correct and what is desired, the next step is to apply the new configuration to the computer. To accomplish this task, select **Security Configuration and**

Analysis and then select **Configure Computer Now**, as shown in Figure 8.44.

Figure 8.44 The Configure Computer Now Selection Screen

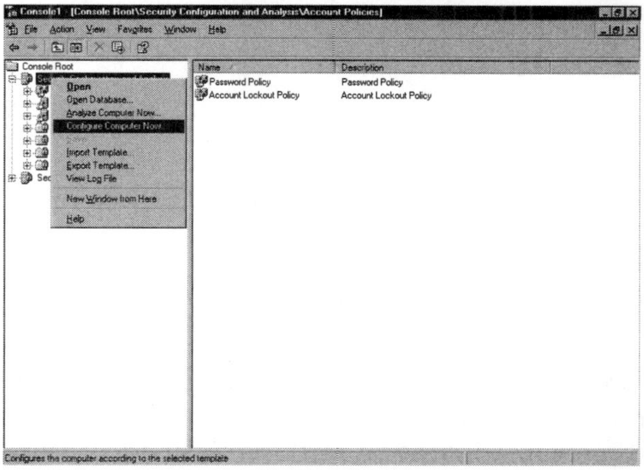

This process applies the contents of the template you created to the machine. Figure 8.45 shows the progress of the configuration process.

Figure 8.45 Showing the Progress of the Application of the New Template

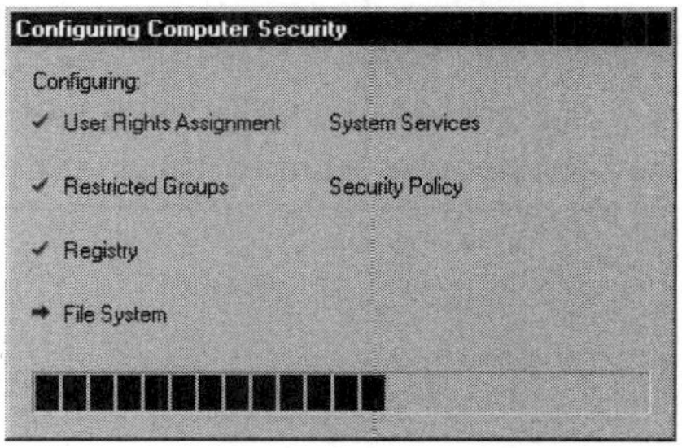

13. When the process is finished, verify the application by performing the analysis process again. As shown in Figure 8.46, the template contents have been successfully applied.

Figure 8.46 A Final Analysis Verifies the Application of the Template

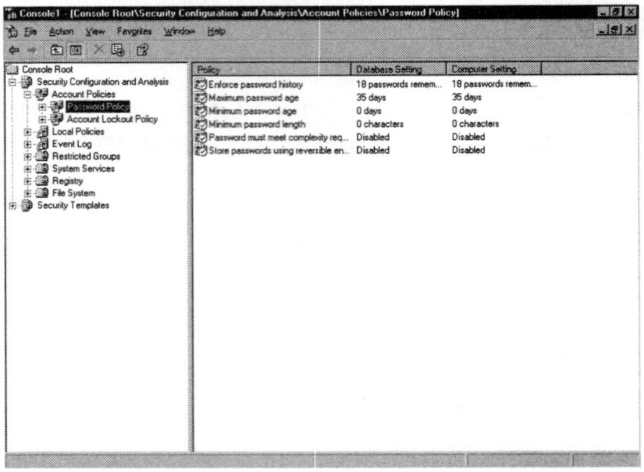

The process for modification of a template is much the same as the process just demonstrated. A template may be opened and modified, saved, and then analyzed prior to application to the machine to ensure that the conditions have been correctly configured.

Test Day Tip

Remember that you should perform a thorough review of the test materials and study materials a number of days ahead of the examination. Be sure to positively reinforce the areas you are comfortable with and practice working with consoles and tools to ensure that you're able to think appropriately under pressure.

EXAM 70-296 OBJECTIVE 4.3 4.3.1 4.3.2

Securing Data Transmission

After performing the security tasks that are required to secure the operating system and file operations, many organizations have found that the data with which they are entrusted for safekeeping is suddenly available to competitors, attackers, and others who were not authorized to view or obtain that information. This security breach is not necessarily because of a weakness in the file systems or authentication or authorization processes but could in fact result from insecure transmission of the data on the network. Through this section of the chapter, we review, discuss, and work with some ways to alleviate that condition to save the aggravation, embarrassment, and financial disasters that can arise from such problems occurring.

Need for Network Security

Network and system administrators have been involved in blocking access to data and resources from external attack points for some time. Unfortunately, many in the profession still do not work proactively within their internal networks to provide the same isolation of resources to protect the information from those who are not entitled to use it. The proliferation of freely accessible tools, many of which were developed as legitimate analysis and diagnostic routines, has provided many users and attackers with automated tools to perform their explorations of our networks. Some potential problems occur daily simply through user error, and often these are unpredictable. Others, however, result from the use and misuse of the freely available tools in internal networks by unauthorized individuals. A disgruntled employee or an employee who believes that they have a "need to know" has ample opportunity to probe your network, examine discovered vulnerabilities, and mount an attack that the system or network administrator might not have anticipated. For this reason, it becomes paramount that we secure not only the physical machines that house the data but also the networks that carry that data from place to place.

EXAM 70-296 OBJECTIVE 4.3.1

Planning for Secure Data Transmission

As we plan for secure data transmission, it is important to get input from the stakeholders of the organization and management to help define the types of information that need to be fully protected from view. Many groups choose to implement plans that secure network transmissions between servers and clients involved with financial transactions. Others choose to secure information transfer involving personnel records or private information about employees or employee relations. Proprietary or developmental materials may be classified as needing protection as well. Each of these types of information requires the implementation of a planning process to determine what needs to be protected and at what level of protection. Generally, data that is public, such as human resources benefits information, or publicly disseminated information need not be protected on the wire.

Other considerations come into play as you begin to develop your plan for securing data. It could be decided that access to POP3 mailboxes needs to be protected, and SPA might need to be enforced, or the use of a PKI infrastructure might be needed to provide encryption or digital signature capabilities for the transmission and verification of e-mail. We could use SSL for authentication from a Web browser to reduce the chance that insecure information is transmitted between host and server. Additionally, we might find that it is important to secure data transmission through the use of VPN technologies, which can include tunneling with PPTP or L2TP. All these scenarios require our best efforts to plan adequately to secure the data being distributed via the network.

EXAM 70-296 OBJECTIVE 4.3.2

IP Security

IP security, and in particular the use of IPSec to provide that protection, has become a popular topic since the introduction of Windows 2000. In Windows Server 2003, improvements have been made to the technology to make it even more usable and capable of protecting data transmitted over networks. IP security has allowed the network and system administrator to more fully secure the data between the server and host machines in the network, at the same time providing a framework for security that is expandable and capable of handling many individual protection scenarios. The capability for multiple uses has proven invaluable in the overall planning and implementation of methods to protect data transmission from spoofing and other alterations and to limit or eliminate casual interception of data from the network media. Additionally, the ability to protect the data has expanded the network's scope from including only the original LAN environment to providing the method to secure data transmission on both trusted and untrusted networks in a global fashion. This, in turn, has allowed the expansion of the workplace to environments that were not able to be secured adequately in the past.

Overview

IPSec in Windows Server 2003 has added a large number of new functions that have improved the performance and usability of the protocol to secure network data transmission. New tools have been added, such as the IP Security Monitor MMC, discussed later in this section. Security improvements have been made, including the use of a stronger cryptographic master key (Diffie-Hellman), better command-line management with the *Netsh* utility on Windows Server 2003 machines, and startup security for IPSec that better controls the function of IPSec during computer initialization. Other new improvements include the removal of default traffic exemptions from filtering, functionality over NAT, integration with Network Load Balancing (NLB), and support for the new Resultant Set of Policy (RSoP) MMC in Windows Server 2003.

Deploying IPSec

Deploying IPSec in Windows Server 2003 installations involves creating appropriate IPSec policies with filters that are configured to permit, block, or negotiate security. The filters examine all inbound or outbound IP packets for compliance with the configured filter rules. Once the filter settings have been configured, they are combined within a policy that defines the traffic that requires security and that which does not. This policy is then matched between the sending and receiving hosts to establish a security association (SA) using Internet Key Exchange (IKE). This establishes a relationship between the two computers, allowing for comparison of policy settings and processing of the defined rules and filters from the policies.

IPSec Management Tools

Windows Server 2003 offers two management methods for performing IPSec configurations and maintenance. The first is a GUI interface available by creating an MMC console, and the second is a command-line extension of the *netsh* command that allows for configuration via scripting and automated functions.

Exercise 8.05

Creating an IPSec Policy

In this exercise, we work through the creation of an IPSec policy. Many options for configuring IPSec policies are available, from creating a policy for an Active Directory domain deployment to policies for a particular OU structure or individual machines. Policies can be applied to either members of the domain or workgroup members. In this exercise, we configure an IPSec policy for a standalone server. The requirement is to allow Telnet communication for administrative purposes. However, knowing the security risks inherent in the use of Telnet, the administrator wants to allow Telnet communication only when security is enforced, and the traffic using Telnet is protected.

1. To begin the exercise, open a blank **MMC**, and add the **IP Security Policy Management** snap-in, as shown in Figure 8.47.

Figure 8.47 Selecting the IP Security Policy Management Snap-in for the MMC

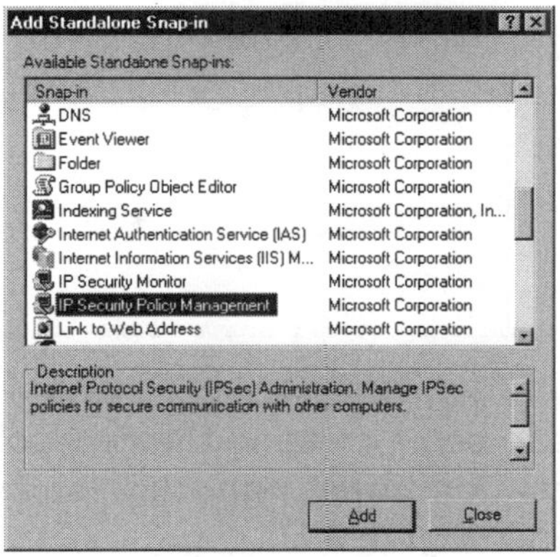

2. When you have selected the snap-in, you must decide on its scope . For this exercise, choose **Local computer** and click **Finish**, as shown in Figure 8.48.

Figure 8.48 Choosing the Scope of the Snap-in

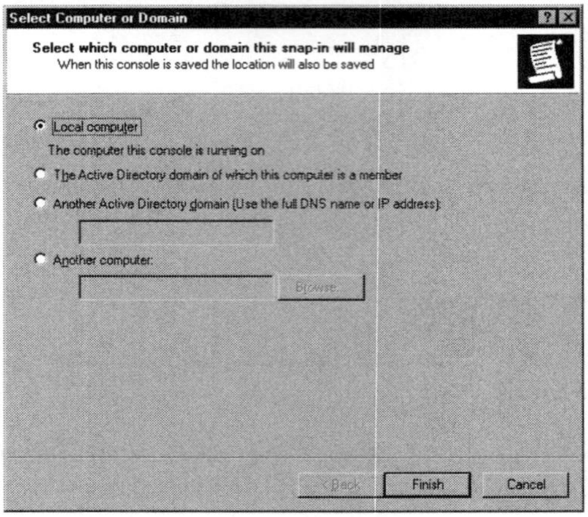

3. After you have made the choice for the scope of the snap-in, you will be returned to the MMC, which will allow you to begin to work with IPSec policies. Before you move on, explore the Properties tabs of the three default sample policies, as shown in Figure 8.49.

Figure 8.49 The IP Security Policies Snap-in

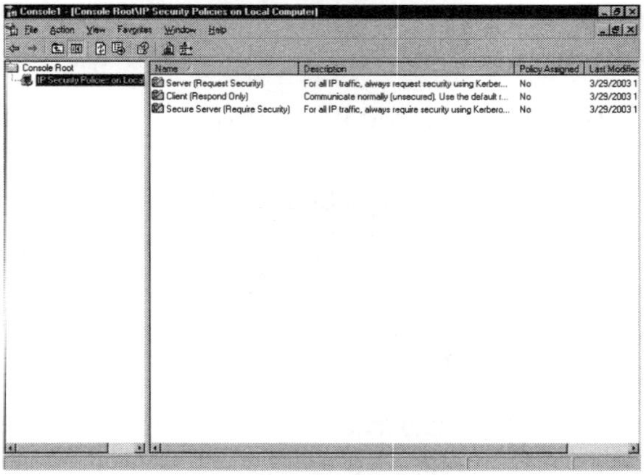

4. Our next task is to begin creating the new policy. Select **IP Security Policies on Local Computer**, right-click, and select **Create IP Security Policy**, as shown in Figure 8.50.

Figure 8.50 Preparing to Create a New IP Security Policy

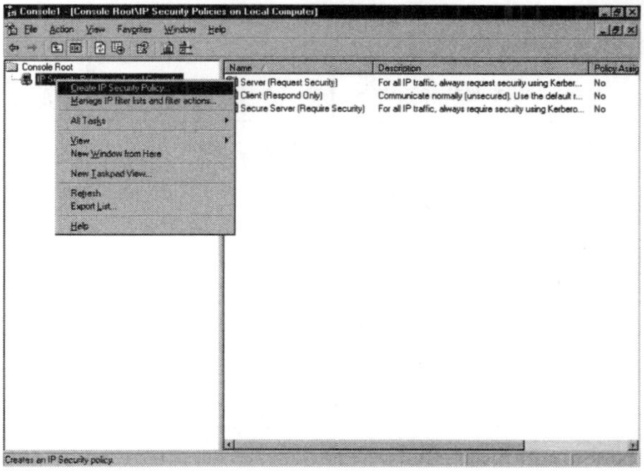

5. This process will launch the IP Security Policy Wizard, as shown in Figure 8.51. Click **Next** to proceed.

Figure 8.51 The IP Security Policy Wizard Welcome Screen

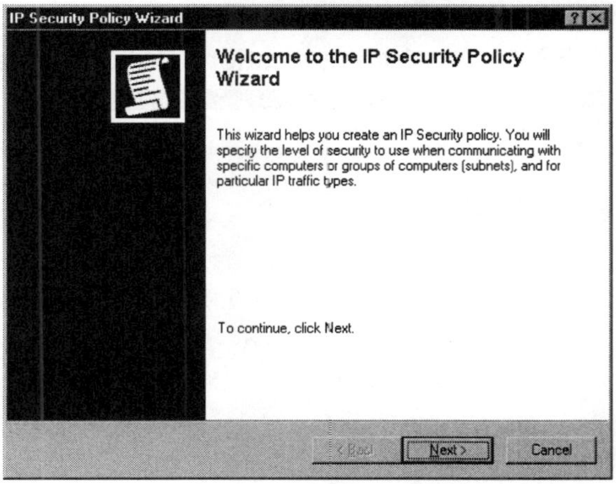

6. The next screen in the process requires an entry for the IP Security policy name and optionally a description of what the policy is for. Enter the information as shown in Figure 8.52, and click **Next**.

Figure 8.52 Enter the Name and Description of the New Policy

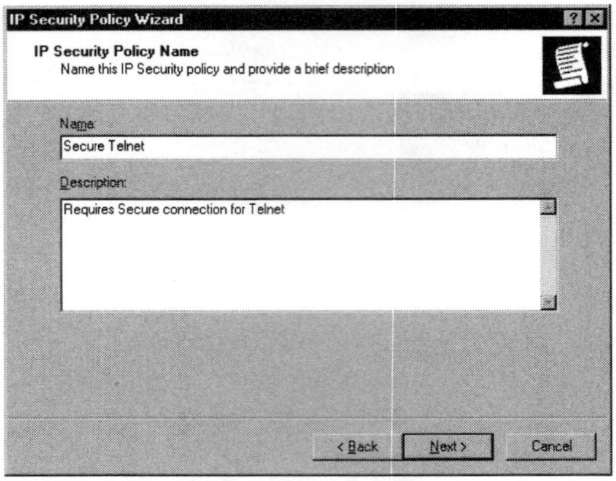

7. The next screen, shown in Figure 8.53, requires that a choice be made about the use of the default response rule. If you deselect the check box, the machine will not communicate securely if other secure conditions have not been established. Leave the rule selected for this exercise, and click **Next**.

Figure 8.53 Secure Communications Options Page

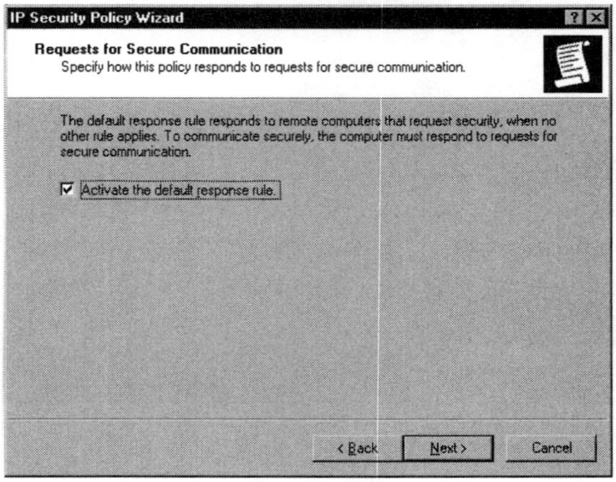

8. Now that we've elected to use the default response rule, we have to choose the method of authentication to be used to secure the connection. If the machine was in an Active Directory domain, we could select to use Kerberos v5. However, this is a standalone machine, so select **Use a certificate from this certification authority (CA):**, as shown in Figure 8.54, and then click **Browse**.

Figure 8.54 Choosing the Authentication Method for the Default Response Rule

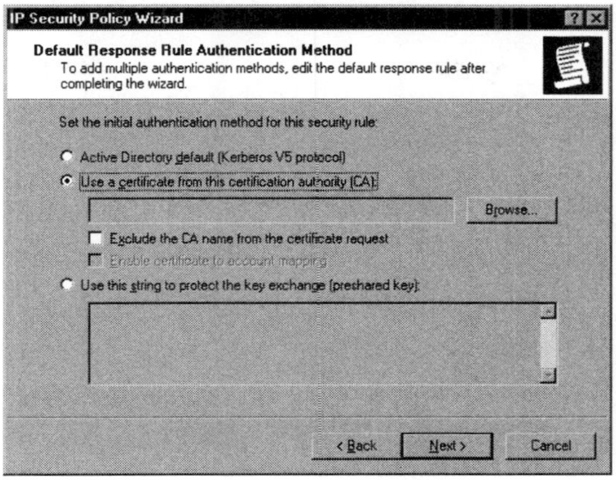

9. For purposes of the exercise, select the first Certification Authority on the list, as shown in Figure 8.55. (In a real-life implementation, it would be preferable to use the certificate provided by your own or a trusted CA.) Following your selection, click **OK**.

Figure 8.55 Selecting the Certification Authority

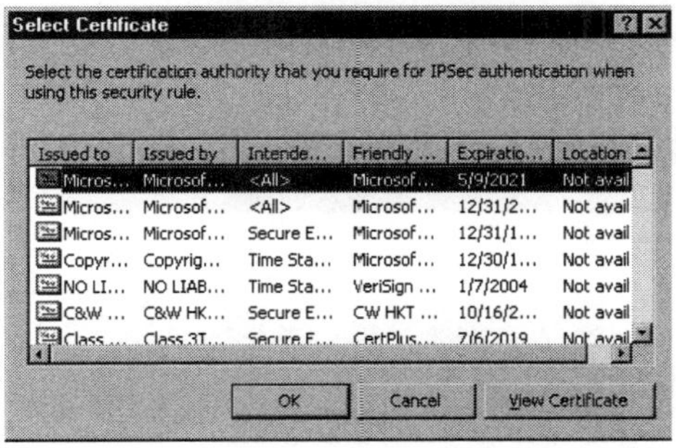

10. You will be returned to the MMC. Select the newly created policy, and then select **Properties** to reach the Properties page illustrated in Figure 8.56. Click **Add** to launch the IPSec Rule Wizard.

Figure 8.56 The Secure Telnet Policy Properties Page

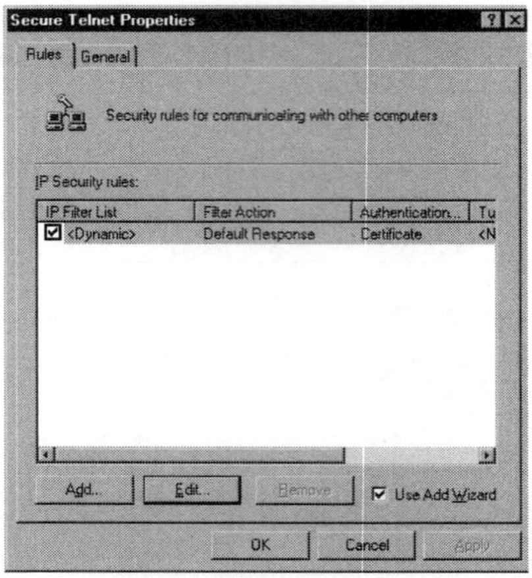

11. As the IPSec Rule wizard launches, read the information presented, and then click **Next**. The following page asks about Tunnel Rules. Accept the default **No Tunnel** selection, and again click **Next**. Another screen will be presented to define the connections to which this policy will apply. Again, select the default **All Connections** selection, and click **Next**. This will launch the IP Filter List wizard, shown in Figure 8.57. Click **Add** to proceed to the next step.

Figure 8.57 The IP Filter List Wizard Screen

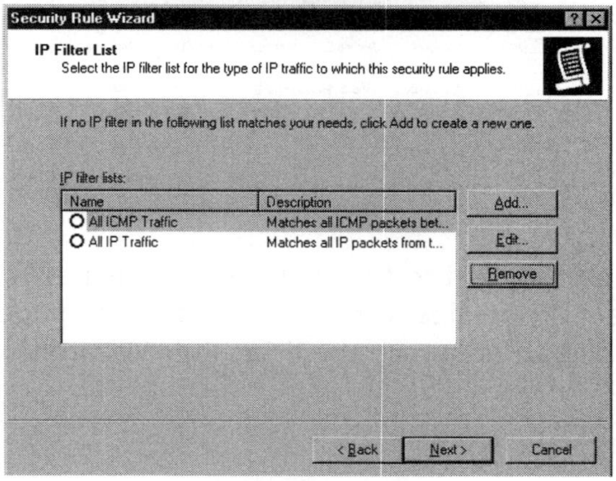

12. This will bring up the screen for defining the IP filter list. Enter the name and description information as shown in Figure 8.58, and then click **Add**.

Figure 8.58 Creating the IP Filter List Entries

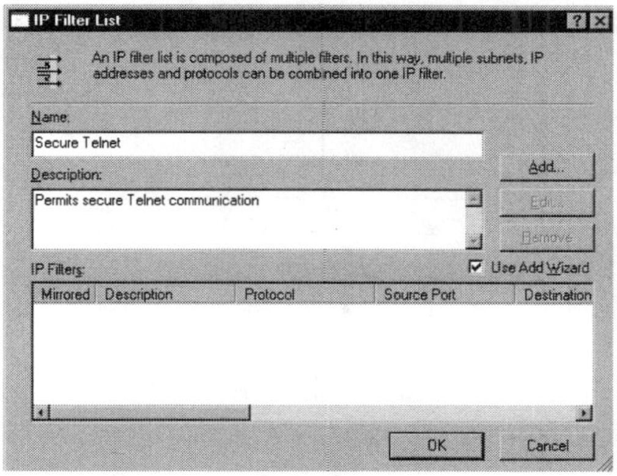

13. In the IP Filter wizard, enter the information about the filter, as shown in Figure 8.59. Leave the default mirrored selection as it is. This provides for filter action in both directions. Click **Next** to proceed.

Figure 8.59 Setting the IP Filter Description

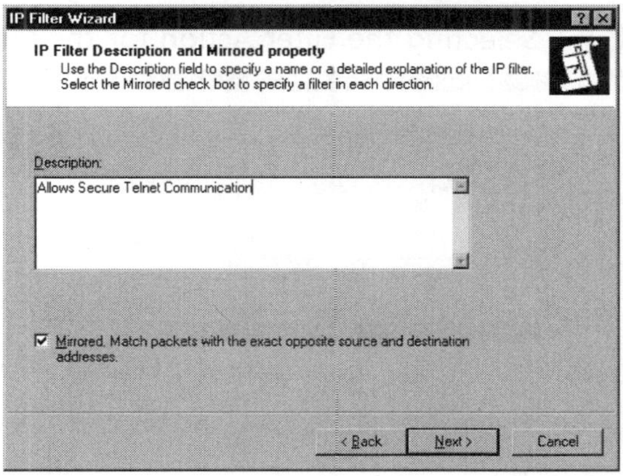

14. After you enter this information, the next page asks for the source and destination information. We want to have traffic from all IPs controlled by this policy, so select **Any IP** in both areas, and click **Next** to proceed. The next page requests information about the protocol you wish to filter. Select **TCP** and click **Next** again. The final page in this portion of the configuration asks for port information. Since we're working with Telnet, enter port **23** in both boxes. Accept the information, and you'll be taken to the screen shown in Figure 8.60. In this screen, select the newly created **Secure Telnet** filter, and then click **Next**.

Figure 8.60 Selecting the Filter to Apply

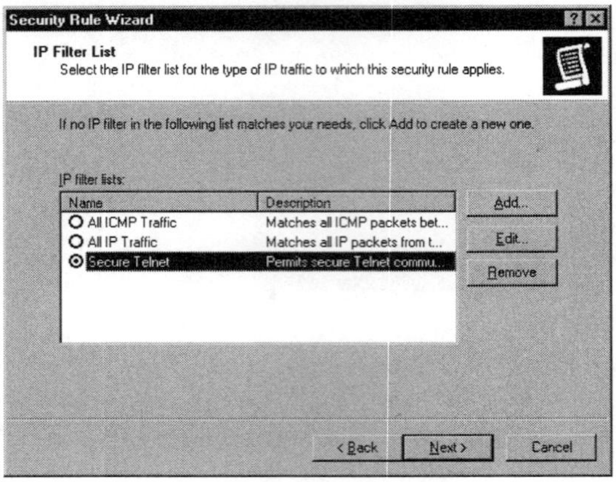

15. Your selection will take you to the screen shown in Figure 8.61, where you will make a choice about the method of connection you want to enforce for this rule. Select **Require Security** and click **Next**, as shown in Figure 8.61.

Figure 8.61 Selecting the Filter Action for the Rule

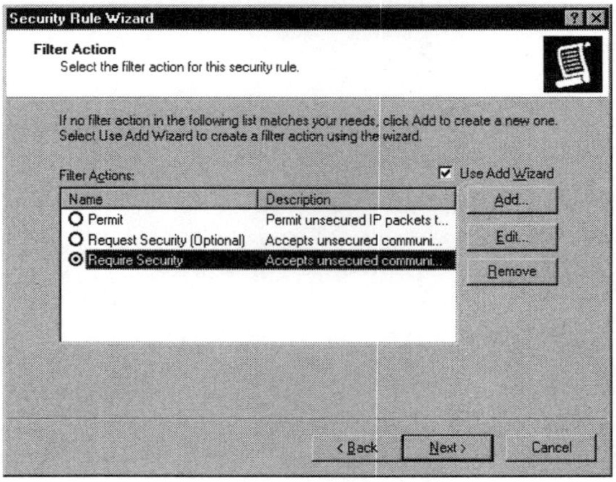

16. You've created an IPSec policy to protect traffic to and from the local machine when Telnet is being used. Your new policy will show up in the list of IPSec policies in the MMC, as shown in Figure 8.62, and can be applied to the machine if desired.

Figure 8.62 The Completed Policy Addition in the IPSec Policies MMC

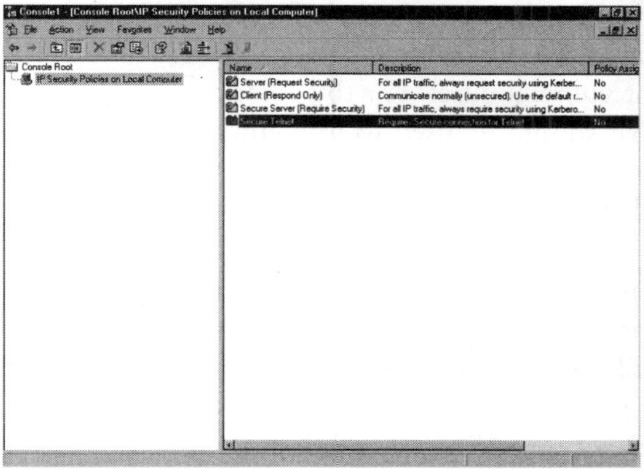

Exam Warning

IPSec policy creation makes rules for what is allowed to pass and may include conditions such as when the traffic is allowed. Be sure to study these and understand the ramifications of creating and ordering filter lists within the policies and how that affects the outcome of the policy's application. This area is fair game for exam scenarios.

EXAM 70-296 OBJECTIVE 5.3

Implementing and Maintaining Security

During the course of the past few years, it has become much more important that each individual working within the network and system administration areas be well versed in the concepts and practices of security in relation to operating systems, various pieces of the network infrastructure, and application vulnerabilities that can affect how resources are accessed and protected. Along with the need for a good understanding of the concepts of security, it is equally important that the system administrator, security professional, and technician all understand the methods used to implement the security infrastructure and rule sets and how to monitor the success and failure of the configurations that have been put in place to assure that the rules and conditions that are established are performing as expected. Additionally, new vulnerabilities are disclosed on a regular basis, and the practitioners must have a working knowledge of the methodologies to detect and combat the weaknesses that are exposed when the vulnerability is announced.

A significant area of vulnerability occurs simply because the day-to-day operation of the system and network often leaves little time for the technician or administrator to adequately track and maintain the environment to accommodate the changes that occur during the disclosure of vulnerabilities. For this reason, it is also important to have knowledge of the methods that should be used to implement change management and the procedures for effectively planning for this change to minimize the danger of unprotected systems. This requires that the individual have an exposure to the methodologies to accomplish this planning.

Finally, it is vitally important that once the processes are understood, the individuals responsible for maintenance of the security levels and equipment understand fully the methods that can be utilized to implement the required updates, service packs, and patches on the equipment that is in need of updating. In the following sections, we explore methods to perform security monitoring and discuss ways to provide for the implementation of change and configuration management. We then explore various ways to accomplish the goal of being up to date with needed patches, service packs, and hotfixes.

EXAM 70-296 OBJECTIVE 5.3.1

Security Monitoring

Security monitoring encompasses the use of a number of processes to assure the integrity of the system. The monitoring of the configurations we have applied must constantly be analyzed and checked to ensure that the defenses we have put in place are not breached.

Many of our day-to-day configurations can substantially affect the security of our enterprise resources as well as the resources that may be in use within the enterprise. We must consider a number of areas as sources of information as we begin to monitor security in our particular operation. Among these, we should consider the use of the following technologies and methodologies to try to achieve the best security possible through constant vigilance:

- Auditing should be enabled and used to monitor access to the systems through logon tracking and to track access to resources as appropriate to our needs. Security logs should be regularly viewed for unusual activity and to compare actual access to configured access values.
- IPSec monitoring should be enabled to assure that the conditions of connection are being met and that the traffic being transmitted on the network is encrypted appropriately if we have configured it to protect the data on the network.
- Group Policy settings should be constantly reviewed for appropriate application and restrictions to access. Group Policy management must be an ongoing process to assure that changes in applications, users, and delegations of authority are appropriate to the conditions that exist in the current environment.
- Network monitoring and analysis should be a continuing effort. It is extremely important to know quickly if unauthorized traffic is occurring in your network.

This includes the necessity to properly encrypt and authenticate all traffic that is carried to and from your network via wireless connections.

- Encrypting File System in Windows Server 2003 domains can be enforced through Group Policy. It is possible in Windows Server 2003 domains to allow sharing of EFS protected folders and files. The stronger encryption capability provided with Windows XP and Windows Server 2003 may be reduced through Group Policy configuration if needed for compatibility with the 168-bit key structure used for Windows 2000 machines.
- Wireless network encryption levels and authentication processes should be controlled through the use of Group Policy within the domain. For instance, it is possible to enforce the use of Internet Connection Firewall (ICF) on wireless connections outside the domain network while not permitting ICF connections within the domain network environment. (For further information, see the Windows Server 2003 Resource Kit at www.microsoft.com/windows/reskits/default.asp.)
- Windows Server 2003 Event logs should be analyzed on an ongoing basis. Depending on the server roles that you have configured, various logs will be added to the Event Viewer. Security-related conditions can be tracked and documented through the use of the Event Viewer reports to further enhance the administrator's ability to monitor security conditions in the domain and on the local machines.

The administrator could also find that it is appropriate to use third-party tools such as intrusion detection system (IDS) packages to monitor the internal network and firewall traffic for appropriate access levels and to report potential abuses. The overall need in this area is the need to maintain the principle of least privilege for access to resources and constant monitoring to assure that the intended controls are effective.

EXAM 70-296 OBJECTIVE 5.3.2

Change and Configuration Management

Change and configuration management has also become an area of responsibility for the network administrator. This process involves participating with a team that is involved with planning updates to network configuration and managing the constant need for updates and patches involving the server and enterprise environment security. It also involves the definition of the procedures for managing these updates and testing prior to application in the production environment.

Change management practices are developed and worked on in a number of different levels. To practice change management, we must be aware of a number of conditions in our operations, including the following:

- We must have an awareness of *why* the change is needed. This can involve change that is occurring due to a newly discovered vulnerability in either software or hardware we control. It could also involve the planning necessary to perform updates to newer technologies or to react to the minimization of the risk involved with vulnerabilities that have been discovered or a change to a newer version of an application because of the perceived benefits of that application.

- We must have an awareness of *how* the change is to be accomplished. This includes planning the use of installation or deployment teams and the planning that is involved to minimize the possibility of update failures or configuration conflicts that could delay the implementation or disrupt the operation of the system we're charged with maintaining.
- We must have an awareness of *what* the problem we're evaluating consists of. This includes the necessary gathering of information and discussions about the type of change that is to be performed during the change management process.
- We must have an awareness of the management team's mindset prior to beginning the change management process. Change management discussions will be ineffective in their implementation if they are not supported by the management team.

Change and configuration management also consists of learning a number of skill sets that might not have been as necessary in prior environments. For instance, there are groups of skills that could be necessary for the person working with change management to acquire or polish. These could include the following:

- System skills, including a working knowledge of everything involved in the network and company operations that could affect the change management implementation or planning.
- Business skills, including the knowledge of company financial condition, overhead costs, and projected availability of funds to implement the changes indicated through the change and configuration analysis process.
- People skills, which need to be developed to a high level to encourage participation in the change management process to more effectively implement the desired level of change.
- Analytical skills, needed to accurately diagnose and predict the need for proactive changes, and to effectively diagnose and resolve reactive changes to conditions as they occur.
- Political skills, needed to work through the various control levels of any organization to promote the implementation of needed change. It is important to realize that as much as many people dislike this area, it is often the most important of the skill sets to develop to accomplish the goals of a change management and implementation program.

Change management skills have become a necessary part of the administrator's skill set. These skills will help keep your environment secure and up to date. In the next section, we begin to look at implementing some of the changes that we might make after the change management process has resulted in decisions about the need and methods to implement the change.

EXAM 70-296 OBJECTIVE 5.4

Updating the Infrastructure

Earlier in the chapter, we discussed the need to install all relevant service packs, updates, and hotfixes to your base server installations and to keep them current as you assigned new roles to them. The process of keeping your servers and workstations up to date has to start somewhere—by identifying the updates you need for each of them. Updates typically come in two different varieties: service packs and hotfixes. (Hotfixes are sometimes known by a variety of other names, such as *security hotfix, security fix,* or *update.*) The bottom line is that there are two major types of updates you need to worry about, differentiated by both size and scope. In the next section we look at the difference between service packs and hotfixes. After we've gotten a good understanding of them and where we can look to find them, we move on to identifying and procuring required updates.

Types of Updates

As mentioned, you need to apply two basic types of updates to your network computers over time: service packs and hotfixes. Both can be found at the Windows Update Web site, located at http://windowsupdate.microsoft.com/. Updates often have very different purposes, reliability levels, and application methods and tools.

Service Packs

Service packs are large executables that Microsoft issues periodically (usually every 6 to 15 months) to keep the product current and correct problems and known issues. Often service packs include new utilities and tools that can extend a computer's functionality. For example, Windows 2000 Service Pack 3 includes the ability to remove shortcuts to Microsoft middleware products (Windows and MSN Messenger, Outlook Express, and the like) from your computer, if desired. Service packs also include updated drivers and files that have been developed for the product after its initial release. Windows 2000 service packs are all-inclusive and self-executing and typically contain all fixes and previous service packs that have been issued for the product.

NOTE

Although the topic is beyond the scope of this exam, you might be wondering just why Microsoft would willingly allow you to remove shortcuts to its middleware products. This action is a result of the settlement of the Microsoft antitrust lawsuit with the U.S. Department of Justice. You can read more about the settlement terms on Microsoft's Press Pass Web site at www.microsoft.com/presspass/trial/nov02/11-12FinalJudgment.asp.

Perhaps one of the greatest improvements in Windows 2000, Windows XP, and Windows Server 2003 service packs is that you can *slipstream* them into the original installation source and create integrated installation media that can be used to install an updated version of the operating system on later new installations without the need to subsequently apply the latest service pack. These updated installation sources can be placed back onto a CD-ROM for a single-instance installation method or can be used for any form of remote installation, including Windows 2000 or Windows Server 2003 Remote Installation Services, or for disk cloning through use of a third-party application.

Although can you get service packs from the Windows Update Web site, the best location to get them for later installation or distribution on your network is directly from the Microsoft Service Packs page at http://support.microsoft.com/default.aspx?scid=fh;EN-US;sp. From there you will be able to download the service pack without having to install it immediately, as you would if you were using Windows Update.

Hotfixes

Hotfixes, also known as *security fixes, security patches, patches,* or *quick-fix engineering*, are small, single-purpose executable files that have been developed to correct a specific critical problem or flaw in a product for which timing is critical. Hotfixes do not typically undergo the same level of testing as service packs to ensure that they are stable and compatible and do not cause further critical issues. Some hotfixes are not made available to the general public and must be obtained directly from Microsoft Product Support (PSS). Others can be found and downloaded from various sources, such as Windows Update, at http://windowsupdate.microsoft.com/ or the TechNet Security page located at www.microsoft.com/technet/security/default.asp.

Hotfixes can be used to correct both client-side and server-side issues. Recently, a fairly even division of client and server hotfixes have been issued as new flaws and weaknesses have been discovered. Perhaps one of the most famous server-side issues that received a hotfix was the Code Red exploitation of the Index service. MS02-018 was issued to correct this problem and stop the propagation of the Code Red worm. You can rely on Windows Update to inform you of missing hotfixes, but you can also use the HFNetChk tool included with the Microsoft Baseline Security Analyzer (MBSA) tool to perform this function for you. The benefit of using HFNetChk is that when it is run against an entire network with a script, it quickly returns the status of all networked Windows Server 2003 computers, thus allowing you to determine the computers that require particular hotfixes.

Exam Warning

As you read this text and through the rest of this chapter, remember the differences between a service pack and a hotfix in terms of what they are designed to do, how they are obtained, and how they are installed. On the exam, you shouldn't expect to be asked directly what a service pack or hotfix is, but your understanding of each will be tested in other, more covert, ways.

Configuring & Implementing...

Get Those Hotfixes!

Because service packs are only issued once in a long while, hotfixes will be your primary means of correcting vulnerabilities and flaws in Windows. You need to make it a regular practice—at least weekly—to check your computers for missing updates. Once you have identified the missing updates, you need to acquire and test them as quickly as you can, but not so quickly that you miss something critical that could cause you new problems down the road. After testing has been completed to your satisfaction, you should take steps to deploy updates as quickly as possible. Sometimes keeping your computers safe from attacks and other vulnerabilities comes down to just a matter of days—perhaps even less. For example, when the Code Red worm struck, it was able to compromise over 250,000 vulnerable systems in less than nine hours. Locating, testing, and deploying required updates as soon as they become available can go great lengths toward keeping your network secure and protected. In the case of the Code Red worm, the vulnerability was known and the fix had been available for some time before the "need" to update and apply fixes and patches was shown to administrators.

Deploying and Managing Updates

Identifying the updates that your computers need might seem like the toughest part of this task; however, that's not the case. Deploying updates, which includes testing them thoroughly before deployment, is in most cases the most time-consuming and problematic part of the update process.

After you have thoroughly tested the updates in a safe environment, usually a lab or an isolated section of the network, you then face the task of actually getting them deployed to the computers that require them. You have a few options available to you when it comes to deployment time, ranging from creating update-integrated installation media, using Group Policy and Remote Installation Service to install updates for you, using other products such as Systems Management Server, or even using scripting.

Of course, all of this assumes that you have actually gone out and gotten the updates you need. You can go about getting the required updates in a variety of ways, some easier than others. How you get the updates you need depends on the method you plan to use to deploy them. The method you use to deploy updates depends on several issues, such as whether the computers are new or existing, the physical location of the computers to be updated, and the number of computers to be updated.

The most common deployment methods for new computers include slipstreaming and scripting. For existing computers, Windows Update, Software Update Services, Automatic Update, Systems Management Server, scripting, and Group Policy are the more common methods. Of these, Automatic Updates (which has recently replaced the now defunct

Critical Notification Service) and Windows Update only apply to the specific computer that they are running on; the rest of the methods can be used to apply fixes and updates to multiple computers.

The Software Update Service, a relatively new service that replaces Windows Corporate Update, can be found at www.microsoft.com/windows2000/windowsupdate/sus/default.asp; however, it only works with Windows 2000, Windows XP, and Windows Server 2003 computers and is not an intelligent updater when it comes to applying patches. Systems Management Server (SMS) has been around for quite some time and is due for a new version release in the near future. SMS can be used to deploy all sorts of fixes and updates to all versions of Windows computers.

Scripting can also apply fixes and updates to all versions of Windows computers and is perhaps the best choice when you have a large number of computers requiring the same updates. The same holds true for Group Policy software installation. Of course, there is always good old-fashioned "sneaker-net," which could utilize collected fixes on transportable media and interactive installations at the machines.

If you need to manually download fixes and patches, you can get them from the following locations:

- For downloading service packs, your best bet is to go straight to the Service Pack homepage located at http://support.microsoft.com/default.aspx?scid=fh;EN-US;sp.
- For hotfixes and other updates, you have several viable options:

    1. You can go directly to the Q article that is listed with the fix. Q articles can be found at http://support.microsoft.com/default.aspx?scid=KB;EN-US;Q*xxxxxx*, where *xxxxxx* is the six-digit Q article number. (*Note:* Microsoft has been changing the numbering of the Q articles to numbers only to provide similar numbering in the company's worldwide operations. Searches may find the information either with or without the Q in the search terms.)
    2. You can look up the specific Security Bulletin that is mentioned at www.microsoft.com/technet/security/bulletin/MS*yy-bbb*.asp, where *yy* is the year and *bbb* is the bulletin number within that year.
    3. You can visit the Windows Catalog, which replaced the Windows Corporate Update Web site, at http://windowsupdate.microsoft.com/catalog. By working through the options and selecting your operating system and type of downloads you are looking for, you can find almost all updates, patches, and hotfixes in one location.

Analyzing Your Computers

Armed with your basic understanding of the types of updates that are available for Windows 2000, Windows XP, and Windows Server 2003, the first step you need to undertake to get your computers up to date (and thus more secure) is to determine their current state. Analyzing your computers can be a very simple task or a difficult one, depending on the size and complexity of your network. If you are responsible for only five computers and they are all located in the same place, your job will be very easy. If you are responsible for several hundred (or thousand) computers spread out over several geographically distant locations, your job is not going to be so easy. The method you choose to analyze your computers will thus depend largely on these factors:

- How many computers are you responsible for updating?
- Where are your computers located?
- What type of network connectivity do you have between locations?
- Do you have knowledgeable help available to you at all your locations?

Let's take a look at some of the methods available to analyze your computers, both manually and via automated methods.

Visiting Windows Update

The Windows Update Web site can be a great asset to you if the number of computers to be managed is relatively low—perhaps five or fewer. Since Windows Update requires you to physically be in front of each computer in order to analyze and download the required updates, this method can be both time and bandwidth intensive. Windows Update, however, could be your best option if the number of computers to be updated is few or if a group of computers are not connected to the company network and thus cannot be analyzed via any other method.

Using Windows Update to analyze a computer for required updates is extremely simple, as outlined in Exercise 8.06.

EXERCISE 8.06

Determining the Need for Updating Using Windows Update

1. Click **Start | All Programs Windows Update** to open an Internet Explorer window pointed to Windows Update. You can also enter **http://windowsupdate.microsoft.com/** into your browser address bar. The Internet Explorer window shown in Figure 8.63 will appear. If you are asked to download and install anything from Microsoft, accept the download; this is a critical part of the process.

Figure 8.63 The Windows Update Web Site

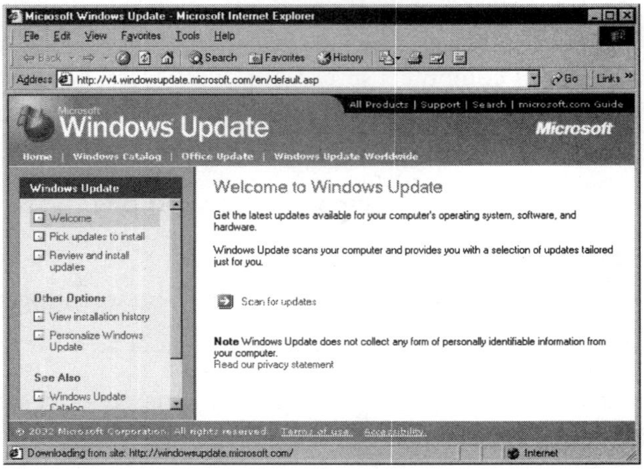

2. Click **Scan for updates** to start the analysis of your computer. After the analysis has completed, you will see the window shown in Figure 8.64.

Figure 8.64 Selecting Required Updates

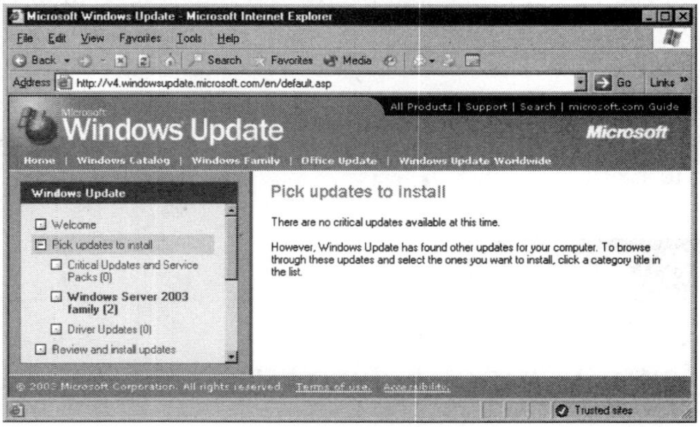

You can navigate through the three categories of updates to determine the updates that Windows Update has found your computer needs. The categories are arranged from most important to least important in regard to computer security and safety; this is why drivers are at the bottom of the list.

3. Another useful tool to help you determine what you have previously applied using Windows Update is the View installation option. Clicking **View installation history** changes the display to that shown in Figure 8.65. (Your installed items will likely be different from those shown here.)

Figure 8.65 Checking Previously Installed Updates

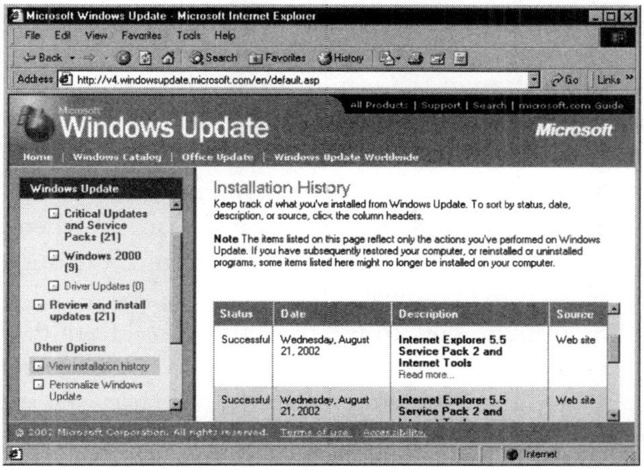

That's all there is to analyzing your computer with Windows Update. Later in this chapter we examine the rest of the steps to use Windows Update to select and install updates onto the local computer.

The Microsoft Baseline Security Analyzer

The Microsoft Baseline Security Analyzer (MBSA) is a GUI-based tool that Microsoft developed to detect common security misconfiguration and weaknesses. The MBSA tool can also be used from the command line if desired. The current version of MBSA, version 1.1, can be run on a Windows 2000, Windows XP, or Windows Server 2003 computer; it scans for missing hotfixes, weaknesses, and vulnerabilities in the following Microsoft products:

- Windows 2000 Professional, Server, and Advanced Server
- Windows XP Professional
- Windows NT Workstation 4.0, Server 4.0, and Enterprise Edition Server 4.0
- SQL Server 7.0
- SQL Server 2000 Standard, Enterprise, and Conferencing Server
- Internet Information Server 4.0
- Internet Information Services 5.0
- Internet Explorer 5.01 and later
- Office 2000
- Office 2002 (XP)

MBSA uses a modified version of the HFNetChk tool to scan for missing hotfixes, service packs, and other updates. At the completion of the scan, an individual XML output report is created for each computer that has been scanned. This report can be viewed immediately after the completion of the scan or later. When MBSA is executed from the GUI, reports are placed in the SecurityScans folder, which is located in the profile of the user who ran the scan.

For example, if a user named Andrea ran the scan, she could expect to find scan reports located at C:\Documents and Settings\Andrea\SecurityScans or wherever her profile path is pointed. You can use the */f* switch to change the location of the output file when you're running the MBSA tool from the command line.

In Exercise 8.07, we examine how to use the MBSA tool from the GUI to examine a local computer and determine its current status. In Exercise 8.08 we perform the same task, this time from the command line. Using the MBSA tool as part of a script or batch file, you could schedule a regular scan of all your network computers and then examine the results after the scan has completed. You should consider performing a scan such as this one at least once per week as your specific situation dictates.

The basic syntax of the MBSA tool from the command line is:

```
msbacli.exe    [/c domainname\computername] [-i ipaddress] [-d domainname]
                [-r range] [/n IIS] [/n OS] [/n password] [/n SQL]
                [/n hotfix] [/o %domain% - %computername% (%date%)]
                [/e] [/l] [/ls] [/lr report name] [/ld report name]
                [/qp] [/qe] [/qr] [/q] [/f]
```

Table 8.4 details the function of each mbsacli.exe switch.

Table 8.4 The mbsacli.exe Switches

Switch	Explanation
/c *domainname\computername*	Performs a scan on the selected computer.
-i *ipaddress*	Specifies the IP address of the computer to be scanned. If not specified, the default is the local computer.
-d *domainname*	Specifies the domain name to be scanned. All eligible computers in the domain will be scanned.
-r *range*	Specifies the inclusive IP address range that is to be scanned in the format *start_IP-end_IP*—for example, 192.168.0.100-192.168.0.199.
/n IIS	Specifies that IIS checks are to be skipped. The */n* options can be added together, such as */n IIS+OS+SQL*.

Continued

Table 8.4 The mbsacli.exe Switches

Switch	Explanation
/n OS	Specifies that operating system checks are to be skipped.
/n password	Specifies that password checks are to be skipped.
/n SQL	Specifies that SQL checks are to be skipped.
/n hotfix	Specifies that hotfix checks are to be skipped.
/e	Lists errors from the latest scan.
/l	Lists all reports available for viewing.
/ls	Lists all reports from the latest scan.
/lr *report name*	Displays an overview of the specified report name.
/ld *report name*	Displays a detailed version of the specified report name.
/qp	Specifies that the progress of the scan is not to be shown.
/qe	Specifies that the error list is not to be shown.
/qr	Specifies that the report list is not to be shown.
/q	Specifies that the progress of the scan, the error list, or the report list are not to be shown.
/f	Specifies that output is to be redirected to a file.

Exam Warning

As with the HFNetChk tool discussed later in the chapter, taking some time to become familiar with the switches that can be used with the command-line version of MBSA could help you on exam day. You might be given one or more answers that require you to know whether or not a particular switch will achieve the desired result.

Exercise 8.07 presents the process to perform a single local computer scan with MBSA from the GUI.

EXERCISE 8.07

USING MBSA TO ANALYZE FOR UPDATES FROM THE GUI

1. Download the Microsoft Baseline Security Analyzer from http://download.microsoft.com/download/e/5/7/e57f498f-2468-4905-aa5f-369252f8b15c/mbsasetup.msi.
2. Double-click the **mbasetup.msi installer**. Click **Next** to progress past the first page of the wizard.
3. Accept the license agreement and click **Next** to continue.
4. Enter the requested information as shown in Figure 8.66 and click **Next** to continue.

Figure 8.66 Configuring the Installation of MBSA

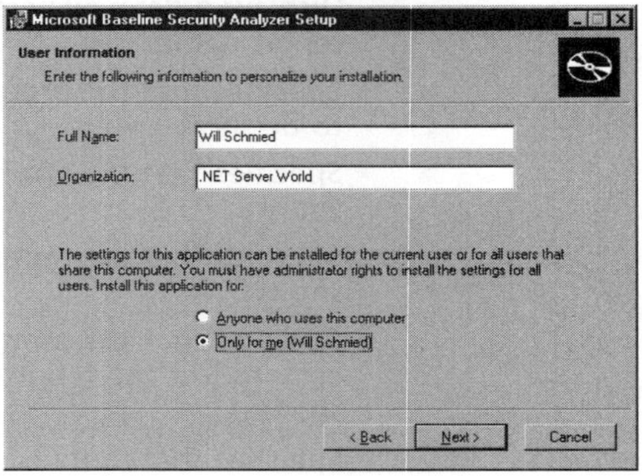

5. On the Destination Folder page, either select a custom installation path or accept the default one and click **Next** to continue.
6. Choose your installation options from the **Choose install options** page and click **Next** to continue.
7. Click **Next** two more times to start the installation.
8. Click **Finish** to complete the installation process.
9. Launch the newly installed MBSA tool and select **Scan a computer**.
10. On the **Pick a computer to scan** page, configure the computer you want to scan and the scan options you want to use, as shown in Figure 8.67. When you're done, click **Start scan**.

Figure 8.67 Configuring the Local Computer Scan Options

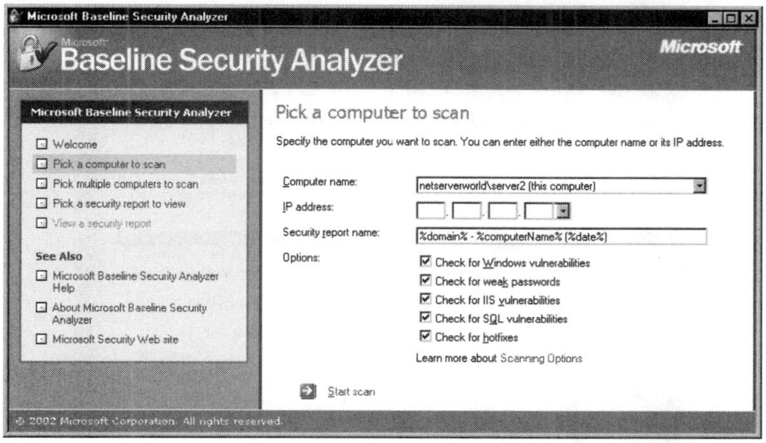

11. You will be asked if you want to install the MSSecureXML file from Microsoft. You must have a copy of the XML file in order for MBSA to work. Note that the file is updated regularly as Microsoft posts new fixes and updates, so you might want to update it each time you run MBSA. Click **Yes** to install the XML file and allow the analysis to continue.
12. After the analysis has been completed, you will receive the results of the scan, as shown in Figure 8.68. It looks as though this server has some serious issues. To examine the specifics of an area, click **Result Details**. The details of the Windows Hotfixes area are shown in Figure 8.69.

Figure 8.68 The MBSA Results

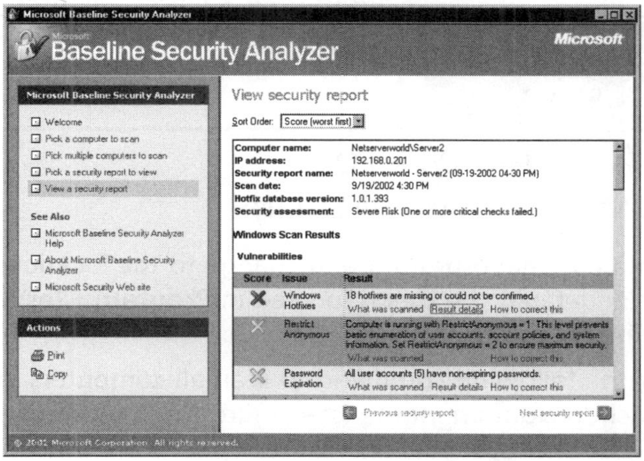

Figure 8.69 Examining Specific Items

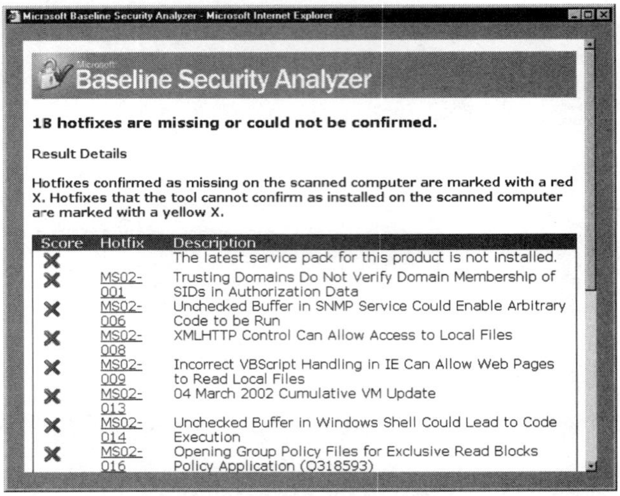

13. Armed with this knowledge, we can now go about getting and installing the required fixes and patches on our computers. That is the topic of the "Deploying and Managing Updates" section later in this chapter.

As mentioned previously, you can also run the MBSA tool from the command line, as demonstrated in Exercise 8.08. This method can be useful in working with scripts and batch files, although with the fairly powerful GUI mode available to the MBSA, you might find yourself shying away from using it at the command line in most cases.

EXERCISE 8.08

Using MBSA to Analyze for Updates from the Command Line

1. Open a command prompt and change to the location of the MBSA tool. By default, the tool is located in **Program Files\Microsoft Baseline Security Analyzer**.
2. Enter the following command to scan all computers in the domain: **mbsacli /d domain_name** (see Figure 8.70) or simply enter **mbsacli** to scan only the local machine. Other options are available for scanning, as detailed in Table 8.4. Press **Enter** after you have entered your scan command.

Figure 8.70 Starting an MBSA Scan from the Command Line

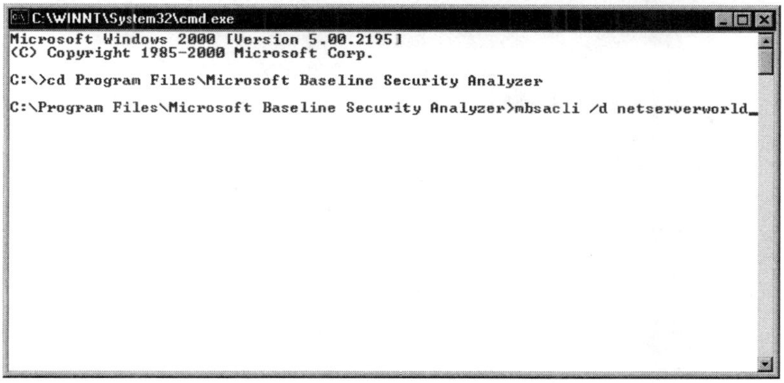

3. You will be asked if you want to install the MSSecureXML file from Microsoft. You must have a copy of the XML file in order for MBSA to work. Note that the file is updated regularly as Microsoft posts new fixes and updates, so you might want to update it each time you run MBSA. Click **Yes** to install the XML file and allow the analysis to continue.
4. After the analysis has been completed, you will receive the results of the scan, as shown in Figure 8.71. You can then open the scan output file in the MBSA GUI version and see exactly what has been found, as shown in Figure 8.72.

Figure 8.71 MBSA Command-Line Scan Is Complete

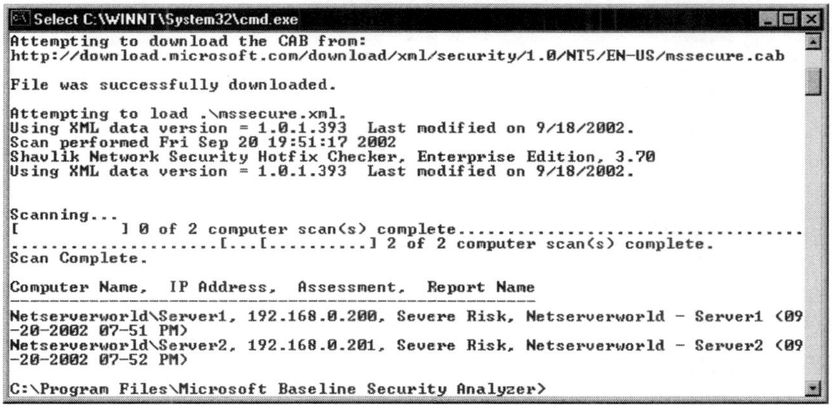

Figure 8.72 Viewing the MBSA Scan Results in the GUI

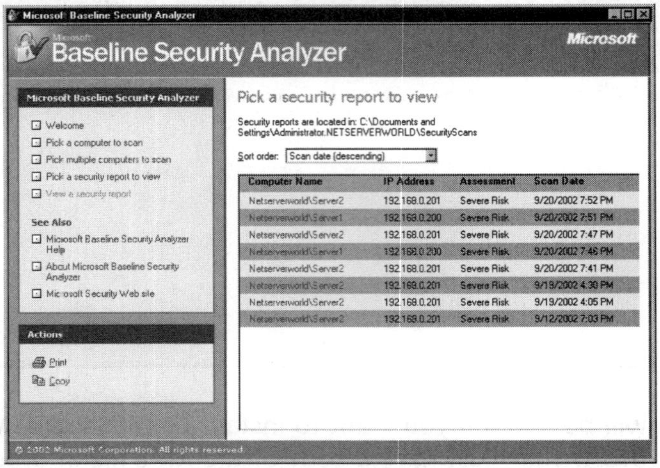

5. Armed with this knowledge, we can now go about getting and installing the required fixes and patches on our computers. That is the topic of the "Deploying and Managing Updates" section later in this chapter.

The next method we examine is the Microsoft Network Security Hotfix Checker, commonly referred to as the *HFNetChk tool.*

The Microsoft Network Security Hotfix Checker

The Microsoft Network Security Hotfix Checker, HFNetChk, is a command-line tool that can be used to quickly analyze one or many computers to determine the installation status of required security patches. In its current versions, it is accessed from and combined with the Microsoft Baseline Security Analyzer Tool (v1.1). Unlike Windows Update, HFNetChk can scan for missing updates from more than one product and can be scripted to perform scans in a number of different configurations, depending on your organization's needs. Products that HFNetChk currently scans include:

- Windows 2000 Professional, Server, and Advanced Server
- Windows XP Professional
- Windows NT Workstation 4.0, Server 4.0, and Enterprise Edition Server 4.0
- SQL Server 7.0
- SQL Server 2000 Standard, Enterprise, and Conferencing Server

- Exchange Server 5.5
- Exchange Server 2000
- Internet Information Server 4.0
- Internet Information Services 5.0
- Internet Explorer 5.01 or later
- Windows Media Player
- Microsoft Data Engine (MSDE) 1.0

NOTE

MBSA v1.1 does not scan Windows Server 2003 platform machines, although it may be installed and used to scan other platforms as indicated in the preceding discussion. Microsoft indicates that the Windows Server 2003 functionality will be available in MBSA v1.2 when it is released.

When the HFNetChk tool is run, it uses an Extensible Markup Language (XML) file containing information about all available hotfixes as its data source. The XML file contains all pertinent information about each product's hotfixes, such as the security bulletin name and title, and other detailed information about the hotfixes, including the file version, Registry keys applied by the hotfix, information about patches that supersede other patches, and various other important types of information about each hotfix.

If the XML file is not found in the directory from which the HFNetChk tool is run or is not specified in the arguments for the HFNetChk tool, it will be downloaded from the Microsoft Web site. The XML file comes in a digitally signed CAB format, and you might be asked to accept the download before the file is downloaded to your computer.

After the CAB file has been downloaded and decompressed, HFNetChk scans the selected computers to determine the operating systems, applications, and service packs you have installed. After this initial scan is completed, HFNetChk parses the XML file to identify any security patches that are required (and not installed) for the configuration of each computer scanned. If a patch is identified as being required but is not currently installed on a computer, HFNetChk returns output informing you so.

By default, HFNetChk displays only those patches and fixes that are necessary to bring your computers up to date. All other nonessential patches are not shown by default. In the event that rollup packages exist, HFNetChk will not report the individual patches that the rollup included as required. When determining the installation status of a patch on a computer, HFNetChk evaluates three distinct items: the file version and checksum of every file that is installed by the patch and the Registry key that is installed by the patch. If the Registry key is not found, HFNetChk assumes the patch is not installed. If the Registry key is found, HFNetChk looks for the files that correspond to that patch, comparing the file version and checksum to the XML file. If any one test fails, the output will be that the patch is not installed. You can, however, disable checking Registry keys as part of the analysis process, as we see later in this section.

The basic syntax of the HFNetChk tool is:

```
mbsacli.exe /hf    [-h hostname] [-i ipaddress] [-d domainname] [-n] [-b]
                   [-r range] [-history level] [-t threads] [-o output]
                   [-x datasource] [-z] [-v] [-s suppression] [-nosum]
                   [-u username] [-p password] [-f outfile] [-about]
                   [-fh hostfile] [-fip ipfile] [-fq ignorefile]
```

Table 8.5 provides the function of each of the HFNetChk switches.

Table 8.5 The HFNetChk Switches

Switch	Explanation
-h *hostname*	Specifies the NetBIOS name of the computer to be scanned. If not specified, the default is *localhost*.
-i *ipaddress*	Specifies the IP address of the computer to be scanned. If not specified, the default is the local computer.
-d *domainname*	Specifies the domain name to be scanned. All eligible computers in the domain will be scanned.
-n	Specifies that the local network is to be scanned. All eligible computers on the local network will be scanned.
-b	Compares the current status of fixes to that of a minimum secure baseline standard.
-r *range*	Specifies the inclusive IP address range that is to be scanned in the format *start_IP-end_IP*—for example, 192.168.0.100-192.168.0.199.
-history *level*	Displays an extremely verbose history of hotfixes as follows: 1. Those that are explicitly installed 2. Those that are explicitly not installed 3. Those that are explicitly installed and not installed MSKB Q303215 (located at http://support.microsoft.com/default.aspx?scid=KB;EN-US;Q303215&) has more information on using this switch.
-t *threads*	Specifies the number of threads to be used for executing the scan. The allowable range is from 1 to 128, with the default being 64.
-o *output*	Specifies the desired output format at the completion of the scan. *Tab* outputs in tab-delimited format. *Wrap* outputs in a word-wrapped format. The default setting is *wrap*.

Continued

Table 8.5 The HFNetChk Switches

Switch	Explanation
-x *datasource*	Specifies the XML data source containing the hotfix information. By default, this is the mssecure.cab file located at http://download.microsoft.com/download/xml/security/1.0/NT5/EN-US/mssecure.cab. This can be changed to any location on your network and can be an XML filename, compressed XML CAB file, or a URL.
-z	Specifies that Registry checking should not be performed.
-v	Displays all available details for "Patch NOT Found," "WARNING," and "NOTE" messages. When *–o tab* is used, this switch is enabled by default.
-s *suppression*	Specifies to suppress "NOTE" and "WARNING" messages as follows: 1. Suppress "NOTE" messages only 2. Suppress both "NOTE" and "WARNING" messages The default setting is to show all messages.
-nosum	Specifies that checksum checking is not to be performed. Performing the checksum test can use large amounts of network bandwidth. If speed or bandwidth usage is a concern, using this option speeds up the scan and reduces bandwidth usage. File version checking is still done.
-u *username*	Specifies an optional username to be used to log into remote computers if required in *DOMAIN\Username* format. *CAUTION: This data is sent in cleartext across the network!*
-p *password*	Specifies the password to be used with the specified username. *CAUTION: This data is sent in cleartext across the network!*
-f *outfile*	Specifies the filename to save the output results to. The default output is to the screen.
-about	Provides information about the version of HFNetChk in use.
-fh *hostfile*	Specifies the file containing a list of NetBIOS computer names to be scanned, one name per line, with a maximum of 256 per file.
-fip *ipfile*	Specifies the file containing a list of IP addresses to be scanned, one IP address per line, with a maximum of 256 per file.
-fq *ignorefile*	Specifies the name of a file that contains Q numbers that you want to suppress on the output. One per line, to suppress output of known note messages or Q numbers of patches you have not approved.

Exam Warning

Take time to become familiar with the HFNetChk switches. Although you will most likely not be required to recall them in bulk during your exam, you could be presented with one or more questions that will require you to display your understanding of the function of a particular switch and how it will or will not provide the desired solution to the problem at hand.

Exercise 8.09 presents the process to perform a simple network scan utilizing the HFNetChk utility, returning the results to a tab-delimited text output file.

EXERCISE 8.09

Using HFNetChk to Analyze for Updates

1. If you haven't already done so, download and install the **MBSA** tool demonstrated in Exercise 8.07.
2. Open a command prompt and change directories to the location where you installed the MBSA files. (This is typically **<driveletter>\Program Files\Microsoft Baseline Security Analyzer**.)
3. From this directory, start the analysis process by entering **mbsacli /hf –v –d domain_name –o tab –f hfnetchk_scan1.txt**. Figure 8.73 shows an example command for a network. Press **Enter** to start the analysis.

Figure 8.73 Starting the Analysis Process with HFNetChk

4. You will see that as the process proceeds, the XML file will be checked and downloaded if an update is needed. Note that the file is updated regularly as Microsoft posts new fixes and updates, so you might want

to update it each time you run HFNetChk. Figure 8.74 illustrates the in-process screen.

Figure 8.74 Getting the XML File

5. Since we have directed the output of the scan to a tab-delimited text file, you should expect to see the output shown in Figure 8.75 at the conclusion of your scan.

Figure 8.75 The Scan Is Complete

6. An examination of the text output file reveals the situation for our computers. Figure 8.76 shows the tab-delimited file imported into Excel for easier viewing and comparison.

Figure 8.76 The Results of the HFNetChk Analysis

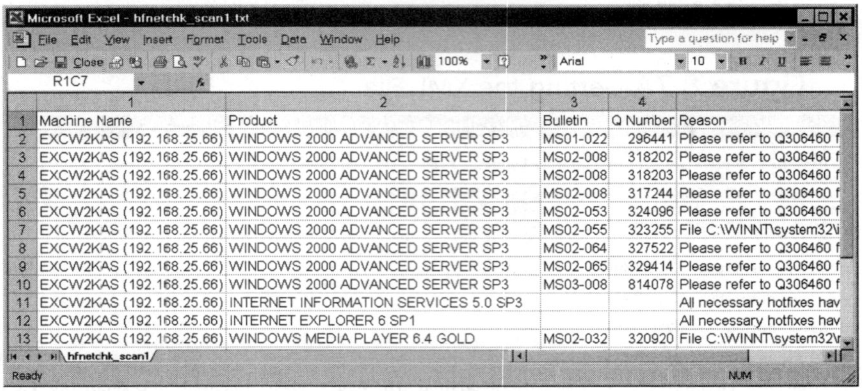

	1	2	3	4	
1	Machine Name	Product	Bulletin	Q Number	Reason
2	EXCW2KAS (192.168.25.66)	WINDOWS 2000 ADVANCED SERVER SP3	MS01-022	296441	Please refer to Q306460 f
3	EXCW2KAS (192.168.25.66)	WINDOWS 2000 ADVANCED SERVER SP3	MS02-008	318202	Please refer to Q306460 f
4	EXCW2KAS (192.168.25.66)	WINDOWS 2000 ADVANCED SERVER SP3	MS02-008	318203	Please refer to Q306460 f
5	EXCW2KAS (192.168.25.66)	WINDOWS 2000 ADVANCED SERVER SP3	MS02-008	317244	Please refer to Q306460 f
6	EXCW2KAS (192.168.25.66)	WINDOWS 2000 ADVANCED SERVER SP3	MS02-053	324096	Please refer to Q306460 f
7	EXCW2KAS (192.168.25.66)	WINDOWS 2000 ADVANCED SERVER SP3	MS02-055	323255	File C:\WINNT\system32\i
8	EXCW2KAS (192.168.25.66)	WINDOWS 2000 ADVANCED SERVER SP3	MS02-064	327522	Please refer to Q306460 f
9	EXCW2KAS (192.168.25.66)	WINDOWS 2000 ADVANCED SERVER SP3	MS02-065	329414	Please refer to Q306460 f
10	EXCW2KAS (192.168.25.66)	WINDOWS 2000 ADVANCED SERVER SP3	MS03-008	814078	Please refer to Q306460 f
11	EXCW2KAS (192.168.25.66)	INTERNET INFORMATION SERVICES 5.0 SP3			All necessary hotfixes hav
12	EXCW2KAS (192.168.25.66)	INTERNET EXPLORER 6 SP1			All necessary hotfixes hav
13	EXCW2KAS (192.168.25.66)	WINDOWS MEDIA PLAYER 6.4 GOLD	MS02-032	320920	File C:\WINNT\system32\r

7. Armed with this knowledge, we can now go about getting and installing the required fixes and patches on our computers. That is the topic of the "Deploying and Managing Updates" section later in this chapter.

Even though we performed a relatively simple scan in Exercise 8.09, you can use HFNetChk's various switches in Table 8.5 to perform very advanced scans on the specific computers of your choosing. By calling the scan from a batch file or script that is scheduled to run weekly, you can easily keep on top of any patches or fixes that your computers require. The only caveat to configuring HFNetChk to run as a scheduled event is that you must specify the location of the XML file—so a small amount of preplanning is required to make it work.

Windows Update

As we discussed earlier in this chapter, Windows Update is a very simple and easy-to-use method of updating one specific computer at a time. Therein lies its drawback: It can be used to update the local computer and requires that updates be downloaded from Microsoft for that computer. Using Windows Update is a good choice if the number of computers to be updated is relatively small or if you do not have Active Directory in your network. As the number of computers and sites increases, so does your workload, and very quickly Windows Update becomes a solution that is not viable. The exact number of computers at which this breaking point occurs is not fixed and can vary from organization to organization, but a good guideline is 10 computers. If you have 10 computers or fewer in your organization, you can, in most cases, get away with using Windows Update without too much administrative effort. If you have more than 10 computers, you should consider another means of keeping them up to date. Another concern with using Windows Update is that each computer downloads the files it requires independently of what any other computer has previously downloaded; this can put quite a hit on your network bandwidth.

Should you need to use Windows Update, the process to scan for required updates was presented earlier in this chapter, in Exercise 8.06. Exercise 8.10 presents the basic process to select and download updates.

Test Day Tip

Don't expect to be tested on a large amount of Windows Update knowledge during your exam. Most likely, you will only see the topic referenced lightly. What you need to take away from the discussion in this chapter is what Windows Update does, how it works, and why it is a limited solution not suitable for enterprise use.

EXERCISE 8.10

Updating a Single Computer Using Windows Update

1. After you've completed the Windows Update scan of your computer (refer back to Exercise 8.06), you need to select and download updates to be applied to your computer. Some updates are mutually exclusive of all other updates, meaning that they must be downloaded and installed separately from any other updates. Most often, this includes any updates to Internet Explorer, service packs, and any sort of security rollup.
2. By default, Windows Update automatically places into your download "basket" any items it finds that fall into the Critical Updates and Service Packs category. This does not mean, however, that it can install them all at once or that you must install them at all. To see what items have been identified and selected as Critical Updates or Service Packs, click the **Critical Updates or Service Packs** link to get the page shown in Figure 8.77. Notice that Internet Explorer Service Pack 1 (the first item selected) is one of those items that is mutually exclusive and must be downloaded and installed separately from the rest of the selected items. In this case, you need to either remove all other items from your download list or remove the one specific item. We recommend checking the entire list to make sure that other items are not mutually exclusive and that the list contains only the items you want to download. You can read more about any item by clicking the **Read more** link at the end of the item's description.

Figure 8.77 Examining the Critical Updates and Service Packs List

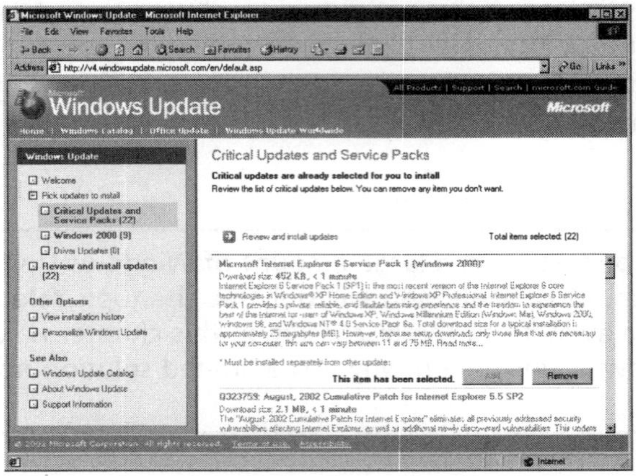

3. The items identified here as Windows 2000 updates are not automatically added to your list of selected items, but they might still be useful or needed for your computer. You should examine this list of items by clicking the **Windows 2000** link and adding to your list any updates you want to have installed.
4. If your scan reveals that you have updated drivers for your computer hardware, they will be listed under **Driver Updates**. You can add any of these updated drivers to your download list as well.
5. Once you have added all the updates that you want (or that you can based on exclusions), click **Review and install updates** to progress to the next step of the Windows Update process (see Figure 8.78).

Figure 8.78 Reviewing Selected Updates

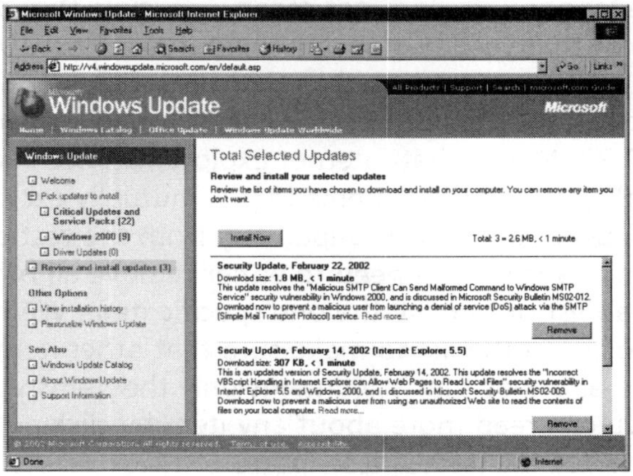

6. Once again you have the option to examine the selected updates you have chosen and remove them from your list. Once you are satisfied with your selections, click **Install Now**.
7. You will be presented with a supplemental licensing agreement like the one shown in Figure 8.79. You must click **Accept** to complete the process.

Figure 8.79 Accepting the Licensing Agreement

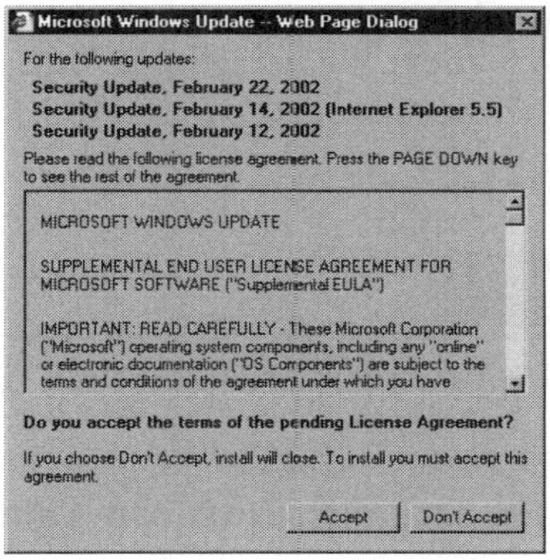

8. Windows Update will now download (see Figure 8.80) and install the selected updates. More often than not, you will be required to restart the computer after the installation to complete the process. Restarting the computer allows files that were in use to be updated. That's all there is to using Windows Update to update a single computer.

Figure 8.80 Windows Update Downloads and Installs the Updates

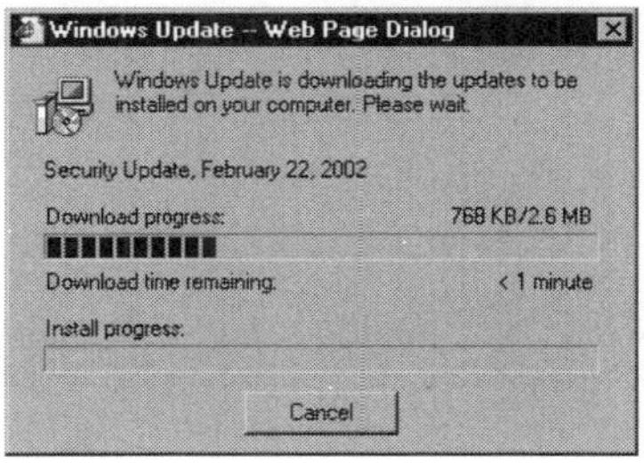

Using Windows Update is a simple, easy way to update a single computer or a few computers. But if you have more than a few computers to update or want to control when and how the updates are applied to your computers, you need to use one of the other methods we discuss in the next few sections.

Windows Update Catalog

The Windows Update Catalog and the Software Update Services have replaced what was once known as Corporate Windows Update. Corporate Windows Update allowed you to browse through all the available updates for your operating system, download the ones you wanted, and then deploy them using any available means, such as scripting or SMS.

Windows Update Catalog pretty much performs the same function as the now defunct Corporate Windows Update site. Software Update Services (SUS) takes the concept a step further by automatically downloading the updates to the SUS server and staging them for you until you are ready to deploy them. We examine SUS in the next section, but for now let's see how the Windows Update Catalog can be used to locate and download updates of our choosing in Exercise 8.11.

EXERCISE 8.11

GETTING UPDATES USING THE WINDOWS UPDATE CATALOG

1. Open Internet Explorer and enter **http://windowsupdate.microsoft.com/catalog** into the address bar. The Windows Update Catalog will open, as shown in Figure 8.81.

Figure 8.81 The Windows Update Catalog

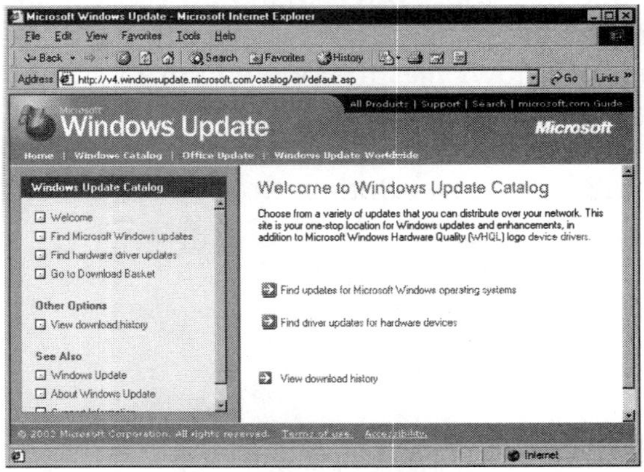

2. Click **Find updates for Microsoft Windows operating systems** to start the process of finding updates for your Windows Server 2003 computers.
3. Choose your operating system from the choices given (see Figure 8.82) to locate all available downloads. If you want to perform an advanced search and only locate specific items, such as service packs or recommended updates, click **Advanced search options**. After you have configured your search parameters, click **Search** to continue.

Figure 8.82 Selecting the Search Criteria

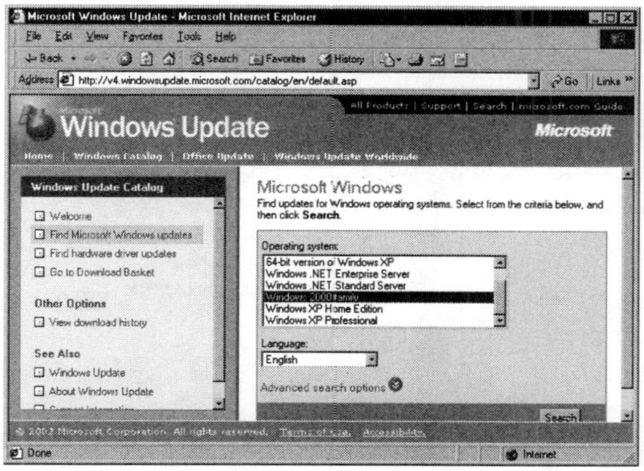

4. Available updates will be enumerated by the category in which you have chosen to search. Clicking **Critical Updates and Service Packs** in our case yields the output shown in Figure 8.83.

Figure 8.83 Listing the Updates

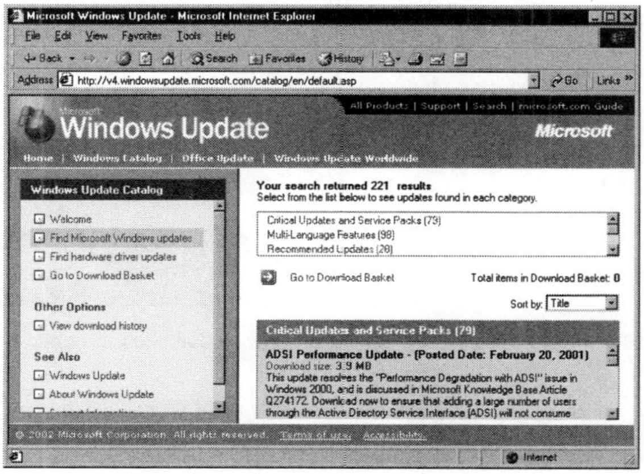

5. Browse through the list of updates in order to determine what you need. You can gain more information about a specific update by clicking the **Read more** link within the update's descriptive text. Click **Add** to place an update into your download basket. When you are done selecting updates, click **Go to Download Basket**.

6. The Download Basket (see Figure 8.84) shows all updates that you have chosen to download and allows you to configure a location to which to download the files. When you are ready to download your chosen files, click **Download Now**.

Figure 8.84 Preparing to Download the Selected Update Items

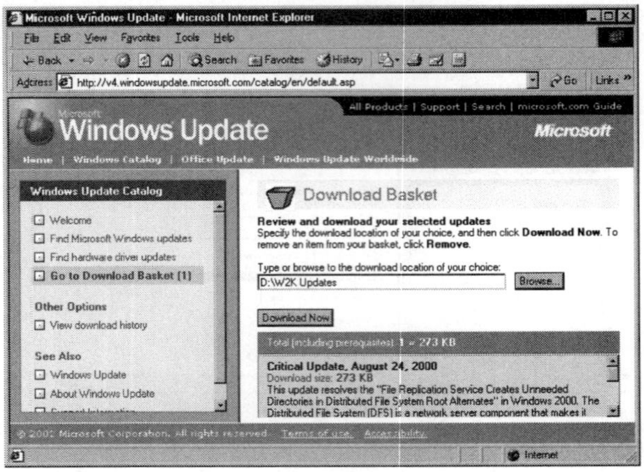

7. When you're prompted to accept the licensing agreement, click **Accept** to complete the download.
8. Downloaded files can be tracked in Download History, as shown in Figure 8.85. Now that you've gotten your updates, you can deploy them via your choice of methods.

Figure 8.85 Keeping Track of Downloaded Updates

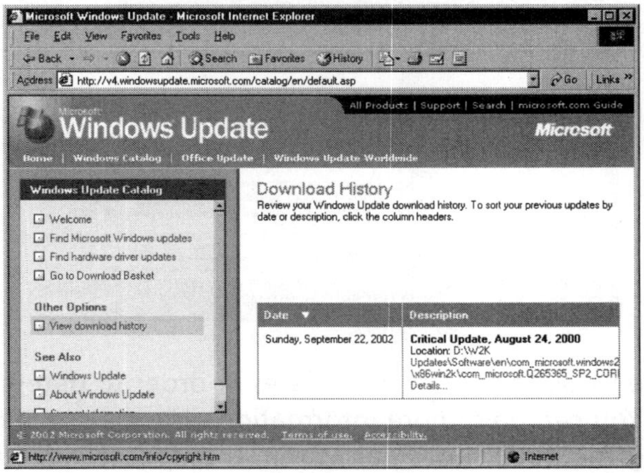

Now let's move on to the Software Update Services, a recent introduction in Windows Server 2003 that allows you to set up the equivalent of a Windows Update server inside your own intranet.

Software Update Services and Automatic Updates

SUS is the other half of the replacement for the discontinued Corporate Windows Update site. Call it what you will, SUS (when paired with the Automatic Updates client) is really just a Windows Update server that lives inside your private network. As the name of this section implies, it is a two-part process: You must install and configure the SUS server component in order to get available downloads from Microsoft, and then you must install and configure Automatic Updates so that available updates will be automatically installed on your client computers.

Before you can use SUS or Automatic Updates on your network, you need to download and install the required files. To get the SUS installer file, see www.microsoft.com/windows2000/downloads/recommended/susserver/default.asp. You should also consider downloading the very good SUS Deployment Guide from that location; it is full of excellent tips and best practices that will help you keep your SUS servers running smoothly. The Automatic Updates client can be downloaded from www.microsoft.com/windows2000/downloads/recommended/susclient/default.asp.

Exercise 8.12 walks you through installing and configuring your first SUS server. It is important to know the restrictions for installing SUS before starting the procedure:

- You must install SUS on Windows 2000 Server Service Pack 2 (or later) or Windows Server 2003.
- The server SUS is installed on must be running IIS 5.0 or later.
- The server SUS is installed on must be running Internet Explorer 5.5 or later.
- SUS must be installed on an NTFS partition, and the system partition on the SUS server must also be using NTFS.
- With the introduction of SUS SP1, it can be installed on domain controllers and Small Business Server servers, which was not previously available.

EXERCISE 8.12

Installing and Configuring Software Update Services

1. Download the **SUS** package from www.microsoft.com/windows2000/downloads/recommended/susserver/default.asp.
2. Double-click the **SUSSetup.msi** file to begin the installation on your new SUS server.
3. Click **Next** to dismiss the opening page of the wizard.

4. After reading the End User License Agreement, select **I accept the terms in the License Agreement** and click **Next** to continue. You must agree to the terms in order to continue the installation of SUS.
5. From the **Choose setup type** page, click **Custom** in order to see all the configurable options available to you.
6. From the **Choose file locations** page (see Figure 8.86), you can configure the location to store the downloaded updates instead of directing clients to a Microsoft Windows Update server. After making your selections (which you can in most cases leave as the defaults), click **Next** to continue.

Figure 8.86 Selecting File Location Options

7. From the Language Settings page, select the language option that you need. In most cases, you can simply select **English only**. This choice also reduces the amount of space required for downloaded updates. After selecting your language, click **Next** to continue.
8. On the **Handling new versions of previously approved updates** page (see Figure 8.87), you are asked to make a seemingly small decision, but really it is a critical one. You should always select **I will manually approve new versions of approved updates** in order to avoid any problems with incompatibilities. Once you have adequately tested the newer version, you can turn it loose on the network. After making your selection, click **Next** to continue.

Figure 8.87 Selecting the Installation Method; Be Wary of Allowing Automatic Approvals

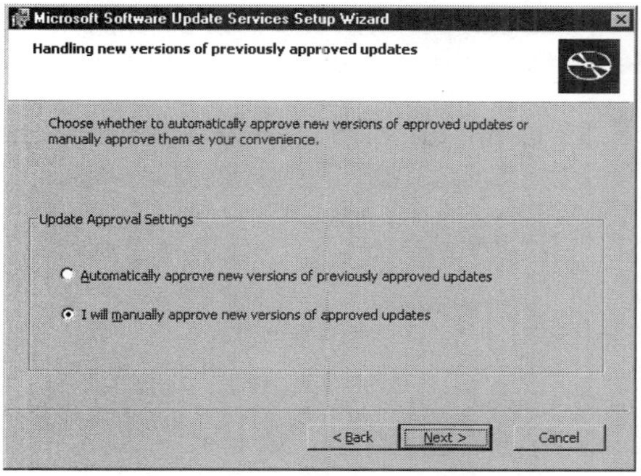

9. The **Ready to install** page provides you with the URL that clients should be targeted toward when configuring the Automatic Updates client. When you are ready to complete the installation of SUS, click **Install**.
10. The setup process will run the IIS Lockdown tool on your Windows Server 2003 in order to secure it as part of its installation process. This includes installing the URLScan ISAPI filter as well.
11. When setup has completed, click **Finish** to close the wizard. You can now administer your SUS server from http://*servername*/SUSAdmin.
12. Open a browser and in the address box, enter the location that corresponds to your SUS server. You should see the SUS server admin page, shown in Figure 8.88.

Figure 8.88 Administering the SUS Server

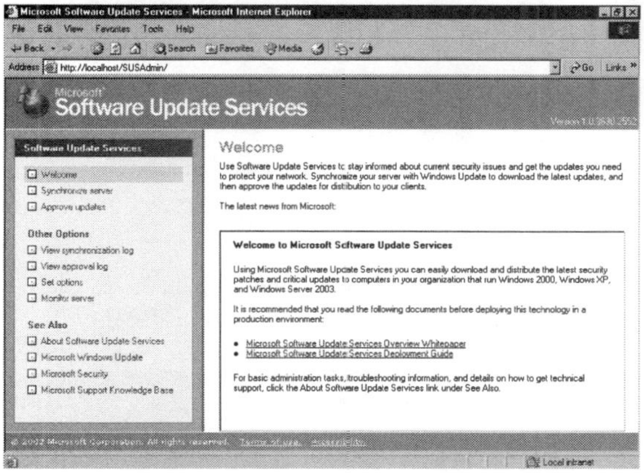

13. To begin, you need to synchronize your server. Click **Synchronize server**. You can, and should, configure a synchronization schedule for your server. You can perform this task by clicking the **Synchronization Schedule** button. This step opens the window shown in Figure 8.89.

Figure 8.89 Configuring the Synchronization Schedule

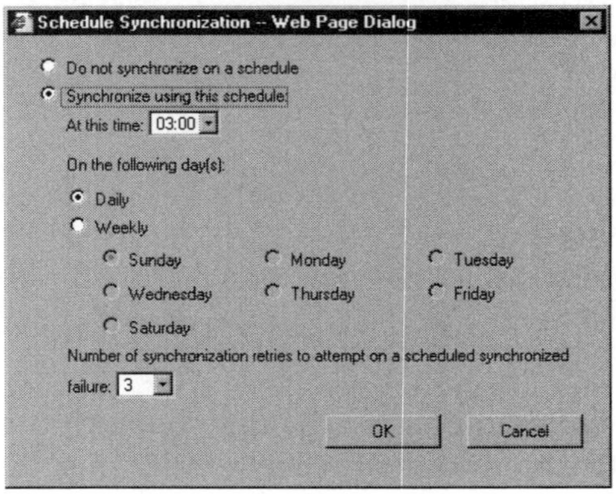

14. If you need to configure options related to a proxy server, click **Set options** from the left pane menu. When you are ready to force a synchronization of your new SUS server to update it, click the **Synchronize Now** button on the Synchronize Server page.
15. Synchronization will run for some time (as shown in Figure 8.90), depending on the number of updates that you need.

Figure 8.90 Downloading Required Updates

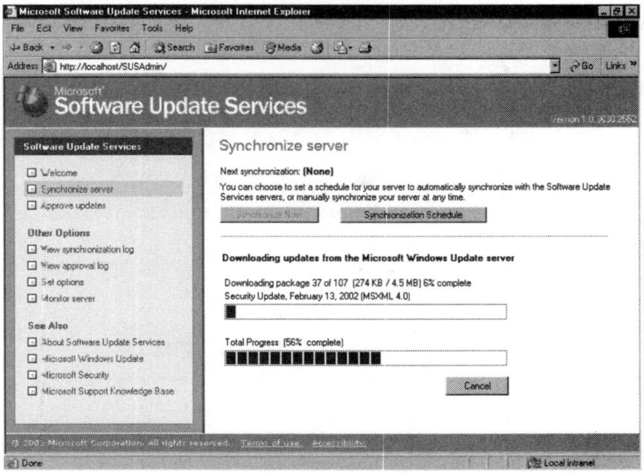

16. After all updates have been downloaded, click **OK**. You are now prompted to test and approve updates. You can do this at your leisure.
17. When you have tested an update and you are ready to approve it, click **Approve updates** to open the Approve Updates window. Select all updates you are ready to approve (see Figure 8.91) and click **Approve**.

Figure 8.91 Selecting the Approved Updates

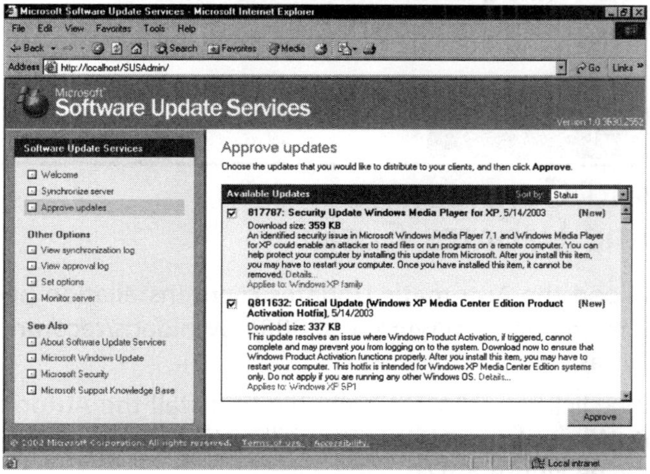

18. You will be asked to verify that the list of updates you are approving is correct, since it will replace the existing approval list. Click **Yes** to allow the list of approved updates to be made available to Automatic Updates clients.
19. You will be presented once again with the familiar supplemental End User License Agreement. Click **Accept** to continue the approval process.
20. Click **OK** when you're informed that the list of updates has been made available to your clients. You have just performed the installation and basic configuration of your first SUS server.

Armed with a functional SUS server, you now need to install the Automatic Updates client software on all your client computers in order for them to take advantage of the service. You can install the Automatic Updates client via any of the traditional methods, including using IntelliMirror and Group Policy, using Systems Management Server (or any other software installation and management application), or by good, old-fashioned sneaker-net.

Since we are going to install only one Automatic Updates client in Exercise 8.13, we will use the sneaker-net method; however, your installation method should be based on the number and location of the client computers on which you want to install the software.

The Automatic Updates client software can be used on the following systems:

- Windows 2000 Professional, Server, or Advanced Server (Service Pack 2 or later). Service Pack 3 includes the Automatic Updates client software.
- Windows XP Home Edition or Professional. Service Pack 1 includes the Automatic Updates client software.

EXERCISE 8.13

INSTALLING AND CONFIGURING THE AUTOMATIC UPDATES CLIENT

1. Download the Automatic Updates client installation package from www.microsoft.com/windows2000/downloads/recommended/susclient/default.asp.
2. Double-click the **WUAU22.msi** file to install the Automatic Updates client. When it completes, you will notice a new applet in the Control Panel (see Figure 8.92).

Figure 8.92 A New Applet Appears

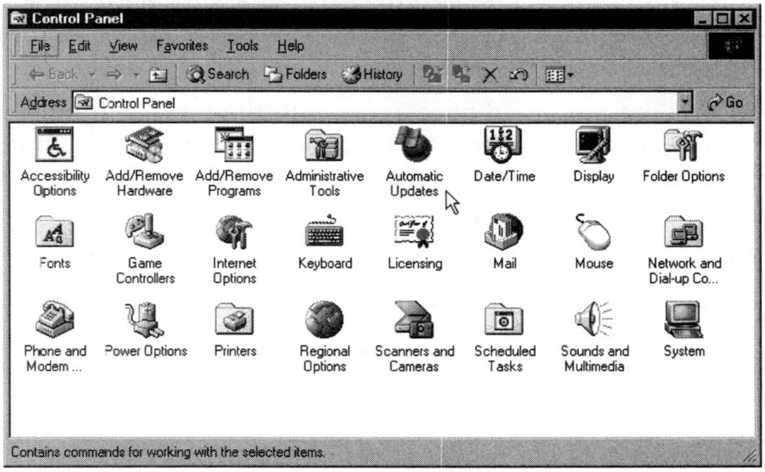

3. By default, the Automatic Updates client is not enabled. If it were (assuming you did no further configuration), it would be able to down-

load updates from the Windows Update server. We are going to configure it to download approved updates from our SUS server instead.

4. Automatic Updates settings for SUS are configured through a special Group Policy administrative template that you must add to the Group Policy object you are editing. Since we are working with one local computer, we will use the Local Computer Policy object. However, you can perform this process for any GPO at any level of Active Directory, as you require.
5. Open the Local Computer Policy window by typing **gpedit.msc** at the command line.
6. Open the Computer Configuration node, right-click **Administrative Templates**, and select **Add/Remove Templates** from the context menu, as shown in Figure 8.93.

Figure 8.93 Adding a New Template

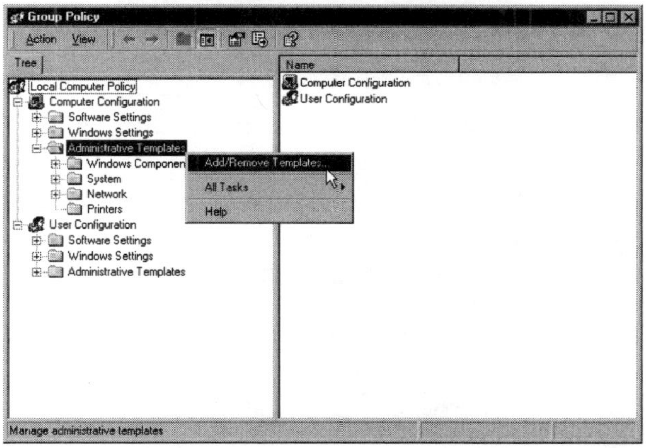

7. Click **Add** and select the **wuau.adm** template, as shown in Figure 8.94. Click **Open**. Click **Close** to close the Add/Remove Templates window.

Figure 8.94 Selecting the New Template

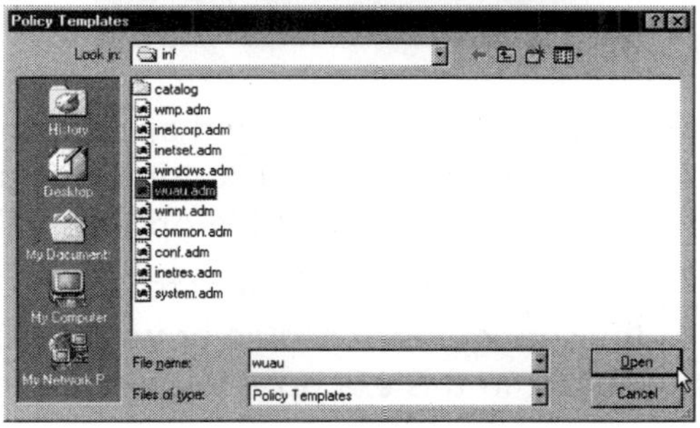

8. Expand the **Administrative Templates** node to the **Windows Updates** node.
9. Configure the **Configure Automatic Updates** and **Specify intranet Microsoft update server location** objects to your requirements, as shown in Figures 8.95 and 8.96.

Figure 8.95 Configuring the Configure Automatic Updates Object

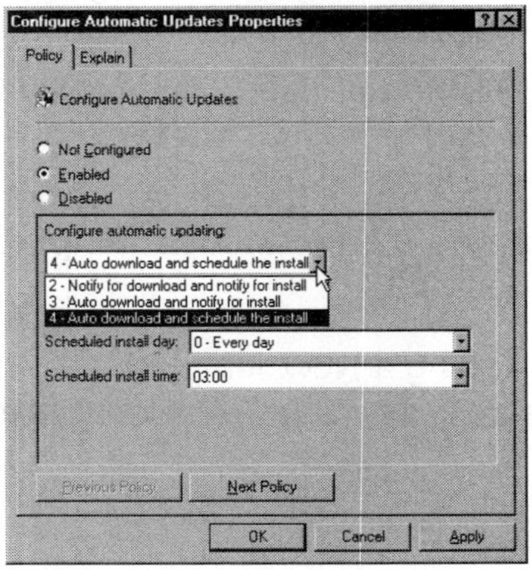

Figure 8.96 Configuring the Specify Intranet Microsoft Update Server Location Object

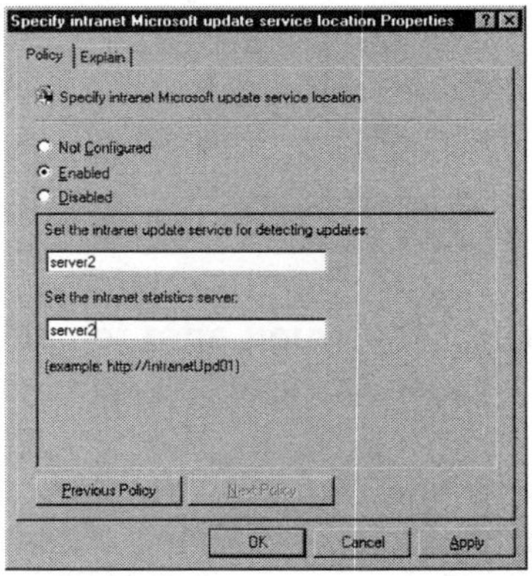

10. After Group Policy has been replicated and taken effect, you will no longer be able to manually control Automatic Updates settings from the Control Panel applet. All available options will be grayed out.
11. Depending on your configuration, updates will either be installed silently according to the configured schedule or will require user intervention to complete the install. In this example, we elected to have updates auto-

matically downloaded and installed. Figure 8.97 shows the result: The update that was approved (see Figure 8.91) was subsequently installed and now shows up in the Add/Remove Programs listing.

Figure 8.97 Inspecting the Work of the Automatic Updates Service

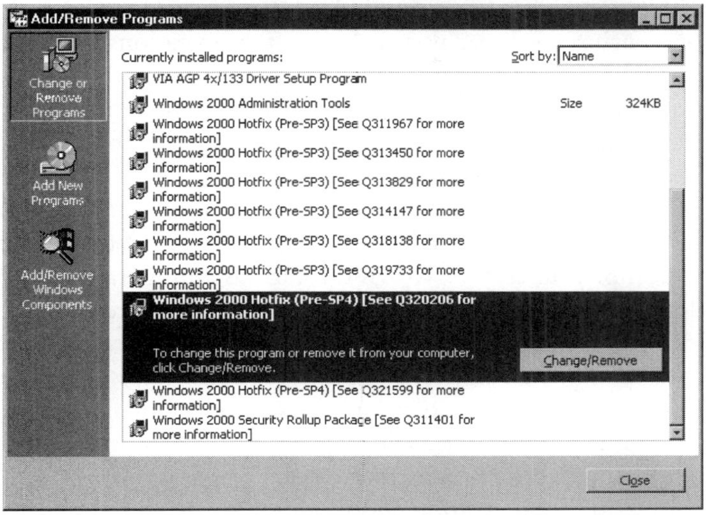

Test Day Tip

Even though it is possible that you will see questions dealing with SUS and the Automatic Updates client on the exam, you should not expect to see detailed installation and configuration questions. Expect to see questions more along the lines of what SUS and Automatic Updates are, how they work, and what you need to do to get them up and running. Remember, SUS is nothing more than a Windows Update server that you run on your internal network to provide your clients a location to automatically get and install required updates.

Summary of Exam Objectives

Our discussion throughout this chapter has been directed at providing you with the opportunity to experience firsthand the thought processes and procedures to enhance the out-of-the-box security that is provided with Windows Server 2003. We introduced the server roles to provide you with a background that should lead to a higher level of understanding of the importance of securing your machines based on the operations for which they are to be used. Microsoft has done a good job of turning around the formerly loose security conditions of past versions of the operating system, providing system and network administrators with much-enhanced functionality for further efforts at security configuration than have ever been available in a Windows platform.

We had a chance to discover that the default configurations are much more secure out of the box, and we discussed recommendations for further review that will enhance the security and operation of your servers. We visited various configurations of the platform and found that along with some specific settings that have been created to limit exposure through unintended service installations, many of the previous operating system features such as IIS have had their authentication and authorization processes dropped to a less privileged state that also enhances security. Through these discussions and exercises, we gained experience that should help in planning and implementing various security measures based on the use we have established for a particular server.

Security templates and their creation and modification provided an opportunity to experience ways to establish different levels of security. We found that the creation of the templates and analysis of their effects are necessary to verify the way they control various user rights and access conditions. Additionally, we found that the templates can be deployed locally (particularly recommended when restoring a machine to a default install level) and can also be distributed as part of Group Policy via Active Directory if the need exists to match the configuration on machines in the domain or OU.

Following our work with the templates, we turned our focus to reviewing the need for security on the network itself. Here we reviewed the processes that are necessary to provide security for data transmission on the network, how to protect it through various means, and then how to protect data through the capabilities exhibited by IPSec. We created an IPSec policy through an exercise, and we found that that process can be handled through either a GUI or command-line interface. This provides us with the knowledge to better protect the data on our network from prying eyes, whether they are looking from outside our network or from the inside.

Our final set of topics included information about implementing and maintaining security and updating the infrastructure. In this area, we looked at the reasons that we need to be concerned with the continued monitoring and evaluation of the security conditions in our network. We found that it is necessary to implement auditing, regularly review logs, and use the available tools such as those provided through Group Policy to provide the security monitoring that we require. We looked then at the change configuration and analysis methodologies and learned that there are a number of questions that must be asked and adequately answered in order to effectively implement a change management solution. Included in this area were the need to know the *why* of the change, the *what* of the change, and the *how* of the change in order to appropriately work with the change management process. After we examined the change management process, we began to explore the various methods we could use to implement the changes we discovered were needed. These included the ability to use tools to analyze the conditions, such as the Microsoft Baseline Security Analyzer and HFNetChk. Additionally, we worked with Windows Update, Windows Update Services (SUS), and the Windows Catalog site to increase our understanding of how the patches, updates, and configurations can be implemented through automatic processes.

Exam Objectives Fast Track

Understanding Server Roles

☑ Server roles are now closely defined by the function that the server will fulfill.

☑ Server roles include tightened security settings out of the box that allow for better configuration and control of access and less vulnerability.

☑ New server roles in Windows Server 2003 versions include application server, mail server, and streaming media server as new capabilities in the platform.

Configuring Server Roles

☑ Server roles may be configured through a new MMC console, Managing Your Server, which provides a new wizard interface to assist you.

☑ Server roles may also be configured using Add/Remove Programs | Add Windows Components. The administrator would be wise to investigate the changes that have been made from previous version configuration defaults.

☑ A major change that has come with Windows Server 2003 is that IIS 6.0 is not installed by default with the exception of Web Server Edition.

Securing Servers by Roles

☑ All Windows Server 2003 platforms are installed with a base security on clean install that is reasonably secure.

☑ Upgrade installs retain their former levels of security, which might be lower than desired in a Windows Server 2003 environment.

- ☑ Each role has additional requirements for security. Servers providing network services, such as DNS, DHCP, WINS, and mail, all require additional configurations for security after they are created.
- ☑ Domain controllers require extra diligence and care to adequately secure their role. Physical security of the machine is of paramount importance.

Securing Data Transmission

- ☑ Network data diversion and interception are not confined to external attacks.
- ☑ Use of encryption technologies and protection of data on the network are configurable and should be used.
- ☑ IPSec and IPSec policy use and planning are encouraged for protection of data on the network.

Implementing and Maintaining Security

- ☑ Security planning and evaluation are necessary components of every network operation today.
- ☑ Monitoring security involves the use of numerous processes, including auditing, evaluation of log files, evaluation of Event Viewer logs, and use of tools appropriate to the area being evaluated, such as IPSec Monitor to evaluate the effectiveness of IP security policies.
- ☑ Group Policy development and creation can be an effective tool for creation of secure environments when you're working with Windows Server 2003 domains.
- ☑ Change management and configuration duties have become part of the skill set that the network administrator must develop.

Updating the Infrastructure

- ☑ Infrastructure updates are a necessary part of maintaining a secure network operation.
- ☑ Individual machines may be updated through the use of Windows Update, provided as an online service by Microsoft.
- ☑ Patch installation and verification can be achieved by the use of the Microsoft Baseline Security Analyzer and complemented by the scriptable HFNetChk tool that is available with MSBA.
- ☑ Updating within the infrastructure (your LAN/WAN environment) is possible through the use of the Software Update Services.

Exam Objectives Frequently Asked Questions

The following Frequently Asked Questions, answered by the authors of this book, are designed to both measure your understanding of the Exam Objectives presented in this chapter, and to assist you with real-life implementation of these concepts. You will also gain access to thousands of other FAQs at ITFAQnet.com.

Q: It seems very complicated to remember all the different roles that are now available. Why are there so many different configurations?

A: It is a bit different when you've worked with default configurations that included many functions that you didn't need. The roles allow you to more closely match the equipment to the needs of your operation.

Q: How can I restore or create the base security settings for the platform if I've performed an upgrade installation?

A: You can import the template setup security.inf in the Security Configuration and Analysis snap-in. Be sure to run a comparative analysis after these processes to be certain that old values have been removed.

Q: Where can I learn more about the configuration of IPSec and how it should be used?

A: Microsoft has an excellent discussion of this topic on the TechNet site. Explore the Windows Server 2003 section and you'll find a wealth of information to help you better understand IPSec.

Q: Why would you change the base security level for Terminal Services encryption on the RDP Settings tab?

A: Depending on your needs, it might be desirable to enhance the security of the transmission channel by raising the level of encryption. This would be particularly true if any part of the connectivity was through an untrusted network, such as the Internet.

Q: When a security template is applied, does it always erase all the previous settings?

A: No. That is why it is important to perform an analysis after applying the template to ensure that the settings have been modified to your specification. Specifically, some settings that are not modified in the template being applied will be left intact and could lead to problems if undetected.

Self Test

A Quick Answer Key follows the Self Test questions. For complete questions, answers, and explanations to the Self Test questions in this chapter as well as the other chapters in this book, see the Self Test Appendix.

1. Your network environment contains file servers that were upgraded from Windows NT 4.0 and Windows 2000 platforms. You have been directed to secure the file servers at a level that would be consistent with the security level provided by a clean install of Windows Server 2003. What template could you import and apply to provide that level of security?

   A. compatws.inf

   B. basicsrv.inf

   C. setup security.inf

   D. basicws.inf

2. Bob in your finance department has requested that a policy be enforced requiring secure communication between a Windows 2000 Professional workstation and a Windows Server 2003 machine that contains confidential data. You have implemented the policy and have not yet established connection between the machines. When you test network connectivity through the use of the *PING* command from the workstation, you find that numerous messages are displayed, that read *negotiating IP security,* but *ping* response messages are not displayed. What could cause this condition? (Choose the *best* answer.)

   A. The IP configuration information is incorrect on one of the machines.

   B. The network is not functional, so communication cannot be established.

   C. The IP security policies on the two machines do not match.

   D. The certificate used for the policy is not valid.

3. You must set the security for the SMTP service on a newly installed Windows Server 2003 machine configured with the mail server role and ensure that mail relaying is not allowed from your server. Where do you find the appropriate tool to accomplish this setting?

   A. Control Panel | Services | SMTP service

   B. Administrative Tools | Services | SMTP service

   C. Administrative Tools | Internet Information Services (IS) Manager | Default Virtual SMTP server | Access tab

   D. Administrative Tools | POP3 Service Manager | Relay tab

4. When you configured your Windows Server 2003 machine as a Web server, you found that the ASPs that had been written could not be served from the server. What must you do to allow the ASP content to be delivered?

   A. Use the IISAdmin IS) Manager | Default Web site | Properties | Content tab to configure the site for use of ASPs.

   B. Use the IISAdmin IS) Manager | Default Web site | Properties | Applications tab to configure the site for use of ASPs.

   C. Use the IISAdmin IS) Manager | *<computer name>* | Web Sites to configure the site for use of ASP content.

   D. Use the IISAdmin IS) Manager | *<computer name>* | Web Service Extensions to configure the site for use of ASPs.

5. You have created a Terminal Services server and have left the configuration in the default state. What additional configuration steps should you take to ensure that the configuration is as secure as possible? (Choose all that apply.)

   A. You should use a RADIUS server for authentication of the clients accessing the terminal server.

   B. You should raise the encryption level of the RDP connections on the server.

   C. You should create new Remote Access Policies and put them in place on the server.

   D. You should add users and groups to the Remote Desktop Users group to allow them access.

6. Your security log contains 100 sequential messages, as shown in the accompanying figure. This is followed by a success audit for the username. What is this most likely to indicate about your server's security? (Choose all that apply.)

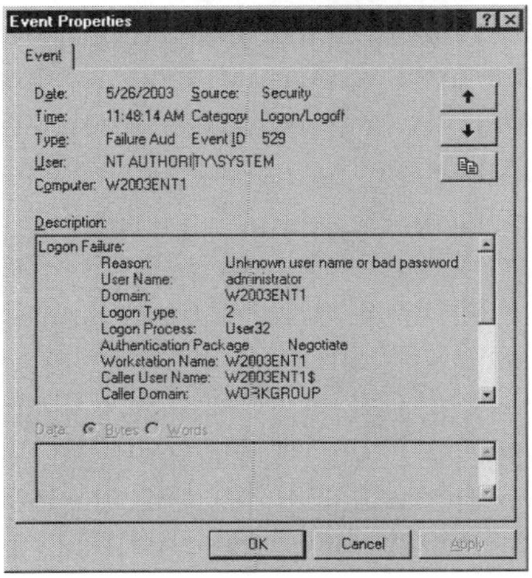

A. The server's security is adequate. The administrator often can't remember the password.

B. The server is most likely compromised. The successful logon after the high number of failed attempts is indicative of the success of a password-cracking attempt.

C. The server's security policy regarding lockout of accounts for failed logon attempts is inadequate.

D. The server's overall security is inadequate because a successful logon using the administrator account was made, and the administrator account should have been renamed before being used in production.

7. You are planning to use HFNetChk in a scripted function to analyze and check the condition of patches and hotfixes on all machines in the domain that can be examined. Pick the correct syntax from the following choices to accomplish this task and output the results as a tab-delimited file named *test_scan1.txt* for a domain named *testdomain* that includes notes about the various patches and hotfixes detected or not detected.

A. *hfnetchk –v –d testdomain –op tab –f test_scan1.txt*

B. *mbsacli /hf –d testdomain –o tab –f test_scan1.txt*

C. *hfnetchk –v –n testdomain –od tab –fip test_scan1.txt*

D. *mbsacli /hf –v –d testdomain –o tab –f test_scan1.txt*

8. You are being sent on a trip to visit various branch offices that are connected to your main corporate site by 56K Frame Relay links, which carry all network traffic and provide Internet access to the branch offices. Each of the branch offices has approximately 10 workstation machines in a mix of Win9*x*, Windows 2000, and Windows XP workstations, and they have not been updated with required security patches in some time. You have only a limited amount of time to perform the updates while at the sites and must pick the most efficient method to deploy the patches when you arrive. Which of the following methods would you choose to accomplish this goal?

A. Software Update Services

B. Windows Update

C. Windows Catalog

D. Group Policy

9. You have developed a customized security template that you want to deploy to all member servers within the domain in a uniform fashion while not affecting the DC servers in the domain. To accomplish this goal, which of the following methods would be appropriate and the *best* choice for this task?

A. Software Update Services

B. Security Configuration and Analysis snap-in for MMC

C. Group Policy

D. Systems Management Server

10. What would be the most appropriate method of distributing software updates, security patches, and hotfixes in a mixed-client Windows environment? (Choose all that apply.)

    A. Windows Update

    B. Software Update Services

    C. Group Policy deployment

    D. Windows Catalog

11. You have a business client that operates a small network consisting of five Windows XP Professional workstations and two Windows Server 2003 servers configured in a workgroup environment. The client wants to secure communication between his workstation and one of the servers, and he also wants to protect some of the data on the servers from some of the users but allow access to the data by the client and one business partner. Which of the following steps would you recommend for this client to provide the level of protection desired?

    A. Deliver EFS policy through the application of Group Policy, which will allow the partners to access the data but protect it from other users. Protect the traffic between the client workstation and the desired server through application of security policy from Group Policy.

    B. Create an EFS policy locally on the member server. Install a certificate for each user who is to access the EFS-protected resources. Protect the traffic between the two desired machines through the creation of matching IPSec policies with a shared key configuration.

    C. Select the "Encrypt Folder to Protect Contents" check box in the Advanced tab of the folder's Properties page. Install security certificates on the local machine for each user who is to be granted access to the secured folder. Add the allowed users to the Security page of the desired resource. Protect the traffic between the two desired machines through the creation of matching IPSec policies with a shared key configuration.

    D. Create an EFS policy locally on the member server. Protect the traffic between the client workstation and the desired server through application of security policy from Group Policy.

12. You have been tasked with performing a change and configuration analysis for your organization. It has been recommended that this process begin with an analysis that creates a configuration benchmark to compare with in future times. What tools should be part of your toolkit for creating this benchmark analysis? (Choose all that apply.)

    A. Performance Monitor

    B. Network Monitor

    C. Microsoft Baseline Security Analyzer

    D. Windows Download Service

13. Look at the accompanying figure. What level of encryption would you recommend for use in a network utilizing network resources that participate in operations requiring the standards required by government security rules?

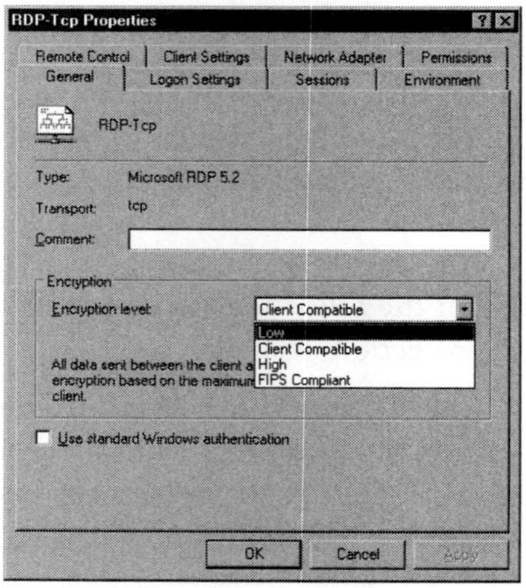

    A. Low

    B. Client compatible

    C. High

    D. FIPS compliant

14. You have been asked to perform a quick single-machine scan for security hotfixes utilizing the command-line function of the Microsoft Baseline Security Analyzer. Of the following, which command would quickly accomplish this task?

    A. mbsalcli.exe /*computername*

    B. mbsacli.exe

    C. mbsacli.exe -d -n

    D. mbsacli.exe /hf

15. In the accompanying diagram, what is the selected template used for? (Choose all that apply.)

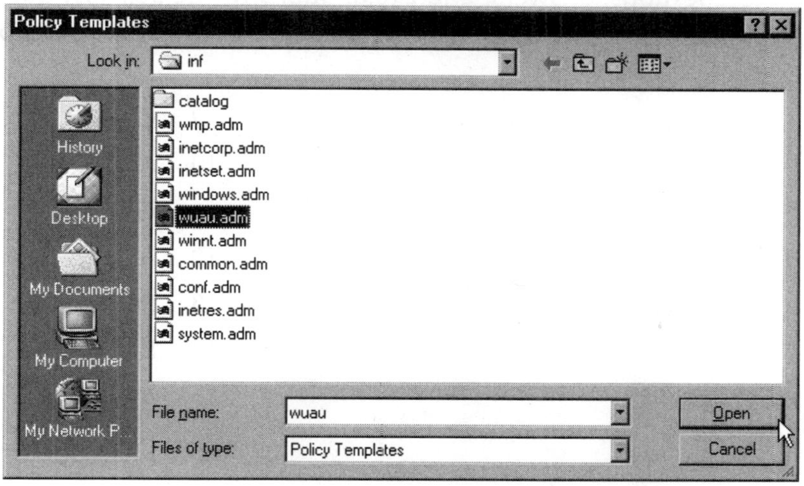

A. Security configuration and analysis

B. Group Policy configuration

C. Windows Update Services automatic update client configuration

D. Automatic Update configuration

Self Test Quick Answer Key

For complete questions, answers, and explanations to the Self Test questions in this chapter as well as the other chapters in this book, see the Self Test Appendix.

1. **C**
2. **C**
3. **C**
4. **D**
5. **B, D**
6. **B, C, D**
7. **D**
8. **C**
9. **C**
10. **A, D**
11. **C**
12. **A, B, C**
13. **D**
14. **B**
15. **B, C**

Chapter 9

MCSA/MCSE 70-296

Planning Security for a Wireless Network

Exam Objectives in this Chapter:

4.2 Plan security for wireless networks.

- ☑ Summary of Exam Objectives
- ☑ Exam Objectives Fast Track
- ☑ Exam Objectives Frequently Asked Questions
- ☑ Self Test
- ☑ Self Test Quick Answer Key

Introduction

Over the past several years, wireless technologies have become more popular as the prices associated with wireless solutions have dramatically decreased. Many companies rely on wireless technologies to give them the freedom they need to become "mobile" within their new environments. As the speed and capabilities of wireless technologies increase and the cost decreases, wireless will in some cases completely replace wired technologies.

In Windows Server 2003, wireless technologies will play a large part in how you manage your network environment. In order to properly manage a wireless environment, you need to familiarize yourself with the technologies available to wireless users, the risks associated with wireless, how to secure a wireless connection, and how to properly configure Windows for use with wireless connectivity. In Windows Server 2003, Microsoft has added several tools and configuration options to make it easier to add a wireless network to your environment.

In this chapter, we begin with a discussion of general wireless concepts. We cover topics such as how wireless works, what a typical wireless architecture might look like, and the protocols and standards associated with wireless technologies. As you have seen throughout this book thus far, security has become a major focal point for Microsoft and its development of the Windows Server 2003 operating system. For that reason, it is important to understand the vulnerabilities and exploits that exist in a wireless environment and what you can do to prevent them from occurring.

Lastly, you will learn how to plan for, configure, and implement wireless technologies in your environment. This chapter lays the groundwork for deciding on the best configuration for Windows for your wireless environment, best practices for implementation, and what you need to know to secure and monitor your wireless network once it is in place.

Wireless Concepts

Wireless local area networks (WLANs) are based on the IEEE 802.11 specification. IEEE 802.11 is not the only wireless networking technology available, but it is certainly the most popular and must be understood in order to gain a solid background for working with wireless networking using recent versions of Windows: Windows 2000 Professional, Server, and Advanced Server; Windows XP Home and Professional; and most important, Windows Server 2003.

The process of connecting to a wireless network is often transparent to users and, from their perspective, is no different from connecting to a copper- or fiber-based Ethernet network, with the exception that no wires are involved. With Windows XP and Windows Server 2003, which boast automatic configuration and seamless roaming from one wireless network to another, the ease with which users can connect to wireless networks further belies the complexity of the technology involved and differences between wired and wireless networks.

Furthermore, because the experience of using a wireless network is identical to that of using a wired Ethernet network, there is a tendency to treat both kinds of networks as though they were the same; however, they are quite different from one another, and an understanding of those differences is critical to providing an informed and effective implementation of a secure wireless network.

Communication in a Wireless Network

Wireless networks, like their wired counterparts, rely on the manipulation of electrical charges to enable communication between devices. Changes or oscillations in signal strength from 0 to a maximum value (*amplitude*) and the rate of those oscillations (*frequency*) allow the encoding and decoding of information.

When two devices understand the method(s) used to encode and decode information contained in the changes to the electrical properties of the communications medium, they can communicate with each other. A network adapter is able to decode the changes in the electrical current it senses on the wire and convert them to meaningful information (bits) that it can subsequently send to higher levels for processing. Likewise, a network adaptor can encode information (bits) by manipulating the properties of the electrical current for transmission on the communications medium (the cable, in the case of wired networks).

Radio Frequency Communications

The obvious and primary difference between wired and wireless networks is that wireless networks use radio waves to transmit their data across an intermediate medium, instead of pushing electrons through a wired connection. Radio waves are created by applying *alternating current (AC)* to an antenna to produce an *electromagnetic (EM)* field. Devices use the resulting *radio frequency (RF)* field for broadcast and reception.

In the case of wireless networks, the medium for communications is the EM *field*, the region of space that is influenced by the electromagnetic radiation. (Unlike audio waves, radio waves do not require a medium such as air or water to propagate.) As with wired networks, amplitude decreases with distance, resulting in the degradation of signal strength and the ability to communicate. However, the EM field is also dispersed according to the properties of the transmitting antenna, not tightly bound, as is the case with communication on a wire. The area over which the radio waves propagate from an electromagnetic source is known as the *Fresnel zone*.

Like the waves created by throwing a rock into a pool of water, radio waves are affected by the presence of obstructions and can be reflected, refracted, diffracted, or scattered, depending on the properties of the obstruction and its interaction with the radio waves. Reflected radio waves can be a source of interference on wireless networks. The interference created by bounced radio waves is called *multipath interference*.

When radio waves are reflected, additional wave fronts are created. These different wave fronts can arrive at the receiver at different times and be in phase or out of phase with the main signal. When the peak of a wave is added to another wave (*in phase*), the wave is amplified. When the peak of a wave meets a trough (*out of phase*), the wave is effectively cancelled.

Multipath interference can be the source of problems that are difficult to troubleshoot. In planning for a wireless network, administrators should consider the presence of common sources of multipath interference. These sources include metal doors, metal roofs, water, metal vertical blinds, or any other source that is highly reflective of radio waves. Antennas could help compensate for the effects of multipath interference, but these have to be carefully chosen. In fact, many wireless access points (APs) have two antennas for precisely this purpose because a single omnidirectional antenna might not be of any use in curbing this kind of interference.

Another source of signal loss is the presence of obstacles. Whereas radio waves can travel through physical objects, they will be degraded according to the properties of the object they travel through. A window, for example, is fairly transparent to radio waves, but it could reduce the effective range of a wireless network between 50 and 70 percent, depending on the presence and nature of coatings on the glass. A solid core wall can reduce the effective range of a wireless network up to 90 percent or greater.

EM fields are also prone to interference and signal degradation by the presence of other EM fields. In particular, 802.11 wireless networks are prone to the interference produced by cordless phones, microwave ovens, and a wide range of devices that use the same unlicensed Industrial, Scientific, and Medical (ISM) or Unlicensed National Information Infrastructure (UNII) bands.

To mitigate the effects of interference from these devices and other sources of electromagnetic interference, RF-based wireless networks employ *spread-spectrum technologies*. Spread-spectrum provides a way to "share" bandwidth with other devices that are operating in the same frequency range. Rather than operating on a single, dedicated frequency, as is the case with radio and television broadcasts, wireless networks use a "spectrum" of frequencies for communication.

Spread-Spectrum Technology

The concept of spread-spectrum communication was first conceived by Hollywood actress Hedy Lamarr and composer George Antheil in 1940 as a method to secure military communications from jamming and eavesdropping during World War II. Spread-spectrum defines methods for wireless devices to simultaneously use a number of narrowband frequencies over a range of frequencies for communication.

The narrowband frequencies used between devices change according to a random-appearing but defined pattern, allowing the use of individual frequencies to contain parts of the transmission. Someone listening to a transmission using spread-spectrum would hear only noise, unless their device "understood" in advance what frequencies were used for the transmission and could synchronize with them.

Two methods to synchronize wireless devices are:

- Frequency-hopping spread-spectrum (FHSS)
- Direct-sequence spread-spectrum (DSSS)

Frequency-Hopping Spread-Spectrum

As the name implies, FHSS works by quickly moving from one frequency to another according to a pseudorandom pattern. The frequency range used by the frequency hop is relatively large (83.5MHz), providing excellent protection from interference. The amount of time spent on any given frequency is known as *dwell time*; the amount of time it takes to move from one frequency to another is known as *hop time*. FHSS devices begin their transmission on one frequency and move to other frequencies according to the predefined pseudorandom sequence and then repeat the sequence after reaching the final frequency in the pattern. Hop time is usually very short (200 to 300?s) and not significant relative to the dwell time (100 to 200ms).

The frequency-hopping sequence creates the channel, allowing multiple channels to coexist in the same frequency range without interfering with one another. Up to 79 FCC-compliant FHSS devices using the 2.4GHz ISM band may be colocated with each other. The expense of implementing such a large number of systems, however, limits the practical number of colocated devices to well below this number. FHSS is less subject to EM interference than DSSS but usually operates at lower rates of data transmission (typically 1.6Mbps but possibly as high as 10Mbps) than networks that use DSSS.

Direct-Sequence Spread-Spectrum

DSSS works somewhat differently from FHSS. With DSSS, the data is divided and simultaneously transmitted on as many frequencies as possible within a particular frequency band (the channel). DSSS adds redundant bits of data known as *chips* to the data to represent binary 0s or 1s. The ratio of chips to data is known as the *spreading ratio*. As the ratio increases, the signal becomes more immune to interference, because if part of the transmission is corrupted, the data can still be recovered from the remaining part of the chipping code. This method provides greater rates of transmission than FHSS, which uses a limited number of frequencies but fewer channels in a given frequency range. In addition, it also protects against data loss through the redundant, simultaneous transmission of data.

However, because DSSS floods the channel it is using, it is also more vulnerable to interference from EM devices operating in the same range. In the 2.4GHz to 2.4835GHz frequency range employed by 802.11b, DSSS transmissions can be broadcast in any one of 14 22MHz-wide channels. The number of center-channel frequencies used by 802.11 DSSS devices depends on the country. For example, North America allows 11 channels operating in the 2.4GHz to 2.4835GHz range, Europe allows 13, and Japan allows 1. Because each channel is 22MHz wide, channels may overlap each other. With the 11 available channels available in North America, only a maximum of three channels (1, 6, and 11) may be used concurrently without the use of overlapping frequencies.

How Wireless Works

The 802.11 standard provides two modes for wireless clients to communicate: Ad Hoc and Infrastructure. The Ad Hoc mode is geared toward an unstructured network of wireless clients within communication range of each other. Ad Hoc networks are created spontaneously between the network participants, resulting in a fully meshed network. In Infrastructure mode, APs provide for a more permanent structure for the network. An *infrastructure* consists of one or more APs as well as a distribution system (such as a wired network) behind the APs, which tie the wireless network to the wired network. Figures 9.1 and 9.2 demonstrate the two modes, Ad Hoc and Infrastructure.

Figure 9.1 Ad Hoc Network Configuration

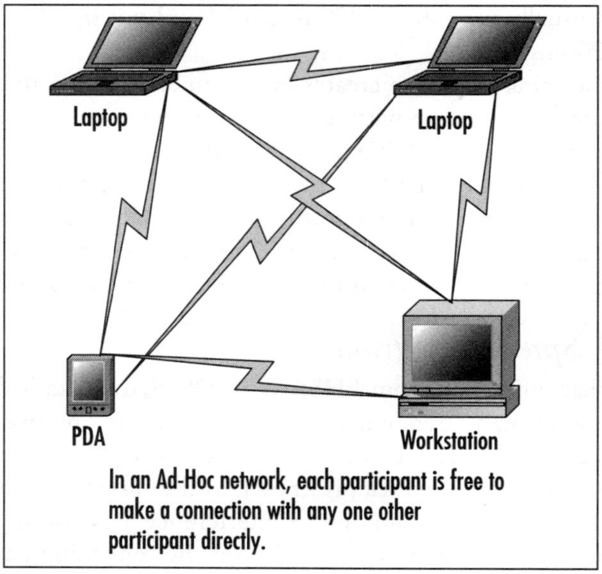

Figure 9.2 Infrastructure Network Configuration

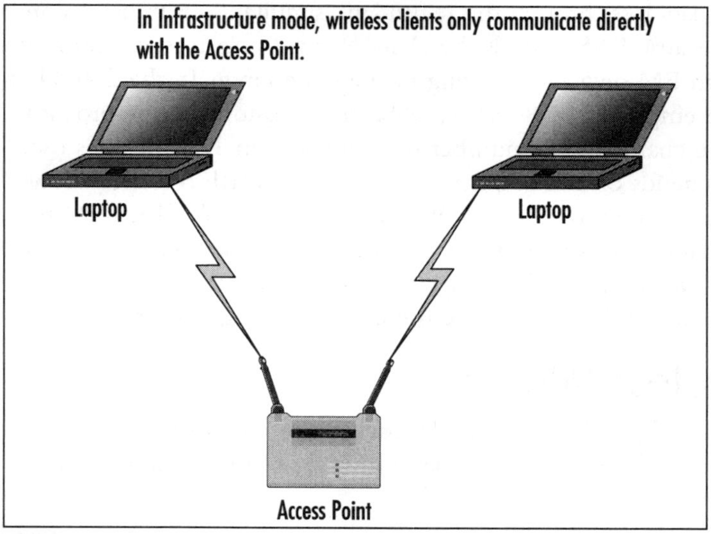

To distinguish different wireless networks from one another, the 802.11 standard defines the Service Set Identifier (SSID). The SSID can be considered the identity element that "glues" together various components of a wireless LAN. Traffic from wireless clients that use one SSID can be distinguished from other wireless traffic using a different SSID. Once the correct network mode has been configured on the wireless client, an AP can determine which traffic is meant for it and which is meant for other wireless networks by using the SSID.

The 802.11 traffic can be subdivided into three parts:

- **Control frames** Control frames include such information as request to send (RTS), clear to send (CTS), and acknowledgement (ACK) messages.
- **Management frames** Management frames include beacon frames, probe request/response, authentication frames, and association frames.
- **Data frames** Data frames are, as the name implies, 802.11 frames that carry data. That data is typically considered network traffic, such as IP encapsulated frames.

These three types of frames can be mapped to different layers within the Open Systems Interconnect (OSI) networking model, which are described in the next section.

Exercise 9.01

Configuring the Network Mode

By default, wireless connections in Windows Server 2003 are set to Infrastructure mode. Exercise 9.01 guides you through the process of changing the network mode from Infrastructure to Ad Hoc. Although this might not be common practice in the real world, it will expose you to the various configuration settings for wireless networking. To change the network mode for an available network:

1. Click **Start | Control Panel | Network Connections**.
2. Double-click the desired Wireless Connection.
3. Click the **Advanced** button.
4. Select the **Wireless Networks** tab.
5. Ensure that **Use Windows to configure my wireless network settings** is checked.
6. Select an SSID from the list of available networks to highlight it.
7. Click the **Configure** button.
8. On the **Association** tab, select **This is a computer-to-computer (ad hoc) network; wireless access points are not used**.
9. Click **OK** twice to accept the changes.

To change the default network mode for all available networks:

1. Click **Start | Control Panel | Network Connections**.
2. Double-click the desired Wireless Connection.
3. In the Wireless Connection window, click the **Advanced** button.
4. In the Wireless Connection Properties window, click the **Advanced** button.
5. Select the **Computer-to-Computer networks only** radio button in the "Networks to access" section.
6. Click **Close** in the Advanced window to accept the changes.
7. Click **OK** in the Wireless Connection Properties window to accept the changes.

Wireless Network Architecture

The Open Systems Interconnect (OSI) Reference Model was developed by the International Standards Organization (ISO). It consists of seven layers that constitute the framework for implementing network protocols. Wireless networks operate at Levels 1 and 2, the Physical and Data Link layers of the OSI model, respectively. The Physical layer is concerned with the physical connections between devices, such as how the medium and low bits (0s and 1s) are encoded and decoded. Both FHSS and DSSS, for example, are implemented at the Physical layer. The Data Link layer is divided into two sublayers: the Media Access Control (MAC) and Logical Link Control (LLC) layers.

The MAC layer is responsible for such things as:

- Framing data
- Error control
- Synchronization
- Collision detection and avoidance

The Ethernet 802.3 standard, which defines the Carrier Sense Multiple Access with Collision Detection (CSMA/CD) method for protecting against data loss as result of data collisions on the cable, is defined at this layer.

TEST DAY TIP

Wireless network security in Windows will be tested on the exam. This whole section on the explanation of wireless, how it works, and what you can do with it is strictly background information to further your understanding of the technology and your education. Exam questions will not be based on FHSS and DSSS technologies, so if this information seems overly technical, do not panic!

However, it is important that you, as a security administrator, know this information. It serves no purpose to pass an exam but not understand the underlying technology. It is our mission to teach you and help you make the transition from the exam to the real world of security analysts who know all the underpinnings of, for example, wireless technologies, so that when you walk into your next position—or stay in the one you have now—you will become a powerhouse of security-related information.

CSMA/CD and CSMA/CA

In contrast to Ethernet 802.3 networks, wireless networks defined by the 802.11 standard do not use CSMA/CD as a method to protect against data loss resulting from collisions. Instead, 802.11 networks use a method known as Carrier Sense Multiple Access with Collision Avoidance (CSMA/CA). CSMA/CD works by detecting whether a collision has occurred on the network and then retransmitting the data in the event of such an occurrence. However, this method is not practical for wireless networks because CSMA/CD relies on the fact that every workstation can hear all the other workstations on the cable segment to determine if there is a collision.

In a wireless network, usually only the AP can hear every workstation that is communicating with it. (For example, both Workstations A and B might be able to communicate with the same AP, but they might be too far apart from each other to hear their respective transmissions.) Additionally, wireless networks do not use full-duplex communication, which is another way to protect data against corruption and loss as a result of collisions. Full-duplex communication occurs when a device is capable of transmitting and receiving simultaneously. Wireless networks work at half duplex, where devices can only transmit or receive at a given time.

CSMA/CA solves the problem of potential collisions on the wireless network by taking a more active approach than CSMA/CD, which kicks in only after a collision has been detected. Using CSMA/CA, a wireless workstation first tries to detect if any other device is communicating on the network. If it senses it is clear to send, it initiates communication. The receiving device sends an ACK packet to the transmitting device, indicating successful reception. If the transmitting device does not receive an ACK, it assumes a collision has occurred and retransmits the data. It should be noted that many collisions could occur and that these collisions can be used to compromise the confidentiality of Wired Equivalent Privacy (WEP) encrypted data—a discussion that we have later in this chapter.

CSMA/CA is only one way in which wireless networks differ from wired networks in their implementation at the MAC layer. For example, the IEEE standard for 802.11 at the MAC layer defines additional functionality, such as virtual collision detection (VCD), roaming, power saving, asynchronous data transfer, and encryption.

The fact that wireless encryption using the WEP protocol is defined at the MAC layer is particularly noteworthy and has significant consequences for the security of wireless networks. This means data at the higher levels of the OSI model, in particular TCP/IP data, is also encrypted. Because many of the TCP/IP communications that occur between hosts contain a large number of frequently repeating and well-known patterns, WEP is more prone to cracking than it would be if implemented in a different fashion, although it does include safeguards against this kind of attack. Later in this chapter we explore in more detail the particular weaknesses of WEP.

EXAM WARNING

Make sure that you completely understand WEP and its vulnerabilities. WEP is discussed in more detail later in this chapter. You will likely be faced with an exam question in which you need to implement WEP.

Wireless Standards

A plethora of wireless standards and subsets of wireless standards are in various states of adoption around the globe. All of them have one basic characteristic in common: They are intended for transferring data over a wireless medium (beam of light, radio wave) to a mobile device. The similarity, however, ends there. Different standards are more or less applicable to different devices, depending on the purposes for which the device was designed. The four most prevalent wireless standards that could be used for wireless IP-based connectivity are:

- Wi-Fi (WLAN or IEE 802.11)
- Infrared (IrDA)
- Bluetooth
- 3G

EXAM WARNING

The exam will not cover networking with infrared, Bluetooth, or 3G. You can expect that all questions on wireless security will pertain to wireless networks that use one of the 802.11 standards.

IEEE 802.11 is the family of wireless standards for connectivity between a client with a wireless LAN adapter and an AP and among wireless clients. The 802.11 standards are comparable to the IEEE 802.3 standard for wired Ethernet networks. This family of standards (802.11a, 802.11b, and 802.11g) is the focus of Windows networking with Windows Server 2003 and is described in detail in the next section, "Windows Wireless Standards."

Windows Server 2003 has built-in support for the Infrared Data Association (IrDA) protocol, which, confusingly enough, is administered by an association of the same name, IrDA. The IrDA protocol is intended for high-speed, short range, line-of-sight, point-to-point cordless data transfer, suitable for high-performance computers, digital cameras, hand-held data collection devices, and so forth. IrDA Control is most commonly used for in-room cordless peripherals that connect to host PCs at low speeds, such as cordless mice and keyboards and synchronizing a personal digital assistant (PDA) with a laptop. The typical range: for continuous data transfer is at least 1 meter; but 2 meters is possible. IrDA is supported by the operating system, but very few, if any, server hardware components come equipped with infrared subcomponents or even with an option to install them. With respect to security, the IrDA standards do not specify any security measures for data transfer; any security for data transfer depends solely on the functionality within applications at each end of the infrared connection.

Bluetooth (www.bluetooth.org) is a short-distance wireless technology designed for low-cost, low-power consumption. Bluetooth is a way to eliminate cables between devices, such as mobile phones, PDAs, digital cameras, and even printers. The Bluetooth specification is an open specification governed by the Bluetooth Special Interest Group (SIG), which is composed of the five founding companies (Ericsson, IBM, Intel, Nokia, and Toshiba) and four new member companies (3Com, Lucent, Microsoft, and Motorola) that were added in 1999. Since Microsoft is one of the newest members, we can probably expect to see more from that company dealing with this emerging technology in the future.

3G (www.fcc.gov/3G) is a generic term that describes a range of emerging wireless network technologies that include W-CDMA, CDMA-2000, TD-CDMA, GPRS, and EDGE. 3G combines high-speed mobile access with IP-based services and will focus on mobile phone technology. 3G enables users to transmit voice, data, and video by improving the data transmission speed up to 144Kbps when moving at high speed, 384Kbps at lower speeds, and 2Mbps when stationary. 3G is being used in Japan and most of Europe because these regions have the high concentrations of antennae required for effective 3G coverage. 3G is proving to be more difficult to deploy in North America, because the population is much more widely dispersed over a larger geographical area.

Windows Wireless Standards

WLANs are covered by the IEEE 802.11 standards. The purpose of these standards is to provide a wireless equivalent to IEEE 802.3 Ethernet-based networks. The IEEE 802.3 standard defines a method for dealing with collisions (CSMA/CD), speeds of operation (10Mbps, 100Mbps, and faster), and cabling types (Category 5 twisted pair and fiber). The standard ensures the interoperability of various devices, despite different speeds and cabling types.

As with the 802.3 standard, the 802.11 standard defines methods for dealing with collisions and speeds of operation. However, because of the differences in the media (air as opposed to wires), the devices used, the potential mobility of users connected to the network, and the possible wireless network topologies, the 802.11 standards differ significantly from the 802.3 standard.

In addition to providing a solution to the problems created by collisions that occur on a wireless network, the 802.11 standard must deal with other issues specific to the nature of wireless devices and wireless communications in general. For example, wireless devices need to be able to locate other wireless devices, such as APs, and be able to communicate with them. Wireless users are, more often than not, mobile and therefore should be able to move seamlessly from one wireless zone to another as required. Many wireless-enabled devices, such as laptops and handheld computers, use battery power and should be able to conserve power when they are not actively communicating with the network. Wireless communication over the air needs to be secure to mitigate both passive and active attacks.

The original 802.11 standard was developed in 1989 and defines the operation of wireless networks operating in the 2.4GHz range using either DSSS or FHSS at the Physical layer of the OSI model. The standard also defines the use of infrared for wireless communication. The intent of the standard is to provide a wireless equivalent for standards, such as 802.3, that are used for wired networks. DSSS devices that follow the 802.11 standard communicate at speeds of 1Mbps and 2Mbps and generally have a range of around 300 feet. Because of the need for higher rates of data transmission and the need to provide more functionality at the MAC layer, other standards were developed by the 802.11 Task Groups (or in some cases, the 802.11 standards were developed from technologies that preceded them).

The IEEE 802.11 standard provides for all the necessary definitions and constructs for wireless networks. The standard defines everything from the physical transmission specifications to the authentication negotiation. Wireless traffic, like its wired counterpart, consists of frames transmitted from one station to another. The primary feature that sets wireless networks apart from wired networks is that at least one end of the communication pair is either a wireless client or a wireless AP.

IEEE 802.11b

The most common standard in use today for wireless networks, the 802.11b standard, defines DSSS networks that use the 2.4GHz ISM band and communicate at speeds of 1, 2, 5.5, and 11Mbps. The 802.11b standard defines the operation of *only* DSSS devices and is backward compatible with 802.11 DSSS devices. The standard is also concerned only with the Physical and MAC layers. Layer 3 and higher protocols are considered payload.

802.11b networks use three frame types: control, management, and data. Each frame has a distinct function on the wireless network and is put together differently. One thing all 802.11b frames share is the maximum size of 2,346 bytes, although they are often fragmented at 1,518 bytes as they traverse an AP to communicate with Ethernet networks.

In general, the frame type provides methods for wireless devices to discover, associate (or disassociate), and authenticate with one another; to shift data rates as signals become stronger or weaker; to conserve power by going into sleep mode; to handle collisions and fragmentation; and to enable encryption through WEP. With regard to WEP, we should note that the standard defines the use of only 64-bit (also sometimes referred to as 40-bit, to add to the confusion) encryption, which can cause issues of interoperability between devices from different vendors that use 128-bit or higher encryption.

IEEE 802.11a

Contrary to its nomenclature, 802.11a is a more recent standard than 802.11b. The standard defines wireless networks that use the 5GHz UNII bands. The 802.11a standard supports much higher rates of data transmission than 802.11b. These rates are 6, 9, 12, 16, 18, 24, 36, 48, and 54Mbps, although higher rates are possible using proprietary technology and a technique known as *rate doubling*.

Unlike 802.11b, 802.11a does not use spread-spectrum and Distributed Quadrature Phase Shift Keying (DQPSK) as a modulation technique at the physical layer; instead, it uses a modulation technique known as Orthogonal Frequency Division Multiplexing (OFDM).

To be 802.11a compliant, devices are only required to support data rates of at least 6, 12, and 24Mbps; the standard does not require the use of other data rates. Although identical to 802.11b at the MAC layer, 802.11a is *not* backward compatible with 802.11b due to its use of a different frequency band and the use of OFDM at the Physical layer, although some vendors are providing solutions to bridge the two standards at the AP.

However, both 802.11a and 802.11b devices can be easily colocated because their frequencies do not interfere with each other, providing a technically easy but relatively expensive migration to a pure 802.11a network. At the time of this writing, 802.11a-compliant devices are becoming more common, and their prices are falling quickly. However, even if the prices for 802.11b and 802.11a devices were identical, 802.11a would require more APs and be more expensive than an 802.11b network to achieve the highest possible rates of data transmission, because higher-frequency 5GHz waves attenuate more quickly over distance.

IEEE 802.11g

In order to provide both higher data rates (up to 54Mbps) in the ISM 2.4GHz bands and backward compatibility with 802.11b, the IEEE 802.11g Task Group members, along with wireless vendors, have recently completed working on the specifications of the 802.11g standard. On June 12, 2003, the IEEE officially ratified 802.11g, although manufacturers have been releasing 802.11g products based on the draft standard for quite some time. For those who purchased products before ratification, most manufacturers will make a firmware update available to upgrade their devices to the latest specification.

To achieve the higher rates of transmission, 802.11g devices use OFDM, in contrast to DQPSK, which is used by 802.11b devices as a modulation technique; however, 802.11g devices are able to automatically switch to DQPSK to communicate with 802.11b devices. The 802.11g standard has the advantage over 802.11a in terms of providing backward compatibility with 802.11b; however, migrating to and coexistence with 802.11b might still prove problematic due to interference in the widely used 2.4GHz band.

Exam Warning

You will not be tested on the content in the following section during your exam. It has been included for your information only.

IEE 802.20

Although it still has a long, bumpy way to go before it is accepted as a standard, IEEE 802.20 could significantly change the landscape for wireless networking. The 802.20 specification marries the increasing speeds of 802.11 networks with the range of 3G. It is intended to support transmission speeds of over 1Mbps for wireless clients traveling up to 250kmph, such as passengers on a high-speed train. At the time of writing, the standard is far from being accepted, because it is running into competition with the direction of future generations of 3G.

Wireless Vulnerabilities

Some might say that a network is a network, but the precautions that must be taken to secure a wireless network are much different than with a wired network. Theoretically, a malicious individual may attempt to connect to an available network jack or tap into an Ethernet cable to compromise a wired network; however, when this individual can compromise a wireless network merely by standing in range of a wireless network, the effort required on the part of that individual is greatly reduced. This section describes the types of attack that can be used to compromise a wireless network and the vulnerabilities of current wireless security technology.

In general, attacks on wireless networks fall into four basic categories:

- Passive attacks
- Active attacks
- Man-in-the-middle attacks
- Jamming attacks

After we examine each of these attack types, we spend some time examining the problems associated with the current wireless security solutions.

Passive Attacks

A *passive attack* occurs when someone listens to or eavesdrops on network traffic. Armed with a wireless network adapter that supports promiscuous mode, the eavesdropper can capture network traffic for analysis using easily available tools, such as Network Monitor in Microsoft products, tcpdump in Linux-based products, or AirSnort (developed for Linux and Windows).

A passive attack on a wireless network might not be malicious in nature. In fact, many in the war-driving community claim their war-driving activities are benign or "educational" in nature. (*War driving* is the act of searching for wireless networks—via car, by foot, or by other vehicle—by means of a roaming wireless client.) Wireless communication takes place on unlicensed public frequencies, which anyone can use. This makes it more difficult to protect a wireless network from passive attacks. However, by its very definition, a *passive* attack cannot be an attack at all. The supposed *passive attacker* is merely a bystander. The relative *passivity* of the interaction completely changes when there is criminal intent to either capture or change data on a network the user is not explicitly authorized to access. *War chalking* is the practice of documenting the networks found while war driving, and the practice has matured to the point where there are even Visio stencils available for download on the Web.

Passive attacks are, by their very nature, difficult to detect. If an administrator is using DHCP on the wireless network (this is *not* recommended), he or she might notice that an unauthorized MAC address has acquired an IP address in the DHCP server logs. Then again, he or she might not notice that. Perhaps the administrator notices a suspicious-looking car sporting an antenna protruding from one of its windows. If the car is parked on private property, the driver could be asked to move or possibly be charged with trespassing. However, the legal response might be severely limited, depending on the laws in your jurisdiction. The circumstance under which the war driver is susceptible to being charged with a data-related crime depends entirely on the country or state in which the activity takes place.

Passive attacks on wireless networks are extremely common, almost to the point of being ubiquitous. Detecting and reporting on wireless networks has become a popular hobby for many wireless war driving enthusiasts. In fact, this activity is so popular that a new term, *war plugging*, has emerged to describe the behavior of people who actually want to advertise both the availability of an AP and the services they offer by configuring their SSIDs with text such as "Get_food_here!"

War Driving to Discover Wireless Networks

Most war driving enthusiasts use a popular freeware program called NetStumbler (www.netstumbler.com). The NetStumbler program works primarily with wireless network adapters that use the Hermes chipset due to its ability to detect multiple APs within range and WEP, among other features. A list of supported adapters is available at the NetStumbler Web site. The most common card that uses the Hermes chipset for use with NetStumbler is the ORiNOCO gold card. Another advantage of the ORiNOCO card is that it supports the addition of an external antenna, which can extend the range of a wireless network by many orders of magnitude, depending on the antenna.

A disadvantage of the Hermes chipset is that it does not support promiscuous mode, so it cannot be used to sniff network traffic. For that purpose, you need a wireless network adapter that supports the PRISM2 chipset. The majority of wireless network adapters targeted for the consumer market (for example, the Linksys WPC network adapters) use this chipset. Sophisticated war drivers arm themselves with both types of cards—one for discovering wireless networks and the other for capturing the traffic.

In spite of the fact that NetStumbler is free, it is a sophisticated and feature-rich product that is excellent for performing wireless site surveys, for legitimate purposes or otherwise. Not only can it provide detailed information on the wireless networks it detects, it can be used in combination with a global positioning system (GPS) to provide exact details on the latitude and longitude of the detected wireless networks. Figure 9.3 shows the interface of a typical NetStumbler session.

Figure 9.3 Discovering Wireless LANs Using NetStumbler

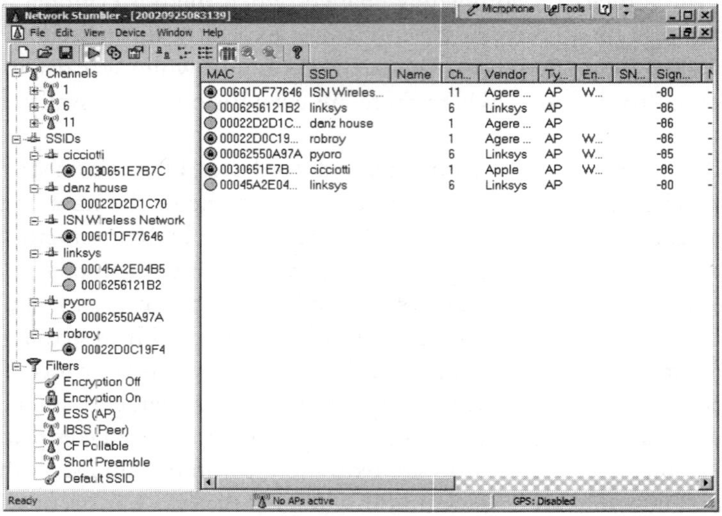

As you can see from Figure 9.3, NetStumbler displays information on the SSID, the channel, and the manufacturer of the wireless AP. A few things about this session are particularly noteworthy. The first is that a couple of APs are still configured with the default SSID supplied by the manufacturer, which should always be changed to a nondefault value on setup and configuration. Another is that at least one network uses an SSID that could provide a clue about the entity that has implemented it; again, this is not a good practice when configuring SSIDs. Finally, we can see which of these networks have implemented WEP.

If the network administrator has been kind enough to provide a clue about the company in the SSID or is not encrypting traffic with WEP, the potential eavesdropper's job is made a great deal easier. Using a tool such as NetStumbler is only a preliminary step for the attacker. After discovering the SSID and other information, the attacker can connect to the wireless network to sniff and capture network traffic. This network traffic can reveal a plethora of information about the network and the company that uses it.

For example, looking at the network traffic, the attacker can determine the DNS servers being used, the default homepages configured on browsers, network names, logon traffic, and so on. The attacker can use this information to determine if the network is of sufficient interest to proceed further with other attacks. Furthermore, if the network is using WEP, the attacker can, given enough time, capture a sufficient amount of traffic to crack the encryption.

NetStumbler works on networks that are configured as *open systems*. This means that the wireless network indicates it exists and will respond with the value of its SSID to other wireless devices when they send out a radio beacon with an "empty set" SSID. This does not mean that the wireless network can be easily compromised, *if* other security measures have been implemented.

To defend against the use of NetStumbler and other programs to easily detect a wireless network, administrators should configure the wireless network as a *closed system*. This means that the AP will not respond to "empty set" SSID beacons and will consequently be "invisible" to programs such as NetStumbler, which rely on this technique to discover wireless networks. However, it is still possible to capture the "raw" 802.11b frames and decode them through the use of programs such as Ethereal and Wild Packet's AiroPeek to determine this information. RF spectrum analyzers can be used to discover the presence of wireless networks. Notwithstanding this weakness of closed systems, you should choose wireless APs that support this feature.

Sniffing

Originally conceived as a legitimate network and traffic analysis tool, *sniffing* remains one of the most effective techniques in attacking a wireless network, whether it's to map the network as part of a target reconnaissance, to grab passwords, or to capture unencrypted data.

Sniffing is the electronic form of eavesdropping on the communications that computers transmit across networks. In early networks, the equipment that connected machines allowed every machine on the network to see the traffic of all others. These devices, repeaters and hubs, were very successful at getting machines connected, but they allowed an attacker easy access to all traffic on the network because the attacker only needed to connect to one point to see the entire network's traffic.

Wireless networks function very similarly to the original repeaters and hubs. Every communication across the wireless network is viewable to anyone who happens to be listening to the network. In fact, the person who is listening does not even need to be associated with the network in order to sniff!

The hacker has many tools available to attack and monitor a wireless network. A few of these tools are AiroPeek (www.wildpackets.com/products/airopeek) in Windows; Ethereal in Windows, UNIX, or Linux; and tcpdump or ngrep (http://ngrep.sourceforg.net) in a UNIX or Linux environment. These tools work well for sniffing both wired and wireless networks.

All these software packages function by putting your network interface card (NIC) in promiscuous mode. When the NIC is in promiscuous mode, every packet that goes past the interface is captured and displayed within the application window. If the attacker is able to acquire a WEP key, he or she can then utilize features within AiroPeek and Ethereal to decrypt either live or post-capture data.

Active Attacks

Once a potential intruder has gained sufficient information from a passive type of attack, he or she has enough "ammunition" to launch an *active attack* against the network. However, you should be aware that a passive attack is not a prerequisite for an active attack. There are a potentially large number of active attacks that an intruder can launch against a wireless network without first performing a reconnaissance passive attack. For the most part, these active attacks are identical to the kinds of active attacks that are encountered on wired networks. These include, but are not limited to, unauthorized access, spoofing, DoS, and flooding attacks, as well as the introduction of *malware* (malicious software) and device theft.

With the rise in popularity of wireless networks, new variations of traditional attacks specific to wireless networks have emerged, along with specific terms to describe them, such as *drive-by spamming,* in which a spammer sends out tens or hundreds of thousands of spam messages using a compromised wireless network.

Due to the nature of wireless networks and the weaknesses of WEP, unauthorized access and spoofing are the most common threats to wireless networks. *Spoofing* occurs when an attacker is able to use an unauthorized station to impersonate an authorized station on a wireless network. A common way to protect a wireless network against unauthorized access is to use MAC filtering to allow only clients that possess valid MAC addresses access to the wireless network. The list of allowable MAC addresses can be configured on the AP, or it can be configured on a Remote Authentication Dial-In User Service (RADIUS) server with which the AP communicates. RADIUS is an access control protocol that uses a challenge/response method for authentication.

Regardless of the technique used to implement MAC filtering, however, it is a relatively easy matter to change the MAC address of a wireless device through software, to impersonate a valid station. In Windows, this is accomplished with a simple edit of the Registry. MAC addresses are sent in cleartext on wireless networks, so it is also a relatively easy matter to discover authorized addresses.

WEP can be implemented to provide more protection against authentication spoofing through the use of shared-key authentication. However, as we discussed earlier, shared-key authentication creates an additional vulnerability. Because shared-key authentication makes visible both a plaintext challenge and the resulting ciphertext version of it, it is possible to use this information to spoof authentication to a closed network.

Once the attacker has authenticated to and associated with the wireless network, he or she can then run port scans, use special tools to dump user lists and passwords, impersonate users, connect to shares, and, in general, create havoc on the network through DoS and flooding attacks. These DoS attacks can be traditional in nature, such as a *ping flood*, *SYN*, *fragment*, or *distributed DoS (DDoS)* attacks, or they can be specific to wireless networks through the placement and use of *rogue APs* to prevent wireless traffic from being forwarded properly (similar to the practice of router spoofing on wired networks).

Spoofing and Unauthorized Access

The combination of weaknesses in WEP and the nature of wireless transmission have highlighted the art of *spoofing*, or interception, as a real threat to wireless network security. Some well-publicized weaknesses in user authentication using WEP have made authentication spoofing just one of an equally well-tested number of exploits by attackers.

One definition of spoofing is an attacker's ability to trick the network equipment into thinking that the address from which a connection is coming is one of the valid and allowed machines from its network. Attackers can accomplish this trick in several ways, the easiest of which is to simply redefine the MAC address of the attacker's wireless or network card to a valid MAC address. This can be accomplished in Windows through a simple Registry edit. Several wireless providers also have an option to define the MAC address for each wireless connection from within the client manager application that is provided with the interface.

There are several reasons that an attacker would spoof. If the network allows only valid interfaces through MAC or IP address filtering, an attacker would need to determine a valid MAC or IP address to be able to communicate on the network. Once that is accomplished, the attacker could then reprogram his or her interface with that information, allowing the attacker to connect to the network by impersonating a valid machine.

IEEE 802.11 networks introduce a new form of spoofing: authentication spoofing. As described in a paper, *Intercepting Mobile Communications: The Insecurities of 802.11*, the authors (Borisov, Goldberg, and Wagner) identified a way to utilize weaknesses within WEP and the authentication process to spoof authentication into a closed network. The process of authentication, as defined by IEEE 802.11, is very simple. In a shared-key configuration, the AP sends out a 128-byte random string in a cleartext message to the workstation that is attempting to authenticate. The workstation then encrypts the message with the shared key and returns the encrypted message to the AP. If the message matches what the AP is expecting, the workstation is authenticated onto the network and access is allowed.

As described in the paper, if an attacker has knowledge of both the original plaintext and the ciphertext messages, it is possible to create a forged encrypted message. By sniffing the wireless network, an attacker is able to accumulate numerous authentication requests, each of which includes the original plaintext message and the returned ciphertext encrypted reply. From this information, the attacker can easily identify the key stream used to encrypt the response message. The attacker can then use the key stream to forge an authentication message that the AP will accept as a proper authentication.

The wireless hacker does not need many complex tools to succeed in spoofing a MAC address. In many cases, these changes either are features of the wireless manufacturers or can be easily changed through a Windows Registry modification. Once a valid MAC address is identified, the attacker needs only to reconfigure his device to trick the AP into thinking he or she is a valid user.

The ability to forge authentication onto a wireless network is a complex process. No known off-the-shelf packages provide these services. Attackers need to either create their own tool or take the time to decrypt the secret key using AirSnort or WEPCrack.

If the attacker is using Windows Server 2003 and his network card supports reconfiguring the MAC address, the network card's MAC address can be changed through the Network Properties window in the System Control Panel. Once the attacker is utilizing a valid MAC address, he is able to access any resource available from the wireless network. If WEP is enabled, the attacker must either identify the WEP secret key or capture the key through malware or by stealing the user's notebook.

Configuring & Implementing...

WEPCrack on Windows

WEPCrack (http://wepcrack.sourceforge.net) is a set of Open Source Perl scripts intended to break 802.11 WEP secret keys. It was the first publicly available implementation of the attack described by Fluhrer, Mantin, and Shamir in their paper, *Weaknesses in the Key Scheduling Algorithm of RC4*. Since a Perl interpreter is not installed by default with Windows Server 2003 (or any version of Windows, for that matter), you need one to run the scripts. One or both of the following freely available solutions will give you what you need: Cygwin (www.cygwin.com) or ActiveState ActivePerl (www.activestate.com/Products/ActivePerl/).

The more robust option is to install Cygwin. Cygwin is a Linux-like environment for Windows that consists of a DLL (cygwin1.dll) to provide Linux emulation functionality and a seemingly exhaustive collection of tools, which provide the Linux look and feel. The full suite of Perl development tools and libraries are available; however, the Perl interpreter is all that is required to run the WEPCrack scripts, as is shown running in Figure 9.4.

Figure 9.4 Executing WEPCrack.pl in Cygwin

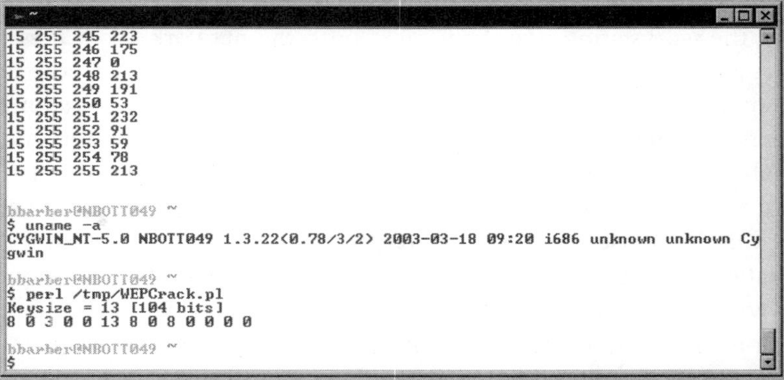

The other option, using a Windows-based Perl interpreter, may be desirable if you have no need for Linux emulation functionality on your workstation or server. ActiveState ActivePerl, available by free download from the ActiveState Web site (www.activestate.com), provides a robust Perl development environment that is native to Windows. WEPCrack was written so that it could be ported to any platform that has a Perl interpreter without needing to modify the code. Figure 9.5 demonstrates the WEPCrack.pl script running natively in Windows without modification from a Windows command prompt.

Continued

Figure 9.5 Executing WEPCrack.pl at the Windows Command Prompt

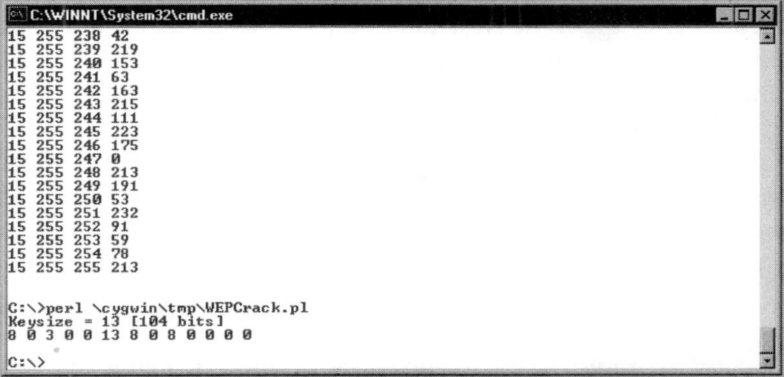

Denial of Service and Flooding Attacks

The nature of wireless transmission, especially via the use of spread-spectrum technology, makes a wireless network especially vulnerable to DoS attacks. The equipment needed to launch such an attack is freely available and very affordable. In fact, many homes and offices contain the equipment that is necessary to deny service to their wireless networks, such as 2.4GHz cordless telephones and microwave ovens.

A DoS occurs when an attacker has engaged most of the resources a host or network has available, rendering it unavailable to legitimate users. One of the original DoS attacks is known as a *ping flood*. A ping flood utilizes poorly configured equipment along with bad "features" within TCP/IP to cause a large number of hosts or devices to send an ICMP echo (ping) to a specified target. When the attack occurs, it tends to use a large portion of the resources of both the network connection and the host being attacked. This makes it very difficult for valid end users to access the host for normal business purposes.

In a wireless network, several items can cause a similar disruption of service. Probably the easiest method is through a conflict within the wireless spectrum, caused by different devices attempting to use the same frequency. Many new wireless telephones use the same frequency as 802.11 networks. Through either intentional or unintentional uses of another device that uses the 2.4GHz frequency, a simple telephone call could prevent all wireless users from accessing the network.

Another possible attack occurs through a massive number of invalid (or valid) authentication requests, known as *flooding*. If the AP were tied up with thousands of spoofed authentication attempts, authorized users attempting to authenticate themselves would have difficulties acquiring a valid session.

As demonstrated earlier, the attacker has many tools available to hijack network connections. If an intruder is able to spoof the machines of a wireless network into thinking that the attacker's machine is their default gateway, not only will the attacker be able to intercept all traffic destined for the wired network, but she would also be able to prevent any of the wireless network machines from accessing the wired network. To do this, the hacker needs only to spoof the AP and not forward connections to the end destination, preventing all wireless users from performing valid wireless activities.

An intruder who wants to launch a DoS attack against a network with a flood of authentication strings in most cases does not need to be a well-skilled programmer. Many tools are available to create this type of attack, so even the most unskilled of black hats, the *script kiddie*, can launch this type of attack with little or no knowledge of how it works or why. A script kiddie is an amateur cracker who tries to illegally break into a system but takes the path of least resistance. For example, the individual may use some known security flaw in certain software to try to exploit that weakness on any server in the Internet without discrimination. Many apartments and older office buildings are not wired for the high-tech networks in use today. To add to the problem, if a large number of individuals are setting up their own wireless networks without coordinating the installations, many problems can occur that will be difficult to detect.

Only a limited number of frequencies are available to 802.11 networks. In fact, once the frequency is chosen, it does not change until it's manually reconfigured. Considering these problems, it is not hard to imagine the following situation occurring.

Say that a person purchases a wireless AP and several network cards for his home network. When he gets home to his apartment and configures his network, he is extremely happy with how well wireless networking actually works. Then suddenly none of the machines on the wireless network is able to communicate. After waiting on hold for 45 minutes to get through to the tech support phone line of the vendor that made the device, he finds that the network has magically started working again, so he hangs up. Later that week, the same problem occurs, except that this time he decides to wait on hold when he calls tech support. While waiting, he goes onto his porch and begins discussing his frustration with his neighbor. During the conversation, his neighbor's kids come out and say that their wireless network is not working. So they begin to do a few tests (while still waiting on hold, of course). First, the man's neighbor turns off his AP (which is usually off unless the kids are online, to "protect" their network). When this is done, the original person's wireless network starts working again. Then they turn on the neighbor's AP and the original user's network stops working again. At this point, a tech support rep finally answers the phone, and the caller describes what has happened. The tech support representative has seen this situation several times and informs the user that he will need to change the frequency used in the device to another channel. He explains that the neighbor's network is utilizing the same channel, causing the two networks to conflict. Once the caller changes the frequency, everything starts working properly.

Man-in-the-Middle Attacks on Wireless Networks

Placing a rogue AP within range of wireless stations is a wireless-specific variation of a man-in-the-middle attack. If the attacker knows the SSID the network uses (which, as we have seen, is easily discoverable) and the rogue AP has enough strength, wireless users have no way of knowing that they are connecting to an unauthorized AP.

Using a rogue AP, an attacker can gain valuable information about the wireless network, such as authentication requests, the secret key that is in use, and so on. Often, the attacker will set up a laptop with two wireless adapters, in which the rogue AP uses one card and the other is used to forward requests through a wireless bridge to the legitimate AP. With a sufficiently strong antenna, the rogue AP does not have to be located in close proximity to the legitimate AP.

For example, the attacker can run the rogue AP from a car or van parked some distance away from the building. However, it is also common to set up hidden rogue APs (under desks, in closets, and so on) close to and within the same physical area as the legitimate AP. Due to their virtually undetectable nature, the only defense against rogue APs is vigilance through frequent site surveys (using tools such as AirMagnet, NetStumbler, and AiroPeek) and physical security.

Frequent site surveys also have the advantage of uncovering the unauthorized APs that company staff members might have set up in their own work areas, thereby compromising the entire network and completely undoing the hard work that went into securing the network in the first place. These unauthorized APs are usually set up with no malicious intent but rather for the convenience of the user, who might want to be able to connect to the network via his or her laptop in meeting rooms or break rooms or other areas that do not have wired outlets. Even if your company does not use or plan to use a wireless network, you should consider doing regular wireless site surveys to see if someone has violated your company security policy by placing an unauthorized AP on the network, regardless of that person's intent.

Hijacking and Modifying a Wireless Network

Numerous techniques are available for an attacker to *hijack* a wireless network or session. Unlike some attacks, network and security administrators might be unable to tell the difference between the hijacker and a legitimate passenger.

Many tools are available to the network hijacker. These tools are based on basic implementation issues within almost every network device available today. As TCP/IP packets go through switches, routers, and APs, each device looks at the destination IP address and compares it with the IP addresses it knows to be local. If the address is not in the table, the device hands the packet off to its default gateway.

This table is used to coordinate the IP address with the MAC addresses that are known to be local to the device. In many situations, this list is a dynamic one that is built up from traffic that is passing through the device and through Address Resolution Protocol (ARP) notifications from new devices joining the network. There is no authentication or verification that the request the device received is valid. Thus a malicious user is able to send messages to routing devices and APs stating that his MAC address is associated with a known IP address. From then on, all traffic that goes through that router destined for the hijacked IP address will be handed off to the hacker's machine.

If the attacker spoofs as the default gateway or a specific host on the network, all machines trying to get to the network or the spoofed machine will connect to the attacker's machine instead of the gateway or host to which they intended to connect. If the attacker is clever, he will only use this information to identify passwords and other necessary information and route the rest of the traffic to the intended recipients. If he does this, the end users will have no idea that this *man in the middle* has intercepted their communications and compromised their passwords and information.

Another clever attack can be accomplished through the use of rogue APs. If the attacker is able to put together an AP with enough strength, the end users might not be able to tell which AP is the authorized one that they should be using. In fact, most will not even know that another AP is available. Using this technique, the attacker is able to receive authentication requests and information from the end workstation regarding the secret key and where users are attempting to connect.

These rogue APs can also be used to attempt to break into more tightly configured wireless APs. Utilizing tools such as AirSnort and WEPCrack requires a large amount of data to be able to decrypt the secret key. An intruder sitting in a car in front of your house or office is noticeable and thus will generally not have time to finish acquiring enough information to break the key. However, if the attacker installs a tiny, easily hidden machine in an inconspicuous location, this machine could sit there long enough to break the key and possibly act as an external AP into the wireless network it has hacked.

Once an attacker has identified a network for attack and spoofed his MAC address to become a valid member of the network, the attacker can gain further information that is not available through simple sniffing. If the network being attacked is using SSH to access the hosts, just stealing a password might be easier than attempting to break into the host using an available exploit.

By simply ARP-spoofing the connection with the AP to be that of the host from which the attacker wants to steal the passwords, the attacker can cause all wireless users who are attempting to SSH into the host to connect to the rogue machine instead. When these users attempt to sign on with their passwords, the attacker is then able to, first, receive their passwords and second, pass on the connection to the real end destination. If the attacker does not perform the second step, it increases the likelihood that the attack will be noticed because users will begin to complain that they are unable to connect to the host.

Jamming Attacks

The last type of attack is the *jamming attack*. This is a fairly simple attack to pull off and can be done using readily available, off-the-shelf RF testing tools (although they were not necessarily designed to perform this function). Whereas hackers who want to get information from your network would use other passive and active types of attacks to accomplish their goals, attackers who just want to disrupt your network communications or even shut down a wireless network can jam you without ever being seen. Jamming a WLAN is similar in many ways to targeting a network with a DoS attack. The difference is that in the case of the wireless network, one person with an overpowering RF signal can carry out the attack.

This attack can be carried out using any number of products, but the easiest is with a high-power RF signal generator, readily available from various vendors.

The jamming attack is sometimes the most difficult type of attack to prevent, since the attacker does not need to gain access to your network. The attacker can sit in your parking lot or even further away, depending on the power output of the jamming device. You might be able to readily determine the fact that you are being jammed, but you could find yourself hard pressed to solve the problem. Indications of a jamming attack include clients' sudden inability to connect to APs where there was not a problem previously.

The problem will be evident across all or most of your clients (the ones within the range of the RF jamming device) even though your APs are operating properly. Jamming attacks are sometimes used as the prelude to further attacks. One possible example includes jamming the wireless network, thereby forcing clients to lose their connections with authorized APs. During this time, one or more rogue APs can be made available, operating at a higher power than the authorized APs. When the jamming attack is stopped, the clients will tend to associate back to the AP that is presenting the strongest signal. Now the attacker "owns" all network clients that are attached to his rogue APs. The attack continues from there.

In some cases, RF jamming is not always intentional and could be the result of other innocuous sources such as a nearby communications tower or another WLAN that is operating in the same frequency range. Baby monitors, cordless telephones, microwave ovens, and many other consumer products can also be sources of interference.

You can take some comfort in knowing that although a jamming attack is easy and inexpensive to pull off, it is not the preferred means of attack. The only real victory with a jamming attack for most hackers is temporarily taking your wireless network offline.

Fundamentals of Wireless Security

Wireless technologies are inherently more vulnerable to attack due to the nature of the network transmissions. Wireless network transmissions are not physically constrained within the confines of a building or its surroundings; thus an attacker has ready access to the information in the wireless networks. As wireless network technologies have emerged, they have become the focus of analysis by security researchers and hackers, who have realized that wireless networks can be insecure and often can be exploited as a gateway into the relatively secure wired networks beyond them.

Understanding and Using the Wireless Equivalent Privacy Protocol

The IEEE 802.11 standard covers the communication between WLAN components. RF poses challenges to privacy in that it travels through and around physical objects. Due to the nature of 802.11 WLANs, the IEEE working group implemented a mechanism to protect the privacy of individual transmissions. The intent was to mirror the privacy found on the WLAN, and the mechanism became known as the Wired Equivalent Privacy protocol, or WEP.

Because WEP utilizes a cryptographic security countermeasure for the fulfillment of its stated goal of privacy, it has the added benefit of becoming an authentication mechanism. This benefit is realized through shared-key authentication that allows the encryption and decryption of wireless transmissions. Up to four keys can be defined on an AP or a client. These keys can be rotated to add complexity for a higher-security standard in the WLAN policy.

WEP was never intended to be the absolute authority in wireless security. The IEEE 802.11 standard states that WEP provides for protection from *casual eavesdropping*. Instead, the driving force behind WEP is privacy. In cases that require high degrees of security, other mechanisms should be utilized, such as authentication, access control, password protection, and virtual private networks.

Despite its flaws, WEP still offers some level of security, provided that all its features are used properly. This means taking great care in key management, avoiding default options, and ensuring that adequate encryption is enabled at every opportunity.

Proposed improvements in the standard should overcome many of the limitations of the original security options and should make WEP more appealing as a security solution. Additionally, as WLAN technology gains popularity and users clamor for functionality, both the standards committees and the hardware vendors will offer improvements. It is critically important to keep abreast of vendor-related software fixes and changes that improve the overall security posture of a wireless LAN.

With data security enabled in a closed network, the settings on the client for the SSID and the encryption keys have to match the AP when you're attempting to associate with the network, or the attempt will fail. The next few sections discuss WEP as it relates to the functionality of the 802.11 standard, including a standard definition of WEP, the privacy created, and the authentication.

WEP provides some security and privacy in transmissions to prevent curious or casual browsers from viewing the contents of the transmissions between the AP and the clients. In order to gain access, an intruder must be more sophisticated and needs to have specific intent to gain access. Some of the other benefits of implementing WEP include the following:

- All messages have a CRC-32 checksum calculated that provides some degree of integrity.
- Privacy is maintained via the RC4 encryption. Without possession of the secret key, the message cannot be easily decrypted.
- WEP is extremely easy to implement. All that is required is to set the encryption key on the APs and on each client.
- WEP provides a very basic level of security for WLAN applications.
- WEP keys are user definable and unlimited. WEP keys can, and should, be changed often.

Creating Privacy with WEP

WEP provides for several implementations: no encryption, 64-bit encryption, and 128-bit encryption. Clearly, no encryption means no privacy. When WEP is set to no encryption, transmissions are sent in cleartext, and they can be viewed by any wireless sniffing application that has access to the RF signal propagated in the WLAN (unless some other encryption mechanism, such as IPSec, is used). In the case of the 64- and 128-bit varieties (just as with password length), the greater the number of characters (bits), the stronger the encryption. The initial configuration of the AP includes the setup of the shared key. This shared key can be in the form of either alphanumeric or hexadecimal strings and must be matched on the client.

WEP uses the RC4 encryption algorithm, a stream cipher developed by Ron Rivest of RSA Security (www.rsasecurity.com). Both the sender and receiver use the stream cipher to create identical pseudorandom strings from a known shared key. The process entails having the sender logically XOR the plaintext transmission with the stream cipher to produce the ciphertext. The receiver takes the shared key and identical stream and reverses the process to gain the plaintext transmission.

The Boolean logic involved in the WEP process can become extremely complex and is not something that most wireless network users, administrators included, will ever get into. The discussion is presented here only for the sake of briefly explaining how WEP functions, which helps to understand how it can be cracked with the right tools and the right amount of time. The steps in the process are as follows:

1. The plaintext message is run through an integrity check algorithm (the 802.11 standard specifies the use of CRC-32) to produce an integrity check value (ICV).
2. The ICV is appended to the end of the original plaintext message.
3. A random 24-bit initialization vector (IV) is generated and *prepended to* (added to the beginning of) the secret key, which is then input to the RC4 Key Scheduling Algorithm (KSA) to generate a seed value for the WEP pseudorandom number generator (PRNG).
4. The WEP PRNG outputs the encrypting cipher stream.
5. This cipher stream is then XOR'ed with the plaintext/ICV message to produce the WEP ciphertext.
6. The ciphertext is then prepended with the IV (in plaintext), encapsulated, and transmitted.

A new IV is used for each frame to prevent the key's reuse weakening the encryption. This means that for each string generated, a different value is used for the RC4 key. Although this is a secure policy in itself, its implementation in WEP is flawed because of due to the nature of the 24-bit space. The space is so small with respect to the potential set of IVs that in a short period of time, all keys are reused. When this happens, two different messages are encrypted with the same IV and key, and the two messages can be XOR'ed with each other using specially crafted WEP cracking tools to cancel out the key stream, allowing an attacker who knows the contents of one message to easily figure out the contents of the other. Unfortunately, this weakness is the same for both the 40- and 128-bit encryption levels because both use the 24-bit IV.

To protect against some rudimentary attacks that insert known text into the stream to attempt to reveal the key stream, WEP incorporates a checksum in each frame. Any frame not found to be valid through the checksum is discarded.

Exercise 9.02

Enabling Privacy with WEP

WEP is far from perfect, but it should be used to at least make things more difficult for the would-be intruder. WEP is disabled by default in Windows Server 2003. In Exercise 9.02, we enable WEP for use with an available network:

1. Click **Start | Control Panel | Network Connections**.
2. Double-click the desired Wireless Connection.
3. Click the **Advanced** button.
4. Select the **Wireless Networks** tab.
5. Ensure that **Use Windows to configure my wireless network settings** is checked.
6. Select an SSID from the list of available networks to highlight it.
7. Click the **Configure** button.
8. On the **Association** tab, ensure that the SSID is correct.
9. Select the **Data Encryption (WEP enabled)** check box.
10. Click **OK** twice to close the open dialog boxes.
11. Double-click the desired Wireless Connection.
12. Enter the network key that your APs are using in the **Network Key** box.
13. Enter the network key again in the **Confirm Network Key** box.
14. Click **OK** to accept the changes.

Head of the Class...

Authentication with WEP

There are two authentication methods in the 802.11 standard:

- Open authentication
- Shared-key authentication

Open authentication is most precisely described as device-oriented authentication and can be considered a null authentication; all requests are granted. Without WEP, open authentication leaves the WLAN wide open to any client who knows the SSID. With WEP enabled, the WEP secret key becomes the indirect authenticator.

The *shared-key authentication* process shown in Figure 9.6 is a four-step process that begins when the AP receives the validated request for association. After the AP receives the request, a series of management frames is transmitted between the stations to produce the authentication. This includes the use of the cryptographic mechanisms employed by WEP as a validation. The four steps break down in the following manner:

1. The requestor (the client) sends a request for association.
2. The authenticator (the AP) receives the request and responds by producing a random challenge text and transmitting it back to the requestor.
3. The requestor receives the transmission, encrypts the challenge with the secret key, and transmits the encrypted challenge back to the authenticator.
4. The authenticator decrypts the challenge text and compares the values against the original. If they match, the requestor is authenticated. On the other hand, if the requestor does not have the shared key, the cipher stream cannot be reproduced. Therefore, the plaintext cannot be discovered, and theoretically, the transmission is secured.

Figure 9.6 Shared-Key Authentication

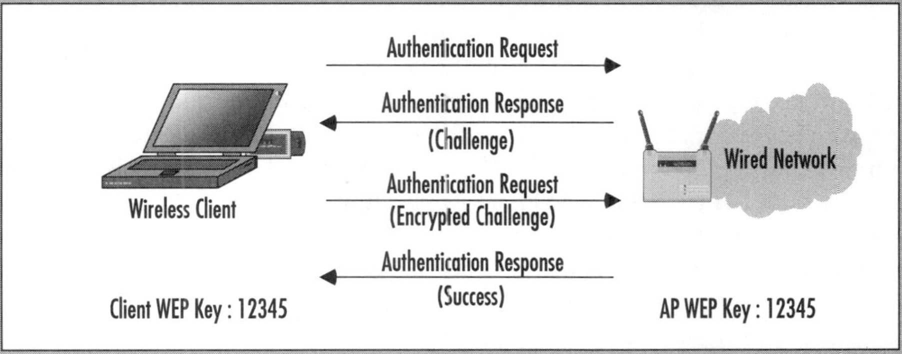

Continued

One of the greatest weaknesses in shared-key authentication is the fact that it provides an attacker with enough information to try to crack the WEP secret key. The challenge, which is sent from authenticator to requestor, is sent in the clear. The requesting client then transmits the same challenge, encrypted using the WEP secret key, back to the authenticator. An attacker who captures both of these packets has two pieces to a three-piece puzzle: the cleartext challenge and the encrypted ciphertext of that challenge. The algorithm, RC4, is also known. All that is missing is the secret key.

To determine the key, the attacker simply tries a brute-force search of the potential key space using a dictionary attack. At each step, the attacker tries to decrypt the encrypted challenge with a dictionary word as the secret key. The result is then compared against the authenticator's challenge. If the two match, the attacker has determined the secret key. In cryptography, this attack is called a *known plaintext attack* and is the primary reason that shared-key authentication is considered slightly weaker than open authentication.

Understanding WEP Vulnerabilities

Like any standard or protocol, WEP has some inherent disadvantages. The focus of security is to allow a balance of access and control while juggling the advantages and disadvantages of each implemented countermeasure for security gaps. WEP's disadvantages include:

- The RC4 encryption algorithm is a known stream cipher. This means that it takes a finite key and attempts to make an infinite pseudorandom key stream in order to generate the encryption.
- Altering the secret must be done across the board. All APs and all clients must be changed at the same time.
- Used on its own, WEP does not provide adequate WLAN security.
- To be effective, WEP has to be implemented on every client as well as on every AP.

WEP is part of the 802.11 standard defined for wireless networks in 1999. WEP differs from many other kinds of encryption employed to secure network communication in that it is implemented at MAC sublayer of the Data Link layer (Layer 2) of the OSI model. Security can be implemented at many layers of the model. IPSec, for example, is implemented at the Network layer (Layer 3) of the OSI model; PPTP creates a secure end-to-end tunnel using the Network layer (GRE) and Transport layer protocols to encapsulate and transport data; HTTP-S and SSH are Application layer (Layer 7) protocols for encrypting data. Due to the complexity of the 802.11 MAC and the amount of processing power it requires, the 802.11 standard made 40-bit WEP an optional implementation.

New & Noteworthy...

Vulnerability to Plaintext Attacks

Right from the outset, knowledgeable people warned that because of the way WEP was implemented, it was vulnerable. In October 2000, Jesse Walker, a member of the 802.11 working group, published his now famous paper, *Unsafe at Any Key Size: An Analysis of WEP Encapsulation*. The paper points out a number of serious shortcomings of WEP and recommends that WEP be redesigned.

For example, WEP is vulnerable to plaintext attacks because it is implemented at the Data Link layer, meaning that it encrypts IP datagrams. Each encrypted frame on a wireless network, therefore, contains a high proportion of well-known TCP/IP information, which can be revealed fairly accurately through traffic analysis, even if the traffic is encrypted. If someone is able to compare the ciphertext (the WEP-encrypted data) with the plaintext equivalent (the raw TCP/IP data), he or she has a powerful clue for cracking the encryption used on the network. To uncover the key stream used to encrypt the data, all the hacker has to do is plug the two values, the plaintext and the ciphertext, into the RC4 algorithm WEP uses. There are a number of ways to speed up the process of acquiring both the plaintext and ciphertext versions: by sending spam into the network, by injecting traffic into the network, using social engineering to get a wireless user to send the hacker e-mail, and so on.

Using IEEE 802.1X Authentication

The IEEE 802.1X standard is still relatively new in relation to the IEEE 802.11 standard, and the security research community has only recently begun to seriously evaluate the security of this standard. One of the first groups to investigate the security of the 802.1X standard was the Maryland Information Systems Security Lab (MISSL) at the University of Maryland at College Park. This group, led by Dr. William Arbaugh, was the first to release a paper (www.missl.cs.umd.edu/Projects/wireless/1x.pdf) documenting flaws in the IEEE 802.1X standard. In this paper, the group noted that 802.1X is susceptible to several attacks, due to the following vulnerabilities:

- The lack of the requirement of strong mutual authentication. EAP-TLS does provide strong mutual authentication, but it is not required and can be overridden.
- The vulnerability of the EAP success message to a man-in-the-middle attack.
- The lack of integrity protection for 802.1X management frames.

These flaws provide avenues of attack against wireless networks. Although the networks are not as vulnerable as they would be without EAP and 802.1X, the "silver bullet" fix designers had hoped for was not provided in the form of 802.1X.

RC4 Vulnerabilities

As suggested in the previous section, another vulnerability of WEP is that it uses a stream cipher called RC4, developed by RSA, to encrypt the data. In 1994, an anonymous user posted the RC4 algorithm to a cipherpunk mailing list; the algorithm was subsequently reposted to a number of Usenet newsgroups the next day with the title "RC4 Algorithm Revealed."

Until August 2001, it was thought that the underlying algorithm RC4 uses was well designed and robust; therefore, even though the algorithm was no longer a trade secret, it was still thought to be an acceptable cipher to use. Scott Fluhrer, Itsik Mantin, and Adi Shamir, however, demonstrated that a number of keys used in RC4 were weak and vulnerable to compromise. They published their findings in a paper, *Weaknesses in the Key Scheduling Algorithm of RC4*. The paper designed a theoretical attack that could take advantage of these weak keys. Because the algorithm for RC4 is no longer a secret and because a number of weak keys were used in RC4, it is possible to construct software that is designed to break RC4 encryption relatively quickly using the weak keys in RC4. Not surprisingly, a number of open-source tools have appeared that do precisely that. Two such popular tools for cracking WEP are AirSnort and WEPCrack.

Some vendors, such as Agere (which produces the ORiNOCO product line), responded to the weakness in key scheduling by making a modification to the key scheduling in their products to avoid the use of weak keys, making them resistant to attacks based on weak key scheduling. This feature is known as *WEPplus*; however, not all vendors have responded similarly.

Planning and Configuring Windows Server 2003 for Wireless Technologies

Embedded wireless capability was introduced with the Windows XP desktop operating system, and it has been enhanced and extended to Microsoft's server line with Windows Server 2003. Many of the new features enhance the security of wireless networking such as the addition of IEEE 802.1X Extensible Authentication Protocol over LAN (EAPOL) for client authentication, Protected Extensible Authentication Protocol (PEAP), and an enhanced Internet Authentication Service (IAS) that simplifies authentication and access control for VPN, dialup, and IEEE 802.1X-based wired or wireless networks. Windows Server 2003 also improved on the operating system's capacity for network bridging of wired and wireless networks that began with Windows XP.

Windows Server 2003's new network-access security capabilities use EAPOL for clients to control access to and protect both wired and wireless networks. Because 802.1X provides dynamic key determination, 802.1X encryption is dramatically improved over previous versions of the standard by addressing many of the known issues associated with WEP. Organizations can now adopt a security model that ensures all physical access is authenticated and encrypted, based on the 802.1X support in Windows Server 2003. Using

802.1X-based wireless APs or switches, companies can be sure that only trusted systems are allowed to connect and exchange packets with secured networks.

Microsoft authored PEAP in an IETF Internet draft to give organizations the option of using Windows domain passwords for authenticated and encrypted wireless communication with any IEEE 802.11 and 802.1X AP without having to deploy a certificate infrastructure. Using IAS, companies can also grant Internet access to "guest" users through 802.1X authentication or bootstrap a system configuration in an authenticated network. Administrators may now quarantine connectivity requests that do not submit valid credentials for authentication, isolating the network communications to specific address ranges or a virtual local area network (VLAN), such as the Internet or a bootstrap configuration network segment.

Network bridging allows administrators to interconnect network segments using computers running Windows Server 2003. In a multisegment network, one or more computers may have multiple network adapters such as a wireless adapter, a dialup adapter, or an Ethernet adapter. By bridging these adapters, the segments can connect to each other over the bridge, regardless of how they connect to the network.

EXAM 70-296 OBJECTIVE 4.2

Planning and Implementing Your Wireless Network with Windows Server 2003

The upside to wireless networking is the freedom of network clients to move about within areas of coverage and its ability to extend the LAN without having to embark on an extensive re-cabling project. The cloud to this silver lining is that planning for a wireless network has many more aspects to it than a traditional wired network. These additional aspects can be grouped into roughly four areas:

- Physical layout
- Network topology
- Network identification
- Wireless security

Because requirements vary from organization to organization, no single plan or network architecture applies to every wireless network or wireless network segment. The following sections introduce the distinctive aspect of wireless network planning and list questions to consider in your planning. It follows that once you've completed the planning for the wireless network, you can confidently proceed with setting it up.

Planning the Physical Layout

With a wired network, clients merely need to be within a cable length of a preinstalled network drop to connect. For wireless networking, however, wireless clients need only be within range of an AP or each other. The physical layout of APs and network clients is critical, not only for the connection speed and performance of each device's wireless connection, but to ensure that roaming within the facilities is possible without dropping the connection and that one network does not interfere with another in a neighboring office. These are some of the questions that need to be answered before setting up your wireless equipment:

- Will the wireless network be Infrastructure mode or Ad Hoc mode?
- Will all the clients be equipped with wireless network adapters, or will there be a mix of wired and wireless clients?
- Are all the clients physically located within close proximity of each other?

The network's physical layout is established by installing the actual required hardware components. The essential pieces of equipment for wireless networking are wireless network adapters and an AP, and in a small office with very few networked devices, an Ad Hoc wireless network might be appropriate where only wireless network adapters are required. In larger organizations, a number of APs may be required to provide wireless network coverage to all desired areas. In a home, where space is at a premium and only basic functionality is required, a combination wireless AP and router would be a good solution. All that is required for setting up an Ad Hoc network is a collection of network clients that are physically in range of each other. For the purposes of this section, we deal with the generic configuration of wireless networking components so that you can apply these principles regardless of the size of your deployment.

The physical placement of the wireless router or APs will have the greatest effect on the effective operating distance and speed of the wireless connections. For best results, you should consider the following location suggestions when placing APs and wireless routers within your facilities:

- Near the center of the area in which your PCs will operate
- In an elevated location, such as a high shelf or fastened to a ceiling or the top of a wall
- Away from potential sources of interference, such as PCs, microwave ovens, and cordless phones
- With the antenna tight and in the upright position
- Away from large metal surfaces

These spots are appropriate for the location of APs and wireless routers, but you can also apply these principles when troubleshooting wireless client connections. For example, the client whose connection drops whenever someone makes microwave popcorn may be located too close to the kitchen.

Planning the Network Topology

A wireless network in Infrastructure mode bears a strong resemblance to a wired network, where all clients connect to a hub or switch and the hubs or switches are connected to each other; however, although the similarity is valid, it is certainly more complex than that. Networking all computers in your organization provides the fundamental "plumbing" for communication and collaboration. The network topology you choose will dictate which devices will be able to participate in the corporate network and how securely they will be able to do so. These are some of the questions that need to be answered before clients can securely connect to each other:

- Will you use a stub network to isolate wireless clients from wired clients?
- Will wired and wireless clients co-exist on the same network?
- Will you use MAC address filtering to restrict wireless access to APs by MAC address?

Once the equipment has been installed and all devices can reliably connect to each other, you face decisions on how to configure your network to facilitate communication and collaboration among your wired and wireless clients. In wireless networking, the topology issues pertain more to security of connections than to their performance. For example, you can create a stub network to isolate wireless clients from wired clients so that data is transmitted among the wireless clients though an AP and across a network bridge when the wireless clients need to communicate to wired network resources. You can also dictate that wireless clients actually connect to the corporate network from outside the firewall using IPSec and VPN technology.

Planning for Network Identification

Some might think that dealing with the network name, or SSID, is a relatively minor issue, but it can be a critical step in eliminating a predictable characteristic of your network. Predictability may be desired if you run an Internet café and you want people to get on your network easily; however, if you are passing corporate data around, you will prefer that only the people who are supposed to be using your network can find and participate on it. These are some of the questions that need to be answered to adequately identify your network:

- Will you change the default SSID?
- Will you use an SSID that is descriptive or one that is generic?
- Will you enable or disable SSID broadcasts?
- Will you permit wireless clients to configure their own preferred networks, or will you enforce that through Group Policy?

As mentioned earlier, network identification is an important issue. The SSID you choose should reflect your wireless clients' connectivity requirements. If you want clients to positively identify your organization, an SSID that uniquely reflects your organization is a good idea; however, you might desire something generic or undecipherable if you prefer to remain anonymous to war drivers and wireless-enabled systems in the offices of neighboring organizations. In addition, you need to decide if you want your APs to broadcast the SSID to all clients in range.

An SSID can be as long as 32 alphanumeric characters, and the value is also case-sensitive. The same SSID must be assigned to all wireless devices in your network. As mentioned earlier in the chapter, APs ship with a preconfigured default SSID. You are free to leave the default SSID in place; however, it is a good idea to change it, especially if the company in the office next to you bought the same equipment and left the default SSID in place. Lists of default SSIDs from wireless equipment manufacturers are readily available on the Internet.

If you decide to allow APs to broadcast the SSID, they will broadcast the SSID name to all wireless clients within range. The broadcast will enable an AP to be scanned by other wireless clients, making connection to an available network much easier than if the wireless client had to manually enter the SSID. This could be alleviated using Group Policy to define the Preferred Networks for wireless clients who authenticate to Active Directory.

Many APs have an option to allow or block access from wireless clients who use an *Unspecified-SSID*. A wireless client without a correct SSID will be denied access to the AP if the AP is set to block access for clients using an SSID that is set to ANY or no SSID at all. This is one way to thwart the use of NetStumbler and similar wireless network-scanning utilities.

Planning for Wireless Security

Your decisions on network topology were the first steps to clients being able to securely connect with each other at a low level, but a host of other security measures specifically for wireless networking protect the integrity of data being transmitted over radio waves. These are some of the questions that need to be answered before clients can be able to securely and confidently interact with each other:

- Will you use WEP? If yes, will you use 64-bit or 128-bit keys?
- Will you use MAC address filtering to restrict wireless access by MAC address?
- Will you enable 802.1X authentication?
- Will you force wireless clients to use IPSec through a VPN tunnel?
- Will you configure wireless client security settings on individual systems, or will you use Group Policy to apply it to all systems?
- What will you use to monitor wireless network activity?

EXAM 70-296 OBJECTIVE 4.2

Implementing Wireless Security on a Windows Server 2003 Network

This chapter covers the exam objective "Plan security for wireless networks." As broad as that topic might seem, the focus of wireless network security is on measures that can be employed once the wireless connection has been made. The sections that follow describe in detail how wireless clients are managed through Group Policy, how they authenticate, and how network traffic is encrypted and monitored.

Using Group Policy for Wireless Networks

One of the new features of Windows Server 2003 is the integration of wireless network configuration to Group Policy. Wireless Network (IEEE 802.11) Policy can be defined for the entire domain, individual OUs, domain controllers, and individual computer accounts. As shown in Figure 9.7, within the Group Policy module of MMC, Wireless Network Policy is located at **[Group Policy Target (Domain, Domain Controllers, Organizational Unit)] | Computer Configuration | Windows Settings | Security Settings | Wireless Network (IEEE 802.11) Policies**.

Figure 9.7 Managing Wireless Network Configuration Through Group Policy

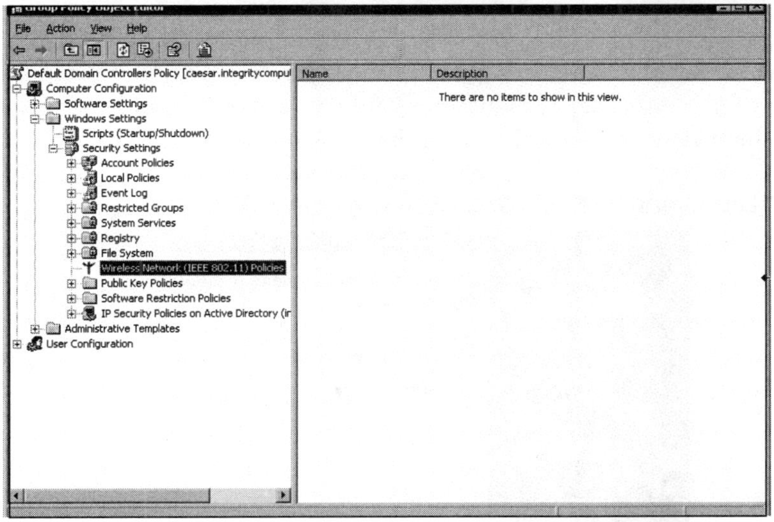

This might sound ridiculously obvious, but there are no default settings for Wireless Network Policies until you've created a Wireless Network Policy by clicking **Wireless Network (IEEE 802.11) Policies**, right-clicking anywhere in the right pane of the MMC window, and left-clicking **Create Wireless Network Policy** in the context menu, as demonstrated in Figure 9.8. This series of steps launches the Wireless Network Policy wizard to create a Wireless Network Policy with default settings.

Figure 9.8 Creating a New Wireless Network Policy

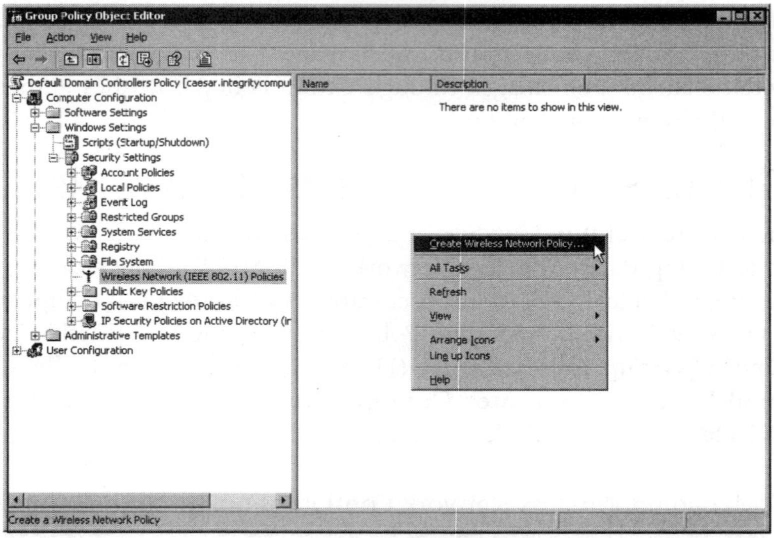

The Wireless Network Policy Wizard creates a generic policy and prompts you to specify a name for it. All other configuration and customization can be performed later, as explained in the Welcome screen shown in Figure 9.9.

Figure 9.9 Launching the Wireless Network Policy Wizard

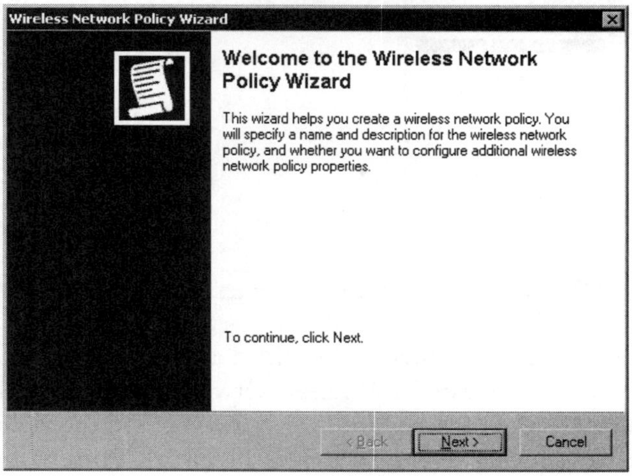

Click **Next** to dismiss the initial screen. This will bring you to the Wireless Network Policy Name window (see Figure 9.10). The name that you specify for the Wireless Network Policy in this screen will appear in the right pane of the window shown previously, in Figure 9.8. Because you can only specify one Wireless Network Policy for each Active Directory object, a fairly specific name would be helpful for distinguishing a particular policy among multiple policies that have been assigned to other objects. In addition, adding a description is also a good practice so that you can record details about the policy for reference at a future date.

Figure 9.10 Choosing a Name for the Wireless Network Policy

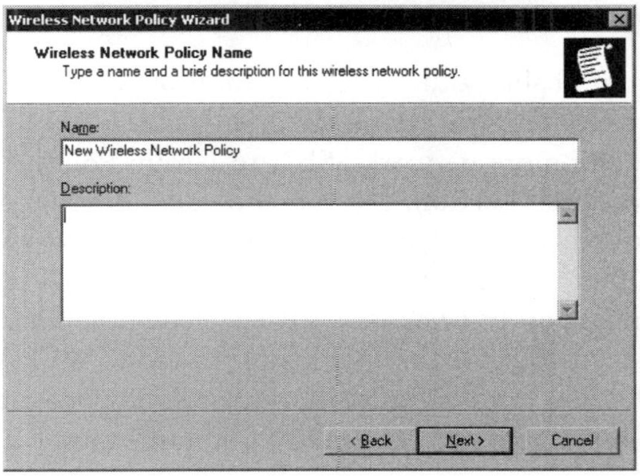

Once you click **Next**, you have essentially completed the process. The completion screen for the wizard, shown in Figure 9.11, will appear. At this point, you have the option of clicking the **Back** button to change the name you specified for the newly created Wireless Network Policy.

Figure 9.11 Completing the Wizard and Preparing to Edit the New Wireless Network Policy

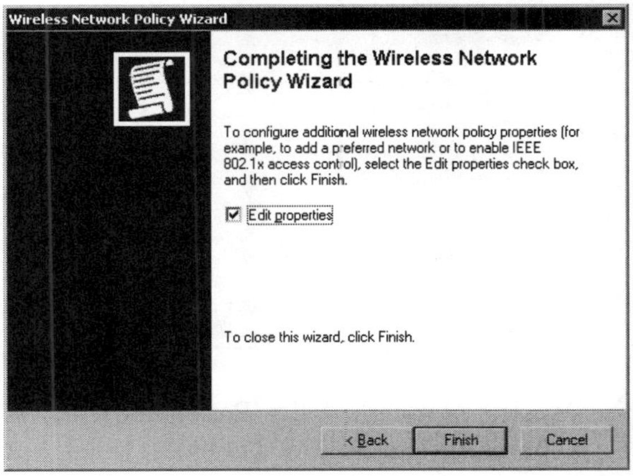

In order to configure the properties of your new Wireless Network Policy, be sure that you have selected the option **Edit properties** prior to clicking the **Finish** button. Once you click the **Finish** button the Properties window, your newly created Wireless Network (IEEE 802.11) Policy will open, as shown in Figure 9.12. In this window, you can:

- Add the default SSID for you organization
- Enable or disable WEP or Shared mode authentication
- Specify if the WEP key is provided automatically or if the client will have to provide one
- Disable Infrastructure mode

There is a very high probability that your organization will only have one wireless network for each site and, therefore, will have only one default SSID to define for each location. The process for adding more network SSIDs to Group Policy is described in the "Defining Preferred Networks" section. You can also add a description for the default wireless network in the text box. Open (WEP-enabled) and shared-key authentication were previously described in the "Authenticating with WEP" section. If possible, you should avoid shared-key authentication in favor of WEP-enabled authentication because if your wireless network is attacked, it can expose your organization's WEP key and other networked resources. Finally, you can configure the wireless network mode to Infrastructure or Ad Hoc by leaving the box unchecked or checking it, respectively. Infrastructure mode is the default.

Figure 9.12 Defining the Default SSID, WEP Settings, and Network Mode

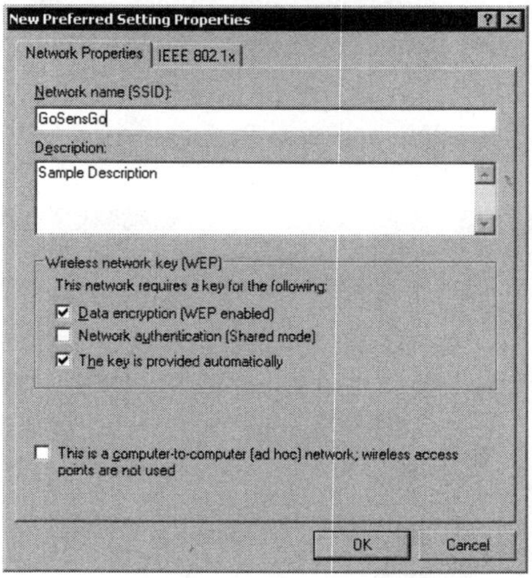

The other tab in the Wireless Network Policy Properties window is for configuring IEEE 802.1X settings; it is shown in Figure 9.13. The 802.1X authentication process and

the meaning of the settings for 802.1X are described in detail in a later section, "802.1X Authentication." The **Authenticate as guest when user or computer information is unavailable** check box, when checked, is useful for providing a wireless client with "guest level" access to the corporate network, without providing access to network resources. The **Authenticate as computer when computer information is available** option provides for automatic 802.1X authentication when all the credentials and other associated data required for 802.1X authentication have been preconfigured on the wireless client.

Figure 9.13 Configuring IEEE 802.1X Parameters

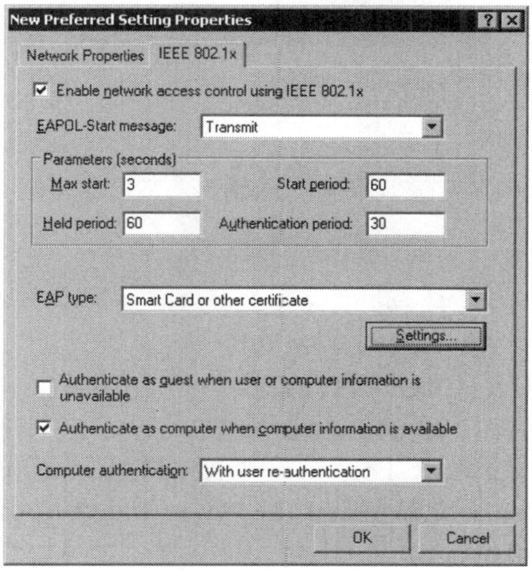

If you click on the **Settings** button under EAP Type, the window in Figure 9.14 opens. For networks that use certificate-based authentication, you can configure the most appropriate settings here. The "When connecting" section of the tab specifies where the client's certificate is stored, either on a smart card in a card reader attached to the wireless client or on a local or removable hard drive.

If **Use a certificate on this computer** is selected, the option to **Validate server certificate** is enabled. At this point you can specify the names or IP addresses of the certificate servers that will provide proof of a positive identity and the type of server that acts as the Trusted Root Certification Authority. Clicking the **View Certificate** button displays the actual certificate and associated information in a separate window. If necessary, you can configure the system to use a different username for the connection, in case the name on the certificate is different from the one being used for the connection. If this is required, put a check mark in the **Use a different user name for the connection** check box.

Figure 9.14 Establishing EAP Authentication Settings

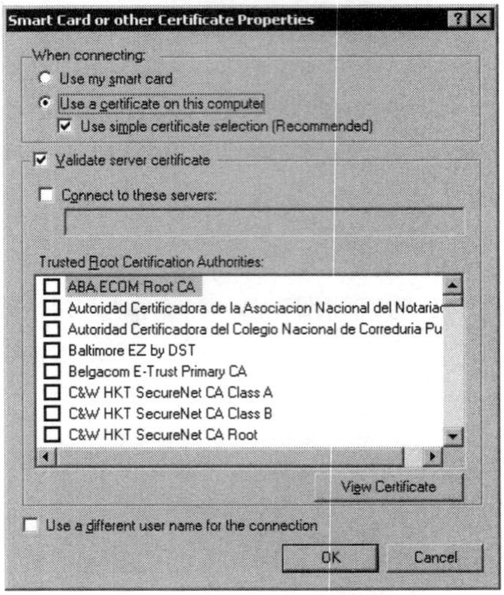

Defining Preferred Networks

The ability to define Preferred Networks makes life easier for wireless clients that connect to more than one wireless network. For example, an IT professional may have a laptop that is used to connect to a wireless network in the office and at home. Preferred Network settings make it possible to store a profile for the networks to which you commonly connect. There are two ways to define Preferred Networks: through the properties of the local wireless network adapter and through Group Policy.

To bring up the wireless network adapter properties, you can right-click the network connection in the system tray, left-click **Status**, and click the **Properties** button. The Preferred Networks settings are on the Wireless Networks tab. Available Networks and Preferred Networks are enabled by default because the **Use Windows to configure my wireless settings** check box is checked by default. As shown in Figure 9.15, the history of the wireless networks to which the system has connected can be configured in the Preferred Networks ordered list. Icons to the left of the network name (SSID) indicate whether the system is in range or out of range of the listed network. Networks that you connect with more frequently can be moved to the top of the list with the **Move Up** button, and you can edit the contents of the list with the **Add** and **Remove** buttons.

Figure 9.15 Defining a Preferred Network in Network Properties

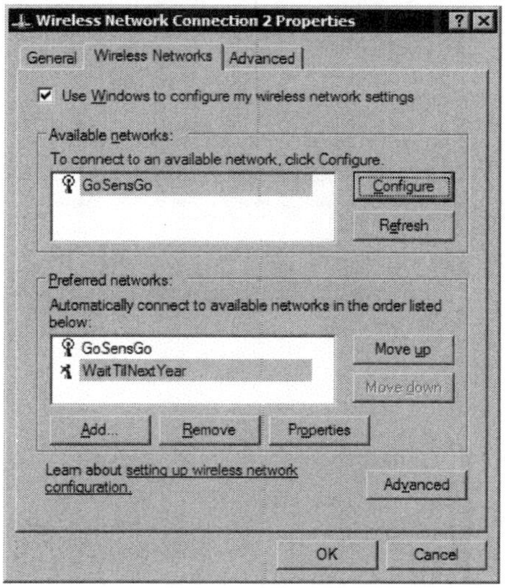

The **Advanced** button configures the preferred wireless network mode for the adapter. As shown in Figure 9.16, the adapter can be set to connect to APs that are in either Infrastructure or Ad Hoc mode using the first radio button. The other two radio buttons restrict the mode to either Infrastructure or Ad Hoc exclusively.

Figure 9.16 Configuring Available Network Settings

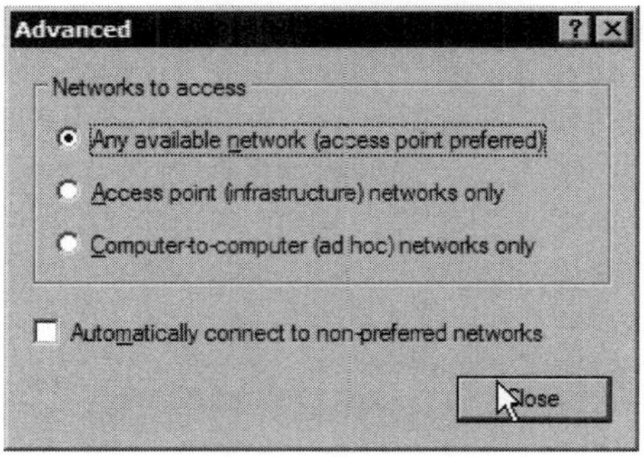

By checking the **Automatically connect to non-preferred networks** check box, your system will automatically attempt to connect to and configure a connection for networks that are not in the list of Preferred Networks. The box is unchecked by default, which means that you will need to manually configure the networks to which you want to connect. This gives you a greater degree of control over to what and how you connect to wireless networks that are in range.

The second method of defining Preferred Networks is to configure the Wireless Network (IEEE 802.11) Policy that you created with the Wireless Network Policy wizard, as shown in Figure 9.17. Using Group Policy facilitates centralized management of wireless network client settings. The cumulative impact of overlapping Group Policies can be assessed using the Resultant Set of Policy snap-in; this is described later in this chapter in the section, "Using RSoP."

Figure 9.17 Defining a Preferred Network in Group Policy

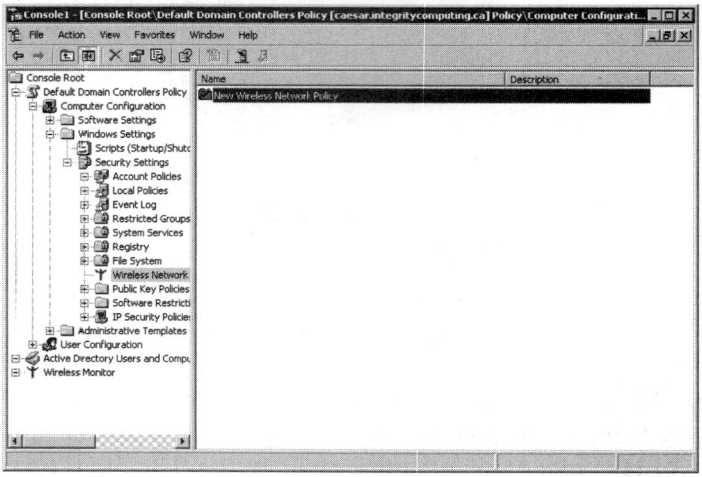

Navigate to **[Group Policy Target (Domain, Domain Controllers, Organizational Unit)] | Computer Configuration | Windows Settings | Security Settings | Wireless Network (IEEE 802.11) Policies** in the left pane of the MMC window, and double-click the name of the wireless network policy for which you want to define a Preferred Network. The New Wireless Network Policy Properties window will open on the General tab; switch to the **Preferred Networks** tab (see Figure 9.18). The buttons for managing Preferred Networks settings are identical in appearance and function to those on the Wireless Networks tab of the local Wireless Connection Properties.

Figure 9.18 Defining a Preferred Network in Group Policy

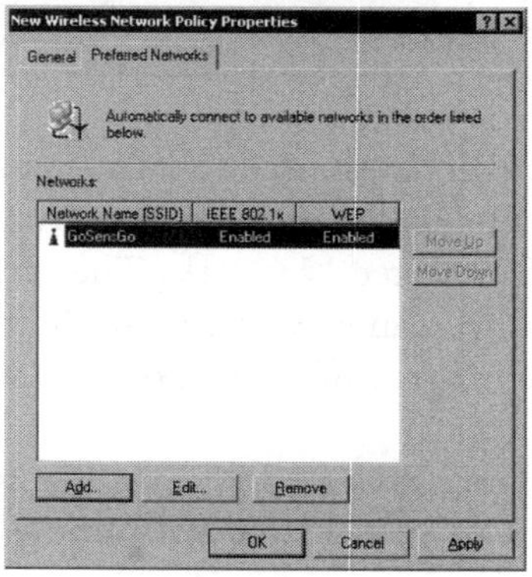

Preferred Networks that are defined in Group Policy override any configuration on all local systems that authenticate to Active Directory. If you choose to disable the **Use Windows to configure my wireless settings** check box on local systems through Group Policy, you can use Group Policy to define Preferred Network settings, and clients who log into affected systems will not be able to define their own settings.

802.1X Authentication

The current IEEE 802.11b standard is severely limited because it is available only for open and shared-key authentication schemes that are non-extensible. To address the weaknesses in the authentication mechanisms we have discussed, several vendors (including Cisco and Microsoft) adopted the IEEE 802.1X authentication mechanism for wireless networks.

The IEEE 802.1X standard was created for the purpose of providing a security framework for port-based access control that resides in the upper layers of the protocol stack. The most common method for port-based access control is to enable new authentication and key management methods without changing current network devices. The benefits that are the end result of this work include the following:

- There is a significant decrease in hardware cost and complexity.
- There are more options, allowing administrators to pick and choose their security solutions.
- The latest and greatest security technology can be installed, and it should still work with the existing infrastructure.
- You can respond quickly to security issues as they arise.

Exam Warning

The 802.1X standard typically is relevant to wireless networks due to the fact that it is quickly becoming the standard method of securely authenticating on a wireless network. However, do not confuse 802.1X with 802.11X.

When a client device connects to a port on an 802.1X capable AP, the AP port can determine the authenticity of the devices. Before discussing the workings of the 802.1X standard, we must define some terminology. In the context of 802.1X, the following terms have these meanings:

- **Port** A port is a single point of connection to the network.
- **Port access entity (PAE)** The PAE controls the algorithms and protocols that are associated with the authentication mechanisms for a port.
- **Authenticator PAE** The authenticator PAE enforces authentication before it will allow access to resources located off that port.

- **Supplicant PAE** The supplicant PAE tries to access the services that are allowed by the authenticator.
- **Authentication server** The authentication server is used to verify the supplicant PAE. It decides whether or not the supplicant is authorized to access the authenticator.
- **Extensible Authentication Protocol Over LAN (EAPOL)** The 802.1X standard defines a standard for encapsulating Extensible Authentication Protocol (EAP) messages so that they can be handled directly by a LAN MAC service. 802.1X tries to make authentication more encompassing rather than enforcing specific mechanisms on the devices. For this reason, 802.11X uses EAP to receive authentication information.
- **Extensible Authentication Protocol over Wireless (EAPOW)** When EAPOL messages are encapsulated over 802.11 wireless frames, they are known as EAPOW.

The 802.1X works in a similar fashion for both EAPOL and EAPOW. As shown in Figure 9.19, the EAP supplicant (in this case, the wireless client) communicates with the AP over an *uncontrolled port*. The AP sends an EAP request/identity to the supplicant as well as a RADIUS access-request to the RADIUS access server. The supplicant responds with an identity packet, and the RADIUS server sends a challenge based on the identity packets sent from the supplicant. The supplicant provides its credentials in the EAP response that the AP forwards to the RADIUS server. If the response is valid and the credentials are validated, the RADIUS server sends a RADIUS access-accept to the AP, which then allows the supplicant to communicate over a *controlled* port. This is communicated by the AP to the supplicant in the EAP-success packet.

Figure 9.19 EAPOL Traffic Flow

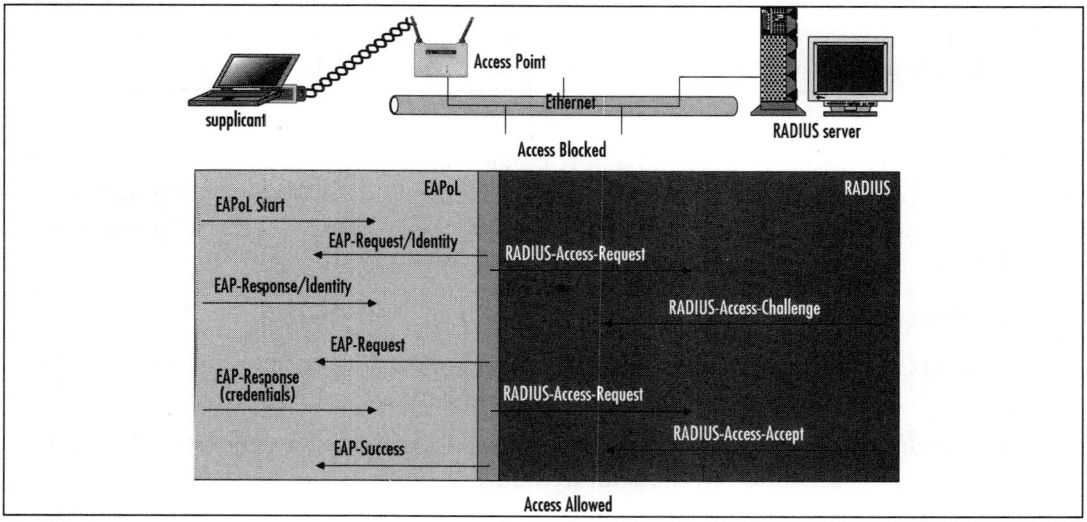

Head of the Class...

So What Are 802.1X and 802.11X, Exactly?

Wireless technology provides convenience and mobility, but it also poses massive security challenges for network administrators, engineers, and security administrators. Security for 802.11 networks can be broken into three distinct components:

- The authentication mechanism
- The authentication algorithm
- Data frame encryption

Current authentication in the 802.11 IEEE standard is focused more on wireless LAN connectivity than on verifying user or station identity. Since wireless can potentially scale so high in terms of the number of possible users, you might want to consider a way to centralize user authentication. This is where the IEEE 802.1X standard comes into play.

User Identification and Strong Authentication

With the addition of the 802.1X standard, clients are identified by usernames, not by the MAC addresses of the devices. This design not only enhances security, it also streamlines the process for authentication, authorization, and accountability for the network. The 802.1X standard was designed so that it could support extended forms of authentication, using password methods (such as one-time passwords, or GSS_API mechanisms such as Kerberos) and nonpassword methods (such as biometrics, Internet Key Exchange [IKE], and smart cards).

Dynamic Key Derivation

The 802.1X standard allows for the creation of per-user session keys. With 802.1X, WEP keys do not need to be kept at the client device or AP. These WEP keys will be dynamically created at the client for every session, thus making it more secure. The Global key, like a broadcast WEP key, can be encrypted using a Unicast session key and then sent from the AP to the client in a much more secure manner.

Mutual Authentication

The 802.1X standard and EAP provide for a mutual authentication capability. This capability makes the clients and the authentication servers mutually authenticating end points and assists in the mitigation of attacks from man-in-the-middle types of devices. Any of the following EAP methods provides for mutual authentication:

- **TLS** This requires that the server supply a certificate and establish that it has possession of the private key.
- **IKE** This requires that the server show possession of a preshared key or private key. (This can be considered certificate authentication.)

- **GSS_API (Kerberos)** This requires that the server can demonstrate knowledge of the session key.

Per-Packet Authentication

EAP can support per-packet authentication and integrity protection, but this authentication and integrity protection are not extended to all types of EAP messages. For example, negative acknowledgment (NAK) and notification messages are not able to use per-packet authentication and integrity. Per-packet authentication and integrity protection work for the following (packet is encrypted unless otherwise noted):

- TLS and IKE derived session key
- TLS ciphersuite negotiations (not encrypted)
- IKE ciphersuite negotiations
- Kerberos tickets
- Success and failure messages that use a derived session key (through WEP)

TEST DAY TIP

You might find it helpful to write out a table showing the various authentication methods used in 802.11 networks (such as open authentication, shared-key authentication, and 802.1X authentication) with the various properties that each of these authentication methods requires. This table will help keep them straight in your mind when you take the test.

Using RSoP

Resultant Set of Policy (RSoP) is an addition to Group Policy that you can use to view wireless network policy assignments for a computer or for members of a Group Policy container. This information can help you troubleshoot policy precedence issues and plan your deployment.

To view wireless network policy assignments in RSoP, you must first open the RSoP MMC console and then run a query. RSoP provides two types of queries: Logging mode queries (for viewing wireless network policy assignments for a computer) and Planning mode queries (for viewing wireless network policy assignments for members of a Group Policy container).

Logging Mode Queries

You can run an RSoP Logging mode query to view all the wireless network policies that are assigned to a wireless network client. The query results display the precedence of each wireless network policy assignment, so you can quickly determine which wireless network policies are assigned but are not being applied and which wireless network policy is being applied. The RSoP console also displays detailed settings (that is, whether 802.1X authentication is enabled, the list of preferred wireless networks that clients can connect to, and wireless network key settings) for the wireless network policy that is being applied.

When you run a Logging mode query, RSoP retrieves policy information from the Windows Management Instrumentation (WMI) repository on the target computer and then displays this information in the RSoP console. In this way, RSoP provides a view of the policy settings that are being applied to a computer at a given time.

Planning Mode Queries

You can run an RSoP Planning mode query to view all the wireless network policies that are assigned to members of a Group Policy container. For example, a Planning mode query can be useful if you are in the midst of planning a corporate restructuring of your organization and you want to move computers from one OU to a new OU. By supplying the appropriate information and then running a Planning mode query, you can determine which wireless network policies are assigned but are not being applied to the new OU and which wireless network policy is being applied. In this way, you can identify which policy would be applied if you were to move the computers to the new OU. As with Logging mode queries, when you run a Planning mode query, the RSoP console displays detailed Group Policy settings for the Wireless Network Policy that is being applied.

When you run a Planning mode query, RSoP retrieves the names of the target user, computer, and domain controller from the WMI repository on the domain controller. WMI then uses the Group Policy Data Access Service (GPDAS) to create the Group Policy settings that would be applied to the target computer, based on the RSoP query settings that you entered. RSoP reads the Group Policy settings from the WMI repository on the domain controller and then displays this information in the RSoP console user interface.

EXAM WARNING

You can run an RSoP Planning mode query only on a domain controller. (When you run a Planning mode query, you must explicitly specify the domain controller name.) However, you can specify any wireless network client as the target for the query, provided you have the appropriate permissions to do so.

Assigning and Processing Wireless Network Policies in Group Policy

Wireless Network Policies can be assigned from and stored in Active Directory, as part of Group Policy, or assigned and stored locally on a computer. When a computer is joined to an Active Directory domain, the domain-level Wireless Network Policy applies. If a computer is not joined to an Active Directory domain, the local Group Policy settings apply.

Group Policy settings are contained in Group Policy objects (GPOs), which are linked with specific Active Directory objects (sites, domains, and OUs). When a Wireless Network Policy is assigned to a GPO for an Active Directory object (such as an OU), that particular Group Policy is propagated to any affected computer accounts.

Multiple GPOs, each of which can contain a Wireless Network Policy, can be assigned to a computer account. When multiple Wireless Network Policies are assigned, the last policy that is processed is the policy that is applied (that is, the last policy takes the highest precedence and overrides the settings of any Wireless Network Policy assignments that were processed earlier).

Policy precedence is based on the Group Policy inheritance model. The policy used is the policy assigned at the lowest level of the domain hierarchy for the domain container of which the computer is a member. For example, if Wireless Network Policies are configured for both the domain and for an OU within the domain, the computers that are members of the domain use the domain Wireless Network Policies. The computers that are members of the OU within the domain use the OU Wireless Network Policies. If there are multiple OUs, members of each OU use the Wireless Network Policy assigned to the OU that is closest in level to their container in the Active Directory hierarchy. If no Wireless Network Policies are configured for Active Directory or if a computer is not connected to an Active Directory domain, the local wireless settings are used.

Wireless Network Policy Information Displayed in the RSoP Snap-in

The RSoP snap-in simplifies the task of determining which Wireless Network Policy is being applied by displaying the following information for each GPO that contains a Wireless Network Policy assignment: the name of the Wireless Network Policy, the name of the GPO that the Wireless Network Policy is assigned to, the Wireless Network Policy precedence (the lower the number, the higher the precedence), and the name of the site, domain, and OU to which the GPO containing the Wireless Network Policy applies (that is, the scope of management for the GPO).

Test Day Tip

When working with Microsoft Management Console (MMC) on a daily basis, you might find it helpful to define and save a console that consists of all your favorite snap-ins or specialized consoles with task-specific snap-ins. This is achieved by selecting **Save as** from the **Action** menu of MMC and using a unique filename to identify the .MSC file. On the exam, there will be no facility to save snap-ins. In performance-based questions, you will need to add any required snap-ins every time you need one.

Exercise 9.03

Using the Resultant Set of Policy Wizard

For every object you want to assess, you need to add the RSoP snap-in and run through the Resultant Set of Policy Wizard. The wizard will prompt you for the information required to adequately assess the cumulative effect of the application of multiple Group Policies. Do the following:

1. *Start to configure RSoP through the wizard*. Once the snap-in has been added, the Resultant Set of Policy Wizard launches automatically. The Welcome screen is displayed in Figure 9.20. Click **Next** to proceed.

Figure 9.20 Launching the RSoP Wizard

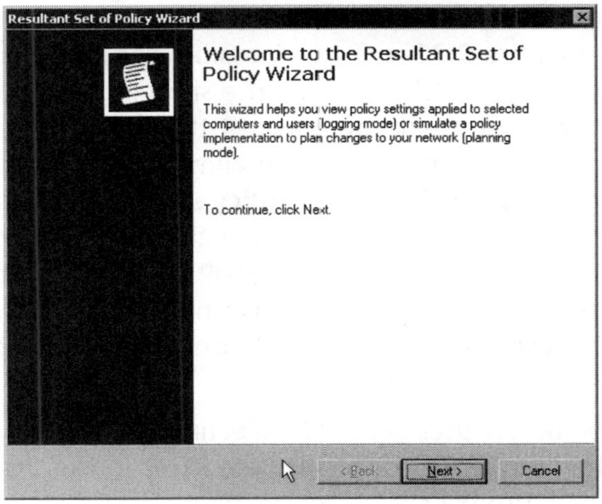

2. *Choose the required RSoP mode*. Logging mode will be the most common choice on a day-to-day basis. Planning mode is used for planning, testing, and assessing the impact of applying various Group

Policies on Users and Computers before they are applied in production. Planning mode can only be selected if the RSoP snap-in is being installed on a domain controller. For this exercise, we want to work with the more common usage of RSoP. Click the **Logging mode** radio button, and then click **Next** to continue (see Figure 9.21).

Figure 9.21 Choosing the RSoP Mode for Group Policy Settings

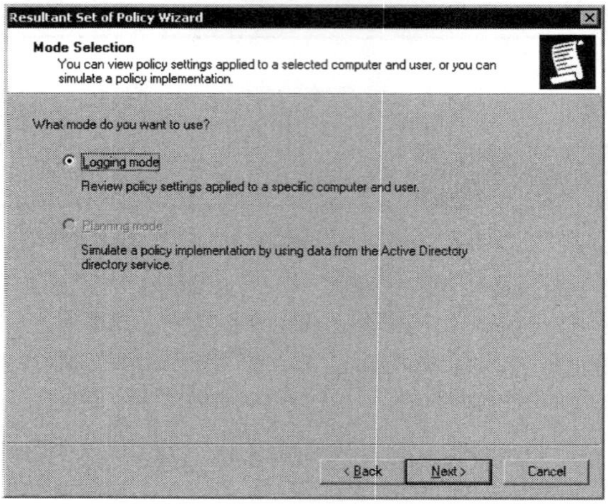

3. *Select the target computer.* Since Group Policy can be targeted at User Accounts and Computer Accounts, the selection of the target computer represents half the required data. In the Computer Selection screen, shown in Figure 9.22, are two possible computer selections: This computer (local machine) on which the snap-in has been installed and Another computer with an account that has been created in Active Directory. You can also decide to eliminate computer-related policies by checking the **Do not display policy settings for the selected computer in the results** check box. For this exercise, we want to select **This computer** as the target for the RSoP snap-in and to *include* computer-related policies; therefore, you also need to clear the **Do not display policy settings for the selected computer** check box, if it is not clear already. Click **Next** to continue.
4. *Select the target user account.* Selecting the target user account completes the data required to calculate RSoP. In the User Selection screen, shown in Figure 9.23, are two possible selections: the Current user (the user who is currently logged in and running the wizard) and Select a specific user (either a local account or one that has been created in Active Directory). You can also decide to eliminate user policy settings by checking the **Do not display user policy settings in the results** check

box. For this exercise, we want to make the current user the target for RSoP and to include user policy settings; therefore, click the **Current user** radio button and clear the **Do not display user policy settings in the results** check box, if it is not clear already. Click **Next** to continue.

Figure 9.22 Selecting the Target System to Analyze

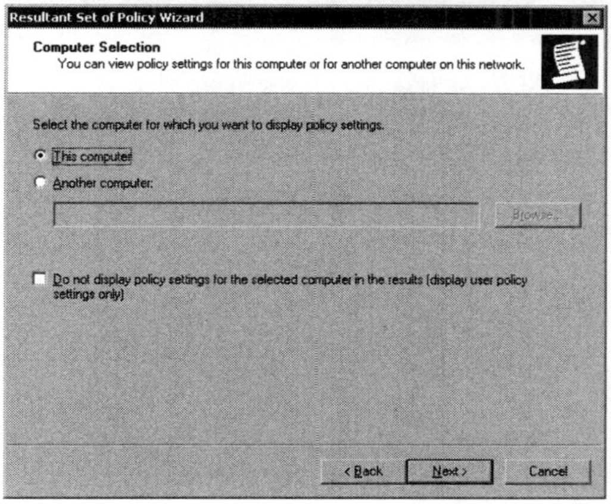

Figure 9.23 Selecting the Target User Account for Analysis

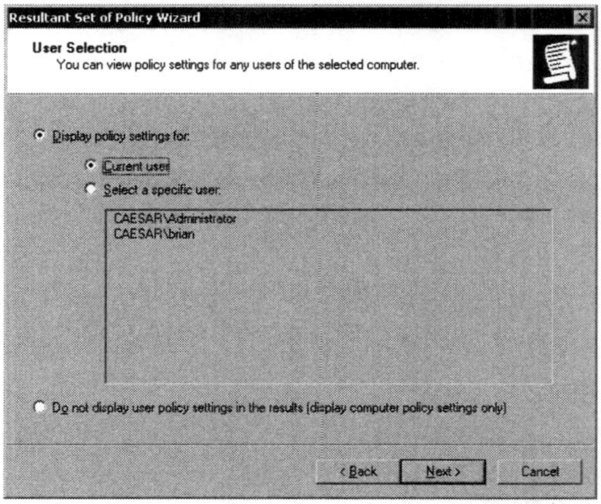

5. *Verify the selections.* The Summary of Selections window (see Figure 9.24) displays a list of the settings that will be used to calculate the Group Policy settings that will be applied to both the User Account and the Computer Account. Read through the summary in the window to verify that everything is correct, and check the **Gather extended error information** check box. This will force the process of calculating RSoP

to conduct an analysis of possible issues and resolutions. If any selections need to be changed, you could click the **Back** button to move to the appropriate screen and make the change. Since everything looks in order, click **Next** to continue.

Figure 9.24 Displaying the Summary of RSoP Selections

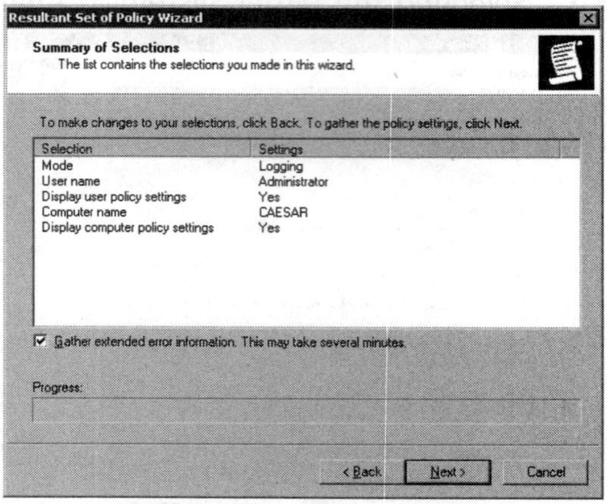

6. *Success.* Once the screen shown in Figure 9.25 is displayed, the system is ready to perform the RSoP calculation. Click **Finish** to set the calculation process in motion, and keep an eye on MMC to see the results. When everything is complete, the console will look like Figure 9.26.

Figure 9.25 Completing the RSoP Wizard

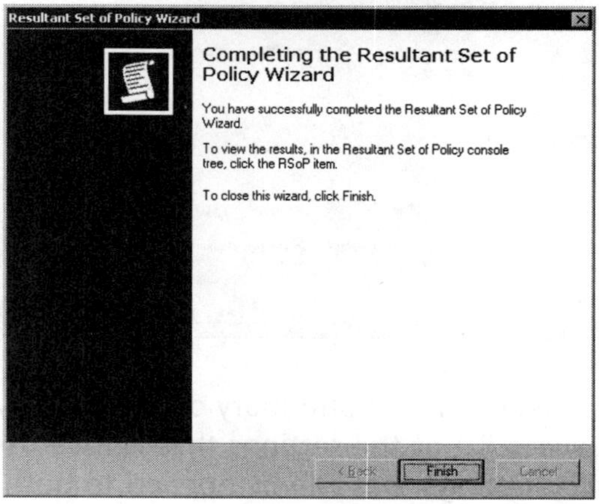

Viewing Wireless Computer Assignments

Once the RSoP snap-in has been added and the Resultant Set of Policy wizard has been completed, you can get down to the business of assessing the impact of all the different Group Policies on the particular computer. Wireless Network (IEEE 802.11) Policy only applies to computer accounts. The wizard calculates the cumulative effects of all the Group Policies that apply to the selected computer and user accounts and produces graphical output in the same format as the Group Policy snap-in, as shown in Figure 9.26.

Figure 9.26 Displaying RSoP Findings

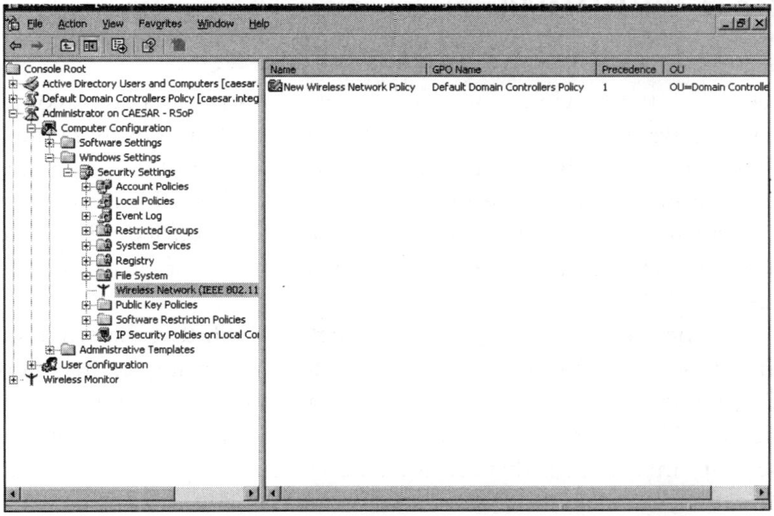

In the example shown in Figure 9.26, any change to the New Wireless Network Policy will be reflected as soon as the change is made. The wizard does not need to run again, unless you decide to change user or computer accounts. To view the RSoP analysis on Wireless Network (IEEE 802.11) Policy in MMC, navigate to **[User Account] on [Computer Account] – RSoP | Computer Configuration | Windows Settings | Security Settings | Wireless Network (IEEE 802.11) Policies** in the left pane of the MMC console. Any Wireless Network (IEEE 802.11) Policies that have been created at the domain and OU levels and associated with the selected computer account will be displayed in the right window. You can double-click the policy to view the cumulative effect of the different policies.

TEST DAY TIP

Wireless Network (IEEE 802.11) Policy can only be applied to computer accounts. Users can move from computer accounts to computer accounts, and the Group Policy settings that are associated with their user account will follow them. If an individual moves from a wireless system to a wired system, the Wireless Network Policy does not need to follow, because the computer, not the user, is wireless.

EXAM 70-296 OBJECTIVE 4.2

Securing a Windows Server 2003 Wireless Network

As we have seen from the previous discussion, wireless security is a large, complex topic. Administrators who want to implement wireless networks should exercise due care and due diligence by becoming as familiar as they can with operation and vulnerabilities of wireless networks and the available countermeasures for defending them. Installing a wireless network opens the current wired network to new threats. The security risks created by wireless networks can be mitigated, however, to provide an acceptably safe level of security in most situations.

In some cases, the security requirements are high enough that the wireless devices require proprietary security features. This might include, for example, the ability to use TKIP and MIC, which is currently only available on some Cisco wireless products but might become available on other products in the near future. In many cases, however, standards-based security mechanisms that are available on wireless products from a wide range of vendors are sufficient.

Even though many currently implemented wireless networks support a wide range of features that can potentially be enabled, the sad fact is that most administrators do not use them. The media is full of reports of the informal results of site surveys conducted by war drivers. These reports provide worrisome information—for example, that most wireless networks are not using WEP and that many wireless networks are using default SSIDs. Many of these networks are located in technology-rich areas such as Silicon Valley, where you would think people would know better, making the information a potential source of serious concern.

There is really no excuse for not minimizing the security threats created by wireless networks through the implementation of security features that are available on most wireless networks. The following is a summary of common best practices that could be employed now on many current or future wireless networks:

- *Carefully review the available security features of wireless devices to see if they fulfill your security requirements.* The 802.11 and Wi-Fi standards specify only a subset of features that are available on a wide range of devices. Over and above these standards, supported features diverge greatly.

- *At a minimum, wireless APs and adapters should support firmware updates, 128-bit WEP, MAC filtering, and the disabling of SSID broadcasts.*
- *Wireless vendors are continually addressing the security weaknesses of wireless networks.* Check the wireless vendors' Web sites frequently for firmware updates and apply them to all wireless devices. You could leave your network exposed if you fail to update even one device with the most recent firmware.
- *In medium- to high-security environments, wireless devices should support EAP-based 802.1X authentication and, possibly, TKIP.* Another desirable feature is the ability to remotely administer the wireless AP over a secure, encrypted channel. Being able to use IPSec for communications between the AP and the RADIUS server is also desirable.
- *Always use WEP.* Although it is true that WEP can be cracked, doing so requires knowledge and time. Even 40-bit WEP is better than no WEP.
- *Always rotate static WEP keys frequently.* If this is too great an administrative burden, consider purchasing devices that support dynamic WEP keys.
- *Always change the default administrative password you use to manage the AP.* The default passwords for wireless APs are well known. If possible, use a password generator to create a difficult and sufficiently complex password.
- *Change the default SSID of the AP.* The default SSIDs for APs from different vendors, such as *tsunami* and *Linksys* for Cisco and Linksys APs, respectively, are well known. A fairly inclusive listing of default SSIDs can be found at http://open-wlan.com/ssids.html.
- *Do not put any kind of identifying information, such as your company name, address, products, divisions, and so on, in the SSID.* If you do so, you provide too much information to potential hackers and let them know whether your network is of sufficient interest to warrant further effort.
- *If possible, disable SSID broadcasts.* This will make your network invisible to site survey tools such as NetStumbler. Disabling SSID broadcasts, however, will cause an administrative burden if you are heavily dependent on wireless clients being able to automatically discover and associate with the wireless network.
- *If possible, avoid the use of DHCP for your wireless clients, especially if SSID broadcasts are not disabled.* Using DHCP, casual war drivers can potentially acquire IP address configurations automatically.
- *Do not use shared-key authentication.* Although it can protect your network against specific types of DoS attacks, it allows other kinds of DoS attacks. Shared-key authentication exposes your WEP keys to compromise.

- *Enable MAC filtering.* It's true that MAC addresses can be easily spoofed, but your goal here is to slow potential attackers. If MAC filtering is too great an administrative headache, consider using port-based authentication available through 802.1X.
- *Consider placing your wireless network in a wireless demilitarized zone (WDMZ), separated from the corporate network by a router or a firewall.*
- *In a WDMZ, restrict the number of hosts on the subnet through an extended subnet mask, and do not use DHCP.*
- *Learn how to use site survey tools such as NetStumbler and conduct frequent site surveys to detect the presence of rogue APs and vulnerabilities in your own network.*
- *Do not place the AP near windows.* Try to place it in the center of the building so that interference will hamper the efforts of war drivers and others trying to detect your traffic. Ideally, your wireless signal would radiate only to the outside walls of the building, not beyond. Try to come as close to that ideal as possible.
- *If possible, purchase an AP that allows you to reduce the size of the wireless zone (cell sizing) by changing the power output.*
- *Educate yourself as to the operation and security of wireless networks.*
- *Educate your users about safe computing practices, in the context of the use of both wired and wireless networks.*
- *Perform a risk analysis of your network.*
- *Develop relevant and comprehensive security policies, and implement them throughout your network.*

Although 802.1X authentication provides good security through the use of dynamically generated WEP keys, security administrators might want to add more layers of security. Additional security for wireless networks can be introduced through the design of the network itself. As we stated previously, a wireless network should always be treated as an *untrusted* network. This fact has implications for the design and topology of the wireless network.

Test Day Tip

The extra security measures and best practices discussed over the next several pages are presented for your reference should you find yourself faced with the task of implementing a wireless network. Do not expect to be directly tested on any of this material during your exam.

Using a Separate Subnet for Wireless Networks

Many wireless networks are set up on the same subnets as the wired network. Furthermore, to make life easier for administrators and users alike, both wired and wireless clients are often configured as DHCP clients and receive IP address configurations from the same DHCP servers. There is an obvious security problem with this approach. This configuration makes it easy for hackers to acquire valid IP address configurations that are on the same subnet as the corporate networks, posing a significant threat to network security.

The solution is to place wireless APs on their own separate subnets, creating, in effect, a kind of DMZ for the wireless network. The wireless subnet could be separated from the wired network by either a router or a full-featured firewall, such as ISA Server. This approach has a number of advantages. When the wireless network is placed on a separate subnet, the router can be configured with filters to provide additional security for the wireless network. Furthermore, through the use of an extended subnet mask on the wireless network, the number of valid IP addresses can be limited to approximately the number of valid wireless clients. Finally, in the case of potential attack on the wireless network, you can quickly shut down the router and prevent any further access to the wired network until the threat has been removed.

If you have to support automatic roaming between wireless zones, you will still want to use DHCP on the wireless subnets. If you do not need to support automatic roaming, you might want to consider not using DHCP and manually configuring IP addresses on the wireless clients, as demonstrated in Figure 9.27. This solution will not prevent an intruder from sniffing the air for valid IP addresses to use on the wireless subnet, but it will provide another barrier for entry and consume time. Additionally, if an intruder manually configures an IP address that is in use by another wireless client, the valid user will receive an IP address conflict message, providing a crude method for detecting unauthorized access attempts.

Figure 9.27 Isolating Wireless Clients on a Separate Subnetwork

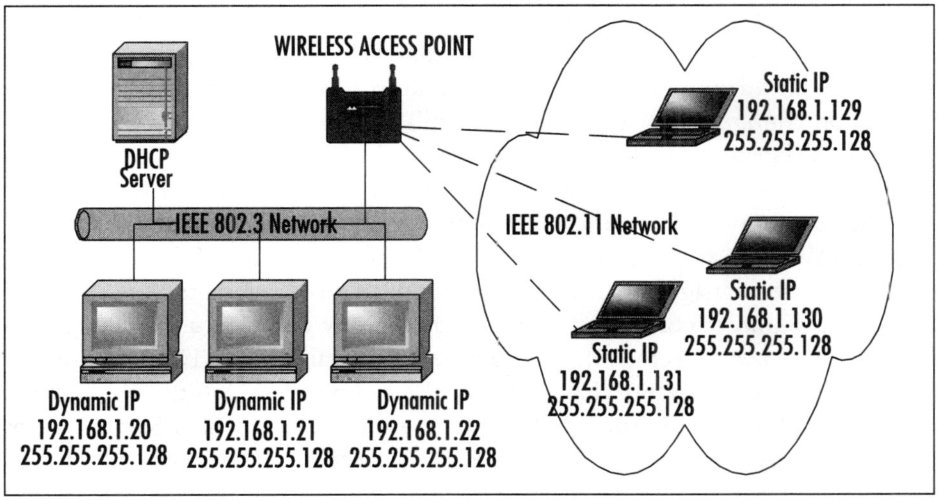

Securing Virtual Private Networks

In high-security networks, administrators might want to leverage the separate subnet by only allowing access to the wired network through a VPN configured on the router or firewall. In order for wireless users to gain access to the wired network, they would first have to successfully authenticate and associate with the AP and then create a VPN tunnel for access to the wired network.

Some vendors, such as Colubris, offer VPN solutions built into wireless devices. These devices can act as VPN-aware clients that will forward only VPN traffic from the wireless network to the wired network, or they can provide their own VPN server for wireless clients. It is not necessary, however, to use a proprietary hardware-based solution. One solution is to use a freeware solution known as Dolphin from www.reefedge.com that will turn a PC into an appliance that will encrypt wireless traffic with IPSec, as described in the next section.

When a VPN is required for access to the corporate network from the wireless network subnet, all traffic between the two networks is encrypted within the VPN tunnel. If you are using static WEP, a VPN will ensure a higher degree of confidentiality for your traffic. Even if the WEP encryption is cracked, the hacker would then have to crack the VPN encryption to see the corporate traffic, which is a much more difficult task. If a wireless laptop is stolen and the theft unreported, the thief would have to know the laptop user's credentials to gain access to the VPN.

EXAM WARNING

It is important to ensure that you do not configure the VPN connection to save the username and password. Although such a configuration makes it more convenient for clients so that they do not have to type the account name and password each time they use a VPN connection, it provides a thief with the credentials needed to access the VPN.

Of course, this kind of configuration is still vulnerable to attack. If, for example, the attacker has somehow acquired usernames and passwords (or the user has saved them in the VPN connection configuration), the hacker can still access the wired network through the VPN. Another consideration is the additional overhead of encryption used in the VPN tunnel. If you are also using WEP, the combined loss of bandwidth as a result of the encryption could easily be noticeable. Again, administrators will have to compare the benefits of implementing a VPN for wireless clients in a DMZ against the cost of deployment in terms of hardware, software, management, loss of bandwidth, and other factors.

Setting up this kind of configuration can be a relatively complex undertaking, depending on a number of factors. If, for example, you are using 802.1X authentication, you might have to ensure that 802.1X-related traffic can pass between the wireless and wired networks without a VPN tunnel. If you were using Microsoft ISA Server to separate the networks, you would have to publish the RADIUS server on the corporate network to the wireless network.

Using IPSec

IP Security (IPSec) is a protocol that provides security for transmission of sensitive information over unprotected networks such as the Internet. IPSec acts at the Network layer (OSI Layer 3) to protect and authenticate IP packets between participating IPSec devices (*peers*). IPSec functions at Layer 3 in IP itself, unlike 802.1X, which is a Data Link layer authentication system. As a result, using it to secure wireless network connections offers better security than 802.1X and other wireless technology. With IPSec, all traffic is encrypted once the connection is established, and any authentication method, such as the use of RSA keys or passwords, can be used through an IPSec tunnel.

For IPSec to be used, both ends of the connection, such as a client and a server, must support IPSec connections. Windows 2000, XP, and Server 2003 all have native support for IPSec; however, it must be enabled because it is not enabled by default. As mentioned earlier, you can create an IPSec gateway software, but you can achieve the same result by installing a second network adapter (wired or wireless), enabling IPSec and creating a bridge with Windows Server 2003.

Implementing Stub Networks for Secure Wireless Networks

According to The Free Online Dictionary of Computing (http://foldoc.doc.ic.ac.uk/), a *stub network* is "a network that only carries packets to and from local hosts. Even if it has paths to more than one other network, it does not carry traffic for other networks." In technical terms, a stub network is an IP-based network segment that uses a subset of an existing parent network address. A router or bridge separates the parent network and the stub network. An example is a parent network with an address range of 89.0.0.1 to 89.255.255.254 and a stub network with an address range of 89.1.0.1 to 89.1.255.254. For this reason, it is also called a *stub subnetwork*.

In the context of wireless networking and especially wireless network security, a stub network is a good way to centralize your wireless clients and isolate them from the rest of the network, as depicted in Figure 9.28. The gateway between the internal (wired) network and the wireless network would be running NAT and will be in bridging mode. As a bridge, the gateway will simply pass traffic between the two networks.

Figure 9.28 Setting Up a Stub Network

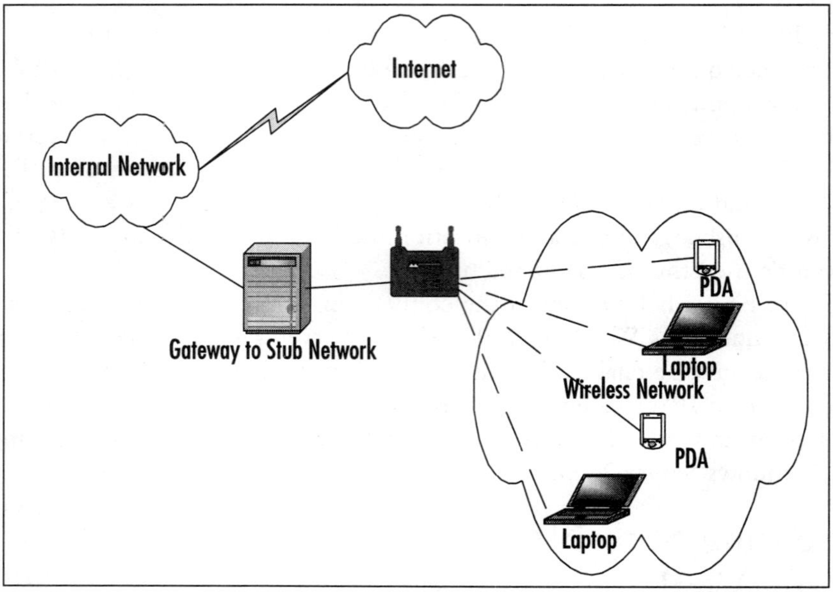

Monitoring Wireless Activity

Windows Server 2003 provides the capability to monitor wireless activity on your local network. The Wireless Monitor snap-in is used to collect and log system information and wireless activity from APs that are within range of the server. This may seem obvious, but in order to use the Wireless Monitor snap-in, the server must be equipped with a wireless network adapter. Windows Zero Configuration for wireless networking, which was introduced with Windows XP, is included with Windows Server 2003 and will support the installation of local wireless network adapters.

Implementing the Wireless Monitor Snap-in

The Wireless Monitor snap-in is the module that is added to MMC to monitor wireless connections to APs on the corporate network. The snap-in accomplishes this job by performing two critical tasks. First, it collects and centralizes information on all APs in range of the server's wireless network adapter, and second, it extracts and aggregates traffic data that has been collected at the APs. To add the snap-in, you simply follow the same procedure as for any other snap-in. The steps for adding the snap-in are:

1. Click **Start | Run**, type **mmc** in the **Open** box, and click **OK**.
2. On the File menu, click **Add/Remove Snap-in** (see Figure 9.29).

Figure 9.29 Adding a Snap-in to MMC

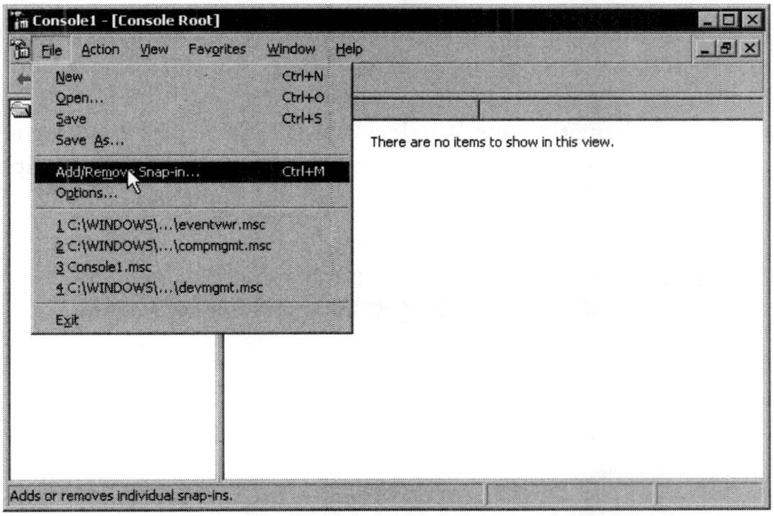

3. In the **Add/Remove Snap-in** dialog box, click **Add**.
4. In the **Add Standalone Snap-in** dialog box, click **Wireless Monitor**, click **Add**, and then click **Close** to finish (see Figure 9.30).

Figure 9.30 Selecting the Wireless Monitor Snap-in

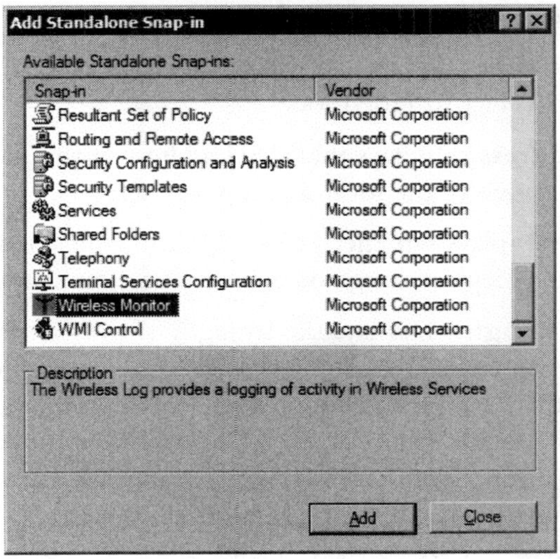

5. Click **Close** in the **Add Standalone Snap-in** dialog box, and click **OK** in the **Add/Remove Snap-in** dialog box.

Monitoring Access Point Data

Once the snap-in has been added to the console, you can click the **Wireless Monitor** entry and navigate to the server that has the wireless network adapter installed. There could be many servers listed; however, only the servers with wireless network adapters will have the Access Point Information and Wireless Client Information subcategories. To monitor AP data for all APs within range of the server's wireless network adapter, click **Access Point Information** and the data will appear in the adjacent window, as shown in Figure 9.31.

Figure 9.31 Monitoring Access Point Information

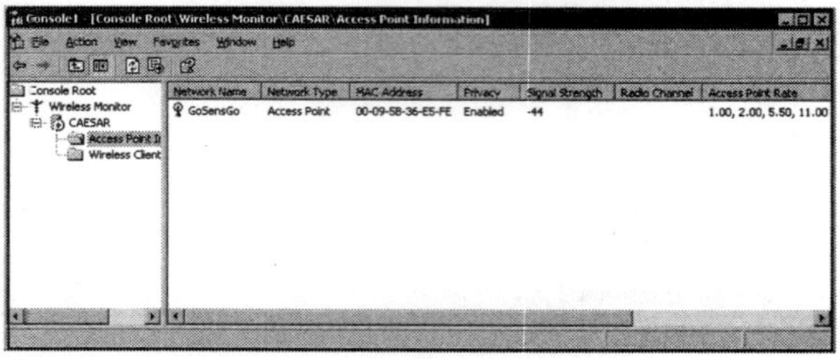

According to the Windows Server 2003 help files on logging and viewing wireless network activity, the following list identifies and describes the fields that are displayed in the Access Point Information window:

- **Network Name** Displays SSIDs of the networks that are within the reception range of the server's wireless adapter.
- **Network Type** Displays the network mode: Access Point (Infrastructure mode) or Peer to Peer (Ad Hoc mode).
- **MAC Address** Displays the MAC address of the networks that are within the reception range of the local wireless adapter.
- **Privacy** Displays whether privacy (WEP) is enabled or disabled for any network within the reception range of the local wireless adapter.
- **Signal Strength** Displays the strength of the signals that are broadcast from the networks that are within the reception range of the local wireless adapter. IEEE specifies that 802.11 wireless devices receive at a signal strength range between -76dBmW (decibel milliwatts) and -10dBmW, with -10dBmW indicating the strongest signal. Some receivers that are more sensitive may be able to accept weaker signals, possibly as weak as -85dBmW to -90dBmW.
- **Radio Channel** Displays the radio channels on which the networks that are within the reception range of the local wireless adapter are broadcasting.
- **Access Point Rate** Displays the data rate that the wireless network will support.
- **Network Adapter GUID** Displays the globally unique identifier (GUID) for each wireless adapter on your computer (not displayed in Figure 9.31).

Using Wireless Logging for Security

Wireless Client Information displays data on the traffic that is flowing through the APs that are in range of the server's wireless network adapter, as well as traffic that is picked up by the adapter itself and not going through an AP. In addition, it displays system information on the status and activity of the local wireless network adapter. Figure 9.32 displays typical logging information. The critical pieces of information in this window are the source, local and remote MAC addresses, network name (SSID), and description, because you will be able to use this data to trace the source of problems and may possibly find clues on how to resolve them.

Figure 9.32 Monitoring Wireless Client Information

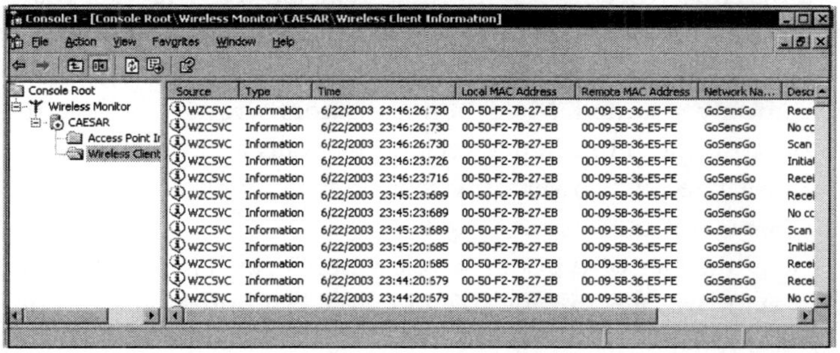

According to the Windows Server 2003 help files on logging and viewing wireless network activity, the following list identifies and describes the fields that are displayed in the Access Point Information window:

- **Source** Identifies the software that generated the event. Events displayed in Wireless Monitor are generated either by the Wireless Zero Configuration service (WZCSVC) or EAPOL.
- **Type** Displays the type of event: Error, Warning, Information, or Packet.
- **Time** Displays the time that the event was logged.
- **Local MAC Address** Displays the MAC address of the local network adapter.
- **Remote MAC Address** Displays the MAC address of the remote network interface. This could be an AP if operating in Infrastructure mode or another wireless computer in an Ad Hoc network.
- **Network Name** Displays the SSID of the wireless network for which the event was generated.
- **Description** Provides a brief summary of the logged event (partially obscured in Figure 9.32).

Summary of Exam Objectives

WLANs are attractive to many companies and home users due to the increased productivity that results from the convenience and flexibility of being able to connect to the network without the use of wires. WLANs are especially attractive when they can reduce the costs of having to install cabling to support users on the network. For these and other reasons, WLANs have become very popular in the past few years. However, WLAN technology has often been implemented poorly and without giving due consideration to the security of the network. For the most part, these poor implementations result from a lack of understanding of the nature of wireless networks and the measures that can be taken to secure them.

WLANs are inherently insecure due to their very nature—the fact that they radiate radio signals containing network traffic that can be viewed and potentially compromised by anyone within range of the signal. With the proper antennas, the range of WLANs is much greater than is commonly assumed. Many administrators wrongly believe that their networks are secure because the interference created by walls and other physical obstructions, combined with the relative low power of wireless devices, will contain the wireless signal sufficiently. Often this is not the case.

You can deploy a number of types of wireless networks. The most popular types employ the 802.11 standard, specifically 802.11a, 802.11b, and 802.11g. The most common type of WLAN in use today is based on the IEEE 802.11b standard; however, with its increased transmission speed and backward compatibility to 802.11b, 802.11g may emerge as the most popular. It also does not hurt that 802.11g devices are being introduced to the market at a lower price point than 802.11a and 802.11b levels when they were introduced.

The 802.11 standard defines the 40-bit Wired Equivalent Privacy (WEP) protocol as an optional component to protect wireless networks from eavesdropping. WEP is implemented in the MAC sublayer of the Data Link layer (Layer 2) of the OSI model.

WEP is insecure for a number of reasons. The first is that because it encrypts well-known and deterministic IP traffic in Layer 3, it is vulnerable to plaintext attacks. That is, it is relatively easy for an attacker to figure out the plaintext traffic (for example, a DHCP exchange) and compare that with the ciphertext, providing a powerful clue for cracking the encryption.

Another problem with WEP is that it uses a relatively short (24-bit) initialization vector (IV) to encrypt the traffic. Because each transmitted frame requires a new IV, it is possible to exhaust the entire IV key space in a few hours on a busy network, resulting in the reuse of IVs. This reuse is known as *IV collisions*. IV collisions can also be used to crack the encryption. Furthermore, IVs are sent in the clear with each frame, introducing another vulnerability.

The final stake in the heart of WEP is the fact that it uses RC4 as the encryption algorithm. The RC4 algorithm is well known; recently it was discovered that it uses a number of weak keys. AirSnort and WEPCrack are two well-known open-source tools that exploit the weak key vulnerability of WEP.

Although WEP is insecure, it does nonetheless potentially provide a good barrier, and its use will slow determined and knowledgeable attackers. For this reason, WEP should always be implemented. The security of WEP is also dependent on how it is implemented. Because the IV key space can be exhausted in a relatively short amount of time, static WEP keys should be changed on a frequent basis.

Securing a wireless network should begin with changing the default configurations of the wireless network devices. These configurations include the default administrative password and the default SSID on the AP.

The Service Set Identifier (SSID) is a kind of network name, analogous to an SNMP community name or a VLAN ID. In order for the wireless clients to authenticate and associate with an AP, they must use the same SSID as the one in use on the AP. The SSID should be changed to a unique value that contains no information that could potentially be used to identify the company or the kind of traffic on the network.

By default, SSIDs are broadcast in response to beacon probes and can be easily discovered by site survey tools such as NetStumbler and recent versions of Windows. It is possible to turn off SSID on some APs. Disabling SSID broadcasts creates a "closed network." If possible, you should disable SSID broadcasts, although doing so will interfere with the wireless client's ability to automatically discover wireless networks and associate with them. Even if SSID broadcasts are turned off, it is still possible to sniff the network traffic and see the SSID in the frames.

Wireless clients can connect to APs using either open system or shared-key authentication. Shared-key authentication provides protection against some DoS attacks, but it creates a significant vulnerability for the WEP keys in use on the network and so should not be used.

MAC filtering is another defensive tactic that you can employ to protect wireless networks from unwanted intrusion. Only the wireless stations that possess adapters that have valid MAC addresses are allowed to communicate with the AP. However, MAC addresses can be easily spoofed, and maintaining a list of valid MAC addresses could be impractical in a large environment.

A much better way of securing WLANs is to use 802.1X technology, originally developed to provide a method for port-based authentication on wired networks. However, it was found to have significant application in wireless networks. 802.1X relies on Extensible Authentication Protocol (EAP) to perform the authentication. The preferred EAP type for 802.1X is EAP-TLS. EAP-TLS provides the ability to use dynamic per-user, session-based WEP keys, eliminating some of the more significant vulnerabilities associated with WEP. However, to use EAP-TLS, you must deploy a public key infrastructure (PKI) to issue digital X.509 certificates to the wireless clients and the RADIUS server.

Other methods that can be used to secure wireless networks include placing wireless APs on their own subnets in wireless DMZs (WDMZs). The WDMZ can be protected from the corporate network by a firewall or router. Access to the corporate network can be limited to VPN connections that use either PPTP or L2TP. New security measures continue to be developed for wireless networks. Future security measures include Temporal Key Integrity Protocol (TKIP) and Message Integrity Code (MIC).

Windows Server 2003 improved on the embedded wireless capability that was introduced with Windows XP. One notable new feature in Windows Server 2003 is the integration of wireless network functionality with Group Policy. Wireless Network (802.11) Policy is available for domains and domain controllers, and it can be used to configure uniform wireless network settings—SSID, encryption levels, preferred networks—for all wireless clients that authenticate to Active Directory. It is important to note that Wireless Network (802.11) Policy only applies to computer accounts.

Resultant Set of Policy (RSoP) is another feature introduced with Windows XP and that has been improved in Windows Server 2003. It is an essential tool for managing Group Policy because it provides a network administrator the ability to calculate the cumulative impact of multiple, overlapping Group Policies. RSoP is available as a snap-in to MMC.

The ability to manage wireless networking is provided by the new Wireless Monitor snap-in. This snap-in enables the collection and aggregation of information on APs within range of the server's wireless network adapter, system information for wireless network clients, and data on wireless traffic that is handled by the AP. All that is required to use the Wireless Monitor snap-in is a wireless network adapter installed on the server; it does not even need to be associated with a particular SSID.

With Windows Server 2003 it is apparent that Microsoft has continued with its intention to integrate all aspects of the operating system and associated services. All aspects of wireless networking for wireless clients can now be managed with Group Policy and administered through MMC using various snap-ins. Wireless networking was clearly the realm of client connectivity in the past. This appears to be changing with Windows Server 2003.

Exam Objectives Fast Track

Wireless Concepts

☑ There are two types of 802.11 network modes: ad hoc and infrastructure. Ad hoc 802.11 networks are peer to peer in design and can be implemented by two clients with wireless network cards. The Infrastructure mode of 802.11 uses APs to provide wireless connectivity to a wired network beyond the AP.

☑ The SSID is the name that uniquely identifies a wireless network. Wireless APs ship with a default SSID, which should be changed as soon as possible.

Fundamentals of Wireless Security

☑ Examining the common threats to both wired and wireless networks provides a solid understanding in the basics of security principles and allows the network administrator to fully assess the risks associated with using wireless and other technologies.

- ☑ Electronic eavesdropping, or sniffing, is passive, undetectable to intrusion detection devices, and gives attackers the opportunity to identify additional resources that can be compromised.
- ☑ Wireless Equivalent Privacy (WEP) is the security method used in IEEE 802.11 WLANs, and Wireless Transport Layer Security (WTLS) provides security in WAP networks.
- ☑ WEP provides for two key sizes: 40-bit and 104-bit secret keys. These keys are concatenated to a 24-bit initialization vector (IV) to provide either a 64- or 128-bit key for encryption. WEP uses the RC4 stream algorithm to encrypt its data.
- ☑ Used on its own, WEP does not provide adequate WLAN security. To be effective, the strongest version of WEP must be implemented on every client as well as every AP. In addition, WEP keys are user definable and unlimited. They do not have to be predefined and can and should be changed often.

Planning and Configuring Windows Server 2003 for Wireless Technologies

- ☑ Many wireless networks that use the same frequency within a small space can easily cause network disruptions and even DoS for valid network users.
- ☑ 802.11 networks use two types of authentication: open system authentication and shared-key authentication. The IEEE 802.1X specification uses the Extensible Authentication Protocol (EAP) to provide for client authentication.
- ☑ Windows 2000, Windows XP, and Windows Server 2003 can support WEP 64 and WEP 128 as well as any third-party solutions on the market.
- ☑ The use of virtual private networks (VPNs), Secure Sockets Layer (SSL), and Secure Shell (SSH) helps protect against wireless interception.
- ☑ External two-factor authentication such as Remote Access Dial-In User Service (RADIUS) or SecureID should be implemented to additionally restrict access requiring strong authentication to access the wireless resources.
- ☑ The Resultant Set of Policy snap-in is used for assessing the cumulative impact of Group Policies. The snap-in can be run in either Logging mode or Planning mode. Logging mode provides RSoP results on a constant basis, as long as the RSoP snap-in is installed. Planning mode can only be used when running the snap-in on a domain controller.
- ☑ The Wireless Monitor snap-in is used for monitoring wireless network traffic. The snap-in aggregates information from both APs and wireless clients to produce valid monitoring data.

Exam Objectives Frequently Asked Questions

The following Frequently Asked Questions, answered by the authors of this book, are designed to both measure your understanding of the Exam Objectives presented in this chapter, and to assist you with real-life implementation of these concepts. You will also gain access to thousands of other FAQs at ITFAQnet.com.

Q: Do I really need to understand the fundamentals of security in order to protect my network?

A: Yes. You might be able to utilize the configuration options available to you from your equipment provider without a full understanding of security fundamentals. However, without a solid background in how security is accomplished, you will never be able to protect your assets from the unknown threats to your network through poor configuration, back doors provided by the vendor, or new exploits that have not been patched by your vendor.

Q: Is 128-bit WEP more secure than 64-bit WEP?

A: Yes, but only to a small degree. WEP vulnerability has more to do with the 24-bit initialization vector than the actual size of the WEP key.

Q: Where can I find more information on WEP vulnerabilities?

A: Besides being one of the sources that brought WEP vulnerabilities to light, www.isaac.cs.berkeley.edu has links to other Web sites that cover WEP insecurities.

Q: If I have enabled WEP, am I now protected?

A: No. Certain tools can break all WEP keys by simply monitoring the network traffic (generally requiring less than 24 hours to do so).

Q: How can I protect my wireless network from eavesdropping by unauthorized individuals?

A: Because wireless devices are half-duplex devices, you cannot wholly prevent your wireless traffic from being listened to by unauthorized individuals. The only defense against eavesdropping is to encrypt Layer 2 and higher traffic whenever possible.

Q: Are wireless networks secure?

A: By their very nature and definition, wireless networks are not secure. They can, however, be made relatively safe from the point of view of security through administrative efforts to encrypt traffic, implement restrictive methods for authenticating and associating with wireless networks, and so on.

Q: My AP does not support the disabling of SSID broadcasts. Should I purchase a new one?

A: Disabling SSID broadcasts adds only one barrier for the potential hacker. Wireless networks can still be made relatively safe, even if the AP does respond with its SSID to a beacon probe. Disabling SSID broadcasts is a desirable feature. However, before you go out and purchase new hardware, check to see if you can update the firmware of your AP. The AP vendor might have released a more recent firmware version that supports the disabling of SSID broadcasts. If your AP does not support firmware updates, consider replacing it with one that does.

Self Test

A Quick Answer Key follows the Self Test questions. For complete questions, answers, and explanations to the Self Test questions in this chapter as well as the other chapters in this book, see the Self Test Appendix.

1. You are opening an Internet café and want to provide wireless access to your patrons. How would you configure your wireless network settings on your AP to make it easiest for your patrons to connect? (Choose all that apply.)

   A. Enable SSID broadcasts.

   B. Disable SSID broadcasts.

   C. Enable WEP.

   D. Set up the network in Infrastructure mode.

   E. Set up the network in Ad Hoc mode.

2. Your company, Company B, has merged with Company A. A new member of the management team has a wireless adapter in her laptop that she used to connect to Company A's wireless network, which was at another location. In her new office, which is located at Company B's headquarters, she cannot connect. Company B's wireless network can accommodate adapters connecting at 11MBps and 54MBps, and she mentions that she could only connect at 54MBps on Company A's wireless network. What do you suspect is happening?

A. The new member of the management team has an 802.11a wireless network adapter and Company B's wireless network is using 802.11g equipment.

B. The new member of the management team has an 802.11b wireless network adapter and Company B's wireless network is using 802.11g equipment.

C. The new member of the management team has an 802.11g wireless network adapter and Company B's wireless network is using 802.11b equipment.

D. The new member of the management team has an 802.11g wireless network adapter and Company B's wireless network is using 802.11a equipment.

3. What are the two WEP key sizes available in 802.11 networks?

A. 64-bit and 104-bit keys

B. 24-bit and 64-bit keys

C. 64-bit and 128-bit keys

D. 24-bit and 104-bit keys

4. Your wireless network does use WEP to authorize users. You use MAC filtering to ensure that only preauthorized clients can associate with your APs. On Monday morning, you reviewed the AP association table logs for the previous weekend and noticed that the MAC address assigned to the network adapter in your portable computer had associated with your APs several times over the weekend. Your portable computer spent the weekend on your dining room table and was not connected to your corporate wireless network during this period of time. What type of wireless network attack are you most likely being subjected to?

A. Spoofing

B. Jamming

C. Sniffing

D. Man in the middle

5. Your supervisor has charged you with determining which 802.11 authentication method to use when deploying the new wireless network. Given your knowledge of the 802.11 specifications, which of the following is the most secure 802.11 authentication method?

A. Shared-key authentication

B. EAP-TLS

C. EAP-MD5

D. Open authentication

6. Bill, a network administrator, wants to deploy a wireless network and use open authentication. His problem is that he also wants to make sure that the network is not accessible by anyone. How can he authenticate users without a shared-key authentication mechanism? (Choose the best answer.)

   A. Use MAC address filters to restrict which wireless network cards can associate to the network.

   B. Deploy a RADIUS server and require the use of EAP.

   C. Set a WEP key on the APs and use it as the indirect authenticator for users.

   D. Use IP filters to restrict access to the wireless network.

7. The 802.1X standard specifies a series of exchanges between the supplicant and the authentication server. Which of the following is not part of the 802.1X authentication exchange?

   A. Association request

   B. EAPoL start

   C. RADIUS-access-request

   D. EAP-success

8. The 802.1X standard requires the use of an authentication server to allow access to the wireless LAN. You are deploying a wireless network and will use EAP-TLS as your authentication method. What is the most likely vulnerability in your network?

   A. Unauthorized users accessing the network by spoofing EAP-TLS messages

   B. DoS attacks occurring because 802.11 management frames are not authenticated

   C. Attackers cracking the encrypted traffic

   D. None of the above

9. In Windows Server 2003, how do you configure WEP protection for a wireless client?

   A. Open the Network Adapter Properties page and configure WEP from the Wireless Networks tab.

   B. Install the high-security encryption pack from Microsoft.

   C. Issue the computer a digital certificate from a Windows Server 2003 Certificate Authority.

   D. Use the utilities provided by the manufacturer of the network adapter.

10. You are attempting to configure a client computer wireless network adapter in Windows Server 2003. You have installed and launched the utility program that came with the adapter, but you cannot configure the settings from it. What is the source of your problem?

    A. You are not a member of the Network Configuration Operators group.

    B. You do not have the correct Windows Service Pack installed.

    C. You do not configure wireless network adapters in Windows Server 2003 through manufacturer's utilities.

    D. Your network administrator has disabled SSID broadcasting for the wireless network.

11. In the past, you spent a lot of time configuring and reconfiguring wireless network settings for clients. You're at the point where you need to prevent wireless clients from configuring their own settings. What can you do to ensure that wireless network settings are configured uniformly for all clients so that they cannot change them?

    A. Configure Local Group Policy.

    B. Configure Site Group Policy.

    C. Configure Domain Group Policy.

    D. Configure Default Domain Controllers Group Policy.

12. Your organization has just implemented Group Policies. On the first morning that Group Policies are applied, you receive a call from a client who can no longer connect to the wireless network at her location. What can you do to figure out the source of her issue?

    A. Use the Resultant Set of Policy Snap-in to assess the impact of Group Policy on her User and Computer Account policy settings.

    B. Use the Resultant Set of Policy Snap-in to assess the impact of Group Policy on her User Account policy settings.

    C. Use the Resultant Set of Policy Snap-in to assess the impact of Group Policy on her Computer Account policy settings.

    D. Block Group Policy inheritance to her User and Computer Accounts.

13. Your company opens five temporary offices for the summer months in different locations every year. To avoid installing network cabling in an office that might not be used in a following year, management has decided to use wireless technology so that the investment in network connectivity can be reused from year to year. One regional manager travels to every office on a regular basis. What is the best solution for enabling the regional manager who needs to connect to the wireless network in every office?

A. Supply the regional manager with a list of SSIDs and WEP keys for every temporary office.

B. Configure Preferred Networks in Network Adapter Properties on the regional manager's laptop.

C. Configure Preferred Networks in Wireless Network (IEEE 802.11) Policy in the Local Group Policy Editor on the regional manager's laptop.

D. Configure Preferred Networks in Wireless Network (IEEE 802.11) Policy for the domain.

14. You want to extend your network to integrate wired and wireless clients; however, you need to isolate wireless clients and encrypt all the network traffic that they generate. What can you do to address these requirements?

    A. Create a separate subnet for all wireless clients by creating a separate zone in DHCP.

    B. Create a separate subnet for all wireless clients by creating a separate zone in DHCP and implement IPSec.

    C. Install a wireless bridge that running IPSec, which connects the wireless segment of the network with the wired section.

    D. Enable IPSec on all wireless clients and APs.

15. You are installing a wireless LAN as part of a wireless pilot project. You want to restrict its use exclusively to those computers that belong to members of the pilot group. What is the best way to begin restricting connections by wireless clients that are not part of the group?

    A. Enable WEP with a 128-bit encryption key.

    B. Disable SSID broadcasts.

    C. Enable MAC address filtering and adding the MAC addresses.

    D. Change the mode from Ad Hoc to Infrastructure.

Self Test Quick Answer Key

For complete questions, answers, and explanations to the Self Test questions in this chapter as well as the other chapters in this book, see the Self Test Appendix.

1. **A, D**
2. **A**
3. **C**
4. **A**
5. **D**
6. **C**
7. **A**
8. **B**
9. **A**
10. **C**
11. **C**
12. **C**
13. **B**
14. **C**
15. **C**

Chapter 10

MCSA/MCSE 70-296

Remote Management

Exam Objectives in this Chapter:

- 4.1 Plan secure network administration methods.
- 4.1.1 Create a plan to offer Remote Assistance to client computers.
- 4.1.2 Plan for remote administration by using Terminal Services.

- ☑ Summary of Exam Objectives
- ☑ Exam Objectives Fast Track
- ☑ Exam Objectives Frequently Asked Questions
- ☑ Self Test
- ☑ Self Test Quick Answer Key

Introduction

With the increasing availability of high-speed Internet connectivity around the globe, workers are increasingly demanding access to corporate resources when they're away from the central office. This demand is coming from users in remote offices, telecommuters, and salespeople who are constantly on the road. Although this ability to access data remotely is great, it creates an additional strain on those who must support this user base. To alleviate some of the burden of supporting these users, it's become necessary to acquire the ability to remotely administer these remote computers.

The concept of remote administration is not new by any means. However, finding the right solution for remotely administering computers has always been a concern for network administrators. Several third-party solutions have been on the market for years, but they typically fell short of administrators' needs. Issues such as security and reliability have been roadblocks on the way to administrators offering their users support via remote administration. Microsoft saw the need for this ability; early on the company offered the Systems Management Server (SMS) tool to assist with remotely assisting clients, but it too fell short of administrators' needs and demands.

In Windows Server 2003, Microsoft has implemented some new technologies but has also expanded on existing technologies, such as Terminal Services, to offer administrators the functionality they need to support remote clients while reducing some of the security risks that were present in earlier applications. In this chapter, you will learn about how to plan, configure, and support remote administration of client computers via the Remote Assistance tool. You will also learn about remotely supporting servers through the use of Terminal Services and its suite of tools. Let's begin with some information on remotely administering client computers.

EXAM 70-296 OBJECTIVE 4.1 4.1.1

Remotely Administering Client Computers

SMS has been Microsoft's weapon of choice for remote control of the desktop since its earliest versions. This began to change when Microsoft Terminal Services was altered so that it could be configured for remote server administration in Windows 2000. Now the Remote Assistance and Remote Desktop Connection capabilities that were introduced in Windows XP have been extended to Microsoft's newest release of the Windows Server 2003 family.

Remote Assistance and Remote Desktop for Administration provide organizations and network administrators with support options that were only available through SMS or third-party applications that provide similar functionality, such as PC Anywhere and Virtual Network Computing (VNC). What sets Remote Assistance apart is that it provides choice and places control over available support options into the hands of the client. Remote Assistance lets the client request assistance from another client so that the remote client (deemed the *expert* in Microsoft parlance) can view and control the local client's desktop and work to resolve any technical issues.

Remote Desktop provides network administrators with the ability to manage a server (or servers) as though they were sitting directly at a server console. This tool is very helpful for administering servers in remote locations, such as the corporate server farm, from any location, such as on a beach in Tahiti, without needing to be physically located in front of the server hardware. Remote Desktop for Administration uses Microsoft Terminal Services technology to open a separate session for each remote client that connects to the system, thereby allowing for management by multiple administrators. It differs from Remote Assistance in that the remotely connected client cannot see what desktop user is doing.

EXAM 70-296 OBJECTIVE 4.1.1

Remote Assistance

Remote Assistance provides the ability for a trusted expert, who could be located anywhere, to make a remote connection to and actively assist someone in need of technical support or instruction. During a Remote Assistance session, the expert can view the client's screen and offer advice or instruction or simply fix the problem. Experts can offer both solicited and unsolicited help, but the act of taking remote control of the client's desktop and addressing the issue or providing the instruction can only be performed once the client has granted his or her permission. Remote Assistance requires that both workstations—the one belonging to the expert and the other to the client—are running Windows XP or Windows Server 2003.

Configuring the Client

By configuring the client system, you provide individuals who use that system with the opportunity to send Remote Assistance invitations and to permit incoming Remote Assistance sessions. To accomplish this task, the server's Remote Assistance properties must be enabled. You can find these properties on the Remote tab of System Properties window (shown in Figure 10.1) by navigating to **Start | Control Panel | System**. Alternatively, you can right-click **My Computer** and left-click **Properties**.

Figure 10.1 Enabling Remote Assistance on the System

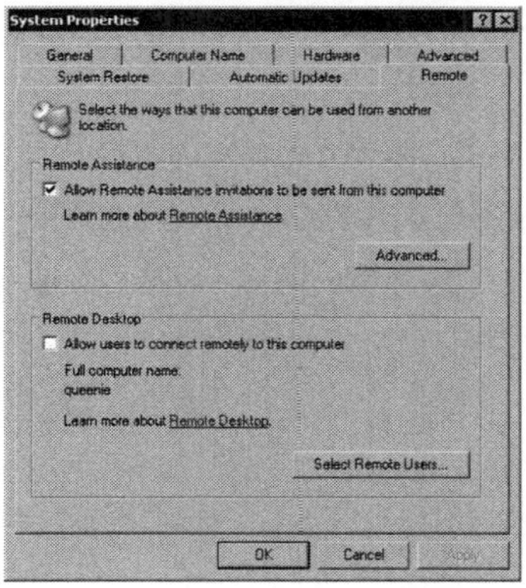

The default setting for Remote Assistance in Windows Server 2003 is that Remote Assistance is disabled and the ability to send and receive invitations is blocked. Click the **Allow Remote Assistance invitations to be sent from this computer** check box in the Remote Assistance portion of the Remote tab to enable Remote Assistance invitations, as demonstrated in Figure 10.1. At this point in the process, the system can send and receive invitations for Remote Assistance, but the experts that provide the assistance cannot take control of the system's desktop.

Clicking the **Advanced** button shown in Figure 10.1 brings up the Remote Assistance Settings dialog box, shown in Figure 10.2. In this dialog box, select the **Allow this computer to be controlled remotely** check box in the Remote Control portion. When you click the **OK** button to accept the change, remote experts then have the ability to take over the desktop and provide assistance. The timeout period for Remote Assistance invitations is set in the Invitations portion of the dialog box. This timeout can be set to a life span of 1 minute up to 99 days; however, the timeout period specified in the Remote Assistance GPO will override the value that is configured in this dialog box if the GPO is enabled for this system.

Figure 10.2 Setting Limits on the Use of Remote Assistance

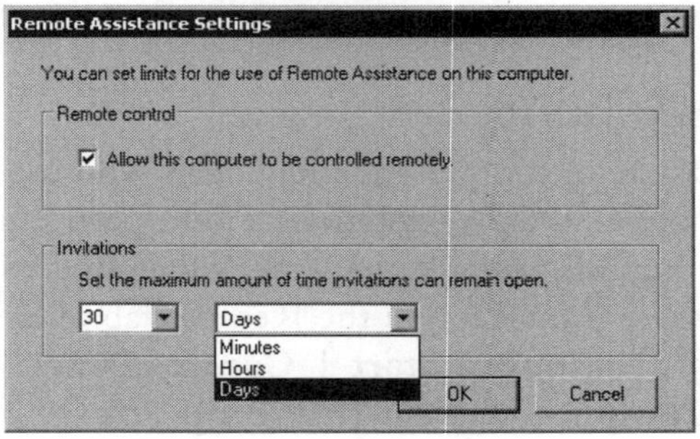

Setting Group Policy for Remote Assistance

Group Policy can be set locally on servers or for all servers that participate in an Active Directory domain. Local Group Policy applies to individual member servers, and domain Group Policy provides comprehensive coverage over all servers in the domain. The local and domain Group Policies that govern Remote Assistance can be found respectively at:

- Console Root/Local Computer Policy/Computer Configuration/Administrative Templates/System/Remote Assistance (as shown in Figure 10.3)
- Console Root/Domain Computer Policy/Computer Configuration/Administrative Templates/System/Remote Assistance

As discussed in Chapter 7, "Managing Group Policy in Windows Server 2003," Group Policy is applied in the following order:

1. Local Group Policies
2. Site Group Policies
3. Domain Group Policies
4. Organizational Unit Group Policies

The order is critical because it means that the local Group Policy object is processed first, followed by GPOs that are linked to the sites, domains, and OU of which the computer or user is a direct member. Whatever GPO is applied last overwrites the GPOs that were applied earlier in the process. The one exception is where a site, domain, or OU Group Policy object is tagged with the No Override attribute. In this case, the object that is highest in the Active Directory hierarchy will "win" and be applied over all others, regardless of processing order. All of this is to say that you need to be careful when you're deciding where to configure a Group Policy, because a domain Group Policy object will override a local object in almost every instance.

Figure 10.3 Accessing the Remote Assistance Group Policy Objects

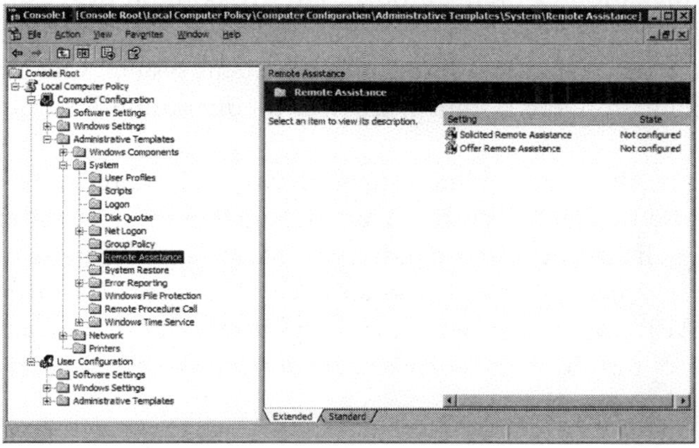

The first Group Policy element is for Solicited Remote Assistance, which dictates whether clients can invite another client to provide technical help through Remote Assistance. If the policy is disabled, clients will not be able to request Remote Assistance and the server will not permit remote control from another workstation; otherwise, Remote Assistance is an available support option. If the status is set to Not Configured, clients have the ability to either enable or disable and configure Remote Assistance according to their own preferences in System Properties (**Start | Control Panel | System**), and the default maximum time that a Remote Assistance invitation can stay open is determined by the Control Panel setting. As depicted in Figure 10.4, if the policy is set to Enabled, there are three settings that you can configure: maximum ticket time, the method for sending e-mail invitations, and permitting remote control of this computer.

Figure 10.4 Configuring Solicited Remote Assistance Properties

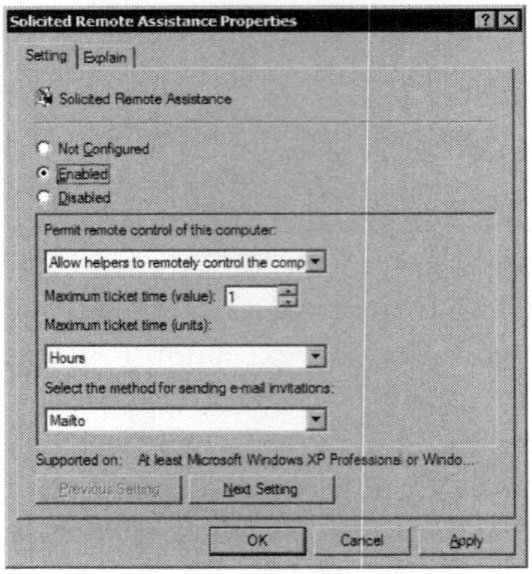

The "Maximum ticket time (value)" setting sets a limit on the amount of time that a Remote Assistance invitation can remain open. The "Maximum ticket time (units)" setting specifies whether the number set in the previous field is the number of minutes, hours, or days. Open invitations are "open windows" into the client system. Once the timeout period has expired for an invitation, the system will reject the incoming Remote Assistance connection attempt.

The "Select the method for sending e-mail invitations" setting dictates the messaging format that will be used to send Remote Assistance invitations. Depending on the preferred electronic messaging client, you can use either the Mailto option, by which the expert will connect through a link that is embedded in an HTML-formatted e-mail message, or the Simple MAPI (SMAPI) standard, in which the expert receives the invitation in a file attachment. For this option to work correctly, the e-mail client must support the mail format standard that is selected.

EXAM WARNING

If you leave Terminal Services Group Policy at the default setting of "Not configured," remote connectivity through Terminal Services will be enabled with minimal security. The best practice is to disable remote connectivity where it is not required and enable Group Policy only when needed.

The "Permit remote control of this computer" setting dictates whether a client on a remote workstation computer can take control of this server. If a client invites an expert to connect to the server and gives that client specific permission to complete the remote connection, the expert can take control of the server. The expert can only make requests to take control during a Remote Assistance session, and the client can terminate the session at any time.

Exercise 10.01

Configuring Security for Remote Assistance

Before you allow an expert to take remote control of your system, it is a good idea to make sure that you define how invitations are sent from your system and how long the invitations are allowed to remain open without being acted on. These invitations represent windows of time when your system is open to receiving inbound remote control sessions. There are two ways to configure these parameters: through Group Policy and through System Properties on the local system. Follow these steps to configure the Remote Assistance GPO:

First you have to add the Remote Assistance snap-in MMC:

1. Click **Start | Run**, type **mmc** in the Open: box, and click **OK**.
2. Click **File | Add/Remove Snap-in....**
3. In the Add/Remove Snap-in dialog box, click **Add.....**
4. In the Add Standalone Snap-in dialog box, click **Group Policy Object Editor**, click **Add**, and then click **Close** to finish.
5. Click **Close** in the **Add Standalone Snap-in** dialog box, and click **OK** in the **Add/Remove Snap-in** dialog box.

Now configure the Remote Assistance GPO:

1. Navigate to the Local Remote Assistance Group Policy Object or the Domain Remote Assistance Group Policy Object, located at **Console Root/Local Computer Policy/Computer Configuration/Administrative Templates/System/Remote Assistance** or **Console Root/Domain Computer Policy/Computer Configuration/Administrative Templates/System/Remote Assistance**, respectively.
2. Double-click **Solicited Remote Assistance**. This action opens the Solicited Remote Assistance Properties window.
3. Click the **Enabled** radio button, which will activate the rest of the fields in the window.
4. Click the drop down box under **Permit remote control of this computer** and select **Allow helpers to remotely control the computer**.
5. We will set the life span of invitations from the default value of 1 hour to 30 minutes. Use the scroll buttons or highlight the field and enter **30** for the Maximum ticket time (value). In the Maximum ticket time (units) drop down box, select **Minutes**.
6. Select **Simple MAPI** from the **Select the method for sending e-mail invitations** drop-down box.

7. Click the **OK** button to accept these changes. The policy will be effective immediately, if you are configuring local Group Policy, or at the next refresh interval if configuring a GPO.

Finally, to configure security on the local system, complete the following steps:

1. Navigate to System Properties (**Start | Control Panel | System**).
2. Click the **Remote** tab to select it.
3. Click the **Allow Remote Assistance invitations to be sent from this computer** check box in the Remote Assistance portion of the Remote tab.
4. Click the **Advanced...** button to bring up the Remote Assistance Settings dialog box.
5. Select the **Allow this computer to be controlled remotely** check box in the Remote control portion of the window.
6. The desired life span for Remote Assistance invitations is set in the Invitations portion of the dialog box. Under **Set the maximum amount of time the invitation can remain open,** select **30** in the first drop-down box and **Minutes** in the second.
7. Click the **OK** button to accept the change. The timeout period specified in the Remote Assistance GPO will override the value that is configured in this dialog box if the GPO is enabled for this system.

Exam Warning

An expert can connect to the server only with the explicit permission of the requestor. If Remote Assistance is set to Disabled or Not Configured and it is disabled in the Control Panel, the Offer Remote Assistance setting will also be disabled.

The other Group Policy element for configuring Remote Assistance is Offer Remote Assistance. This setting is used to dictate whether or not an expert can offer Remote Assistance to this computer without a user explicitly initiating the request through a file, e-mail, or Windows Messenger. Using this setting, an expert can offer Remote Assistance to the server. Although the expert can initiate Remote Assistance, he or she cannot connect to the server unannounced or take remote control without permission from the requestor, in a process that consists of two steps. When the expert tries to make the remote connection, the requestor is still given the opportunity to accept or deny the connection. If the connection is accepted, the expert has view-only permissions for the server. Once the connection has been accepted, the client has to explicitly grant the expert permission to remotely control the desktop.

If this option is set to Enabled, you as the expert can offer Remote Assistance. When you configure this setting, you can select either "Allow helpers to only view the computer" or "Allow helpers to remotely control the computer," as shown in Figure 10.5. In addition to making this selection, when you configure this setting you also specify "helpers," a list of users or groups that will be allowed to offer Remote Assistance. To configure the list of helpers, click **Show**. This opens a new window in which you can enter the names of the helpers. Each user or group can only be added one at a time, using one of the following formats:

- *<Domain Name>\<User Name>*
- *<Domain Name>\<Group Name>*

Figure 10.5 Enabling Offer Remote Assistance Properties

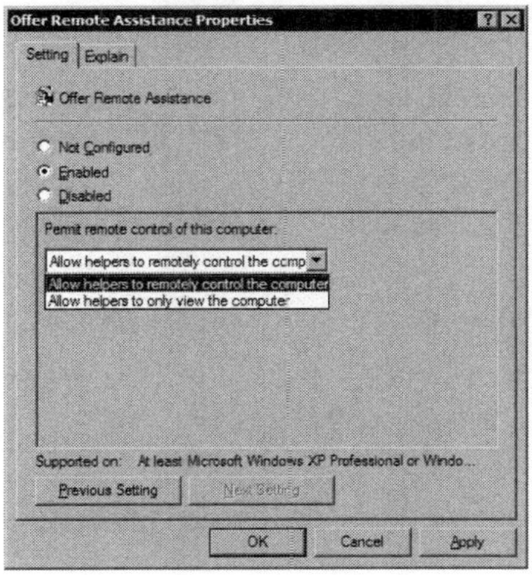

Test Day Tip

If Offer Remote Assistance is enabled on the client's workstation, an expert can offer Remote Assistance to that client without an explicit invitation. The expert must be added as an expert on the client's workstation in Group Policy or be a member of the local Administrators group.

If this policy is set to Disabled or Not Configured, users or groups cannot offer unsolicited Remote Assistance to the server.

Requesting Help Using Remote Assistance

Depending on the technology at their disposal, clients have two avenues though which they can request Remote Assistance:

- Windows Messenger
- Electronic mail

In Windows Server 2003, Windows Messenger is not part of the default installation; it must be deliberately installed after the fact. Outlook Express is installed by default, which makes e-mail the most probable choice if you decide to enable Remote Assistance.

New & Noteworthy...

Leveraging Support Resources Outside the Service Desk

Remote Assistance provides an additional avenue for clients to request and receive technical support. If a client has the opportunity to ask a colleague for help with a problem that is common or that the individual has recently experienced, the individual can relay the knowledge that he or she has received from the "official" service desk. The ability to request and receive help from anyone extends the reach of the service desk without increasing its workload, because Remote Assistance provides the capability for knowledge imparted by the service desk to be passed on by anyone in the organization, not just those who work in client support roles.

Remote Assistance is also a good facility for individuals who are "in the know" to demonstrate techniques for solving common problems. Remote experts can take control of the desktop when the client is watching and following along with verbal instruction that the expert is giving over the phone or even through the server's audio system. The functionality of Remote Assistance mirrors the saying "Give a man a fish and he eats for a day; teach a man to fish and he eats for a lifetime." Anyone can use this tool to implement the quick fix without leaving their desks, and it can be used to show people how to implement a solution themselves so that they can be self-sufficient.

Requesting help from an expert begins in the Help and Support Center (**Start | Help and Support**). The opening screen is shown in Figure 10.6. Clicking the **Invite someone to help you** link takes you to the next screen (shown in Figure 10.7), where you can choose your preferred method of Remote Assistance. The number beside the "View installation status" link indicates the number of outstanding Remote Assistance invitations.

Figure 10.6 Beginning the Process of Requesting Remote Assistance

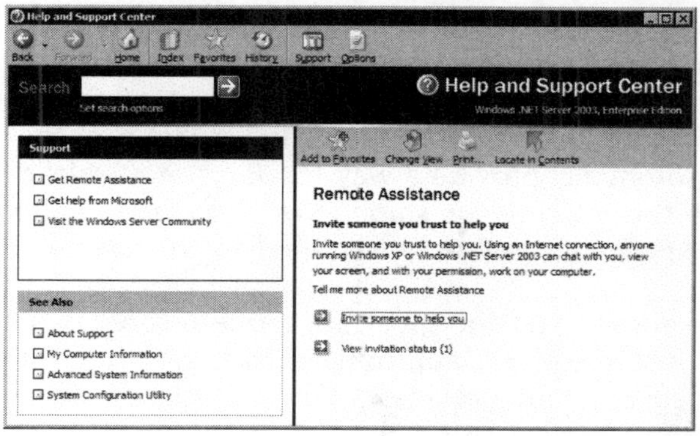

As shown in Figure 10.7, invitations for Remote Assistance can be sent from the Help and Support Center through Windows Messenger, if it is installed, or through e-mail. If your e-mail client and that of your preferred expert supports messages sent in HTML format, a hyperlinked URL can be embedded in the body of a message and sent to the desired expert. If not, you have the option of creating a file that contains the invitation that can then be attached to a message and sent. The recipient only needs to click the hyperlink or open the file to invoke the Remote Assistance session.

Figure 10.7 Choosing an Invitation Method

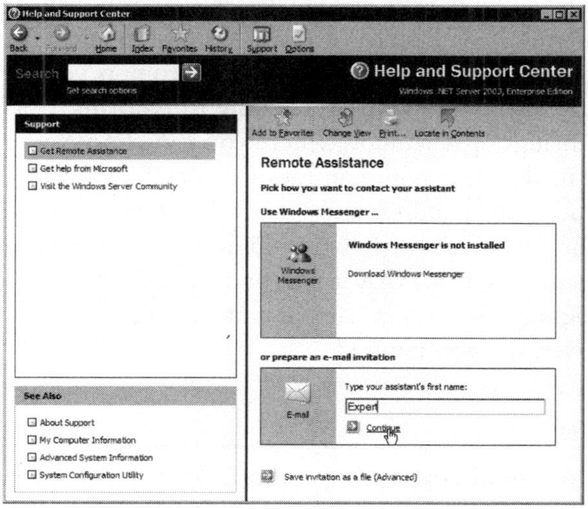

Configuring & Implementing...

Server Software Packages

From a security standpoint, the maxim is that if something is not required, it should not be installed. After all, every piece of software is a component that must be tested, secured, maintained, and updated. In addition, every installed software component can potentially provide a way for someone to deliberately or accidentally compromise the integrity or stability of a system. Limiting the number of installed software packages to what is required mathematically reduces the risk of compromise.

One way to ensure that the most appropriate services and applications are installed is to select the most appropriate role, or roles, for your server. The Windows Server 2003 family provides 11 preconfigured server roles. To apply a server role, you can install it using the Configure Your Server Wizard, which is accessed from the Manage Your Server utility.

In the context of remote administration for servers, you might be tempted to choose the Terminal Server role when configuring your system. Remote assistance and remote administration for servers use the functionality provided by Terminal Services, but your server does not need any additional software to administer the system from a remote workstation.

Unlike Windows XP, Windows Messenger is an optional Windows Server 2003 component and is neither installed by default nor inextricably intertwined with the operating system. If Windows Messenger is installed on your system, clicking the **Windows Messenger** option launches Windows Messenger and prompts you to sign in, if you're not already authenticated. At this point, you can navigate to **Actions | Ask for Remote Assistance...**, which brings up a window where you can choose an expert from your contacts who is signed in to the same communications service as you are in the My Contacts tab, or you can enter the e-mail address and specify the instant-messaging service of your expert of choice on the Other tab, as shown in Figure 10.8. If the expert is outside your organization, there is a good chance that it will be the .NET Messenger Service; however, other electronic messaging systems that have instant-messaging capability, such as Microsoft Exchange 2000 or newer, can also be used.

Exam Warning

Make sure that you read any exam questions concerning Windows Messaging clients very carefully. There is no Remote Assistance functionality in the current version of MSN Messenger, only in Windows Messenger, which is only available to Windows XP desktops and newer. If you get a question on Remote Assistance through MSN Messenger or through Windows Messenger on another version of Windows, do not fall for the trap.

Figure 10.8 Asking for Remote Assistance Using Windows Messenger

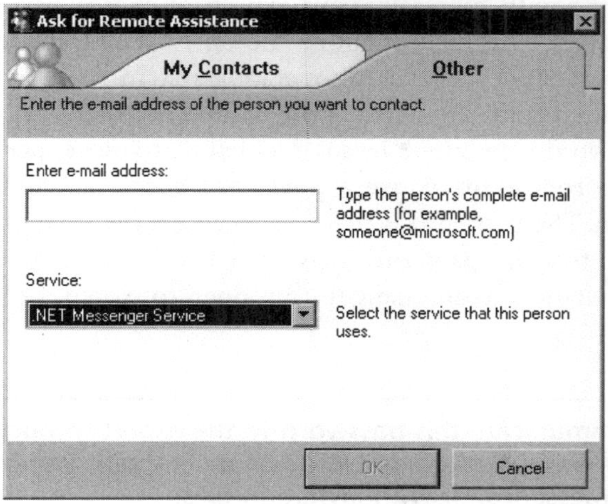

You can also request Remote Assistance through an active instant-messaging conversation within Windows Messenger, as shown in Figure 10.9. The option to ask for Remote Assistance is just beneath the Send E-Mail link and just above any options to collaborate on important applications. Once the invitation is made, the expert must accept the request, and the Remote Assistance window will open. The requestor must explicitly grant the expert permission to take control of the client desktop and can terminate a Remote Assistance session at any time.

Figure 10.9 Initiating the Invitation from Within a Windows Messenger Conversation

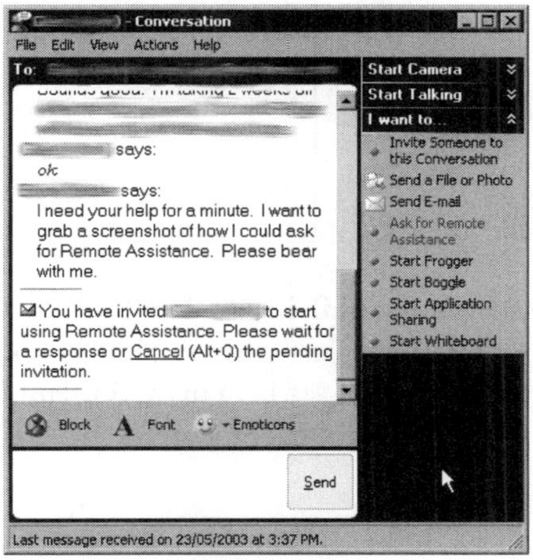

The other avenue for requesting Remote Assistance is through e-mail. Just about everyone you are dealing with, especially your experts of choice, have e-mail, and a Remote Assistance request by e-mail might be the only method for receiving assistance from an expert who works with a different operating system. As shown in Figure 10.10, the only information required from the client is the desired life span and a decision as to whether or not a password is required. If it is decided that your expert needs a password, click the **Require the recipient to use a password** check box and enter the password twice for confirmation. The password is required to access the Remote Assistance window. It is important to note that this password is associated with this particular invitation and is only valid until the invitation status changes from open to closed.

Test Day Tip

You need to communicate this password to the expert through a separate communication channel because the password is not sent with Remote Assistance invitations, in e-mail messages, or with invitation files.

Figure 10.10 Creating an E-Mail Remote Assistance Invitation

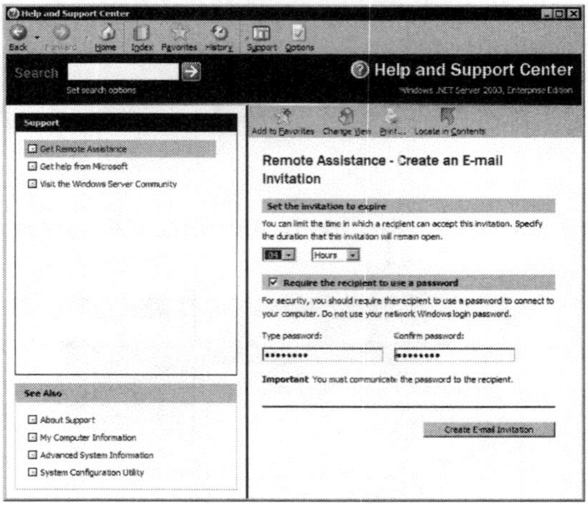

Once you click the **Continue e-mail invitation** button, the default e-mail client is launched and a new message window opens with an already composed invitation message and embedded URL, as shown in Figure 10.11. This URL launches the Remote Assistance window and leads the expert to the target client system.

Figure 10.11 Sending the Invitation Through an E-Mail Message

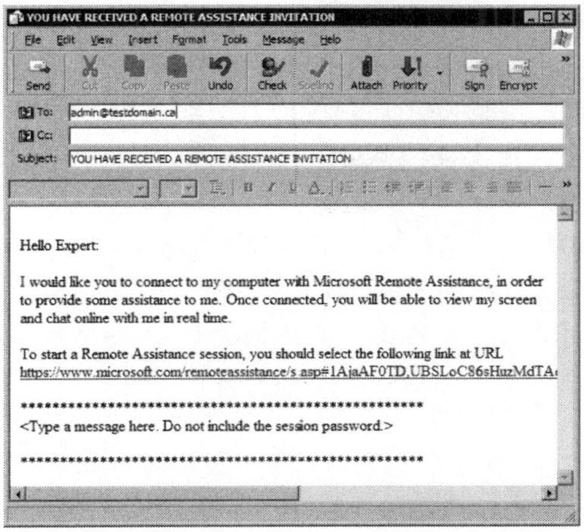

There are several circumstances in which an e-mail message is not an appropriate method of requesting Remote Assistance. There could be Windows Server 2003 servers that do not have a default mail client installed or that have a mail client that does not support or permit HTML-formatted messages. Furthermore, your expert or experts of choice might not prefer or accept HTML-formatted messages. In these circumstances, you have the ability to create an invitation file, which can only be executed in Microsoft Windows XP and Server 2003 systems. As demonstrated in Figures 10.12 and 10.13, the only information required for a Remote Assistance invitation file is the name that will appear on the invitation, the life span of the invitation, and a password, if desired.

EXERCISE 10.02

CREATING AND SENDING A REMOTE ASSISTANCE INVITATION

In order to receive Remote Assistance, you must first make a request for it. Walk through the following steps to create a Remote Assistance invitation within the body of an e-mail message:

1. Navigate to the Help and Support Center (**Start | Help and Support**).
2. Click the **Remote Assistance** link. The link is highlighted in bold text in the first bullet point of the list on the right side of the window.
3. Click **Invite someone to help you**.
4. Since we want to send the invitation in an e-mail message, enter the recipient's name in the field beside the e-mail icon under **or** prepare an e-mail invitation. Click the **Continue** link.

5. In keeping with Exercise 10.1, under **Set the invitation to expire**, select **30** in the first drop-down box and **Minutes** in the second.
6. Click the **Require the recipient to use a password** check box to ensure that a password is used for Remote Assistance, and enter the password in the Type password field. Re-enter the password in the Confirm password field.
7. Click the **Create E-mail Invitation** button to accept these settings and to continue sending the invitation.
8. When the default e-mail client launches, a new message window opens with a formatted invitation message and embedded URL for Remote Assistance. Enter the recipient's e-mail address and, if you have no changes to the body of the message, click the **Send** button.

Figure 10.12 Creating a Remote Assistance Invitation File

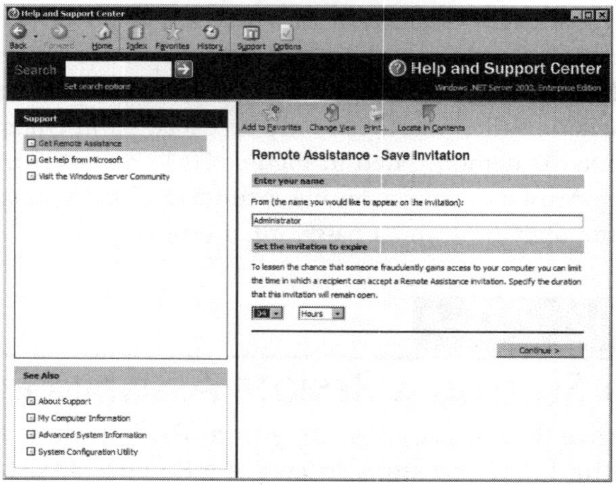

The file can be saved to any folder and then transferred to another system by the most appropriate means at a convenient time. The file can be transferred by e-mail, sent through an instant-messaging client, or transferred on a diskette by "sneaker-net." The best method is the efficient one on which both you and your expert of choice agree.

Figure 10.13 Saving the Invitation File

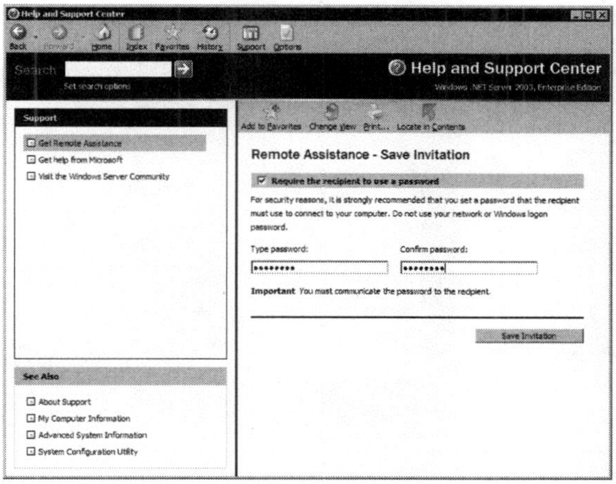

As soon as the file is saved, the number of open invitations for the requestor's system is increased by one.

Providing Help Using Remote Assistance

When you receive an invitation for Remote Assistance through Windows Messenger, e-mail, or a transferred invitation file and you accept it, the Remote Assistance window is launched. The client is always in control of the session, and the client must explicitly grant permission for any activity you want to conduct before you proceed. This includes starting the session, sending files, communicating over a voice connection, and taking control of the desktop. At any point during the session, the client can terminate it.

As shown in Figure 10.14, the Remote Assistance window is divided into three main areas:

- A Remote Assistance taskbar
- The Chat History panel
- A Remote Control panel

The taskbar at the top of the window contains buttons for every type of activity that you need to conduct to provide Remote Assistance. Arguably the most important and most used button is Take Control. This button, when clicked by the expert and when the client grants permission, provides the expert with full control of the client's desktop, except where Terminal Services Group Policy limits access. (Please refer to the "Securing Remote Assistance" section later in the chapter for more information on this topic.) The Send a File and Start Talking buttons are discussed in the "Sending Files" and "Talking Via Remote Assistance" sections, respectively.

Figure 10.14 Starting a Remote Assistance Session

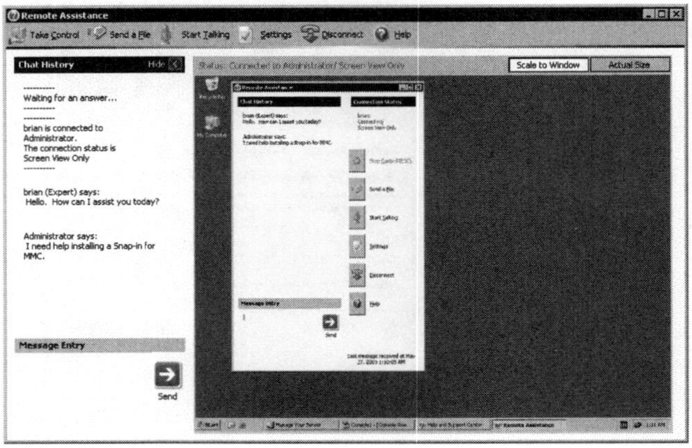

The Chat History section of the Remote Assistance window provides for real-time interaction between the expert and the client through instant-messaging. In addition to text messages sent back and forth, the chat history records any events that occur during the session, such as changes in status, transferred files, and permission being granted for various activities.

The Remote Control panel is where the expert does what he or she has been invited to do. As mentioned earlier, the client must grant permission before the expert can take control of the client desktop. When the Remote Assistance session opens, you will see two Start menu buttons: the one in the bottom left for your workstation and the other inside the Remote Control panel for the system that you are assisting. If you click the Actual Size button at the top right of the panel and the remote system's screen resolution is the same or greater than that of your workstation, the Remote Control panel will take over your screen real estate; be very certain that you know whose Start button you are using to provide assistance. You could end up reconfiguring your own workstation.

Sending Files

On occasion, a solution could require installing new driver files or a hotfix, and the Remote Assistance window provides the facility to transfer files within a session. As demonstrated in Figure 10.15, clicking the **Send a File** button opens a dialog box to browse for, select, and send a file. When you click the **Send File** button in the dialog box, a window to Accept or Reject the file appears on the remote system. Once the client accepts this action, the file the transfer begins. A confirmation message appears once the file has been sent successfully or in the event that the file transfer fails or is rejected.

Figure 10.15 Sending a File through the Remote Assistance Window

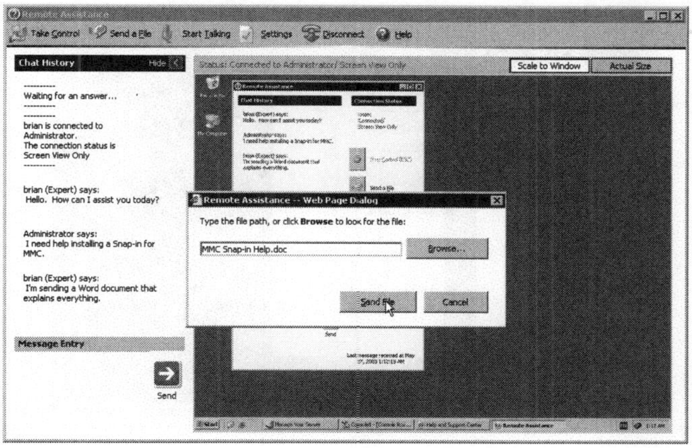

Talking Via Remote Assistance

Much of the Remote Assistance functionality has been derived from Microsoft NetMeeting. This becomes evident when you're working with communications functionality. A Remote Assistance session in which the expert has remote control of a client's desktop is more comfortable for the client if the expert can interact with the client, announce what he or she is doing, and ask questions before proceeding. It is pretty unnerving to watch someone else do things to your workstation when you do not know what is going on in the mind of the person who is doing the work.

Communication during a Remote Assistance session can be conducted by real-time interactive text messaging similar to Windows Messenger (see Figure 10.16) and through an actual voice conversation using the audio capability of the expert and client's systems and the network that connects the two. Instant-messaging traffic occurs within the Remote Assistance session and does not require Windows Messenger or another instant-messaging client. This feature is very beneficial for environments in which instant-messaging violates company policy.

The facility for voice communication comes directly from NetMeeting and uses the same familiar wizards for calibrating the microphone and audio playback. If your terminal is not equipped with a microphone or even a sound card, voice communication is not an option. For voice communication to be effective, you must have a fairly reliable network connection to produce good sound quality.

Blocking Remote Assistance Requests

To block Remote Assistance requests, you must do the reverse of what was discussed in the "Configuring the Client" section. Again, you will find the properties that need to be disabled on the Remote tab of System Properties by navigating to **Start | Control Panel | System**. Alternatively, you can right-click **My Computer** and left-click **Properties**. Clear

Figure 10.16 Chatting Through the Remote Assistance Window

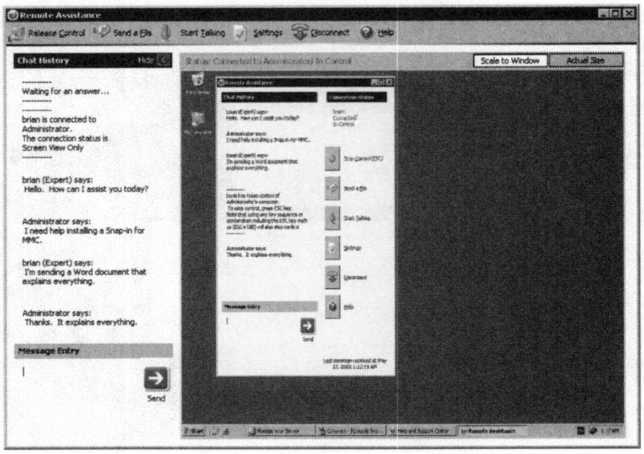

the check box in the **Remote Assistance** portion of the Remote tab and, as shown in Figure 10.17, the Advanced button will become disabled.

Figure 10.17 Disabling Remote Assistance to Block Remote Assistance Requests

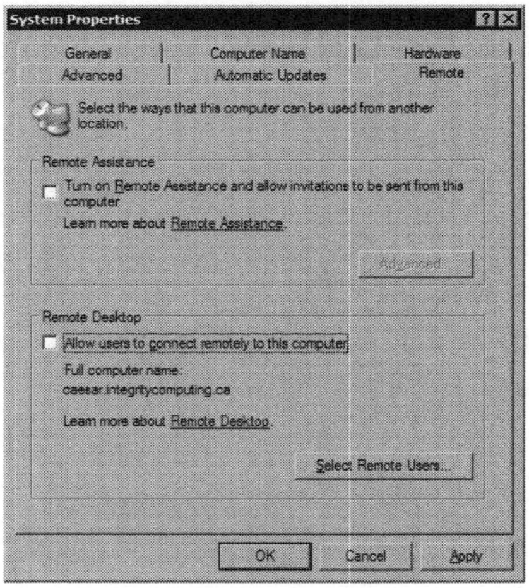

Once Remote Assistance has been disabled, invitations cannot be sent to experts nor can experts make unsolicited offers for assistance.

Head of the Class...

Blocking Remote Assistance: Three Lines of Defense

For any number of reasons, an organization might want to block Remote Assistance invitations. Perhaps the organization wants all technical support requests to be channeled through the central service desk, or perhaps concerns over security prompt an organization to prevent prying eyes from outside taking control of its corporate workstations. Depending on the degree to which you enable or disable Remote Assistance in your organization, you can allow or block the tool at any or all of the following places:

- Local system
- Internal network
- Public gateway

Remote Assistance can be enabled or disabled on the local system through the local Remote Assistance Group Policy or on the Remote tab of System Properties. If you want to block members of the local Users group, you should disable Remote Assistance using the Remote Assistance GPO, and the Remote tab will become fully enabled in System Properties.

For the internal network, Active Directory and domain level Group Policy can be used together to enable and configure or to completely disable Remote Assistance in a consistent manner across the enterprise. A GPO configured with the appropriate Remote Assistance settings can be applied at the site, domain, or OU level within Active Directory to carefully target where the settings are applied.

Preventing assistance from experts from outside the organization is very straightforward. Have the administrator of the firewall that guards your public gateway to the Internet block TCP port 3389. Once 3389 is blocked, Remote Assistance invitations cannot be replied to from external experts because the request for a session is dropped when it hits the organization's firewall.

Securing Remote Assistance

The first step to securing the Remote Assistance tool is to disable or prevent access to all services that are not required for a Remote Assistance session. This can be accomplished using the Local Terminal Services Group Policy, or if you want the same security precautions applied to all domain controllers in an Active Directory domain, to the domain, which are located in Console Root\Local Computer Policy\Computer Configuration\Administrative Templates\Windows Components\Terminal Services and Console Root\Default Domain Controller Policy\Computer Configuration\Administrative Templates\Windows Components\Terminal Services, respectively. The two key Group Policy settings for securing the activities that are directly associated with Terminal Services are Client/Server data redirection and Encryption and Security.

To enhance security, you can use the settings under Client/Server data redirection to disable the use of a number of system components across a Remote Assistance session and any other session that uses Terminal Services in the background. Disabling the use of any or all of these components not only enhances the security of the session—it also makes the session performance more efficient. As shown in Figure 10.18, you can disable:

- Clipboard redirection
- Smart card device redirection
- COM port redirection
- Client printer redirection
- LPT port redirection
- Drive redirection
- Audio redirection

Figure 10.18 Configuring Client/Server Data Redirection

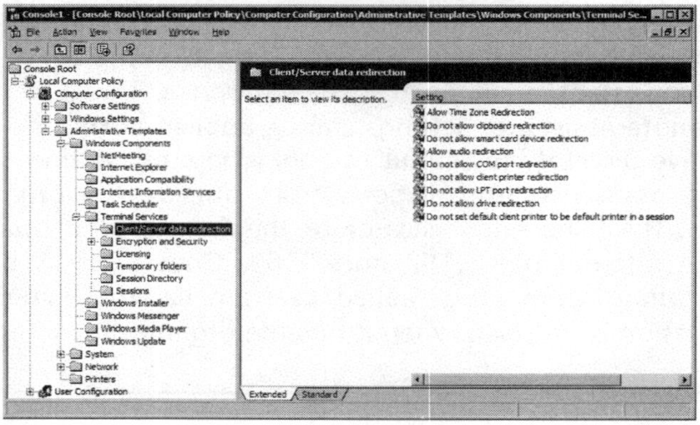

The actual session can be protected by enforcing password security, establishing an appropriate encryption level for all data transmitted between the client system and the expert's system, and setting the duration of the life span of an open Remote Assistance invitation before it expires.

Password Security

We all know that the Internet is a dangerous place, and one of the best places to start securing Remote Desktop sessions is by requiring that all users supply a password. It is recommended that you go one step further and prevent automatic password passing—the automatic transfer of the logged-on client's authentication credentials from the local session to the Remote Desktop session. To accomplish this task, you should enable the **Always prompt client for password upon connection in the Terminal Services Group**

Policy setting. When this setting is enabled, the client must supply a password in the Windows Logon dialog box whenever a Remote Desktop session is initiated. The ability to transfer authentication credentials could be desirable in secure environments. It is possible to configure something similar to single sign-on so that clients have the ability to quickly and securely access other systems without having to re-enter a username and password.

To access Terminal Services Group Policy, the following steps must be completed to add the Group Policy snap-in:

1. Click **Start | Run**, type **mmc** in the Open: box, and click **OK**.
2. On the **File** menu, click **Add/Remove Snap-in...**.
3. In the Add/Remove Snap-in dialog box, click **Add...**.
4. In the Add Standalone Snap-in dialog box, click **Group Policy Objects Editor**, click **Add**, and then click **Finish** to complete the Group Policy wizard.
5. Once back in the Add Standalone Snap-in dialog box, click **Close** to finish, and click **Close** in the Add Standalone Snap-in dialog box to complete the process.
6. In the Console Root pane, double-click **Computer Configuration | Administrative Templates | Windows Components | Terminal Services**.

In the list of Group Policy options that is displayed in the right-hand pane is a folder item called **Encryption and Security**. It contains the option "Always prompt client for password upon connection policy," as shown in Figure 10.19.

Figure 10.19 Enabling Password Security for Terminal Services

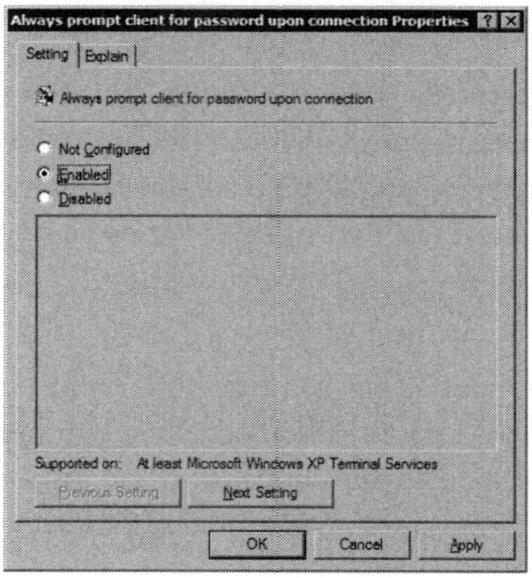

Password security can be greatly enhanced by password policies such as password retention and complex passwords. Policies can be set to ensure that passwords expire at predetermined intervals and that past passwords cannot be reused. Passwords are considered complex if they meet the following criteria:

- Contain at least eight characters
- Not a word found in the dictionary
- Mixture of upper- and lowercase letters
- Include numbers
- Include special characters, such as punctuation

Passwords that meet these criteria are not easily guessed and are less likely to be cracked quickly by brute-force or dictionary-based attacks.

Client Connection Encryption Levels

The "Set client connection encryption level" Group Policy setting specifies whether or not all traffic sent between the client workstation and the remote system during a Terminal Services session is encrypted and assigns the strength of the encryption that will be used.

TEST DAY TIP

You cannot change the encryption level using other Group Policy or Terminal Services configurations if FIPS compliance has already been enabled by the "System cryptography: Use FIPS-compliant algorithms for encryption, hashing, and signing" GPO.

If the status is set to Enabled, encryption for all connections to the server is set to the level you specify. By default, encryption is set to High. As demonstrated in Figure 10.20, the following encryption levels are available:

- **FIPS Compliant (not shown)** Encrypts data sent from client to server and from server to client to meet the FIPS 140-1 standard, a security implementation designed for certifying cryptographic software. Use this level when Terminal Services connections require the highest degree of encryption. FIPS 140-1 validated software is required by the U.S. Government and requested by other prominent institutions.
- **High** Encrypts data sent from client to server and from server to client using strong 128-bit encryption. Use this level when the remote system is running in an environment containing 128-bit clients only (such as Remote Desktop Connection clients). Clients that do not support this level of encryption cannot connect.
- **Client Compatible** Encrypts data sent from client to server and from server to client at the maximum key strength supported by the client. Use this level when the remote system is running in an environment containing mixed or legacy clients.
- **Low** Encrypts data sent from the client to the server using 56-bit encryption. Data that is sent from the server to the client is not encrypted.

Figure 10.20 Setting the Client Connection Encryption Level

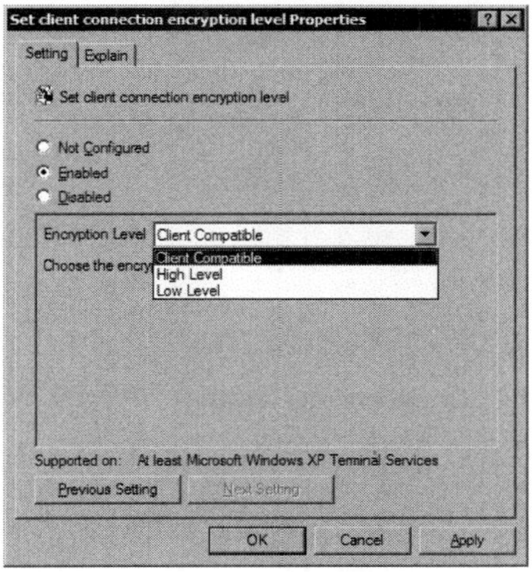

If the status is set to Disabled or Not Configured, the encryption level is not enforced through the GPO being modified. However, administrators can set the encryption level on the server using the Terminal Services Configuration tool, or another GPO.

Setting Remote Assistance Timeout

The life span of Remote Assistance invitations should be appropriately configured. The best practice is to keep the invitations open long enough for the chosen expert to respond but short enough to ensure that invitations are not left open beyond their usefulness. Because an invitation provides an open door to at least view the server, having a bunch of open invitations to potentially more than one expert makes it difficult to keep track of who has been invited to take control and increases the chances that your network will be breached.

From the Terminal Services Group Policy, shown in Figure 10.21, the value and units that set maximum ticket life can be configured down to a minimum of one minute and up to 9999 days. The invitation timeout can also be configured by the client behind the Advanced button on the Remote tab of System Properties. In Figure 10.22, in the Invitations section of the Remote Assistance Settings dialog box, the same type of time adjustment can be made as that of the Terminal Services Group Policy.

Firewalls and Remote Assistance

The Remote Assistance tool uses Remote Desktop Protocol (RDP) to connect the desktops of the client who is requesting help and the expert who is coming to the rescue. RDP uses TCP port 3389 for this connection. If you want to allow users within an organization to receive help through Remote Assistance from experts outside your organization, port 3389 must be opened on the firewall, as shown in Figure 10.23. Closing port 3389 prevents clients from receiving external help.

Figure 10.21 Adjusting the Life Span of a Remote Assistance Invitation

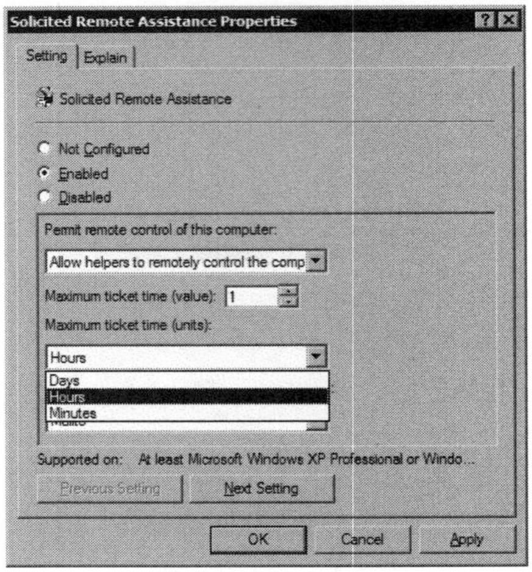

Figure 10.22 Setting Limits on the Use of Remote Assistance

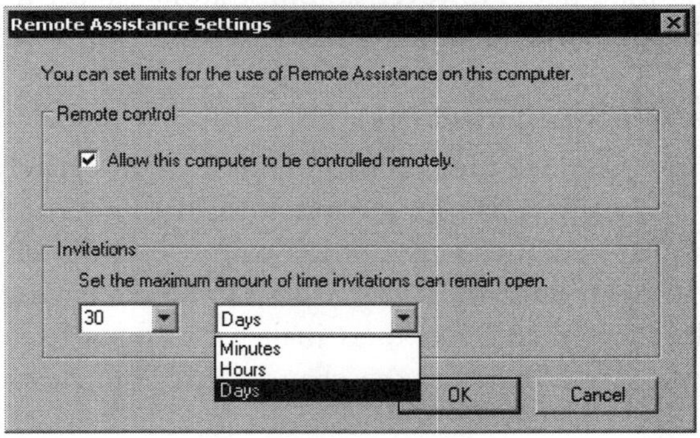

Exam Warning

The TCP port for RDP (3389) is different from the TCP port required for Windows Messenger (1863). Windows Messenger is not required for communication during a Remote Assistance session. To support voice communications in both directions through the firewall, you must open all UDP ports between 5004 and 65535 to accommodate signaling (SIP) and media streams (RTP) because dynamic ports are used. Opening ports 6891 through 6900, inclusive, will enable file transfer.

Figure 10.23 Managing Firewall Ports to Accommodate Remote Assistance

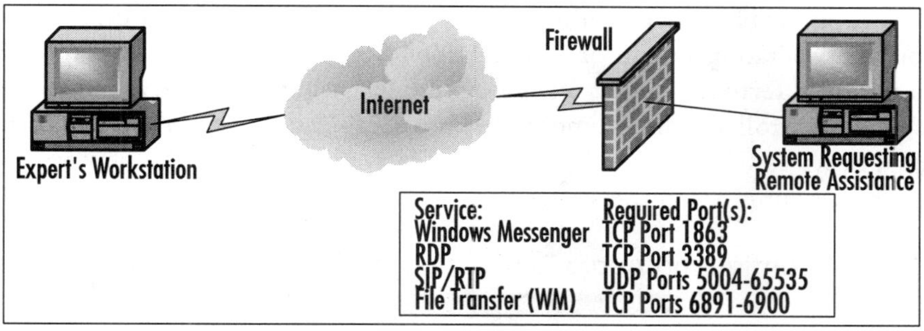

If port 3389 is closed, you will prevent all Remote Desktop and Terminal Services traffic from passing through your firewall. To permit these services, use Group Policy to limit Remote Assistance requests.

Terminal Services Remote Administration

EXAM 70-296 OBJECTIVE 4.1.2

If you are familiar with new features that were introduced with Windows 2000, you will recall that they gave you the ability to remotely manage a Windows 2000 server using Terminal Services in Remote Administration mode. With Windows Server 2003, Terminal Services in Remote Administration mode has evolved into Remote Desktop for Administration. With Remote Desktop for Administration, you still have the ability to manage a computer from virtually any computer on your network; however, the new version is specifically designed for server management because you can now log on remotely to the actual console of the server as though you were physically located at the server console, using the Remote Desktop snap-in.

New Features in Terminal Services

Several new features greatly enhance the experience and security of Terminal Services and Remote Desktop for Administration. The most prominent features are:

1. Redirection of sounds from the server to the management workstation within the Remote Desktop for Administration session
2. Enhanced integration of Terminal Services in Group Policy
3. Display enhancements, including greater color depth and screen resolution

Audio Redirection

Audio redirection enables the reproduction of system-generated sounds on a client workstation from the operating system or running applications that attempt to play a .WAV sound file within a Terminal Server session. As shown in Figure 10.24, audio redirection is configured and controlled from Remote Desktop Connection—the newest incarnation of the Terminal Services Client—yet the functionality is embedded in the new version of Terminal Services running on the server.

Figure 10.24 Configuring Audio Redirection from the Remote Server to the Client

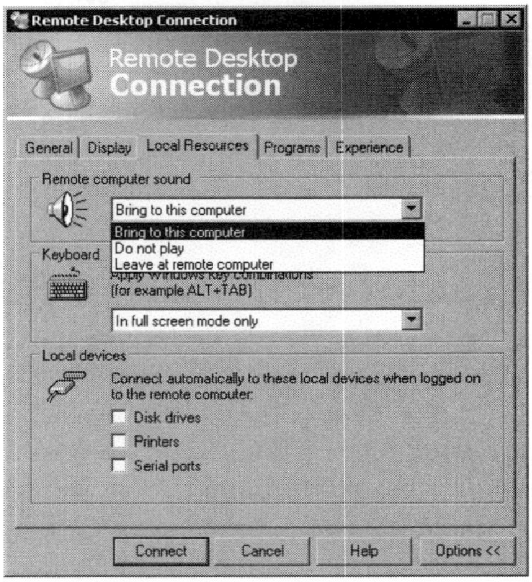

In the context of server administration, this is a feature that could prove very useful. If you are the kind of network administrator who prefers to keep a few Remote Desktop Connection sessions open on your desktop, having audio redirection enabled will provide you with audible cues when something pops up in one of the sessions. Since all Windows audio notifications are stored in .WAV audio format, any sounds that are triggered by information or an error will be redirected to the client workstation.

Group Policy Integration

In Windows Server 2003, Terminal Services continues to be more deeply integrated with Group Policy. By integrating Terminal Services with Group Policy, we are now able to define the configuration of Terminal Services on both a local server and for the the multiple Terminal Services servers that are members of a domain in the forest using Group Policy. In addition, the Resultant Set of Policy snap-in provides the ability to gauge the impact of Terminal Services Group Policy in conjunction with other Group Policies.

As shown in Figure 10.25, with Windows Server 2003 you can manage the behavior of Terminal Services by enforcing component redirection, password policies, and color depth, among many other settings.

Figure 10.25 Integrating Terminal Services with Local and Domain Group Policies

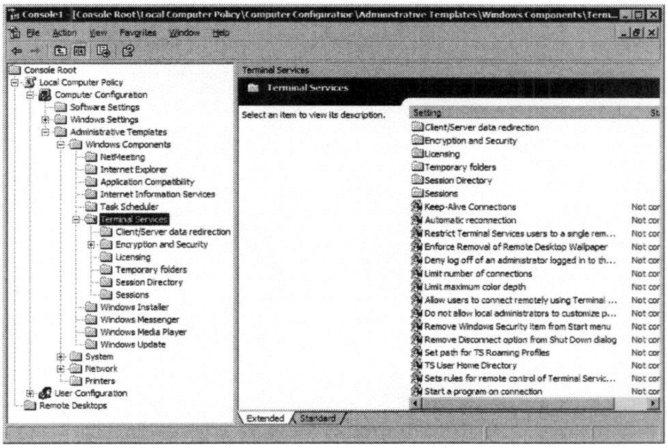

When using Terminal Services for remote administration, many of the policies will not be applicable. The performance-oriented policies, such as "Limit maximum color depth," and security-oriented polices, such as "Sets rules for remote control of Terminal Services user sessions," are very relevant for establishing boundaries around the behavior of network administrators who will be managing servers remotely. The other settings are essential when using Terminal Services to deliver a desktop environment to thin clients on which the performance and security of applications and clients' desktop interface are the primary concern.

Exam Warning

When configuring Terminal Services Group Policy for Remote Desktop for Administration, make sure that you accommodate for Remote Assistance if you know that it is required. The services use the same set of Group Policy settings, and caution must be exercised that a balance among usability, performance, and security is struck when accommodating for both services.

Resolution and Color Enhancements

Terminal Services in Windows Server 2003 now permits a range of screen resolutions and color depths, as demonstrated in Figure 10.26. Using Remote Desktop Connection, you can set the screen resolution from 640x480 to the highest level supported by the client, and color depth ranges from 256 colors to True Color (24 bit). These settings should be adjusted for optimal performance of Remote Desktop Connection over the network used for the remote administration session.

Figure 10.26 Setting Screen Resolution and Color Depth in Remote Desktop Connection

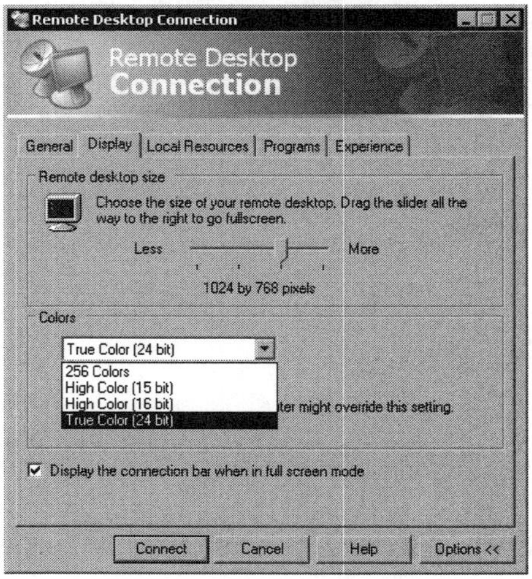

Regardless of what is possible for screen resolution and color depth, running Remote Desktop Connection at Full Screen and True Color over a 28.8 dialup connection will produce a pretty frustrating experience. The limits for screen resolution and color depth must be enabled on both the server and the client and should be tuned so that remote administration sessions actually make remote administration easier and do not gobble up bandwidth required by other network applications.

Remote Desktop for Server Administration

Remote Desktop for Server Administration provides a Terminal Services session across LAN and WAN connections and even the Internet. All the processing activity is performed at the server, and only keystrokes, mouse, and display data are transmitted between the client workstation running Remote Desktop Connection and the remote server. The Remote Desktop Connection client can be found at **Start | All Programs | Accessories | Communications | Remote Desktop Connection**. Note that the Terminal Services Client that shipped with Windows 2000 is not compatible with the new generation of Terminal Services that comes with Windows Server 2003.

Understanding Remote Desktop for Administration

Remote Desktop for Administration is used to remotely manage servers running any versions of the Windows Server 2003 family of products. It has been designed to provide network administrators with remote access to systems that are typically locked away in a secure, climate-controlled environment, such as a corporate data center. Through Remote Desktop for Administration, the administrator has access to the GUI tools that are available in the Windows environment, even if he or she is not using a Windows-based computer to administer the server.

Remote Desktop for Administration allows server management from any location without affecting server performance or application compatibility. In addition to the console session, up to two remote administration sessions are supported. Since this is meant as a single-user remote access solution, no Terminal Server Client Access License (CAL) is required when a server has the Terminal Server role installed and is being used as an application server for clients.

New & Noteworthy...

Remote Administration Saves Time and Money

Network administrator, imagine your world if every tool you need is always at your fingertips and you can manage every server for which you are responsible without leaving your chair. This is exactly the functionality that Remote Desktop for Administration provides to you. What keyboard, video, mouse (KVM) switches contributed to centralized server management within a single data center, Remote Desktop for Administration has extended to servers located anywhere in the world. Although it will not do wonders for your fitness level, you will definitely save time and be more productive if you do not have to continually move from your desk to the data center to make changes, especially those minute changes that you forgot to make during your last visit but that you remembered as soon as you got back to your desk.

In addition to reducing the amount of travel time and increasing convenience, Remote Desktop for Administration enables an organization to assign resources to the vast majority of specific server management tasks and responsibilities without needing to physically deploy or dispatch the required personnel. For example, if there is a messaging server in a troublesome state in Montreal and the best individual to handle it is located in Paris, that individual can connect to the server using the Remote Desktop Connection client without having to fly from France to Canada. The organization not only saves the travel expenses, but the response and resolution time will be quicker and the downtime of the server or service does not depend on international flight schedules.

Configuring Remote Desktop for Administration

The configuration of Remote Desktop for Administration is performed at each end of the desired connection—on the remote server and on the client workstation. The System Properties on the server must be altered from their defaults so that Remote Desktop is enabled and Remote Desktop Connection must be configured to make the connection to the target server at an optimum level of performance.

Roughly the same process is followed for Remote Desktop for Administration as it was for configuring Remote Assistance. Navigate to the Remote tab of System Properties (**Start | Control Panel | System**). Click the **Allow users to connect remotely to this computer** check box in the Remote Desktop portion of the window, as shown in Figure 10.27.

Figure 10.27 Enabling Remote Desktop on the Target Server

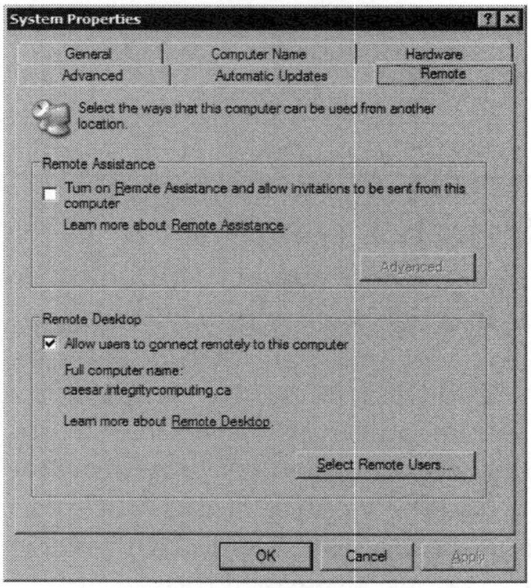

Once Remote Desktop for Administration has been enabled, any members of the local Administrators group can connect. To add additional users who can connect to the system, click the **Select Remote Users** button. This will open the Remote Desktop Users window, shown in Figure 10.28, where other client accounts on the local system can be added or deleted.

Once Remote Desktop for Administration has been enabled and clients have been added (if required), you will receive a warning about password securities and ports on the firewall that need to be opened (see Figure 10.29). Refer to earlier sections of this chapter that address these issues.

Now that the system is configured to receive inbound Remote Desktop for Administration connections, the Remote Desktop connection must be configured on the workstations or servers that will be used to manage other servers.

Figure 10.28 Adding Names of Clients Who Can Connect Remotely

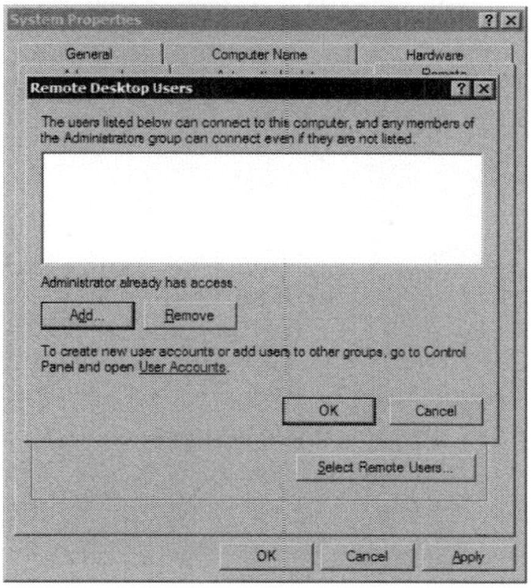

Figure 10.29 Finalizing the Configuration of Remote Administration

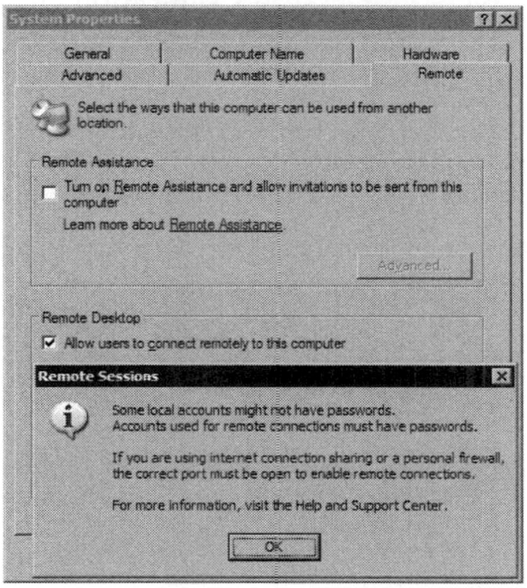

To configure Remote Desktop for Administration, you must configure Remote Desktop Connection for remote administration. To launch Remote Desktop Connection, click **Start | All Programs | Accessories | Communications | Remote Desktop Connection**.

When you open Remote Desktop Connection, click the **Options>**button to expand the window and expose the tabs with all the configuration settings. The General tab, shown in Figure 10.30, is where you enter the name of the server to which you will be connecting and the local or domain account credentials that you will use to authenticate. Any settings that you configure on this tab or any others can be saved into individual profiles. This is useful for tailoring individual connections to various network conditions and configurations.

Figure 10.30 Configuring General Options for Remote Desktop Connection

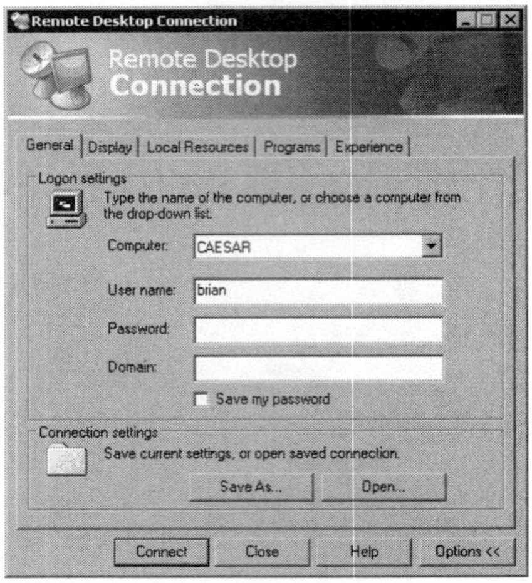

As described in an earlier section and displayed in Figure 10.31, the Display tab defines the display properties for the Remote Desktop Connection client. The screen resolution can be set from 640x480 to the highest level supported by the server video configuration, and a color depth range's from 256 colors to True Color (24 bit). These settings should be adjusted for optimal performance of Remote Desktop Connection over the network used for the remote administration session.

Figure 10.31 Setting Remote Administration Display Properties

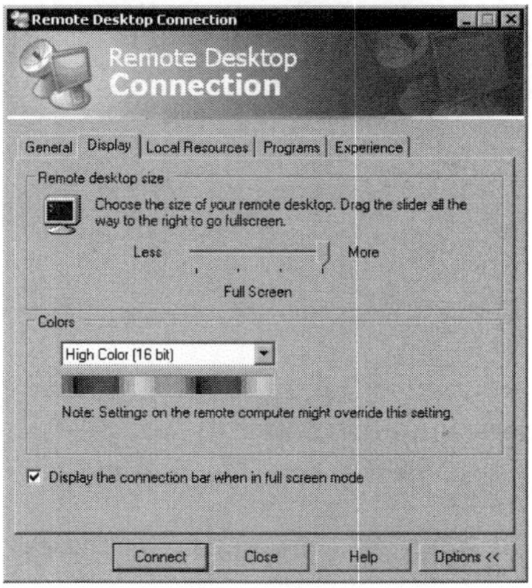

One of the key aspects of Remote Desktop for Administration that completes the client's experience is the redirection of input and output devices from the remote system to the client workstation. In the "Remote computer sound" section, you can select "Bring to

this computer," "Do not play," or "Leave at remote computer." **Bring to this computer** redirects audio output from the server to the client; **Do not play** disables the server's audio at both ends of the connection; and **Leave at remote computer** has audio output play back at the server.

In the Keyboard portion of the window, the **Apply Windows key combinations** property specifies how keystroke combinations, such as **Ctrl + Esc** or **Alt + Tab**, behave on the client workstation when Remote Desktop Connection windows are open and active. The three options are "On the local computer," "On the remote computer," or "In full screen mode only." The option you select depends on the way you work and what you expect to happen when you issue Windows keystroke combinations. If you expect to switch applications on your workstation when you issue an **Alt + Tab** command and a Remote Desktop for Administration session window is active, **On the local computer** and **In full screen mode only** are your best choices. If you expect the keystroke combination to switch applications on the remote system, **On the remote computer** is the best choice. For the **In full screen mode only** option, the remote system executes keystroke combinations only when the remote session has taken over the entire display on the client workstation.

The "Local devices" section permits you to redirect all configured disk drives, printers, and serial ports from the client for use in the session. This section enables, for example, the user to have the default printer in their session to be the same as the default pinter on their local workstation, as shown in Figure 10.32. This holds true for serial devices and all physical and mapped storage.

Figure 10.32 Configuring Local Input and Output Redirection

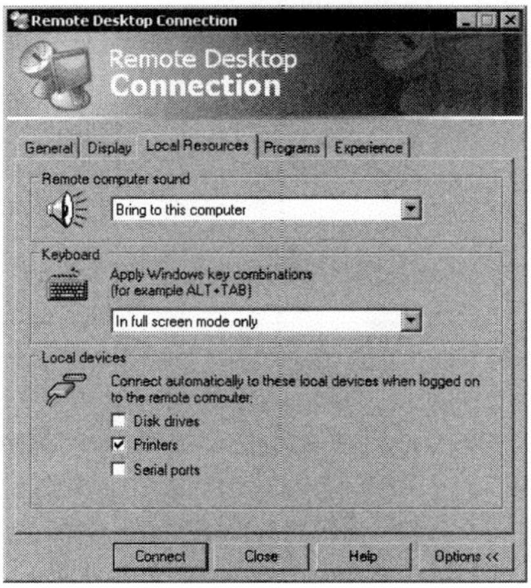

You can specify a program to execute when a Remote Desktop for Administration session opens, on the **Programs** tab shown in Figure 10.33. Click the **Start the following program on connection** check box and enter the path and filename of the desired program. in the **Program path and file name** field and the working directory for the program in the **Start in the following folder** field.

Figure 10.33 Selecting Programs to Execute When a Remote Desktop for Administration Is Launched

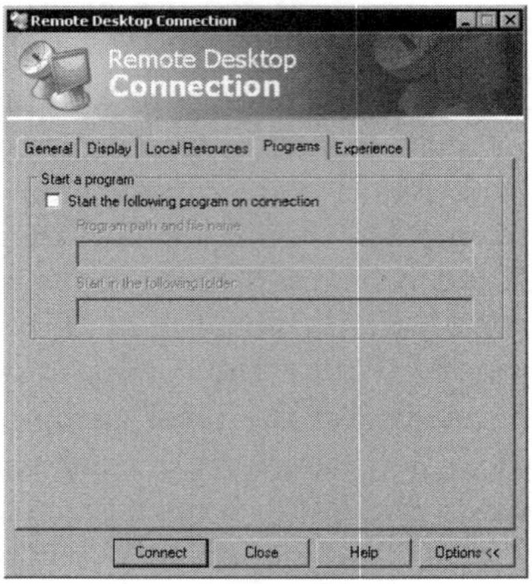

The Experience tab is used to improve the performance of the Remote Desktop for Administration connection. You can configure certain characteristics of the remote Windows session so that it appears that they are enabled on the remote compute, and these characteristics can be changed depending on the speed of your connection:

- Desktop background
- Show window contents while dragging
- Menu fading and sliding
- Themes
- Bitmap caching

Test Day Tip

Any customization of Remote Desktop for Administration connection information is saved in a connection (.RDP) file. These .RDP files can then be transferred from one server or workstation to another or stored in a shared drive or on removable media for access to your personalized settings from any system that uses Remote Desktop Connection.

The default connection speed is modem (56Kbps), which offers good performance for most networks. As shown in Figure 10.34, the most basic speed setting is modem (28.8Kbps), which does not transfer any graphical features and uses bitmap caching to optimize the connection by only transferring images from the server once and caching them at the local client workstation. Where it is appropriate, you can use the faster speed settings, such as LAN (10Mbps or higher), to enable richer graphical features such as desktop wallpaper or menu sliding and fading, as demonstrated in Figure 10.35. To select a combination of individual effects, use the Custom setting.

Figure 10.34 Optimizing the Performance (Client Experience) for a Slow Dialup Connection

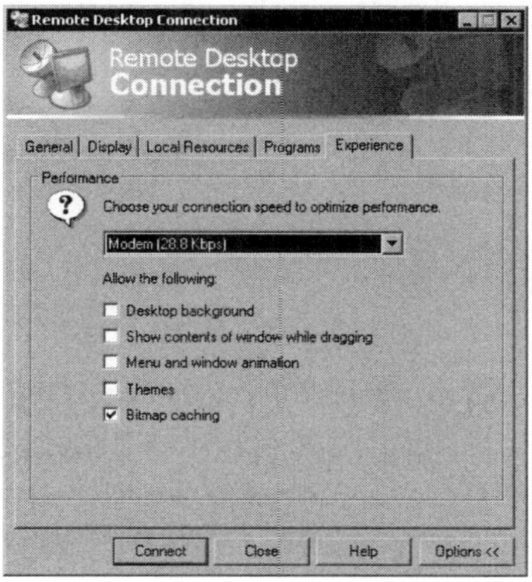

Figure 10.35 Optimizing the Performance for a Local Area Network Connection

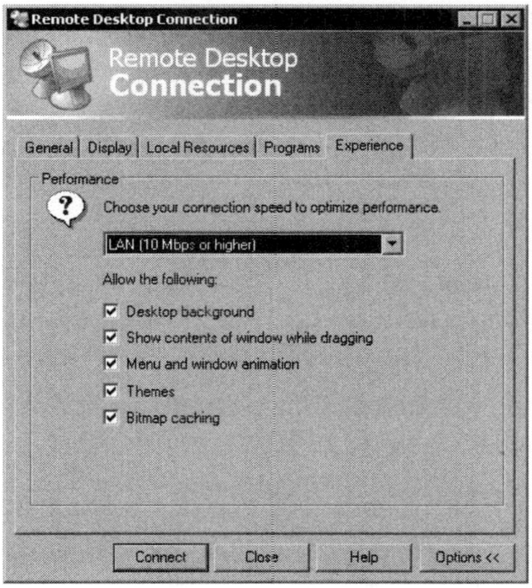

EXAM WARNING

If you are asked about optimizing a Remote Desktop for Administration connection, do not be tempted to clear all the check boxes on the Experience tab. Clearing the boxes for the graphical features is great for performance; however, the bitmap caching option is also a performance-enhancing feature and should be enabled. When it comes to performance, graphics mean a decrease in performance, and caching means an increase in performance.

EXERCISE 10.03

OPTIMIZING REMOTE DESKTOP CONNECTION FOR A SLOW OR CONGESTED NETWORK

There is little that is more frustrating that having to wait. This exercise helps the most impatient Remote Desktop for Administration clients. Follow these steps to speed up your connection to a remote server on a slow or congested network:

1. Click **Start | All Programs | Accessories | Communications | Remote Desktop Connection** to launch Remote Desktop Connection.
2. Click the **Options** button to extend the window and reveal the configuration options.
3. Click the **Experience** tab.
4. From the **Choose your connection speed to optimize performance** drop-down box, select **Custom**.
5. Two options are selected: Themes and Bitmap Caching. This is actually the same configuration as Modem (56Kbps), which offers good performance over just about all but the slowest dialup connections. For our purposes, disable **Themes** by clicking the **Themes** check box to clear it.
6. Verify that the **Reconnect if connection is dropped** check box has a check mark in it.
7. Click **OK** to accept the changes.

As many or as few options as you like can be checked to optimize the connection to the remote server. The key is finding the most satisfactory balance between the visual effects that are displayed on the client system and the performance of the connection.

Deploying Remote Desktop for Server Administration

The Remote Desktop Connection client is installed by default on Windows XP workstations and Windows 2003 Servers and can be launched from exactly the same location, **Start | All Programs | Accessories | Communications | Remote Desktop Connection**. The client is available for Macintosh OS X, Windows 95, Windows 98 and 98 Second Edition, Windows Me, Windows NT 4.0, Windows 2000, and Windows Server 2003. There is even an open-source implementation of an RDP client for Linux called *rdesktop*.

Exam Warning

Remote Desktop Connection can be used to connect to Windows 2000 servers running Terminal Services, Windows XP workstations, and Windows Server 2003. The Terminal Services Client that shipped with Windows 2000 cannot be used with Windows Server 2003

For workstations running down-level versions of Windows, you have several options for deploying Remote Desktop Connection:

- Microsoft SMS or Active Directory Group Policy can publish or assign the Windows Installer-based Remote Desktop Connection.
- Share the %systemroot%\system32\clients\tsclient\win32 directory on Windows Server 2003.
- Install Remote Desktop Connection directly from the Windows XP or Windows Server 2003 CD-ROM. Insert the installation CD-ROM and select **Set up Remote Desktop Connection** from the list of activities in the Perform Additional Tasks selection from the CD's Autoplay menu. The actual installation file is located on the CD-ROM at \Support\Tools\MSRDPCLI.EXE.
- Download the latest version of Remote Desktop Connection from www.microsoft.com/windowsxp/remotedesktop/ and install it from **Start | Run**.

Using Remote Desktop for Administration

Now that we know how to configure Remote Desktop Connection, we should start using it to manage a remote server. To initiate a Remote Desktop for Administration session, click **Start | All Programs | Accessories | Communications | Remote Desktop Connection**. This will bring up the windows displayed in Figure 10.36. The system to which you last connected will be displayed in the Computer field; a list of all other systems is available in the drop-down box by clicking the down arrow at the right of the field. If there are no other options to be configured for this session, click the **Connect** button to initiate the Remote Desktop for Administration session.

Depending on how the particular session has been configured, it will run in either full screen mode or in a window. Running a session in a window gives you direct access to your own desktop and enables you to select between several Remote Desktop for Administration sessions that you may have open at the same time. If you decide that you need to change one of the session settings, you need to terminate the session, change the settings, and reconnect with the new settings.

Figure 10.36 Opening Remote Desktop Connection

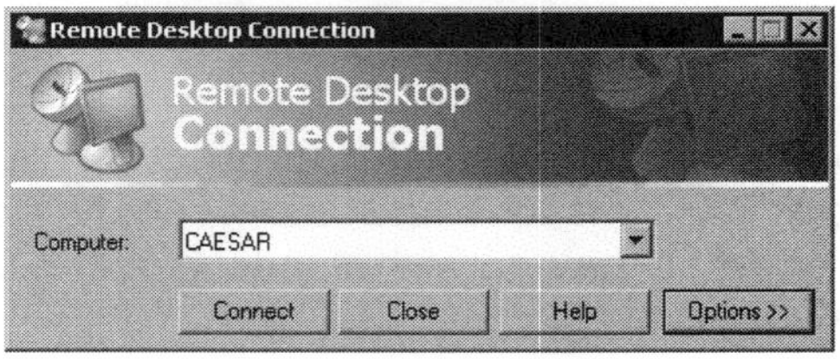

When you are finished with your Remote Desktop for Administration session, you can terminate it by clicking **Log Off** on the session's Start menu or disconnect by clicking the **Close** button at the top right of the session window. If you disconnect from the session without logging off, all the programs you started will continue to run, and you will be able to reconnect to the same session again at a later time. This could be useful for occasionally launching programs that have a long running time without having to leave a session open. Although this session is still running on the remote system, it will not be accessible to anyone other than the one who originally logged into it.

Configuring & Implementing...

Administering Remote Connections Through a Firewall

A collection of protocols enables Remote Assistance and Remote Desktop for Administration. The protocols you choose to use will have a direct impact on the experience of the individual who connects to the remote system and on security if that individual happens to dwell outside your internal network. Table 10.1 lists the various protocols, their primary purposes, and their associated TCP and UDP port numbers.

The primary protocol is Remote Desktop Protocol (RDP), which is used to connect the desktops of the clients who request assistance with their expert of choice or the remote network administrator with the server of his or her choice. RDP uses TCP port 3389 for this connection, and if you want to allow users within an organization to receive help through Remote Assistance from experts outside your organization, port 3389 must be opened on the firewall. If port 3389 is closed, no individual outside your network will be able to connect to a system behind the firewall.

Table 10.1 Protocols, Purposes, and Port Numbers

Service	Purpose	TCP Port(s)	UDP Port(s)
Remote Desktop Protocol (RDP)	Remote control data transfer between	3389	
Windows Messenger	Instant-messaging	1863	
Windows Messenger File Transfers	File transfer through instant-messaging	6891-6900	
Session Initiation Protocol (SIP)	Internet voice communications		5004-65535
Real-time Transport Protocol (RTP)	Internet voice communications		5004-65535

Windows Messenger is not required for instant-messaging communication during a Remote Assistance session; however, by blocking port 1863, you eliminate an avenue for requesting support. To maintain control over the application of software updates and the like, blocking ports 6891 through 6900 might not be a bad idea. Finally, for bi-directional voice communications through the firewall, all UDP ports between 5004 and 65535 must be opened to accommodate SIP and RTP. The large number of open ports is required because SIP and RTP use dynamic ports for data transfer.

Remote Desktop Snap-in

The Remote Desktops snap-in is the module that is added to MMC to manage Remote Desktop sessions with Terminal Servers and other computers that are a part of the Windows Server 2003 family. It is not available on Windows XP or other down-level operating systems. To add the snap-in, simply follow the same procedure as you would for any other snap-in. The steps for adding the snap-in are:

1. Click **Start | Run**, type **mmc** in the Open: box, and click **OK**.
2. On the File menu, click **Add/Remove Snap-in...** (see Figure 10.37).
3. In the Add/Remove Snap-in dialog box, click **Add...**.
4. In the Add Standalone Snap-in dialog box, click **Remote Desktops**, click **Add**, and then click **Close** to finish (see Figure 10.38).
5. Click **Close** in the Add Standalone Snap-in dialog box, and click **OK** in the Add/Remove Snap-in dialog box.

Figure 10.37 Adding a Snap-in to Microsoft Management Console (MMC)

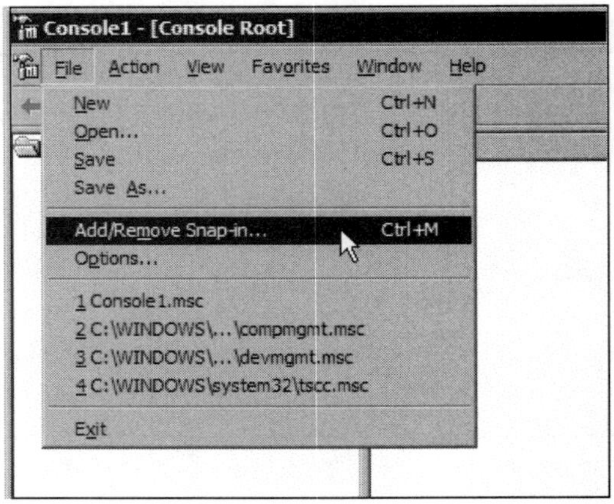

Figure 10.38 Selecting the Remote Desktops Snap-in

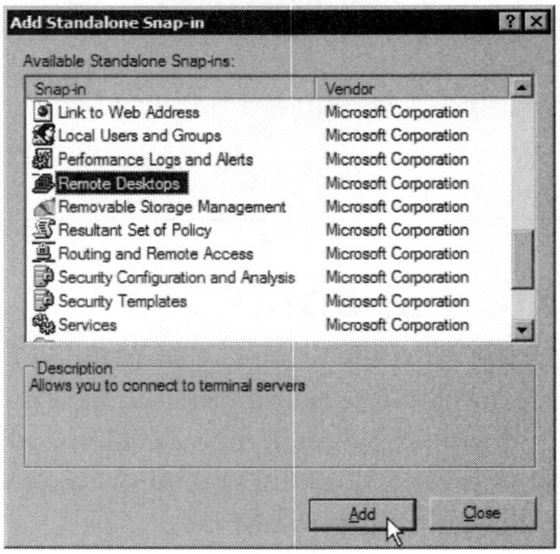

Once the Remote Desktop Snap-in has been added, you can add new Remote Desktop connections to be managed. You can select **Add new connection...** from the Action menu or right-click anywhere in the right pane, as demonstrated in Figure 10.39. This will bring up the Add New Connection dialog box.

You need to provide all the requested information about the new Remote Desktop connection in the Add New Connection dialog box (shown in Figure 10.40). Enter the hostname of the server or its IP address in the appropriate box and a familiar, descriptive name in the Connection name box; this is the name that will be displayed once the connection has been configured. Provide the credentials required to authenticate to the server during the Remote Desktop session, and click **OK** to accept the information that you entered.

Figure 10.39 Adding a New Remote Desktop Connection to Manage

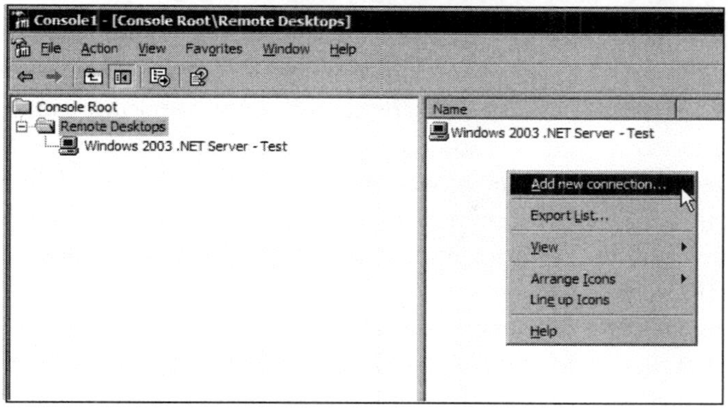

Figure 10.40 Configuring the New Remote Desktop Connection

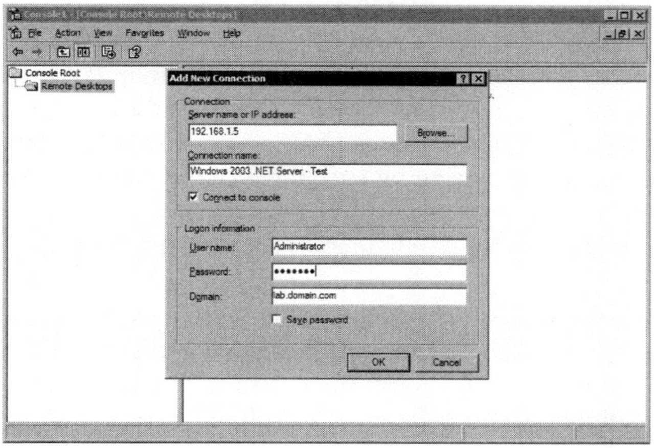

The "Connect to console" option forces network administrators using that particular connection to connect directly to console session 0. If the option is unchecked, an administrator can connect to another virtual session; however, it is best to connect directly to the console session so that the client can interact with the server as though he or she were using a keyboard, mouse, and display that are physically connected to the server. For example, all messages that appear on the physical server console will be visible remotely through the Remote Desktop for Administration session as long as the administrator is in that console session. To ensure the security of the session, the console at the actual server will be automatically locked to prevent passersby from monitoring the network administrator's remote administration activities.

Once you click **OK**, the connection appears in both the left and right panes. Double-clicking the connection produces statistics on the connection and enables the client to force a disconnection, among other actions.

Summary of Exam Objectives

We began this chapter with the overall objective to plan the use of secure remote network administration methods. Specifically we were looking to create a plan to offer Remote Assistance to client computers and to plan for remote administration using Terminal Services. Remote Assistance and Remote Desktop for Administration use Terminal Services as the underlying technology and Terminal Services Group Policy is at the heart of configuring the performance and environment for each service. Both involve connecting a knowledgeable individual to a remote system; however, they are used for very different purposes and in different ways.

The Remote Assistance tool involves the user on the system reacting to some adverse behavior on his or her system by asking another individual to help resolve the issue. The user creates and sends an invitation and the expert connects to the client system and begins to assess (and hopefully solve) the problem. The client is completely in control of the session and must grant permission to the remote expert before the expert can take control of or send files to the system or initiate a voice conversation from his or her system to the local client. The client can disconnect at any time. All this activity—both the client's and the expert's—can be configured using Remote Assistance and Terminal Services Group Policy.

Remote Desktop for Administration is the evolution of the Terminal Services Administration Mode that was introduced with Windows 2000. The newest incarnation greatly enhances remote administration by enabling a richer remote desktop environment via graphical features and audio redirection within the session and integration with Group Policy to manage Terminal Services configuration and security. Remote Desktop for Administration involves a network administrator connecting to a remote system to manage or administer it. Connections can be customized and optimized to provide the remote administrator with the most effective desktop environment possible, striking a balance between robustness and performance across the network. The Remote Desktop snap-in has been added so that multiple Remote Desktop for Administration sessions can be managed through Microsoft's single point of administration, an MMC. When using the Remote Desktops snap-in to connect to the console session, the administrator sees the same desktop in the session as they would see if they were physically seated in front of the actual server.

The administrator's task is to define the boundaries around and the limitations within each of these types of remote connectivity session. The key is to continually monitor the use of each service to ensure that remote connectivity is as full featured as possible without compromising network and system performance and security.

Exam Objectives Fast Track

Remotely Administering Client Computers

- ☑ Invitations for Remote Assistance can be sent through Windows Messenger, e-mail, and the transfer of invitation files.
- ☑ The operator of the client workstation, the individual receiving Remote Assistance, is in complete control of the Remote Assistance session.
- ☑ Terminal Services and Remote Assistance Group Policy settings can govern configuration and security for all remote connectivity that relates to Remote Assistance. No local configuration settings can override those that are set in Terminal Services and Remote Assistance Group Policy.
- ☑ Remote Assistance can be blocked at the firewall by closing TCP port 3389; across the network, or on the local system through Remote Assistance Group Policy by disabling Solicit Remote Assistance and Offer Remote Assistance. This can also be completed at the client by clearing the "Allow Remote Assistance invitations to be sent from this computer" check box.
- ☑ For external clients to connect to systems on an internal network, TCP port 3389 must be opened, at a minimum. Windows Messenger (TCP port 1863) is not required for remote connectivity associated with Remote Assistance or Remote Desktop for Administration.

Terminal Services Remote Administration

- ☑ Several new features greatly enhance the experience and security of Terminal Services and Remote Desktop for Administration. The most prominent features are audio redirection, Group Policy integration, and display enhancements that include greater color depth and screen resolution.
- ☑ Terminal Services GPOs govern configuration and security for all remote connectivity that relates to Remote Desktop for Administration. No local configuration settings can override those set in Terminal Services Group Policy.

Remote Desktop for Server Administration

- ☑ Any member of the local Administrators group can connect to the server through Remote Desktop for Administration without being explicitly listed as a Remote Desktop User.

- ☑ Remote Desktop Connection is used for Remote Desktop for Server Administration. Older versions of the Terminal Services client will not work. All that is required on the remote host is that Remote Desktop is enabled in **Start | Control Panel System Properties | Remote**.
- ☑ Enabling bitmap caching for all types of network connections, and only the graphical features that do not degrade the session performance can optimize Remote Desktop for Administration connections.
- ☑ Logging off will terminate a Remote Desktop for Administration session, closing all running applications that were started by the remote network administrator. Disconnecting from a session leaves all applications running, but the session is not accessible by other clients.
- ☑ Remote Desktop Connection sessions can be created through the Remote Desktops snap-in of the MMC. The "Connect to console" option allows a network administrator to connect directly to the server's console session.

Exam Objectives Frequently Asked Questions

The following Frequently Asked Questions, answered by the authors of this book, are designed to both measure your understanding of the Exam Objectives presented in this chapter, and to assist you with real-life implementation of these concepts. You will also gain access to thousands of other FAQs at ITFAQnet.com.

Q: What is the difference between Remote Assistance and Remote Desktop for Administration?

A: Both Remote Assistance and Remote Desktop for Administration use Terminal Services as the underlying technology, and Terminal Services Group Policy is at the heart of configuring the performance and environment for each service. In addition, both involve connecting a knowledgeable individual to a remote system; however, the services are used for different purposes and in different ways. Remote Assistance involves the client on the system asking another individual to help in resolving a system problem. Remote Desktop for Administration involves a network administrator connecting to a remote system to manage or administer it; administrators see the same desktop in a Remote Desktop for Administration session as they would see if they were physically seated in front of the actual server. In a manner of speaking, Remote Assistance is reactive, whereas Remote Desktop for Administration could be considered proactive in nature.

Q: What are the disadvantages of allowing clients the ability to issue Remote Assistance invitations?

A: The key disadvantage to allowing clients the ability to issue Remote Assistance invitations is the potential loss of control over management of corporate workstations and servers. If clients can solicit support from other clients, notably clients who are outside the organization, the ability to maintain standard configurations and consistent software versions for workstations and servers and to apply consistent solutions to known problems can be severely compromised.

Q: If I enable the "Always prompt client for password upon connection" Group Policy, do other password-related Group Policies apply?

A: The short answer is yes and no. Since local and domain accounts are used for Remote Desktop for Administration, all password-related Group Policies apply. This includes policies for password expiration, complexity, and retention, among others. For Remote Assistance, a password that is specified when the invitation is created is associated with the invitation and expires once the Remote Assistance session is closed. Password-related Group Policies do not apply to Remote Assistance invitation passwords.

Q: What is the difference between connecting to the console session and connecting to any other session in Remote Desktop for Administration?

A: When a client remotely connects to the console session the client connects to the same console that he or she would connect to if physically seated in front of the actual server. A Windows Server 2003 can run multiple sessions. If the "Connect to console 0" check box is clear in the Remote Desktop snap-in, the client will connect to a separate console.

Q: How can I issue an **Alt+Tab** or **Ctrl+Esc** keystroke combination on the remote system?

A: On the Local Resources configuration tab in Remote Desktop Connection, you can configure "Apply Windows key combinations" to be enabled "On the remote computer" when working in windowed mode. Alternatively, you can configure Windows key combinations to work "In full screen mode only." In either instance, when you issue a Windows key combination on the local system, Remote Desktop Connection grabs the keystrokes and sends them to the remote system.

Self Test

A Quick Answer Key follows the Self Test questions. For complete questions, answers, and explanations to the Self Test questions in this chapter as well as the other chapters in this book, see the Self Test Appendix.

1. You are assigning the newest member of your staff responsibility for a new file server running Windows Server 2003. He will be an Administrator on the server, and you want him to be able to ask for help from his coworkers so that they can walk him through steps to resolve any issues that arise. How would you have the new server configured so that this new administrator can request Remote Assistance?

   A. Check the Remote Assistance box on the Remote tab in System Properties, and enable remote control in the Remote Assistance Settings dialog box.

   B. Check the Remote Desktop box on the Remote tab in System Properties.

   C. Check the Remote Assistance box on the Remote tab in System Properties, and add him as a Remote User in the Add New Users window.

   D. Enable Remote Assistance through Local Remote Assistance Group Policy.

2. You just recently finished configuring the properties for Solicited Remote Assistance in Remote Assistance Group Policy, and you start receiving complaints that certain experts outside the organization cannot respond to the invitations that are embedded in the body of e-mail messages. You verify that the correct ports on the firewall are open and that the property for the format of e-mail invitations is set to Mailto. What could be the problem?

   A. The experts do not have the Remote Assistance client installed.

   B. The experts' e-mail client cannot read HTML-formatted messages.

   C. The Remote Assistance timeout period is too short.

   D. The experts do not have the correct password.

3. You want to restrict who can offer remote assistance to immediate members of the server support team in your IT organization. You decide that creating a group is the most efficient way to manage this function. What kind of group is required, and where do you create it?

   A. Create a Local group on each server that could request remote assistance, and add the group to the Local Administrators group.

   B. Create a Domain group and add it to the Local Administrators group on each server that could request remote assistance.

   C. Create a Universal group and add it to the Offer Remote Assistance Group Policy.

   D. Create a Domain group and add it to the Offer Remote Assistance Group Policy.

4. You have given the ability to offer unsolicited Remote Assistance to members of the server support team. However, they find that they can connect but not take control of the servers they are supposed to manage. What is the most efficient way of enabling the server support team members to take control of the servers they manage through unsolicited Remote Assistance while controlling the amount of access they have?

   A. Add the members of the server support team to the Domain Administrators group, and add the Domain Administrators group to the Local Administrators group on each server that could request Remote Assistance.

   B. Add the Domain group for the server support team members to the Local Administrators group on each server that could request Remote Assistance.

   C. Add the Domain account for each member of the server support team to the Local Administrators group on each server that could request Remote Assistance.

   D. Create Local accounts for each member of the server support team and add them to the Local Administrators group on each server that could request Remote Assistance.

5. You work for a consulting firm that has just installed Windows Server 2003. While at your office, you receive a Remote Assistance invitation to resolve a hardware issue from your client. You connect to the remote server without any problems; however, during the Remote Assistance session, your attempt to send a file with an updated driver is unsuccessful. What is the most probable cause for the lack of success?

   A. The client is refusing to accept the file.

   B. The required ports on one or both firewalls are closed.

   C. The client has insufficient rights to accept the file.

   D. Windows Messenger is not installed on the remote server.

6. The corporate service desk is overloaded, and management wants to leverage technical knowledge that exists throughout the organization. However, due to concerns over the security of corporate data, managers are wary of providing access to the organization's desktop and laptop systems to individuals outside the organization. They are also wary of allowing individuals who do not possess the required knowledge to provide "help." What strategy would you recommend to satisfy management's requirements with the least amount of effort? (Choose all that apply.)

   A. Block Remote Assistance at the firewall.

   B. Enable Remote Assistance in domain Group Policy and restrict it to members of the IT group.

   C. Enable Remote Assistance in System Properties on every desktop and laptop, and add the appropriate users.

   D. Enable Remote Assistance in local Group Policy on every desktop and laptop.

7. You receive your first Remote Assistance invitation from a colleague who works in a highly secure unit within your organization, and you immediately respond. Every time you try to connect, however, your connection attempt is refused. You are on the same subnet and can ping to verify that you can "see" the remote server. There is no Domain Remote Assistance Group Policy; therefore, you verify the settings in your Local Remote Assistance Group Policy. Everything looks normal to you. You notice that Client Connection Encryption Levels is set to Client Compatible. What do you suspect is happening?

   A. Port 3389 is closed on the firewall.

   B. The client is refusing your request to take control of the remote server.

   C. The Client Connection Encryption Level is set to High Level.

   D. The Client Connection Encryption Level is set to Low Level.

8. A network administrator is experiencing difficulty with one of his Windows Server 2003 servers and sends a Remote Assistance invitation via Windows Messenger to a colleague who works in another office. The colleague accepts the invitation and attempts to connect to the remote system, but he is unsuccessful. All offices are interconnected using VPN connections over the Internet, and each office's private network is protected by its own firewall that is not running NAT. What should be done to enable the Remote Assistance session? (Choose all that apply.)

   A. Have the firewall administrators in each office open the TCP/IP ports for Windows Messenger on their firewalls.

   B. Have the firewall administrators in each office open the TCP/IP ports used by Remote Desktop on their firewalls.

   C. Instruct the network administrator to enable Remote Assistance in the Terminal Services section of the local Group Policy Object Editor.

   D. The network administrator should create a Remote Assistance invitation file, attach it to an electronic mail message, and send it to his colleague.

9. You are experiencing a series of problems with a particular server that you manage remotely, and the hardware vendor is asking you for the system configuration. You know you can display the data on screen using msinfo32.exe, but the vendor is requesting a paper copy. What is the best way to print the information?

   A. Save the information from msinfo32.exe as a text file and copy it to your workstation to print it on your default printer.

   B. Configure printer redirection in Remote Desktop Connection, reconnect to the server, and print the output of msinfo32.exe to your default printer.

   C. Have msinfo32.exe print to the server's default printer.

   D. Display the output of msinfo32.exe in a Remote Desktop for Administration window and capture the window to your default printer.

10. You decide to start using Remote Desktop for Administration to manage the servers for which you have direct responsibility. Because you expect to have several Remote Desktop Connection windows open, you configure Audio Redirection in your Remote Desktop Connection client to "Bring to this computer." This seems to be working well because you notice that sound is being directed to your workstation for all your servers except one. The sound system on your workstation is fully operational. What are the possible reasons that audio features are not being redirected from this one server? (Choose all that apply.)

    A. The server does not have a sound system or the sound system is disabled.

    B. The "Allow audio redirection" setting in local Terminal Services Group Policy on your workstation is set to Disabled.

    C. The "Allow audio redirection" setting in local Terminal Services Group Policy on the server is set to Disabled.

    D. The "Allow audio redirection" setting in domain based Terminal Services Group Policy is set to Disabled.

11. You take responsibility for a mission-critical server that absolutely has to be available on a 24/7 basis. As a result, you are issued a laptop computer so that you can manage the server whenever the need arises. You decide to use Remote Desktop for Administration to connect remotely to the server. At the office you can use the LAN, but at home only a dialup connection is available. How should you configure Remote Desktop Connection on your laptop to work efficiently from both locations? (Choose all that apply.)

    A. Before you attempt a Remote Desktop for Administration session, click the **Experience** tab and select **LAN (10Mbps or higher)** when connecting at the office or **Modem (28.8Kbps)** when connecting from home.

    B. Before you attempt a Remote Desktop for Administration session, click the **Experience** tab and select **Custom** and check the appropriate boxes depending on your location.

    C. Click the **Experience** tab, select **Custom** from the drop-down box, check the appropriate boxes for your location, and save the settings with a unique name on the **General** tab for future use.

    D. Use the default setting for Remote Desktop Connection—**Modem (56Kbps)**—for all connections.

12. You find that you consistently keep several Remote Desktop Connection sessions open during the course of your workday. You are beginning to get a little frustrated when you issue Windows keystroke combinations, expecting them to execute on your desktop but they end up executing on a remote server, or vice versa. What can you do to ensure that when you issue Windows keystroke combinations, they execute where you expect them to?

    A. Configure Apply Windows key combinations in Remote Desktop Connection to **On the local computer**.

    B. Configure Apply Windows key combinations in Remote Desktop Connection to **In full screen mode only**.

    C. Configure Apply Windows key combinations in Remote Desktop Connection to **On the remote computer**.

    D. Disable keyboard redirection in Local Terminal Services Group Policy on the remote servers that you manage.

13. Your organization has implemented VPN technology in support of the IT department's new on-call policy for network administrators. As part of this policy, network administrators have the ability to connect to and manage corporate servers using their own ISPs. You find that the performance of Remote Desktop for Administration connections degrades in the early evening when utilization of your cable ISP's services are at their highest. What can you do improve the performance of Remote Desktop for Administration on those rare occasions when you need to manage a server during your ISP's busy times?

    A. Select **Broadband (128Kbps–1.5Mbps)** on the **Experience** tab in Remote Desktop Connection.

    B. Select **Custom** on the **Experience** tab in Remote Desktop Connection and accept the items that are checked by default.

    C. Select **LAN (10Mbps or higher)** on the **Experience** tab in Remote Desktop Connection.

    D. Select **Custom** on the **Experience** tab in Remote Desktop Connection and clear all check boxes.

14. You have been asked to take primary responsibility for a server that is used to perform systems management and track software licensing for your organization's entire network. Due to the number of servers to which you need to connect, you need an efficient way to store the different connection configurations to the various servers. For some servers you need direct access to the server console; for others you need a workspace to enter data or generate reports. How can you manage remote access to each server for different levels of access?

    A. Install the Remote Desktop snap-in on the server and create connections for every server which you need to access remotely, configuring some connections to connect to the console and others to connect to individual sessions.

    B. Install the Remote Desktops snap-in on the workstation you will use to connect to the servers, configuring some connections to connect to the console and others to connect to individual sessions.

    C. Edit the Local Terminal Services Group Policy on the workstation you will use to connect to the servers, configuring some connections to connect to the console and others to connect to individual sessions.

    D. On the workstation you will use to connect to the servers, create a connection profile for each server, and save the profiles as .RDP files in your home directory.

Self Test Quick Answer Key

For complete questions, answers, and explanations to the Self Test questions in this chapter as well as the other chapters in this book, see the Self Test Appendix.

1. **A**
2. **B**
3. **D**
4. **B**
5. **B**
6. **A, B**
7. **C**
8. **B**
9. **B**
10. **A, C**
11. **C ,D**
12. **B**
13. **B**
14. **A**

Chapter 11

MCSA/MCSE 70-296

Disaster Recovery Planning and Prevention

Exam Objectives in this Chapter:

- 3.1 Plan services for high availability
- 3.1.1 Plan a high availability solution that uses clustering service
- 3.1.2 Plan a high availability solution that uses Network Load Balancing
- 3.2 Plan a backup and recovery strategy
- 3.2.1 Identify appropriate backup types. Methods include full, incremental, and differential.
- 3.2.2 Plan a backup strategy that uses volume shadow copy.
- 3.2.3 Plan system recovery that uses Automated System Recovery (ASR).

- ☑ Summary of Exam Objectives
- ☑ Exam Objectives Fast Track
- ☑ Exam Objectives Frequently Asked Questions
- ☑ Self Test
- ☑ Self Test Quick Answer Key

Introduction

Our final topic for discussion is disaster recovery. We could dedicate an entire book to this topic simply because it is an issue that can make or break your company. Having a disaster recovery plan in place is crucial to an organization's livelihood. Many companies have felt the pain of being unprepared for a major catastrophe. For example, let's say that one of your critical database servers suffers a major hardware catastrophe. All your company's customer records and order information are stored on this system. If you do not have a backup of the information stored on this server, how do you plan to fulfill your customer's orders and bill them for your products if your server is destroyed?

While certain aspects of disaster recovery are beyond the scope of this book, one area that you must be familiar with for the 70-296 exam is backup and recovery. You need to understand the types of backup strategies that are available in Windows Server 2003, how to develop a plan for backing up your data, and the security concerns associated with doing so. Aside from backup and recovery, you also need to know some of the additional tools that Microsoft provides to aid you with disaster recovery issues, such as Automated System Recovery and the Recovery Console.

In this chapter, you will learn about these topics as well as the various types of clustering services available in Windows Server 2003 to help reduce the impact of a disaster. Microsoft offers tools such as Network Load Balancing and Server Clustering in Windows Server 2003 to give you another degree of fault tolerance in your networking environment. By the time you reach the end of this chapter, you will be able to plan, configure, and implement these clustering services within your environment. Let's begin this chapter with a discussion of the general concepts of disaster recovery.

EXAM 70-296 OBJECTIVE 3.2.3

Understanding Disaster Recovery

Disaster recovery could be described as the Rodney Dangerfield of IT—it gets no respect. The irony here is that disaster recovery can be your best friend if you give it the attention that it requires. Too many times we've seen environments in which IT staff diligently swap tapes on a daily basis while otherwise ignoring their disaster recovery plans—assuming they have even developed them. As a networking professional, you should make it a priority to stay diligent in *all* aspects of disaster recovery.

Perhaps the most common reason that IT professionals do not pay attention to all aspects of disaster recovery is lack of understanding. This section covers two specific areas relating to disaster recovery. First, we discuss planning for disaster recovery and the fundamentals of disaster recovery, as well as the steps you need to consider when planning a disaster recovery strategy. Then we discuss some of the ways that Microsoft assists you in the recovery of your Windows Server 2003 environment. Let's begin with a discussion of disasters and define the types of disaster.

Planning for Disaster Recovery

If you follow current events, the widespread effects of any disaster will become clear to you rather quickly. Equipment, data, and personnel can be destroyed and staggering amounts of money lost by individual businesses, the economic after-effects of which can be felt internationally on a regular basis. Some companies can tolerate a certain amount of downtime, but some never recover and find themselves out of business. A disaster recovery plan identifies potential threats against your network, including terrorism, fire, and flood, in order to provide employees guidance on how to deal with such events when they occur.

Disasters can also result from the actions of people. Such disasters can occur as a result of employees accidentally or maliciously deleting data, system intrusions by hackers, viruses and malicious programs that damage data, and other events that cause downtime or damage. As with environmental disasters, a disaster recovery plan can be used to prepare and deal with such "human catastrophes."

Preparation for disaster recovery begins long before a disaster actually occurs. Data backups must be performed daily to ensure that data can be recovered, plans need to be created that outline the tasks that need to be performed and by whom, and other issues need to be addressed as well. Of course, we hope that such preparation will never be needed, but it is vital that you put a strategy in place to deal with incidents that could arise. The disaster recovery plan should identify as many potential threats as possible and include easy-to-follow procedures. In greater detail, a plan should provide countermeasures that address each threat effectively.

Disaster recovery plans are documents that are used to identify potential threats and outline the procedures necessary to deal with various types of threats. When creating a disaster recovery plan, administrators should try to identify all the types of threats that could affect their company. For example, a company in California would need to be concerned about earthquakes, fire, flood, power failures, and other kinds of natural disaster but would need to worry less about blizzards. Once the administrators have determined the disasters that their company could face, they can create procedures to minimize the risk of such disasters.

Disasters are not limited to acts of nature but can be caused by electronic means. For example, DoS attacks occur when large numbers of requests are sent to a server, which overloads the system and causes legitimate requests for service to be denied. When an e-commerce site experiences such an attack, the losses can be as significant as any natural disaster.

Risk analysis should be performed to determine the company resources that are at risk when a disaster occurs. This analysis should include such elements of a system as:

- Loss of data
- Loss of software and hardware
- Loss of personnel

Software can be backed up, but the cost of applications and OSs can make up a considerable part of a company's operating budget. Thus, copies of software and licenses should be kept offsite so that they can be located and implemented when systems need to be restored. Configuration information should also be documented and kept offsite so that it can be used to return the system to its previous state.

Additional hardware should also be available. Because hardware might not be easily installed and configured, administrators might need to involve outside parties. You should check any such vendor agreements to determine whether they provide onsite service within hours or days, because waiting for outsourced workers can present a significant delay in restoring a system.

A person working for a company could have distinct skill sets that can cause a major loss if that person is unavailable. If a person is injured, dies, or leaves a company, the employee's knowledge and skills are also gone. Imagine a network administrator getting injured in a fire with no one else fully understanding how to perform that job. This would have a major impact on any recovery plans. Thus, it is important to have a secondary person with comparable skills who can step in for important personnel, documentation on systems architecture and other elements related to recovery, and clear procedures to follow to perform important tasks.

When considering the issue of personnel, administrators should designate members who will be part of an incident response team to deal with disasters when they arise. Members should have a firm understanding of their roles in the disaster recovery plan and the tasks they need to perform to restore systems. A team leader should also be identified, so a specific person is responsible for coordinating efforts.

Recovery methods discussed in the plan should focus on restoring the most business-critical requirements first. For example, if a company depends on sales from an e-commerce site, restoring this server would likely be a high priority. This would allow customers to continue viewing and purchasing products while other systems are being restored.

Another important factor in creating a disaster recover plan is cost. When planning for disaster recovery, you need to plan for alternate sites in the event of a disaster. There are three common types of sites: hot sites, warm sites, and cold sites. A *hot site* has all the equipment needed for a company to continue operation, including computer equipment, utilities, telephone systems, and furniture. A *cold site* provides office space but does not have the equipment and other features of the hot site. A *warm site* falls somewhere in the middle, not providing as much "plug-and-play" functionality as a hot site but not quite as bare-bones as a cold site. Hot, warm, and cold sites require additional cost such as rent, hardware that might not be used until a disaster occurs (if one ever does), office supplies, and other elements that allow a business to run properly. This can present a dilemma; you do not want to spend more money on preparation than it would cost to recover from a disaster, but you also do not want to be overly frugal and not be able to restore systems in a timely manner. Finding a balance between these two extremes is the key to creating a disaster recovery plan that is affordable and effective.

EXAM 70-296 OBJECTIVE 3.2.3

Windows Disaster Recovery

As a Windows Server 2003 MCSE, you need to know the various methods of disaster recovery that Microsoft provides. Aside from Windows backup and restore (which we talk about in the next section), several other options are available in Windows Server 2003 that can assist you in recovering a downed server. Three options that we discuss in this section are:

- Startup options
- Recovery Console
- Automated System Recovery

Let's start our discussion of Windows disaster recovery tools with a look at the Windows startup options, a feature you're probably familiar with from past versions of the Windows operating system.

Startup Options

At some point, you will undoubtedly come across a server that is unable to start the Windows Server 2003 operating system normally. A *normal startup* implies that the server can perform a reboot and bring up all startup services and applications without user intervention. When you encounter a system that cannot start up normally, you can choose to start up in one of eight different modes:

- Safe mode
- Safe mode with networking support
- Safe mode with command prompt
- Enable boot logging
- Enable VGA mode
- Last known good configuration
- Directory services restore mode
- Debugging mode

Safe Mode

When you start a server in Safe mode, Windows defaults to the most basic settings for running a server, including the Microsoft mouse driver, VGA video display, and other system-specific drivers (such as SCSI controller drivers) that are needed to start Windows. Safe mode can be used for a variety of reasons. For example, let's say that you download and install a new device driver for your video card. After installing the device driver, your screen resolution changes or your machine freezes, making it impossible to view the screen. By rebooting into Safe mode, you can change your video settings and remove the newly installed driver that is causing the problem. Certainly, an improperly installed video driver might not be considered a "disaster," but you can see the need for Safe mode on your servers.

Safe Mode with Networking Support

We can use Safe mode to recover from situations such as malfunctioning software or device drivers, but what if we need access to resources on the network in order to recover the system? You can use Safe mode with networking. This startup mode allows to access resources on your network as well as the Internet. Safe mode with networking offers the same functionality of Safe mode plus additional drivers needed to support network connectivity.

Safe Mode with Command Prompt

Safe mode with command prompt starts using basic files and drivers, but unlike the other two Safe mode variants, it displays a command prompt instead of the Windows desktop after you've logged onto the system. Safe mode with command prompt might be used in situations in which you need to perform command-level functions that Windows will not let you use in the GUI environment. For example, you might need to replace a system file that would be protected by the operating system in Safe mode or Safe mode with networking support. In another example, if a file is locked for exclusive use when the Windows GUI is present, you can manipulate this file using the command-level functions.

EXAM WARNING

Make sure you know how the three types of Safe mode differ from one another:

- **Safe mode** Defaults to the most basic settings for running a server, including the Microsoft mouse driver, VGA video display, and other system-specific drivers.
- **Safe mode with networking support** Defaults to the most basic settings for running a server, including the Microsoft mouse driver, VGA video display, and other system-specific drivers, but also adds networking capabilities.
- **Safe mode with command prompt** Defaults to a command prompt to allow you to use command-level functions that Windows will not let you use in the GUI environment.

Enable Boot Logging

When you choose to enable boot logging, Windows logs all drivers and services that were loaded (or failed to load) during startup in a file called ntbtlog.txt, which is located in the %systemroot% directory. Boot logging is helpful when you're not exactly sure what is causing your server problems. You can see a sample ntbtlog.txt file in Figure 11.1; take special note of the lines in bold text that indicate drivers that failed to load during system startup.

Figure 11.1 A Sample ntbtlog.txt File

```
Microsoft (R) Windows (R) Version 5.2 (Build 3790)
 5 18 2003 20:48:05.500
Loaded driver \WINDOWS\system32\ntoskrnl.exe
Loaded driver \WINDOWS\system32\hal.dll
Loaded driver \WINDOWS\system32\KDCOM.DLL
Loaded driver \WINDOWS\system32\BOOTVID.dll
Loaded driver pci.sys
Loaded driver isapnp.sys
Loaded driver intelide.sys
Loaded driver \WINDOWS\system32\DRIVERS\PCIIDEX.SYS
Loaded driver MountMgr.sys
Loaded driver ftdisk.sys
Loaded driver \WINDOWS\system32\DRIVERS\WMILIB.SYS
Loaded driver dmload.sys
Loaded driver dmio.sys
Loaded driver volsnap.sys
Loaded driver PartMgr.sys
Loaded driver atapi.sys
Loaded driver disk.sys
Loaded driver \WINDOWS\system32\DRIVERS\CLASSPNP.SYS
Loaded driver Dfs.sys
Loaded driver KSecDD.sys
Loaded driver Ntfs.sys
Loaded driver NDIS.sys
Loaded driver Mup.sys
Loaded driver agp440.sys
Loaded driver crcdisk.sys
Loaded driver \SystemRoot\system32\DRIVERS\audstub.sys
Loaded driver \SystemRoot\system32\DRIVERS\rasl2tp.sys
Loaded driver \SystemRoot\system32\DRIVERS\ndistapi.sys
Loaded driver \SystemRoot\system32\DRIVERS\ndiswan.sys
Loaded driver \SystemRoot\system32\DRIVERS\raspppoe.sys
Loaded driver \SystemRoot\system32\DRIVERS\raspptp.sys
Loaded driver \SystemRoot\system32\DRIVERS\ptilink.sys
Loaded driver \SystemRoot\system32\DRIVERS\raspti.sys
Loaded driver \SystemRoot\system32\DRIVERS\wlbs.sys
```

Continued

Figure 11.1 A Sample ntbtlog.txt File

```
Loaded driver \SystemRoot\system32\DRIVERS\atimpae.sys
Loaded driver \SystemRoot\system32\DRIVERS\cdrom.sys
Loaded driver \SystemRoot\system32\DRIVERS\usbuhci.sys
Loaded driver \SystemRoot\system32\DRIVERS\el90xbc5.sys
Loaded driver \SystemRoot\system32\DRIVERS\rdpdr.sys
Loaded driver \SystemRoot\system32\DRIVERS\termdd.sys
Loaded driver \SystemRoot\system32\DRIVERS\kbdclass.sys
Loaded driver \SystemRoot\system32\DRIVERS\mouclass.sys
Loaded driver \SystemRoot\system32\DRIVERS\swenum.sys
Loaded driver \SystemRoot\system32\DRIVERS\update.sys
Loaded driver \SystemRoot\system32\DRIVERS\i8042prt.sys
Loaded driver \SystemRoot\system32\DRIVERS\parport.sys
Loaded driver \SystemRoot\system32\DRIVERS\serial.sys
Loaded driver \SystemRoot\system32\DRIVERS\serenum.sys
Loaded driver \SystemRoot\system32\DRIVERS\fdc.sys
Loaded driver \SystemRoot\System32\Drivers\NDProxy.SYS
Did not load driver \SystemRoot\System32\Drivers\NDProxy.SYS
Loaded driver \SystemRoot\system32\DRIVERS\usbhub.sys
Loaded driver \SystemRoot\system32\DRIVERS\flpydisk.sys
Did not load driver \SystemRoot\System32\Drivers\Sfloppy.SYS
Did not load driver \SystemRoot\System32\Drivers\i2omgmt.SYS
Did not load driver \SystemRoot\System32\Drivers\Changer.SYS
Loaded driver \SystemRoot\System32\Drivers\Fs_Rec.SYS
Loaded driver \SystemRoot\System32\Drivers\Null.SYS
Loaded driver \SystemRoot\System32\Drivers\Beep.SYS
Loaded driver \SystemRoot\System32\drivers\vga.sys
Loaded driver \SystemRoot\System32\Drivers\mnmdd.SYS
Loaded driver \SystemRoot\System32\DRIVERS\RDPCDD.sys
Loaded driver \SystemRoot\System32\Drivers\Msfs.SYS
Loaded driver \SystemRoot\System32\Drivers\Npfs.SYS
Loaded driver \SystemRoot\system32\DRIVERS\rasacd.sys
Loaded driver \SystemRoot\system32\DRIVERS\msgpc.sys
Loaded driver \SystemRoot\system32\DRIVERS\ipsec.sys
Loaded driver \SystemRoot\system32\DRIVERS\tcpip.sys
Loaded driver \SystemRoot\system32\DRIVERS\wanarp.sys
Loaded driver \SystemRoot\system32\DRIVERS\netbt.sys
```

Continued

Figure 11.1 A Sample ntbtlog.txt File

```
Loaded driver \SystemRoot\system32\DRIVERS\netbios.sys
Did not load driver \SystemRoot\system32\DRIVERS\redbook.sys
Loaded driver \SystemRoot\system32\DRIVERS\rdbss.sys
Loaded driver \SystemRoot\system32\DRIVERS\mrxsmb.sys
Did not load driver \SystemRoot\system32\DRIVERS\imapi.sys
Loaded driver \SystemRoot\System32\Drivers\Fips.SYS
Loaded driver \SystemRoot\System32\Drivers\Cdfs.SYS
Loaded driver \SystemRoot\System32\drivers\afd.sys
Loaded driver \SystemRoot\system32\DRIVERS\ndisuio.sys
Did not load driver \SystemRoot\system32\DRIVERS\rdbss.sys
Did not load driver \SystemRoot\system32\DRIVERS\mrxsmb.sys
Loaded driver \SystemRoot\system32\DRIVERS\parvdm.sys
Loaded driver \SystemRoot\system32\DRIVERS\srv.sys
Loaded driver \SystemRoot\System32\Drivers\Fastfat.SYS
```

Test Day Tip

For the exam, remember that the ntbtlog.txt file is stored in the %systemroot% directory. Read the question carefully, because the answer choices might include different %systemroot% directories than the Windows default.

Enable VGA Mode

The difference between Safe mode and Enable VGA mode is that Enable VGA mode starts the computer using the currently installed video driver at the lowest possible resolution instead of the Microsoft VGA driver. You could use VGA mode when you require the additional functionality of your video card. For example, if you needed a higher resolution than the regular Safe mode provides, you could boot into VGA mode instead.

Last Known Good Configuration

This is an option that is probably very familiar to you if you've worked with Windows NT and Windows 2000. The last known good configuration starts by using Registry information that was saved during the previous logon. Rather than using Safe mode to remove a faulty driver that was installed, you can restart using the last known good configuration, which stores information about the drivers that were installed previous to the faulty configuration. The only downside to using the last known good configuration option is that *any* changes made after the previous logon, not just the faulty configuration, will be lost.

Directory Services Restore Mode

Directory services restore mode is an option that is only available on domain controllers and is used in restoring the SYSVOL directory and Active Directory. Directory services restore mode was covered in depth in Chapter 3, "Managing and Maintaining and Active Directory Infrastructure."

Debugging Mode

Debugging mode is one of those options that you might use only infrequently, but you should still be aware of it should the need arise. When you boot a server in Debugging mode, debugging information is sent to another computer using a device known as a *null modem*. A null modem is a serial cable that connects two computers and simulates a connection similar to that of a standard analog modem. You might use Debugging mode when you're working with a Microsoft technical support representative to troubleshoot a server. The debugging information can be captured by the other computer and sent to Microsoft for analysis.

Recovery Console

In some situations, you might not be able to boot your server into any of the startup modes we've just discussed. If this situation arises, all is not lost. Using the Windows Recovery Console, you have the ability to read and write data on a local drive, enable and disable system services, format drives, and perform other types of tasks.

Recognizing the potential for the Recovery Console to be exploited if a malicious user gained access to a server console, Microsoft developers made sure to keep security in mind they designed this function. When you start a Recovery Console session, you are required to provide the password for the administrator account. On a domain controller, this will be the username and password for the *domain* user account. For standalone servers, the administrator account is the *local* administrator account. The Recovery Console interface looks like a standard command-line interface but also provides you a help file for the commands that are available in the Recovery Console.

TEST DAY TIP

If you get a question about the Recovery Console on your exam, read it carefully. If you are asked about logging into the Recovery Console, check to see if the question mentions that the server is a domain controller or a standalone server. This information will determine which administrator account to use.

New & Noteworthy...

The Recovery Console in Real Life

I have only found the need to use the Recovery Console twice in my time as a networking professional. However, on both occasions it saved me from hours of troubleshooting and system recovery. On the first occasion, I was attempting to remove an application from a Windows 2000 server. The application failed to uninstall properly and left several files behind on the server. This might not have seemed like a big issue, but we were uninstalling the application to install a newer version. Unfortunately, the newer version was not configured to overwrite the older application and required the older application to be completely removed. When I tried to manually delete the files, I received a sharing violation error message on the files. Even in Safe mode, I was unable to remove the files due to this error. Rather than reinstalling the OS or spending hours on the phone with the application developer's technical support staff, I booted the server into Recovery Console and was able to change to the directory where the files were stored and remove them.

The second occasion was a little bit scarier. One of the Oracle servers at my company failed to start properly, claiming that the OS could not be found. Obviously, in this situation Safe mode was not an option. By booting into the Recovery Console, I was able to determine that the boot.ini file had become corrupted and was causing the server to fail on boot. I manually recreated the boot.ini file on another computer and copied it onto the downed server via a diskette. After replacing the boot.ini file, the server started normally on the next reboot.

Exercise 11.01

Starting the Recovery Console

In this exercise, we restart a Windows Server 2003 computer using the Recovery Console. Start this process by inserting the Windows Server 2003 CD into your CD-ROM drive. In addition, ensure that your server is set to boot from the CD-ROM as the primary device.

1. Reboot your computer.
2. During the boot process, you may be prompted to press a key to boot to the CD. Press any key.
3. Windows begins running through the Windows Server 2003 installation process, then prompts you to make a decision on how to proceed.
4. Press **R** to select "Repair a Windows installation using Recovery Console."

5. The installation process terminates and begins launching the Recovery Console.
6. You will be prompted to select a Windows installation. In our example, choose option **1, C:\WINDOWS**.
7. Next you may need to enter the administrator password for this computer. If this is not required, press **Enter** to continue.
8. Once you have entered the correct password, you will receive a DOS prompt. From here, you can navigate various directories on the drive, or you can pull up a list of Recovery Console commands by typing **HELP**. You can also find out more information about a particular command by typing **HELP <command>**, where *<command>* is the name of a particular Recovery Console command.

EXAM 70-296 OBJECTIVE 3.2.3

Automated System Recovery

In terms of Windows disaster recovery options, use Automated System Recovery (ASR) only as a last resort. ASR can be used to back up the system state data, system services, and all other files associated with the operating system. Along with the information itself, ASR creates a "road map" to the data on a diskette, which contains information about the ASR backup, the logical disk configurations, and how to perform an ASR restore. When you initiate an ASR restore, the system reads the information on the diskette and restores all the disk signatures, volumes, and partitions on the disks that are needed to start Windows. Once the disk information is restored, ASR installs a stripped-down installation of Windows and automatically starts to restore from backup using the backup ASR information. ASR should be used as a last resort only, because its purpose is to essentially rebuild from scratch previously stored information about the server. By using ASR, you will lose any user data that is stored on the system drive unless it has been backed up through other methods. Although ASR is a great tool and a nice addition to Windows Server 2003, you should exhaust all other recovery methods prior to using it.

EXERCISE 11.02

CREATING AN ASR BACKUP

In Exercise 11.02, we create an ASR backup to diskette. This diskette backs up all our critical system data in case we need to completely restore the system information:

1. Click **Start | All Programs | Accessories | System Tools | Backup**.

2. When the Backup or Restore Wizard (see Figure 11.2) opens, click **Advanced Mode**.

Figure 11.2 The Backup or Restore Wizard

3. Select **Automated System Recovery Wizard** from the Backup Utility window (see Figure 11.3).

Figure 11.3 Backup Utility

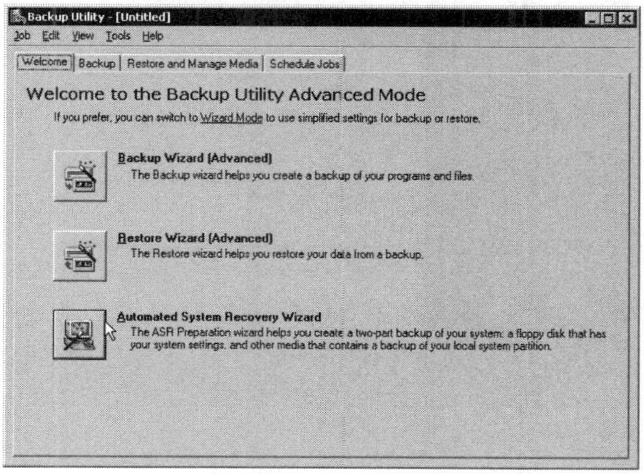

4. When the Automated System Recovery Preparation Wizard starts, click **Next** to continue.
5. Select a backup location for your ASR files (see Figure 11.4). Here we use a mapped drive from another server to store the actual files. However, we also need a diskette to store the actual system settings that would be read during the recovery process. Make sure you have a diskette in the disk drive.

Figure 11.4 Selecting a Backup Location

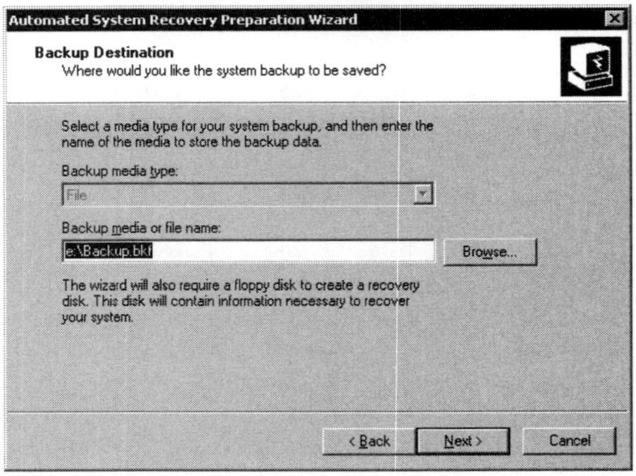

6. Once the ASR preparation process is complete (see Figure 11.5), click **Finish** to begin backing up your system files. Depending on the amount of data, you might be asked to insert several disks.

Figure 11.5 Completing the ASR Preparation

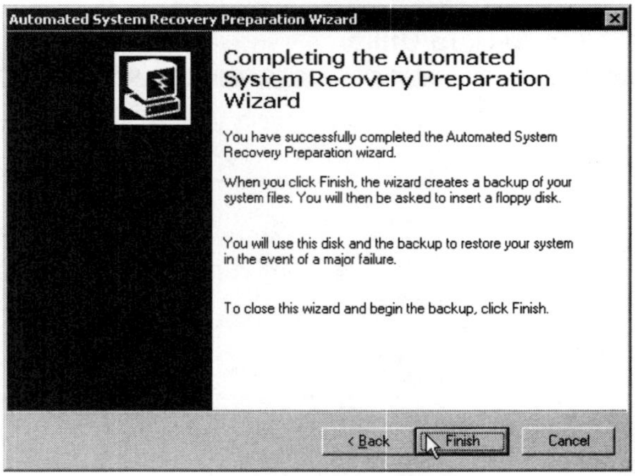

7. The files will begin copying to your diskette(s), as shown in Figure 11.6.

Figure 11.6 Copying the ASR Files to Diskette

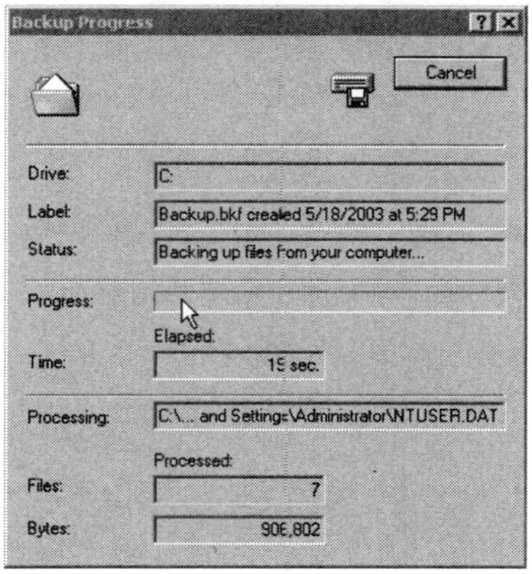

8. You will be prompted to insert a blank diskette into your drive; the system then copies the system settings and backup media information to the diskette. This completes the ASR backup process.

Exam Warning

ASR is *not* a full-system recovery option. In other words, it can be used to restore the Windows OS and all vital OS information, but it does not back up any data files. If you are presented with a question about ASR on your exam relating to the restoration of user data, remember that ASR cannot perform this function.

EXAM 70-296
OBJECTIVE
3.2
3.2.1
3.2.2

Backup and Recovery

Data backup and recovery is the one area of disaster recovery with which networking professionals are most familiar. Everyone knows that they must back up their servers (and in some cases, workstations) to removable media in case anything should ever happen to their hardware. However, changing tapes on a regular basis is not enough; there are several other factors that you should consider in case such a disaster does occur. As a Microsoft networking professional, you will want to establish a backup and recovery plan for your Windows Server 2003 servers.

Establishing a Plan

After deciding *what* data will be backed up, the two most important decisions you must make in terms of backup and recovery are *how* you will back up your data and *where* you will store it. When establishing a backup and recovery plan, you want to consider tape rotation and offsite storage.

Tape Rotation

It is important to keep at least one set of backup tapes offsite so that all tapes are not kept in a single location. If backup tapes were kept in the same location as the servers that were backed up, all the data (on the server and the backup tapes) could be destroyed in a disaster. By rotating backups between different sets of tapes, data is not always being backed up to the same tapes, and a previous set is always available in another location.

A popular rotation scheme is the grandfather-father-son (GFS) rotation, which organizes rotation into a daily, weekly, and monthly set of tapes. With a GFS backup schedule, at least one full backup is performed per week, with Differential or Incremental backups performed on other days of the week. At the end of the week, the daily and weekly backups are stored offsite and another set is used through the next week. To better understand this concept, assume a company is open Monday through Friday. As shown in Table 11.1, a full backup of the server's volume is performed every Monday, with Differential backups performed Tuesday through Friday. On Friday, the tapes are moved to another location, and another set of tapes is used for the following week.

EXAM WARNING

Since GFS is such a popular rotation scheme, expect this term to come up somewhere on the exam.

Table 11.1 Sample Weekly Backup Schedule

Sun.	Mon.	Tues.	Wed.	Thurs.	Fri.	Sat.
None	Full backup	Differential backup	Differential backup	Differential backup	Differential backup, with week's tapes moved offsite	None

NOTE

We discuss Full, Differential, and other types of backups in our discussion of backup strategies.

Because it is too expensive to continually use new tapes, old tapes are often reused for backups. A tape set for each week in a month is rotated back into service and reused. For example, at the beginning of each month, the tape set for the first week of the previous month is rotated back into service and used for that week's backup jobs. Because one set of tapes is used for each week of the month, most sets of tapes are kept offsite. Even if one set was corrupted, the set of tapes for the previous week could still be used to restore data.

In the GFS rotation scheme, the full backup is considered the "father," and the daily backup is considered the "son." The "grandfather" segment of the GFS rotation is an additional full backup that is performed monthly and stored offsite. The grandfather tape is not reused but is permanently stored offsite. Each grandfather tape can be kept for a specific amount of time (such as a year) so that data can be restored from previous backups, even after the father and son tapes have been rotated back into service. If someone needs data restored from several months ago, the grandfather tape enables a network administrator to retrieve the required files.

A backup is only as good as its ability to be restored. Too often, backup jobs are routinely performed, but the network administrator never knows whether the backup is performed properly until the data needs to be restored. To ensure that data is being backed up properly and can be restored correctly, administrators should perform test restores of data to the server. This testing can be as simple as attempting to restore a directory or small group of files from the backup tape to another location on the server.

Offsite Storage

Once backups have been performed, administrators should not keep all the backup tapes in the same location as the machines they have backed up. After all, a major reason for performing backups is to have the backed-up data available in case of a disaster. If a fire or flood occurred and destroyed the server room, any backup tapes in that room would also be destroyed. This would make it pointless to have gone through the work of backing up data. To protect data, the administrator should store the backups in a different location so that they will be safe until they are needed.

Offsite storage can be achieved in a number of ways. If a company has multiple buildings in different cities, for example, the backups from City A can be stored in a building in City B, and vice versa.. If this is not possible, there are firms that provide offsite storage facilities. The key is to keep the backups away from the physical location of the original data.

When deciding on an offsite storage facility, administrators should ensure that the facility is secure and has the environmental conditions necessary to keep the backups safe. They should also ensure that the site has air conditioning and heating, because temperature changes may affect the integrity of data. The facility should also be protected from moisture and flooding and have adequate fire protection. The backups need to be locked up, and policies must be in place that detail who is authorized to pick up the data when it's needed.

EXAM 70-296 OBJECTIVE 3.2.1

Backup Strategies

Backing up data is a fundamental part of any disaster recovery plan. When data is backed up, it is copied to a type of media that can be stored in a separate location. The type of media will vary depending on the amount of data being copied, but can include digital audio tape (DAT), digital linear tape (DLT), compact disks, both recordable and rewritable (CD-R/CD-RW), or diskettes. If data is unintentionally destroyed, it can be restored to its original state from the media.

When making backups, the administrator needs to decide what data will be copied to alternative media. Critical data such as trade secrets that a business relies on to function and other important data crucial to a business's needs must be backed up. Other data such as temporary files and applications might not be backed up since it can easily be reinstalled or missed in a backup. Such decisions, however, vary from company to company. Once the administrator has decided what information needs to be backed up, he or she can determine the type of backup that will be performed. Common backup types include:

- **Full backup** Backs up all data in a single backup job. Generally, this includes all data, system files, and software on a system. When each file is backed up, the archive bit is changed to indicate that the file has been backed up.
- **Incremental backup** Backs up all specified data that was changed since the last backup. Because only files that have changed are backed up, this type of backup takes the least amount of time to perform. When each file is backed up, the archive bit is changed to indicate that the file has been backed up.
- **Differential backup** Backs up all specified data that has changed since the last full backup. When this type of backup is performed, the archive bit is not changed, so data on one Differential backup contains the same information as the previous Differential backup plus any additional files that have changed.
- **Volume shadow copy** A mirror image of a disk volume, including files that are in an "open" state. This is a new feature in Windows Server 2003.

Because different types of backups copy data in different ways, the methods used to back up data may vary between businesses or even from server to server. One company might do Daily full backups, whereas another might use a combination of Full and Incremental backups or Full and Differential backups.

Volume Shadow Copy

Let's take a few moments to discuss how volume shadow copy works, then we will walk through a couple of backup exercises. As we mentioned, volume shadow copy is the latest addition to the built-in backup functionality of Windows Server 2003. Unlike other types of backups, you can now back up files and volumes, including files that are open or in use by another user or system process. This was not previously possible without third-party backup software. Another advantage of volume shadow copy is that backups can be performed at any time (although it's still best to perform backups during off-hours) without locking users out of the storage areas that you are trying to back up.

TEST DAY TIP

Remember that the key to volume shadow copy is that it can back up open files, which is not possible with the other backup methods.

Now that we've discussed the backup types available in Windows Server 2003, let's take a few minutes to perform a Differential backup in Exercise 11.03.

EXERCISE 11.03

CREATING A DIFFERENTIAL BACKUP

In this exercise, we create a Differential backup set using the Windows Server 2003 Backup utility. Let's begin by opening the Backup Utility:

1. Click **Start | All Programs | Accessories | System Tools | Backup.**
2. When the Backup or Restore Wizard (see Figure 11.7) opens, click **Advanced Mode.**

Figure 11.7 The Backup or Restore Wizard

3. From the Backup Utility menu (see Figure 11.8), select **Tools**, and click the **Backup Wizard (Advanced)** option.

Figure 11.8 The Backup Utility

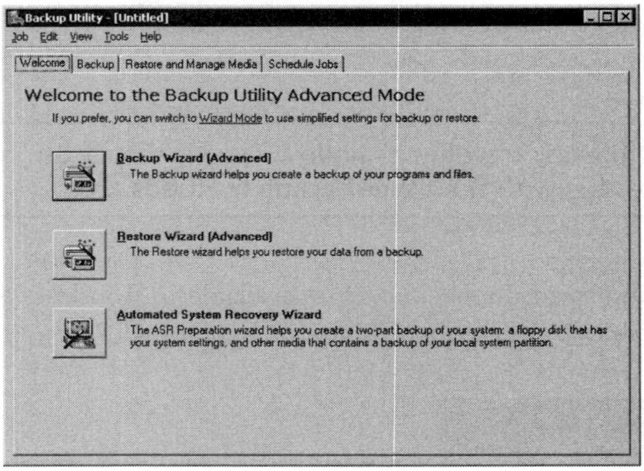

4. When the Backup Wizard starts, click **Next.**
5. When you are prompted on what you want to backup, select **Backup everything on this computer** (see Figure 11.9) and click **Next**.

Figure 11.9 Selecting Data for Backup

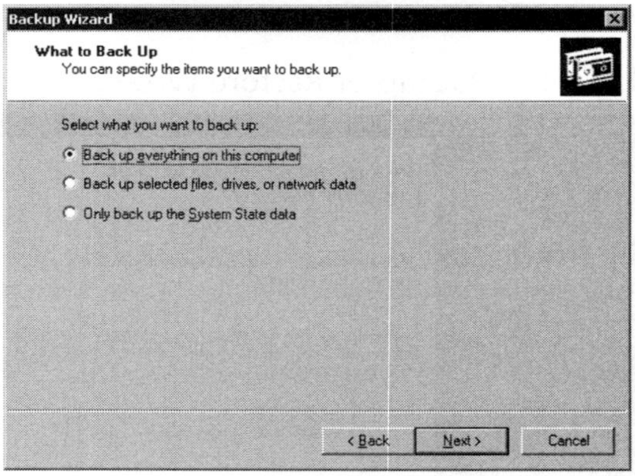

6. Choose a location to store your backup. If you have a tape device, select it here. Otherwise, you can use a network share. You can also name your backup, and then click **Next** to continue.
7. When you reach the completion of the Backup Wizard (see Figure 11.10), do not click Finish; click **Advanced** instead.

Figure 11.10 Completing the Backup

8. Now we will select the type of backup (see Figure 11.11). Since we are using a differential backup for this exercise, click the down arrow beneath **Select the type of backup** and choose **Differential**.

Figure 11.11 Selecting a Type of Backup

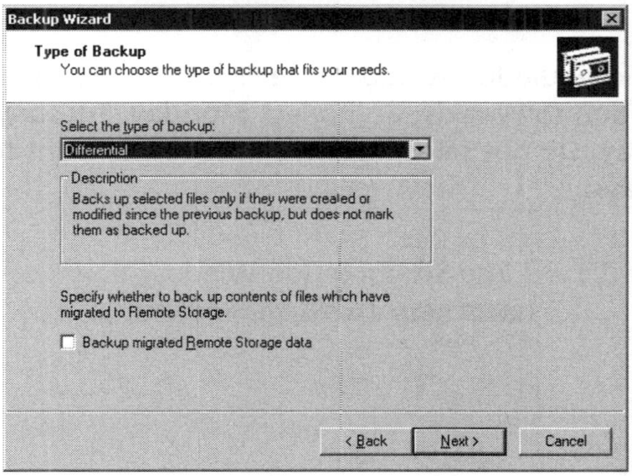

9. Click **Next**.
10. When prompted with additional selections on how to back up, click **Next**.
11. If you are using previously used media for backup, you can select to append to the media or overwrite. For this exercise, leave this the default of **Append** and click **Next**.

12. Now you will be prompted to select when the backup job will run (see Figure 11.12). Select **Later**.

Figure 11.12 Selecting When the Backup Will Run

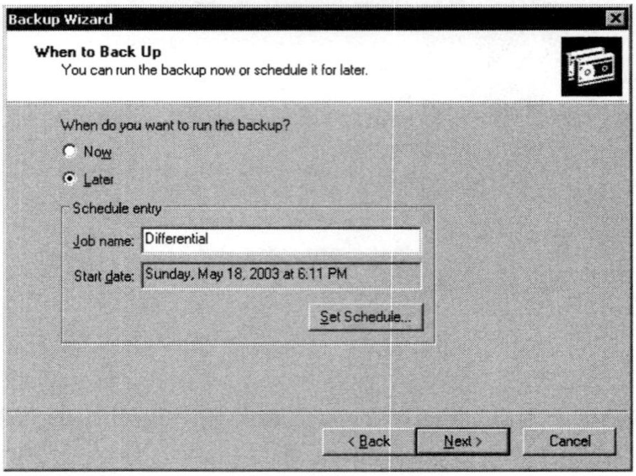

13. Enter a name for your job. We called ours **Differential**.
14. Click the **Set Schedule** button to set the dates and times for the backup.
15. In the Schedule Job window (see Figure 11.13), change the Schedule Task option to **Weekly**, and select **Monday, Tuesday, Wednesday,** and **Thursday**. Do not select Friday, since we will want to run a full backup on Fridays.

Figure 11.13 The Schedule Job Window

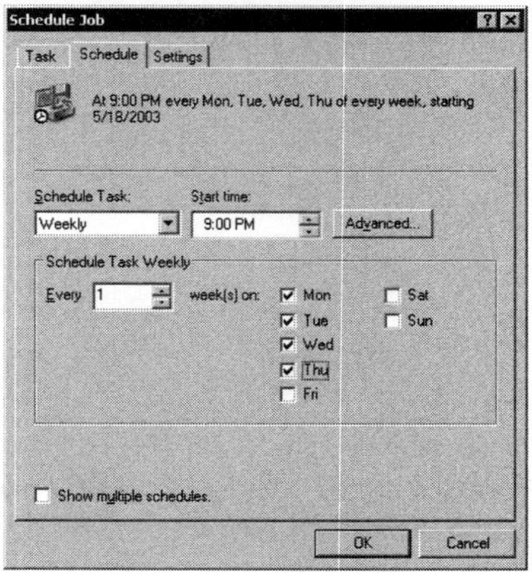

16. Next, set the Start time to 9:00P.M.
17. Click **OK** to continue.
18. You will be prompted to select an account to run as. In a real-world configuration, you would create a separate backup account, but for this exercise just use the **administrator** account. Once you have entered the account information, click **OK**.
19. Click **Finish** to complete the Backup wizard.

The Need for Periodic Testing

In the previous two exercises, we spent a lot of time talking about backups. However, backing up data is only half the battle. You also need to perform periodic testing on your backups to verify that data has been backed up properly. Performing periodic testing provides for two very important points in disaster recovery:

- **Verification of backup** This is the most obvious advantage to testing. By verifying your data that has been backed up, you are verifying not only the data on the tape media but also the integrity of the media itself. Too often media is left in rotation too long and fails to properly back up the data.
- **Verification of backup plan** Although it might not be as necessary to perform verification of the plan itself as often as verifying the actual data, checking your backup plan for inconsistencies is nonetheless a critical matter. By testing your backup plan, you ensure yourself and other members of your organization that your plan will work in case of a real disaster.

When possible, you might also want to perform periodic testing on "test" equipment. It's one thing to be able to recover a few Excel or Word files; it's another to be able to recover an entire server. If you have the equipment, you should consider testing your backup and recovery plan on it to verify that you can recover the contents of an entire server based on the configuration of a production machine.

Security Considerations

We've discussed security considerations throughout this book, and now comes the time that we must discuss security for backups. One consideration in planning a backup strategy is separation of duties. This means that one user is authorized to back up data, and another user is authorized to restore data. By separating duties, you prevent one user from having total control over the backup strategy and potentially exploiting the process. Beyond access rights, you also have to take physical security into consideration. You want to make sure that the backup media you are using is stored in a safe place. This includes both onsite and offsite storage. If you are sending your media offsite, consider locking the media in a tamperproof lockbox. If you place the media in a lockbox, it will be apparent if someone tries to access the media while it's offsite or in transit. When the media is onsite, make sure that the tapes are locked in either a fireproof safe or at minimum a locked cabinet.

TEST DAY TIP

Expect a question on access rights and backup/restore on the exam. You'll probably see a question involving separation of duties and the inability of one user to restore backups he or she has made.

Using Windows Clustering

Developing a backup and recovery strategy is important to provide a means of recovering a system if it should fail. However, wouldn't it be great if you could circumvent a failure before it even occurred? The good news is that there are many ways to offer disaster recovery prevention to your users and your network infrastructure. Some third-party hardware and software solutions can provide for this type of fault tolerance, but why use a third-party solution if you can do this within the Windows OS itself? As you are aware from Windows 2000, high-availability solutions were included in the operating system for your convenience. In this section, we discuss some of the features and benefits of high-availability solutions that are now available in Windows Server 2003.

Clustering Technologies

High-availability features such as Windows clustering technologies have been around since the days of Windows NT but are primitive in comparison to those found in Windows Server 2003. Microsoft states that "clustering technologies are the key to improving availability, reliability, and scalability," meaning that these clustering tools provide a higher level of system uptime than can be offered if your network possesses a *single point of failure*. A single point of failure occurs when the degradation or failure of a single device (whether a hub, a switch, a router, a server, or the like) causes a system or service to become unavailable.

For example, say that you have an Active Directory domain that contains only one domain controller. This would be considered a single point of failure because if that domain controller fails for any reason, it will bring down your network infrastructure by preventing your users from logging on and accessing needed network resources. Another example is a single file and print server that contains all your system printers and user files. Losing this server and restoring from backup would not only be time consuming, it also greatly decreases user productivity during the time required to perform the restore operation.

In the following section, we spend some time planning a high-availability solution for our Windows Server 2003 network, but for now we dedicate a few pages to discussing the three-part clustering strategies that are included in Windows Server 2003.

Availability and Features

As with Windows 2000, clustering is available only in the Enterprise and Datacenter versions of the Windows Server 2003 operating system. Along with Windows Server Clustering, Windows Server 2003, Enterprise Edition offers support for expanded memory and additional processors, allowing applications to run faster, which in turn provides better response for your users. Because of the additional horsepower that the Enterprise version of Windows Server 2003 provides, it is a better candidate for clustering services than Standard Edition. On the other hand, Network Load Balancing is available in any of the four Windows Server 2003 editions (Web, Standard, Enterprise, or Datacenter). As we mentioned, the clustering services provide for a two-part clustering strategy:

- Network Load Balancing
- Server Clustering

Network Load Balancing

NLB, unlike Server Clustering, is available in all versions of Windows Server 2003 (Web, Standard, Enterprise, and Datacenter Editions). NLB provides failover support for IP-based applications and services. Using NLB, you can group 2 to 32 servers together to build Server Clusters that support load balancing of TCP, UDP, and GRE traffic between them. Load-balanced servers are recommended for many server installations, including Web servers, Terminal servers, and media servers. Using this technology eliminates the possibility of a single point of failure on a server that provides such a crucial service. In an NLB cluster, a client requests a service from a *virtual IP* (an IP address that is not assigned to one specific machine) that is shared by all the servers within the cluster, as illustrated in Figure 11.14. In this configuration, should one of the servers fail for any reason, the other servers in the cluster take over. Using NLB is not only a way to provide high availability—it also offers you the ability to take a mission-critical server (such as a company Web or e-commerce server) offline for maintenance without impacting business functionality.

Server Clustering

The second type of clustering strategy is a Server Cluster. A Server Cluster consists of one or more Windows Server 2003 (Enterprise or Datacenter Edition) servers that work together as a single "server" so that applications and services remain available to clients and other servers. Each server in a Server Cluster is a *node*; each cluster can consist of up to eight nodes. With servers clustered together, users access the nodes as though they were a single system rather than unrelated individual computers. In Windows Server 2003, you can configure three types of Server Clusters:

Figure 11.14 A Network Load-Balanced Cluster

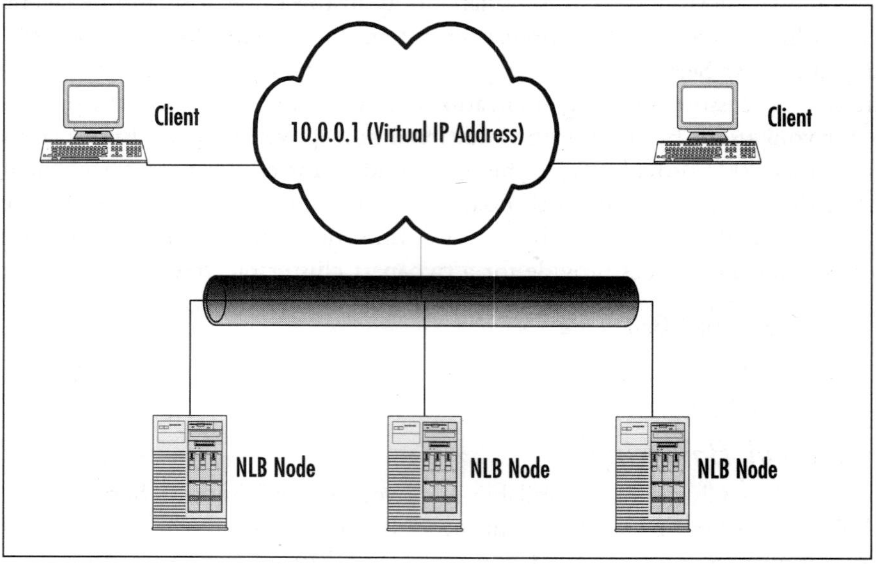

- **Single-node Server Clusters** A single-node Server Cluster has only one node and can be configured to use external storage or local hard disks configured as a clustered storage device.
- **Single quorum device Server Clusters** A single quorum device Server Cluster has two or more nodes in which each node is attached to a cluster storage device. In a single quorum device Server Cluster, the configuration information for the cluster is kept on a single storage device.
- **Majority node set Server Clusters** A majority node set Server Cluster has two or more nodes, but the nodes may or may not be attached to one or more storage devices. Unlike the single quorum device Server Cluster, the configuration information for this cluster is stored on multiple storage devices within the cluster and is kept consistent by the clustering service.

You can learn more about choosing a cluster type at www.microsoft.com/technet/treeview/default.asp?url=/technet/prodtechnol/windowsserver2003/proddocs/entserver/SAG_MSCS2planning_6.asp.

EXAM 70-296 OBJECTIVE 3.1 3.1.1 3.1.2

Planning a High-Availability Solution

In this section, we use the information on using Windows clustering to plan for a high-availability solution using the two high-availability services. Within our plans, we take a look at some of the considerations that you must assess prior to implementing a server cluster solution and what a typical Server Cluster deployment might look like. Then we examine the factors for planning a load-balanced solution and create a new network load-balanced cluster.

EXAM 70-296 OBJECTIVE 3.1.1

Clustering Services

In the previous section, we discussed the two types of clustering technologies available for Windows Server 2003. The first step in planning a high-availability solution is to decide on the type of cluster you need for your organization. Again, the two types of available clustering technologies are:

- Network Load Balancing clusters
- Server Clusters

Each of these technologies has its own features and benefits; they can be used individually or together to provide an even more robust high-availability solution. However, several considerations will help you make a decision as to which solution is the best fit for you.

Considerations

Unfortunately, Server Clustering is not available in Windows Server 2003 Standard Edition. In order to realize the benefits of Server Clusters, you must have Windows Server 2003 Enterprise Edition or Datacenter Edition installed on your servers. Beyond the limitation of OS version, you must take other items into consideration prior to the deployment of your server cluster, including the hardware to be used within your cluster. Check Microsoft's list of supported hardware for clustering technologies, which you can find at www.microsoft.com/whdc/hcl/scnet.mspx. You must also make sure that all the servers within your cluster are running the same version of the operating system. This means that a cluster cannot have a mixture of Windows Server 2003 Enterprise Edition and Windows 2003 Datacenter Edition. Before deploying your cluster, make sure you understand which version you need for your installation.

Typical Deployments

Microsoft recognizes the need for Server Clusters in many types of environments but specifically recommends Server Clusters for mission-critical installations that may include Microsoft SQL Server, Exchange Server, and file and print servers. Generally, you will want to deploy a cluster server in any organization in which a particular application or service cannot be unavailable for any reason.

In many configurations, the servers in the Server Clusters reside in the same physical location. However, you might find it necessary to create Server Clusters in separate physical locations. You might install several servers in remote offices that are physically separated, perhaps on different sides of the country, which can be used to provide local access to users who are closer to a particular office. Another important reason for the physical separation of servers within a cluster is for disaster recovery purposes. For example, if one of the offices where one of the clustered servers is located is destroyed by a natural disaster, the applications and services would still be available on the server in the second location.

Installing a Server Cluster

Before we begin our installation of a Server Cluster, we have to discuss the server location settings. Each server within the cluster must have the same location configuration, meaning that they must all be using the same language, country, and region set during the installation of Windows Server 2003. You must also have the proper rights to the local computer or be a member of the Domain Admins group in order to perform a Server Cluster installation. Once you have verified the server locale information and that you have proper rights to complete the Server Cluster installation, you can install your Server Cluster.

TEST DAY TIP

Expect at least one question about access rights and clustering services. Read the question carefully, and make sure that the exam question is depicting the proper rights.

Securing a Server Cluster

As you might expect, there are certain security considerations in installing a Windows Server 2003 Server Cluster. One of the first security points is the use of the service accounts for the Server Cluster. If you plan to have multiple Server Clusters, avoid using the same service accounts. This will keep users who might know the account information for one cluster from being able to manipulate administrative functions of another cluster. You will also want to avoid placing the cluster service account in the Domain Admins group to avoid any chance of unauthorized changes to your domain. In addition, restrict physical access to the Server Cluster and any infrastructure relating to the cluster. This is not only an important part of securing a Server Cluster—it is good practice for overall network security. Lastly, you will want to enable auditing for all security-related events in the cluster. By logging and auditing these events, you can keep track of authorized and unauthorized access to the Server Cluster.

EXAM 70-296 OBJECTIVE 3.1.2

Network Load Balancing

Although NLB works on any version of the Windows Server 2003 operating system, your server must meet certain hardware requirements. Besides the minimum requirements for a Windows Server 2003 server (which you can find at www.microsoft.com/windowsserver2003/evaluation/sysreqs/default.mspx), you also need between 750KB and 2MB of additional RAM per network adapter. Although you can use just one network adapter for load balancing, you will get much better performance by using a second network adapter.

When your servers are configured in this way, you can use the first network adapter for general network traffic, and the second network adapter can be dedicated to communications between the various nodes in the load-balanced cluster. Besides server components, we must discuss one other consideration prior to installation: sizing of the load-balanced cluster.

EXAM WARNING

Read questions relating to hardware requirements and the installation of load balancing carefully. You might see a question that asks you to calculate the necessary amount of RAM based on Microsoft's hardware recommendations.

Sizing a Load-Balanced Cluster

When you are planning a load-balanced cluster, you must take into consideration the number of clients that will be using the load-balanced cluster. The anticipated number of clients (or *client load*) directly affects the number of nodes that are participating within the cluster. Although you can only have up to 32 nodes within a load-balanced cluster, you can maximize your cluster's performance using servers with a more powerful configuration. For example, if you were reaching the 32-node limitation within your cluster, you could remove the four slowest servers and replace them with four faster and more powerful servers.

Head of the Class...

Licensing and NLB

One area that usually falls through the cracks in load-balancing efforts is application licensing. Most application packages offer only a one-for-one licensing configuration. This means that a client license for an application only allows you to install the application onto a single machine. Even though you are only using the application in a load-balanced configuration to support additional users, installing the application onto multiple servers might be in violation of the end-user license agreement. If you are unsure of the licensing for an application, read the end-user license agreement (which is either displayed during the installation process or is available in hard copy supplied with the software) before installation. If you are still not sure whether you can use the application without purchasing additional licenses, contact the software vendor. It's always a better idea to know about licensing issues before installation than it is to find out down the road, during an IT audit.

Typical Deployment

There are four options for deploying a network load-balanced cluster in Windows Server 2003. These models offer different features and functionality, but in the end they all serve the same purpose: balancing the client load for a particular service or application. The different NLB installation models are:

- **Single network adapter in unicast mode** This model is used in situations in which traffic to the nodes within a network cluster is low and the overhead of communications between the nodes of the cluster is not an issue. You can also use this configuration when normal network traffic between the cluster nodes is low or nonexistent.
- **Multiple network adapters in unicast mode** This model is used in situations in which network traffic from clients to server nodes within the cluster must not be compromised or degraded by traffic within the cluster. In this configuration, the cluster management traffic (or *heartbeat traffic*) would be transmitted over the second adapter.
- **Single network adapter in multicast mode** This model is used when network traffic between the cluster nodes is necessary but is not generally affected by traffic outside the cluster subnet.
- **Multiple network adapters in multicast mode** This model is used when network communication among cluster hosts is necessary and there is a great deal of traffic from outside the cluster subnet to the cluster nodes.

EXAM WARNING

Watch for a question that involves cluster nodes that have mixed configurations of unicast and multicast. If a test question presents a Server Cluster that has one server using unicast and another server using multicast, that is very likely the reason that the cluster is functioning improperly.

You can learn more about the advantages and disadvantages of each of these modes at www.microsoft.com/technet/treeview/default.asp?url=/technet/prodtechnol/windowsserver2003/proddocs/entserver/planning_choosing_an_NLB_model.asp. In the following exercise, we install a network load-balanced cluster using the single network adapter in unicast mode model.

Configuring & Implementing...

Using a Single Network Adapter

Although you can install a network load-balanced cluster using only one network adapter in unicast mode, there are two limitations to this solution:

- Ordinary network communication among cluster hosts is not possible. This means that if these servers need to share information with one another for any reason (say, SQL servers within a load-balanced cluster sharing database information), you should consider using either a single network adapter in Multicast mode or multiple network adapters in unicast or multicast mode.
- Network traffic intended for any individual computer within the cluster generates additional networking overhead for all computers in the cluster.

If you are not sure that you should use multiple network adapters, you can always configure your cluster using a single network adapter prior to installing additional network adapters for operational purposes.

Installing Network Load Balancing

As with Server Clusters, you must use an account that is in the Administrators group on each host to perform a Network Load Balancing cluster install. You might also want to set up a dedicated account that will be used for the cluster rather than using an administrative account, but you need to set the credentials for such an account. When (and if) you create such an account, make sure that this account is not used for any other purpose. You will also want to make sure that the password for this account does not expire, since it will be used by the NLB cluster after the installation process as well. Let's move on to Exercise 11.04 and set up the first node in a NLB cluster.

Exercise 11.04

Configuring Load Balancing

In this exercise, we put two servers, SERVER1 and SERVER2, together in a Network Load Balancing cluster. The first thing we need to do to enable and configure our Load Balancing cluster is to start the Network Load Balancing Manager.

1. To start Network Load Balancing Manager, click **Start | Run**, and type **NLBMGR**.
2. When the Network Load Balancing Manager (see Figure 11.15) opens, right-click **Network Load Balancing Clusters** and select **New Cluster**.

Figure 11.15 The Network Load Balancing Manager

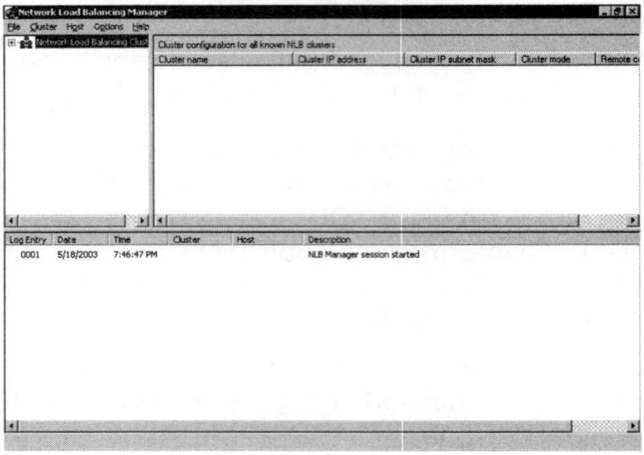

3. Next we need to enter the cluster parameters (see Figure 11.16). The first parameter is the IP address of the cluster. Keep in mind that this must be a unique address and not one in use by another network node. Here we use **192.168.0.100**.

Figure 11.16 The Cluster Parameters

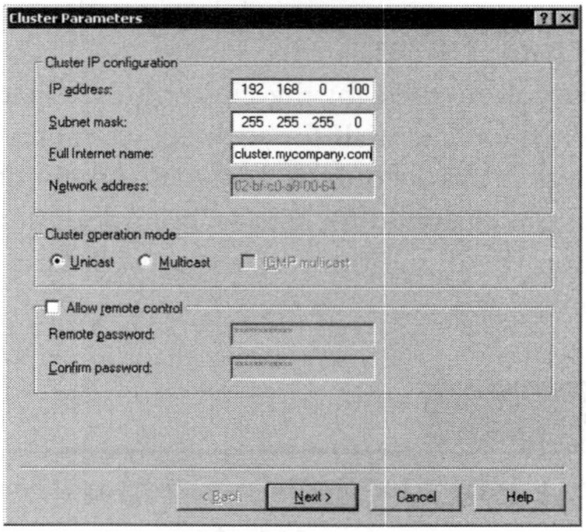

4. Next enter the subnet mask for the cluster. We use **255.255.255.0**.
5. Lastly, enter the full Internet name for the cluster. For this example, we use **cluster.mycompany.com**.
6. Leave the rest of the options at the defaults, and click **Next**.
7. Now we can specify additional IP addresses for our cluster if it is necessary. Since we will use only the primary address, click **Next**.

8. We are now allowed to select the ports we want to load balance between these servers (see Figure 11.17). Assume that these servers will be hosting Web pages (secured and unsecured). We can limit the traffic to these servers by first clicking **Remove** to delete the default selection of all ports.

Figure 11.17 NLB Port Rules

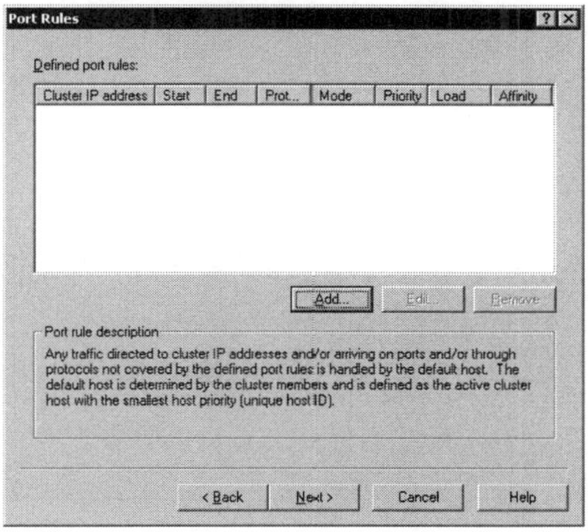

9. Next, click the **Add** button to add a port rule.
10. In the Add/Edit Port Rule window (see Figure 11.18), change the port range from **0** to **65535** to **80** to **80** and click **OK**. This will allow HTTP traffic to be load balanced.

Figure 11.18 The Add/Edit Port Rule Window

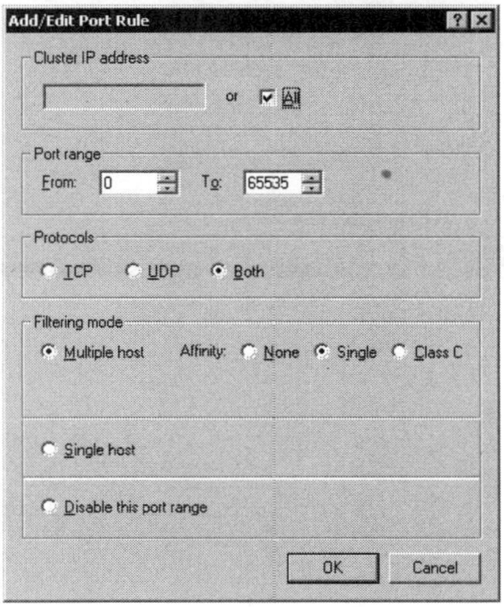

11. Repeat this process for adding port 443 (SSL) to be load balanced. When you are done, your Port Rules window should look like the one shown in Figure 11.19.

Figure 11.19 The Port Rules Window After Adding HTTP and SSL Rules

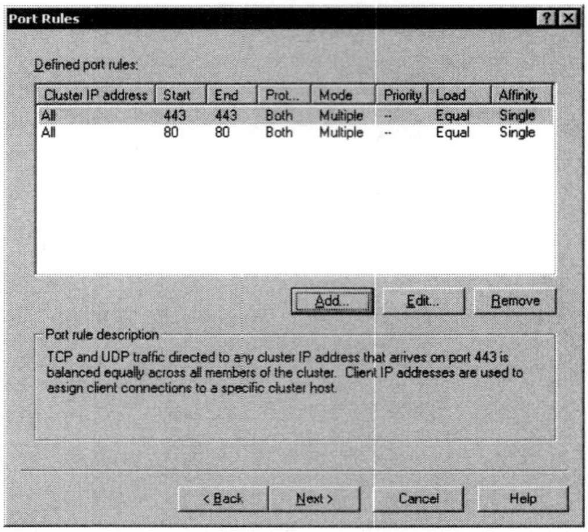

12. Click **Next** to continue.
13. Now we need to select the hosts that will be part of the cluster (see Figure 11.20). For our example, we use SERVER2. Enter the server name in the Host field and click **Connect**.

Figure 11.20 Selecting the Cluster Hosts

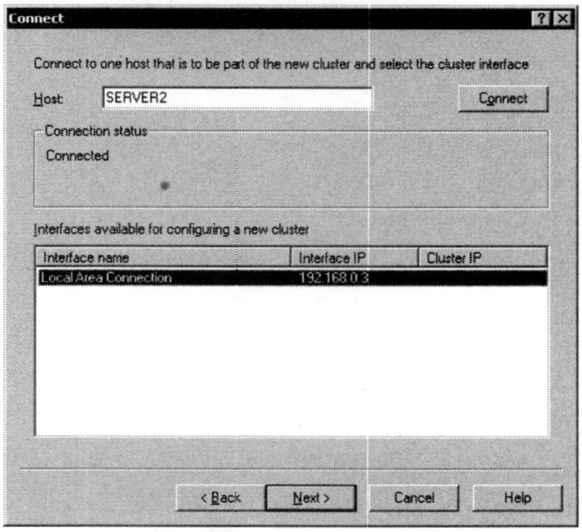

14. After you click Connect, the network adapters that are available on the host that you typed will be listed at the bottom of the dialog box. Click the network adapter that you want to use for Network Load Balancing, and then click **Next**.
15. When asked about the host parameters, click **Next**.
16. You can add a second node to your cluster by right-clicking the **cluster.mycompany.com cluster** and selecting **Add Host to Cluster**.
17. Once you have added a second host, your NLB cluster is complete.

Securing Network Load Balancing

Just as there were security considerations in establishing a Server Cluster, there are security considerations with a load-balanced cluster. First, you need to make sure that the applications that reside on the NLB cluster have been secured. For example, if you are using IIS on the servers within the cluster, make sure that IIS has been locked down and secured and that all unnecessary services (such as FTP) have been turned off. Lastly, you will want to turn on auditing for all security-related events in the cluster. By logging and auditing these events, you can keep track of authorized and unauthorized access to the Server Cluster.

Summary of Exam Objectives

In this chapter, we covered a variety of topics relating to disaster recovery planning and prevention. Early in the chapter, we talked about the various aspects of disaster recovery, including the tools that Microsoft offers in the Windows Server 2003 operating system. Each of these tools gives you a different method to recover your server from a potential disaster state. One of those tools that we covered in great depth was Windows Backup Utility. We examined the planning process for developing a backup strategy and the various backup methods that are built into Windows Server 2003.

Typically, disaster recovery tools are used after a disaster has occurred, but we also discussed tools that we can use to prevent the business from being impacted by a disaster. Specifically, we discussed the different types of Windows clustering technologies. We examined how Server Clusters and network load-balanced clusters differ from one another and how each of them provides reliability and availability to your servers and services. Overall, the planning, prevention, and recovery of disasters cannot be ensured by any one solution. It requires a mix of various solutions, including the ones that we discussed in this chapter. It is your job as a Windows Server 2003 MCSE to find the balance between each of these solutions.

Exam Objectives Fast Track

Understanding Disaster Recovery

- ☑ Disaster recovery plans are documents that are used to identify potential threats and outline the procedures necessary to deal with different types of threats.
- ☑ When creating a disaster recovery plan, administrators should try to identify all the types of threats that could affect their company.
- ☑ When you encounter a system that cannot start up normally, you can choose to start up in one of eight different modes: Safe mode, Safe mode with networking, Safe mode with command prompt, Enable boot logging, Enable VGA mode, last known good configuration, Directory services restore mode, and Debugging mode.
- ☑ Using the Windows Recovery Console, you have the ability to read and write data on a local drive, enable and disable system services, format drives, and perform other types of tasks.

Backup and Recovery

- ☑ Windows Server 2003 backup types include Full backups, Incremental backups, Differential backups, and volume shadow copy.

- ☑ When choosing an offsite storage facility, administrators should ensure that the site is secure and has the environmental conditions necessary to keep the backups safe. They should also ensure that the site has air conditioning and heating, because temperature changes can affect the integrity of data. The facility should also be protected from moisture and flooding and have fire protection. The backups need to be locked up, and policies must be in place specifying who can pick up the data when needed.
- ☑ Automated System Recovery (ASR) can be used to back up the System State data, system services, and all other files associated with the operating system.

Using Windows Clustering

- ☑ Microsoft states that "clustering technologies are the key to improving availability, reliability, and scalability," meaning that using Microsoft's clustering tools provides a higher level of system uptime than can be offered by a single point of failure.
- ☑ Windows Server Clustering is only available in the Enterprise and Datacenter versions of the Windows Server 2003 operating system.
- ☑ Network Load Balancing, unlike Server Clustering, is available in all versions of Windows Server 2003 (Web, Standard, Enterprise, and Datacenter Editions).

Planning a High-Availability Solution

- ☑ Microsoft recognizes the need for Server Clusters in many different types of environments, but the company specifically recommends Server Clusters for mission-critical installations that include Microsoft SQL Server, Exchange Server, and file and print servers.
- ☑ Load-balanced servers are recommended for many types of implementation, including Web servers, terminal servers, and media servers, eliminating the possibility of a single point of failure on a server that provides such a crucial service.
- ☑ You might need to purchase additional licensing for applications hosted in a network load-balanced cluster, since many applications require a license per node.
- ☑ If you are planning to have multiple Server Clusters, avoid using the same service accounts. This will keep users who know the account information for one cluster from being able to manipulate administrative functions of another cluster.

Exam Objectives Frequently Asked Questions

The following Frequently Asked Questions, answered by the authors of this book, are designed to both measure your understanding of the Exam Objectives presented in this chapter, and to assist you with real-life implementation of these concepts. You will also gain access to thousands of other FAQs at ITFAQnet.com.

Q: When should the Windows Recovery Console be used?

A: The Recovery Console is typically used when booting into any of the other modes fails.

Q: Which backup strategy is the best for me—Full, Differential, or Incremental?

A: This is really an organizational decision. One strategy might work for one company, but it might not for another. For example, a smaller company with less data on its servers might be able to perform Full backups nightly, whereas a company with more data to back up might not have enough time to perform a full backup and therefore must use Differential or Incremental backups.

Q: My servers only have one network card in them. Should I buy a secondary card if I want to use Network Load Balancing?

A: You don't have to buy a second card, but since they are so inexpensive and you have the ability to move the "heartbeat" traffic off the main NIC, it's typically the recommended method.

Q: What is the benefit of using ASR versus a typical backup?

A: Using ASR will give you the quickest recovery time to get a server back online. Once the server is brought back online using ASR, you can use your typical backup method (Full, Incremental, Differential) to recover any user data.

Q: I'm planning my disaster recovery strategy for my company. What type of disaster recovery site is best—a hot site, a warm site, or a cold site?

A: It's a matter of cost, and it's going to come down to how long your company can survive without operating on a near-normal level. If your organization cannot afford any down time, a hot site is probably best. However, there is a high cost associated with this type of setup. You need to work with your management team to decide what option is best suited to your company.

Self Test

A Quick Answer Key follows the Self Test questions. For complete questions, answers, and explanations to the Self Test questions in this chapter as well as the other chapters in this book, see the Self Test Appendix.

1. Bill is having problems starting his Windows Server 2003 server after updating a variety of device drivers. Bill wants to be able to record the drivers and services that are loaded when his server starts. Which startup mode can Bill use to do this?

   A. Safe mode

   B. Last known good configuration

   C. Boot logging

   D. This can't be done in Windows Server 2003; it is only a feature of Windows 2000

2. Bill has logged the drivers and services that have loaded (or have failed) during the startup of a bad server. What file stores the logged information?

   A. %systemroot%\ntbtlog.txt

   B. c:\ntblog.txt

   C. c:\temp\ntblog.txt

   D. %systemroot%\system32\ntbtlog.txt

3. Pedro is configuring three Windows Server 2003 servers to be part of a Server Cluster. He wants the configuration information for the cluster to be stored on multiple storage devices within the cluster. Which Server Cluster should he use to achieve this?

   A. Majority node set Server Cluster

   B. Single-node Server Cluster

   C. Network Load Balancing Server Cluster

   D. Single quorum device Server Cluster

4. In terms of outlining potential risks to your organization, which of the following is used to identify potential threats of terrorism, fire, flood, and other incidents as well as provide guidance on how to deal with such events when they occur?

   A. Disaster recovery plan

   B. Backup strategy

   C. Business continuity plan

   D. Risk analysis plan

5. You can select from many Windows startup options during a computer's boot process. Which startup option is only available on a domain controller?
   A. Debugging mode
   B. Safe mode with command prompt
   C. Recovery Console
   D. Directory services restore mode

6. Drew is attempting to load Server Clustering on his Windows Server 2003 Standard Edition servers. However, he cannot find the installation option on his server or his Windows Server 2003 CD-ROM. Why is he having difficulty installing Server Clustering?
   A. The installation files for Server Clustering are on the Windows Server 2003 Resource Kit CD.
   B. Windows Server Clustering is only available in the Enterprise and Datacenter versions of the Windows Server 2003 operating system.
   C. Drew would have to reinstall the operating system in order to create a Server Cluster, because this option must be selected during the initial server configuration.
   D. Drew needs to purchase the Server Cluster software separately from the Windows Server 2003 software.

7. Each server within a cluster must have the same location configuration set during the installation of Windows Server 2003. What are the components of the location configuration? (Choose all that apply.)
   A. Language
   B. Country
   C. Region
   D. State
   E. Company

8. John is planning a Server Cluster using Windows Server 2003. He is trying to measure the number of servers that he will need for this cluster. By measuring the number of clients that can be anticipated to use the Server Cluster, John is able to determine the number of servers he needs. What is the name of the measurement of clients versus server nodes?
   A. Client load
   B. Client traffic
   C. Client bandwidth
   D. Client analysis

9. Brittany has configured three servers for NLB. She wants to limit the type of network traffic that is balanced between the servers. What window in the Network Load Balancing Manager allows her to do this?

   A. Cluster Parameter window

   B. Add/Edit Port Rule window

   C. Port Configuration window

   D. Port Filter window

10. What type of Server Cluster has two or more nodes in which each node is attached to a cluster storage device?

    A. Single quorum device Server Cluster

    B. Major node set Server Cluster

    C. Single-node Server Cluster

    D. Network Load Balancing cluster

    E. None of the above

11. Luke wants to back up his files at any time during the business day, but he's afraid that he could lock users out of storage areas during the backup. What type of backup can Luke use to back up data during the day without locking out users?

    A. Full backup

    B. Differential backup

    C. Incremental backup

    D. Volume shadow copy backup

    E. Automated System Recovery

    F. None of the above; users will always be locked out when a storage device is being backed up

12. Owen is analyzing the security of his Server Cluster. He notices that security logging is not turned on in the Server Cluster. Of the following choices, which is the *best* reason for Owen to consider logging and auditing security-related events on his cluster?

A. By logging and auditing these events, he can watch files being accessed by users of the Server Cluster.

B. By logging and auditing these events, he can watch for any DoS attacks against the Server Cluster.

C. By logging and auditing these events, he can keep track of unauthorized access to the Server Cluster.

D. By logging and auditing these events, he can keep track of authorized access to the Server Cluster.

E. Answers **C** and **D**

F. Answers **B** and **C**

G. None of the above

13. Sean has created a backup job for one of his servers. He has also opened the advanced settings for the backup job and configured it to run as an Incremental backup. What other setting can he configure in the advanced settings for this backup job?

A. What type of media to use

B. When to start the backup

C. End-of-job notification

D. Copying the backup job to create another job

14. Brian is describing to his boss the differences between a Server Cluster and a Network Load Balancing cluster. He explains that an NLB cluster can support up to 32 nodes. His boss asks him how many nodes can be configured within a server cluster. How many nodes does he tell his boss can be configured?

A. 8

B. 10

C. 32

D. Infinite number

15. Automated System Recovery is a new disaster recovery solution in Windows Server 2003. It can be configured to back up specific data from a server. Which of the following types of data can be backed up (and restored) using ASR? (Choose all that apply.)

A. User data

B. System State data

C. OS-related data

D. System services

Self Test Quick Answer Key

For complete questions, answers, and explanations to the Self Test questions in this chapter as well as the other chapters in this book, see the Self Test Appendix.

1. **C**
2. **A**
3. **A**
4. **A**
5. **D**
6. **B**
7. **A**, **B**, **C**
8. **A**
9. **B**
10. **A**
11. **D**
12. **E**
13. **B**
14. **A**
15. **B**, **C**, **D**

Appendix

MCSA/MCSE 70-296

Self Test Questions, Answers, and Explanations

This appendix provides complete Self Test Questions, Answers, and Explanations for each chapter.

Chapter 1 Implementing DNS in a Windows Server 2003 Network

1. Stephen is creating a standard primary zone for his company on a Windows Server 2003 DNS server. Stephen wants to enable secure-only dynamic DNS updates on his standard primary zone for clients within his office. Stephen opens the DNS management console and opens the Properties window of the primary zone. He notices that the only options available for dynamic updates are None and Nonsecure and Secure. Why can't Stephen enable secure-only dynamic DNS updates on this zone?

   A. Stephen cannot use secure-only dynamic DNS updates unless his zone is an Active Directory integrated zone.

   B. The Secure Dynamic Updates feature is not available in Windows Server 2003.

   C. After creating the zone, Stephen must stop and restart the DNS server service.

   D. Stephen can just use the Nonsecure and Secure option, since clients will attempt to use secure dynamic updates first.

   ☑ **A**. Secure-only dynamic updates are available only on zones that have been configured as Active Directory integrated.

   ☒ **B, C, D**. Answer **B** is incorrect because secure dynamic updates are available in Windows Server 2003, but secure-only dynamic updates require Active Directory integration. Answer **C** is incorrect because the DNS service does not require a restart. Answer **D** is incorrect because clients will always attempt an unsecured dynamic update prior to attempting a secure dynamic update.

2. Your manager is concerned that the DNS servers in your network could be susceptible to name spoofing and wants to implement DNS security in your environment. He asks you to research the implementation of DNSSEC onto your existing Windows Server 2003 DNS servers. After researching DNSSEC, you explain to your boss that your Windows Server 2003 DNS servers can only act as secondary servers while running DNSSEC. Why is this so?

   A. A Windows Server 2003 DNS server can only run as a secondary server when using DNSSEC because it only meets the basic requirements of DNSSEC.

   B. A Windows Server 2003 DNS server can only run as a secondary server when using DNSSEC because a DNSSEC primary server can only run on BIND.

   C. A Windows Server 2003 DNS server can only run as a secondary server when using DNSSEC because you must purchase the additional DNSSEC module for Windows Server 2003 in order for your server to function as a primary DNS server.

   D. A Windows Server 2003 DNS server can indeed run as a primary or secondary server when using DNSSEC, as long as it is configured correctly.

☑ **A**. The basic support functionality as described in the RFC states that a DNS server must possess the ability to store and retrieve SIG, KEY, and NXT resource records. Although a Windows Server 2003 DNS can meet these requirements, it cannot sign zones or resource records, nor can it validate SIG resource records.

☒ **B, C, D**. Answer **B** is incorrect because although DNSSEC will run on a BIND server, it can also function on other non-Microsoft DNS servers. Answer **C** is incorrect because there is no additional package that you can purchase from Microsoft in order to make DNSSEC run as a primary server. Answer **D** is incorrect because a Windows Server 2003 DNSSEC-enabled DNS server cannot function as a primary server under any configuration.

3. One of your coworkers, Sam, has been tasked with finding various ways to reduce the amount of network traffic that passes over your wide area network. Sam comes to you with the idea of setting up DNS Notify for your Active Directory integrated DNS zones. You tell Sam that although this is a good idea for reducing DNS traffic, it will not work in your environment. Why is this true?

   A. DNS Notify is used to notify secondary servers of changes to the DNS database on the primary server. Since secondary servers do not exist in Active Directory integrated zones, DNS Notify cannot be implemented.

   B. DNS Notify is not available on the Windows Server 2003 operating system; however, an Active Directory integrated zone can function as a secondary server using DNS Notify on a BIND server that functions as the primary server.

   C. DNS Notify cannot run on your Windows Server 2003 server *unless* you place your zone files into an application directory partition.

   D. This is not true. You can use DNS Notify in your environment as long as you add the list of secondary servers to notify in the properties of the primary server.

   ☑ **A**. Answer **A** is correct because, by definition, an Active Directory integrated DNS zone does not need secondary zones, so DNS Notify would serve no purpose within this configuration. Therefore, DNS Notify cannot be implemented for Active Directory integrated zones.

   ☒ **B, C, D**. Answer **B** is incorrect because DNS Notify is indeed available on the Windows Server 2003 operating system. Answer **C** is incorrect because DNS Notify will not function in an Active Directory integrated zone, regardless of it being stored in an application directory partition. Answer **D** is incorrect because adding secondary DNS servers to the notify list will make an Active Directory-integrated zone use DNS Notify.

4. You are configuring your parent DNS server to delegate authority for your child domains to authoritative DNS servers in remote offices. However, you want to know about any additional DNS servers brought online in these remote offices without having to manually

enter resource records for the DNS servers. What can you create in your parent DNS server to support this scenario?

A. Conditional forwarders

B. Primary zone

C. Secondary zone

D. Stub zone

☑ **D**. A stub zone can be configured on your parent domain's DNS server that will retrieve resource records from the child domain for any new authoritative DNS servers that are brought online within that domain.

☒ **A, B, C**. Answer **A** is incorrect because conditional forwards are used to force replication directly to a DNS server within a particular domain but will not automatically become aware of any new DNS servers that are brought online. Answers **B** and **C** are incorrect because primary and secondary zones are used when a server has authority over a particular zone. In our example, the remote offices have control over their individual zones.

5. You have just started a new job as the network administrator for a software development company. You are reviewing the resource records in the Windows Server 2003 DNS server and notice that there are NXT and SIG resource records in the zone file. Upon further research, you discover that this server is functioning as a secondary server. What else would this DNS server need to have configured in order to produce these types of records?

A. Stub zones

B. Secure dynamic updates

C. Conditional forwarders

D. DNSSEC

☑ **D**. When a Windows Server 2003 DNS server is configured to support basic functionality as a secondary server for DNSSEC, it will allow for the replication of NXT and SIG records that will appear in the DNS zone file.

☒ **A, B, C**. All three of these answers are incorrect because none of them will create these additional DNS resource record types in the DNS server.

6. DNS spoofing occurs when a DNS server uses information from a host that has no authority to pass along resource information. In this scenario, the unauthorized host is intentionally supplying incorrect data to be added to the cache of the DNS server. What type of attack is DNS spoofing a form of?

A. Footprinting

B. Cache poisoning

C. Cache implantation

D. Cache registration

E. None of the above

☑ **B**. DNS spoofing is a form of cache poisoning. Spoofing attacks can cause users to be directed to an incorrect Internet site or e-mail servers to route e-mails to mail servers other than that for which they were originally intended.

☒ **A, C, D, E**. Answer **A** is incorrect because DNS footprinting is a separate type of attack from DNS spoofing. Answers **C** and **D** are incorrect because these terms do not exist in relation to DNS spoofing. Since **B** is the correct answer, Answer **E** (none of the above) cannot be the correct answer.

7. On occasion, clients need to resolve DNS records for external resources. When this occurs, the client sends its query to its appropriate internal DNS server. The DNS server sends additional queries to external DNS servers, acting on behalf of the client, and returns the query information to the client once the server obtains it. What type of query occurs when a DNS server is used as a proxy for DNS clients that have requested resource record information outside their domain?

   A. Recursive query

   B. Iterative query

   C. Reverse lookup query

   D. External query

   ☑ **A**. A recursive query occurs when a DNS server is used as a proxy for DNS clients that have requested name resolution for a host outside their domain.

   ☒ **B, C, D**. Answer **B** is incorrect because an iterative query occurs when a client is not requesting the use of recursive lookup from external DNS servers. Answers **C** and **D** are incorrect because these types of queries do not exist.

8. Kaitlyn wants to change the replication scope of her Active Directory integrated DNS zones so that they can replicate with Windows 2000 DNS servers. Which replication scope does she need to use in order for her Windows Server 2003 servers to replicate with Windows 2000 servers?

   A. DNS servers within an Active Directory domain

   B. DNS servers within an Active Directory forest

   C. Domain controllers within an Active Directory domain

   D. Domain controllers within an application directory partition

   ☑ **C**. This scope type allows for replication of zone data to all domain controllers within a domain, including Windows 2000 DNS servers.

   ☒ **A, B, D**. Answer **A** is the default setting for Windows Server 2003 DNS servers, which replicates zone data to all Windows Server 2003 DNS servers running on domain controllers in the Active Directory domain. Answer **B** is incorrect because this replicates zone data to all Windows Server 2003 DNS servers running in the forest. Answer **D** is incorrect because this uses application directory partitions, which do not exist on Windows 2000 servers.

9. Michael is creating a new standard primary zone for the law firm that he works for, Jones and Associates, using the domain jones.firm. Michael creates the zone through the DNS management console, but he wants to view the corresponding DNS zone file, jones.firm.dns. Where would Michael need to look in order to find this file?

   A. Michael cannot view the zone file because it is stored in Active Directory.

   B. Michael can look in the C:\Windows\system32\dns folder.

   C. Michael cannot view the DNS file except by using the DNS management console.

   D. The DNS zone file is actually just a key in the Windows Registry. Michael needs to use the Registry Editor if he wants to view the file.

   ☑ **B**. Michael can use Windows Explorer to drill down to the C:\Windows\system32\dns folder and open the .dns file with a text editor.

   ☒ **A, C, D.** Answer **A** is incorrect because this is a standard zone; it is stored in a zone file instead of Active Directory. Answer **C** is incorrect because Michael can use a text editor to view the .dns file. Answer **D** is incorrect because the DNS zone file is not stored in the system registry.

10. Windows Server 2003 offers legacy support for NETBIOS names. If the fully qualified domain name for a Windows Server 2003 fileserver were fileserv1.parentdomain.com, what could the corresponding NETBIOS name be?

   A. FILESERV1

   B. FILESERV1PARENT

   C. FILESERV

   D. Whatever you want it to be

   ☑ **B**. A NETBIOS name in Windows Server 2003 is derived from the first 15 characters of the FQDN.

   ☒ **A, C, D**. Answers **A** and **C** are incorrect because these names are fewer than 15 characters. Answer **D** is incorrect because the NETBIOS name is derived from the FQDN.

11. David is planning his DNS namespace for his new Windows Server 2003 network and is deciding what top-level domain to use for his internal network. He has decided that he will use a top-level domain that falls outside the Internet standard. Which of the following top-level domains should David use if he isn't going to use one of the Internet standard top-level domains?

A. .com

B. .biz

C. .net

D. .corp

☑ **D.** Answer **D** is correct because .corp is not currently a top-level domain that has been accepted and in use on the Internet, but it can still be used for David's internal network.

☒ **A, B, C.** Answers **A, B,** and **C** are incorrect because they are all top-level domains currently in use on the Internet.

12. Before DNS was developed, DNS resolution was controlled via special files to translate friendly names to IP addresses. Names and IP addresses were entered into these files, and computers used copies of these files for name resolution. What is the name of these files?

A. DNS zone text

B. LMHOSTS

C. HOSTS

D. WINS

☑ **C.** Prior to the implementation of DNS, IP-based networks used HOSTS files for name resolution. These files became oversized and unmanageable and were replaced by DNS servers.

☒ **A, B, D.** Answer **A** is incorrect because the DNS zone file is what DNS servers use to store zone information. Answer **B** is incorrect because LMHOSTS files were used in earlier version of Windows to resolve NETBIOS names. Answer **D** is incorrect because there is and was no such thing as a WINS file. WINS servers were used similar to DNS servers for centralized NETBIOS name resolution.

13. Active Directory integrated zones store their zone data in the Active Directory tree under the domain or application directory partition. Each zone is stored in a container object, which is identified by the name of the zone that has been created. What is the name of this type of container object?

A. dnsZone

B. dns-Zone

C. .dnsZone

D. Active Directory zone

☑ **A.** Active Directory integrated zone data is stored in a container object known as a *dnsZone* container.

☒ **B, C, D.** Answers **B, C,** and **D** are incorrect because they are nonexistent variations of the correct container name, dnsZone.

14. Active Directory uses DNS as a locator service to resolve domains, sites, and service names to their corresponding IP addresses. In order to log onto a computer that is part of an Active Directory domain, the client must send a message to his or her DNS server to obtain the address of an available domain controller. What is the name of the message that is sent to the DNS server?

    A. Broadcast request

    B. DNS query

    C. DC query

    D. Recursive query

    ☑ **B**. Clients who want to log on to an Active Directory domain must first send a DNS query to their DNS server (which is known either through DHCP or static entry) to locate a domain controller.

    ☒ **A, C, D**. Answers **A** and **C** are incorrect because no such queries exist in terms of network logon requirements. Answer **D** is incorrect because recursive queries are used to resolve queries for resources that exist outside the domain.

15. David is planning his DNS zones for his company. The company has 12 regional offices within the United States, with smaller branch offices that report to the regional offices. Three key issues David will need to take into consideration when planning DNS zones are which of the following? (Choose all that apply.)

    A. Use of caching-only servers

    B. The version of Windows DNS that is being used in the regional offices

    C. Link speed

    D. Traffic patterns

    E. Use of conditional forwarders

    F. Client configuration

    ☑ **A, C, D**. Three key elements must be taken into consideration when planning DNS zones and namespaces. First is the use of caching-only servers for smaller offices (such as the branch offices) that do not require full DNS servers. The second is the speed of the links between offices for purposes of lookups and replication. The third is traffic patterns. If a high percentage of network traffic passing over his WAN is to other offices for DNS resolution, David might want to place a full DNS server in that office rather than a caching server or no server at all. For these reasons, Answers **A**, **C**, and **D** are correct.

    ☒ **B, E, F**. Answer **B** is incorrect because of DNS version in terms of server and zone placement and management. Answer **E** is incorrect because conditional forwarders are not a critical part of a DNS hierarchy design. Answer **F** is incorrect because the client OS configuration will not affect how and where DNS servers are placed.

Chapter 2 Planning and Implementing an Active Directory Infrastructure

1. Your network currently uses a single Windows NT 4.0 domain named EXAMPLE, which is used by 2000 people at 12 different offices. The company has registered the name exampleinc.com for e-mail purposes. You have a PDC and seven BDCs. You discover that none of your domain controllers can support Windows Server 2003. You decide to install a new domain for Windows Server 2003 Active Directory using all new equipment, then migrate users, computers and data after the new domain is established. Which of the following names should you select for your root domain?

   A. Example.local

   B. Exampleinc.com

   C. Sub.example.local

   D. Sub.exampleinc.com

   ☑ **B**. Given that the company has registered the exampleinc.com name and only uses it for e-mail, it is the most likely candidate for a root domain. From here, you can create subdomains in the same domain tree or other domain trees fairly easily.

   ☒ **A, C, D**. Answer **A** is incorrect mainly because the company did not indicate a reason for not using the exampleinc.com name. A second issue would possibly arise if the company used the EXAMPLE portion as the domain's NetBIOS name, which would conflict with the existing Windows NT 4.0 domain. Answer **C** is incorrect because if you had selected a root domain with a different namespace, you would start at the top of the tree. Answer **D** is incorrect because using a subdomain of the registered domain name, although a valid selection, is usually only indicated by security reasons and none was given here.

2. You have a Windows 2000 Active Directory forest with 14 domains. The company has undergone some changes, many of which have streamlined administrative duties. Instead of several different administrative groups heading up their own divisions, the company now has a central administrative unit with three subunits that handle help desk and password changes, deskside support and computer account management, and installations and deployments, respectively. The company has decided to restructure the domains so that the forest root domain is empty except for forest management. You are now designing the child domains. How many should you design?

   A. 0

   B. 1

   C. 3

   D. 13

☑ **B**. The prior domain structure had been established based on administrative separation. With the administrative separation replaced by administrative delegation, there is only the need for one child domain within which you can design an OU hierarchy so that administrative duties can be delegated to match the various groups' responsibilities.

☒ **A, C, D**. If the forest root is empty and there are 0 child domains, no one would have user accounts, therefore Answer **A** is incorrect. Answer **C** is incorrect because the three subgroups mentioned are responsible for the same users and computers, just different administrative rights concerning those users, so you couldn't really split the users into different domains. Answer **D** is incorrect because that would essentially leave the original 14 domains, and you wouldn't really restructure the domains as the question requires.

3. You have been hired as a consultant to review an Active Directory design for Example Inc. The company hands you its WAN map, an organizational chart, and its Active Directory design. Headquarters for Example Inc. are in Boston. You immediately notice that the WAN map has a Boston location, a New York location, and a Philadelphia location. In addition, you discover that the Active Directory root name is intended to be NY.example.com. The child domains are intended to be named Boston.example.com and philly.example.com. What is wrong with this design?

   A. The names of cities cannot be the same as a site, which you assume they will use.

   B. Boston.example.com should be the root of the forest, since it is the headquarters.

   C. The root domain namespace and the child domains are at the same level.

   D. The name example.com was not registered.

   ☑ **C**. The name of the child domains would best be at a lower level from the forest root in order to create a true domain tree. The names themselves are somewhat troubling because the domain structure is intended to be logical. Sites are supposed to reflect the physical network, whereas domains should be logical. That doesn't prevent the domains from being arranged by a physical location, but when domains are designed, an actual business or technical need should drive the number of domains and the resources contained within them.

   ☒ **A, B, D**. Answer **A** is incorrect. You can use city names for domains if you would like, and they could even match the names of the sites, although we wouldn't recommend it because it would be confusing. Answer **B** in incorrect because the location of the headquarters and the forest root domain do not need to have the same name. Answer **D** is incorrect because DNS names ending in .com should be registered with InterNIC before being used on the Internet, but the question did not state whether example.com was registered or not.

4. You are an administrator for an automotive parts company. Your manufacturing plant is located in Flint, Michigan, and you have a large office in Detroit, Michigan. You have small offices on site at your main business partner, an automotive company. Your headquarters is in Paris, France. You have three names registered with InterNIC: autoparts.net, autoparts.fr, and autoparts.co.uk. The autoparts.fr and autoparts.co.uk names are used on the Web to sell automotive parts to European and Pacific Rim countries and for research and development, respectively. The autoparts.net name is not used. Which of the following names will you select for the forest root domain?

   A. autoparts.fr

   B. autoparts.co.uk

   C. autoparts.local

   D. autoparts.net

   ☑ **D**. Autoparts.net is both registered and currently unused making it an ideal forest root domain name.

   ☒ **A, B, C**. Answer **A** is incorrect. Autoparts.fr is currently used as a Web site. Although you can use this as the forest root domain, you would either have to implement a form of split DNS to secure the internal forest root domain or you would leave the forest root domain open to a security hole. Answer **B**, autoparts.co.uk, is used for research and development, which means that your forest root domain could become a test domain for developers and that could potentially cause a network outage. Therefore, this is not your best choice. Answer **C**, autoparts.local, is a valid choice, but it is not a registered name that is unused, which makes autoparts.net the best choice for the forest root domain name.

5. Your help desk staff have decided to implement a new TAPI application that will integrate with Active Directory. The application will only be used at the help desk location in Atlanta. They require fault tolerance for the application. You have seven other branches and do not want any excess traffic on your WAN links to them. How do you assist the help desk staff with their request?

   A. Deny the request for the application. It will overwhelm the WAN links.

   B. Implement the TAPI application with extensions to the schema and new objects to be replicated across the network.

   C. Create an application directory partition on an Atlanta domain controller.

   D. Create one application directory partition and two replicas on three separate Atlanta domain controllers.

   ☑ **D**. The application directory partition will enable the TAPI application to integrate with Active Directory but maintain the information locally. The replicas provide fault tolerance.

☒ **A, B, C.** Answer **A** is incorrect because you can use an application directory partition to localize the TAPI application's data. Answer **B** is incorrect because this will add the excess WAN traffic that you did not want. Answer **C** is incorrect because a single application directory partition does not provide fault tolerance.

6. You have a Windows NT 4.0 network with three domains that you will be migrating to an Active Directory Windows Server 2003 forest. You will also create a mirrored Windows Server 2003 lab forest for research and development. You want to allow users in the lab forest to have access to the production forest's resources. How do you enable this ability?

   A. Create a one-way forest trust in which the production forest trusts the lab forest.

   B. Create an explicit external trust relationship in which the lab forest root domain trusts the production forest root domain.

   C. Create a two-way forest trust between the production and lab forests.

   D. Create a one-way explicit trust in which the production forest root trusts the lab forest root.

   ☑ **A.** The production forest must trust the lab forest in order for resources in the production forest to be accessible by users anywhere in the lab forest.

   ☒ **B, C, D.** Answer **B** is incorrect because this will only enable lab root domain resource access to the production forest root users. Answer **C** is incorrect because there is no need given to allow production users access to lab resources. Answer **D** is incorrect because this will only enable production root domain resource access to the lab forest root users, preventing access from child domains to child domains.

7. You have a Windows NT 4.0 network with three domains that you will be migrating to a Windows Server 2003 Active Directory forest. Your domain controllers are not able to support the Windows Server 2003 operating system. You create a new forest and migrate users and computers to the new forest. During the migration, you create a trust relationship so that users who are in the new forest can access resources on member servers of the old domains. What type of trust relationships will you need to create?

   A. A forest trust relationship

   B. Explicit external trust relationships

   C. Implicit Kerberos trust relationships

   D. Shortcut trust relationships

   ☑ **B.** You need to create explicit external trust relationships in which the old Windows NT 4.0 domains trust the domains in the new forest.

   ☒ **A, C, D.** Answer **A** is incorrect because you only have a single forest. A forest trust requires two forests. Answer **C** is incorrect because implicit Kerberos trust relationships only exist between domains within the same forest. Answer **D** is incorrect because a shortcut trust relationship is used to speed up access to resources across a forest.

8. Your Windows 2000 Active Directory forest has just been upgraded to Windows Server 2003. You have added seven new domains because you are merging with another company. Users in your sub.child.trunk.root.local domain are having lengthy access times for resources in the new.child.trunk.other.co.local domain, whose resources are in the same building as the users trying to access them. How can you speed up access?

   A. Move the users to a new building.

   B. Create an explicit external trust relationship between the domains.

   C. Raise the domain functional level to Windows Server 2003.

   D. Create a shortcut trust relationship.

   ☑ **D**. Given that the users and resources are local to each other, the access time latency is likely due to the resolving of the implicit Kerberos trusts. To make this process faster, you simply need to create a shortcut trust between the two domains.

   ☒ **A, B, C**. Answer **A** is incorrect because the resources and users are in the same building, so moving the users will probably increase the latency. You do not create explicit external trusts between domains within the same forest, therefore Answer **B** is incorrect. Raising the domain functional level will not increases resource access, therefore Answer **C** is incorrect.

9. You are designing an Active Directory network. There will be two forests in the final design. Forest A will trust Forest B in the final configuration. You will have several member servers that will run Windows NT 4.0 and several that will run Windows Server 2000. Which forest functional level should you select?

   A. None; you cannot configure this forest

   B. Windows 2000

   C. Windows Server 2003 interim

   D. Windows Server 2003

   ☑ **D**. You can only create a forest trust when the forest functional level of both forests is at Windows Server 2003. Member servers can be any operating system, but all domain controllers must be running Windows Server 2003.

   ☒ **A, B, C**. Answer **A** is incorrect because it is possible to configure this forest. Answer **B** is incorrect because it will not support a forest trust. Answer **C** is incorrect because it is used only in upgrading Windows NT 4.0 domains to Windows Server 2003.

10. You have an Active Directory network with three domains. Domain 1 is at the domain functional level of Windows 2000 native. Domain 2 is at the domain functional level of Windows Server 2003 interim. Domain 3 is at Windows Server 2003. What is the highest level you can have for the forest functional level?

   A. Windows 2000

   B. Windows Server 2003 interim

C. Windows Server 2003

D. None; this forest cannot be configured

☑ **A.** The only forest functional level that will support all three of these domain functional levels is Windows 2000.

☒ **B, C, D.** The Windows Server 2003 interim forest functional level only supports domains at the Windows Server 2003 and Windows Server 2003 interim functional levels, therefore Answer **B** is incorrect. Answer **C** is incorrect because the Windows Server 2003 forest functional level only supports domains with the Windows Server 2003 functional level. The forest can be configured at Windows 2000 forest functional level, causing Answer **D** to be incorrect as well.

11. You are upgrading a Windows NT 4.0 domain and a Windows 2000 Active Directory forest with two domains to Windows Server 2003. In your final forest configuration, you will have domain controllers with either Windows 2000 server or Windows Server 2003 operating systems. Which domain functional levels are the highest you can reach?

A. Windows 2000 mixed

B. Windows 2000 native

C. Windows Server 2003 interim

D. Windows Server 2003

☑ **B.** The highest level you can raise a domain that contains both Windows 2000 and Windows Server 2003 domain controllers is Windows 2000 native.

☒ **A, C, D.** Answer **A** is incorrect because this is the default domain functional level for a domain. Answer **C**, Windows Server 2003 interim, is incorrect because it does not allow Windows 2000 domain controllers. Answer **D**, Windows Server 2003, would only be correct if you had a single domain that only contained Windows Server 2003 domain controllers, but the question does not give you enough information to know that.

12. You have a network with four locations: NY, PHX, LA, SEA. You have three domains that contain both users and network resources. You install a new printer in the SEA location. The printer is in the root domain, which has most of its other resources in the NY location. Several users in a child domain at the SEA location complain that it takes a long time to access the printer. What steps can you take to speed up access to the printer?

A. Create a shortcut trust to the root domain from the child domain.

B. Add a global catalog server to the NY location.

C. Add a global catalog server to the SEA location.

D. Enable universal group membership caching at SEA.

☑ **C.** When you add a global catalog server, it will speed up queries to resources in other domains.

☒ **A, B, D**. Answer **A** is incorrect because the root domain and its child already have an immediate trust relationship with each other. The shortcut trust would not reduce the latency. Answer **B** is incorrect because the global catalog server needs to be placed in the location where queries are taking place—in other words, next to the users—in order to speed up query time. Answer **D** is incorrect because the problem is not concerned with credentials.

13. You have a network with five locations. You have configured four sites, one of which combines the offices at two locations and is named COMBO. There is one global catalog server at each site and domain controllers at all five locations. At COMBO's Office A, users are periodically complaining that they cannot log on. However, at COMBO's Office B, there have been no problems. In what two ways can you fix this problem? (Select two answers.)

    A. Install another domain controller at COMBO's Office A.

    B. Enable a global catalog server at COMBO's Office A.

    C. Enable a global catalog server at COMBO's Office B.

    D. Enable universal group membership caching for the entire COMBO site.

    ☑ **B, D**. Answers **B** and **D** are both options for this situation. It is likely that users are periodically unable to log on because they have lost network access to a functioning global catalog server to resolve their credentials in universal groups. You can either add a global catalog server to the local network or enable group membership caching. Both of these are options because the office has a domain controller on site.

    ☒ **A, C**. Answer **A** is incorrect because the domain controller will not help process logons for universal groups. Answer **C** is incorrect because the COMBO Office B is not experiencing problems.

14. You have two forests. Each of these forests is used across your five office locations. You have users who access resources in both forests. You have explicit external trust relationships between certain domains to allow access. These users often complain that they cannot query for resources in one of the forests in the same window that they browse the other forest. What can you do to fix this problem?

    A. Add a global catalog server.

    B. Enable universal group membership caching.

    C. Create a new trust.

    D. Nothing.

    ☑ **D**. The global catalog cannot be shared between forests.

    ☒ **A, B, C**. Answers **A**, **B**, and **C** are all incorrect because they would not combine the browsing capabilities of two separate forests.

15. You are designing a Windows Server 2003 forest. You will have a single domain in the forest. You will have three sites with over 400 users each. You will not be using UPN names. How many global catalog servers should you plan for?

   A. 0

   B. 1

   C. 2

   D. 3

   ☑ **B**. You should plan for at least one global catalog server. The first server installed into the root domain of a forest is always a global catalog server. If you add domains in the future, you can add more global catalog servers, but you won't need them until that point.

   ☒ **A, C, D**. Answer **A** is incorrect because you will automatically be given one global catalog server. Answer **C** is incorrect because there is no need for fault tolerance for the global catalog servers as the question is written. Answer **D** is incorrect because the users will not be using any of the features that a global catalog server offers, so you will not need to place one at each site.

Chapter 3 Managing and Maintaining an Active Directory Infrastructure

1. Your Windows Server 2003 Active Directory structure contains multiple domains and child domains, as shown in the following illustration. Many of your users need to work from different locations at various points throughout the week, and they are having difficulty remembering the information that they need to enter when logging onto different domains within the network. What is the most efficient way for you to make the login process simpler for your users when they are logging onto the network from different domains?

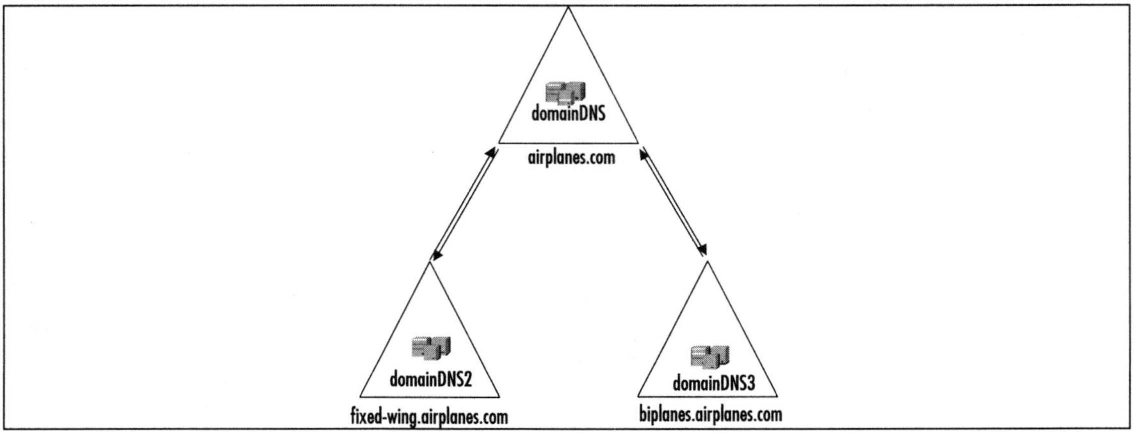

A. Create local accounts in each domain from which roaming users need to log in.

B. Create two-way transitive trusts between all domains within your Active Directory forest.

C. Create a single common UPN suffix so that users can log in simply by entering their usernames, regardless of where on the network they attempt to log in from.

D. Implement a RADIUS database to handle login requests from multiple domains.

☑ **C**. Creating a common UPN suffix simplifies the login process for users in a large, multidomain environment.

☒ **A, B, D**. Answer **A** is incorrect because it will create unnecessary administrative overhead. Each user only requires an Active Directory user object in order to access resources across the network. Answer **B** is incorrect because the existence of trust relationships is not directly related to UPN suffixes. Answer **D** is incorrect because an external RADIUS application would be unnecessary and redundant.

2. Your organization includes a large sales department, with many representatives who only come into the corporate headquarters a few times a month. For this reason, many of them forget their network passwords. You would like Jane, a power user in the sales department, to be able to reset passwords for the members of her department. What is the best way to implement this solution without allowing Jane any more administrative access than necessary?

A. Make Jane a member of the Domain Admins group.

B. Install a domain controller in the sales department and run *dcpromo* to create a new domain in your organization's Active Directory forest.

C. Create a separate OU for the sales department and delegate the authority to reset passwords to Jane's user account.

D. For each user account in the sales department, grant Jane's account the Change Password right.

☑ **C**. OUs provide the most efficient way to delegate specific administrative tasks for a collection of Active Directory objects. The Delegation of Control wizard makes it simple to assign permissions to perform common tasks such as creating and deleting user accounts or resetting passwords.

☒ **A, B, D**. Answer **A** is incorrect because it would grant far too much administrative authority to Jane's user account. Answer **B** is incorrect because it would unnecessarily complicate your company's Active Directory implementation, especially since the creation of an OU will accomplish exactly what you need to do. Answer **D** is incorrect because it will allow Jane to reset passwords for the existing users within the department but will force you to assign that permission to every new user in the department. This solution is not at all efficient.

3. You are the administrator of the fixed-wing.airplanes.com Windows Server 2003 domain. You are installing an Active Directory-aware database application that has created an application partition directory called application25 on the dc1.fixed-wing.airplanes.com domain controller as a child domain of the fixed-wing.airplanes.com domain. If there are no other application partition directories within your domain, what is the fully qualified DNS name of this partition directory?

   A. application25.dc1.fixed-wing.airplanes.com

   B. application25.airplanes.com

   C. application25.fixed-wing.airplanes.com

   D. application25.com

   ☑ **C.** Application partition directories use the same naming standards as the rest of your DNS naming scheme. This partition will be created as a child of the existing domain directory partition, fixed-wing.airplanes.com.

   ☒ **A, B, D.** Answer **A** is incorrect because the DNS syntax will not include the name of the controller that is housing the application partition directory. Answer **B** is incorrect because it has dropped the fixed-wing portion of the fully qualified DNS name. Answer **D** is incorrect because it is how the application partition directory might appear if it had been created as the root of a new forest.

4. You are attempting to raise the functional level of your domain to Windows Server 2003 in order to take advantage of the advanced Active Directory features that it offers. You are able to authenticate and browse the network, and you access Active Directory Domains and Trusts using the login credentials of your user account in the Enterprise Admins group. When you attempt to raise the forest functional level, you receive an error message, and the functional level is not raised to Windows Server 2003. Of the following, which is the most likely cause of this failure?

   A. Your forest still contains Windows NT 4.0 and/or Windows 2000 domain controllers.

   B. TCP/IP is not running on your network.

   C. Your user account is not a member of the Schema Admins group.

   D. Your workstation has a failed NIC.

   ☑ **A.** You cannot raise the functional level of your forest to Windows Server 2003 unless all domain controllers in the forest are running Windows Server 2003. Any remaining NT 4.0 and 2000 controllers need to be upgraded or demoted to member server status.

   ☒ **B, C, D.** Answer **B** is incorrect because network protocol has no direct bearing on raising your forest functional level so long as you can access network resources. Answer **C** is incorrect because you do not need to be a member of the Schema Admins group to raise the functional level of a Windows Server 2003 forest; rather, you need to be a member of the Enterprise Admins group. Answer **D** is incorrect because you are able to log onto your network and browse network resources, which indicates that your NIC is functioning properly.

5. You need to make some alterations to the schema in your Active Directory forest. You've used the regsvr32 utility to register schmmgmt.dll on your administrative workstation. However, when you open the Administrative tools folder, the Active Directory Schema snap-in does not appear. What do you need to do in order to manage the Active Directory schema from your workstation?

   A. You cannot manage the schema from your workstation. You need to log onto the server that holds the schema master operational role.

   B. Open a blank Microsoft Management Console and add the Active Directory Schema snap-in.

   C. Run schmmgmt.exe from your workstation command prompt.

   D. Use the ADSI Editor in the Windows Server 2003 Resource Kit.

   ☑ **B**. After you've registered the schmmgmt.dll on your workstation, you can add the Active Directory Schema snap-in to any MMC. Because of the potential hazards of editing the schema, the Schema snap-in is not installed by default.

   ☒ **A, C, D**. Answer **A** is incorrect because, although the Active Directory Schema snap-in will attach to the schema master to perform its management functions, you do not need to log onto the console of the schema master itself in order to manage the schema. Using administrative tools from your workstation allows for better physical security for your domain controllers since you're not logging onto them locally. Answer **C** is incorrect because the schmmgmt.exe file does not exist; it is a reference to the .DLL file that you need to register in order to access the Active Directory Schema snap-in. Answer **D** is incorrect because ADSI Edit allows administrators and developers to access and modify the Active Directory attributes of individual Active Directory objects, not the underlying schema.

6. Your forest is structured according to the following illustration. You have a group of developers in the east.fixed-wing.airplanes.com domain who need to access files in the development.central.biplanes.airplanes.com domain on a regular basis. The users are complaining that accessing the files in the development domain is taking an unacceptably long time. What can you do to improve their response time?

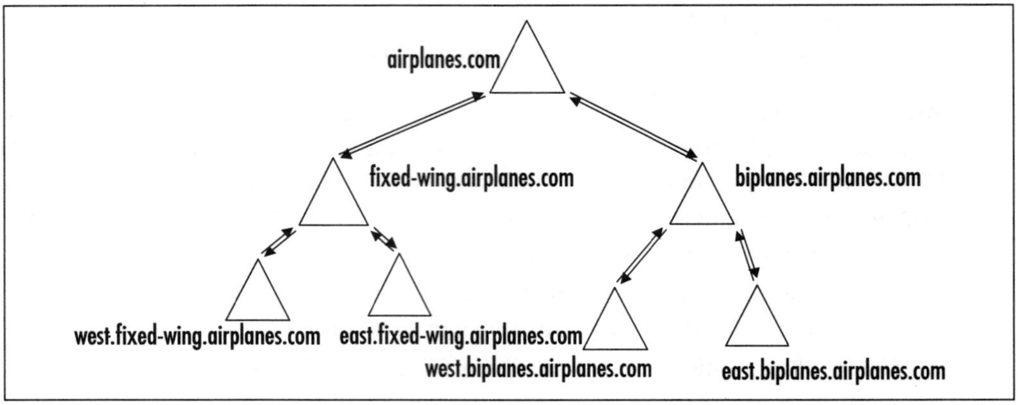

A. Create a domain local group in the development domain and add the developers' user accounts to it.

B. Create a shortcut trust between the east.fixed-wing.airplanes.com domain and the development.central.biplanes.airplanes.com domain.

C. Place the resources in the development domain into an OU. Use the Delegation of Control wizard to grant the users in the east.fixed-wing.airplanes.com domain the appropriate permissions.

D. Create an external trust between the fixed-wing.airplanes.com domain and the biplanes.airplanes.com domain.

☑ **B**. A shortcut trust will allow logon and resource requests to process more quickly by bypassing the usual traversal of domain trusts.

☒ **A, C, D**. Answer **A** is incorrect because creating a domain local group will not speed the logon request process. Answer **C** is incorrect because grouping the resources into a separate OU will not improve logon requests from other domains in the network. Answer **D** is incorrect because an external trust is used to establish a trust relationship between a Windows Server 2003 Active Directory forest and a Windows NT4 or 2000 domain. In this case, the two domains in question are part of the same Windows Server 2003 forest.

7. You need to perform an authoritative restore on a domain controller on your network. From the Windows Server 2003 Windows Advanced Options menu, you select the option for Directory Services Restore Mode. When prompted, you enter the username and password of your individual account that is a member of the Domain Admins and Enterprise Admins groups. You are unable to log onto the server. What is the cause of the login failure?

A. You need to log onto the server using the local administrator account and the Directory Services Restore Mode password that you specified when you ran the Active Directory Installation wizard.

B. Your account does not meet the password complexity requirements of the local system policy.

C. Your account has been locked out.

D. Your account needs to be a member of the Schema Admins group.

☑ Answer **A.** When you log onto a domain controller in Directory Services Restore Mode, you need to provide the local administrator account and password, not any domain-level administrator accounts.

☒ **B, C, D.** Answers **B**, **C**, and **D** are incorrect because they are irrelevant to being able to log onto your controller in Directory Services Restore Mode.

8. You are the administrator of the network shown in the following figure. You have just installed an Active Directory-aware enterprise resource planning (ERP) application on your network, which has created an application directory partition on dc1.biplanes.airplanes.com. You perform nightly backups of the data contained in this partition, but you are still concerned that a server failure will leave your mission-critical ERP application unavailable to your network users for an unacceptable length of time. What is the most efficient way to increase the fault tolerance of this application?

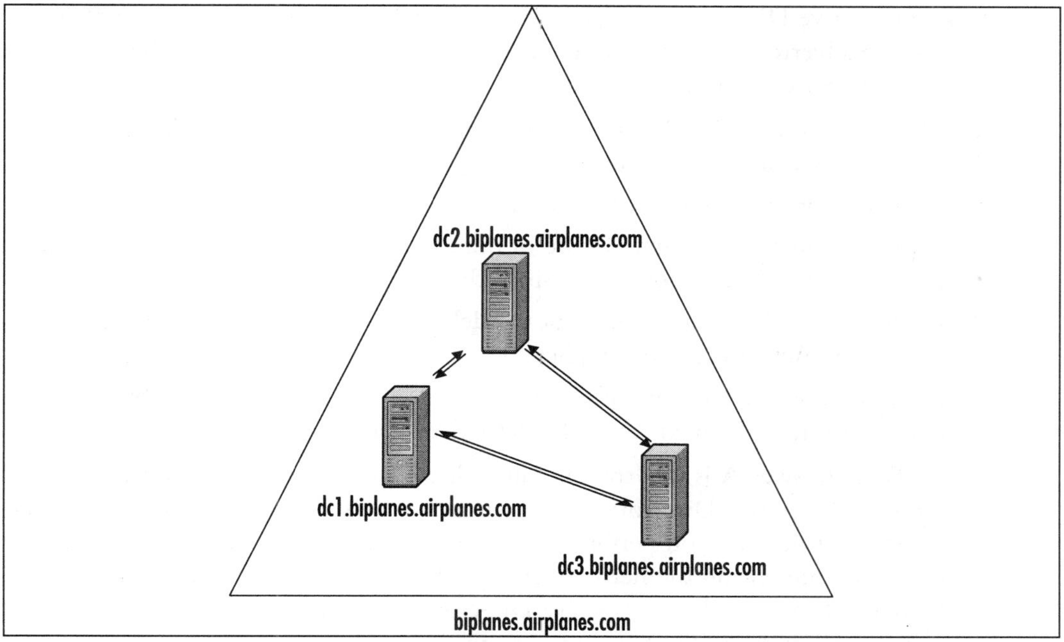

A. Increase the frequency of your backups.

B. Configure a second application directory partition on dc2.biplanes.airplanes.com, and configure the partition directory on dc1 to replicate its information to the new partition directory.

C. Store a local copy of the application's data on each user's workstation so that they can work from the local copy in case the server goes down.

D. Create a duplicate installation of the ERP application on a test server and restore the previous evening's production backups to the test server on a daily basis.

☑ **B**. Creating a second application partition directory will create fault tolerance in case the server hosting the first directory suffers an outage. It will also improve performance for clients that are physically closer to the second partition.

☒ **A, C, D**. Answer **A** is incorrect because it will do nothing to increase the fault tolerance of the application. Answer **C** is incorrect because it is not possible, and even if it were, it would create data inconsistencies between the individual workstations. Answer **D** is incorrect because it is incredibly labor-intensive and would still allow the possibility of data loss between the time of the server failure and the time of the last production backup.

9. You are the administrator of a Windows Server 2003 network with three domain controllers; a portion of the network is shown in the following illustration. You perform a full backup of Active Directory on a nightly basis. On Monday afternoon, a member of your help desk inadvertently deletes the Human Resources OU. What is the best way to restore this information while losing as little information as possible?

A. Manually recreate the OU and its contents. Any permissions associated with deleted user groups will automatically transfer over to the recreated OU.

B. Perform a primary restore of the entire Active Directory database.

C. Perform a nonauthoritative restore of the deleted OU so that it will receive any updates that had been performed since the OU was deleted.

D. Perform an authoritative restore of the deleted OU so that it will not be deleted again at the next Active Directory replication.

☑ **D**. An authoritative restore of the deleted OU will ensure that the object will not be deleted again at the next Active Directory replication.

☒ **A, B, C**. Answer **A** is incorrect because all permissions would be lost if you manually recreated an Active Directory object, since the GUIDs would be different. Answer **B** is incorrect because you perform a primary restore only if there is a single domain controller present on the network. Answer **C** is incorrect because the OU will simply be deleted again at the next Active Directory replication, since the other domain controllers will replicate the deletion back to the restored OU.

10. The domain controller on your network that held the domain naming master operations role suffered a failed power supply. Since you needed to create new domains because of a recent corporate merger, you immediately seized the domain naming role to another domain controller. Your hardware technicians have replaced the power supply on the original domain naming master. What do you need to do before you return the original domain controller to the network?

    A. Use *ntdsutil* to seize the domain naming master role back to the original domain controller.

    B. Nothing. Simply return the server to production as normal.

    C. Reformat the machine and reinstall the operating system.

    D. Use Active Directory Domains and Trusts to reassign the domain naming master back to the original domain controller.

    ☑ **C.** You need to reformat any machine from which you've seized the schema master, the RID master, or domain naming master roles before you return them to your network.

    ☒ **A, B, D.** Answers **A**, **B**, and **D** are all incorrect because the original domain naming master can never return to the network once the role has been seized and assigned to another domain controller.

11. You have a comma-separated text file containing updated account information for existing users on your network. How can you add this information to your Active Directory database as quickly as possible?

    A. Using the text file as a reference, update the user accounts using the Active Directory Users and Groups management console.

    B. Use the LDIFDE command-line utility to import the .CSV information directly into Active Directory.

    C. Purchase a third-party add-on utility to import the information into Active Directory.

    D. Delegate control over the Users container and have a help desk associate enter the information using Active Directory Sites and Services.

    ☑ **B.** The LDIFDE utility allows you to import information contained in .CSV files directly into Active Directory.

    ☒ **A, C, D.** Answer **A** is incorrect because this will be too time-consuming and inefficient. Answer **C** is incorrect because you don't need to spend additional money on an external utility when the functionality to import information exists within the CSVDE utility. Answer **D** is incorrect because Active Directory Sites and Services is used to manage the physical layout of Active Directory, not the information contained in user accounts.

12. You have two user accounts on your Windows Server 2003 network: one account that belongs to the Domain Admins and Enterprise Admins group that you use to perform sensitive administrative tasks, and one nonadministrative user that you use for everyday logins and activities. What is the most efficient and secure way to access the Windows Server 2003 Administrative Tools using your "superuser" account?

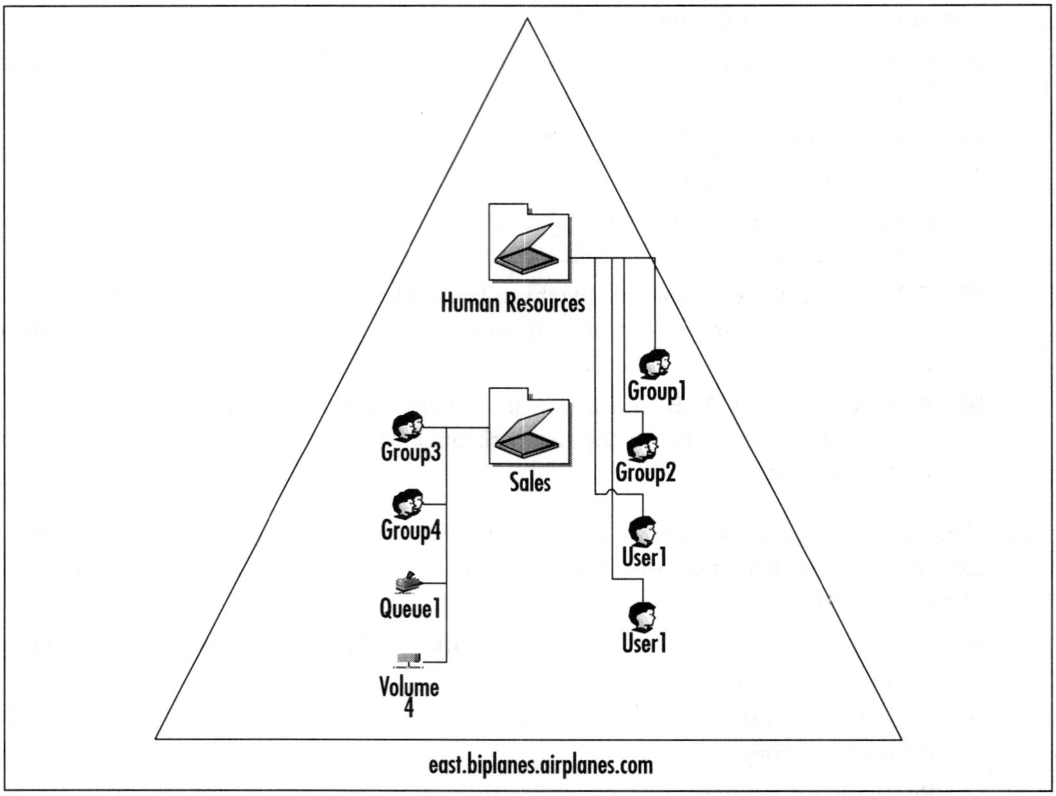

A. Use the *RunAs* function to launch the Administrator Tools using your administrator account's login information.

B. Log out of your workstation and log back in with your administrator account whenever you need to perform a management task.

C. Walk over to a server to access the administrative tools.

D. Log onto your workstation using your administrator account at all times; you shouldn't maintain two user accounts within your domain.

☑ **A**. Microsoft recommends as a security best practice that you use the *RunAs* feature to launch administrative tools using the security context of an administrative user, without necessitating that you remain logged in as that user at all times.

☒ **B, C, D**. All three of these options allow you to perform administrative tasks, but the question is looking for the method that would offer the *best* security and efficiency in performing network management functions. Answer **B**, although certainly an option that would work, is not the most efficient way to perform administrative tasks, because it wastes time during repeated logon/logoff operations. You also run the risk of forgetting to log back on as a normal user after you've finished performing the administrative task at hand. Answer **C** is incorrect because it too is inefficient and will interfere with the physical security of your domain controllers by forcing you to work directly from the console when it isn't necessary to do so. Answer **D** is a security risk to your network because leaving yourself logged in as an administrator means that anyone who gains access to your workstation has obtained the "keys to the kingdom" and can wreak havoc on your network at will.

13. You have just created a child domain on your Windows Server 2003 network. What type of trust relationship exists by default between the parent and child domains?

    A. One-way: outgoing from the parent domain to the child domain

    B. Two-way transitive

    C. One-way: incoming from the parent domain to the child domain

    D. One-way: outgoing from the child domain to the parent domain

    E. One-way: incoming from the child domain to the parent domain

    ☑ **B**. By default, a two-way transitive trust exists between a newly-created child domain and its parent.

    ☒ **A, C, D, E**. Answers **A**, **C**, **D**, and **E** are all incorrect because none of these options is the default trust relationship that is created when you add a child domain to an existing parent domain.

14. You have just been informed that your company's training department, whose resources are currently housed in their own domain called *training.mycompany.com*, is changing its department name to Staff Development. The vice president of the department would like their Active Directory domain renamed to staffdevelopment.mycompany.com. All domain controllers are running Windows Server 2003. How can you meet the vice president's request? (Choose all that apply.)

    A. Rename the training.mycompany.com domain using Active Directory Domains and Trusts.

    B. Raise the domain functional level of the training.mycompany.com domain to Windows Server 2003.

    C. Use the *DomainRename* Resource Kit utility to rename training.mycompany.com to staffdevelopment.mycompany.com.

D. Raise the forest functional level of your Active Directory forest to Windows Server 2003.

☑ **B, C.** You'll need to raise the functional level of the domain to Windows Server 2003 before using the *DomainRename* utility. You will be able to do this because all domain controllers in the target domain are running Windows Server 2003..

☒ **A, D.** Answer **A** is incorrect because you will use the *DomainRename* utility to rename the domain in question. Answer **D** is incorrect because, although raising the forest functional level would allow you to use the *DomainRename* utility, the environment described in the question would not allow this. You cannot raise the forest functionality level of an Active Directory domain that still contains Windows NT and/or 2000 controllers.

15. You have five domain controllers in your Windows Server 2003 domain, each of which maintains an operations master role. Your domain is operating at the Windows Server 2003 domain functional level. PDC1.AIRPLANES.COM, the machine that hosts the PDC emulator role, fails. Your hardware technicians estimate that it will be out of service for 48 hours. Your Windows NT 4.0 Workstation clients report that they cannot log onto the network. How can you resolve this situation as quickly as possible?

A. Wait for your hardware technicians to repair the PDC emulator.

B. Upgrade a Windows NT 4.0 member server to Windows Server 2003 and assign it the PDC emulator role.

C. Install a Windows NT 4.0 domain controller to handle down-level client authentication until the PDC emulator is repaired.

D. Use *ntdsutil* to seize the PDC emulator role and assign it to another domain controller.

☑ **D.** You'll use the *ntdsutil* utility to seize the operations master role of any server that has failed and will be unavailable for an extended length of time. In the case of the PDC emulator, you can return the original operations master to the network without incident.

☒ **A, B, C.** Answer **A** is incorrect because it will cause unnecessary aggravation for your down-level clients because they will be unable to authenticate to the domain until the PDC emulator is repaired. Answer **B** is incorrect because it will be too time-consuming, since planning a controller upgrade is not something that should be done on a moment's notice. Answer **C** is incorrect because your domain is operating at the Windows Server 2003 domain functional level, which prohibits you from adding any NT4 controllers to the domain.

Chapter 4 Implementing PKI in a Windows Server 2003 Network

1. You have installed certificate services on a Windows Server 2003 server named CA101.somecompany.com. Your boss has decided that he wants to change all the servers to a naming convention that is more descriptive to the organization. He wants to rename CA101.somecompany.com to certserver.somecompany.com. You explain to your boss that renaming a server with certificate services is not a good idea. Which of the following answers best describes the reason that you should not rename the server?

   A. Once a server has joined an Active Directory domain, you cannot change the name without reloading the server.

   B. The server name is bound to the CA information in Active Directory, and changing the name would invalidate certificates that have been issued by the server.

   C. DNS will not allow for the renaming of a CA server.

   D. You can change the name of the CA server, as long as you use the certutil.exe *–R* option prior to the server rename, so that all the clients and subordinate servers are aware of the name change.

   E. None of the above.

   ☑ **B**. Since the CA's own certificate is based on the server information, changing the server name would invalidate the machine names stored within the certificate.

   ☒ **A, C, D, E**. Answer **A** is incorrect because you can change a server name as long as you have the appropriate credentials. Answer **C** is incorrect because DNS does not have authority to allow or deny a server rename. Answer **D** is incorrect because there is no *–R* switch for the certutil.exe utility that allows for the renaming of a CA server.

2. You have installed certificate services on a Windows Server 2003 server, but after installation you are unable to open the Web enrollment Web site. What must you do in order to run Web enrollment on the server?

   A. You must stop and restart certificate services or restart the computer before Web enrollment will work.

   B. You must run certutil.exe *–w [servername]* to activate Web enrollment.

   C. Prior to installing certificate services, you must install IIS on the server.

   D. You must open the Certificate Services management tool, right-click the servername, open the **Properties** for the server, and check off **Web enrollment** on the **General** tab.

   E. Web Enrollment is a Windows 2000 feature and was not carried over to Windows Server 2003.

☑ **C**. IIS must be installed on the server prior to the installation of certificate services. If you don't have IIS installed, you can still install certificate services, but users will not be able to use Web enrollment.

☒ **A, B, D, E.** Answer **A** is incorrect because stopping and restarting the service or rebooting the PC will have no effect on Web enrollment. Answer **B** is incorrect because there is no such switch for the certutil.exe tool. Answer **D** is incorrect because there is no check box in the properties for the server in the Certificate Services management tool. Answer **E** is incorrect because Web enrollment is indeed a part of Windows Server 2003 certificate services.

3. You want to create an issuer policy statement for your Windows Server 2003 certification authority. What file must you place in the %systemroot% directory prior to the certificate services install?

   A. The name of the server with a file extension of .inf—for example, certserv.inf

   B. IssuerPolicy.inf

   C. CAPolicy.txt

   D. CAPolicy.inf

   E. None of the above

   ☑ **D**. Before installing certificate services on a Windows Server 2003 server, you must place the CAPolicy.inf file in the %systemroot% directory.

   ☒ **A, B, C.** Answers **A**, **B**, and **C** are incorrect because none of these answers provides the correct filename necessary to create an issuer statement.

4. You want to back up your CA information using the Certificate Services management tool. Which items can you backup using this method? (Choose four answers.)

   A. Private key

   B. Group policies

   C. CA certificate

   D. Certificate database

   E. System state

   F. Certificate database log

   ☑ **A**, **C**, **D**, and **F**. The private key and CA certificate are backed up as one combined selection, and the certificate database and certificate database log are another combined backup selection; therefore Answers **A**, **C**, **D**, and **F** are correct.

   ☒ **B, E**. Answers **B** and **E** are incorrect because these items would be part of a full system backup but not a CA backup.

5. A Microsoft Windows PKI has four fundamental components. Each of these components serves a separate function within the PKI configuration. What are the four fundamental components of the Windows PKI? (Choose four answers.)

   A. Microsoft Certificate Services

   B. Web enrollment

   C. CryptoAPI

   D. CAPICOM

   E. DCOM

   F. Active Directory

   ☑ **A, C, D, F**. Microsoft Certificate Services, CyptoAPI, CAPICOM, and Active Directory are the four fundamental components that are used in the Windows Server 2003 PKI; therefore Answers **A**, **B**, **C**, **D**, and **F** are correct.

   ☒ **B, E.** Answer **B** is incorrect because Web enrollment is a feature of certificate services. Answer **E** is incorrect because it is another type of COM different from CAPICOM.

6. There are several differences and similarities between standalone CA servers and enterprise CA servers. However, there is one key difference between the two as well. What is this difference?

   A. Web enrollment

   B. Issuer policies

   C. Active Directory integration with certificates for standalone CA servers

   D. Active Directory integration with certificates for enterprise CA servers

   ☑ **D**. Enterprise CAs have the ability to integrate certificates with Active Directory.

   ☒ **A, B, C.** Answers **A** and **B** are incorrect because both are features that are available for standalone or enterprise CAs. Answer **C** is incorrect because standalone CA servers cannot integrate certificates with Active Directory.

7. In Windows Server 2003, you can separate the front end of the Web enrollment services from the back-end Certificate Services server. What must you do in order to use Web enrollment on a server separate from the CA server?

   A. You must configure the computer account for the front-end server to be trusted for delegation within Active Directory.

   B. You must configure the computer account for the front-end server to be trusted for delegation within the Certificate Services management tool.

   C. You must configure the computer account for the back-end server to be trusted for delegation within Active Directory.

   D. You must configure the computer account for the back-end server to be trusted for delegation within the Certificate Services management tool.

E. None of the above; the Web enrollment services cannot be on a separate machine.

☑ **A**. If you should choose to install the Web enrollment pages on a separate computer from the CA, the computer account must be trusted for delegation within Active Directory.

☒ **B, D.** Answers **B** and **D** are incorrect because delegation is handled in Active Directory. Answer **C** is incorrect because the front-end (Web) server, not the back-end server, must be trusted for delegation. Answer **E** is incorrect because you can indeed separate the Web enrollment functionality.

8. David is mapping out his CA servers for his PKI. David decides that he will need one root CA, four intermediate CAs, and three leaf CAs beneath each of the four intermediate CAs. Based on this configuration, which is depicted in the following figure, what type of CA model has David designed?

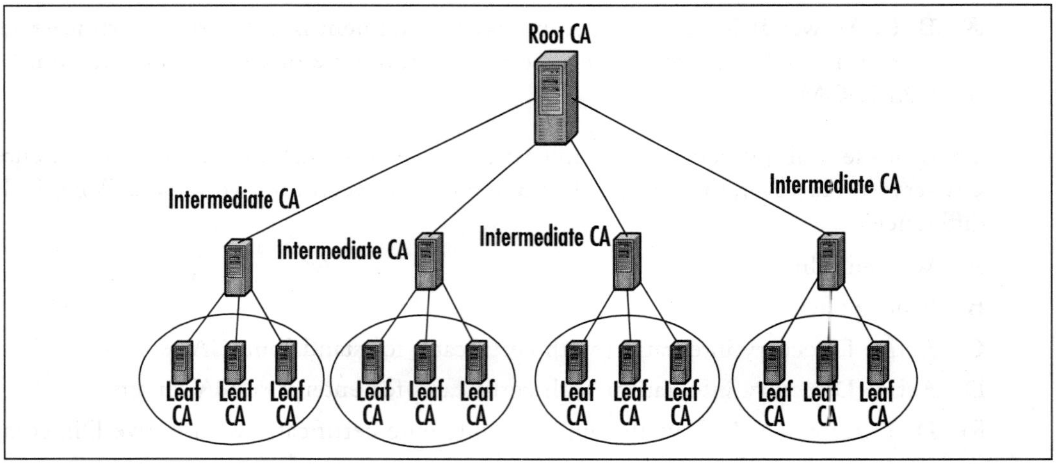

A. Standalone CA

B. Chain of trust

C. CA hierarchy

D. CA tree

☑ **C**. In a hierarchical model, a *root CA* functions as a top-level authority over CAs beneath it, called *intermediate CAs*.

☒ Answer **A** is incorrect because a standalone CA model has only one CA, with the possibility of an RA. Answer **B** is incorrect because there is no defined hierarchy in a chain of trust. Answer **D** is incorrect because there is no CA model known as a CA tree.

9. Denise, an employee in XYZ Corporation, is returning from her honeymoon and has decided to take her husband's last name. Denise works in the accounting department for

XYZ, which requires the use of smart cards to store certificates for department employees. You explain to Denise that you need to revoke her old certificate and create a new one for her. Why do you need to revoke her old certificate and create a new one?

A. You do not have to revoke the certificate and create a new one; you can just change her name on the certificate and the CA server.

B. Denise's account was deactivated while she was on her honeymoon, which requires the creation of a new certification.

C. There has been a change in the name of the public key subject.

D. There has been a change in the name of the certificate subject.

☑ **D**. Denise has changed her last name, which affects the certificate subject name.

☒ **A, B, C.** Answer **A** is incorrect because you do in fact need to revoke her certificate and issue her a new certificate. Answer **B** is incorrect because disabling a Windows user account would have no affect on the digital certificate. Answer **C** is incorrect because there isn't a "subject" associated with the public key.

10. What feature of a Windows Server 2003 PKI can programmers use to develop software to communicate with other applications using encryption?

A. Certificate services

B. CryptoAPI

C. Active Directory

D. CAPICOM

☑ **B**. Through the use of CryptoAPI, programmers can develop software applications than can communicate with the operating system or other applications through encrypted means.

☒ **A, C, D.** Answer **A** is incorrect because a certificate service allows you to issue, store, publish, and manage certificates. Answer **C** is incorrect because in a Windows Server 2003 PKI, Active Directory is used for storing certificates and CRLs and to publish root CA certificates and cross-certificates. Answer **D** is incorrect because CAPICOM is a COM client that uses CryptoAPI and PKI to perform cryptographic operations such assigning data, verifying digital signatures, encrypting data for specific receivers, and managing digital certificates.

11. Jeff wants to simplify the process for user enrollment into his company's PKI by allowing users to automatically obtain, store, and update their certificates without administrator or user intervention. What feature of Windows Server 2003 PKI can Jeff use to accomplish this task?

A. Automatic certificate enrollment

B. Autoenrollment

C. Web enrollment

D. CAPICOM

☑ **B**. Autoenrollment is a process for obtaining, storing, and updating the certificates for subjects without administrator or user intervention.

☒ **A, C, D.** Answer **A** incorrect because it relates to the enrollment of computers, not users. Answer **C** is incorrect because Web enrollment requires the intervention of the user. Answer **D** is incorrect because CAPICOM is a COM client that uses CryptoAPI and PKI to perform cryptographic operations such assigning data, verifying digital signatures, encrypting data for specific receivers, and managing digital certificates.

12. What does a PKI provide to make it possible for one entity to trust another? (Select the *best* answer.)

A. Privacy

B. Integrity

C. Authentication

D. Nonrepudiation

E. All of the above

F. None of the above

☑ **E**. PKI makes it possible for one entity to trust another by providing privacy, authentication, nonrepudiation, and integrity.

☒ **A, B,C, D.** Answers **A**, **B**, **C**, and **D** are all correct, but the *best* answer is the one that includes all four. Since the correct answer is all of the above, Answer **F** is incorrect by default.

13. Matthew is explaining certificate revocation lists (CRLs) to his coworker Jenna. Jenna asks Matthew how a CRL can be distributed within a Windows Server 2003 PKI. What options are available in a Windows Server 2003 PKI for distribution of CRLs?

A. Manual distribution

B. Automatic distribution

C. Scheduled distribution

D. Forced distribution

E. Answers A and C

F. Answers B and D

G. None of the above

☑ **E**. In a Windows Server 2003 PKI, you can either use scheduled replication or force a manual distribution of the CRL as needed.

☒ **A, B, C, D, F,G.** Answers **A** and **C** are incorrect because both manual and scheduled distribution are possible. Answers **B, D,** and **F** are incorrect because there is no automatic distribution or forced distribution types. Since Answer **E** is correct, none of the above (Answer **G**) is incorrect.

14. Brittany has been tasked by her supervisor to develop a process plan for the development of her public key infrastructure. What five steps does Microsoft recommend for designing a PKI? (Choose all correct answers.)

A. Define the certificate requirements

B. Install certificate services

C. Install Active Directory

D. Create a certification authority infrastructure

E. Extend the certification authority infrastructure

F. Configure sites and services

G. Configure certificates

H. Create a management plan

☑ **A**, **D**, **E**, **G**, and **H**. In planning a PKI, Microsoft recommends that you define the certificate requirements, create a certification authority infrastructure, extend the certification authority infrastructure, configure certificates, and create a management plan; therefore Answers **A**, **D**, **E**, **G**, and **H** are correct.

☒ **B, C, F.** Answer **B** is incorrect because the installation of certificate services is part of the creation of the certification authority infrastructure. Answer **C** is incorrect because a PKI does not necessarily require the installation of Active Directory, although it will offer additional functionality. Answer **F** is incorrect because sites and services do not need to be planned for or configured for a Windows Server 2003 PKI.

15. You are the network administrator for International Tea Leaves Inc. and have been tasked with creating a PKI for the company. Tea Leaves Inc. has offices in several locations across the globe. You are trying to determine where CAs should be placed within your infrastructure. Which of the following answers will most likely affect your decision?

A. WAN link speed

B. Internet connectivity

C. Server processor speed

D. Number of users in an office

☑ **A.** The speed of your WAN connections can affect where CA servers should be placed. For example, an office in Europe that can only connect to the WAN at 56Kbps and needs to use the PKI would likely require its own CA server.

☒ **B**, **C**, **D**. Answer **B** is incorrect because a remote office doesn't need an Internet connection in order to be part of a company PKI. Answer **C** is incorrect because the speed of the processor on the server would not directly affect where you place the CA servers. Answer **D** is incorrect because even though the number of users can be a factor, an office could have only a few users but also have several servers that require a CA server to be present.

Chapter 5 Managing User Authentication

1. You have created an e-commerce Web application that allows your customers to purchase your company's products via the Internet. Management is concerned that customers will not feel comfortable providing their credit card information over the Internet. What is the most important step to secure this application so that your customers will feel confident that they are transmitting their information securely and to the correct Web site?

   A. Use IP restrictions so that only your customers' specific IP addresses can connect to the e-commerce application.

   B. Issue each of your customers a smart card that they can use to authenticate to your e-commerce Web site.

   C. Place your company's Web server behind a firewall to prevent unauthorized access to customer information.

   D. Install a Secure Sockets Layer (SSL) certificate on your Web server.

   ☑ **D**. Installing an SSL certificate provides *mutual authentication* so that your customers will know that they are communicating with the correct Web site and not being redirected to another site that's being used to steal their information.

   ☒ **A**, **B**, **C**. Answer **A** is impractical because your customers (and their associated IP addresses) will change from day to day as you gain new referrals. Answer **B** is incorrect since smart cards are not used for Web authentication. It is also impractical because the costs associated with supporting smart cards for your customers would be quite high compared to how often they would make purchases on your site. Answer **C**, although a good security practice, is incorrect because it will not protect your customers' data while it is being transmitted to and from your Web site. Protecting data during transit requires the kind of encryption offered by an SSL certificate.

2. What is a potential drawback of creating a password policy on your network that requires user passwords to be 25 characters long?

   A. Users will be more likely to write down a password that is so difficult to remember.

   B. User passwords should be at least 30 characters long to guard against brute-force password attacks.

C. There are no drawbacks; this solution creates network passwords that will be impossible for an unauthorized user to penetrate.

D. Windows Server 2003 will not allow a password of more than eight characters.

☑ **A.** A 25-character password is perhaps unreasonably long and could prompt your users to write them down on their monitors or in their wallets. This creates another avenue of attack that can easily render such a strong password meaningless.

☒ **B, C, D.** Answer **B** is incorrect because a password length of 8 to 14 characters is usually sufficient to guard against most brute-force attacks. Answer **C** is incorrect because a 25-character password will create the issues described in Answer **A**. Answer **D** is incorrect because Windows passwords can be up to 255 characters in length.

3. Your network configuration includes a Terminal Server designed to allow users at remote branches to access network applications. The Terminal Server often becomes overloaded with client requests, and you have received several complaints regarding response times during peak hours. You have recently issued smart cards for the users located at your corporate headquarters and would like to prevent those users from using their smart cards to access the Terminal Server. How can you accomplish this goal in the most efficient manner possible?

A. Enable auditing of logon/logoff events on your network to determine which smart card users are accessing the Terminal Server, then speak to their supervisors individually.

B. Create a separate OU for your Terminal Server. Create a global group containing all smart card users, and restrict the logon hours of this group for the Terminal Servers OU.

C. Enable the "Do not allow smart card device redirection" policy within Group Policy.

D. Create a global group containing all smart card users, and deny this group the "Log on locally" right to the computers on your network.

☑ **C.** The "Do not allow smart card device redirection" only allows smart card users to use their smart card credentials for their local workstations. Their credentials would not be forwarded to a Terminal Services session.

☒ **A, B, D.** Answer **A** is incorrect because it requires too much administrative overhead and has no guarantee of being effective. Answer **B** is incorrect because account policies such as logon hours can only be set at the domain level, not at the OU level. Answer **D** is incorrect because this will prevent smart card users from logging onto *any* machine on your network, not just the Terminal Server.

4. You have recently begun a new position as a network administrator for a Windows Server 2003 network. Shortly before he left the company, your predecessor used the syskey utility on one of your domain controllers to create a password that needed to be entered when the machine is booted. You reboot the controller, only to discover that the password that the previous administrator recorded is incorrect, and he cannot be reached to determine the correct password. How can you return this controller to service as quickly as possible?

A. Reformat the system drive on the server and reinstall Windows Server 2003.

B. Boot the server into Directory Services Restore Mode and restore the controller's Registry from a point before the previous administrator ran the *syskey* utility.

C. Boot the server into Safe Mode and run *syskey* again to change the password.

D. Use *ntdsutil* to seize the PDC emulator role and transfer it to another controller.

☑ **B**. If you misplace the password or diskette that's created when you run the *syskey* utility, your only option is to restore the system Registry from a point before the *syskey* utility was run.

☒ **A, C, D**. Answer **A** is not the quickest way to restore the controller to service, because you will lose any application and Registry data stored on the system drive; all applications will need to be reinstalled and any shares recreated. Answer **C** is incorrect because you cannot change the *syskey* password without knowing the original password. This is designed so that an attacker cannot circumvent *syskey* security by simply rebooting the server. Answer **D** is incorrect because transferring the PDC emulator role, although necessary to authenticate any down-level clients, will do nothing to return this controller to service.

5. Your Active Directory domain contains a mixture of Windows Server 2003, Windows 2000 Server, and Windows NT 4.0 domain controllers. Your clients are similarly heterogeneous, consisting of Windows XP and Windows 2000 Professional along with NT 4.0 Workstation. What is the most secure network authentication method available to you in this environment?

A. Password Authentication Protocol (PAP)

B. NTLM

C. NTLMv2

D. Kerberos version 5

☑ **C**. In the environment described here, all server and client operating systems are capable of using NTLMv2 to communicate.

☒ **A,B, D**. Answer **A** is incorrect because PAP is a remote access protocol used for dialup access and is not used for LAN communications. Answer **B** is incorrect because, although all the servers and clients listed are capable of using NTLM, NTLMv2 provides a more secure authentication option. Answer **D** is incorrect because Kerberos authentication is only available for machines running at least Windows 2000. Windows NT4 Server and Workstation cannot communicate using Kerberos authentication.

6. According to Microsoft, which of the following would be considered weak passwords for a user account named *jronick*? (Choose all that apply.)

A. S#n$lUsN7

B. soprano

C. ronickrj

D. Oo!dIx2

E. new

☑ **B**, **C**, **E**. Microsoft considers a password weak if it is all lowercase, contains any portion of the user's account name (in this case, *jronick*), or contains a word found in the English dictionary (such as *soprano* or *new*); therefore Answers **B**, **C**, and **E** are correct.

☒ **A D**. Answers **A** and **D** are incorrect because both of these passwords meet the criteria for strong passwords. They are at least seven characters long and contain a mix of upper- and lowercase letters and alphanumeric and nonalphanumeric characters.

7. You are the network administrator for the Windows Server 2003 domain diagrammed in the following illustration. Your boss has been reading about Kerberos authentication and is concerned that your KDC represents a single point of failure for your company's network authentication. How should you respond to this concern?

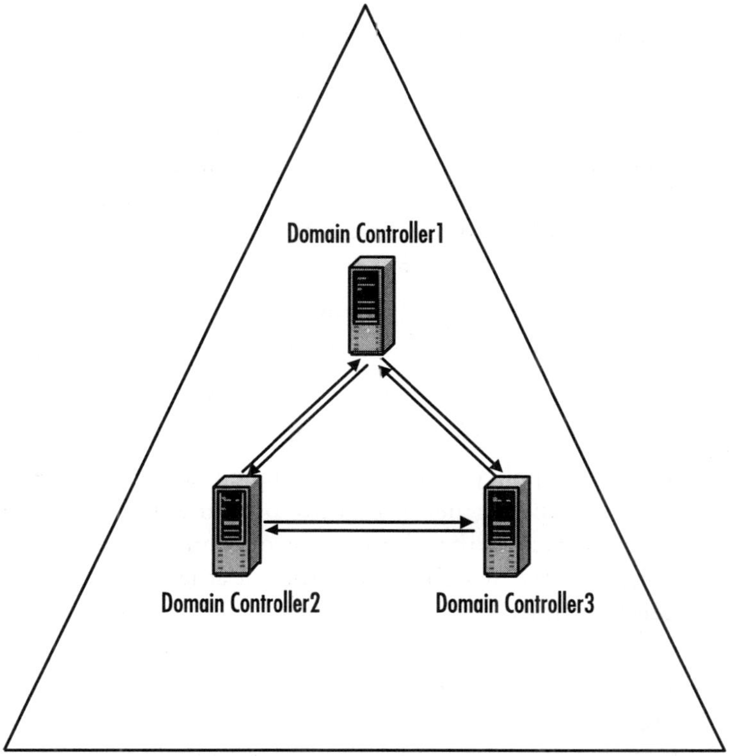

A. Every Windows Server 2003 domain controller acts as a KDC. If your DC1 controller fails, DC2 and DC3 will still perform the KDC functions.

B. Your network requires only one KDC to function since you are only using a single domain.

C. The KDC function is a single master operations role. If the machine that houses the KDC role fails, you can use *ntdsutil* to assign the role to another server.

D. If the KDC fails, your network clients will use DNS for authentication.

☑ **A**. The Windows implementation of Kerberos has built-in redundancy as long as your network contains more than one domain controller. Each Windows Server 2003 controller in your domain can process Kerberos authentication and ticket-issuing functions.

☒ **B, C, D**. Answer **B** is incorrect because every Active Directory implementation should contain more than one domain controller to provide fault tolerance for user authentication and logons. Answer **C** is incorrect because Kerberos functions are not FSMO roles like those discussed in Chapter 3. If a domain controller fails, the remaining DCs in your domain will take over the KDC functionality. Answer **D** is incorrect because DNS is used for name resolution, not authentication.

8. You have implemented a password policy that requires your users to change their passwords every 30 days and retains their last three passwords in memory. While sitting in the lunch room, you hear someone advise his coworker that all she needs to do to get around that rule is to change her password four times so that she can go back to using the password that she is used to. What is the best way to modify your domain password policy to avoid this potential security liability?

A. Increase the maximum password age from 30 days to 60 days.

B. Enforce password complexity requirements for your domain users' passwords.

C. Increase the minimum password age to seven days.

D. Increase the minimum password length of your users' passwords.

☑ **C**. If your password policy retains three unique passwords in memory, this will prevent your users from changing their passwords four times in rapid succession so that they can change them back to their initial passwords on the fifth change. A minimum password age of seven days will force users to wait at least seven days before they can change their passwords.

☒ **A, B, D**. Answer **A** is incorrect because increasing the maximum password age will not circumvent the security breach of maintaining the same password for an extended period of time. Answer **B** is incorrect because password complexity has nothing to do with how often a password can be changed. Answer **D** is incorrect because the minimum password length setting has nothing to do with how often a password can be changed.

9. You have created a Web application that relies on digest authentication. You check the account properties of one of the user accounts and see the following screen. What is the most likely reason that your users cannot authenticate?

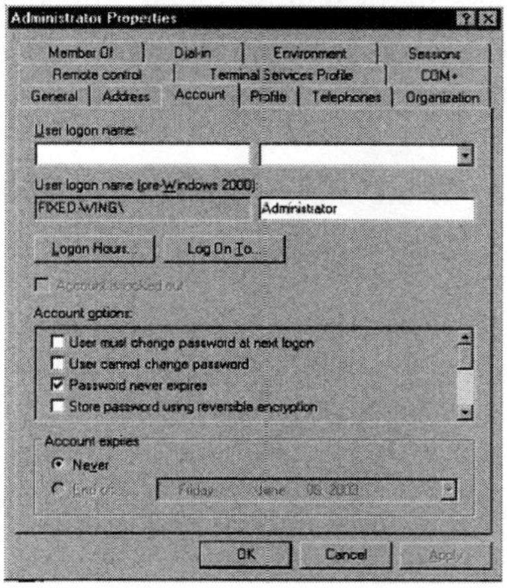

A. When you log on using digest authentication, the Windows username is case-sensitive.

B. To use digest authentication, users must be running Internet Explorer version 6.

C. Your users' passwords are set to expire every 60 days, which is causing digest authentication to fail.

D. You must enforce the "Store passwords using reversible encryption" setting for all users who need to authenticate using digest authentication.

☑ **D**. In order for digest authentication to function properly, you must select this option for the user accounts that need to use digest authentication, either manually or through a policy. Once you've enabled this setting, the users in question will need to change their passwords so that the reversibly encrypted value can be recorded in Active Directory.

☒ **A**, **B**, **C**. Answer **A** is incorrect because a user's password is case sensitive when accessing any Windows application but the username is not. Answer **B** is incorrect because digest authentication functions under Internet Explorer version 5.0 or later. Answer **C** is incorrect because digest authentication will not fail simply because a user changes his Active Directory password.

10. A developer on your network uses a workstation that is not attached to the corporate domain. He phones the help desk to report that he has forgotten the password to his local user account. If he has not previously created a password reset disk, what information will he lose when the password for his local account is reset? (Choose all that apply.)

A. Local files that the user has encrypted

B. E-mail encrypted with his public key

C. His Internet Explorer favorites and links

D. The entries in the Recent Documents dialog box

☑ **A, B**. All three of these items will be lost if a user needs his or her local user account password reset. Creating a password reset disk beforehand will prevent the user from losing any data if they forget their local account passwords; therefore Answers **A**, and **B** are correct.

☒ **C, D**. Answers **C** and **D** are incorrect because neither of these items will be lost if a user needs to have his or her local user account password reset.

11. You have attached a smart card reader to your Windows XP Professional workstation's serial port. The reader is not detected when you plug it in and is not recognized when you scan for new hardware within Device Manager. The smart card reader is listed on the Microsoft Web site as a supported device, and you have verified that all cables are connected properly. Why is your workstation refusing to recognize the smart card reader?

A. You need to run the manufacturer-specific installation routine.

B. The workstation needs to be rebooted before it will recognize the card reader.

C. Smart card readers are only supported on machines running Windows Server 2003.

D. You are not logged on as a member of the Domain Admins group.

☑ **B**. If the smart card reader attaches via a serial port, the workstation needs to be rebooted before Windows Server 2003 will recognize the new hardware.

☒ **A, C, D**. Answer **A** is incorrect because smart card readers that are supported under Windows Server 2003 will be either automatically detected or installed via the Hardware Installation wizard. Answer **C** is incorrect because smart card readers are supported under both the client and server editions of the Windows Server 2003 family. Answer **D** is incorrect because this would not preclude the need to reboot the workstation.

12. You are a new network administrator for a Windows Server 2003 domain. In making user support calls, you have noticed that many users are relying on simplistic passwords such as their children's or pets' names. Passwords on this network are set to never expire, so some people have been using these weak passwords for months or even years. You change the default Group Policy to require strong passwords. Several weeks later, you notice that the network users are still able to log on using their weak passwords. What is the most likely reason that the weak passwords are still in effect?

A. You must force the users to change their passwords before the strong password settings will take effect.

B. The Group Policy settings have not replicated throughout the network yet.

C. Password policies need to be set at the OU level, not the domain level.

D. The users reverted back to their passwords the next time that they were prompted to change their passwords.

☑ **A**. Password policies only apply to new and/or changed passwords within the domain; they are not applied retroactively to existing passwords. If your users' passwords are set to never expire, they will never be forced to change to strong passwords.

☒ **B**, **C**, **D**. Answer **B** is incorrect because Active Directory replication should not take several weeks to replicate, even on the largest of networks. Answer **C** is incorrect because it is stated backward: Password policies can only be set at the domain level, not on individual OUs. Answer **D** is incorrect because Windows would reject the users' original passwords for not meeting the new complexity requirements of the password policy.

13. You were walking through your server room when you noticed that a contractor had plugged his laptop directly into one of your network switches and was using your company bandwidth to download pirated software onto his hard drive. You have recently upgraded your network switches and routers to the most up-to-date hardware available. What is the best way to prevent this sort of illegitimate access to your network in the future?

    A. Install smart card readers on all your users' desktops.

    B. Implement the Internet Authentication Service's ability to authenticate Ethernet switches on your network.

    C. Do not allow outside contractors to bring any hardware into your building.

    D. Disable the Guest account within Active Directory.

    ☑ **B**. Most modern Ethernet switches can request authentication before a user is allowed to plug into a network port. In Windows Server 2003, IAS provides the ability to manage this type of authentication.

    ☒ **A**, **C**, **D**. Answer **A** is incorrect because having smart card readers on existing user desktops would not have prevented this contractor from plugging his own machine into an empty port on an Ethernet switch. Answer **C**, although it would have prevented this contractor from accessing your network, is not the best answer because many contractors have legitimate reasons to bring outside hardware in to perform the functions for which they were hired. Answer **D**, although a security best practice, would not have prevented the scenario described in this question.

14. You have recently deployed smart cards to your users for network authentication. You configured the smart card Logon certificates to expire every six months. One of your smart card users has left the company without returning her smart card. You have disabled this user's logon account and smart card, but management is concerned that she will still be able to use the smart card to access network resources. How can you be sure that the information stored on the former employee's smart card cannot be used to continue to access network resources?

    A. Monitor the security logs to ensure that the former employee is not attempting to access network resources.

B. Use the smart card enrollment station to delete the user's smart card Logon certificate.

C. Deny the Autoenroll permission to the user's account on the smart card Logon Certificate template.

D. Add the user's certificate to the CRL on your company's CA.

☑ **D**. Every CA maintains a CRL that denies access to users in situations such as this one. Even if the former employee found a way to use her smart card, the Windows Server 2003 domain would not accept her certificate as valid.

☒ **A**, **B**, **C**. Answer **A**, although a security best practice, takes no proactive actions to prevent the former employee from accessing network resources. Answer **B** is incorrect because the user did not return her smart card, so the existing certificate is still stored in memory on it. Answer **C** is incorrect because this will not disable the existing certificate that is stored on the user's smart card.

15. The account lockout policy on your Windows Server 2003 domain is set up as shown in the following illustration. You come into work on a Monday morning and are informed that many of your users' accounts were locked out over the weekend. Your company's help desk staff have unlocked the user accounts in question, but they are now reporting that your Exchange server and Microsoft SQL databases are not accessible by anyone in the company. Network utilization is at normal levels. What is the most likely reason that these applications are not responding?

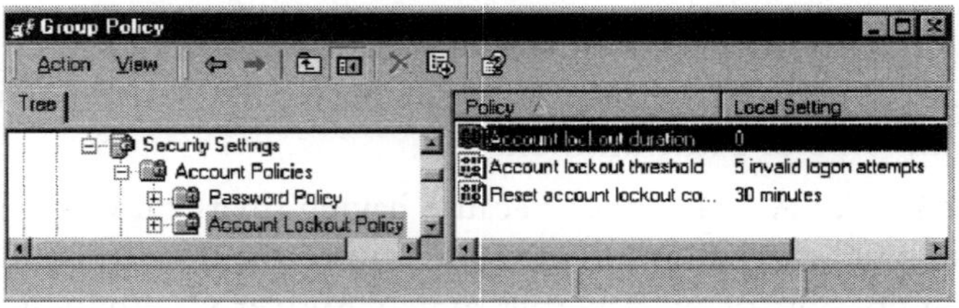

A. An attacker has deleted the Exchange and SQL executables on your production servers.

B. The accounts that Exchange and SQL use to start or connect to the network have been locked out and need to be manually unlocked.

C. The users whose accounts were unlocked by the help desk need to reboot their workstations to access these applications.

D. An attacker is perpetrating a DOS attack against your network.

☑ **B**. When you configure your account lockout policy so that accounts must be manually unlocked, applications that rely on service accounts to function can become unresponsive if the service accounts become locked out.

☒ **A**, **C**, **D**. Answer **A** is possible but not as likely as Answer **B**, given the way your account lockout policy is configured. Answer **C** is incorrect because the applications are inaccessible to all network users, not just those users whose accounts had been unlocked. Answer **D** is incorrect because a DoS attack "floods" your network with traffic, rendering it unusable. In this case, your network utilization is normal.

Chapter 6 Developing and Implementing a Group Policy Strategy

1. You are the network administrator for Vinca Jams. The company is a large food manufacturing and distribution corporation with locations all over the world. As a result, you have over 36 sites configured. You have three domains in Active Directory: vincajams.com, corp.vincajams.com, and food.vincajams.com. In each domain you have identical sets of 10 OUs, beginning with All, followed by Exec, Mgmt, Admins, and Standard. Within Standard, you have Finance, Accounting, Sales, Production, and Maintenance. You are developing a Group Policy strategy for user passwords. What will be the maximum number of different policies that you can configure for users who log on to the domain?

   A. 1

   B. 3

   C. 10

   D. 36

   ☑ **B**. The key to this question is that you are looking only at Password Policies that will apply to users who log on to the domain. You can configure exactly one Password Policy for each domain in your network. Since you have three domains, you can configure three different Password Policies.

   ☒ **A, C, D**. Answer **A** is incorrect because you can have more than one Password Policy in a forest if you have more than one domain in the forest. Answer **C** is incorrect because although you can configure 10 different Password Policies for each of the OUs within a domain, these will only affect users who log on locally, not users who log on to the domain. Answer **D** is incorrect because the site-attached policies will not be used to establish the domain's Password Policy.

2. Your network has a single domain named saddlebags.org, with two sites, named Boston and NY, and four OUs. A single top OU named Corp contains three OUs named Admins, Mgmt, and Org, which are all configured as peers. You have created a GPO named POL1 that distributes Office XP to computer objects. You have also created a GPO named POL2 that redirects the My Documents folders to a network share. You want to make certain that Office XP is deployed to every user in the network. You want to make sure that folder redirection is performed for management and the rest of the organization, but not for administrators. To which of the following should POL1 be applied?

A. Saddlebags.org

B. Boston

C. Mgmt

D. Admins

☑ **A**. You should apply the Group Policy to saddlebags.org because you want everyone in the entire network to receive Office XP.

☒ **B, C, D**. Answer **B** is incorrect because by deploying POL1 to Boston, none of the users in NY will receive Office XP. Answer **C** is incorrect because by deploying POL1 to Mgmt, none of the rest of the users will receive Office XP. Answer **D** is incorrect because Office XP should be deployed to more users than just those who are in the Admins OU.

3. You have a single domain with a single site. You are in the process of planning Group Policy for your network. During your testing phase, you have finally created the perfect desktop, Password Policy, redirected folders, and secured computer and user objects. You have made so many changes, blocked and enforced a variety of policies, and have applied so many GPOs in your test OU structure that you are not certain which Group Policies have been finalized. Which of the following actions can you take to make certain that the user object's Group Policies are documented and can be recreated in the production portion of the OU tree?

A. In Active Directory Sites and Services, right-click the site and select **All Tasks | Resultant Set of Policy (Planning)**.

B. In Active Directory Users and Computers, right-click the test OU at the top of the OU hierarchy and select **All Tasks | Resultant Set of Policy (Planning)**.

C. In Active Directory Domains and Trusts, right-click the domain and select **All Tasks | Resultant Set of Policy (Logging)**.

D. In Active Directory Users and Computers, right-click the user object and select **All Tasks | Resultant Set of Policy (Planning)**.

☑ **D**. You can query a user's Group Policies by right-clicking the user object from within Active Directory Users and Computers, then selecting **All Tasks | Resultant Set of Policy (Planning)**.

☒ **A, B, C**. Answer **A** is incorrect because this level will only show the policies that were applied at the site level, not at the domain or OU level, and certainly would not include any policy inheritance enforcement or blocking information. Answer **B** is incorrect because the OU at the top of the hierarchy might have Group Policy settings that are overridden by Group Policies established at points lower in the OU hierarchy. Answer **C** is incorrect because you would not conduct a query in the Active Directory Domains and Trusts console, aside from the fact that the domain Group

Policies would not show any Group Policies set in the OU hierarchy or any of the changes that might have been made through blocking or enforcement.

4. You have deployed a set of several Group Policies to the domain, the site, and the OU hierarchy. The various Group Policies consist of folder redirection, Password Policies, and locking down the desktop and Control Panel. Password Policy is applied to the domain. Desktop lockdown is applied to the Upgrade OU. Control Panel lockdown is applied to the Corp OU. Folder redirection is applied to the Clerical OU. You perform an RSoP query on a user and computer object that are both in the OU tree of All\Corp\Mgmt\LA\Upgrade. Which Group Policies will you not see in this query?

   A. Password Policy

   B. Desktop lockdown

   C. Control Panel lockdown

   D. Folder redirection

   ☑ **D**. The user object is not located in the OU tree that contains the Clerical OU, so the Folder redirection group policies will not appear in the RSoP query.

   ☒ **A, B, C**. Answer **A** is incorrect because the Password Policy is applied at the domain level and should be seen in the query. Answer **B** is incorrect because the desktop lockdown is applied to the Upgrade OU, which directly contains the user and computer objects. Answer **C** is incorrect because the Control Panel lockdown is applied to the Corp OU, which is within the OU hierarchy containing the user and computer objects.

5. You are the network administrator of a domain with a complex OU hierarchy. About a dozen users have been moved out of the marketing department into sales. You move the user accounts into the new OU. You provide the users with new computers that are members of their new Sales OU. The marketing department and the sales department have different configurations for folder redirection, software applications that are distributed to users and computers, Control Panel lockdown, and autoenrollment of certificates. When you move the user objects from the Marketing to the Sales OU, which should you follow up with further configuration?

   A. Folder redirection

   B. Software distribution

   C. Control Panel lockdown

   D. Autoenrolled certificates

   ☑ **A**. Folder redirection could be a problem for the users since the Sales OU and the Marketing OU have different configurations for the folder redirection Group Policy. If both OUs have configured the folders to be redirected to different locations on the network, when you simply move the user objects, their data will still be located in the old network location. You should then move the data to the new location.

☒ **B, C, D**. Answers **B**, **C**, and **D** are incorrect because when you move the user objects to the Sales OU, they will automatically inherit the correct configuration for the new OU and will not require further configuration.

6. You are the network administrator for a large forest. You have recently hired on an assistant. You decide to grant your new assistant the rights to perform RSoP queries in the test OU structure of the domain. Which of the following wizards will you need to use to provide your assistant with the correct rights?

   A. Resultant Set of Policy wizard

   B. Delegation of Control wizard

   C. Active Directory Installation wizard

   D. Group Policy Editor wizard

   ☑ **B**. You will use the Delegation of Control wizard to grant the assistant the correct rights in conducting RSoP queries in the test OU structure.

   ☒ **A, C, D**. Answer **A** is incorrect because the RSoP wizard does not inherently provide a user with rights to conduct RSoP queries. Answer **C** is incorrect because the Active Directory Installation wizard is used to promote or demote domain controllers. Answer **D** is incorrect because there is no such wizard.

7. Users in the Corp OU have the need for a software application named FINANCE. However, you discover that all users who are in the Corp\General OU should not receive FINANCE. Which two of the following actions should you take?

   A. Assign FINANCE to Corp users

   B. Assign FINANCE to Corp\General computers

   C. Block inheritance to Corp

   D. Block inheritance to Corp\General

   ☑ **A, D**. You should assign FINANCE to the Corp OU users, then you should block the inheritance of the policy so that it is not inherited by the users in Corp\General; therefore Answers **A** and **D** are correct.

   ☒ **B, C**. Answer **B** is incorrect because it is likely that Corp\General computers are used by Corp\General users, who should not receive FINANCE. Answer **C** is incorrect because blocking inheritance to Corp will prevent the Corp users from receiving FINANCE.

8. You have a set of Group Policies that function well in your test lab. You want to see how these policies will work for users who log on using remote access through dialup or VPN across the Internet. Which of the following RSoP options should you select?

   A. Loopback processing

   B. Linked WMI filters

C. Slow network connection

D. Logging mode

☑ **C**. You should select slow network connection when you perform an RSoP query in Planning mode. This choice allows you to simulate the policies when using dialup or slow network links.

☒ **A, B, D**. Answer **A** is incorrect because loopback processing is used for circumstances in which the computer requires special user configuration policies that should either override or merge with the logged-on user's policies. Answer **B** is incorrect because WMI is not discussed in the question. Answer **D** is incorrect because you cannot simulate a slow network connection in Logging mode.

9. You are planning the computer environment for a set of kiosks that you will place at pharmacies. You require that each of the kiosks is locked down and prevented from accessing any network resources other than the application that you are making available to the public. Each kiosk should be identical to the others. There are 10 kiosks, one for each pharmacy site. The pharmacies each have one to five other networked computers onsite. Each pharmacy has its own OU that is below the Pharm OU. Where should you place the kiosk computer objects?

   A. In an OU that is analogous to the site the kiosk is in

   B. In the pharmacy OU where it is located

   C. In the Pharm OU

   D. In a Kiosks OU below the Pharm OU

   ☑ **D**. Each kiosk computer object should be placed together with the others in the Kiosks OU. This placement ensures that you can apply specific Group Policies to lock down those computers and that they will be configured identically.

   ☒ **A, B, C**. Answers **A** and **B** are incorrect because placing the kiosks in separate OUs as each of these answers indicates will not ensure that the kiosks will be identical. Answer **C** is incorrect because placing the kiosks in the Pharm OU will either cause the pharmacy computers to have the wrong Group Policies or require you to create several inheritance blocks to prevent those Group Policies from affecting the other pharmacy computers.

10. You are the network administrator for an Active Directory forest. You have three domains and seven sites. Each site contains users from each domain. Users in the Atlanta site require an application called PROJ. Users in the root domain, vincajax.com, require a strict Password Policy. Users in the JOBs OU within the corp.vincajax.com domain require folders to be redirected to a network share. To which of the following locations will you apply the GPO that distributes PROJ?

A. Vincajax.com

B. Corp.vincajax.com

C. Atlanta

D. JOBs

☑ **C**. Since all the users in Atlanta require the PROJ application, you should apply that GPO to the Atlanta site.

☒ **A, B, D**. Answers **A** and **B** are incorrect because applying the GPO for PROJ's distribution would affect users from other sites and would neglect to affect all the users in the Atlanta location. Answer **D** is incorrect because the JOBs OU was not mentioned in conjunction with the users who require the PROJ application.

11. The manager of your company's service department has just invested in a new software application that she asks you to deploy to all 234 service department members. This application does not use Windows Installer. Currently the service department members are located in an OU that they share with the maintenance and file room departments. These departments do not require the new software application. Users in the service department often use computers belonging to the sales and file room departments. Which of the following actions should you take in deploying this application? (Select all that apply.)

A. Install each service department computer separately.

B. Create a .ZAP file for the application and deploy it by publishing it to users.

C. Move all service department users into an OU that is nested within their current OU.

D. Create a transform for the application and deploy it by publishing it to computers.

☑ **B, C**. Answer **B** is correct because applications that do not use the Windows Installer must use the .ZAP file for software distribution via Group Policy. Answer **C** is correct because you need to separate the users in the service department from users in other departments and then publish the software to the users so that they can access the application when using computers from other departments.

☒ **A, D**. Answer **A** is incorrect because it is very time consuming and can be done in a better way. Answer **D** is incorrect because you can only create a transform for applications that use Windows Installer.

12. You have three groups of users in your company. Administrators have full access to everything within their computer and have no Group Policies aside from the domain's Password and Account Policies. The second group is power users, who have partial access to their computers and are able to configure desktop, Start menu, and printers. Power users are not allowed to install any software that is not approved. The third group is regular users. Regular users do not have access to any Control Panel or desktop configuration options. No one in the network should have to wait to log on to a computer because it impacts productivity, but users typically turn their computers on in the morning and then grab a cup of coffee. If you deploy a software application to all users, which of the following is the best method if you use Group Policy?

A. Assign the application to users.

B. Assign the application to computers.

C. Publish the application to users.

D. Publish the application to computers.

☑ **B.** The best method is to assign the application to the computers, because this will make certain that all computers in the network have the application. Since users have the habit of turning their computers on and leaving their desks before logging on in the morning, the installation of the software will have little impact on productivity.

☒ **A, C, D.** Answer **A** is incorrect because assigning an application to users will impact logon time and productivity. Answers **C** and **D** are incorrect because publishing the software will make it available in the Control Panel, which is not accessible to the third group, the regular users.

13. You have configured a GPO for the folder redirection of the Start menu. A user calls up and claims that his Favorites menu items keep appearing and then disappearing from his Start menu. What could be the problem?

A. The user has accidentally received someone else's Group Policy.

B. The Group Policy is refreshing on a periodic basis.

C. The user's computer is periodically disconnecting from the network.

D. The user has accidentally deleted the Favorites option from the Start menu.

☑ **C.** It is most likely that the user's computer is periodically disconnecting from the network. When the user logs on locally, the folder is no longer redirected and the user sees the options on the computer locally. To overcome this problem, you can synchronize offline files between the redirected folder and the local one.

☒ **A, B, D.** Answer **A** is incorrect because Group Policy application is not accidental (aside from administrator error, of course). Answer **B** is incorrect because the Group Policy refresh period would not cause this particular behavior. Answer **D** is incorrect because the user reported that the Favorites items both appear and disappear from the menu.

14. You are the network administrator for Vinca Ink, a small company. In your network, you have created the following OU structure. The Corp OU is at the top of the hierarchy. Within Corp, you have the Admins OU and the General OU. Members of the production department, who are members of a security group that receives full access to the PROD server, want to have their My Documents folders redirected to the \\PROD\DESKTOP share. Which options do you select to configure this setting without affecting the other users in the General OU?

A. Not configured

B. Basic: Redirect everyone's folder to the same location

C. Advanced: Specify locations for various user groups

D. Cannot be done

☑ **C.** When you select the Advanced option, you can then add the Production security group and specify that the My Documents folders should be redirected to the \\PROD\DESKTOP share.

☒ **A, B, D.** Answer **A** is incorrect because you need to configure this option. Answer **B** is incorrect because the Basic option will affect all users within the General OU. Answer **D** is incorrect because you can use the Advanced option to achieve the desired results.

15. You are configuring the Password Policy for the users within All Corp OU (which is the top of the OU tree) in the vincajax.com domain. There is only one site in Atlanta. To which of the following locations will you configure this policy?

A. All Corp OU and create a new GPO for Password Policies

B. The Domain Controllers OU, editing the Default Domain Controllers Policy

C. The vincajax.com domain, editing the Default Domain Policy

D. The Atlanta site, creating a new GPO for Password Policies

☑ **C.** Password Policies are configured on a domainwide basis. You would need to configure the Password Policy for the Default Domain Policy on the vincajax.com domain.

☒ **A, B, D.** Answers **A**, **B**, and **D** are incorrect because configuring the Password Policies in any other GPO will affect the way that users log on locally to machines that are not connected.

Chapter 7 Managing Group Policy in Windows 2003

1. You have created and linked a single GPO to your Windows Server 2003 domain to apply various security settings to your client workstations, as well as redirecting the contents of each user's C:\Documents and Settings\%username%\My Documents folder to a central server location of \\FILESERVER1\DOCS\%username%\My Documents. This server share is backed up every night; no client systems are included in the backups. You have several users in a remote branch office that is connected to the corporate headquarters via a 128Kbps ISDN line. One of your branch users calls the help desk needing a file in his My Documents folder restored from backup after he deleted it accidentally. You are dismayed to find that his information does not exist on the FILESERVER1 share. Most other GPO settings have been applied to the client workstation, including event log auditing and account lockout settings. What is the most likely reason that the branch user's files have not been redirected to the central file server?

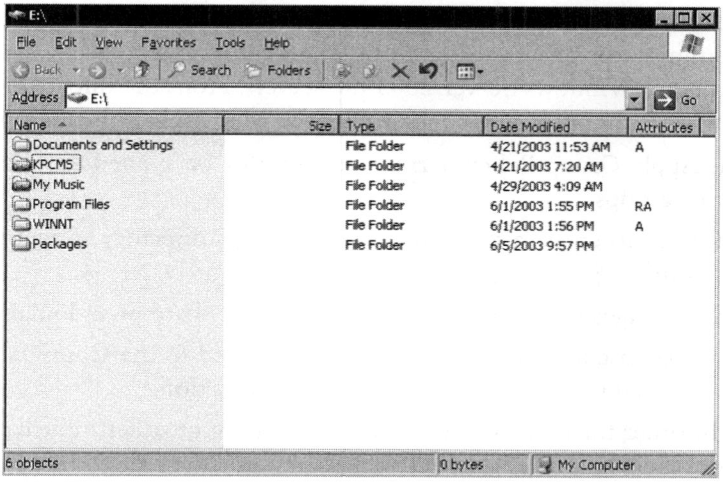

A. Folder Redirection settings are not applied by default when a user logs onto the network using a slow link.

B. The branch users do not have the Apply Group Policy permission assigned to them for the GPO.

C. You need to link the GPO to the OU that the user objects belong to, not just the domain.

D. The GPO is being applied synchronously when the branch users log onto their workstations.

☑ **A.** When GPOs are applied over a slow link (less than 500Kbps), Software Installation, Folder Redirection, and scripts are not applied by default. Security Settings and Administrative templates are still applied over a slow link.

☒ **B, C, D.** Answer **B** is incorrect because other GPO information such as security settings have been successfully applied to the branch user's computer. This indicates that the user is able to access the policy, which he would not be able to do without the Apply Group Policy permission. Answer **C** is incorrect because the GPO linked to a domain will filter down to all objects within the domain, even those contained within other OUs. Answer **D** is incorrect because the timing with which the GPO is being applied is not what is causing Folder Redirection not to be applied.

2. You have created an MSI installer package to distribute GPMC to your help desk. You have added the package information to the User Configuration | Software Settings section of the Default Domain GPO, and you have enabled the Apply Group Policy permission to the HelpDesk global group. You've saved the GPMC.MSI file to the E:\PACKAGES directory of the W2K-STD Windows Server 2003 file server, as shown in the following figure. Your help desk staff is reporting that the GPMC software has not

been installed on their workstations, despite several reboots. Each help desk staffer is a local administrator on his or her workstation and is able to access shared directories on this and other Windows Server 2003 file servers. From the information shown in the figure, what is the most likely reason that the MSI package is not being distributed?

A. The Apply Group Policy permission can only be applied to individual user accounts, not to groups.

B. You need to create a share for the e:\packages directory so that the help desk staff can access the MSI package over the network.

C. MSI packages must be stored in the SYSVOL share on a domain controller.

D. Software Installation settings need to be applied to the Computer Configuration section of a GPO, not the User Configuration section.

☑ **B**. In order for users to access an MSI package or other information during startup or login, the files must be stored on a shared directory that is accessible by all users who require it. In the illustration, the E:\PACKAGES directory has not been shared and would not be accessible by the help desk staff when they log onto the network.

☒ **A**, **C**, **D**. Answer **A** is incorrect because NTFS permissions such as Apply Group Policy not only *can* be applied to groups, but it is a best practice that they *should* be applied that way to ease network administration. Answer **C** is incorrect because the SYSVOL share is replicated between all domain controllers and should be kept as small as possible, used only to store scripts, GPOs, and other pertinent Active Directory information. Answer **D** is incorrect because Software Installations can be applied equally well to a user or a computer.

3. You have a test lab consisting of four Windows XP Professional workstations that you use to investigate new software packages and security settings before rolling them out to a production environment. This lab exists in a separate TEST domain with its own domain controller, DC1.TEST.AIRPLANES.COM. You are making many changes to security settings on the Default Domain Policy on DC1 and would like to test the results immediately so that you can implement the security setting on your production network as quickly as possible. What is the most efficient way to accomplish this goal?

A. Use GPOMonitor to indicate when the Group Policy objects perform a background refresh.

B. Update the GPO to force Group Policies to refresh every 60 seconds.

C. Reboot the test lab workstations after each change that you want to test.

D. Run GPUpdate.exe from the command line on the test workstations after each change that you want to test.

☑ **D**. GPUpdate is the Windows Server 2003 update to the *secedit /refresh_policy* command under Windows 2000. It immediately refreshes the Group Policy settings on a machine to reflect the most recent changes to all relevant GPOs.

☒ **A**, **B**, **C**. Answer **A** is incorrect because GPOMonitor only monitors Group Policy information; it does not do anything to force a refresh of policy information on a network client. Answer **B** is incorrect because performing a background refresh every 60 seconds generates a great deal of unnecessary network traffic, impeding network performance. Answer **C** is incorrect because running GPUpdate is a far more efficient way of updating GPO settings than performing multiple reboots.

4. You have a new accounting software package that you would like to install for the Payroll OU of your Windows Server 2003 domain. You would like this software to be available to any user who logs onto each Windows XP Professional workstation in the payroll department. You create a new GPO and assign the MSI package to the Computer Configuration section, and then link the new GPO to the Payroll OU with the appropriate security filtering permissions. You send an e-mail to the payroll department staff instructing them to log off their workstations and log back in to prompt the software installation to begin. Your help desk begins to receive calls from the users in the payroll department, saying that the accounting package has not been installed, even though they have logged off and onto their workstations several times. What is the most likely reason that the software package has not been installed?

   A. The workstations in the payroll department need to be rebooted before the software package will be installed.

   B. Software Installation packages can only be assigned at the domain level.

   C. The software can be installed using the Add New Programs section of the Add/Remove Programs Control Panel applet.

   D. Logon scripts are running asynchronously; they must be reconfigured to run synchronously.

   ☑ **A**. When a software installation package is assigned through the Computer Configuration section of a GPO, it will only be installed when the computer starts up. The logoff/logon process is not sufficient to launch the installation process.

   ☒ **B**, **C**, **D**. Answer **B** is incorrect because software installation packages can be published or assigned at the site, domain, or OU. Answer **C** is incorrect because only *published* software packages are available through Add/Remove Programs; this package was *assigned*. Answer **D** is incorrect because the software will be installed at startup, not logon.

5. You are the network administrator for a Windows Server 2003 network that has a corporate headquarters and several remote sales offices, each connected to the main office via 56K dialup modems. After a recent bout of attempted hacker attacks at the remote sites, your firewall administrator has decided to block NetBIOS, ICMP, and IGMP traffic from entering or leaving any remote site. Shortly after this solution is implemented, you receive several complaints from users at the remote sites that the logon times to their Windows XP Professional workstations have increased dramatically, often timing out and forcing them to reboot their machines. What is the most likely reason that this is occurring?

A. Each remote site should have its own domain controller to handle logon processing.

B. Group Policy does not function in environments that include firewalls.

C. Windows XP Professional requires NetBIOS to connect to a Windows Server 2003 domain controller.

D. Group Policy is no longer able to detect slow network links.

☑ **D**. Group Policy uses ICMP to detect slow network links. The remote sites' workstations are having difficulties logging in because the GPO is attempting to transmit all GPO settings over the slow link rather than withholding scripts, Software Installation, and Folder Redirection settings, as is the default behavior over slow links.

☒ **A, B, C**. Answer **A** is incorrect because having a domain controller at each remote site is an unneeded expense and unnecessarily increases administrative overhead. Answer **B** is incorrect because Group Policy functions properly as long as the firewall is properly configured. Answer **C** is incorrect because Windows XP Professional uses DNS to connect to Windows domain controllers by default.

6. You are a network administrator for an accounting firm with 200 employees that has been contracted to perform an audit of data stored in a proprietary 16-bit data entry application that was never upgraded to a 32-bit format. The application will only be used for the duration of this contract and does not have any option for a network or Terminal Services installation. How can you install this application on each workstation most efficiently?

A. Use a ZAP file published via a GPO to automate the installation process.

B. Contract a software developer to upgrade the application to an Active Directory-aware platform such as Visual Basic.

C. Send a broadcast e-mail with installation instructions and the location of the setup files to all users who require the software.

D. Install the software once on the domain controller and create a link to the program on each user's desktop.

☑ **A**. If an MSI file is not available and cannot be created for a legacy application, you can package it using a ZAP installer, which uses a text file to automate the installation process. You can then distribute this installer automatically via Group Policy.

☒ **B, C, D**. Answer **B** is incorrect because such a project would be extremely time-consuming and inefficient, since the application in question is only needed for a short period of time. Answer **C** is incorrect because it is prone to user error and is less efficient than using a GPO to automate the installation. Answer **D** is incorrect because the application itself would not function correctly in this scenario.

7. You have recently begun a new position as a network administrator for a Windows Server 2003 domain. Your predecessor created a number of GPOs, and it seems as if each network user has different policy settings applied to his or her account. You would like to

simplify the GPO implementation on your network, and you want to begin by creating a baseline report of exactly which GPOs are in effect for the various users on the network. What is the most efficient means of accomplishing this goal?

A. Use the Resultant Set of Policy snap-in to view the GPO settings for each user/computer combination on the network.

B. Use the Group Policy Results report in the GPMC to export the GPO settings of each user/computer combination to a single XML file for analysis.

C. Use the GPResults.exe command-line utility to generate a report for all users on the domain.

D. Export the Event Viewer Security logs from each workstation and collate the results for analysis.

☑ **C.** The GPResults command-line utility will quickly produce a report detailing each user's effective GPO settings, as well as which GPO has taken precedence in an environment with multiple policy objects. Running GPResults from the command line will allow you to quickly enumerate all accounts within the domain.

☒ **A, B, D.** Answer **A** is incorrect because you would be required to run the RSoP snap-in for each user individually, making it extremely inefficient. Answer **B** is inefficient since each report would need to be run manually from the GPMC. Answer **D** is incorrect because the workstation Security logs would not contain the necessary information regarding effective Group Policy settings.

8. You are the network administrator for a Windows Server 2003 domain with network resources from each department grouped into separate OUs: Finance, IT, Sales, Development, and Public Relations. You have assigned the MSI package shown in the following figure to the Development OU. User EMandervile is a telecommuting user who is transferring from development to public relations. What is the most efficient way to remove this application from *EMandervile's* workstation?

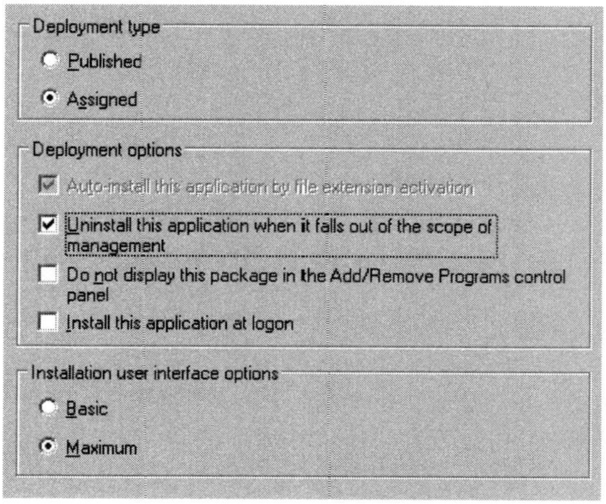

A. Visit *EMandervile's* home office and manually uninstall the application from his home workstation.

B. Redeploy the MSI package to the Development OU after moving *EMandervile's* user account.

C. Email *EMandervile* instructions to uninstall the application from his home office workstation.

D. Since "Uninstall this application when it falls out of the scope of management" is selected, the application will automatically be uninstalled after you move *EMandervile's* account from the Development OU to the Public Relations OU.

☑ **D.** The "Uninstall this application when it falls out of the scope of management" option automatically uninstalls a deployed application when the GPO that installed it no longer applies to the user in question.

☒ **A, B, C.** Answer **A** is incorrect because the Software Installation package in question has been configured to automatically uninstall itself in this situation. A site visit to a remote user would be inefficient and unnecessary. Answer **B** is incorrect because redeploying the application is unnecessary to remove it from a single workstation. Answer **C** is incorrect because the application will be uninstalled automatically and without any end-user intervention.

9. Your have been reading about the new features offered by GPMC and would like to use it to manage your Windows environment, shown in the following figure. Your administrative workstation is located in Domain A, and you have administrative control over Domain A, Domain B, and Domain C. Which of the following would allow you to use GPMC from your present location? (Choose all that apply.)

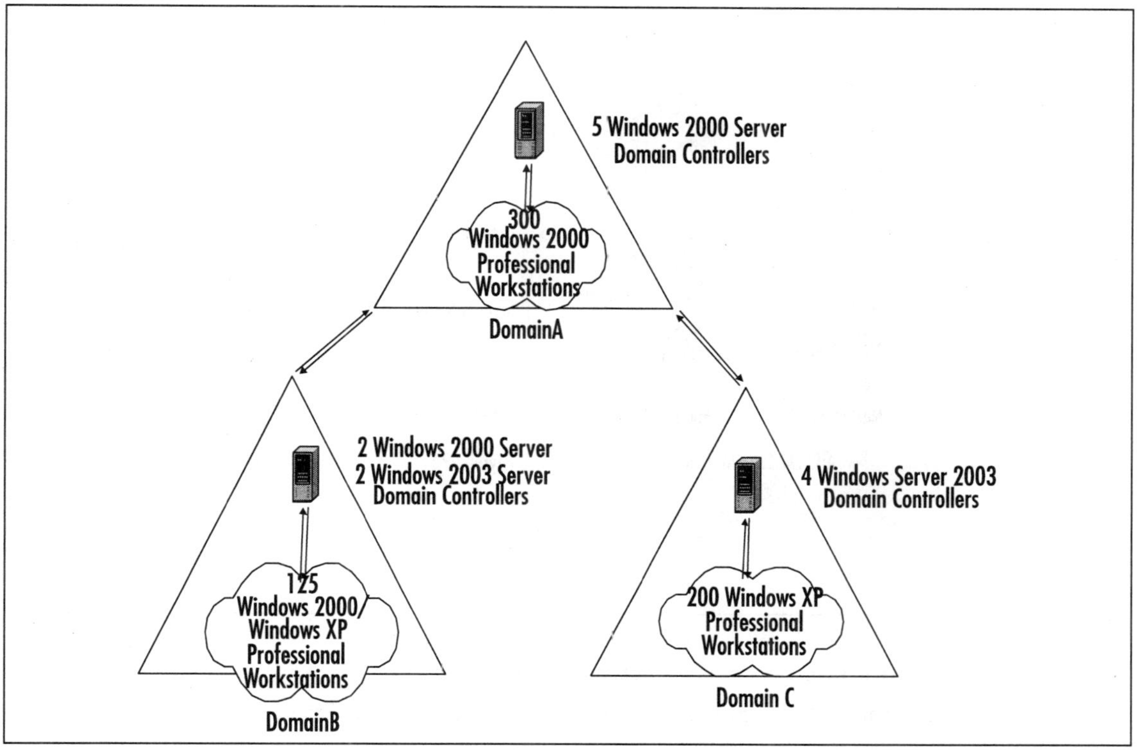

A. Install GPMC on your existing Windows 2000 Professional workstation.

B. Upgrade your administrative workstation to Windows XP Professional, SP1, and install the necessary hotfix from Microsoft before installing GPMC.

C. Install a Windows Server 2003 member server in Domain A, and install GPMC on the member server.

D. Install the GPMC onto a Windows 2000 Server in Domain A, and use the GPMC from the server console.

☑ **B**, **C**. You can use GPMC to administer a Windows 2000 domain, but the utility itself requires Windows Server 2003 or Windows XP Professional with SP1 and a gpedit.dll hotfix to install properly. Therefore, Answers **B** and **C** are correct.

☒ **A**, **D**. Answer **A** is incorrect because the GPMC requires Windows XP Professional or Windows Server 2003 to run properly. Answer **D** is incorrect because the GPMC will not install on a Windows 200 Server, even though it will allow you to administer a Windows 2000 domain.

10. Your Active Directory domain is configured like the one shown in the following figure. Which GPO settings would be applied to a computer located in the Marketing OU? (Choose all that apply.)

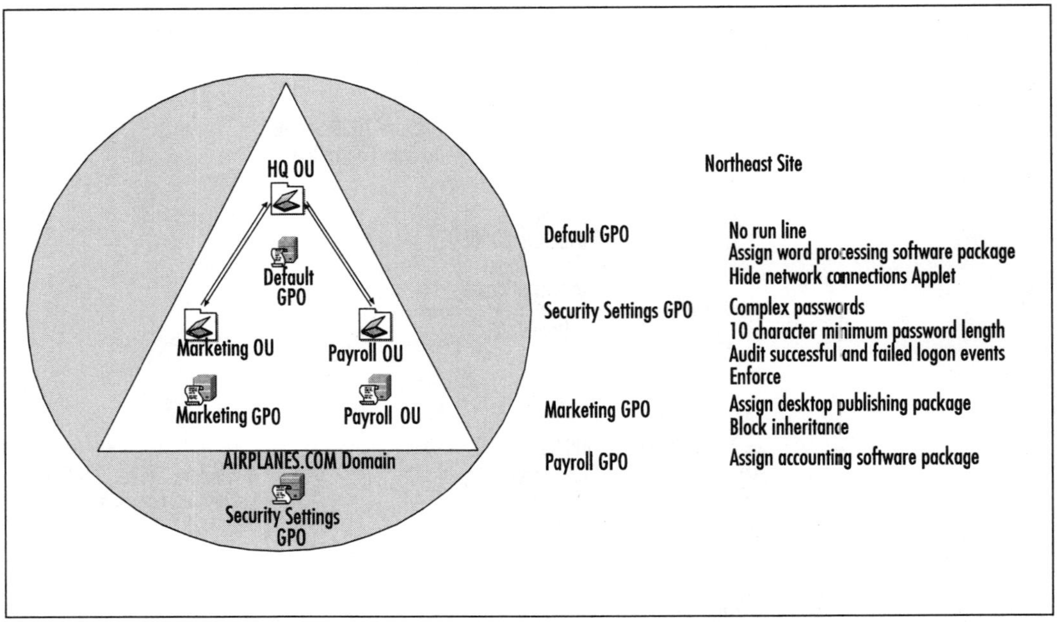

A. The Network Connections applet will be hidden.

B. Successful and failed logon events will be recorded to the Event Log.

C. A desktop publishing software package will be assigned.

D. The Run line will not be visible.

☑ **B**, **C**. Because the Security Settings GPO has the Enforce property enabled, the settings enforced by this GPO will be applied to all containers within the domain. Therefore, Answer **B** is correct. The desktop publishing package is assigned by the Marketing OU GPO itself.

☒ **A**, **D**. Answer **A** is incorrect because the Marketing OU GPO has the Block Inheritance property enabled. Since the Default GPO does not have Enforce enabled, its settings are not propagated to the Marketing OU. Answer **D** is incorrect because hiding the Run line is enabled through the Default GPO whose settings are not inherited by the Marketing OU.

11. You are the administrator of the Windows Server 2003 domain shown in the following figure. The Executive OU and Payroll OU each contain the domain user accounts for the employees in each department. Which GPO settings would be applied to clients in the Executive OU? (Choose all that apply.)

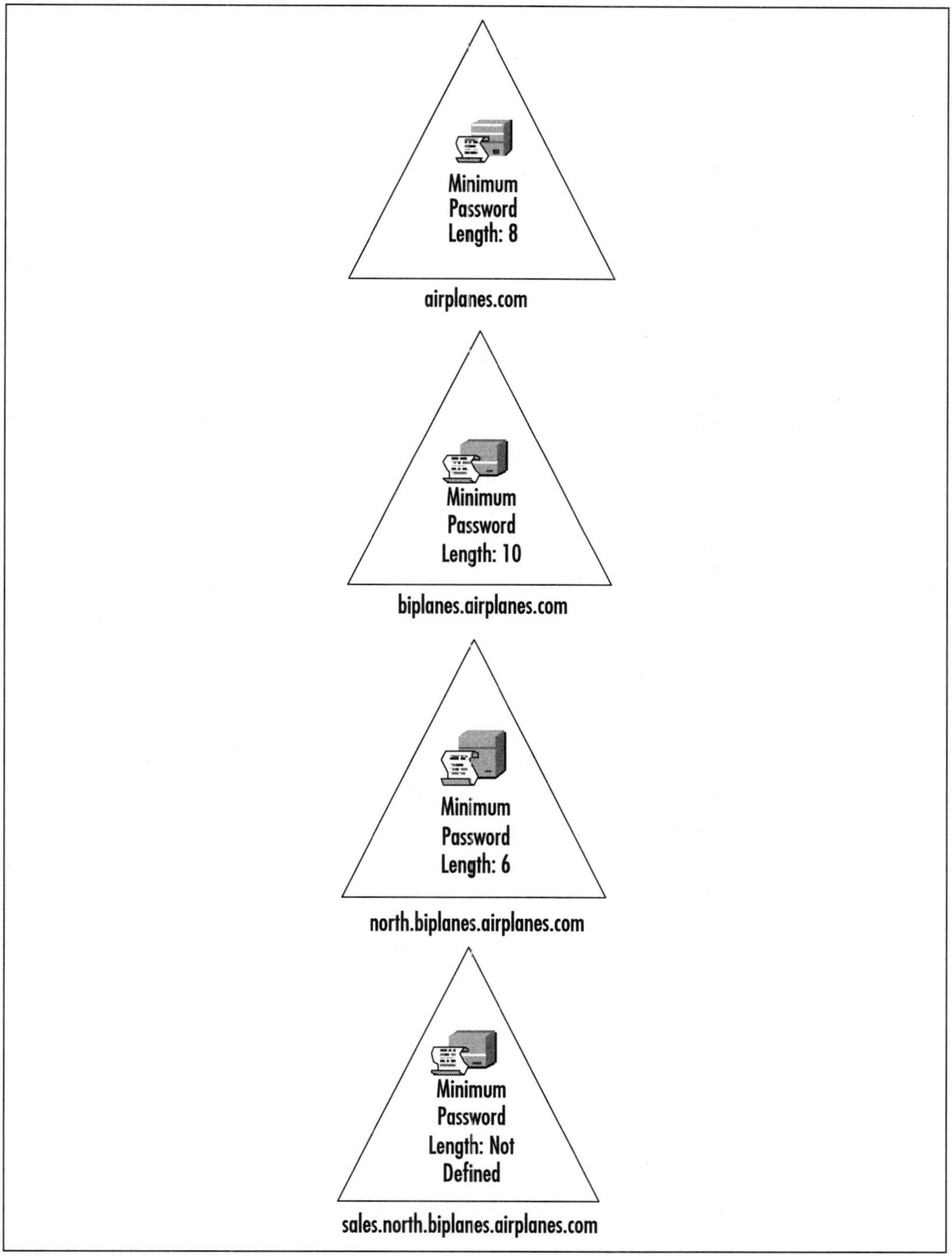
Minimum
Password
Length: 8
airplanes.com
Minimum
Password
Length: 10
biplanes.airplanes.com
Minimum
Password
Length: 6
north.biplanes.airplanes.com
Minimum
Password
Length: Not
Defined
sales.north.biplanes.airplanes.com

A. A 10-character minimum password length

B. A four-character minimum password length

C. No Run line

D. Enable Run line

☑ **A**, **D**. Minimum password length is assigned at the domain level and cannot be overridden by a conflicting setting at the OU level. Therefore Answer **A** is correct. Since the default GPO inheritance rules apply, the Run Line setting enabled at the Executive OU overrides the No Run Line setting established higher in the processing hierarchy at the HQ OU.

☒ **B**, **C**. Answer **B** is incorrect because minimum password length cannot be set at the OU level; the Executive OU inherits the minimum password length setting from the Security Settings GPO linked to the domain. Answer **C** is incorrect because the Enable Run Line setting established through the Executive GPO overrides the conflicting setting established by the HQ OU.

12. You are the network administrator of the Windows Server 2003 forest shown in the following figure. Which of the following Password Policy values will be in effect for clients in the sales.north.biplanes.airplanes.com domain?

A. Six characters

B. Eight characters

C. Ten characters

D. Not defined

☑ **D**. Although child OUs inherit policy settings from their parent OUs, child *domains* do not inherit GPO settings from parent domains.

☒ **A**, **B**, **C**. Since the minimum password setting must be established at each domain, the minimum password length for the sales.north.biplanes.airplanes.com domain has not been defined. Therefore, Answers **A**, **B**, and **C** are incorrect.

13. By default, how does Windows Server 2003 process GPO settings at startup and at logon? (Select all correct answers.)

A. Startup: Synchronous

B. Startup: Asynchronous

C. Logon: Asynchronous

D. Logon: Synchronous

☑ **B**, **C**. Windows Server 2003, by default, processes Group Policies simultaneously at both computer startup and user logon. Therefore, Answers **B** and **C** are correct.

☒ **A, D**. Answers **A** and **D** are incorrect because Windows Server 2003 processes GPOs synchronously at startup and logon. Windows XP Professional processes these settings asynchronously, as a background process after startup and/or logon have completed.

14. Your Active Directory environment is configured as shown in the following figure, with two conflicting Enforces. Which setting(s) will be applied to a client in the Collections OU? (Choose all that apply.)

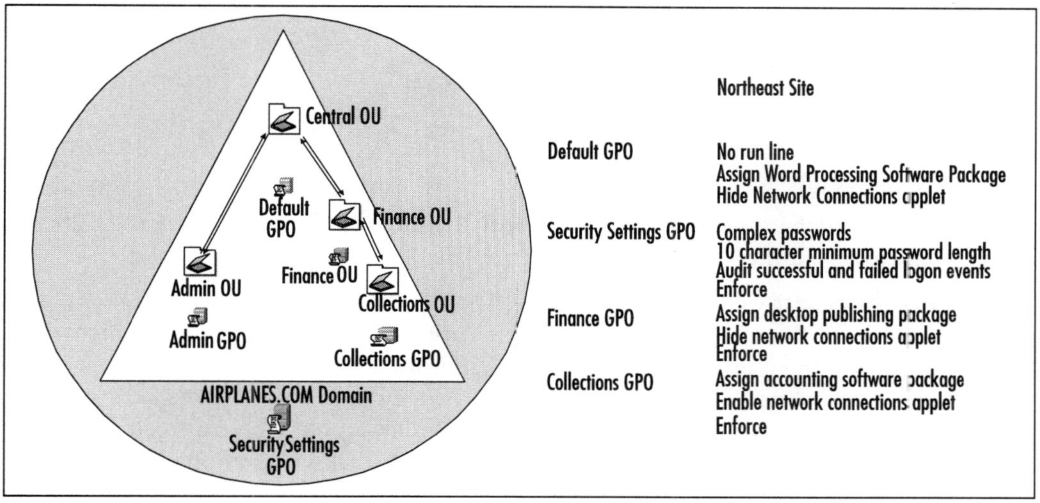

A. The desktop publishing package will be assigned.

B. The Network Connections applet will be hidden.

C. The Network Connections applet will be visible.

D. The Run line will be hidden.

☑ **A, B, D**. Since the Collections GPO does not have the Block Inheritance property set, it will inherit the desktop publishing package installation from the Finance GPO. Therefore, Answer **A** is correct. Although the Collections GPO has the Enforce property set, the Finance GPO (which exists at a higher level in the OU hierarchy) *also* has the Enforce property set. In the case of conflicting enforced settings, the setting that occurs *higher* in the hierarchy takes precedence. This is the reverse of the usual GPO inheritance rules. Therefore, Answer **B** is correct. The Marketing OU will also inherit the No Run Line property from the Default GPO. Therefore, Answer **D** is correct.

☒ **C**. Answer **C** is incorrect because even though the Marketing GPO has enabled the Network Connections applet enabled along with the Enforce property, it is overridden by the Enforce property in the Finance GPO.

Chapter 8 Securing a Windows Server 2003 Network

1. Your network environment contains file servers that were upgraded from Windows NT 4.0 and Windows 2000 platforms. You have been directed to secure the file servers at a level that would be consistent with the security level provided by a clean install of Windows Server 2003. What template could you import and apply to provide that level of security?

   A. compatws.inf

   B. basicsrv.inf

   C. setup security.inf

   D. basicws.inf

   ☑ **C.** The default settings for a clean install condition for Windows Server 2003 are included in the setup security.inf template.

   ☒ **A, B, D.** Answer **A** is incorrect because the compatws.inf template lowers security to allow for the operation of legacy applications. Answers **B** and **D** are incorrect because they are the names of templates for Windows 2000 installations.

2. Bob in your finance department has requested that a policy be enforced requiring secure communication between a Windows 2000 Professional workstation and a Windows Server 2003 machine that contains confidential data. You have implemented the policy and have not yet established connection between the machines. When you test network connectivity through the use of the PING command from the workstation, you find that numerous messages are displayed, reading *negotiating IP security*, but ping response messages are not displayed. What could cause this condition? (Choose the best answer.)

   A. The IP configuration information is incorrect on one of the machines.

   B. The network is not functional, so communication cannot be established.

   C. The IP security policies on the two machines do not match.

   D. The certificate used for the policy is not valid.

   ☑ **C.** In establishing IP security policies, both machines must have identical policies configured. If the policies are not identical, you will receive the negotiating IP security message and fail to establish communication; therefore Answer **C** is the best answer.

   ☒ **A, B, D.** Answers **A** and **B** are incorrect because if the IP configuration is incorrect or the network is not functional, you will not receive the message indicated. Answer **D** is a possible cause of policy mismatch but is incorrect because it is not the best answer.

3. You must set the security for the SMTP service on a newly installed Windows Server 2003 machine configured with the mail server role and ensure that mail relaying is not allowed from your server. Where do you find the appropriate tool to accomplish this setting?

   A. Control Panel | Services | SMTP service

   B. Administrative Tools | Services | SMTP service

   C. Administrative Tools | Internet Information Services Admin | Default Virtual SMTP server |Access tab

   D. Administrative Tools | POP3 Service Manager | Relay tab

   ☑ **C**. The IIS Admin MMC is added to the Administrative Tools menu when the mail server role is added, and the Access tab contains a Relay button to configure relay parameters.

   ☒ **A, B, D**. Answer **A** is incorrect because the Services MMC is not available from the Control Panel. Answer **B** is incorrect because the relay settings are not configurable from the services configuration area. Answer **D** is incorrect because only the POP3 settings are configurable from within the POP3 Service Manager MMC.

4. When you configured your Windows Server 2003 machine as a Web server, you found that the ASPs that had been written could not be served from the server. What must you do to allow the ASP content to be delivered?

   A. Use IISAdmin MMC | Default Web site | Properties | Content tab to configure the site for use of ASPs.

   B. Use IISAdmin MMC | Default Web site | Properties | Applications tab to configure the site for use of ASPs.

   C. Use IISAdmin MMC | *<computer name>* | Web Sites to configure the site for use of ASPs.

   D. Use IISAdmin MMC | *<computer name>* | Web Service Extensions to configure the site for use of ASPs.

   ☑ **D**. The new MMC for IIS 6.0 contains a different structure and highly restricted functionality until the administrator configures the individual servers and virtual Web sites for use.

   ☒ **A, B, C**. **A** is incorrect because the folder structure within the IIS 6.0 MMC is changed from IIS 5.0, and this path would not reach the area for configuration of the services to be allowed on the Web server. Answer **B** is incorrect because the applications are not configured in this area. Answer **C** is incorrect because this is the location of the content of the Web site rather than the configuration of the application extensions that are allowed.

5. You have created a Terminal Services server and have left the configuration in the default state. What additional configuration steps should you take to ensure that the configuration is as secure as possible? (Choose all that apply.)

   A. You should use a RADIUS server for authentication of the clients accessing the terminal server.

   B. You should raise the encryption level of the RDP connections on the server.

   C. You should create new Remote Access Policies and put them in place on the server.

   D. You should add users and groups to the Remote Desktop Users group to allow them access.

   ☑ **B, D**. The encryption level should be raised to more fully protect the information being shared between the client and server machines, and all users or groups that are to be allowed access to the Terminal Server must be added to the Remote Desktop Users group or they will be denied access to the server; therefore Answers **B** and **D** are correct.

   ☒ **A, C**. Answers **A** and **C** are incorrect because RADIUS and Remote Access Policies are possible components in the installation and configuration of the Remote Access/VPN server role but are not used in the Terminal Services role.

6. Your security log contains 100 sequential messages, as shown in the accompanying figure. This is followed by a success audit for the username. What is this most likely to indicate about your server's security? (Choose all that apply.)

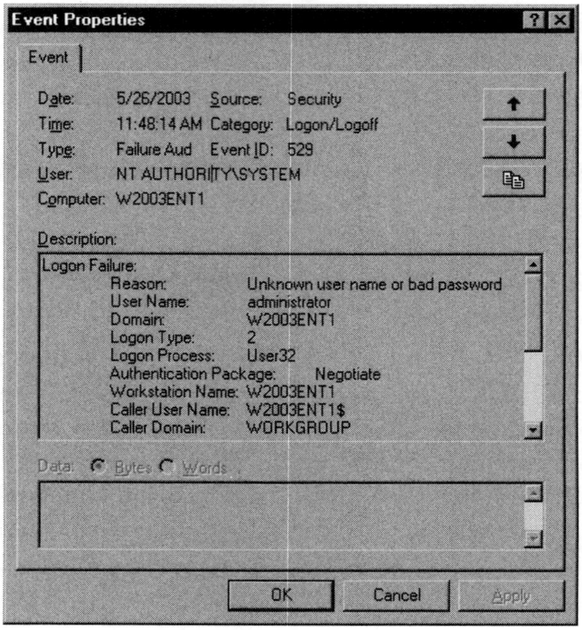

A. The server's security is adequate. The administrator often can't remember the password.

B. The server is most likely compromised. The successful logon after the high number of failed attempts is indicative of the success of a password-cracking attempt.

C. The server's security policy regarding lockout of accounts for failed logon attempts is inadequate.

D. The server's overall security is inadequate because a successful logon using the administrator account was made, and the administrator account should have been renamed before being used in production.

☑ **A, B, D**. In this scenario, it would be highly likely that a breach had occurred, requiring a complete reinstall of the server. Failed logon attempts should result in lockout in all cases, not just for user accounts. The administrator account should have been renamed as a best practice prior to introducing the server to the production environment; therefore Answers **B**, **C**, and **D** are all correct.

☒ **A**. Answer **A** is incorrect because the inability of an administrator to remember a password should never result in this volume of logon attempts. It is obvious from the pattern that the security settings are not adequate.

7. You are planning to use HFNetChk in a scripted function to analyze and check the condition of patches and hotfixes on all machines in the domain that can be examined. Pick the correct syntax from the following choices to accomplish this task and output the results as a tab-delimited file named *test_scan1.txt* for a domain named testdomain that includes notes about the various patches and hotfixes detected or not detected.

A. *hfnetchk –v –d testdomain –op tab –f test_scan1.txt*

B. *mbsacli /hf –d testdomain –o tab –f test_scan1.txt*

C. *hfnetchk –v –n testdomain –od tab –fip test_scan1.txt*

D. *mbsacli /hf –v –d testdomain –o tab –f test_scan1.txt*

☑ **D**. The HFNetChk tool is now run as a component of the Microsoft Baseline Security Analyzer and is initiated with the command line *mbsacli /hf*. In this case, the *–v* switch provides the notes we require, the *–d* switch designates the domain to be checked, the *-o* tab indicates an output file that is tab delimited, and *–f* designates the name of the output file.

☒ **A**, **B**, **C**. Answers **A** and **C** are incorrect because the HFNetChk utility is now run from within the MBSA installation folder and thus is not called directly with the *hfnetchk* command-line function as in previous versions. Answer **B** is incorrect because it does not contain the *–v* switch to include the notes and patch information that was requested.

8. You are being sent on a trip to visit various branch offices that are connected to your main corporate site by 56K Frame Relay links, which carry all network traffic and provide Internet access to the branch offices. Each of the branch offices has approximately 10 workstation machines in a mix of Win9*x*, Windows 2000, and Windows XP workstations, and they have not been updated with required security patches in some time. You have only a limited amount of time to perform the updates while at the sites and must pick the most efficient method to deploy the patches when you arrive. Which of the following methods would you choose to accomplish this goal?

   A. Software Update Services

   B. Windows Update

   C. Windows Catalog

   D. Group Policy

   ☑ **C.** The Windows Catalog allows you to download the appropriate fixes prior to departure and transfer them to media such as CD-R disks to use for the various platform installations; therefore Answer **C** is the best answer for this scenario.

   ☒ **A, B, D.** Answers **A** and **B** would not be the best choices in this situation due to the relatively slow link speeds that would limit simultaneous deployment of patches during your limited stay. Answer **D** is not a viable choice because not all the machines will participate in Group Policy.

9. You have developed a customized security template that you want to deploy to all member servers within the domain in a uniform fashion while not affecting the DC servers in the domain. To accomplish this goal, which of the following methods would be appropriate and the best choice for this task?

   A. Software Update Services

   B. Security Configuration and Analysis snap-in for MMC

   C. Group Policy

   D. Systems Management Server

   ☑ **C.** Group Policy deployment in this case would allow the administrator to distinguish between classes of machines on which the newly created template was to be deployed.

   ☒ **A, B, D.** Answer **A** is incorrect because SUS contains no provision for installing components not provided through Windows Update. Answer **B** is possible, but not efficient, because it would require being interactively attached to each machine, requiring many more hours of administrative time. Answer **D** is incorrect because although Systems Management Server is a possibility, it includes a cost factor that would not be favorable unless already in use.

10. What would be the most appropriate method of distributing software updates, security patches, and hotfixes in a mixed-client Windows environment? (Choose all that apply.)

A. Windows Update

B. Software Update Services

C. Group Policy deployment

D. Windows Catalog

☑ **A, D**. In a mixed environment, this would require use of one or the other of the services or a combination of them, since Win9*x* clients and Windows NT 4.0 clients cannot participate in Group Policy or SUS configurations; therefore Answers **A** and **D** are both correct answers.

☒ **B, C**. Answers **B** and **C** are incorrect because down-level clients cannot utilize either SUS or Group Policy deployments.

11. You have a business client that operates a small network consisting of five Windows XP Professional workstations and two Windows Server 2003 servers configured in a workgroup environment. The client wants to secure communication between his workstation and one of the servers, and he also wants to protect some of the data on the servers from some of the users but allow access to the data by the client and one business partner. Which of the following steps would you recommend for this client to provide the level of protection desired?

    A. Deliver EFS policy through the application of Group Policy, which will allow the partners to access the data but protect it from other users. Protect the traffic between the client workstation and the desired server through application of security policy from Group Policy.

    B. Create an EFS policy locally on the member server. Install a certificate for each user who is to access the EFS-protected resources. Protect the traffic between the two desired machines through the creation of matching IPSec policies with a shared key configuration.

    C. Select the "Encrypt Folder to Protect Contents" check box in the Advanced tab of the folder's Properties page. Install security certificates on the local machine for each user who is to be granted access to the secured folder. Add the allowed users to the Security page of the desired resource. Protect the traffic between the two desired machines through the creation of matching IPSec policies with a shared key configuration.

    D. Create an EFS policy locally on the member server. Protect the traffic between the client workstation and the desired server through application of security policy from Group Policy.

    ☑ **C**. In the absence of Active Directory, it is necessary on Windows Server 2003 standalone servers to install a certificate for each user allowed to access the resource. Additionally, it is necessary to utilize NTFS and to enable EFS by selecting the appropriate box on the Advanced tab of the Properties sheet for the resource, and then add the user account to the Security tab of the resource. Finally, IPSec policies must be matched between the client machine and the server. In the case of standalones, it is usual practice to utilize a preshared key to establish the common authentication between the two machines.

☒ **A, B, D.** Answer **A** is incorrect because in the noted absence of Active Directory, Group Policy application is not possible. Answers **B** and **D** are incorrect because it is not possible to create a local EFS policy on a machine.

12. You have been tasked with performing a change and configuration analysis for your organization. It has been recommended that this process begin with an analysis that creates a configuration benchmark to compare with in future times. What tools should be part of your toolkit for creating this benchmark analysis? (Choose all that apply.)

    A. Performance Monitor

    B. Network Monitor

    C. Microsoft Baseline Security Analyzer

    D. Windows Download Service

    ☑ **A, B, C.** Performance Monitor and Network Monitor are regularly used for creating baseline analyses, and the Microsoft Baseline Security Analyzer performs the analysis of current patch and service pack conditions for all NT 4.0, Windows 2000, and Windows XP machines in the network; therefore Answers **A, B,** and **C** are all reasonable components of the change and configuration analysis task.

    ☒ Answer **D** is incorrect. The Windows download service will be of little or no help in this activity.

13. Look at the accompanying figure. What level of encryption would you recommend for use in a network utilizing network resources that participate in operations requiring the standards required by government security rules?

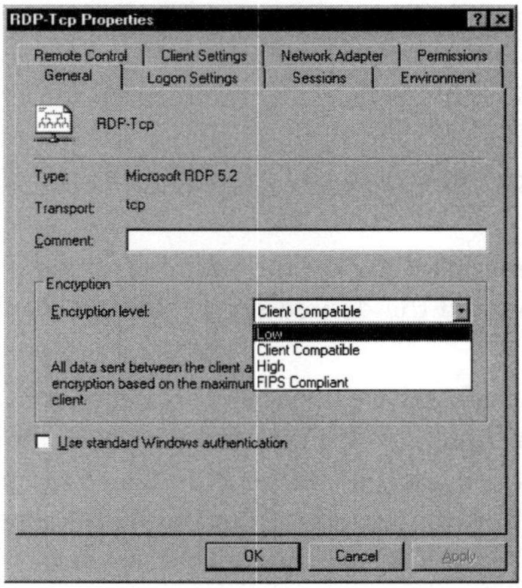

A. Low
B. Client compatible
C. High
D. FIPS compliant

☑ **D**. In order to use Terminal Services in an environment requiring compliance with government security standards, it would be appropriate to use FIP-compliant encryption, which meets or exceeds the specification.

☒ **A**, **B**, **C**. Answers **A**, **B**, and **C** are incorrect because they do not provide the necessary level of encryption required by government security standards.

14. You have been asked to perform a quick single-machine scan for security hotfixes utilizing the command-line function of the Microsoft Baseline Security Analyzer. Of the following, which command would quickly accomplish this task?

A. mbsalcli.exe /*computername*
B. mbsacli.exe
C. mbsacli.exe -d -n
D. mbsacli.exe /hf

☑ **B**. Simply entering the command at the command line will perform the task on the local machine.

☒ **A**, **C**, **D**. Answer **A** is incorrect because it involves more than is required to perform the task. Answer **C** is incorrect because it contains incorrect parameters. Answer **D** is incorrect because it causes HFNetChk to be used rather than the MBSA tool.

15. In the accompanying diagram, what is the selected template used for? (Choose all that apply.)

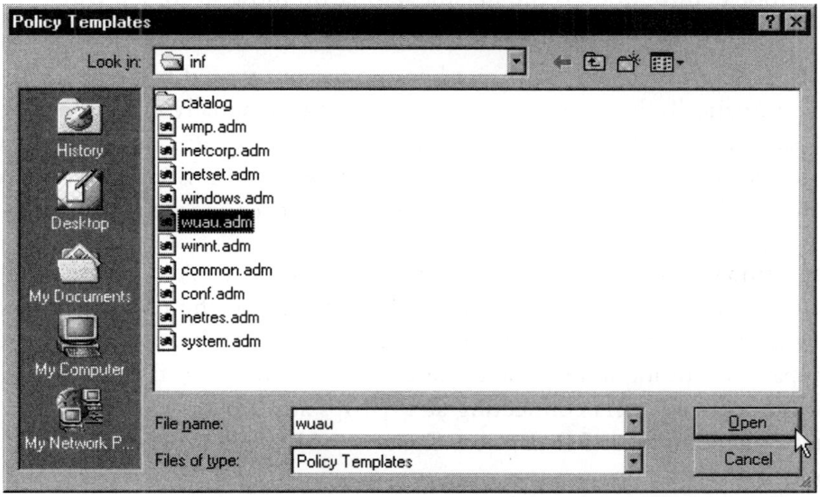

A. Security configuration and analysis

B. Group Policy configuration

C. Windows Update Services automatic update client configuration

D. Automatic Update configuration

☑ **B, C.** The template can be applied to individual machines through the local computer policy object, or through Group Policy in an Active Directory domain to configure multiple client machines; therefore Answers **B** and **C** are correct answers.

☒ **A, D.** Answer **A** is incorrect because this template is not used for security configuration. Answer **D** is incorrect because the template would not be applied unless the need existed for configuration of the Windows Update Service in the local intranet environment.

Chapter 9 Planning Security for a Wireless Network

1. You are opening an Internet café and want to provide wireless access to your patrons. How would you configure your wireless network settings on your AP to make it easiest for your patrons to connect? (Choose all that apply.)

   A. Enable SSID broadcasts.

   B. Disable SSID broadcasts.

   C. Enable WEP.

   D. Set up the network in Infrastructure mode.

   E. Set up the network in Ad Hoc mode.

   ☑ **A, D.** Answer **A** is correct because wireless clients will be able to scan for and detect the SSID when they start configuring their devices. Answer **D** is correct because infrastructure mode is the default setting on most, if not all, wireless devices, and you will be using an AP.

   ☒ **B, C, E.** Answer **B** is incorrect because patrons would not be able to detect the SSID automatically, hence they would be forced to manually enter the SSID once they have asked you for it. Answer **C** is incorrect because WEP is not required and can be tricky to set up for a wireless-challenged patron. Answer **E** is incorrect because an AP will be used, and in Ad Hoc networks, wireless clients connect to each other, not to an AP.

2. Your company, Company B, has merged with Company A. A new member of the management team has a wireless adapter in her laptop that she used to connect to Company A's wireless network, which was at another location. In her new office, which is located at Company B's headquarters, she cannot connect. Company B's wireless network can accommodate adapters connecting at 11MBps and 54MBps, and she mentions that she could only connect at 54MBps on Company A's wireless network. What do you suspect is happening?

A. The new member of the management team has an 802.11a wireless network adapter and Company B's wireless network is using 802.11g equipment.

B. The new member of the management team has an 802.11b wireless network adapter and Company B's wireless network is using 802.11g equipment.

C. The new member of the management team has an 802.11g wireless network adapter and Company B's wireless network is using 802.11b equipment.

D. The new member of the management team has an 802.11g wireless network adapter and Company B's wireless network is using 802.11a equipment.

☑ **A**. 802.11a equipment and 802.11g equipment are incompatible. Because 802.11g and 802.11b equipment both work on the 2.4GHz band and 802.11g is backward compatible for use with equipment that conforms to the 802.11b standard, 802.11b and 802.11g equipment can be used together on the same network.

☒ **B, C, D.** Answer **B** is incorrect because 802.11a is not compatible with 802.11g, although both work at speeds up to 54MBps. Answer **C** is incorrect because the new member of the management team indicated that she only had the option of connecting at 54MBps, which would indicate that Company A was using 802.11a equipment. Answer **D** is incorrect because Company Bs equipment can accommodate wireless client connecting at 11MBps and 54MBps, which would indicate that it is using 802.11g equipment, not 802.11a.

3. What are the two WEP key sizes available in 802.11 networks?

   A. 64-bit and 104-bit keys

   B. 24-bit and 64-bit keys

   C. 64-bit and 128-bit keys

   D. 24-bit and 104-bit keys

   ☑ **C.** The 802.11 specification calls for 64-bit keys for use in WEP. Later the specification was amended to allow for 128-bit keys as well.

   ☒ **A, B, D.** The actual key size of the secret key is 40 bits and 104 bits. When these are added to the 24-bit IV, you wind up with WEP key sizes of 64 bits and 128 bits; thus Answers **A**, **B**, and **D** are incorrect.

4. Your wireless network does use WEP to authorize users. You use MAC filtering to ensure that only preauthorized clients can associate with your APs. On Monday morning, you reviewed the AP association table logs for the previous weekend and noticed that the MAC address assigned to the network adapter in your portable computer had associated with your APs several times over the weekend. Your portable computer spent the weekend on your dining room table and was not connected to your corporate wireless network during this period of time. What type of wireless network attack are you most likely being subjected to?

A. Spoofing

B. Jamming

C. Sniffing

D. Man in the middle

☑ **A**. You are the victim of a MAC spoofing attack whereby an attacker has captured valid MAC addresses by sniffing your wireless network. The fact that you have no other protection in place has made becoming associated with your APs an easy task for this attacker.

☒ **B**, **C**, **D**. Jamming attacks are those in which high-power RF waves are targeted at a wireless network installation with the hope of knocking it out of operation by overpowering it; thus Answer **B** is incorrect. Although your network has been sniffed previously to obtain the valid MAC address, you are currently being attacked using a spoofing attack; thus Answer **C** is incorrect. A man-in-the-middle attack is one in which an attacker sits between two communicating parties, intercepting and manipulating both sides of the transmission to suit his or her own needs; thus Answer **D** is incorrect.

5. Your supervisor has charged you with determining which 802.11 authentication method to use when deploying the new wireless network. Given your knowledge of the 802.11 specifications, which of the following is the most secure 802.11 authentication method?

A. Shared-key authentication

B. EAP-TLS

C. EAP-MD5

D. Open authentication

☑ **D**. Open authentication is actually more secure than shared-key authentication because it is not susceptible to a known plaintext attack, to which the shared-key authentication method is susceptible.

☒ **A**, **B**, **C**. Shared-key authentication is susceptible to a known plaintext attack if the attacker can capture the random challenge the AP sends to the client, as well as the encrypted response from the client. The attacker can then try to brute-force the WEP key by trying to decrypt the encrypted response and comparing it to the random challenge sent by the AP; thus Answer **A** is incorrect. EAP-TLS and EAP-MD5 are authentication methods specified in the 802.1X standard, not the 802.11 standard; thus Answers **C** and **D** are incorrect.

6. Bill, a network administrator, wants to deploy a wireless network and use open authentication. His problem is that he also wants to make sure that the network is not accessible by anyone. How can he authenticate users without a shared-key authentication mechanism? (Choose the best answer.)

A. Use MAC address filters to restrict which wireless network cards can associate to the network.

B. Deploy a RADIUS server and require the use of EAP.

C. Set a WEP key on the APs and use it as the indirect authenticator for users.

D. Use IP filters to restrict access to the wireless network.

☑ **C**. Use the WEP key as an indirect authenticator for open networks. Unlike shared-key authentication, open authentication does not provide for a challenge/response exchange and therefore does not expose the WEP key to a known plaintext cryptographic attack.

☒ **A**, **B**, **D**. MAC filtering does not absolutely authenticate a user, since MAC addresses are easily spoofed. In addition, MAC filtering is an administrative burden; thus Answer **A** is incorrect. Deploying RADIUS server or IP filters are both beyond the scope of the question; thus Answers **B** and **D** are incorrect.

7. The 802.1X standard specifies a series of exchanges between the supplicant and the authentication server. Which of the following is not part of the 802.1X authentication exchange?

   A. Association request

   B. EAPoL start

   C. RADIUS-access-request

   D. EAP-success

   ☑ **A**. The association request is part of the 802.11 standard, not the 802.1X standards.

   ☒ **B**, **C**, **D**. The EAPoL start, RADIUS-access-request, and EAP-success messages are all part of the 802.1X authentication exchange; thus Answers **B**, **C**, and **D** are incorrect.

8. The 802.1X standard requires the use of an authentication server to allow access to the wireless LAN. You are deploying a wireless network and will use EAP-TLS as your authentication method. What is the most likely vulnerability in your network?

   A. Unauthorized users accessing the network by spoofing EAP-TLS messages

   B. DoS attacks occurring because 802.11 management frames are not authenticated

   C. Attackers cracking the encrypted traffic

   D. None of the above

   ☑ **B**. One of the biggest problems identified in a paper discussing 802.1X security is the lack of authentication in the 802.11 management frames and that 802.1X does not address this problem.

   ☒ **A**, **C**, **D**. Spoofing EAP-TLS is not possible, because the attacker needs the user's certificate and passphrase; thus Answer **A** is incorrect. Cracking encrypted traffic is possible but unlikely, since EAP-TLS allows for WEP key rotation; thus Answer **C** is incorrect. The lack of authentication in 802.11 is the most likely vulnerability; thus Answer **B** is incorrect.

9. In Windows Server 2003, how do you configure WEP protection for a wireless client?

   A. Open the Network Adapter Properties page and configure WEP from the Wireless Networks tab.

   B. Install the high-security encryption pack from Microsoft.

   C. Issue the computer a digital certificate from a Windows Server 2003 Certificate Authority.

   D. Use the utilities provided by the manufacturer of the network adapter.

   ☑ **A**. In about 95 percent or more of the cases, Windows Server 2003 integrates control and management of wireless network adapters into the Network Adapter Properties page.

   ☒ **B, C, D**. Installing the high encryption pack from Microsoft just raises the encryption strength supported by the computer itself to 128 bits; thus Answer **B** is incorrect. Issuing the computer a digital certificate will not configure it for WEP protection in a wireless network; thus Answer **C** is incorrect. In about 95 percent or more of the cases, Windows Server 2003 integrates control and management of wireless network adapters into the Network Adapter Properties page, so you cannot configure network adapters using the manufacturer's utilities; thus Answer **D** is incorrect.

10. You are attempting to configure a client computer wireless network adapter in Windows Server 2003. You have installed and launched the utility program that came with the adapter, but you cannot configure the settings from it. What is the source of your problem?

    A. You are not a member of the Network Configuration Operators group.

    B. You do not have the correct Windows Service Pack installed.

    C. You do not configure wireless network adapters in Windows Server 2003 through manufacturer's utilities.

    D. Your network administrator has disabled SSID broadcasting for the wireless network.

    ☑ **C**. In Windows Server 2003, you must use the Network Adapter Properties page to perform wireless network configuration.

    ☒ **A, B, D**. Being a member of the Network Configuration Operators group is not required to make configuration changes to wireless network adapter properties; thus Answer **A** is incorrect. The Service Pack level has no bearing on being able to configure the network adapter properties; thus Answer **B** is incorrect. Closed networks, those that do not broadcast the SSID, have no effect on being able to configure the network adapter properties; thus Answer **D** is incorrect.

11. In the past, you spent a lot of time configuring and reconfiguring wireless network settings for clients. You're at the point where you need to prevent wireless clients from configuring their own settings. What can you do to ensure that wireless network settings are configured uniformly for all clients so that they cannot change them?

A. Configure Local Group Policy.

B. Configure Site Group Policy.

C. Configure Domain Group Policy.

D. Configure Default Domain Controllers Group Policy.

☑ **C.** Domain Group Policy is the only Group Policy that has the Wireless Network (802.11) Group Policy object and applies uniformly to all clients.

☒ **A, B, D.** Answer **A** is incorrect because Local Group Policy does not have Wireless Network (802.11) and only applies to the local system. Answer **B** is incorrect because Site Group Policy applies to individual sites only. Answer **D** is incorrect because it applies to domain controllers only.

12. Your organization has just implemented Group Policies. On the first morning that Group Policies are applied, you receive a call from a client who can no longer connect to the wireless network at her location. What can you do to figure out the source of her issue?

A. Use the Resultant Set of Policy Snap-in to assess the impact of Group Policy on her User and Computer Account policy settings.

B. Use the Resultant Set of Policy Snap-in to assess the impact of Group Policy on her User Account policy settings.

C. Use the Resultant Set of Policy Snap-in to assess the impact of Group Policy on her Computer Account policy settings.

D. Block Group Policy inheritance to her User and Computer Accounts.

☑ **C.** Wireless Network (IEEE 802.11) Policy only applies to Computer Accounts, and the RSoP Snap-in can assess the cumulative impact of Wireless Network Policy on her Computer Account.

☒ **A, B, D.** Answers **A** and **B** are incorrect because Wireless Network (802.11) Policy does not apply to User Accounts. Answer **D** is incorrect because it is a measure that is far too extreme, given that the RSoP Snap-in can provide the required information.

13. Your company opens five temporary offices for the summer months in different locations every year. To avoid installing network cabling in an office that might not be used in a following year, management has decided to use wireless technology so that the investment in network connectivity can be reused from year to year. One regional manager travels to every office on a regular basis. What is the best solution for enabling the regional manager who needs to connect to the wireless network in every office?

A. Supply the regional manager with a list of SSIDs and WEP keys for every temporary office.

B. Configure Preferred Networks in Network Adapter Properties on the regional manager's laptop.

C. Configure Preferred Networks in Wireless Network (IEEE 802.11) Policy in the Local Group Policy Editor on the regional manager's laptop.

D. Configure Preferred Networks in Wireless Network (IEEE 802.11) Policy for the domain.

☑ **B**. All the configurations for the various wireless networks can be stored in one place, prioritized and used by the wireless network adapter with minimal intervention by the regional manager.

☒ **A**, **C**, **D**. Answer **A** is not necessarily incorrect, but it is not the best answer; defining the various wireless networks as Preferred Networks in the properties of the network adapter is more efficient for the regional manager and eliminates a potential security risk if the list falls into the wrong hands. Answer **C** is incorrect because Wireless Network (IEEE 802.11) Policy is not available in Local Group Policy. Answer **D** is incorrect because only the regional manager requires wireless network configurations for other offices' wireless networks.

14. You want to extend your network to integrate wired and wireless clients; however, you need to isolate wireless clients and encrypt all the network traffic that they generate. What can you do to address these requirements?

A. Create a separate subnet for all wireless clients by creating a separate zone in DHCP.

B. Create a separate subnet for all wireless clients by creating a separate zone in DHCP and implement IPSec.

C. Install a wireless bridge that running IPSec, which connects the wireless segment of the network with the wired section.

D. Enable IPSec on all wireless clients and APs.

☑ **C**. The actions in Answer **C** actually create a stub network (or stub subnetwork). It is the only response that isolates the wireless clients and encrypts the traffic they generate. The wireless bridge transfers IPSec-encrypted traffic that is directed from wireless clients towards the "wired" network, which might or might not have clients that use IPSec.

☒ **A**, **B**, **D**. Answer **A** is incorrect because using a separate subnetwork could isolate the wireless clients, but network traffic is not encrypted. Answer **B** is incorrect because IPSec would be required on all clients, wired and wireless, for data from the wireless clients to be encrypted; IPSec has to be enabled on both ends of the connection for a secure tunnel to be established. Answer **D** is incorrect because IPSec cannot be configured on the current generation of APs.

15. You are installing a wireless LAN as part of a wireless pilot project. You want to restrict its use exclusively to those computers that belong to members of the pilot group. What is the best way to begin restricting connections by wireless clients that are not part of the group?

A. Enable WEP with a 128-bit encryption key.

B. Disable SSID broadcasts.

C. Enable MAC address filtering and adding the MAC addresses.

D. Change the mode from Ad Hoc to Infrastructure.

☑ **C**. Answer **C** is correct because it provides control to whomever is running the pilot over the network adapters that are allowed to connect to an AP. The wireless network would still be vulnerable to MAC address spoofing; however, it is the best first step.

☒ **A**, **B**, **D**. Answer **A** is incorrect because, although they will not be able to authenticate, enabling WEP will still allow a wireless client to connect to an AP. Answer **B** is incorrect because a wireless client will be able to connect if he or she discovers the SSID through another means, such as asking a member of the pilot group. Answer **D** is incorrect because changing the mode from Ad Hoc to Infrastructure will permit a wireless client to connect to the network once the client's wireless network adapter has been configured to Infrastructure mode.

Chapter 10 Remote Management

1. You are assigning the newest member of your staff responsibility for a new file server running Windows Server 2003. He will be an Administrator on the server, and you want him to be able to ask for help from his coworkers so that they can walk him through steps to resolve any issues that arise. How would you have the new server configured so that this new administrator can request Remote Assistance?

   A. Check the Remote Assistance box on the Remote tab in System Properties, and enable remote control in the Remote Assistance Settings dialog box.

   B. Check the Remote Desktop box on the Remote tab in System Properties.

   C. Check the Remote Assistance box on the Remote tab in System Properties, and add him as a Remote User in the Add New Users window.

   D. Enable Remote Assistance through Local Remote Assistance Group Policy.

   ☑ **A**. Once the Remote Assistance box on the Remote tab in System Properties is checked and Remote Control is checked in the Remote Assistance Settings dialog box, the new administrator will be able to request Remote Assistance. Those from whom he will receive assistance will be able to take remote control of the server with his permission.

   ☒ **B**, **C**, **D**. Answer **B** is incorrect because, apart from the underlying technology, Remote Desktop is unrelated to Remote Assistance; it is used for remote control and has no functionality for inviting assistance. Answer **C** is incorrect because there is no Add New User window for Remote Assistance; Add New Users is for Remote Desktop. Answer **D** is incorrect because enabling Remote Assistance in thee Local Remote Assistance Group Policy permits remote assistance for all local accounts; Remote Assistance is not configured by default, which makes it an option for all local accounts.

2. You just recently finished configuring the properties for Solicited Remote Assistance in Remote Assistance Group Policy, and you start receiving complaints that certain experts outside the organization cannot respond to the invitations that are embedded in the body of e-mail messages. You verify that the correct ports on the firewall are open and that the property for the format of e-mail invitations is set to Mailto. What could be the problem?

   A. The experts do not have the Remote Assistance client installed.

   B. The experts' e-mail client cannot read HTML-formatted messages.

   C. The Remote Assistance timeout period is too short.

   D. The experts do not have the correct password.

   ☑ **B**. When the format for sending e-mail is set to Mailto, the link the expert will use to connect to the client system is embedded in the body of an HTML-formatted message. Changing the format to SMAPI will resolve this issue.

   ☒ **A, C, D**. Answer **A** is incorrect because there is no such thing as a Remote Assistance Client. Answers **C** and **D** are incorrect because the expert would have to be able to connect first before realizing that the invitation had expired or that the password was incorrect.

3. You want to restrict who can offer remote assistance to immediate members of the server support team in your IT organization. You decide that creating a group is the most efficient way to manage this function. What kind of group is required, and where do you create it?

   A. Create a Local group on each server that could request remote assistance, and add the group to the Local Administrators group.

   B. Create a Domain group and add it to the Local Administrators group on each server that could request remote assistance.

   C. Create a Universal group and add it to the Offer Remote Assistance Group Policy.

   D. Create a Domain group and add it to the Offer Remote Assistance Group Policy.

   ☑ **D**. All that is required to enable Offer Remote Assistance is that a Domain group or individual Domain users be added to the list behind the Show button. This opens a new window where you can enter the names of the experts.

   ☒ **A, B, C**. Answers **A** and **C** are incorrect because only Domain groups can be used in this situation. Answer **B** is incorrect because the Domain group needs to be added to the Remote Assistance Group Policy so that remote assistance can be offered, not to the servers that will be managed. The accounts for the members of the server support teams need to be added as Local Administrators to take control during a Remote Assistance session; however, this is not necessary to make the offer.

4. You have given the ability to offer unsolicited Remote Assistance to members of the server support team. However, they find that they can connect but not take control of the servers they are supposed to manage. What is the most efficient way of enabling the server support team members to take control of the servers they manage through unsolicited Remote Assistance while controlling the amount of access they have?

   A. Add the members of the server support team to the Domain Administrators group, and add the Domain Administrators group to the Local Administrators group on each server that could request Remote Assistance.

   B. Add the Domain group for the server support team members to the Local Administrators group on each server that could request Remote Assistance.

   C. Add the Domain account for each member of the server support team to the Local Administrators group on each server that could request Remote Assistance.

   D. Create Local accounts for each member of the server support team and add them to the Local Administrators group on each server that could request Remote Assistance.

   ☑ **B**. The server support team members need to be Local Administrators on each of the servers that they manage. The most efficient way to manage this function is to create one group at the Domain level and add it to the Local Administrators group on each server.

   ☒ **A, C, D**. Answer **A** is incorrect because the members of the server support team will be granted a much greater degree of access than is required for Remote Assistance. Answer **C** is incorrect because adding individual Domain accounts to the Local Administrators group means that access has to be managed on an individual basis; this could prove especially difficult if the team's membership changes and former members are left with Administrator access to servers that they no longer manage. Answer **D** is incorrect because Domain accounts are required.

5. You work for a consulting firm that has just installed Windows Server 2003. While at your office, you receive a Remote Assistance invitation to resolve a hardware issue from your client. You connect to the remote server without any problems; however, during the Remote Assistance session, your attempt to send a file with an updated driver is unsuccessful. What is the most probable cause for the lack of success?

   A. The client is refusing to accept the file.

   B. The required ports on one or both firewalls are closed.

   C. The client has insufficient rights to accept the file.

   D. Windows Messenger is not installed on the remote server.

   ☑ **B**. Port 3389 needs to be open on each firewall for the Remote Assistance session, and TCP ports 6891 through 6900 need to be opened on each firewall to enable the transfer of files from the client workstation to the remote server.

☒ **A, C, D**. Answer **A** is incorrect because the expert would be able to send the file and if the client were refusing to accept it, the expert would receive a message that the client is rejecting the file transfer. Answer **C** is incorrect because, beyond having the ability to request remote assistance, client permissions in the system are not a factor. Answer **D** is incorrect because Windows Messenger is not required for remote assistance.

6. The corporate service desk is overloaded, and management wants to leverage technical knowledge that exists throughout the organization. However, due to concerns over the security of corporate data, managers are wary of providing access to the organization's desktop and laptop systems to individuals outside the organization. They are also wary of allowing individuals who do not possess the required knowledge to provide "help." What strategy would you recommend to satisfy management's requirements with the least amount of effort? (Choose all that apply.)

   A. Block Remote Assistance at the firewall.

   B. Enable Remote Assistance in domain Group Policy and restrict it to members of the IT group.

   C. Enable Remote Assistance in System Properties on every desktop and laptop, and add the appropriate users.

   D. Enable Remote Assistance in local Group Policy on every desktop and laptop.

   ☑ **A, B**. By blocking port 3389 on the firewall and restricting responsibility for Remote Assistance to members of IT through domain Group Policy, you will prevent anyone outside the organization and outside IT from providing Remote Assistance; therefore Answers **A** and **B** are correct.

   ☒ **C, D**. Answers **C** and **D** are incorrect because both measures would involve making a series of configuration changes to every individual system in your organization. Even in a small organization, the management burden will be significant, and if clients have administrative privileges on their systems, you would have a difficult time ensuring that your configuration changes remain intact.

7. You receive your first Remote Assistance invitation from a colleague who works in a highly secure unit within your organization, and you immediately respond. Every time you try to connect, however, your connection attempt is refused. You are on the same subnet and can ping to verify that you can "see" the remote server. There is no Domain Remote Assistance Group Policy; therefore, you verify the settings in your Local Remote Assistance Group Policy. Everything looks normal to you. You notice that Client Connection Encryption Levels is set to Client Compatible. What do you suspect is happening?

   A. Port 3389 is closed on the firewall.

   B. The client is refusing your request to take control of the remote server.

   C. The Client Connection Encryption Level is set to High Level.

   D. The Client Connection Encryption Level is set to Low Level.

☑ **C.** The remote server has its Client Connection Encryption Level set to High Level and is rejecting your connection because your system is not set to High Level as well. This would not be a factor if you were using Remote Desktop Connection; however, Remote Assistance requires that clients and servers have compatible levels of encryption.

☒ **A, B, D.** Answer **A** is incorrect because you are not going through a firewall. Answer **B** is incorrect because you would have been able to establish the connection before you would have been able to make a request to take remote control. Answer **D** is incorrect because the local system would have been able to connect to any server with a Client Encryption Level of Client Compatible or Low Level.

8. A network administrator is experiencing difficulty with one of his Windows Server 2003 servers and sends a Remote Assistance invitation via Windows Messenger to a colleague who works in another office. The colleague accepts the invitation and attempts to connect to the remote system, but he is unsuccessful. All offices are interconnected using VPN connections over the Internet, and each office's private network is protected by its own firewall that is not running NAT. What should be done to enable the Remote Assistance session? (Choose all that apply.)

   A. Have the firewall administrators in each office open the TCP/IP ports for Windows Messenger on their firewalls.

   B. Have the firewall administrators in each office open the TCP/IP ports used by Remote Desktop on their firewalls.

   C. Instruct the network administrator to enable Remote Assistance in the Terminal Services section of the local Group Policy Object Editor.

   D. The network administrator should create a Remote Assistance invitation file, attach it to an electronic mail message, and send it to his colleague.

   ☑ **B.** The only port required for the actual Remote Assistance session is TCP port 3389. By opening the ports on the firewalls, the remote workstation or server will be able to connect directly to the system that issued the invitation. Other ports can be opened to enable file transfer and voice communication, but they are optional.

   ☒ **A, C, D.** Answer **A** is incorrect because Windows Messenger is not required for Remote Assistance. If it were, the Remote Assistance session would have happened because the two colleagues were already able to communicate using it. Answer **C** is incorrect because the network administrator was able to issue a Remote Assistance invitation; therefore, Remote Assistance must already be enabled for him in local or domain Group Policy. Answer **D** is incorrect because the problem is with the connection, not with the invitation. Sending the invitation in a different way will not resolve the connection problem, but opening the appropriate ports will.

9. You are experiencing a series of problems with a particular server that you manage remotely, and the hardware vendor is asking you for the system configuration. You know you can display the data on screen using msinfo32.exe, but the vendor is requesting a paper copy. What is the best way to print the information?

   A. Save the information from msinfo32.exe as a text file and copy it to your workstation to print it on your default printer.

   B. Configure printer redirection in Remote Desktop Connection, reconnect to the server, and print the output of msinfo32.exe to your default printer.

   C. Have msinfo32.exe print to the server's default printer.

   D. Display the output of msinfo32.exe in a Remote Desktop for Administration window and capture the window to your default printer.

   ☑ **B**. Using the printer redirection functionality in Remote Desktop Connection, you can print documents from the server on any of your configured printers as though the printers were directly connected to the server.

   ☒ **A**, **C**, **D**. All these answers are not necessarily incorrect, because you could use each of these methods to get the output of msinfo32.exe to a printer; however, they are definitely not as quick, effective, and efficient as using printer redirection. Answer **A** is incorrect because it involves unnecessary steps, given that printer redirection functionality is available. Answer **C** is incorrect because it involves a trip to the server's default printer, if the server even has a default printer installed. Answer **D** is incorrect because if you do not have a large-screen monitor, it might be difficult or even impossible to display all the information in one window in a font size that is easy to read.

10. You decide to start using Remote Desktop for Administration to manage the servers for which you have direct responsibility. Because you expect to have several Remote Desktop Connection windows open, you configure Audio Redirection in your Remote Desktop Connection client to "Bring to this computer." This seems to be working well because you notice that sound is being directed to your workstation for all your servers except one. The sound system on your workstation is fully operational. What are the possible reasons that audio features are not being redirected from this one server? (Choose all that apply.)

   A. The server does not have a sound system or the sound system is disabled.

   B. The "Allow audio redirection" setting in local Terminal Services Group Policy on your workstation is set to Disabled.

   C. The "Allow audio redirection" setting in local Terminal Services Group Policy on the server is set to Disabled.

   D. The "Allow audio redirection" setting in domain-based Terminal Services Group Policy is set to Disabled.

   ☑ **A, C**. This might seem too obvious, but Answer **A** is correct because Windows will disable system sounds if the server does not have a sound card or if it does have a card and it is disabled in Device Manager. Answer **C** is correct because Local Terminal Services Group Policy on the server determines if the server will redirect audio from its local sound system to inbound Remote Desktop for Administration sessions.

☒ **B**, **D**. Answer **B** is incorrect because Local Terminal Services Group Policy controls the parameters of incoming sessions in which the local system is the host, not outbound sessions in which the local system is the client. Answer **D** is incorrect because if Domain Terminal Services Group Policy was set to disabled, you would not be hearing system sounds on any of your Remote Desktop for Administration sessions.

11. You take responsibility for a mission-critical server that absolutely has to be available on a 24/7 basis. As a result, you are issued a laptop computer so that you can manage the server whenever the need arises. You decide to use Remote Desktop for Administration to connect remotely to the server. At the office you can use the LAN, but at home only a dialup connection is available. How should you configure Remote Desktop Connection on your laptop to work efficiently from both locations? (Choose all that apply.)

   A. Before you attempt a Remote Desktop for Administration session, click the **Experience** tab and select **LAN (10Mbps or higher)** when connecting at the office or **Modem (28.8Kbps)** when connecting from home.

   B. Before you attempt a Remote Desktop for Administration session, click the **Experience** tab and select **Custom** and check the appropriate boxes depending on your location.

   C. Click the **Experience** tab, select **Custom** from the drop-down box, check the appropriate boxes for your location, and save the settings with a unique name on the **General** tab for future use.

   D. Use the default setting for Remote Desktop Connection—**Modem (56Kbps)**—for all connections.

   ☑ **C, D**. Both Answers **C** and **D** are correct because they provide you with the ability to recall the settings whenever necessary or use the perfectly acceptable default settings, respectively, on an ongoing basis.

   ☒ **A**, **B**. Answers **A** and **B** are incorrect because any settings that you configure are for that particular instance and are not preserved for future use; the requirement for the settings to be used on an ongoing basis would suggest that the settings be persistent.

12. You find that you consistently keep several Remote Desktop Connection sessions open during the course of your workday. You are beginning to get a little frustrated when you issue Windows keystroke combinations, expecting them to execute on your desktop but they end up executing on a remote server, or vice versa. What can you do to ensure that when you issue Windows keystroke combinations, they execute where you expect them to?

   A. Configure Apply Windows key combinations in Remote Desktop Connection to **On the local computer**.

B. Configure Apply Windows key combinations in Remote Desktop Connection to **In full screen mode only**.

C. Configure Apply Windows key combinations in Remote Desktop Connection to **On the remote computer**.

D. Disable keyboard redirection in Local Terminal Services Group Policy on the remote servers that you manage.

☑ **B**. Answer **B** is correct because it will give you absolute control over how and where Windows keystroke combinations will execute. The "In full screen mode only" option forces Windows keystroke combinations to execute on the remote system only when the remote session has taken over the entire display on the client workstation. When Remote Desktop for Administration windows are restored or minimized, Windows keystroke combinations execute normally on the local workstation.

☒ **A, C, D**. Answer **A** is incorrect because the "On the local computer" option disables Windows keystroke combinations on the remote server. Answer **C** is incorrect because the "On the remote computer" option disables Windows keystroke combinations on the local workstation when a Remote Desktop for Administration session is open. Answer **D** is incorrect because there is no option for keyboard redirection in Terminal Services Group Policy.

13. Your organization has implemented VPN technology in support of the IT department's new on-call policy for network administrators. As part of this policy, network administrators have the ability to connect to and manage corporate servers using their own ISPs. You find that the performance of Remote Desktop for Administration connections degrades in the early evening when utilization of your cable ISP's services are at their highest. What can you do improve the performance of Remote Desktop for Administration on those rare occasions when you need to manage a server during your ISP's busy times?

A. Select **Broadband (128Kbps–1.5Mbps)** on the **Experience** tab in Remote Desktop Connection.

B. Select **Custom** on the **Experience** tab in Remote Desktop Connection and accept the items that are checked by default.

C. Select **LAN (10Mbps or higher)** on the **Experience** tab in Remote Desktop Connection.

D. Select **Custom** on the **Experience** tab in Remote Desktop Connection and clear all check boxes.

☑ **B**. The best answer is Answer **B**, where the connection will only send Themes over the connection and where "Bitmap caching" is enabled. The first three check boxes—"Background," "Show contents of windows while dragging," and "Menu and window animation"—consume a lot of bandwidth and should only be enabled on higher-capacity, more reliable network connections.

☒ **A**, **C**, **D**. Answer **A** would have been appropriate if the speed of the network connection was guaranteed; however, because speed degrades during peak traffic times, the options for "Show contents of windows while dragging" and "Menu and window animation" will further degrade performance without adding functionality. Answer **C** is incorrect because all options are enabled, notably the bandwidth hog "Background" option. Answer **D** is incorrect because although disabling Themes will improve performance, disabling "Bitmap caching" will force the entire screen image generated by the screen capture functionality within Remote Desktop Connection to be continually refreshed and sent across the network connection, rather than storing the image locally and refreshing only the portions of the screen that change.

14. You have been asked to take primary responsibility for a server that is used to perform systems management and track software licensing for your organization's entire network. Due to the number of servers to which you need to connect, you need an efficient way to store the different connection configurations to the various servers. For some servers you need direct access to the server console; for others you need a workspace to enter data or generate reports. How can you manage remote access to each server for different levels of access?

    A. Install the Remote Desktop snap-in on the server and create connections for every server which you need to access remotely, configuring some connections to connect to the console and others to connect to individual sessions.

    B. Install the Remote Desktops snap-in on the workstation you will use to connect to the servers, configuring some connections to connect to the console and others to connect to individual sessions.

    C. Edit the Local Terminal Services Group Policy on the workstation you will use to connect to the servers, configuring some connections to connect to the console and others to connect to individual sessions.

    D. On the workstation you will use to connect to the servers, create a connection profile for each server, and save the profiles as .RDP files in your home directory.

    ☑ **A**. The most efficient way of managing many connections from your server to other servers is to use the Remote Desktop snap-in to create connections for each server that you need to manage. For the servers where you need to connect directly to the server console (console 0), check the **Connect to console** box in the Add New Connection window. For the other servers, leave **Connect to console** unchecked.

    ☒ **B**, **C**, **D**. Answers **B**, **C**, and **D** are incorrect because the Remote Desktops snap-in is only available for servers. More specifically, Answer **C** is incorrect because Terminal Services Group Policy is used to configure the parameters within which Remote Desktop for Administration can take place. Answer **D** is incorrect because .RDP files are used to store behavior and performance configuration parameters for Remote Desktop Connection, not the session on the server to which Remote Desktop Connection connects.

Chapter 11 Disaster Recovery Planning and Prevention

1. Bill is having problems starting his Windows Server 2003 server after updating a variety of device drivers. Bill wants to be able to record the drivers and services that are loaded when his server starts. Which startup mode can Bill use to do this?

   A. Safe mode

   B. Last known good configuration

   C. Boot logging

   D. This can't be done in Windows Server 2003; it is only a feature of Windows 2000

   ☑ **C**. In order to log the drivers and services that are loaded during the boot process, Bill must enable boot logging during startup.

   ☒ **A, B, D**. Answers **A** and **B** are incorrect because even though each of these modes will help you troubleshoot a problem server, neither will allow you to log the drivers and services. Answer **D** is incorrect because boot logging can be used on a Windows Server 2003 server.

2. Bill has logged the drivers and services that have loaded (or have failed) during the startup of a bad server. What file stores the logged information?

   A. %systemroot%\ntbtlog.txt

   B. c:\ntblog.txt

   C. c:\temp\ntblog.txt

   D. %systemroot%\system32\ntbtlog.txt

   ☑ **A**. The list of drivers and services that are loaded during boot is stored in *%system-root%\ntbtlog.txt*.

   ☒ **B, C, D**. Answers **B, C,** and **D** are incorrect because the ntbtlog.txt file is only stored in the %systemroot% directory.

3. Pedro is configuring three Windows Server 2003 servers to be part of a Server Cluster. He wants the configuration information for the cluster to be stored on multiple storage devices within the cluster. Which Server Cluster should he use to achieve this?

   A. Majority node set Server Cluster

   B. Single-node Server Cluster

   C. Network Load Balancing Server Cluster

   D. Single quorum device Server Cluster

   ☑ **A**. A majority node set Server Cluster has two or more nodes, but the nodes might or might not be attached to one or more storage devices. Unlike the single quorum device Server Cluster, the configuration information for this cluster is stored on multiple storage devices.

☒ **B, C, D**. Answers **B**, **C**, and **D** are incorrect because none of these cluster modes allows you to store the cluster configuration across multiple storage devices.

4. In terms of outlining potential risks to your organization, which of the following is used to identify potential threats of terrorism, fire, flood, and other incidents as well as provide guidance on how to deal with such events when they occur?

   A. Disaster recovery plan

   B. Backup strategy

   C. Business continuity plan

   D. Risk analysis plan

   ☑ **A**. A disaster recovery plan is used to identify potential threats of terrorism, fire, flood, and other incidents, and it provides guidance on how to deal with such events when they occur.

   ☒ **B, C, D**. Answer **B** is incorrect because a backup strategy is only concerned with how, when, and where backups (and restores) are performed. Answer **C** is incorrect because a business continuity plan is used for continuing normal business in the face of disaster, not for outlining risks. Answer **D** is incorrect because risk analysis is mainly concerned with outlining the potential risks to an organization. This information is used in the disaster recovery plan to determine a course of action to respond to the various risks.

5. You can select from many Windows startup options during a computer's boot process. Which startup option is only available on a domain controller?

   A. Debugging mode

   B. Safe mode with command prompt

   C. Recovery Console

   D. Directory services restore mode

   ☑ **D**. Directory services restore mode is an option that is only available on a domain controller and is used in restoring the SYSVOL in Active Directory.

   ☒ **A**, **B**, **C**. Answers **A** and **B** are incorrect because both Debugging mode and Safe mode with command prompt are available in member servers as well as domain controllers. Answer **C** is incorrect because the Recovery Console is also available on member servers.

6. Drew is attempting to load server clustering on his Windows Server 2003 Standard Edition servers. However, he cannot find the installation option on his server or his Windows Server 2003 CD-ROM. Why is he having difficulty installing server clustering?

A. The installation files for Server Clustering are on the Windows Server 2003 Resource Kit CD.

B. Windows Server Clustering is only available in the Enterprise and Datacenter versions of the Windows Server 2003 operating system.

C. Drew would have to reinstall the operating system in order to create a Server Cluster, because this option must be selected during the initial server configuration.

D. Drew needs to purchase the Server Cluster software separately from the Windows Server 2003 software.

☑ **B.** Windows Server Clustering is only available in the Enterprise and Datacenter versions of the Windows Server 2003 operating system.

☒ **A, C, D.** Answer **A** is incorrect because Server Clustering is not on the Resource Kit CD. Answer **C** is incorrect because Server Clusters can be installed after the initial server configuration—as long as that server is running Enterprise or Datacenter Edition. Answer **D** is incorrect because Server Clustering is not purchased separately.

7. Each server within a cluster must have the same location configuration set during the installation of Windows Server 2003. What are the components of the location configuration? (Choose all that apply.)

A. Language

B. Country

C. Region

D. State

E. Company

☑ **A, B, C.** Each server within the cluster must have the same location configuration, meaning that they must all be using the same language, country, and region set during the installation of Windows Server 2003; therefore Answers **A, B**, and **C** are correct.

☒ **D, E.** Answers **D** and **E** are incorrect because the state that a server resides in and the company that owns the server are not part of the location configuration.

8. John is planning a Server Cluster using Windows Server 2003. He is trying to measure the number of servers that he will need for this cluster. By measuring the number of clients that can be anticipated to use the Server Cluster, John is able to determine the number of servers he needs. What is the name of the measurement of clients versus server nodes?

A. Client load

B. Client traffic

C. Client bandwidth

D. Client analysis

☑ **A.** The client load can directly affect the number of nodes that are participating within a cluster.

☒ **B, C, D.** Answers **B**, **C**, and **D** are incorrect because none of these terms exists in relation to the number of nodes within a cluster.

9. Brittany has configured three servers for NLB. She wants to limit the type of network traffic that is balanced between the servers. What window in the Network Load Balancing Manager allows her to do this?

   A. Cluster Parameter window

   B. Add/Edit Port Rule window

   C. Port Configuration window

   D. Port Filter window

   ☑ **B.** The Add/Edit Port Rule window is used to limit the type of traffic that is to be balanced between servers in a Network Load Balanced cluster.

   ☒ **A, C, D.** Answer **A** is incorrect because this window is used for setting the parameters for the cluster (including IP address of the cluster, subnet, and name). Answers **C** and **D** are incorrect because these windows do not exist.

10. What type of Server Cluster has two or more nodes in which each node is attached to a cluster storage device?

    A. Single quorum device Server Cluster

    B. Major node set Server Cluster

    C. Single-node Server Cluster

    D. Network Load Balancing Server Cluster

    E. None of the above

    ☑ **A.** A single quorum device cluster has two or more nodes in which each node is attached to a cluster storage device. In a single quorum device Server Cluster, the configuration information for the cluster is kept on a single storage device.

    ☒ **B, C, D, E.** Answers **B**, **C**, **D**, and **E** are incorrect because only a single quorum device cluster allows you to have configuration information kept on a single storage device.

11. Luke wants to back up his files at any time during the business day, but he's afraid that he could lock users out of storage areas during the backup. What type of backup can Luke use to back up data during the day without locking out users?

    A. Full backup

    B. Differential backup

    C. Incremental backup

    D. Volume shadow copy backup

E. Automated System Recovery

F. None of the above; users will always be locked out when a storage device is being backed up

☑ **D**. One advantage of volume shadow copy is that backups can be performed at any time (although it's still best to perform backups during off-hours) without locking users out of the storage areas that you are trying to back up.

☒ **A**, **B**, **C**, **E**, **F**. Answers **A**, **B**, and **C** are incorrect because these backup methods lock users out of storage areas during the backup process. Answer **E** is incorrect because ASR only backs up system-related information, not user data. Answer **F** is incorrect because a volume shadow copy backup can back up without user lockout.

12. Owen is analyzing the security of his Server Cluster. He notices that security logging is not turned on in the Server Cluster. Of the following choices, which is the *best* reason for Owen to consider logging and auditing security-related events on his cluster?

A. By logging and auditing these events, he can watch files being accessed by users of the Server Cluster.

B. By logging and auditing these events, he can watch for any DoS attacks against the Server Cluster.

C. By logging and auditing these events, he can keep track of unauthorized access to the Server Cluster.

D. By logging and auditing these events, he can keep track of authorized access to the Server Cluster.

E. Answers **C** and **D**

F. Answers **B** and **C**

G. None of the above

☑ **E**. By logging and auditing these events, he can keep track of authorized (and unauthorized) access to the Server Cluster.

☒ **A**, **B**, **C**, **D**, **F**, **G**. Answers **A** and **B** are incorrect because neither of these are advantages of logging and auditing a Server Cluster. Answers **C** and **D** are correct, but the *best* answer is *both* **C** and **D**. Answer **F** is incorrect because although Answer **C** is part of the correct answer, Answer **B** is not.

13. Sean has created a backup job for one of his servers. He has also opened the Advanced settings for the backup job and configured it to run as an Incremental backup. What other setting can he configure in the advanced settings for this backup job?

A. What type of media to use

B. When to start the backup

C. End-of-job notification

D. Copying the backup job to create another job

☑ **B**. In the advanced settings of the backup job, Sean can schedule when the job is going to kick off.

☒ **A**, **C**, **D**. Answers **A**, **C**, and **D** are incorrect because none of these answers is an option that can be configured in the advanced settings.

14. Brian is describing to his boss the differences between a Server Cluster and a Network Load Balancing cluster. He explains that an NLB cluster can support up to 32 nodes. His boss asks him how many nodes can be configured within a Server Cluster. How many nodes does he tell his boss can be configured?

A. 8

B. 10

C. 32

D. Infinite number

☑ **A**. A Server Cluster can have up to eight nodes.

☒ **B**, **C**, **D**. Answers **B**, **C**, and **D** are incorrect because a Server Cluster can be configured for up to eight nodes, and each of these answers exceeds this number.

15. Automated System Recovery is a new disaster recovery solution in Windows Server 2003. It can be configured to back up specific data from a server. Which of the following types of data can be backed up (and restored) using ASR? (Choose all that apply.)

A. User data

B. System State data

C. OS-related data

D. System services

☑ **B**, **C**, **D**. Automated System Recovery, or ASR, can be used to back up the System State data, system services, and all other files associated with the operating system; therefore Answers **B**, **C**, and **D** are correct.

☒ **A.** Answer **A** is incorrect because ASR cannot be used to back up or restore user data; it is only meant to back up system-critical data.

Index

Symbols and Numbers

A

B

C

E

F

H

I

M

N

O

P

Q

R

T

U

V

X

Z